Cultural Meanings of News

To My Family

Cultural Meanings of News

A Text-Reader

EDITOR
DANIEL A. BERKOWITZ
University of Iowa

Los Angeles | London | New Delhi
Singapore | Washington DC

For information:

SAGE Publications, Inc.
2455 Teller Road
Thousand Oaks, California 91320
E-mail: order@sagepub.com

SAGE Publications Ltd.
1 Oliver's Yard
55 City Road
London EC1Y 1SP
United Kingdom

SAGE Publications India Pvt. Ltd.
B 1/I 1 Mohan Cooperative Industrial Area
Mathura Road, New Delhi 110 044
India

SAGE Publications Asia-Pacific Pte. Ltd.
33 Pekin Street #02-01
Far East Square
Singapore 048763

Printed in the United States of America

Library of Congress Cataloging-in-Publication Data

Cultural meanings of news: A text-reader/editor, Daniel A. Berkowitz.
p. cm.
Includes bibliographical references and indexes.
ISBN 978-1-4129-6765-5 (pbk.)
1. Journalism—Social aspects. 2. Journalism. 3. Journalism—Objectivity. I. Berkowitz, Daniel A. (Daniel Allen)

PN4749.C85 2011
302.23—dc22 2009037881

Printed on acid-free paper

10 11 12 13 14 10 9 8 7 6 5 4 3 2 1

Acquiring Editor: Todd R. Armstrong
Editorial Assistant: Nathan Davidson
Production Editor: Astrid Virding
Copy Editor: Megan Bell
Proofreader: Wendy Jo Dymond
Indexer: Kathleen Paparchontis
Typesetter: C&M Digitals (P) Ltd.
Cover Designer: Gail Buschman
Marketing Manager: Helen Salmon

CONTENTS

ACKNOWLEDGMENTS

Students have always been my best teachers. It becomes a learning experience when I explain a concept to them, when they challenge the ideas we are discussing, when they offer a new interpretation of what I *thought* I had understood. When I explained this to a graduate student several years ago, she told me she felt uneasy about this "role reversal." Nonetheless, it's true.

But my acknowledgments need to go a few steps further. Over the years, I have worked with several graduate students—as dissertation advisor and research collaborator with culturally oriented studies—and these encounters have pushed me to better understand the material that this book presents. I'm afraid to start naming them for fear of forgetting somebody, but I should at least mention Sarah Burke, Matt Cecil, Dina Gavrilos, Mirerza Gonzalez-Velez, Josh Grimm, Charles Hays, Amani Ismail, Robin Johnson, Arlecia Simmons, Jim TerKeurst, Vitalis Torwel, Jim Trammell, Tim Vos, and Mervat Youssef. The same goes for all the colleagues I have known and worked with over the years—especially Hillel Nossek, who introduced me to the concept of mythical narrative (and collaborated with me on some projects), and Oren Meyers, who got me thinking about the idea of collective memory as it relates to media.

To assemble this collection, I began with articles I had added to my courses and cited in my research published after my previous reader, *Social Meanings of News,* came out in 1997. I then asked my research assistant, Mervat Youssef, to put together the tables of contents from journals in the field over the last several years. She then gathered files for the articles I chose from and eventually settled on. Mervat was a former student in my Sociology of News class and had a pretty good idea of how my turf was defined. At times, it was difficult to decide what made a piece of research "cultural" instead of "sociological" or even just plain journalistic common sense. That is where the Introduction to this book proved helpful as I worked to define the terrain and distinguish it from earlier trends in the field. The table in this book's Introduction grew out of several iterations of graduate courses I taught. The first time I presented these ideas for systematically understanding research, I remember students clustering around later that day telling me that, for the first time, they could actually explain why two studies had reached two different answers to similar questions. Once the table took form, I introduced the current working version at the start of my next course and incorporated our discussions and suggestions into a new version.

Without a few helpful people, this book would not have reached fruition. First, I want to thank my editor at SAGE, Todd Armstrong, for selling the idea to his committee, and to Todd's assistant, Aja Baker and later, Nathan Davidson, for providing information I needed along the way. My plans to complete the book on Todd's schedule went awry twice. First, I accepted a position in university administration that took far more of my time than I had expected. Second, on a rainy Friday the 13th in June 2008, my house was inundated by a flood that hit my entire neighborhood and made my family transients for the next six months while we prepped our house for reconstruction and learned more about painting, plumbing, wiring, cabinets, and flooring than I ever really wanted to. Through it all, Todd patiently adjusted the schedule and waited for my updates. A second thank-you goes to the Graduate College and the School of Journalism & Mass Communication at the University of Iowa. Thanks to Robert E. Gutsche, Jr. for his eagle-eye proofreading. Without their support and flexibility, I never would have found time to finish the project. Finally, I must thank SAGE's reviewers listed below, who commented on my proposal and a first draft of the book's key elements; these ideas were greatly helpful in refining the basic concept and making it feel all the more cohesive.

Matthew C. Ehrlich, University of Illinois at Urbana-Champaign

James S. Ettema, Northwestern University

Maura Jane Farrelly, Brandeis University

Amani Ismail, American University, Cairo

Carolyn Kitch, Temple University

Therese L. Lueck, The University of Akron

Daniel Riffe, Ohio University

Carl Sessions Stepp, University of Maryland

Christa J. Ward, University of Georgia

Introduction

From Sociological Roots to Cultural Perspectives

Let us begin with two simple questions:

- What is news?
- Why does news turn out like it does?

That is where my earlier reader—*Social Meanings of News*—began. This book continues to address those questions and adds one more question:

- What does news tell us about the professional culture and the society that produces it?

These are deceptively simple questions with deceptively complex answers. For many people, these questions require a personal paradigm shift, a change of mind-set about the meaning of news and journalism.

Here is an example. In April 2007, a troubled student at Virginia Tech went on a shooting rampage, going from classroom to classroom and randomly firing his weapons at the students and professors inside. By the time he ended his own life, 32 people had been killed and many more were wounded. Among them were several professors who sacrificed themselves to save their students. In particular, one elderly professor who had survived the Holocaust held his classroom door closed while his students jumped out the classroom window to safety—ultimately, the gunman forced his way into the classroom and shot the professor.

Two points of view can be applied to this example: One could be called the *journalism critic,* the other the *cultural scholar.* From the perspective of the journalism critic, a discussion might focus on depth and details of the coverage, of ethics and sensitivity to the people interviewed and to the families who were affected. Ultimately, the discussion would close in on an assessment of how well the media did in this situation and what flaws lay in the news they covered. There might be an ethical discussion, for example, judging whether the television networks should have broadcast video materials the gunman taped and sent to them. Or there could have been a debate about whether mental illness should have been incorporated into the story.

This book moves away from the journalistic answers and toward the perspective of the cultural scholar of journalism, considering the work of journalists in their news organizations and the texts that they produce. The cultural scholar sees journalists as people living and working within the culture of a newsroom, a media organization, and a society. And it views the texts that news organizations produce as an artifact of the culture that represents key values and meanings. This is quite different than the role of the journalism critic, because the cultural scholar steps aside from professional judgments to consider journalism as a human phenomenon like any other. The cultural scholar of journalism realizes that a particular study produces one of several possible answers shaped by the conceptual premise guiding that inquiry.

The cultural scholar of journalism might therefore study news stories about the Virginia Tech shootings and discuss how they correspond to long-standing cultural narratives of The Hero and how this narrative represents key values of the culture. The cultural scholar of journalism might consider how American collective memory of the Holocaust added meaning to the story by placing the event into a historical perspective. Or the scholar could argue for how both of these cultural elements serve as tools for the journalist, providing a way to facilitate writing news about a broad, multifaceted event in a way that can be accomplished more quickly while retaining the appearance of how a news story "is supposed to go."

A key goal of this book, then, is to help readers begin to ponder cultural meanings of news, considering a variety of answers to "What is news?"—which flow from several perspectives that cultural scholars of journalism have explored. The book is organized into six key conceptual parts. As a prelude, the Introduction sets up the exploration through three frameworks. The *first framework* considers the underlying vantage points that have guided research about journalism—some conversations about meanings of news that have emerged from ongoing research over time. By understanding these conversations, it becomes possible to sense the worldview that has shaped those research findings. The *second framework* considers meanings of the term *cultural,* which help locate the basis for the selected readings; the term has been used so often in so many ways that it has begun to lose its meaning. The *third framework* offers six dimensions for understanding why research about news has asked certain kinds of questions, and subsequently, why a specific study has arrived at a particular answer (these dimensions have broader application for mass communication research as well). Taken together, the three frameworks place the readings that follow into better perspective, helping show why one answer to "What is news?" comes out differently from some others.[1]

---

[1]The intent here is not to call for considering news in a multidimensional grid built from a combination of the three frameworks: That would be an unwieldy and counterproductive exercise. In general, these three frameworks should be used distinctly to better understand the foundations that shaped the authors' questions and their resulting answers.

Vantage Points in the Study of News

Over the years, thinking and research about news and how it comes to be has passed through three central vantage points: the *journalistic* position, moving to an emphasis on *sociological organization,* and then on to a consideration of the *cultural* dimensions. These three vantage points are roughly chronological, yet all three continue to exist today among those who study the news and news media. Each vantage point has a different worldview about journalism, each asks different questions, and each shapes its answer in a different direction. Ultimately, each vantage point also represents a shift in thinking about what journalism means in a society, generating three discussions that are essentially incompatible.

From the *journalistic* vantage point, the core tenets focus on the ideals of objectivity and the "mission" of a journalist as standard-bearer of a Fourth Estate that protects a society from corruption in government and business. As such, questions about news tend to center around possible bias in reporting, on stories that are missed or misreported, and on other elements that might lead to less than a full and accurate truth. For example, a study in this vein might examine newspaper content involving people with Hispanic surnames to see if the news is favorable or unfavorable to that social group—the assumption underlying such a study might be that news about minority groups could be biased against them. Or a study of news selection in local television might consider which of a textbook range of news values—impact, timeliness, conflict, prominence, and proximity—is most closely related to news that has been broadcast. In general, these kinds of questions shaped inquiry into journalism and news from the founding of the discipline on through the 1960s. Answers about the nature of news from this vantage point could be considered normative (judged by a shared standard) or administrative (designed to improve the news media institution). The chief weakness of this journalistic position is that it centers on passing judgment about how journalism has dealt with issues, texts, and actions rather than on working toward understanding and explanation of news as a human phenomenon.

In all, the journalistic perspective on news can be considered an *ideology*—a taken-for-granted belief system that accepts a dominant form of practice as natural and right. Relying on this professional ideology to understand news actually *masks* understanding by making normative judgments about what is good and bad about journalism. A news article can be depicted as a good story or a bad story. Likewise, the article's writer can be called "a good journalist" if the story is seen by other journalists as "right" or as "not a good journalist" if a story does not conform to professional convention (but oddly, not as a "bad journalist"). As a professional ideology, the journalist's perspective may be applied to criticize the accuracy or slant of the news we encounter, but underlying this critique rests the unspoken belief that news can ideally represent the real world, presenting an accurate picture of what is really out there.

To get beyond this, professional critique first requires a shift to two different vantage points—that news is a socially and culturally created product like any other—and then to explore the social working arrangements and culturally agreed upon meanings that shape this product. From this perspective, news is constructed by workers who unavoidably put a bit of themselves, their organization, their profession, and their society into what they produce. These news workers interface with others in their organization as they do their jobs, learning norms for what they should be doing, receiving criticism and praise for what they have done. Within an organization, resources are limited in terms of staff and equipment; production demands related to deadlines, space, time, and competition further dictate how news turns out. And as news is gathered and manufactured, its end result is shaped by unspoken expectations about which meanings are acceptable within the profession and within the society. All of this ends up being packaged within the tacitly accepted meanings of the culture of journalism and the culture of the society to which they belong.

Although an answer stemming from journalistic ideology might acknowledge these limitations on the news, it would still argue that eliminating those limitations is ideally possible and would allow an accurate presentation of reality to prevail. To go beyond *judging* news and move toward *understanding* it, we must step aside from professional ideology, avoiding the notion that news can be neutral.

The *sociological organization* vantage point surfaced most clearly in the late 1960s when sociologists began studying journalism from the perspective of the accomplishment of work—journalists make a product agreed to be "good" within a conventional time frame and allocation of resources (mainly staff and equipment). This perspective views journalists as similar to other workers who face expectations from their organizations and regularly develop strategies that allow them to accomplish their work in a predictable way. Because the backgrounds and theory of these researchers were based in sociology rather than in the discipline they were studying—journalism—they were not as intellectually bound by the professional ideology of journalism. To somebody thinking within the journalistic vantage point, this basic assumption becomes dissonant; journalists are supposed to have a higher societal mission than workers in factories or service industries.

Questions in this vein of study depict journalists in a struggle between the ideals of journalism and the tensions created within the journalism workplace, further tempered by the behavioral norms and ethics of the profession at large. Key to these arguments are the working arrangements and the constraints that they impose on a journalist's ability to fulfill their professional ideals. The ultimate argument is that this clash leads not to an approximation of reality but instead to a *constructed* reality that emerges from the imperatives of a journalist's everyday life. In a way, this argument was more about the shape and rhythms of journalistic work than it was about the meaning of the work—and its outcomes—to those involved in its construction. Along the way, it became clear that life and work in the news organization and the journalistic profession subsumed much of the differences that individuals could accomplish. For example, a study drawing on the sociological vantage point might look at the unspoken rules in the newsroom and how new reporters learn them. Or a study could explore the strategies that reporters use to gather information for news stories and what they do to ensure their stories will be done by deadline with the appropriate level of quality.

The *cultural* vantage point for studying news and its production shifted the emphasis away from the process, constraints, and structures of "making news" to an exploration of what doing journalism meant to those who worked in it. That is, the act of accomplishing journalistic work in itself carries meanings—when journalists do their work, the values and significance of that work both follows from that enactment and also leads toward work done in a way that yields those rewards. For example, when local television journalists produce stories and newscasts during rating periods (sweeps), their working as a competitive team in itself becomes part of the larger cultural activity. Just the act of engaging in this special kind of work carries important meanings for those within the culture. Likewise, when disaster strikes, journalists become part of a storytelling community, functioning as "bards" of the times to help society reflect on itself and join together for healing from the trauma that has been created. And when the integrity of the journalistic institution is threatened by an individual journalist or news organization that has violated professional principles, the broader institution comes together to show how the aberration was isolated to one person or organization—the institution as a whole is thus not represented as flawed, and the blame is just placed on those who have deviated.

In each of these three examples, the emphasis is on the culture of journalism, blending the meanings of the product that journalists create with the meanings they see in the production work itself. But the term *cultural* still seems blurry and needs further attention.

Toward Three Meanings of *Cultural* for News

As used in this book, three meanings of the term *cultural* are in regular use; all are relevant and will be included even though they focus on quite different concerns. The first meaning of cultural—and most central to this book—corresponds to an anthropological position that explores the meanings of lived cultures of news production. In other words, this version of the term considers what it means for journalists to engage in their work. This position also explores how news texts in their various forms reflect both the cultures of news production and the cultural values of the society where that news production takes place. To explain these ideas more fully, imagine that you are a reporter working in a newsroom of a television station. You interact with others in the newsroom as you work on your story assignments, and over the course of time, the news you produce begins to carry meanings beyond the news itself. Some stories predictably foretell the progress of society's events throughout the year, such as news of recurring holidays and the changing of the seasons. Other news stories tell society's great tales—joys, tragedies, successes, and traumas. Yet other news stories signify meanings about the profession of journalism itself—its professional values, its challenges, its successes and failures.

Over time, the act of creating news begins to shape the news itself not intentionally but simply by living out the meanings that emerge from everyday life in an organization that is part of a profession, an institution, and a society. It is a life bound with regular, familiar rituals with ongoing conflicts and with meanings that are readily recognized by those who participate in it. In all, news reflects the culture of its creation, both within and outside of a news organization.

A second meaning of cultural refers to how news is shaped by its global context. Most simply, journalism in countries as different as Korea, India, Germany, Kenya, Egypt, and the United States has some degree of commonality as a profession and a social institution. Yet all differ from each other because of how they have been impacted by historical, political, economic, religious, and other factors. Because much of the research on sociological and cultural dimensions of news is based in the West—and specifically in the United States—asking questions about the first meaning of cultural from another country's perspective both broadens inquiry and offers a comparative sense that enriches understanding. This meaning of cultural cannot simply be reduced to "international"—news made in another country—because it is the influence of a specific country's culture and its press system on news that becomes important.

A third meaning of cultural is less central to this book's mission, but it still needs to be addressed. Here, the term comes from the British cultural studies tradition that focuses on power and hegemony. This meaning of cultural argues that cultures develop subconscious understandings about who is considered powerful and who is subservient, and how meanings embedded in that culture—and conveyed by the media—serve to reinforce that social structure. By doing so, social power is wielded and maintained. This meaning of cultural clearly contrasts with the first, where power is not a central purpose and the concern is more about understanding how human interactions carry meanings—although the meanings could, in turn, bring messages about a society's power structure.

Introductions to each part of the readings weave these three meanings of cultural into the discussion. Also key are six dimensions of a typology for understanding meanings of research. By doing so, the selections can be placed into their contexts, guiding the interpretation of what these readings contribute and illuminating how they differ.

A Systematic, Conceptual Approach to the Study of News

In retrospect, then, the purpose of this book is to further a growing and maturing trend in the study of news by developing key themes in the cultural dimensions. Even within this smaller realm, a systematic approach is helpful for sorting out equally appealing answers to "What is news?" and "Why does news turn out like it does?" Studies addressing these kinds of questions can be analyzed through six dimensions that help sort out why different studies arrive at different but valid answers. Table 1 presents a summary of the six dimensions. These are helpful to keep in mind while reading culturally oriented studies, as well as with studies based in other traditions. It is also important to mention that it would be too difficult to separate studies by matching them up on all six dimensions at once, so Table 1 should be considered as a guide for interpretation rather than as an organizing scheme for this book.

Considering news through its *topic of study* is probably the least productive route for understanding this book's key questions—answers in the topic dimension tend to mainly describe a phenomenon. At the same time, this is the part that many scholars—especially newer ones—respond to when asked what a study is about. Answers might come back like, "It's a case study of news about a student who went on a campus shooting spree" or "I want to learn about women journalists." The challenge here is to temporarily omit the topic itself and see what is left. That is, what does news about a specific campus shooting spree represent in the abstract about the interface between news and society? Or, what does it mean, more broadly, to study women journalists? Does this really represent how journalists with lower social power cover the news compared to those with greater authority and social power? Can such a study help inform research about Hispanic journalists or journalists just starting their careers? In sum, the topic dimension serves as a beginning of thinking about news but needs to be connected to something larger and more abstract that shows what the topic represents conceptually.

Focus of research tends to be selected as an offshoot of choosing a research topic: Some questions concern the production of news, some the reception of news by its audiences, and other questions concern the texts of news that move from producer to audience. We don't always outwardly consider the focus of research in these terms, but this decision—whether purposive or not—directly shapes both the direction of the research and the outcome of what is learned. An important point is that news content production can be studied by examining the outcome of that production: the news text. In culturally oriented studies especially, textual analysis of news is commonplace, even though assertions about production are the aim.

Turning back to Table 1, concerns about *level of analysis* become integrated into the bigger picture. The concept looks to specific social aggregations as the foundation of an

Table 1 A Typology for Understanding the Meanings of Research

This table offers a set of dimensions by which a reader can evaluate the meaning of research. Key here is understanding the positions, purposes, and assumptions that have gone into shaping a study. These may be either consciously or subconsciously chosen by the research but shape the process and outcome of research in either case.

Dimension	Sample Categories	Utility
1. Topic of study	Campus shootings, women journalists, presidential campaigns	Sets up the basic area of exploration. Working only at this dimension tends to create descriptive work. Try to ask what this topical exploration helps exemplify conceptually.
2. Focus of research	Producer, texts, audience	Identifies where the concerns might lie or where the data might be gathered.
3. Level of analysis	Individual, organizational, professional, institutional, cultural, etc.	Addresses the kind of social aggregation related to the focus of research. Data can be gathered from one level of observation to develop an understanding of a different level of analysis, such as individual survey questionnaires to study organizations.
4. Paradigm	Positivism, constructivism, postpositivism, critical, etc.	Relates to the kind of assumptions about truth, knowledge, reality, etc. that have shaped a researcher's exploration and the understandings that have been gleaned from it. Also guides potential theory to be applied.
5. Methodological choices	Qualitative, quantitative	The nature of the data collection scheme is somewhat linked to the four previous dimensions yet not necessarily so. For example, positivism would usually employ quantitative methodology, but qualitative research could also be conducted from a positivist perspective.
6. Purpose	Describe, predict, explain, understand	Helps assess the role of theory in the research and the perceived utility that the research attempted to bring to the work. Purely descriptive work tends not to incorporate theory into its design. Research aiming toward explanation or understanding uses theory more for interpretive vision. Predictive research uses theory to set up a framework for likely expectations.

explanation. For example, an individual-level answer would focus on the psychological dimensions that shape how a journalist accomplishes work, such as the way that schema influence the processing of information and telling stories. Higher levels all largely remove the individual from the equation while also exerting a stronger homogenizing force on lower levels of analysis. Introducing the notion of level of analysis is a key part—but just one part—of explaining how news comes to be.

Questions about level of analysis are interwoven with the topic of study and purpose of research. Considering the level of analysis also helps to look ahead toward paradigm questions, methods that are chosen, and even purpose of the research. Cultural approaches tend toward more macro social kinds of questions that texts can represent. Psychologically framed questions, in contrast, will by necessity focus on the individual journalist. Sociological studies will be based more on the news organization, along with the interactions among media workers and the ways that they strategically accomplish their jobs. There is no officially prescribed or agreed upon set of levels. Some scholars consider just three: individual, organizational, and societal. Some have included many more, so that within organizations, working subgroups might be considered in addition to the organization as a whole. In any case, what is key is how a particular social aggregation becomes a driving force in shaping outcomes.

- *Individual level* would consider cognitive processing of information, as well as questions about the degree of journalists' individual autonomy and agency.
- *Organizational level* looks at the way that individuals interact within an organization, how life within a news organization shapes the news that is produced, and the interplay between layers of reporters, editors, and managers.
- *Professional level* begins to examine larger homogenizing forces that present commonalties among, for example, broadcast journalists, or even more broadly, across journalists regardless of their medium.
- *Institutional level* suggests that forces from the media as a social institution carry common influences on the nature of news because of variations in kinds of ownership, press freedom, and financing arrangements. The media institution's mission is also important, such as the differences between furthering a nation's development, maintaining political authority, or informing the citizenry.
- *Cultural level* speaks to larger meanings that might span a nation or even a region. At the cultural level, these meanings are taken for granted and either unquestioned or positioned within an insider–outsider binary. Considering the cultural level helps understand why images in the news, for example, tend to be cast in similar ways—ways essentially matching systems of beliefs and meaning.

Looking at *paradigm* takes discussions of news in specific directions, again based on assumptions that might not be specifically acknowledged. Three basic directions are helpful to outline. First, positivism most closely corresponds to a social science perspective that a knowable reality exists—if a study can be designed well enough, it can come close to explaining a knowable truth. The positivist paradigm is a poor fit to a cultural approach to news, because culture can be considered intangible while positivist research focuses on tangible objects of study. The positivist paradigm contrasts with constructivism, which argues that the world consists of multiple realities, each based on a construction that comes from the research design and the study context. In contrast to positivism, constructivism argues that there are several "truths" that can be learned and that more than one truth can provide meaningful insights—in these multiple answers, the researcher's questions and the methods used to explore them are acknowledged as leading toward one answer rather than another. A postpositivist position straddles these two polar opposites, designing research *toward* a truth yet acknowledging that the outcome of the research design represents a construction nonetheless.

A critical paradigm contrasts with these two positions by actually asking a different kind of question—one that deals with social power, class differences, and control by social elites. These kinds of concerns become the theoretical framework for designing critical research. In a sense, critical research assumes a truth about power arrangements and then adopts an interpretive, constructivist approach to support that assumption. By doing so, critical research carries attributes of both positivistic and constructionist paradigms.

Ultimately, paradigm has a connection to level of analysis. More micro levels of analysis (individual, organizational, professional) tend to fit best with positivistic perspectives. Constructivist and critical paradigms, in contrast, fit best with more macro levels (societal, cultural) because the questions falling from these perspectives better align with these levels. At the same time, these distinctions are not absolutes—any level can be explored as having knowable truths, and any level can also have results acknowledged to be a construction.

As with the other dimensions, *methodological choices* do not stand alone. In particular, methodological choices especially connect with the research paradigm a researcher adopts. For example, a scholar with a constructivist orientation would likely draw on qualitative methods (based on words and meanings) because that kind of analysis lends itself more toward open-ended findings that allow for multiple realities to be considered. A scholar more focused on a positivist paradigm would commonly draw on quantitative methods (employing computer analysis and statistical tests) for the perceived precision of numerical measurement of the phenomena under study—at the same time working to create more and more resonant measurement schemes that get closer to a singular, knowable truth. Although many researchers may explain a methodological choice based on preference for words or numbers, concern for paradigm tends to be lurking beneath the surface, even if not explicitly expressed.

Finally, the *purpose* of the research connects topic of study, focus of research, level of analysis, paradigm, and methodological choices. Strictly descriptive research may be nearly devoid of theory, with paradigm concerns also taking a backseat—data tend to either be qualitative or based on simple counts of some kind. On the other end of the spectrum, research directed toward building predictive models tends toward a positivistic paradigm (the ability to model outcomes within a single reality), quantitative methods (belief in the science of numbers), and a focus on the micro level (particularly on the individual). In between these two polarities are postpositivism, constructivism (or interpretive), and critical approaches. For each of these, explanation and understanding are the more likely research purposes, because both are compatible with paradigm beliefs (data guided by theory) and the nature of the data (tending toward the qualitative that allows interpretation).

Applying the Typology to This Book

The six dimensions of the typology for understanding the meanings of research serve this book in two ways. First, the typology provides a systematic framework for understanding why readings seem different in their outcomes. One of the difficult aspects of reading a variety of articles on the same topic is understanding why they have drawn equally plausible conclusions. For a scholar looking for *the* answer, this can be frustrating. However, for somebody accepting the notion that research represents multiple answers constructed by the way a study has been designed, conducted, and analyzed, the framework can provide some clear guidance. When it becomes clear that key choices have been made in at least six dimensions, contrasts between studies can be understood more systematically. Competing answers no longer become contradictory but instead illuminating.

A second benefit of the typology is that it helps locate the emphasis of this book and the various parts within the broader terrain of the field. Here are some ways that the selected readings fit these six dimensions:

- *Topic of study:* This book centers on two key questions. First, what is news? Second, how do the cultures of the news organization, the journalism profession, and the society influence the way that news turns out?
- *Focus of research:* This dimension has two centers. One center is the news producer; the other is the news product in forms of print, broadcast, and online content.
- *Level of analysis:* The book considers midrange and higher levels of analysis, from the organization to the profession, the media institution, and—more broadly—to the society and culture.
- *Paradigm:* The key guiding paradigm is constructivism but with a few forays into the critical realm. This direction comes from the nature of culture itself—it is more intuitive than it is observable. To study culture is to acknowledge a construction of reality is at work.
- *Method:* Readings come from qualitative foundations, a decision that follows especially from the choice of paradigm and the focus of research.
- *Purpose:* The central purpose of these readings is toward explanation and understanding. Description alone would not be particularly helpful in exploring the role of culture in the nature of news. Prediction would require the paradigmatic assumption that culture can be known and measured precisely.

Plan of the Book

The six parts of readings in *Cultural Meanings of News* each present a different thematic aspect of studying news from a cultural perspective. All selections are original studies that build a conceptual foundation and explore their topic through textual or ethnographic data. All readings have been chosen from journals in order to provide concise, complete packages of ideas. In keeping with the cultural paradigm's focus, all studies engage in qualitative analysis. An introduction begins each part, setting up the theme, highlighting key concepts, and bringing out ideas that connect the selections. These introductions also show how the selections fit into the book's larger purpose.

At times, a selection may be reinterpreted to tease out an idea lurking within the study but not emphasized by the study's author—a study is often open to multiple interpretations. For example, sometimes an author provides a good example but uses a different conceptual label. For many of us, that is the norm, as we often take away something different from each new reading of the same text. Likewise, an important way to develop conceptual approaches is to fuse together ideas. Drawing from existing studies provides a strategic benefit for creating this kind of book, because readings can be chosen purposively to build a diverse, yet cohesive, group of ideas. Following from this train of thought, it is also important to mention that because of the common paradigmatic base across this book's selections, some readings could be equally well located in more than one part. As a reader of this book, keep an eye open for how ideas from one part can inform concepts central to another. Pay attention, too, for key elements that differentiate parts.

Part I, "A Framework for Thinking About the Meanings of News," offers three readings that address big-picture questions about news, setting up what distinguishes the cultural perspective from the journalistic one. The discussion of levels of analysis formalizes and further develops the basic ideas about news in global contexts, while the other two readings call for a fresh look at what it means to be a journalist.

Part II, "Cultural Practice of Journalism," moves ahead from the framework readings to place the work of journalists and the news they produce into settings that demonstrate how culture at several levels of analysis interacts with journalistic practice. These selections consider settings in new media, cross-national comparison, and crisis news work.

Part III, "Making Meaning in the Journalistic Interpretive Community," places news as a site of meaning making, where journalists work within a shared sense of both events and the work that they accomplish. Again, these readings consider scenarios at both macro and midrange levels of analysis, incorporating settings in multiple nations and both traditional and new media forms. Ultimately, news appears as a construction that results from the meanings that journalists share and maintain.

Part IV, "Repairing the Journalistic Paradigm," returns to the notion that journalists work within a professional paradigm that dictates norms for journalistic practice. The concept of paradigm repair is illustrated not only through failures in applying traditional methods for attaining objectivity but also by how the news institution polices the culture into which it is embedded.

Part V, "News Narratives as Cultural Text," picks up on the term often applied to news articles—*stories*—and asks if news could be treated literally as a story, that is, as a conventional tale that both rings true with the larger realm of a culture's stories about itself while also incorporating elements of the current instance of that story. This part develops the idea that news resonates with a culture by retelling a culture's stories the way they have traditionally been told, complete with all the ongoing mythical characters and cultural values.

Part VI, "News as Collective Memory," uses interpretive community as a point of departure but also can be considered a special case of news narrative that anchors the narrative in a tangible context of a historical moment. Collective memory helps journalists judge the magnitude of current occurrences in light of how things have unfolded in the past, which guides the news gathering process and provides a means for journalists to assess if their news stories have been presented "correctly." The concept of collective memory also ties to a story's resonance with the journalistic paradigm that expects news to be based in the present rather than drawing from story templates from the past.

The Epilogue provides an opportunity to revisit the starting point of this book, considering the initial frameworks, analytic perspectives, and belief systems that shape both presuppositions and new insights about the cultural meanings of news. This part also looks beyond the readings to assess what questions they did not directly address, as well as their implications for larger questions that consider the intersections of culture and news.

I hope that as you work through this book, you will experience some moments of discomfort as your beliefs about news get twisted around and recast, along with some moments of pleasure as new insights about news begin to appear on the horizon. The discomfort can be seen as "growing pains," while the pleasure follows from the joy of discovery. Sometimes, though, joy of discovery hits a moment of dissonance when a perfectly satisfactory answer to "What is news?" or "Why does news turn out like it does?" or "What does news tell us about the professional culture and the society that produces it?" confronts another equally plausible answer. That is a time when the scholar of news and journalism can turn back to the frameworks of this chapter—particularly Table 1, which outlines a researcher's choice points—to understand why these answers are different. It is also a time when *the* answer begins to appear as *an* answer that is both satisfying and open-ended.

PART I

A Framework for Thinking About the Meanings of News

An important thread runs through this book: Studies about news can be better understood if there are some guiding frameworks in place. The Introduction presented three frameworks for approaching cultural meanings of news, a way of locating a specific study within the broader body of research. On their own, those frameworks offer helpful perspective but lack contextualization to the study of news. That is where this part fits in—by providing a broad look at the scope of news research, raising larger questions that challenge how news and journalism have been studied in the past.

What was once called Sociology of News, or something similar, has grown into what is now known as Journalism Studies. Along with a broadening of the questions about news and how it comes to be, Journalism Studies has also expanded the ways in which news can be studied. Sociology of News, for example, was centered largely on ethnographies of newspaper journalists in the United States and the United Kingdom. For Journalism Studies, the realm has grown beyond newspapers to incorporate other media and has expanded to create a global network of scholars exploring news production in a variety of press systems.

Stephen D. Reese's "Understanding the Global Journalist: A Hierarchy-of-Influences Approach" begins the call to drop a single national norm for understanding news and instead to consider journalism's context in a larger perspective. Reese raises the example of professional norms, explaining how they are heavily dependent on their working contexts. These norms are difficult to see on their own, but they start to become visible in comparison across nations. Sometimes seemingly similar national press arrangements encompass larger fundamental differences. A useful tool that Reese introduces to sort out these differences is the "hierarchy of influences model," where influences on the production of news can be considered at different levels of analysis. He offers five levels—individual, routines, organizational, extra-media, and ideological—arguing that "each successive level [is] viewed as subsuming the one(s) prior." Reese applies these levels to build a refined understanding of journalistic professionalism not as a constant standard but as something that adapts itself to its cultural contexts related to nation and press system. Through these levels, commonalities can be found to show where shared explanations may lie. Although the hierarchical model does not necessarily provide answers to questions about the nature of news, it does provide a helpful organizing scheme for understanding how questions posed and answers found may share roots in common lenses of interpretation.

Mark Deuze's "What is Journalism? Professional Identity and Ideology of Journalists Reconsidered" expands on Reese's discussion of professionalism, claiming that journalism represents a "consensual occupational ideology." This consensus is not globally uniform but rests in the particulars of national and regional cultures—there is not *one journalism* but many *journalisms.* The ideology of any single journalism represents a consensus of who is a "real" journalist and which parts of news media should be considered as "real" journalism. As journalists learn and share their occupational ideology, they simultaneously "self-legitimize their position in society." Deuze operationalizes the ideology of journalism through five values: public service, objectivity, autonomy, immediacy, and ethics. He then explains that this ideology becomes threatened when the contexts of journalism—such as technology and society—undergo fundamental change. Adapting journalism to these social pressures creates a conflict with the consensus of professional ideology, and change becomes difficult. At the same time, journalism needs to change to remain virile within a society under flux. In all, Deuze takes on the concept of professionalism and translates it effectively away from a natural entity into a human construction that attempts to remain steadfast when its worldview is challenged.

In "Deconstructing Journalism Culture: Toward a Universal Theory," Thomas Hanitzsch picks up where Reese and Deuze left off by offering a set of continuums to dissect key elements of journalistic culture. These continuums represent part of what Hanitzsch refers to as elements of "journalism culture," "journalistic culture," or the "cultural identity of journalism." When probing journalistic belief systems across cultural identities, a clear lack of consensus quickly becomes apparent. However, Hanitzsch concludes that journalism culture goes beyond ideology to represent a struggle for the roles and meanings of journalism in society. By doing so, Hanitzsch encompasses all three meanings of culture that were presented in the Introduction to this book. A key to this reading is Figure 1, which offers three dimensions—and seven polar considerations—that constitute journalism culture. Essentially, the model looks behind a single professional ideology to consider the positions that underlie the sociopolitical contexts of the many journalistic cultures. By probing journalism through these dimensions, Hanitzsch breaks down professional norms, helping to remove them from ongoing reification.

Taken together, the pieces by Reese, Deuze, and Hanitzsch begin this book's conversation about news, its professional cultures, and the societies that produce it. It would be too much to ask, though, for the reader to sort out all the dimensions that these authors raise and then begin to systematically compartmentalize each of the selections that follow into the folds of a vast, multidimensional net. More practically, the readings serve as thought points, asking us not to blanketly accept a single journalism as *the* journalism but instead to consider it as one of many answers to why news appears as it does and how it is shaped by the culture in which it is enmeshed. By taking this perspective, a reader can begin to develop a better sense of the foundations, traditions, and assumptions that have shaped the inquiry of each author's work and understand the differing yet potentially satisfying conclusions that they drew from their inquiries.

1

Understanding the Global Journalist

A Hierarchy-of-Influences Approach

Stephen D. Reese

Introduction

We study journalists and their profession to find insights into the ultimate shape of their work. We find this group worthy of our interest and research because of the crucial role it plays in the quality of the world's press. Particularly now, with the globalization of media through major corporate conglomerates, the professionalism of these journalists may be crucial in preserving standards of journalism. Although it is not often explicitly stated, many media scholars would share the conviction that there should be an international standard of journalistic professionalism with basic shared values. The global media have attracted a similarly global group of media scholars who study them. The European Union movement, in particular, recently has inspired a strong interest in collaborative media research that cuts across national boundaries. Shared theoretical perspectives allow these scholars to address comparative research issues as they bring their own national experiences to these questions.

Another factor leading to the popularity of journalists as a research subject is the rise of professional journalism and communication education, which has become more firmly established in the United States and elsewhere. Not only does this represent an important phenomenon for research, but it means increasing numbers of scholars have been trained in these areas as their home discipline. Thus, it is natural that they want to know more about journalism professionals and have begun to approach this study systematically. It is also natural that these scholars attribute social importance to journalism and wish to enhance its status as a profession. This transnational view of the profession has found the social survey a natural methodological approach, allowing scholars to make general descriptive statements about the nature of these journalists and their adherence to certain professional tenets. Indeed, the attraction of this survey approach is that it is easily exported, making it tempting to apply it without sufficient conceptual attention to different cultural settings.

In this article, I will consider the issues raised by this increasing research interest in global journalism and propose a model to help guide these studies. This "hierarchy of influences" model proposes important distinctions between levels of analysis and locates the individual journalist within a web of organizational and ideological constraints. Such a model is particularly important in comparative research, because it helps to place the phenomena of interest within a structural context. Understanding journalism through these levels of analysis helps untangle many of the critiques of press performance, identify their implicit normative and theoretical assumptions, and suggest appropriate kinds of evidence. Ultimately, press practices must be viewed against normative standards. A multi-perspectival approach helps us sort out how different press professionals, practices, and systems work to advance these basic social goals and reminds us that professionalism is a problematic concept, consisting of many values held in tension, which different national groups balance in their own way.

The issues I take up here may be broadly described as a sociology-of-media view, which considers how media power functions within a larger social context. More narrowly, "media sociology" is often equated with the newsroom ethnographies carried out by many scholars trained in the sociological discipline. I mean it more broadly, as I think scholars in Europe and South America would as well, to refer to a broader social structural context of press practice. Although no phrase is entirely adequately, "media sociology" certainly suggests that we must tackle the structural context of journalism, moving beyond the more narrow attempt to psychologize the media through the attitudes and values of individual practitioners. By this phrase, I do also mean to distinguish my questions of interest from traditional audience-and-effects studies. In agenda-setting terminology, for example, researchers have frequently considered how successful media are in setting the agenda of the public; in the media sociology view we are more interested in those forces which set the media's agenda (Reese, 1991). Because it is such a crucial concept with regard to international journalistic practice, I will first review the notion of professionalism within a media sociology framework, before considering some issues raised in comparative media research. I will then present and explain the hierarchy of influences model as a way of addressing these issues.[1]

The Problematic Concept of Professionalism

Before we consider how best to understand and compare the work of journalists we must consider more carefully the profession to which they belong. Fundamentally, our assessment of journalism is based on its contributions to a democratic society. Is journalism indeed a profession? It does not resemble the traditional learned professions with required credentials and licensing procedures, but does have many professional features. It aspires to an important social role and ascribes to ethical codes of conduct. To that extent journalism benefits from its practitioner laying claim to professional membership. Indeed, the idea of professionalism is highly normative. As McQuail (1992) discusses, we evaluate media performance against the major social values of freedom, equality, and order. We assume that journalists must have a high degree of professional freedom and autonomy to carry out their function, and we gauge their work against some standard of fairness, or equal representation of relevant social features. Ethically, we trust that journalists will observe standards that do not violate expectations of social order. We wish that journalists would adhere to certain roles and ethical conduct because we think that doing so benefits the larger society. Thus, an important objective of our analysis is to find the conditions that either encourage or threaten the professional conduct and press quality that we would desire.

I have argued elsewhere that "professionalism" is a problematic concept, with attempts to define it often linked to specific interests. In journalism education, for example, the news media wish to play an influential role in encouraging universities to train students in a "professional" sense. As the prestige of the journalism profession slips in society, the media are driven to shore up their prestige through a number of channels, including by exerting influence on university campuses. Important journalistic foundations, such as the Freedom Forum (established with an endowment derived from the largest U.S. newspaper chain), have taken a much more proactive stance in shaping future faculty-hiring and curricular decisions. The media industry might prefer workers trained with basic entry-level skills, but university education must construct a broader professionalism of civic engagement if students are to contribute effectively to a democratic society (Reese, 1999; Reese and Cohen, 2000). Thus, professionalism is a contested terrain, and continually being renegotiated in response to social shifts.

Hallin (1992), for example, considers how U.S. journalism reached a "high modernism" stage, characterized by the independent insider, a journalistic role with its model in the national security corespondent. This role broke down with the collapse of political consensus and economic support for media reporting, to give way to an interpretive, but largely technical analysis, role. He recommends that a further role shift is needed from a "mediating" position to one that assists in opening up the public sphere. So far I have been discussing professionalism within my own American context. To what extent are these same issues applicable cross-culturally?

In recent years more attention has been devoted to universal principles of human rights. Is it similarly possible to establish principles of journalistic practice acceptable to the diverse world nations? Many studies certainly have proceeded with that implicit assumption. U.S. government and media initiatives have worked to encourage the adoption of the "objective" press model in the emerging democracies of South America and Eastern Europe. They implicitly assume that U.S.-style journalism is a natural and inevitable world model. This movement has been viewed by many Third World nations, however, as a thinly disguised attempt for the multi-national communication firms to dominate the flow of media products, a threat to indigenous media production, and often contrary to nation-building goals. The post-Cold-War environment has brought a more receptive climate for internationalizing the concept of press professionalism, making it especially important that we monitor the shape it is taking.

Freedom is perhaps the most vigorously articulated international professional value. The Freedom Forum, among other groups, has worked to promote press freedom around the world, especially in emerging democracies. The Interamerican Press Association, for example, has developed a basic principle of journalistic freedom, which they promote to the world community. The 1994 Declaration of Chapultepec states that "no law or act of government may limit freedom of expression or of the press whatever the medium." The Declaration is based on the idea that a free press is necessary to enable societies to function as effective democracies. Often this emphasis on official restraint may simply translate as the ability for the news organization and its employees to go where they want and transmit information across national boundaries. Less often emphasized is the freedom of journalists to follow their own professional dictates against organizational pressure.

Thus, our initial concern should be with the problematic issue of professionalism itself. What interests are implicated in supporting one view of professionalism over another. What normative goals are professional practices designed to achieve, and are they meeting those goals? What functions does professionalism serve from different perspectives of the media system? To what extent do professional characteristics of journalists affect the way they shape media content? A model is needed to help us sort out these questions, which are brought into sharper focus when considered cross-culturally.

Comparative Research on Journalists

As mentioned above, the global media are studied by a correspondingly global group of scholars.

Multi-country studies and collaborative research have become more common, making it all the more important that we have a clear model and well-defined set of research questions to guide these investigations. Studies of professional journalists have been perhaps most easily adaptable to comparative analysis. Survey methodology permits replicating the same questionnaire in a variety of national settings, yielding results that can be located within a comparative framework. As indicated in books like Weaver's (1998) *The Global Journalist,* surveys of professional attitudes have proved a successful export to many countries. By contrast, media sociology more generally may be criticized for its overemphasis on explaining specific national, usually North American or British, systems—that is, focusing on a single case and context. The newsroom ethnography studies that have come to exemplify this style of research have been done primarily in U.S. media organizations. A more comparative approach would be useful in calling into question the features of these systems: what is common versus idiosyncratic? If research is to be comparative, however, we must be clear about how this comparison is to be carried out. A brief discussion of the issues raised by comparative research shows the importance of the model I will introduce below.

"Comparative" refers to research "across two or more geographic and historical (spatially/temporally) defined systems, in which the phenomena of interest are embedded in a set of interrelations, relatively coherent, patterned comprehensive, distinct, and bounded" (Blumler et al., 1992). In one sense we are always comparing people and groups based on their location on various social measurement scales, but that doesn't mean that the comparison are necessarily at the appropriate, macrosocietal systemic level. Comparing across systems yields different insights than comparing within and calls for crucial distinctions between the phenomenon of interest and its surrounding structural context. It considers the interplay of theories about substance—the phenomenon of real interest and theories about organization of systems—the surrounding context (Blumler et al., 1992).

Thus, the first task of comparative media sociology is to clearly define the media system in which journalists of interest work. Comparative research includes two important kinds of questions. First-order questions ask "how much?" and "how many?" in various systems, which are by definition less interesting for being atheoretical. Second-order questions move beyond the frequency of things to ask about the relationships among them. Establishing these relationships allows us begin to theorize about causal connections rather than transitory features. What is being compared in comparative research? Most common is the most basic, comparing things. Less self-evidently available to the researcher would be structures formed by things, processes within structures, and, finally, functions of seemingly different things, structures, and processes (Blumler et al., 1992).

Comparative media research is often equated with being cross-national, where the nation becomes the "defined system" and the basis for organizing analysis. Kohn (1989, pp. 22–24) identifies four main approaches to cross-national research based on the role the "nation" plays in the analysis: as object, context, unit of analysis, or as component of a larger system. These can easily be related to media sociology research.

When the goal is to understand the nation system itself as the object and its closely related media system, we may find analyses such as Sigal's (1973) comparison of reporting practices in the United States and Britain. Hallin and Mancini (1994) have provided a similar comparison of U.S. and Italian journalists in their orientation to the state. The nation is perhaps most frequently viewed as a context for some other phenomenon of interest, as with the studies by Weaver and colleagues, mentioned above, of professional attitudes in a number of countries (Weaver, 1998). In this approach, the journalists' host country takes a secondary position, as a marker of certain factors of interest that can help explain comparative differences in journalists. Little emphasis is placed on explaining how the national press system and its special historic and cultural role—although these may be described in passing— are connected to professional practices.

Nations may become the unit of analysis in a broader examination of media patterns. Nations, for example, may be organized along a continuum of press freedom to examine its predictors. Finally, we may view nations as components of a larger system. Indeed, media will increasingly be operating across national boundaries, forming systems that have less and less to do with specific national cultures. Scholars have begun to examine the "global newsroom," to consider how decisions made in supranational news organizations in cities like London affect coverage of other countries.

This discussion suggests that when conducting comparative research it is tempting to rely on the nation system as the natural organizing principle. We need to carefully consider, however, how we are viewing journalists and their professional systems as relating to these national contexts. If we do choose to compare on a national level, we implicitly assume that countries are relatively homogeneous internally, that the variation in the phenomenon of interest is greater across rather than within countries. Increasingly, however, the stratifications of professional conduct may be more varied within than across countries, as a global media professionalism continues to emerge. The results of the Weaver studies, for example, show as many differences as similarities in professional features of journalists. These differences argue against emerging professional standards, as Splichal and Sparks (1994) have argued based on an analysis of journalism students in several countries. Elite journalists will likely have more in common with each other, across national boundaries, than with many of their more localized compatriots. More interesting questions may involve considering how this emerging class of "cosmopolite" journalists shares a common standard and understanding of journalism. As transnational commercialism grows, exemplified by firms like McDonald's and Disney, a common monoculture is developing, with media products moving easily across national borders. Global journalism is part of this development, supporting increasingly common understandings of what constitutes the international news agenda.

Comparative research should also make us cautious in assuming that the meaning of basic concepts is self-evident and comparable across cultures. The meaning of "professionalism," for example, needs to be understood in relation to its specific cultural context. Other media features and practices may be less problematic, but in each case an attempt to specify the structural pattern within a given system helps to guard against prematurely assuming that something means the same thing in one cultural setting as another. Indeed, the interesting question may be not how professional one country's journalists are compared with another's, but how professionalism comes to mean something different in different cultures, or how different journalistic practices are employed to accomplish the same normative goals? In addressing these questions, it is useful to identify the available perspectives, and so I turn now to describing a model that provides such an orientation.

Hierarchy-of-Influences Model

I have found it valuable to consider the forces that shape media messages as a "hierarchy of influences," a model that is the basis for the book *Mediating the Message: Theories of Influences on Mass Media Content* (Shoemaker and Reese, 1996). This volume, developed with my colleague Pamela Shoemaker, establishes a theoretical framework for analyzing media based on levels of analysis, which help classify influences operating both separately and in conjunction with each other. In brief, these levels range from the most micro to the most macro: individual, routines, organizational, extra-media, and ideological, with each successive level viewed as subsuming the one(s) prior. This model helps to meaningfully organize a vast array of eclectic research by considering the level or perspective at which explanation is primarily sought.

The hierarchical aspect draws attention to the idea that these forces operate simultaneously at different levels of strength in any shaping of media content. While it is tempting to gravitate toward monocausal explanatory models depending on one's political and disciplinary leanings, reality shows that in a web of interconnected forces, our analytical choices are a matter of emphasis Thus, theoretically we must ask which explanation is most parsimonious and successful in making sense of media phenomena. Empirically, this hierarchical model suggests that the investigator's task is to determine under which conditions certain factors are most determinative and how they interact with each other. And it reminds us that the evidence presented in support of empirical propositions should be appropriate to the level of analysis. Inferences must be ventured carefully when made at a lower or higher level of abstraction than the level of measurement.

Individual Level

At the individual level, we view the attitudes, training, and background of the journalist (or media worker more generally) as influential. Conceptually, we would locate here the many studies that attempt to describe the individual characteristics of this occupational group, perhaps the most common approach to conducting research on professional issues. At one time, little was known about journalists compared with other professionals. Hindering this systematic study was the tendency in the United States for journalists to encourage a certain mythic image of their distinctive role in society, while, paradoxically, the objectivity concept implied that the nature of these workers mattered little to their actual product. Viewing this product as a construction, like those produced in any other complex organization, was antithetical to the ostensible goal of the media to reflect reality and tell the truth.

In a politically based counter-perspective, much energy has been expended in the U.S. policy arena by conservative thinktanks and advocacy groups to establish the (liberal) bias of the American journalist. For these groups, the tendency of journalists to favor Democratic over Republican candidates is sufficient to explain what in their view is a leftward slant in news content. Critics on the left, however, are more likely to view this bias as lodged elsewhere, especially in the power of media ownership. Indeed, the individual level provides an attractive explanatory perspective for both the public and journalists alike. News consumers may prefer to put a human face on their views of media power, while the journalists' biographical genre must attribute to themselves enough influence to make a fit literary subject.

Rosten (1937) was perhaps the first to try to describe journalists in his study of Washington correspondents, but not until the 1970s did sociologists begin to apply the same occupational and organizational insights to this as to any other professional group. Johnstone and colleagues are frequently cited as the first major empirical effort to describe U.S. journalists as a whole (Johnstone et al., 1972). Since that time, the work of Weaver and Wilhoit (1991) has inspired a host of other efforts around the world to examine journalism professionals empirically. These country studies were sufficient to inspire regular presentations at international conferences and a recent volume, *The Global Journalist* (Weaver, 1998). These surveys are large-scale and difficult undertakings and have provided valuable empirical description. They have provided a valuable counterweight to those who would make sweeping generalizations about journalists based on a few high-profile but unrepresentative cases.

At the individual level we can see that this choice of the population sampled becomes especially important. U.S. conservative media critics, for example, have focused on the sociopolitical views of members of the so-called "elite" media concentrated in the northeastern major urban centers of New York and Washington. Lichter and colleague (1986), for example, conclude that journalists were more likely to vote Democratic, to express left-of-center political views, and to be non-religious than the American public as a whole. Of course, their sample was not of elite journalists, as they claimed, but journalists employed at elite media (defined as including *The New York Times, Newsweek,* and the major television news networks). This obviously urban and northeastern sample showed predictable differences with the nation as a whole. More academically based surveys, such as those by Weaver, have examined the professional views of a broader population, showing that American journalists, across the entire country, are much more like the American public than the Lichter study would suggest.

As seen above, this level allows easy comparison of journalists and the public at large, providing the unsurprising finding that they do differ in many ways. Supporting these comparisons, is often an implicit normative assumption that journalists should be socially representative, reflecting the beliefs of the public. No other profession is held so strictly to this evaluative standard, which even if met would still leave larger forces affecting media quality unaddressed. Although, studies like these may be criticized for being overly descriptive and largely atheoretical, we may see that an implicit theory does underlie all of the research described above. Whether political or academic, power to shape news is held by the individual journalist, and journalist studies attribute great importance to individual characteristics in shaping the news product. Even so, these individual predictive factors are not often linked to specific outcomes.

While choice of population must be evaluated in considering research claims, the probability-survey approach has its general tradeoffs. These studies treat journalists as typically undifferentiated with regard to their location in the organization, and the influence of elite journalists and key gatekeepers is understated by the attempt to emphasize the broad occupational features of this group. The "group" quality of this survey perspective means attributing the major influence to its professional features rather than to the power of specific individuals within the group who have advantageous structural "gatekeeper" locations.

Routines Level

Individuals do not work alone, however, or use rules they invent themselves. The routines level of analysis considers the constraining influences of work practices. "Routines" are patterned practices that work to organize how we perceive and function within the social world. Thus, here we look to those ongoing, structured, deeply naturalized rules, norms, procedures that are embedded in media work (e.g., Reese and Buckalew, 1995). We recognize that individuals do not have complete freedom to act on their beliefs and attitudes, but must operate within a multitude of limits imposed by technology, time, space, and norms. We naturally are often led to view these routines in a negative light, as constraints on individual agency, but they can just as appropriately be viewed as inevitable features of any human activity. Creativity is exercised through the structure made available through these routines, which in terms of Giddens' notion of "structuration" may be viewed as both constraining and enabling.

Analysis taking this perspective often finds the ethnographic method valuable because it allows the impact of these practices to be observed over time and in their natural setting. We assume that journalists are often not aware of how their outlooks are so "routinely" structure and would be unable to self-report honestly about it. And indeed we assume that much of what journalists provide as reasons for their behavior are actually justifications for what they have already been obliged to do by forces outside their control. Because field observation also allows these practices to unfold over time, it suits our concern with the ongoing and structured rather than the momentary or sporadic. The routines attracting most interest have been those involving frontline reporters. While everyone faces routines in their work (publishers, owners, etc.), the routines of newsworkers themselves are perhaps more visible, and more open to scholarly access and attention. This routine structuring of the newsgathering task also gives us important clues about how the media have chosen to deploy their resources, telling us something about the rest of the media structure as well.

Organizational Level

At the organizational level we may consider the goals and policies of a larger social structure and how power is exercised within it. If the routines are the most immediate environment within which a journalist functions, the organizational level considers the imperatives that give rise to those routines and how individuals are obliged to relate to others within that larger formal structure. The major questions addressed at this level are suggested by an organizational chart, which maps the key roles and their occupants and how those roles are related to each other in formal lines of authority. The chart additionally suggests that the organization must have ways to enforce and legitimize the authority of its hierarchy and calls our attention to the organization's main goals (economic in relation to journalistic), how it is structured to pursue them, and how policy is enforced. Editorial policy, in particular, allows the organization to shape what stories are considered newsworthy, how they are prioritized, and how they are framed.

Newsroom studies often contain elements of both the routines and the organizational perspective, which are clearly related. This more macro level, however, reminds us that news is an organizational product, produced by increasingly complex economic entities, which seek ever more far-reaching relationships in their ownership patterns and connections to non-media industries. While journalists have long needed to be concerned with business considerations influencing their work, now these concerns may stretch far beyond their immediate organization. As news companies become part of large, global conglomerates, it is often difficult to anticipate the many conflicts of interest that may arise, and journalists find it difficult to avoid reporting that has a relationship to one or more aspects of their parent company's interests. Thus, this level has within it a number of layers that may need sorting out depending on the case: the news organization itself, the larger company to which it belongs, and the still more complex ownership network of firms (media and otherwise) that may subsume both.

The organizational level brings different challenges for analysis than the previous two levels. Organizational power is often not easily observed and functions in ways not directly indicated by the formal lines of authority describe in accessible documents. As Breed (1955) emphasizes in his classic observation of social control in the newsroom, power is not often overtly expressed over the news product because it would violate the objectivity notion, that news is something "out there" waiting to be discovered. Enforcing policy about what the news is to be would contradict this principle. At this level we are curious about how decisions are made, and how they get enforced. By definition, we are concerned with power that is exercised periodically, implicitly, and not overtly, and, as a result, is not so readily available to direct observation; indeed, a journalist anticipates organizational boundaries, the power of which is manifested in self-censorship by its members. Thus, journalists may accurately state that no one told them to suppress a story. This self-policing is more effective than direct censorship, however, because outsiders are often not even aware that anything has taken place. Thus, the analyst must be careful to fully understand the organizational structure and its control mechanisms in order to make an accurate assessment of how news is shaped.

Extra-Media Level

At the extra-media level we consider those influences originating primarily from outside the media organization. This perspective considers that the power to shape content is not the media's alone, but is shared with a variety of institutions in society, including the government, advertisers, public relations influential news sources, interest groups, and even other media organizations. This latter factor may be seen in the form of competitive market pressures. From a critical perspective, the extra-media level draws our attention to the way media are subordinated to elite interests in the larger system. While individual journalists may scrupulously avoid conflicts of interest that may bias their reporting, maintaining a professional distance from their subject, their employers may be intimately linked to larger corporate interests through interlocking boards of directors and other elite connections.

At this level, then, we assume that the media operate in structured relationships with other institutions that function to shape media content. We further assume that these relationships can be coercive but more often are voluntary and collusive. Normative concerns at this level are for press autonomy, assuming often that it is not desirable for the media to be so dependent on other social institutions. Conceptually, this level encompasses a wide variety of influences on the media, but we are particularly concerned with those systemic, patterned, and ongoing ways media are connected with their host society. Here we can see that the vantage point of the researcher makes an important difference. Observation from within the news organization may lead one to conclude (as does Gans [1979], for example) that news sources and associated public relations efforts exert great influence on the news agenda; a similar analysis from the vantage point of the public relations organization may suggest that most of their efforts do not have an immediate payoff. Judging the result depends on against whose professional standards (public relations or journalistic) they are being evaluated.

Ideological Level

Each of the preceding levels may be thought to subsume the one before, suggesting that the ultimate level should be an ideological perspective. The diverse approaches and schools of thought in media studies that may be deemed "ideological" make them difficult to summarize. Here we at least are concerned with how media symbolic content is connected with larger social interests, how meaning is constructed in the service of power. This necessarily leads us to consider how each of the previous levels functions in order to add up to a coherent ideological result. In that respect, a critical view would consider that the recruitment of journalists, their attitudes, the routines they follow, their organizations' policy, and those organizations' positions in the larger social structure work to support the *status quo,* narrow the range of social discourse, and serve to make the media agencies of social control.

Perhaps we need not take a critical view to examine the media as ideological institutions, but typically that is the case. Ideological analysis involves assumptions about power and how it is distributed in society. In the liberal pluralist tradition, this power is viewed as spread around such that a balance is maintained. If elites are favored, then those elites will circulate actively enough to minimize any concerns about concentrated power (e.g., Reese, 1991). A critical view is more likely to be concerned with how power is exerted by the natural workings of the media system, creating a process of hegemony which may be defined as the "systematic (but not necessarily or even usually deliberate) engineering of mass consent to the established order" (Gitlin, 1980, p. 253). At this level we ask how a system of meanings and common-sense understandings is made to appear natural through the structured relationship of the media to society. In a broader sense this level resembles the "culturological" approach outlined by Schudson (1989), which is concerned with the relations of ideas to symbols. The "cultural air" thus provides the larger environment that journalists and their institutions occupy. In this sense it may be seen to encompass more questions than are typically associated with the "ideological," especially the ideological viewed as a particular process within late capitalism.

Hierarchy of Influences and Professionalism

Having identified the five levels of this model, it may be helpful to return briefly to the concept of professionalism and consider some of the questions and issues raised by these different perspectives. Here the interesting questions may become definitional issues, as we ask what different functions are served by professionalism at each level? The hierarchical model also helps identify a variety of causal factors that may be more explicitly tied to professionalism and ultimately to the shape of professional work.

The idea of professionalism, for example, can be considered an individual-level value that journalists espouse, and an occupational calling to which they belong. Codes of ethics are ultimately guides to individual action for those who call themselves "professionals." Individuals value their profession to the extent it provides protection from unwarranted interference and a shared sense of socially desirable goals. Here we might ask, to what extent are expressions of professional roles meaningful to the individual and beneficial in helping resist other pressures?

Alternatively, to the extent that it embodies a set of procedures on how to report a story, professionalism may be viewed from a routines perspective. Tuchman's "strategic ritual" of news work shows that journalists are considered professional to the extent that they are following accepted practices, adhering to deadlines and getting the work done. To the extent that objectivity is a core professional value, she shows how it may be routinely satisfied by attributing opinion to sources, handling quotations correctly, and other basic practices (Tuchman, 1978). Following the procedures provides a defense against audience and peer critics.

Within the organization we can ask how professionalism is a negotiated set of values that must be worked out to satisfy the organization's needs. Commercial ownership and individual bias are both rendered less threatening to credibility by the invocation of professionalism in what Hallin (1992) called the fully rationalized "high modernism" of American journalism. As less overtly political U.S. journalists have self-selected into the profession, and as owners have become less partisan, and more corporate and managerial, the internal clashes over what professionalism properly requires have become less direct. Here we might ask questions like the following: What organizational changes have worked to value different professional norms? How is professionalism negotiated within an organization to facilitate both owner and journalistic needs? To what extent are organizational goals in harmony with the professional norms of individual journalists? How does the increasing complexity of media organizations affect the definition of "professionalism"?

Weaver and Wilhoit (1991) have proposed three major roles that may be said to characterize journalists: adversarial, interpretive, and disseminator. Many changes in these roles that they observe can be understood in relation to changes in the organizational setting. The disseminator role appears to be most on the rise and is most consistent with the current nature of corporate journalism. Finding that less importance is now given by journalists to analysis, challenging government authority and investigative reporting, is consistent with the greater emphasis given by mainstream news media to entertainment and celebrity journalism. Finding that journalists have given increasing value to getting information to the public quickly is not surprising given the neutral quality of that professional value. Speed is a feature of news that transcends any cultural setting and suits the global nature of newsgathering with its emphasis on speed and commonly accepted understandings of news, but the global newsroom has taken a professional step backward when speed is the ascendant value compared with more interpretive and adversarial functions.

The extra-media level reminds us that professionalism is worked out at many levels. The independence of the reporter may be offset by the close relationships of owners with other institutions, through elite networking, common board memberships, and so forth. As news organizations have increasingly been merged with other even non-media conglomerates, invoking some vision of professionalism works to protect their unique claim to societal protection. To some extent I have this level in mind when I consider how the media in general, in a way similar to other corporate sectors, have sought through their philanthropy, subsidies and other institutional ties to affect how universities define and pursue being "professional," namely, to better serve the needs of industry and the private sector (Reese, 1999). Here we might ask what aspects of professionalism are invoked by audience and interest groups to criticize the press. In addition, we must question whether these professional roles make sense in isolation, or whether journalists are always positioning themselves relative to specific other social institutions. Blumler and Gurevitch (1995), for example, discuss whether journalists adopt a "sacerdotal," or priestly, attitude toward government officials as opposed to a more pragmatic view. The former perspective would be more likely to accept the institution's right to speak for itself. From a critical ideological perspective, we may see that the professionalism of journalists often leads them to accept the conservative critique of their work, which blames their biases for the shortcomings of news coverage. While they may not appreciate being criticized, it would be professionally unacceptable for them to embrace their critics on the left who view them as subservient to the powers-that-be with little individual autonomy (e.g., Reese, 1990). Thus, the predictable ideological result is that more energy is spent responding to critics on the right than on the left, a process that Herman and Chomsky (1988) refer to as "flakking." At this level we may ask, for example, how tenets of professionalism are used to justify media ownership patterns?

Seeing how professionalism varies in meaning across levels alerts us to challenges in making comparisons across systems. As suggested earlier, the comparative perspective as applied to such journalistic issues encourages us to think across levels, and to consider the systemic context of our phenomena of interest. As Blumler et al. (1992, p. 8) note, comparative research

> creates a need to think structurally, to conceptualize in macro terms, to stretch vertically across levels and horizontally across systems . . . to adjust to the embeddedness of phenomena within a system to keep an eye out for the relevant principles of its organization.

Thus, the model described above helps in this process. I have already suggested that a comparative view calls us to not take our national context for granted, as a static and universal feature. It requires us to be especially clear about those things we are comparing and whether they mean the same thing in different contexts. Cross-national studies should carefully consider what routines and organizational differences, for example, the country contexts represent. Where possible, comparative cases can be chosen to show contrasts in some features (e.g., cultural, normative traditions) while holding others constant (e.g., media systems). Considered cross-nationally we may question in which setting a particular level is strongest: in which country, for example, are professional dictates more likely to override organizational business pressure? A levels-of-analysis approach also may draw our attention to relational differences. How do journalists relate to their employers in one setting compared with another? How do organizational routines differ in the ways that they relate to professional values? What seemingly different national press practices may serve the same function of maintaining professional autonomy for journalists?

Conclusion

My goal in this essay has been to pose some important questions for research questions on journalism and the professionals who practice it from a media sociology perspective. The hierarchy-of-influences framework is presented not as a complete theoretical explanation, but as a model that helps sort out the crucial concepts and identify connections that research questions may address. I have suggested a number of questions to show how these levels of analysis lead to pursuing different kinds of research. Of course, this conceptual work is in some ways the easy part, considering the time and resources required by large-scale empirical research. On the other hand, time and effort are well spent ensuring theoretical precision and avoiding effort wasted by prematurely jumping into the data-gathering process.

It is a positive development that so many scholars around the world are pursuing research on media professional questions. The great interest in the multi-country studies of journalist mentioned earlier suggests that we will see a continued rise in this style of research. The many opportunities available for cross-national research have the potential for providing important new insights into global journalism, particularly as U.S. and British media sociology is compared and tested against experience and evidence from other systems. This comparative approach should also valuably highlight the normative aspects of press performance, which are often implicitly embedded in research. Especially in the ethnocentrism of U.S. research there is a strong tendency to take such values for granted.

Few discussions of international news can avoid acknowledging the economics of transnational corporations, which have worked to concentrate increasing power in the hands of fewer and fewer organizations. The study of professional journalists cannot take place without recognizing these realities, and indeed an authentic professionalism (as opposed to one manufactured for the purpose of media image management) may be one of the most important counterweights to the economics of global newsgathering. The joining together of journalists in support of desirable democratic goals can be an important movement, worthy of our attention and monitoring. Ultimately, if we want to connect professional features to professional work, it will mean relating the "hierarchy of influences" factors to textual and content analysis. This may mean considering effects of various factors on the press agenda (its emphasis on various issues and features) as well as on how issues are "framed" (how social life is organized, visually and verbally) (Reese et al., 2001).

As we begin to link these individual and structural factors to media content, this examination of the work professionals produce will also be highly normative. We need better understandings of what may be taken to represent journalistic "quality" in these agendas and frames. We need to be concerned also with what is underreported or kept out of the news, in addition to the content that is available for us to measure. Finally, from a cross-national perspective, each country may be considered a different laboratory for press performance, as we evaluate the conditions that contribute to enhancing professional autonomy and good journalism. Clear definitions, questions and a systematic framework for comparative research will ensure that research in this area is cumulative and contributes to both better understanding and good social policy.

Note

1. I will immodestly refer to a number of my own works in this essay to illustrate some topics that have appealed to me in my own efforts to tackle these issues. Although my work has dealt with U.S. media and issues, I have been fortunate to have the opportunity to explore these questions in recent years with colleagues and students in a number of countries, including Finland, Germany, Hong Kong, Japan, Mexico, The Netherlands, and Spain. As I have taken on administrative positions within journalism education, I have thought particularly about professional issues, especially as they relate to higher education. I especially appreciate the opportunity to work with the faculty at the University of Navarra in Pamplona, Spain, where in the summer of 1999 I taught a doctoral seminar.

References

Blumler, Jay and Gurevitch, Michael (1995) *The Crisis of Public Communication,* London: Routledge.

Blumler, Jay, McLeod, Jack and Rosengren, Karl E. (1992) *Comparatively Speaking: Communication and Culture across Space and Time,* Newbury Park, CA: Sage.

Breed, Warren (1955) "Social control in the newsroom," *Social Forces* 33, 326–35.

Gans, Herbert (1979) *Deciding What's News,* New York: Random House.

Gitlin, Todd (1980) *Whole World Is Watching,* Berkeley: University of California Press.

Hallin, Daniel (1992) "The passing of the 'high modernism' of American journalism," *Journal of Communication,* 42(3), 14–25.

Hallin, Daniel and Mancini, Paolo (1994) "Speaking of the president: political structure and representational form in U.S. and Italian television news," in: Daniel Hallin (Ed.), *We Keep America on Top of the World,* London: Routledge, pp. 113–32.

Herman, Edward and Chomsky, Noam (1988) *Manufacturing Consent: The Political Economy of the Mass Media,* New York: Pantheon.

Johnstone, John W., Slawski, Edward J. and Bowman, William W. (1972) "The professional values of American newsmen," *Public Opinion Quarterly* 36, 522–40.

Kohn, Melvin (Ed.) (1989) *Cross-national Research in Sociology,* Newbury Park, CA: Sage.

Lichter, S. Robert, Rothman, Stanley and Lichter, Linda S. (1986) *The Media Elite,* Bethesda, MD: Adler.

McQuail, Denis (1992) *Media Performance: Mass Communication and the Public Interest,* Newbury Park, CA.: Sage.

Reese, Stephen and Buckalew, Bob (1995) "The militarism of local television: the routine framing of the Persian Gulf War," *Critical Studies in Mass Communication,* 12, pp. 40–59.

Reese, Stephen (1990) "The news paradigm and ideology of objectivity: a socialist at the Wall Street Journal," *Critical Studies in Mass Communication,* 7(4), pp. 390–409.

Reese, Stephen (1991) "Setting the media agenda: a power balance perspective," in: James Anderson (Ed.), *Communication Yearbook* 14, Beverly Hills: Sage, pp. 309–340.

Reese, Stephen (1999) "The progressive potential of journalism education: recasting the academic vs. professional debate," *Harvard International Journal of Press Politics,* 4(4), pp. 70–94.

Reese, Stephen and Cohen, Jeremy (2000) "Educating for journalism: the professionalism of scholarship," *Journalism Studies* 1(2), pp. 21 3–27.

Reese, Stephen, Gandy, Oscar and Grant, August (Eds.) (2001) *Framing Public Life,* Hillsdale, NJ: Erlbaum.

Rosten, Leo (1937) *Washington Correspondents,* New York: Harcourt Brace.

Schudson. Michael (1989) "The sociology of news production," in: *Media. Culture & Society.* London: Sage. pp. 263–82.

Shoemaker, Pamela and Reese, Stephen (1996) *Mediating the Message: Theories of Influences on Mass Media Content,* 2nd edn, White Plains, NY: Longman.

Sigal, Leon (1973) *Reporters and Officials: The Organization and Politics of Newsmaking,* Lexington, MA: DC Heath.

Splichal, Slavko and Sparks, Colin (1994) *Journalists for the 21st Century,* Norwood, NJ: Ablex.

Tuchman, Gaye (1978) *Making News: A Study in the Construction of Reality,* New York: Free Press.

Weaver, David (Ed.) (1998) *The Global Journalist: News People around the World,* Creskill, NJ: Hampton.

Weaver, David and Wilhoit, G. Cleveland (1991) *The American Journalist: A Portrait of U.S. News People and Their Work,* 2nd edn, Bloomington: Indiana University Press.

Source: From "Understanding the Global Journalist: A Hierarchy-of-Influences Approach," 2001, by S. D. Reese, *Journalism Studies, 2*(2), 173–187. Reprinted by permission of Taylor & Francis/Routledge.

2

What Is Journalism?

Professional Identity and Ideology of Journalists Reconsidered

Mark Deuze

Journalism is and has been theorized, researched, studied and criticized worldwide by people coming from a wide variety of disciplines. Indeed, research about journalism and among journalists has been established as a widely acknowledged field, particularly in the second half of the 20th century. Worldwide one can find universities, schools and colleges with dedicated departments, research and teaching programs in journalism. The field even has its own international and national journals. This suggests journalism as a discipline and an object of study is based on a consensual body of knowledge, a widely shared understanding of key theories and methods, and an international practice of teaching, learning and researching journalism. Alas, this is not the case. Several authors in various parts of the world have signaled a lack of coherence in the field of journalism (education and studies), and have sought to offer overviews into different conceptual approaches to theory and methodology—see for example Breen (1998) in Australia, Löffelholz (2000) in Germany and Austria, McNair (2003) in the United Kingdom, Schudson (2003) and Zelizer (2004b) in the United States, Deuze (2004b) in the Netherlands, and De Beer and Merrill (2004) internationally.

A lack of (international) consensus and disciplinary dialogue in journalism studies can be attributed to several factors. Journalism as an academic discipline is still very much under critical debate (Fedler et al., 1998). Throughout the history of journalism (education and studies), the field has had to balance between industry and university, each with its own institutionalized expectations and assumptions, leading observers to conclude: '[J]ournalism education [. . .] has ended up as neither fish nor fowl; it feels itself unloved by the industry and tolerated, barely, by the academy' (Raudsepp, 1989: 9). If one furthermore considers the variety of disciplines and paradigms deployed to understand journalism, another contentious factor emerges: the perceived clash of perspectives coming from scholars trained in the (critical) humanities, with those in the social sciences (Zelizer, 2000). Between and within these backgrounds there exists such a variety of approaches to journalism, that authors like Rühl (2000) in Germany or Schudson (2003) in the USA lament the 'folkloric' inconsistency of the field as well as the impossibility to generate a more or less consensual body of knowledge out of the existing literature. It is therefore safe to say that many scholars, educators and students all over the world are involved in journalism studies and education, but only rarely do their approaches, understandings or philosophies meet.[2]

In this article I explore the concept of journalism as an occupational ideology as a possible meeting point for journalism studies and education, operationalizing it to analyze how emerging sociocultural and socioeconomic issues stand to transform ways of thinking about and doing journalism. Although the ideology of journalism is an approach widely used in the literature, only rarely has it been adequately defined and operationalized to fit immediate concerns in a pragmatic way. As pressing contemporary case studies in point I investigate how new media and multiculturalism (which I understand to be two key social issues recognized in media industries across the globe at the start of the 21st century) interface with contemporary journalisms. I argue that this approach is inspiring because it helps us to look beyond infrastructures (as in computer hardware and software) or representationalism (as in the number of minority journalists in a newsroom) when assessing what journalism as a profession is (or can be) in a context of fast-changing technology and society.

In choosing new media and multiculturalism as conceptual case studies I temporarily turn a blind eye towards other areas of change and challenge for journalism that warrant critical inquiry; one could think of economic issues (corporate colonization of the newsroom, media concentration), and political issues (localization and globalization, press freedom, media law). This article does not aim to establish a hierarchy of pressing issues, after all. While acknowledging the selectivity of my approach, I argue that multimedia and multiculturalism can be considered valid developments of how the ideology of journalism takes shape and is shaped by internationally acknowledged relevant issues of the day.[3]

Journalism as Ideology

The 20th-century history of (the professionalization of) journalism can be typified by the consolidation of a consensual occupational ideology among journalists in different parts of the world. Conceptualizing journalism as an ideology (rather than, for example, other options offered in the literature such as a profession, an industry, a literary genre, a culture or a complex social system) primarily means understanding journalism in terms of how journalists give meaning to their newswork. Although most scholarly work on journalism is reduced to studies of institutional news journalism, research on other more feminine or so-called 'alternative' journalisms suggests journalists across genres and media types invoke more or less the same ideal-typical value system when discussing and reflecting on their work (Van Zoonen, 1998).[4]

In decades of journalism studies, scholars refer to the journalists' professionalization process as a distinctly ideological development, as the emerging ideology served to continuously refine and reproduce a consensus about who was a 'real' journalist, and what (parts of) news media at any time would be considered examples of 'real' journalism. These evaluations shift subtly over time; yet always serve to maintain the dominant sense of what is (and should be) journalism. Schlesinger (1978) for example writes about 'newsmen's occupational ideology', Golding and Elliott (1979) speak broadly of 'journalism's occupational ideology', while a decade later Soloski (1990) talks about an 'ideology of professionalism', and Zelizer (2004a) mentions 'journalists' professional ideology'; yet most of these authors do not make explicit what this ideology consists of, other than claiming it contains 'self-contradictory oppositional values' (Reese, 1990). Schudson describes the occupational ideology of journalism as 'cultural knowledge that constitutes 'news judgment', rooted deeply in the communicators' consciousness (2001: 153). Elliott (1988) and McMane (1993: 215) locate journalism's ideology in a 'class spirit,' whereas Zelizer (2004a: 101) refers to the 'collective knowledge' journalists employ. This understanding also trickles down to the way journalism is taught, as Brennen (2000: 106) concludes in her study of U.S. journalism textbooks published in the 1980s and 1990s: '[a]ll of them address the practice of journalism from an identical ideological perspective that neglects to consider all the changes in journalism that have occurred over time.'

In the particular context of journalism as a profession, ideology can be seen as a system of beliefs characteristic of a particular group, including—but not limited to—the general process of the production of meanings and ideas (within that group). This kind of thinking about journalists and journalism builds on an international tradition of journalism research, surveys among and interviews with journalists (Weaver, 1998). Comparing 21 countries, Weaver found support for claims that the characteristics of journalists are largely similar worldwide (1998: 456). A cross-national comparison of findings from surveys among journalists in different and more or less similar countries yields results that to some extent suggest similar processes of professionalization as expressed through the measured characteristics of media practitioner populations (Weischenberg and Scholl, 1998). Weaver however concludes there is too much disagreement on professional norms and values to claim an emergence of 'universal occupational standards' in journalism (1998: 468). Other scholars have addressed this variety of views on how important certain universal standards are in terms of what their meanings can be in (country-)specific circumstances and different cultural contexts (Donsbach and Klett, 1993; Deuze, 2002a). What these overall findings and conclusions suggest is that journalists in elective democracies share similar characteristics and speak of similar values in the context of their daily work, but apply these in a variety of ways to give meaning to what they do. Journalists in all media types, genres and formats carry the ideology of journalism. It is therefore possible to speak of a dominant occupational ideology of journalism on which most newsworkers base their professional perceptions and praxis, but which is interpreted, used and applied differently among journalists across media (Shoemaker and Reese, 1996: 11).

Ideology is seen here as an (intellectual) process over time, through which the sum of ideas and views—notably on social and political issues—of a particular group is shaped, but also as a process by which other ideas and views are excluded or marginalized (Stevenson, 1995: 37–41; Van Ginneken, 1997: 73). Although the notion of a 'dominant' ideology (or 'dominant discourses' through which the ideology is perpetuated as suggested by Dahlgren, 1992: 9) denotes a worldview of the powerful, the term is chosen here not in terms of a struggle, but as a collection of values, strategies and formal codes characterizing professional journalism and shared most widely by its members. This ideology is generally referred to as a dominant way in which news people validate and give meaning to their work.[5] Journalism's ideology has, for example, been analyzed as a 'strategic ritual' to position oneself in the profession vis-a-vis media critics and publics (Tuchman, 1971). Ideology has also been identified as an instrument in the hands of journalists and editors to naturalize the structure of the news organization or media corporation one works for (Soloski, 1990). Especially when faced with public criticism, journalists apply ideological values to legitimate or self-police the recurring self-similar selection and description of events and views in their media (Molotch and Lester, 1974; Golding and Elliott, 1979; Hall, 1982; Hallin, 1986; Reese, 1990; Zelizer, 1993; Bennett, 2001). This criticism also comes from within the profession, as, for example, supporters of the public journalism movement blame this ideological way of thinking for the news media's inability to engage citizens (Merritt, 1995; Rosen, 1999).

In short, there seems to be a consensus among scholars in the field of journalism studies that what typifies more or less universal similarities in journalism can be defined as a shared occupational ideology among news-workers which functions to self-legitimize their position in society. Even though scholars are comfortable to refer to journalism as an occupational ideology, the distinct building blocks of such an ideology are sometimes left to the imagination of the reader. Indeed, some scholars tend not to venture much further than an acknowledgment that there exists a professional ideology and that it is not a 'set of things' but an active practice and that it is continually negotiated (Reese, 1990). In the context of this article the core characteristics of this ideology have been identified, as these can be located in the concept and historical development of journalism professionalism (Soloski, 1990: 208).

Hallin (1992) sees the ongoing professionalization process and the corresponding development of a shared occupational ideology as a period of 'high modernism' in journalism. Hallin in particular mentions the sense of wholeness and seamlessness in the practitioner's vision of professional journalism in this period (roughly between the 1960s and 1990s). Indeed, research by Russo (1998) suggests that journalists identify themselves more easily with the profession of journalism than for example with the medium or media company that employs them. Key characteristics of this professional self-definition can be summarized as a number of discursively constructed ideal-typical values. Journalists feel that these values give legitimacy and credibility to what they do. The concepts, values and elements said to be part of journalisms' ideology in the available literature can be categorized into five ideal-typical traits or values.[6] Colleagues like Golding and Elliott (1979), Merritt (1995), and more recently Kovach and Rosenstiel (2001) describe these as

- Public service: journalists provide a public service (as watchdogs or 'newshounds', active collectors and disseminators of information);
- Objectivity: journalists are impartial, neutral, objective, fair and (thus) credible;
- Autonomy: journalists must be autonomous, free and independent in their work;
- Immediacy: journalists have a sense of immediacy, actuality and speed (inherent in the concept of 'news');
- Ethics: journalists have a sense of ethics, validity and legitimacy.

Reese (2001) suggests the ideological perspective can be seen as a global factor of influence on journalistic decision-making processes, enabling us to analyze how media symbolic content is connected with larger social interests, and how meaning is constructed in the service of power. Power in the context of an occupational ideology must be understood as the power to define what ('real') journalism is, enacted for example through access to mainstream debates about journalistic quality.

One has to note that these values can be attributed to other professions or social systems in society as well, and that these values—as I will show hereafter—are sometimes inevitably inconsistent or contradictory. To journalists this generally does not seem to be a problem, as they integrate such values into their debates and evaluations of the character and quality of journalism. In doing so, journalism continuously reinvents itself—regularly revisiting similar debates (for example on commercialization, bureaucratization, 'new' media technologies, seeking audiences, concentration of ownership) where ideological values can be deployed to sustain operational closure, keeping outside forces at bay. I move on by briefly operationalizing the five ideal-typical values of journalism's ideology.

Journalists Provide a Public Service

The public-service ideal can be seen as a powerful component of journalism's ideology. It is an ideal that journalists aspire to, and use to legitimize aggressive (Clayman, 2002) or increasingly interpretive (Patterson, 1997) styles of reporting. Journalists share a sense of 'doing it for the public', of working as some kind of representative watchdog of the status quo in the name of people, who 'vote with their wallets' for their services (by buying a newspaper, watching or listening to a newscast, visiting and returning to a news site). One may find evidence of such a value by specifically examining journalists' images of their audience, and by looking at their views on what they do and how their work may affect (intended) publics—as citizens or consumers. The expanding body of literature on the public journalism movement has actualized this value, serving to rethink journalism's role in society by invoking old or new notions of the public service ideal through 'people's journalism' (Merrill et al., 2001). Woodstock (2000) and Schudson (1999) indicate that practices of public journalists tend to reinforce the dominant position of news media in communities while at the same time endorsing a more responsive attitude towards publics, indeed showing how an age-old ideological value can serve to maintain the status quo in journalism while its practitioners adapt to a changing media culture.

Journalists Are Neutral, Objective, Fair and (thus) Credible

American authors in particular have identified objectivity as a key element of the professional self-perception of journalists (see Schudson, 1978 and 2001; Reese, 1990; Ognianova and Endersby, 1996; Mindich, 1998). Although objectivity has a problematic status in current thinking about the impossibility of value-neutrality, academics and journalists alike revisit this value through synonymous concepts like 'fairness', 'professional distance', 'detachment' or 'impartiality' to define and (re-)legitimize what media practitioners do. Objectivity may not be possible but that does not mean one should not strive for it, or redefine it in such a way that it in fact becomes possible, as Ryan (2001) argues. Other voices lament this kind of detachment as an overriding reflex of journalism that makes its professionals immune to any kind of comment or critique, and therefore failing in journalism's task of promoting democratic deliberation (paraphrasing Merritt, 1995: 127–30). Feminist media scholars argue, however, that subjectivity does not contradict objectivity as both values can be considered as constitutive elements of a professional identity of journalists (Van Zoonen, 1998). The point is that the embrace, rejection as well as critical reappraisal of objectivity all help to keep it alive as an ideological cornerstone of journalism.

Journalists Must Enjoy Editorial Autonomy, Freedom and Independence

Reporters across the globe feel that their work can only thrive and flourish in a society that protects its media from censorship; in a company that saves its journalists from the marketers; in a newsroom where journalists are not merely the lackeys of their editors; and at a desk where a journalist is adequately supported through, for example, further training and education (Weaver, 1998). Any kind of development from perceived extra-journalistic forces—be it public criticism, marketing or corporate ownership—tends to get filtered through this overriding concern to be autonomous to tell the stories you want to. Research by McDevitt et al. (2002) suggests that this notion of autonomy as a building block of journalists' professional identity serves as a way to preclude attempts by individual news people to be more interactive and supportive of community engagement in their work. Most if not all innovations in journalism tend to be met by doubts regarding their perceived impact on editorial autonomy (see for example Singer, 2004 and Boczkowski, 2004 on journalists and newsroom convergence). This elevates editorial independence to the status of an ideological value in that it functions to legitimize resistance to (as well as enabling piecemeal adaptation of) change.[7]

Journalists Have a Sense of Immediacy

According to journalists, their work is reporting the news. This lends the work of journalists an aura of instantaneity and immediatism, as 'news' stresses the novelty of information as its defining principle. The work of journalists therefore involves notions of speed, fast decision-making, hastiness, and working in accelerated real-time. Stephens (1988), Nerone and Barnhurst (2003) and Lule (2001) note that from its earliest days journalism has relied on certain forms, archetypes, themes and routines enabling its practitioners to manage an ever-increasing volume of information within the confounds of continuous deadlines. Working under time pressure is acknowledged in surveys among journalists in the USA and elsewhere, as respondents are specifically asked how important it is to them to deliver the news 'as quickly as possible' (Weaver and Wilhoit, 1996: 263). The scholarly literature has rekindled this notion of speed regarding emerging journalistic practices and genres on the Internet, signaling the implications this medium has as it propels journalists to work in a so-called 'non-stop' 24/7-digital environment (Pavlik, 1999; Hall, 2001). When experienced through the eyes of journalists, speed can be seen as both an essentialized value and a problematized side effect of newswork.

Journalists Have a Sense of Ethics and Legitimacy

Parallel to the history of 20th century professionalization of journalism runs the history of professional codes of ethics—especially since the adoption of the Code of Bordeaux by the International Federation of Journalists in 1956 (Nordenstreng and Topuz, 1989). Although journalists worldwide disagree on whether a code of ethical conduct should be in place or not, they do share a sense of being ethical—which in turn legitimizes journalists' claims to the position as (free and fair) watchdogs of society. A comparison of ethics codes in a number of European and Middle Eastern countries shows that even though political and social systems in these countries may vary considerably, ethical guidelines reflect a broad intercultural consensus on certain key elements such as a commitment to truth and objectivity (Hafez, 2002). Ryan (2001) even goes as far as to claim ethics as the all-encompassing value in journalism. In doing so, these academics confuse the function of ethical behavior as a legitimizing value with its concrete meaning or interpretation in a given situation or setting.

Hallin referred to the period of the 1930s to the late 1960s when describing high modernism in the professionalization process of journalism. Ever since, he argued, 'all of this was beginning to change [. . .] substantially' (1992: 18). Hallin (1996) suggests the collapse of political consensus and the increased commercialization of news were prime movers of these changes. In recent years, these trends can be seen as accelerated by the widespread proliferation of new media technologies and the twin forces of globalization and localization, uprooting or outsourcing peoples, ideas and industries across the globe (Bauman, 2000). The high modernism of journalistic professionalization has moved to a liquid modern state of affairs of feverish journalistic differentiation across media genres (including popular, tabloid, and infotainment journalisms), platforms, and industries. The hotly debated emergence of multimedia newsrooms (Stone and Bierhoff, 2002; Deuze, 2004a) or pro-active diversity awareness policies (Campbell, 1998; Bealor Hines, 2001; Rich, 2005: 336ff) in media organizations can be seen as good examples of changes and challenges in journalistic praxis at the beginning of the 21st century. My argument is based on the assumption that the global picture of journalism is constantly and perhaps exponentially changing to such an extent that one has to analyze and discuss the main attributes of such (potential) changes in order to successfully study, describe and explain contemporary journalism. These changes are here selectively operationalized as coming to terms with the convergence of media technologies (multimedia) and sociocultural complexity (multiculturalism).

Journalism and Technology: Multimedia

Parallel to the professionalization process of journalism in the 20th century runs a history of ongoing computerization and digitalization in all sectors of society (Lievrouw and Livingstone, 2002). Distributed technologies, such as the Internet and the proliferation of computer networks, inspired training programs all over the world to develop courses, curricula or even entire institutes devoted particularly to teach and study journalism in a 'new media' environment. The literature on the impact of converging technologies on the practice and education of journalists is expanding rapidly. Digital media and, more recently, multimedia newsrooms are transforming training and education of journalism worldwide (Castaneda, 2003). The disparity of approaches and models of teaching and researching multimedia reveal one thing at least: multimedia means different things to different people (Boczkowski, 2004). Wise (2000) claims digital media, new media, information and communications technologies, Internet, interactivity, virtuality and cyberspace are all used interchangeably with multimedia. The convergence process that characterizes multimedia poses challenges to departmentalized news organizations, and is generally considered to threaten a news culture that prefers individual expert systems and 'group think' over teamwork and knowledge-sharing (Singer, 2004). Professional experience and the literature suggest that new media technologies challenge one of the most fundamental 'truths' in journalism, namely, the professional journalist is the one who determines what publics see, hear and read about the world (Fulton, 1996; Singer, 1998). The combination of mastering newsgathering and storytelling techniques in all media formats (so-called 'multi-skilling'), as well as the integration of digital network technologies coupled with a rethinking of the news producer-consumer relationship tends to be seen as one of the biggest challenges facing journalism studies and education in the 21st century (Bardoel and Deuze, 2001; Pavlik et al., 2001; Teoh Kheng Yau and Al-Hawamdeh, 2001).

Discussing the emergence of 'cyberjournalism' in the early 1990s, Dahlgren (1996) suggests we look at its online media logic as the particular institutionally structured features of a medium, the ensemble of technical and organizational attributes which impact on what gets represented in the medium and how it gets done, including the cultural competences of the producers and consumers of that medium. Seen in this light, one would have to consider the elements defining multimedia logic (Deuze, 2004a). The institutionally structured features of multimedia would assume some kind of cross-media ownership, participation or access to multiple platforms for storytelling. This convergence of communication modalities leads to an integration and possible specialization of information services, where the existing unity of production, content and distribution within each separate medium will cease to exist (Bardoel, 1996). The multimedia journalist has to make decisions about what kind of platforms to utilize when practicing his or her craft, and in the case of multimedia productions has to be able to oversee story 'packages' rather than repurposing single stories in multiple formats. This relates to organizational features of convergent media and the competences of journalists working in such new media contexts. Applied research suggests the necessity for multimedia operations to organize people in teams, and to arrange these working units in cross-departmentalized ways (Huang et al., 2003). This advice is underscored by the experiences of multimedia newsrooms such as *Tampa Bay Online* (TBO.com) in the U.S. where the convergence process met with the resistance of reporters, who did not want to give up their established way of doing things, and in particular refused to work in synergy with colleagues in other parts of the media organization (Stevens, 2002). Similar accounts can be found in case studies elsewhere as well, as a recent report on the state of European multimedia news shows in detail (Stone and Bierhoff, 2002). Research among reporters in various converging newsrooms in the

U.S. by Singer (2004) and Boczkowski (2004) shows similar experiences, citing turf wars and a general reluctance of journalists to innovate, share knowledge, embrace the new technology—even though those that do reportedly think they are better for it. A survey by multimedia consulting firm Innovation—commissioned by the World Association of Newspapers and conducted in 2001 among media executives worldwide—cited as the biggest obstacle to media convergence 'the individualistic nature of journalists' (mentioned by 31% of all respondents). On the basis of these studies and considerations one may argue that the shift from individualistic, 'top-down' mono-media journalism to team-based, 'participatory' multimedia journalism creates particular tensions in the industry and among journalists, and potentially challenges the ideal-typical values in journalism's ideology (Bowman and Willis, 2003).

Journalism and Society: Multiculturalism

Recognition of cultural diversity is generally seen as a function of multiculturalism, even though the normative implications for thinking about societies consisting of a plurality of cultures vary in different parts of the world (Parekh, 1997). Whether it functions as a celebration of migrant communities and thus challenges journalism in a particular country to become more international in its outlook, or whether it operates as an acknowledgment of the rural in an otherwise rather urban program of journalism, multiculturalism impacts upon all levels of editorial decision-making processes—and particularly challenges a notion of journalism as if it could or would operate outside society (Cottle, 2000). Multiculturalism can therefore be seen as one of the foremost issues in journalism where media professionals are confronted by their real or perceived responsibilities in contemporary society. This consideration is independent of whether such a society is seen as a melting pot of supposedly inherently different cultures, or as a society where culture is understood as actively and continuously negotiated over time (Baumann, 1999: 81ff). The multicultural society indeed shifts the focus and news values of today's media professionals:

> [o]rientation points for journalists are now the multicultural society, in which the position of minorities will have to be redefined. Race, language, ethnic background, religion, all these factors are present and potential battlegrounds and generate a constant stream of events. (Bierhoff, 1999)

In many Western democracies, such as Australia, the USA, Great Britain and the Netherlands, several organizations, universities, scholars and media groups have put discussions on the role of the media in a multicultural society on top of the professional agenda in the last decade or so (see, for example, Jakubowicz et al. 1994; Cottle, 2000). Discussions are framed according to specific contexts and histories of the countries involved. In the Netherlands and Great Britain, for example, multiculturalism is related to discussions of the different histories of slave trade and colonialism as well as to preoccupations with Eurocentrism and nationalism or regionalism in the context of the European Union. Multiculturalism therefore assumes a variety of forms and meanings. Issues regarding the relevance of media and multiculturalism to journalism can be framed in terms of three central issues: knowledge of journalists about different cultures and ethnicities, issues of representation (pluriformity or diversity), and perceived social responsibilities of journalists in a democratic and multicultural society.

Knowledge can be seen as a resource of information, sources, experiences and contacts journalist may (or may not) have regarding different and overlapping cultures. A core aspect of professional knowledge is sourcing: who are included or excluded as news actors in the media. Knowledge also relates to a journalist's awareness of different modes of intercultural communication when working in a culturally diverse society. Knowledge in the context of the impact it may have on journalism can therefore be seen as an inventory and discussion of one's frames of reference, one's resources of information and life experiences when it comes to multicultural issues.

It can be argued in the context of the media that resources of information and experience (cf. knowledge), interpretation and explanation (cf. responsibilities of journalists), and social delegation are in fact all questions of representation. In an educational course or curriculum in journalism, issues of representation can be isolated to the ways in which journalists reflect ethnic and cultural diversity in terms of the labor force, the construction of their networks, and in the portrayal of minorities in still and moving images, spoken and written word. This may oversimplify the complex nature of representation, as it has different meanings in various disciplines such as art (cf. ways to depict and portray), or politics (cf. representing constituencies). However, in journalism studies, this has been an effective way to address the issue as in, for example, the multicultural hiring practices of news media organizations (see Becker et al., 1999; Ouaj, 1999), and content analyses of the way news media write about or depict minorities (see for example Van Dijk, 1991; Entman and Rojecki, 2000).

The social responsibilities of news media have been well documented and established as the public service doctrine in contemporary journalism. Costera Meijer (2001: 13) summarizes this responsibility as 'informing citizens in a way that enables them to act as citizens'. As modern democracies have developed in the context of increased globalization and corresponding migration and the emergence of diasporic communities, the notion of cultural or multicultural citizenship has become a central consideration in today's social-political formation of society (Kymlicka, 1995). One may therefore expect today's journalism to develop equivalent cultural or multicultural sensibilities. This in turn problematizes journalists' role perceptions in contemporary society: an active awareness of multicultural sensibility contradicts a cherished independence of special interests. A valued detachment of society, however, may result in disconnections with certain publics and oversimplified representations of social complexity. Multiculturalism is a felt responsibility among media professionals everywhere—whether they like it or are opposed to it—and thus forces them to face their ideology and rethink their value system.

Discussion

If news organizations opt for convergence or are striving to be more inclusive they also invite changes beyond hiring a couple of 'backpack' journalists or 'non-white' reporters. As shown in the admittedly brief discussions of the impact multimedia and multiculturalism have on the attributes, organization, culture and practices of journalists, there is more to these developments than issues of technology and representation alone. Such changes have also to do with editorial organization patterns, and challenges to established journalistic ways, norms and values of storytelling. Living up to the characteristics and potential added value of multimedia and multiculturalism challenges perceptions of the roles and functions of journalism as a whole.

Although an expanding body of scholarly work addresses technological and cultural issues regarding journalism, few authors combine such insights and research into a broader framework of thinking about journalism and media production processes as a whole. The literature on media and multiculturalism generally assumes more civic engagement or involvement by journalists and media organizations, seeking a reconnection of (predominantly white, both in terms of news coverage and news people) media with society (see Cottle, 2000; Wilson and Gutierrez, 2003). Similarly, work on new media and journalism signals increased interactivity and a further blurring of the hierarchical relationships between producers and users of news as the main characteristics of the changes digitalization and convergence bring to conceptualizing journalism (Löffelholz, 2000; Hall, 2001; Pavlik, 2001).

What sets the sketched developments in society and technology apart in their impact upon contemporary journalism are related issues of control and transparency. Control, as in initiatives to remove primacy of authority over the news agenda or even the storytelling experience from the hands of (professional) journalists in favor of more responsive, interactive and inclusive journalistic practices. Transparency, as in the increasing ways in which people both inside and external to journalism are given a chance to monitor, check, criticize and even intervene in the journalistic process. One element enables and follows the other, of course: more shared control over newsgathering and storytelling increases opportunities for surveillance and processual criticism. The point here is that a rethinking of journalism and the professional identity of journalists is necessary not so much because there is something wrong with the profession, but rather because it is essential in order to maintain a conceptually coherent understanding of what journalism is in an increasingly complex and liquid modern society (Bauman, 2001). It is my contention that ideology in this process of change and adaptation serves as the social cement of the professional group of journalists—following Carey (1989) and Zelizer (2004a: 101) where she writes how journalists use it 'to become members of the group and maintain membership over time'. In the concluding section of this article I therefore explore how multiculturalism and multimedia potentially challenge historically embedded views in journalism.

Public Service

Providing a service to publics in a multimedia and multicultural environment is not the same safe value to hide behind like it used to be in the days of print and broadcast mass media. After all this is the age of individualization, audience fragmentation and attention spans ranging from minutes while watching to seconds while surfing. Some early consequences for newswork have been documented. For instance, the practice of multimedia journalism presupposes teamwork and sharing expertise to produce story packages that can be delivered across media, including (but not limited to) interactive components (Deuze, 2004a). Multicultural journalism suggests actively seeking out new angles and voices from undercovered communities, engaging actively in public life among diverse peoples—whether some authors like it (Wilson, Gutierrez and Chao, 2003) or not (McGowan, 2001). A slow and subtle shift occurs in the consensual notion of serving the public, as it moves from a primary top-down meaning to an increasingly bottom-up application. It is a move from 'telling people what they need to know' to Carey's (1989 [1975]) ideal of amplifying conversations society has with itself. In this context the public journalism movement can be understood as a way to bridge the gap between these oppositional expectations of reporters and editors: it maintains its primacy on storytelling while cautiously embracing the wants and needs of an audience.

Objectivity

The strategic ritual of 'objective' detachment has been described in much of the (critical) literature as one of the causes for the divide between journalism and its publics (Schudson, 2001). Interestingly, studies in new media newsrooms as well as on multicultural reporting offer an alternate interpretation of objectivity. The discourse of professional distance clearly stands in stark contrast to the rhetoric of inclusivity (regarding diverse media and minorities). A multicultural sensitivity challenges objectivity as it is commonly understood, and supposedly offers a way out of the binary paradigm of 'getting both sides of the story' in favor of a more complex or multiperspectival reading of events. Multimedia's careful embrace of interactivity as well as a merging of different cultures (print, broadcast, online; 'hard' and 'soft' news, marketing and editorial) within the news organization—a perceived necessary byproduct of convergence—confronts the individual professional with multiple interpretations of objectivity. It is therefore not surprising that journalists' main response to such changes and challenges is nostalgia (and stress). Yet at the same time reporters involved in the frontlines claim to have gained a new appreciation of different ways to do things, reaching out to different communities (and colleagues), enacting their agency in the process of change. In other words, an active awareness of (the potential added value of) new media technologies and cultural plurality makes the core value of objectivity more complex.

Autonomy

Journalists all over the world voice concerns regarding their freedom to work as they please. Editorial autonomy is invoked in the face of any extra-journalistic or management-driven force. In an increasing transparent and sometimes even participatory news ecology, 'autonomy' as an individual-level concept is quite problematic. Working in multimedia news teams, journalists have to at least learn to share autonomy. Engaging people with ethnicities, religious beliefs or nationalities assumed to be different than one's own challenges the age-old ways of doing things in many newsrooms where only peers tend to be seen as legitimate sparring partners for creating credible newswork. The literature addressing multiculturalism calls for more community-based reporting, signals the need for journalists to become much more aware of entrenched inequalities in society, and expects media professionals to become active agents in reversing these (Cottle, 2000). Journalistic autonomy in this context is collaborative (with colleagues and publics) in its implications, and thus begets a distinctly different understanding.

Immediacy

The 'right here, right now' credo of journalism is challenged by normative claims made by advocates of both multicultural and multimedia journalism: these styles of reporting apparently bring more depth to journalistic storytelling by packaging news and information across media and throughout diverse communities. As mentioned before, this potential of multi-perspective news narratives adds more complexity to journalistic storytelling. According to some critics, investing time to get to know different communities (networking without necessarily pursuing a news story), or cross-platform storytelling (without the depth provided by specialization in a single medium) is a luxury not available when practicing, studying or researching journalism (Campbell, 1998; Castaneda, 2003). The question becomes, what kind of immediacy are we talking about. The digital media environment allows reporters to constantly edit and update their story packages, and even to include end-users in this process (for example by offering options for feedback, postings to discussion platforms, uploading files). On the other hand, studies of organizational journalistic cultures suggest that it is exactly the predisposition to fast work according to set ways of doing things (like the day-to-day deadline schedule of programming and printing) that effectively prevents journalism from becoming more open to diversity—both in terms of newsroom diversity (including and accommodating different voices like younger, female, disabled, and ethnic minority colleagues), and sourcing (allowing different languages, grass-roots spokesperson, seeking alternate interpretations) (Cottle, 2000). In short, immediacy in a multimedia and multicultural environment entails the sense of speed inherent in the 24/7 deadline structure of online publishing to a potential worldwide audience. Yet it also means exactly the opposite in that it offers depth, inclusiveness and more than two polarized perspectives.

Ethics

Of all these values, a sense of ethics is probably the most researched—even though scholars like Starck (2001) criticize the expanding volume of journalism ethics research, in particular for its lack of cross-cultural perspectives, and lament the apparent gap between theory and practice in the field. Ethics, however situational, based on casuistry, or principled, can and have been used by journalists and scholars alike to claim higher moral ground when judging the quality of reporting (Iggers, 1999; Ryan, 2001: 18). Indeed, scholars and media professionals in both fields tend to advocate a turn to ideal journalistic values that supposedly supersede medium-specific particularities or cultural complexities. It is important to note how ethics can be both a flag behind which to rally the journalistic troops in defense of commercial, audience-driven or managerial encroachments, as well as an emblem of newsworkers' legitimacy when reporting on complex events involving the wants and needs of different media, different people and different ways to be inclusive.

Conclusion

The argument as outlined in this article builds on similar arguments in the contemporary literature in favor of a 'catholic' (Sparks, 1992), or 'comprehensive' (Morgan, 1998) and 'holistic' (Skinner et al., 2001) understanding of journalism. I deliberately ignored real or perceived differences between mainstream and alternative news media, between serious and popular journalism or between hard and soft news. For one, the cultural inquiry of journalism suggests such distinctions to be part of journalists' 'modernist bias of its official self-presentation' (Zelizer, 2004a: 112). On the other hand, if one chooses to accept for a moment that this representation is very real to a lot of journalists across the globe, I would perceive these and other binary oppositions increasingly untenable in our liquid modern news times. The analyses of the ideal-typical values of journalism, and how these vary and get meanings in different circumstances, have shown that any definition of journalism as a profession working truthfully, operating as a watchdog for the good of society as a whole and enabling citizens to be self-governing is not only naïve, but also one-dimensional and sometimes nostalgic for perhaps the wrong reasons. It is by studying how journalists from all walks of their professional life negotiate the core values that one can see the occupational ideology of journalism at work.

In this article I hope to have shown how revisiting an 'old' concept can provide added value to a more comprehensive theorizing of what journalism is, or could be. The key to this attempt has been to make explicit what the literature too often takes for granted—as in the operationalization of the values that journalism's ideology consists of—and to update this in terms of the immediate. The significance of this contribution also lies in its rejection of utopian or anti-utopian discourses when analyzing the impact of emerging sociocultural and socioeconomic issues on journalism. Instead I have pushed for a more holistic argument based on the assumption that multimedia developments and multiculturalism are indeed similar forces of change when seen through the lens of journalists' perceptions of themselves. Ultimately this combination of insights may prove helpful both to the education and practice as well as the academic discipline of journalism.

Notes

1. Key international journals: *Journalism Quarterly, Journalism: Theory, Practice and Criticism, Journalism Studies.* Some examples of national journals devoted to journalism: *Australian Journalism Review, British Journalism Review, Ecquid Novi* (South Africa), *Brazilian Journalism Research.*

2. A similar conclusion formed the basis of the Journalism Studies Interest Group (JSIG), started in Summer 2004 as part of the International Communication Association. The JSIG manifesto for example states: 'The Interest Group is intended to facilitate empirical research and to bring more coherence to research paradigms, and in so doing, to further support the professionalization of journalism studies and journalism education. Furthermore, while journalism is presently studied across the field, often the individuals behind these different research endeavors do not have a place to speak with each other'.

3. See Hall (2001) and Pavlik (2001) for an international appreciation of new media and journalism; Cottle (2000) is a similar global overview regarding news media and multiculturalism.

4. I refer to two case studies I did that show how 'alternative' reporters for Indymedia websites (Platon and Deuze, 2003) as well as journalists working for Dutch tabloids (Deuze, 2002b: 156ff) indeed use the same values in their work as mainstream 'hard' news journalists. For a similar argument see Eliasoph (1988).

5. For a classic reference in this respect see the work of Herbert Gans (1979: 183). Carey (1989 [1975]: 47–8) suggests—following the work of Clifford Geertz—that ideology should be seen as providing answers to the invariably contradictory and inconsistent situations one finds oneself in as an individual between the 'chronic malintegration' of the personality and society. This interpretation of ideology—called strain theory—seems to be most fruitful for the argument at hand.

6. I argue that these values can indeed be seen as ideal-typical in the Weberian sense, in that they involve an accentuation of (arche-)typical courses of conduct for the professional group of journalists—one might say serving as a yardstick or measuring rod to ascertain similarities as well as deviations in concrete cases—and thus contributing to the exclusory potential of ideology—without necessarily being 'real'.

7. Indeed this function goes for all ideal-typical values in the ideology of journalism.

References

Bardoel, J. (1996) 'Beyond Journalism: A Profession between Information Society and Civil Society', *European Journal of Communication* 11(3): 283–302.

Bardoel, J. and M. Deuze (2001) '"Network Journalism": Converging Competencies of Old and New Media Professionals', *Australian Journalism Review* 23(2): 91–103.

Bauman, Z. (2000) *Liquid Modernity.* Cambridge: Polity Press.

Baumann, G. (1999) *The Multicultural Riddle: Rethinking National, Ethnic, and Religious Identities.* London: Routledge.

Bealor Hines, B. (2001) *Into the 21st Century: The Challenges of Journalism and Mass Communication Education. Report of the AEJMC Subcommittee on Inclusivity in the New Millennium.* URL (consulted August 2002): http://www.aejmc.org/pubs/2001.html

Becker, L., E. Lauf and W. Lowrey (1999) 'Differential Employment Rates in the Journalism and Mass Communication Labor Force Based on Gender, Race, and Ethnicity: Exploring the Impact of Affirmative Action', *Journalism Quarterly 76(4):* 631–45.

Bennett, W. Lance (2001) *News: The Politics of Illusion,* 4th edn. New York: Addison Wesley Longman.

Bierhoff, J. (1999) 'Journalism Training in Europe: Trends and Perspectives', Paper presented at the 'Media Minority's Message' conference at the Universitat Autonoma de Barcelona, 11–13 June.

Boczkowski, P. (2004) *Digitizing the News: Innovation in Online Newspapers.* Boston: MIT Press.

Bowman, S. and C. Willis (2003) *We Media: How Audiences Are Shaping the Future of News and Information.* The Media Center at The American Press Institute, URL (consulted June 2005): http://www.mediacenter.org/mediacenter/research/wemedia/http://www.hypergene.net/wemedia/ download/we media.pdf

Breen, M. (ed.) (1998) *Journalism: Theory and Practice.* Paddington: Macleay Press.

Brennen, B. (2000) 'What the Hacks Say: The Ideological Prism of US Journalism Texts', *Journalism* 1(1): 106–13.

Campbell, K. (1998) 'News Media Coverage of Minorities', in D. Sloan and E. Erickson Hoff (eds) *Contemporary Media Issues,* pp. 90–104. Northport: Vision Press.

Carey, J. (1989 [1975]) *Communication as Culture: Essays on Media and Society.* Boston: Unwin Hyman.

Castaneda, L. (2003) 'Teaching Convergence', *Online Journalism Review* 6 March 2003, URL (consulted June 2005): http://www.ojr.org/ojr/education/1046983385.php

Clayman, S. (2002) 'Tribune of the People: Maintaining the Legitimacy of Aggressive Journalism', *Media, Culture and Society* 24(2): 197–216.

Costera Meijer, I. (2001) 'The Public Quality of Popular Journalism: Developing a Normative Framework', *Journalism Studies* 2(2): 189–205.

Cottle, S. (2000) 'Media Research and Ethnic Minorities: Mapping the Field', in S. Cottle (ed.) *Ethnic Minorities and the Media: Changing Cultural Boundaries,* pp. 1–30. Ballmoor: Open University Press.

Dahlgren, P. (1992) 'Introduction', in P. Dahlgren and C. Sparks (eds) *Journalism and Popular Culture,* pp. 1–23. Thousand Oaks, CA: Sage.

Dahlgren, P. (1996) 'Media Logic in Cyberspace: Repositioning Journalism and its Publics', *Javnost/The Public* 3(3): 59–72.

De Beer, A. S. and J. Merrill (eds) (2004) *Global Journalism: Survey of International Communication,* 4th edn. New York: Longman.

Deuze, M. (2002a) 'National News Cultures: A Comparison of Dutch, German, British, Australian and US Journalists', *Journalism Quarterly* 79(1): 134–49.

Deuze, M. (2002b) *Journalists in the Netherlands.* Piscataway, NJ: Transaction.

Deuze, M. (2004a) 'What is Multimedia Journalism?', *Journalism Studies* 5(2): 139–52.

Deuze, M. (2004b) *Wat is journalistiek?* [What is journalism?] Amsterdam: Spinhuis.

Donsbach, W. and B. Klett (1993) 'Subjective Objectivity. How Journalists in Four Countries Define a Key Term of their Profession', *Gazette* 51(1): 53–83.

Eliasoph, N. (1988) 'Routines and the Making of Oppositional News', *Critical Studies in Mass Communication* 5(4): 313–34.

Elliott, D. (1988) 'All is Not Relative: Essential Shared Values and the Press', *Journal of Mass Media Ethics* 3(1): 28–32.

Entman, L. and A. Rojecki (2000) *The Black Image in the White Mind: Media and Race in America.* Chicago, IL: University of Chicago Press.

Fedler, F., A. Carey and T. Counts (1998) 'Journalism's Status in Academia: A Candidate for Elimination?', *Journalism Educator* 53(1): 4–13.

Fulton, K. (1996) 'A Tour of our Uncertain Future', *Columbia Journalism Review* (March! April), URL: http://www.cjr.org/year/96/2/tour.asp

Gans, Herbert (1979) *Deciding What's News.* New York: Vintage Books.

Golding, P. and P. Elliott (1979) *Making the News.* London: Longman.

Hafez, K. (2002) 'Journalism Ethics Revisited: A Comparison of Ethics Codes in Europe, North Africa, the Middle East, and Muslim Asia', *Political Communication* 19(2): 225–50.

Hall, J. (2001) *Online Journalism: A Critical Primer.* London: Pluto Press.

Hall, S. (1982) 'The Rediscovery of Ideology: Return of the Repressed in Media Studies', in M. Gurevitch, T. Bennet, J. Curran and J. Woollacott (eds) *Culture, Society and the Media,* pp. 5 6–90. London: Methuen.

Hallin, D. (1986) *The 'Uncensored War': The Media and Vietnam.* Berkeley: University of California Press.

Hallin, D. (1992) 'The Passing of the "High Modernism" of American Journalism', *Journal of Communication* 42(3): 14–25.

Hallin, D. (1996) 'Commercialism and Professionalism in American News Media', in J. Curran and M. Gurevitch (eds) Mass *Media and Society,* pp. 243–64. London: Arnold.

Huang, E., S. Shreve, T. Davis, A. Nair, E. Bettendorf, K. Davison and A. Meacham (2003) 'Bridging Newsrooms and Classrooms: Preparing the Next Generation of Journalists for Converged Media', Presentation at the AEJMC conference in Kansas, August.

Iggers, J. (1999) *Good News, Bad News: Journalism Ethics and the Public Interest.* Boulder, CO: Westview.

Innovation (2001) *Innovations in Newspapers: The 2001 World Report.* URL (consulted April 2003): http:// www.innovaion.com/english/eng_report2001.htm

Jakubowicz, A., J. Goodall, T. Marin, L. R. Mitchell and K. Seneviratne (1994) Racism, *Ethnicity and the Media.* St. Leonards: Allen and Unwin.

Kovach, B. and T. Rosenstiel (2001) *The Elements of Journalism.* New York: Crown Publishers.

Kymlicka, W. (1995) *Multicultural Citizenship: A Liberal Theory of Minority Rights.* Oxford: Clarendon Press.

Lievrouw, L. and S. Livingstone (eds) (2002) *Handbook of New Media: Social Shaping and Consequences of ICTs.* London: Sage.

Löffelholz, M. (ed.) (2000) *Theorien des Journalismus.* Opladen: Westdeutscher Verlag.

Lule, J. (2001) *Daily News, Eternal Stories.* New York: The Guilford Press.

McDevitt, M., B. M. Gassaway and F. G. Perez (2002) 'The Making and Unmaking of Civic Journalists: Influences of Professional Socialization', *Journalism Quarterly* 79(1): 87–100.

McGowan, W. (2001) *Coloring the News.* San Francisco, CA: Encounter Books.

McMane, A. A. (1993) 'A Comparative Analysis of Standards of Reporting among French and US Newspaper Journalists', *Journal of Mass Media Ethics* 8(4): 207–18.

McNair, B. (2003) *Sociology of Journalism.* London: Routledge.

Merrill, J. C., P. J. Gade and F. R. Blevens (2001) *Twilight of Press Freedom: The Rise of People's Journalism.* Hilisdale, NJ: Lawrence Erelbaum.

Merritt, D. (1995) 'Public Journalism – Defining a Democratic Art', *Media Studies Journal* 9(3): 125–32.

Mindich, D. (1998) *Just the Facts: How 'Objectivity' Came to Define American Journalism.* New York: New York University Press.

Molotch, H. and M. Lester (1974) 'News as Purposive Behavior: On the Strategic Use of Routine Events, Accidents, and Scandals', *American Sociological Review* 39(1): 10 1–12.

Morgan, F. (1998) 'Recipes for Success: Curriculum for Professional Media Education', *Asia/Pacific Media Educator* 8(1): 4–21, URL (consulted): http://www.uow.edua.au/crearts/journalism/APME/contents8.morgan.htm [2000, Dec.5]

Nerone, J. and K. Barnhurst (2003) 'News Form and the Media Environment: A Network of Represented Relationships', *Media, Culture and Society* 25(1): 111–24.

Nordenstreng, K. and H. Topuz (eds) (1989) *Journalist: Status, Rights and Responsibilities.* Prague: International Organization of Journalists.

Ognianova, E. and J. Endersby (1996) 'Objectivity Revisited: A Spatial Model of Political Ideology and Mass

Communication', *Journalism and Mass Communication Monographs* 159.

Ouaj, J. (1999) *More Colour in the Media: Employment and Access of Ethnic Minorities to the Television Industry in Germany, the UK, France, the Netherlands and Finland.* Düsseldorf: The European Institute for the Media.

Parekh, B. C. (ed.) (1997) *Rethinking Multiculturalism.* Basingstoke: Palgrave.

Patterson, T. E. (1997) 'The News Media: An Effective Political Actor?', *Political Communication* 14(4): 445–55.

Pavlik, J. (1999) 'New Media and News: Implications for the Future of Journalism', *New Media and Society* 1(1): 54–9.

Pavlik, J. (2001) *Journalism and New Media.* New York: Columbia University Press.

Pavlik, J., G. Morgan and B. Henderson (2001) *Information Technology: Implications for the Future of Journalism and Mass Communication Education.* Report of the AEJMC Task Force on Teaching and Learning in the New Millenium, URL (consulted May 2001): http://www .aejmc.org/pubs/2001.html

Platon, S. and M. Deuze (2003) 'Indymedia Journalism: A Radical Way of Making, Selecting and Sharing News?', *Journalism* 4(3): 343–62.

Raudsepp, E. (1989) 'Reinventing Journalism Education', *Canadian Journal of Communication* 14(2): 1–14.

Reese, S. (1990) 'The News Paradigm and the Ideology of Objectivity: A Socialist at the *Wall Street Journal', Critical Studies in Mass Communication* 7(4): 390–409.

Reese, S. (2001) 'Understanding the Global Journalist: A Hierarchy-of-influences Approach', *Journalism Studies* 2(2): 173–87.

Rich, C. (2005) *Writing log ond Reporting News.* 4th edn. Belmont: Wadsworth.

Rosen, J. (1999) *What are Journalists* for? New Haven, CT: Yale University Press.

Rühl, M. (2000) 'Des Journalismus vergangene Zukunft: zur Theoriegeschichte einer kuenftigen Journalismus-forschung [The Past Future of Journalism: A History of Theory of a Future Journalism Studies]', in M. Löffelholz (ed.) *Theorien des Journalismus,* pp. 65–80. Opladen: Westdeutscher Verlag.

Russo, T. C. (1998) 'Organizational and Professional Identification: A Case of Newspaper Journalists', *Management Communication Quarterly* 12(1): 72–111.

Ryan, M. (2001) 'Journalistic Ethics, Objectivity, Existential Journalism, Standpoint Epistemology, and Public Journalism', *Journal of Mass Media Ethics* 16(1): 3–22.

Schlesinger, P (1978) *Putting 'Reality' Together.* London: Methuen.

Schudson, M. (1978) *Discovering the News: A Social history of American Newspapers.* New York: Basic Books.

Schudson, M. (1999) 'What Public Journalism Knows about Journalism but Doesn't Know about "Public", in T. Glasser (ed.) *The Idea of Public Journalism,* pp. 118–34. New York: Guilford Press.

Schudson, M. (2001) 'The Objectivity Norm in American Journalism', *Journalism* 2(2): 149–70.

Schudson, M. (2003) *Sociology of News.* New York: W.W. Norton.

Shoemaker, P. J. and S. D. Reese (1996) *Mediating the Message: Theories of Influences on Mass Media Content.* New York: Longman.

Singer, J. (1998) 'Online Journalists: Foundation for Research into their Changing Roles', *Journal of Computer–Mediated Communication* 4(1), URL: http://jcmc.huji.ac.il/vol4/issue1/singer.html

Singer, J. (2004) 'Strange Bedfellows: The Diffusion of Convergence in Four News Organizations', *Journalism Studies* 5(1): 3–18.

Skinner, D., M. J. Gasher and J. Compton (2001) 'Putting Theory to Practice: A Critical Approach to Journalism Studies', *Journalism* 2(3): 341–60.

Soloski, J. (1990) 'News Reporting and Professionalism: Some Constraints on the Reporting of the News', *Media, Culture and Society* 11(4): 207–28.

Sparks, C. (1992) 'Popular Journalism: Theories and Practice', in P. Dahlgren and C. Sparks (eds) *Journalism and Popular Culture,* pp. 24–44. Thousand Oaks, CA: Sage.

Starck, K. (2001) 'What's Right/Wrong with Journalism Ethics Research?', *Journalism Studies* 2(1): 133–52.

Stephens, M. (1988) *A History of News.* New York: Penguin.

Stevens, J. (2002) 'Backpack Journalism is Here to Stay', *Online Journalism Review,* April 2, URL (consulted Jun. 2005): http://www.ojr.org/ojr/workplace/1017771575 . php

Stevenson, N. (1995) *Understanding Media Cultures: Social Theory and* Mass *Communication.* London: Sage.

Stone, M. and J. Bierhoff (2002) 'The State of Multimedia Newsrooms in Europe', Presentation at the 'Media in Transition 2' conference, May 10–12, MIT, Cambridge, MA, URL (consulted Apr 2003): http://cms.mit.edu/conf/ mit2/Abstracts/ JanBierhoff.pdf

Teoh Kheng Yau, J. and S. Al-Hawamdeh (2001) 'The Impact of the Internet on Teaching and Practicing Journalism', *Journal of Electronic Publishing* 7(1), URL (consulted Sep. 2001): http://www .press.umich.edu/jep/07–01/ al-hawamdeh.html

Tuchman, G. (1971) 'Objectivity as Strategic Ritual: An Examination of Newsmen's Notions of Objectivity', *American Journal of Sociology 77(4)*: 660–79.

Van Dijk, T. A. (1991) *Racism and the Press.* New York: Routledge.

Van Ginneken, J. (1997) *Understanding Global News: A Critical Introduction.* London: Sage.

Van Zoonen, L. (1998) 'A Professional, Unreliable, Heroic Marionette (M/F): Structure, Agency and Subjectivity in Contemporary Journalisms', *European Journal of Cultural Studies* 1(1): 123–43.

Weaver, D. H. (ed.) (1998) *The Global Journalist: News People around the World.* New Jersey: Hampton Press.

Weaver, D. H. and G. C. Wilhoit (1996) *The American Journalist in the 1990s: US News People at the End of an Era.* Mahwah, NJ: Erlbaum.

Weischenberg, S. and A. Scholl (1998) *Journalismus in der Gesellschaft: Theorie, Methodologie und Empirie.* Opladen: Westdeutscher Verlag.

Wilson, C., F. Gutierrez and L. Chao (2003) *Race, Multiculturalism and the Media: From Mass to Class Communicaiton,* 2nd edn. London: Sage.

Wise, R. (2000) *Multimedia: An Introduction.* London: Routledge.

Woodstock, L. (2000) 'Public Journalism's Talking Cure: An Analysis of the Movement's "Problem" and "Solution" Narratives', *Journalism* 3(1): 37–55.

Zelizer, B. (1993) 'Has Communication Explained Journalism?', *Journal of Communication* 43(4): 80–8.

Zelizer, B. (2000) 'What is Journalism Studies?', *Journalism* 1(1): 9–12.

Zelizer, B. (2004a) 'When Facts, Truth and Reality are God-terms: On Journalism's Uneasy Place in Cultural Studies', *Communication and Critical/Cultural Studies* 1(1): 100–19.

Zelizer, B. (2004b) *Taking Journalism Seriously: News and the Academy.* London: Sage.

Source: From "What Is Journalism? Professional Identity and Ideology of Journalists Reconsidered," 2005, by M. Deuze, *Journalism, 6*(4), 442–464. Reprinted by permission of Sage Publications, Ltd.

3

Deconstructing Journalism Culture

Toward a Universal Theory

Thomas Hanitzsch

International journalism research has produced much evidence in support of the view that the onward march of globalization coincides with a convergence in journalistic orientations and practices. The traditional ideals of objectivity and impartiality seem to dominate many newsrooms across the globe, and one can find many similarities in professional routines, editorial procedures, and socialization processes in countries as diverse as Brazil (Herscovitz, 2004), Germany (Weischenberg, Scholl, & Malik, 2006), Indonesia (Hanitzsch, 2005), Tanzania (Ramaprasad, 2001), and the United States (Weaver et al., 2007), to name just a few examples. In his compilation of more than 20 surveys of journalists all over the world, Weaver (1998b, p. 478) concludes that the "typical journalist" is young, male, college-educated, and comes from the established and dominant cultural group. Splichal and Sparks (1994, p. 179), in their survey of first-year journalism students in 22 countries, found a striking similarity in the desire for independence and autonomy. Deuze (2005, pp. 446–447) sees these more or less universal traits as an articulation of a "shared occupational ideology among newsworkers," consisting of five ideal-typical elements. These elements are that journalists (a) provide a public service; (b) are impartial, neutral, objective, fair, and credible; (c) ought to be autonomous, free, and independent in their work; (d) have a sense of immediacy, actuality, and speed; and (e) have a sense of ethics, validity, and legitimacy.

However, in his concluding chapter, Weaver (1998b) concedes that substantial differences between national journalistic cultures persist. Similar conclusions have been made in a number of comparative studies (e.g., Berkowitz, Limor, & Singer, 2004; Donsbach & Patterson, 2004; Esser, 1998; Shoemaker & Cohen, 2006). Given the differences in work roles and editorial control mechanisms between German and U.S. newsrooms, Donsbach (1995) even refers to both cultures as "two very different professional worlds." In conceptualizing the differences in the professional orientations and practices of journalists, researchers refer to a considerable array of concepts, including "journalism culture" (Campbell, 2004, p. 80; Gurevitch & Blumler, 2004, p. 337), "journalistic culture" (Donsbach & Patterson, 2004, p. 252; Hollifield, Kosicki, & Becker, 2001, p. 112; Keeble, 2005, p. 57; Waisbord, 2000, p. 93), "news culture" (Deuze, 2002), "newspaper cultures" (Knott, Carroll, & Meyer, 2002, p. 26), or the "culture of news production" (Schudson, 2003, p. 186), to name just a few. All these concepts are widely used and serve multiple purposes: They are employed to capture the cultural diversity of journalistic values and practices, and they sometimes suggest an all-encompassing consensus among journalists toward a common understanding and cultural identity of journalism.

References to journalism's "professional" or "occupational cultures" (Pasti, 2005, p. 101; Viall, 1992, p. 48) resonate with earlier conceptualizations of professional and "occupational ideologies" (Golding, 1977, pp. 298–300; Golding & Elliott, 1979, p. 214; Schudson, 1990, p. 24). Although this occupational ideology, associated with the values of impartiality, objectivity, and accuracy (Golding & Elliott, 1979), is often granted universal status by journalists and researchers, the rise of counterhegemonic articulations and practices (e.g., public or civic journalism, development journalism, and peace journalism) raises many challenging questions, including the following two: Does such a common professional culture really exist in "the West," in Europe, in Asia, or anywhere else? Is there any class of "cosmopolite" journalists (Reese, 2001, p. 178) who share a common occupational ideology and understanding of journalism?

To be able to address these questions systematically, one will need at hand a clear conceptualization of journalism culture that works properly in diverse cultural contexts. The lack of consensus on the concept of culture and the way in which it should be applied to research has, however, produced a scattered body of literature. There is clearly a need for an elaborated theoretical foundation on which the concept of journalism culture can be conceptualized and operationalized. Secondly, this key concept in the cultural analysis of journalism must be established in a way that ensures a maximum of conceptual stability and validity in diverse cultural contexts.

The purpose of this paper is, therefore, to propose a theoretical foundation on which systematic and comparative research on journalism cultures is feasible and meaningful. By doing so, this essay sets out to provide a central point of reference in a field where concepts are often used in many different ways. In the following sections, existing notions of professional culture will be reviewed and transformed into a truly global concept. We will deconstruct the concept of journalism culture in terms of its constituents and principal dimensions that are able to tap the existing cultural diversity of journalisms.

Deconstructing Journalism Culture

Culture is defined in many ways, driving the cultural analysis of journalism to further disperse into a highly heterogeneous field. Commonly used definitions of culture in the social sciences and humanities range broadly between "national cultures" (Hofstede, 1980) on the most macro level, and attitudes, values, and beliefs (Smith & Schwartz, 1997) on the most micro level. Williams' (1958, p. 18) definition of culture as the "whole way of life" was echoed by Hall (1959, p. 31) who referred to culture as "the way of life of a people." Wallerstein (1991, p. 159) defined culture as "a way of summarizing the ways in which groups distinguish themselves from other groups," whereas Alvesson (2002, p. 3) laments that culture is a "tricky concept" that is "easily used to cover everything and consequently nothing." Given the ever-growing number of definitions, Archer (1996, p. 2) noticed that "[w]hat culture is and what culture does are issues bogged down in a conceptual morass from which no adequate sociology of culture has been able to emerge."

Although a large number of studies are broadly concerned with the cultures of news production, they rarely attempt to tackle journalism culture and its dimensional structure at the conceptual level. One can generally speak of culture as a set of *ideas* (values, attitudes, and beliefs), *practices* (of cultural production), and *artifacts* (cultural products, texts). Journalism culture becomes manifest in the way journalists think and act; it can be defined as a particular set of ideas and practices by which journalists, consciously and unconsciously, legitimate their role in society and render their work meaningful for themselves and others. In the chain of news production, journalism cultures are articulated at three basic levels of analysis:

> At the cognitive level, they shape the foundational structure on the basis of which the perception and interpretation of news and news work take place (e.g., the attribution of news values to events).
>
> At the evaluative level, they drive the professional worldviews of journalists (e.g., role perceptions) as well as occupational ideologies (e.g., "objective journalism," "investigative journalism").
>
> At the performative level, they materialize in the way journalists do their work (e.g., methods of reporting, use of news formats). Journalistic practices are shaped by cognitive and evaluative structures, and journalists—mostly unconsciously—perpetuate these deep structures through professional performance.

Although *culture* and *ideology* are often used interchangeably, both terms should be distinguished for the sake of conceptual clarity. Generally, ideology can be understood in two basic ways: as a system of ideas and in terms of struggle over dominance, both notions being highly relevant to the cultural analysis of journalism. In the first view, ideologies are organized thoughts that form internally coherent ways of thinking and that become manifest as a set of values, orientations, and predispositions (Lull, 1995). Although ideology is generally seen as a cohesive and integrating force in society (Shoemaker & Reese, 1996), a shared occupational ideology is believed to serve as the "cultural cement" (Deuze, 2005, p. 455) that holds journalists together as a profession and that, therefore, forms the foundation of journalism's identity.

In a critical view, and this includes Marxist and Gramscian perspectives, ideology does also evoke concerns of social domination and hegemony. For some, occupational ideology is seen as a bold expression of cultural hegemony of Western professional norms over local modes of practicing journalism, as indicated by the Asian values debate (see Masterton, 1996; Xiaoge, 2005). Professional ideologies in journalism thus can be understood as crystallizations of distinctive arrays of journalism-related values, orientations, and predispositions that articulate themselves as dominant professional culture (e.g., objective journalism) or as a counterhegemonic set of values (e.g., civic journalism and peace journalism). These professional ideologies occupy specific positions within the space of journalism culture; they live in journalism culture and articulate themselves against other ideologies relevant to the conduct of journalism. Journalism culture is more than ideology; it is the arena in which diverse professional ideologies struggle over the dominant interpretation of journalism's social function and identity.

To speak of any journalism culture only makes sense if we assume that there exist other (not necessarily journalistic) cultures to which the former could be compared. Cross-cultural comparative research should therefore be a principal venue of the inquiry in journalism culture. One of the challenges in comparative research is that it ultimately requires functional equivalence of constructs, which means that constructs must display sufficient overlap across cultures and can be equivalently integrated into theories (van de Vijver & Leung, 1997; Wirth & Kolb, 2004).

There are basically two popular strategies to come to an operational definition in comparative research, and they often refer to the work of linguist Kenneth Pike who suggested an emic–etic distinction for the analysis of human communication. The *etic* approach, emphasizing the universal and cross-cultural, examines the constitutive elements of culture from the perspective of a common denominator of theoretical terms and concepts (Jensen, 1998). The *emic* approach, on the other hand, pays attention to the culture specific and explores a culture from the view of its members or participants. An emic approach to journalism culture would develop its conceptualizations in a specific cultural context. This inductive bottom-up strategy would necessarily produce culture-bound definitions that do not easily translate from one cultural context to another. The cross-national variation in definitions of who is a journalist is quite revealing to this fact (see Weaver, 1998a). In order to ensure that concepts work properly in a variety of cultures, an etic strategy seems much more powerful. It would start from a common theoretical denominator of journalism culture that can be applied to the diverse national and organizational contexts in which news production takes place around the globe. Such a deductive top-down strategy would not only guarantee a high degree of conceptual equivalence, it would also produce definitions that are likely to withstand the test of time, particularly as journalism culture is a fast-changing object of inquiry. Any etic strategy, however, would have to be accompanied by an emic component to render comparative findings meaningful across different cultural contexts.

Therefore, journalism culture needs first to be deconstructed in terms of its constituents and conceptual dimensions. Because it is practically impossible to identify all facets of journalism culture, we will use a deductive and etic method to identify the principal dimensions that show the largest cultural overlap. By highlighting differences at the expense of similarities, the present approach seeks to provide an analytical grid to map diverse journalism cultures onto a set of universal dimensions of global variance. Based on the existing and accessible body of research, this paper proposes a conceptualization of journalism culture that has three essential constituents: institutional roles, epistemologies, and ethical ideologies (see Figure 1). These three constituents further divide into seven principal dimensions: interventionism, power distance, market orientation, objectivism, empiricism, relativism, and idealism.

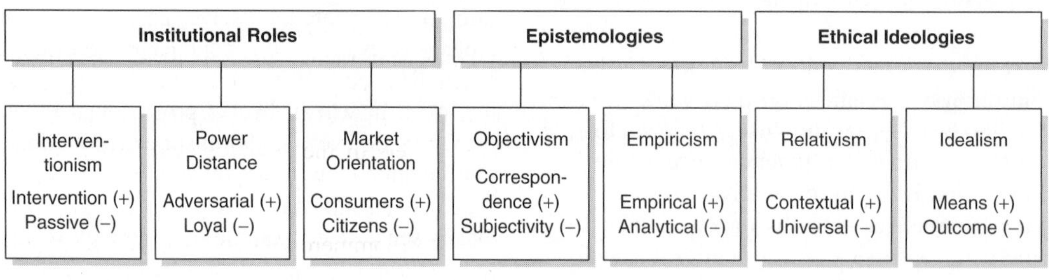

Figure 1 The constituents and principal dimensions of journalism culture.

Each of the seven dimensions spans two ideal-typical extremes that rarely become manifest in the "real" world of journalistic practice. Most of the time, the truth lies somewhere between the poles. Although the various dimensions of journalism culture do more or less surface in all nations and media organizations, the relative importance of these dimensions is likely to vary. Many journalists, for instance, follow the neutral-objective paradigm, whereas others prefer the advocacy approach. These relative differences in the extent to which journalists endorse these dimensions reveals a universe of diverse and coexisting worlds of journalism.

Institutional Roles

The first constituent of journalism culture is prescriptive and refers to the institutional roles of journalism in society, both in terms of its normative responsibilities and its functional contribution to society. More than 40 years of research have produced an impressive body of literature in this area, but terminology varies considerably (e.g., "news functions," "media roles," "role perceptions"). Janowitz's (1975) classification of gatekeeper and advocate roles echoed the distinction between neutral and participant roles, which Cohen (1963) had suggested earlier. Although the gatekeeper orientation emphasized objectivity and separation of facts from opinion, the role of the advocate is to "participate" in the advocacy process. Donsbach and Patterson (2004) proposed a theory-driven model that organized role models according to two analytical dimensions: The passive-active dimension refers to the extent to which journalists act independently of those who have interests in the story, whereas the neutral-advocate dimension reflects the extent to which the journalist takes a stand on a certain issue. Studies in Bangladesh (Ramaprasad & Rahman, 2006), Brazil (Herscovitz, 2004), Egypt (Ramaprasad & Hamdy, 2006), Germany (Scholl & Weischenberg, 1998), Indonesia (Hanitzsch, 2005), Nepal (Ramaprasad & Kelly, 2003), Switzerland (Marr, Wyss, Blum, & Bonfadelli, 2001), and Tanzania (Ramaprasad, 2001), employed factor analysis to identify the dimensional structure of the concept.

Still, the conceptualization of journalism's institutional roles is deeply colored by a Western understanding of news making and does not echo cultural variation across the globe. Many studies borrowed items from the "American journalist" studies of Weaver and Wilhoit (1991), but the normative expectations of the professional model that have molded the questionnaire may also have shaped the answers (Josephi, 2006). By taking the above-mentioned approaches further, we suggest a new multidimensional structure that allows us to capture the global variance in the journalists' role perceptions, consisting of three basic dimensions: interventionism, power distance, and market orientation.

Interventionism

This dimension reflects the extent to which journalists pursue a particular mission and promote certain values. The interventionism dimension, which Himelboim and Limor (2005, p. 9) labeled "involvement sequence," stretches from "passive" (low) to "intervention" (high). The distinction tracks along a divide between two types of journalist; the one interventionist, socially committed, and motivated, the other detached and uninvolved, dedicated to objectivity and impartiality. The passive pole of this dimension is ideal-typically associated with roles like the "neutral disseminator" and "gatekeeper" (Cohen, 1963; Janowitz, 1975; Weaver & Wilhoit, 1991). Journalism cultures on this side of the continuum stick to the principles of objectivity, neutrality, fairness, detachment, and impartiality, which are deeply rooted in the history of Western, and particularly U.S., journalism.

Whenever such a professional culture dominates the newsroom, journalists primarily subscribe to the ideology of "professionalism" and to the information function of journalism. They perceive themselves merely as disinterested transmitters of the news who contribute mostly to vertical communication in society. Although these values and professional views emerged from the commercial logic of media businesses in most liberal democracies, with the neutrality and impartiality of reporting being built into the notion of the institutional separation of the media from the state, media organizations in many other countries (e.g., in China or Russia) tend to be ideologically bound with certain political groups (Golding, 1977; Hallin & Mancini, 2004; Lee, 2001). In some nations (e.g., in large parts of South America), the transition from a politically active journalism to the more passive pole of the continuum is still taking place; journalists in these countries are likely to endorse a more interventionist approach to reporting.

The intervention pole of the continuum becomes manifest in role models like the "participant," "advocate," and "missionary" (Cohen, 1963; Donsbach & Patterson, 2004; Janowitz, 1975; Köcher, 1986), with journalists taking a more active and assertive role in their reporting. Journalism cultures that follow an interventionist approach may act on behalf of the socially disadvantaged or as mouthpiece of a political party and other groups whose interests are at stake. The impetus behind interventionist journalism is not to stay apart from the flow of events, as does the neutral and disinterested observer, but to participate, intervene, get involved, and promote change. An interventionist impulse can be found in normative concepts such as peace journalism and even more so in development(al) journalism, as well as civic or public journalism as its "Western counterpart" (Gunaratne, 2006, p. 17).

Power Distance

The second dimension refers to the journalist's position toward loci of power in society and shows some similarity to Himelboim and Limor's (2005, p. 10) "adversary sequence." The term *power distance* was originally coined by Hofstede (1980) to label one of the basic dimensions of cultural variance. In journalism, one end of the power distance dimension is represented by the "adversary" pole (high); the other end should be labeled "loyal" (low). The adversary pole of the continuum captures a kind of journalism that openly challenges the powers that be. Adversarial journalism has a long tradition in liberal democracies and is often understood in terms of serving as "fourth estate" or as countervailing force of democracy. Journalists of this type posture themselves as "watchmen" or "watchdogs" and as agents of social control (Gans, 1979, p. 295; Schramm, 1964, p. 127). They are relentless cross-examiners who provide an independent and radical critique of society and its institutions, and they are skeptical of or even hostile to every assertion made by those who are in power (Fuller, 1996; McQuail, 2000).

The normative appeal of journalism functioning as fourth estate is clearly situated within the nexus of liberal democracy. Although many journalists in the West do outspokenly celebrate their adversarial stance, any such attitude might be difficult to detect among "news people" in other cultures. Although in some, especially Asian, cultures, an adversarial understanding of journalism may conflict with a preference for consensus and harmony, in other contexts, tight press restrictions might prohibit journalists from openly challenging those in power. In some of these countries, for example, in China, journalists can nonetheless convey criticisms between the lines of censored media texts by ways of "double coding," and the audience can skillfully decode these messages by subversive reading (Ma, 2000). In Soeharto-ruled Indonesia, this has been a way of "saying serious things nonseriously" (Nasution, 1996, p. 53).

The other extreme end of the power distance dimension is a form of journalism that positions itself as "loyal" to those in power. This kind of journalism can be bluntly loyal: taking on a "propagandist role" (Pasti, 2005, p. 99), practicing "agitator journalism" (Wu, Weaver, & Johnson, 1996, p. 544), being defensive of authorities, routinely engaging in self-censorship, and serving as mouthpiece of the government or the party. To the extent that these journalists sometimes remain highly paternalistic toward "the people," they see themselves as "guiding public opinion" and "bringing the influence of public opinion to bear on the government" (Lee, 2001, p. 249).

The lighter variant of low power distance is less visible, however. It is a sort of journalism that serves as an ideological state apparatus in an Althusserian sense. It never challenges the legitimacy of the powers that be and, as such, tends to lend support to established authority and norms, although not in an explicit and straightforward manner. In the tradition of the Mexican "oficialista" (Hallin, 2000, p. 99) or "protocol news" in Uganda (Mwesige, 2004, p. 87), these journalists pay disproportionately high attention to the authorities and rarely question the official version of the story. Instead, they accept information provided by government sources as authoritative, credible, and trustworthy, and they often become public relations channels for the transmission of government messages to the public.

Market Orientation

The third dimension of institutional roles is reflective of the primary social focus that guides news production. Market orientation is high in journalism cultures that subordinate their goals to the logic of the market; it is low in cultures that produce the news primarily in the "public interest." Such a distinction—market-oriented journalism versus a role model that is geared toward public needs—has been proposed by Marr et al. (2001) in their survey of journalists in Switzerland. Generally, the large number of scholarly publications and conference papers on this particularly crucial issue in the discussion of journalism's function in society shows that market orientation as a dimension of journalistic culture goes to the very heart of journalism studies. It ultimately boils down to the fact that the media can address the people in two seemingly antagonistic ways, in their role as citizens or consumers, with the former being increasingly displaced by the latter.

In journalism cultures that give priority to the public interest, the audience is clearly addressed in its role as citizenry. It is assumed that the primary purpose of journalism is to provide citizens with the information they need to be free and self-governing (Kovach & Rosenstiel, 2001). Journalism is seen as a communicator-driven activity that is central to the functioning of democratic societies through the creation of an informed citizenry and the encouragement of political participation. The negative pole of the market orientation dimension incorporates some of the basic tenets of social responsibility theory in journalism, as it was originally articulated by the Commission on Freedom of the Press (1947). However, Gunaratne (2006) rightly points out that social responsibility is a concept that is understood differently in the East and the West. As indicated in the Asian values debate, the responsibility of the media is often linked to the preservation of social harmony and respect for leadership, and it urges the media to restrain from coverage that could potentially disrupt social order (Masterton, 1996; Xiaoge, 2005). The idea of journalism acting in the public interest is also inherited by the idea of public or civic journalism, which originated in the United States as an effort to reconnect Americans to the public life from which they have become disengaged. Public or civic journalism sees people as citizens and helps them participate in civic activity and political conversation (Rosen, 2000).

When market orientation is high, journalism gives emphasis to what the audiences want to know at the expense of what they should know. Journalism cultures on this pole of the dimension champion the values of consumerism; they focus on everyday life issues and individual needs. Audiences are not addressed in their role as citizens concerned with the social and political issues of the day but in their role as clients and consumers whose personal fears, aspirations, attitudes, and emotional experiences become the center of attention (Campbell, 2004). Market-oriented journalism is driven by a rating mentality and does largely take place in commercial media where the perspective of the individual is increasingly privileged (Bourdieu, 1998; Hallin & Mancini, 2004).

A journalistic orientation to the logic of the marketplace crystallizes in a journalistic culture that provides help, advice, guidance, and information about the management of self and everyday life (Eide & Knight, 1999). To the extent that such a kind of service journalism is partly a reaction to the demand for greater individual autonomy, it gives prominence to consumer news and "news-you-can-use" items (Underwood, 2001, p. 102). Empirical studies in Germany and Indonesia have shown that service journalism harmonizes readily with entertainment-oriented popular journalism, and both aspects, as indicated by results from factor analyses, constitute a common dimension (Hanitzsch, 2005; Scholl &

Weischenberg, 1998). The materialization of infotainment news and lifestyle journalism exemplifies this trend toward a blending of information with advice and guidance as well as with entertainment and relaxation.

Epistemologies

Epistemology is commonly defined as the study of knowledge and the justification of belief (Dancy, 1985). It is "the inquiry into the character of knowledge, the nature of acceptable evidence, and the criterion of validity that enables one to distinguish the false from the truth, the probable from the actual" (Anderson & Baym, 2004, p. 603). In the study of journalism, epistemology is crucial because "the legitimacy of journalism is intimately bound up with claims to knowledge and truth" (Ekström, 2002, p. 260). Still, it is common sense to say that journalism's "first obligation is to the truth" (Kovach & Rosenstiel, 2001, p. 37).

The epistemology constituent of journalism culture is concerned with the philosophical underpinnings of journalism that are instrumental in doing news work. Epistemological considerations in journalism raise the question of whether or not the news can provide an objective and value-free account of the truth and, if so, how such truth claims are to be justified. Epistemologies of journalism can be classified with respect to two fundamental dimensions: objectivism and empiricism.

Objectivism

The first dimension, related to the question of how truth can be attained, is concerned with a philosophical or absolute sense of objectivity rather than with a procedural sense of objectivity as method. The division tracks along a divide between the correspondence pole (high), which assumes that there is a correspondence between "what is said" and "what exists" (Merill & Odell, 1983, p. 70), and a subjectivism pole (low), which adheres to the view that all news is selective and that human beings perceive reality based on judgments.

Journalism cultures that are close to the correspondence pole of the continuum entail a totalitarian understanding of "truth," for they endorse the principles of epistemological foundationalism, which holds knowledge as the correspondence between mental impression and the true shape of the existent actual, and perceptual realism, in which the perceived objects are seen as independent of the existence of any perceiver (Anderson & Baym, 2004; Dancy, 1985). Journalists claim the existence of an objective and ultimate truth "out there" that ought to be "mirrored" and not be created, invented, or altered in any way. The observer and the observed are seen as two distinct categories, and it is assumed that reality, in principle, can be perceived and described "as it is" and tested against the "genuine reality." Consequently, reality has to be described as accurately and precisely as possible; advocates of the precision journalism philosophy even suggest that truth should be pursued by means of scientific inquiry. At any rate, commonly accepted is a definition of objectivity as the view that one can and should separate facts from values.

Extreme subjectivism, on the other hand, entails the constructivist idea that there is no absolute truth, and journalists inescapably create their own realities. Subjectivist journalists believe that there is no such thing as an objective reality, news are just a representation of the world, and all representations are inevitably selective and require interpretation (Schudson, 2003). Truth, and its pursuit, cannot be separated from context and human subjectivity, rendering it impossible for journalists to produce value-free accounts of events. Such an epistemological stance resonates quite well with Eastern philosophy, which sees the objective reality and its phenomenal representation—substance and form—as inextricably bound (Cheng, 1987). This can, at least partly, explain the reluctance of many Asian journalists to implement any Western-style objective journalism (see Masterton, 1996).

Although subjectivist journalists agree on the view that truth must be pursued, they believe that truth ultimately emerges from the combination of—or competition between—a potentially infinite number of subjective accounts. As Oleg Poptsov, the former head of the Russian state-run TV channel RTR, put it, "[T]here is no such thing as objectivity. Objectivity is a sum total of subjectivities" (quoted in McNair, 2000, p. 90). Very much like the ideology of objectivity, the idea of pluralist subjectivity as a way to move toward truth has a long history, which can be traced back to the report of the Commission on Freedom of the Press (1947) and to early sociological studies of the news (e.g., Golding & Elliott, 1979). Such an understanding of a discursive approximation of truth foregrounds explicit and open competition in the public domain, which means competition in the marketplace of ideas as well as competition between mainstream news and alternative accounts.

Empiricism

The second dimension of the epistemology constituent is concerned with the means by which a truth claim is ultimately justified by the journalist. Journalists consistently make truth claims that need to be justified in order to appear valid to the audience. There are basically two ideal-typical ways of justifying truth claims in the epistemology of journalism: Journalists can justify truth claims empirically (high) or analytically (low).

Journalism cultures that prioritize an empirical justification of truth strongly emphasize observation, measurement, evidence, and experience. Central to these cultures is the view, as articulated in classical foundationalism, that all knowledge is derived from experience (Dancy, 1985). Journalists who score high on the empiricism dimension believe that truth essentially needs to be substantiated by facts; they give priority to factual knowledge over a priori (analytical) knowledge (Merill & Odell, 1983). The procedural and methodological aspects of proper reporting (investigation, fact checking, etc.) are highly valued, which makes this epistemological position compatible with precision journalism. In its most radical form, this pole of the empiricism dimension leads journalists to merely record events and let "the facts speak for themselves."

The negative end of the empiricism continuum, where journalism cultures stress the analytical justification of truth claims, accentuates reason, ideas, values, opinion, and analysis. Journalists who tend to this pole of the empiricism dimension give priority to analytic knowledge with truth being independent of the facts (Merill & Odell, 1983). Analytical journalism, which becomes manifest in commentary and opinion journalism, does not require its practitioners to be neutral. The credibility of commentary journalists and columnists is not rooted in conventional standards like accuracy, fairness, and balance, but in their ability to persuade the audience. However, the two extremes, empirical and analytical journalism, rarely appear in practice. In reality, most news coverage occupies a middle ground, as in the case of interpretative journalism.

The distinction between the two epistemological dimensions may appear puzzling at times. Although high empiricism is strongly associated with the correspondence pole of the objectivism dimension, the analytical end is somewhat related to the subjectivism pole. Nevertheless, both dimensions, objectivism and empiricism, cannot be collapsed into a single factor, as the former is concerned with the perception of reality and the latter relates to the importance of facts versus analysis. Although it seems counterintuitive at first sight, journalists who score high on the objectivity dimension can engage in commentary journalism. There are values that can be objectified in the sense that they are almost universally true (peace, human dignity, etc.), and that can be consequently treated as "facts."

Ethical Ideologies

Ethical ideologies are the third constituent of journalism culture. In general ethics theory, one can distinguish between ethical ideologies and moral values, both being evaluative with respect to whether or not a certain practice can be justified or considered ethical. Moral values are specific to the cultural context in which they are embedded; they should therefore be treated as contextual dimensions of journalism culture. Some of these factors are believed to be the prototype values of a "universal" code of ethics in journalism, though most of these principles have evolved in a Western cultural context. These values include "aboveboard" (straightforward, transparent), "avoiding harm," "completeness," "freedom, independence, and self-esteem," "fairness," "honesty," "just," "respect of privacy and honor," and "truth" (Herrscher, 2002, pp. 280–281; Plaisance & Skewes, 2003, p. 839). Many non-Western cultures, however, give priority to the concepts of social harmony and unity, which may render ineffective some of the above ethical values in certain cultural contexts (Perkins, 2002). Berkowitz et al. (2004), as well as Weaver (1998b), conclude from comparative evidence that the national context of news making may be most important in shaping ethical decisions of journalists.

As moral values are inevitably culture-bound and far too specific to serve as a common denominator of the global variations in professional practice, a more abstract and humanocentric strategy is needed. Instead of focusing on the distinctive content of ethical values in journalism, an approach that points our attention to how journalists respond to ethical problems seems more fruitful. In this regard, Keeble (2005) distinguished four mainstream approaches in journalism ethics: While the "standard professional approach" stresses the journalists' commitment to agreed-upon codes of ethics and editorial guidelines, the "liberal professional approach" criticizes this standard perspective from a range of standpoints. For those who follow the "cynical approach," ethical issues have little relevance to journalists, whereas "ethical relativists" promote ad hoc responses to ethical dilemmas.

Another, more general approach to classify distinct ethical perspectives in journalism has been proposed by Plaisance (2005), who was inspired by the work of the psychologist Donelson R. Forsyth. Forsyth (1980, 1981) organized ethical ideologies along two basic continuous dimensions: Relativism focuses on the extent to which individuals base their personal moral philosophies on universal ethical rules. Some individuals tend to reject the possibility of relying on universal moral rules (high), whereas others believe in and make use of moral absolutes (low). The second dimension, idealism, refers to the consequences in the responses to ethical dilemmas. Ideal-typically, there are individuals who assume that desirable outcomes should always be obtained with the "right" action (high, means oriented), whereas less idealistic individuals are more outcome-oriented, for they admit that harm will sometimes be necessary to produce good (low).

When these two dimensions are crossed, they yield a classification off our ethical ideologies (see Figure 2): Situationists are idealistic, but they are also relativistic, for they tend to reject moral rules and to advocate individualistic analysis of each act in each situation. Absolutists are also idealistic, but they feel that the best possible outcome can always be achieved by following universal moral rules. Subjectivists, like situationists, base their judgments on personal values and perspectives rather than universal ethical principles. However, unlike situationists they feel that negative behavior is sometimes necessary to produce good. Finally, exceptionists allow moral absolutes to guide their judgments but remain pragmatically

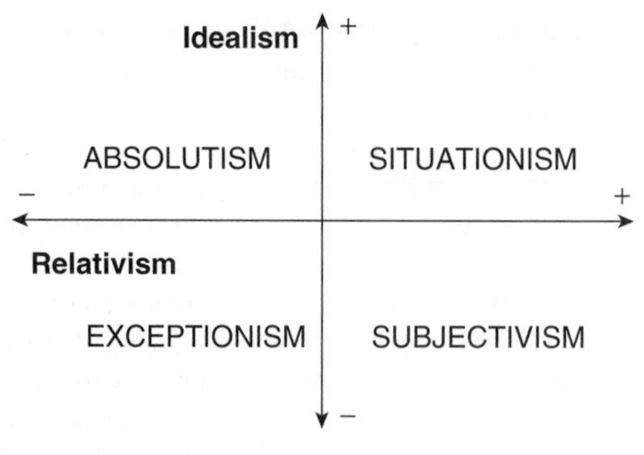

Figure 2 Classification of ethical ideologies according to Forsyth (1980, p. 176).

open to exceptions in so far as these help to prevent negative consequences. Although Forsyth did not address his use of *ideology* in his work, it is quite obvious that he understands ideology in terms of distinct sets of values and attitudes.

The four ethical ideologies resonate well with the journalism literature. The situationism approach has been the subject of extensive discussion (e.g., Merill & Odell, 1983) and partly resembles Keeble's (2005) "ethical relativist approach." Situationist journalists believe that ethical issues cannot be decided in the abstract and that decisions must be grounded in the concrete of actual situations. Absolutism mirrors the "deontologist" and "standard professional approach," whereas subjectivism approximates the "cynical approach" in journalism (Keeble, 2005; Sanders, 2003). Applied to the justification of unconventional and potentially harmful practices of reporting (e.g., badgering informants, paying for information), situationist journalists would feel that these judgments are highly contingent on the actual details of a given situation, whereas subjectivists would tend to justify these methods provided they yield the best possible outcome. Absolutist journalists would always reject critical methods of reporting as long as these methods run counter to agreed-upon ethical principles. Exceptionist journalists, on the other hand, would agree that universal ethical principles in journalism, are necessary, but exceptionists are also utilitarian, for they feel that unconventional practices of reporting may be allowable in very exceptional cases.

Conclusion

One strength of the presented approach to journalism culture is that it combines relatively diverse and sometimes isolated scholarly discourses. Professional ideologies, such as "objective journalism" or "civic journalism," are mostly discussed with reference to journalism's social function and epistemological concerns (and sometimes also with respect to ethical issues), but often enough there is not much conceptual overlap between these perspectives. The theory-driven approach offered by this paper allows us to systematically map, compare, and classify professional ideologies within a seven-dimensional space of journalism cultures. Table 1 presents a selection of popular professional ideologies in journalism along with their theoretical classifications.

The dimensional structure we propose can, of course, always be contested on the grounds that journalism culture is inherently multidimensional. Any choice of its principal constituents is contingent, thus inevitably selective—but not necessarily arbitrary. The object of this paper was professional news production, which excludes many alternative communication activities that are sometimes referred to as "participatory" or "citizen" journalism. The incorporation of these communication modes is likely to require a different dimensional structure, probably one that includes a dimension that taps into the conceptualization of the audience as either active or passive.

The three constituents of journalism culture have been selected according to their prominence in the literature and in the public domain. They are central to our understanding of journalism and have generated most ofthe debate, among journalists themselves and scholars alike. The seven dimensions take account of the normative and actual functions of journalism in society (institutional roles), the accessibility of reality and the nature of acceptable evidence (epistemologies), as well as responses to ethical problems (ethical ideologies). These constituents of journalism cultures encompass some of the "essential shared values" that give journalists a group identity (Elliott, 1988, p. 30) and that help create a "collective conscience for the profession" (Keeble, 2005, p. 55).

It is true that the selection of the dimensional components of journalism culture and the work cited in this essay is inevitably constrained by the limited access to the (mainly U.S.-centric) literature and unavoidably ethnocentric perspective of the author. The Anglo-Saxon dominance of

Table 1 Classification of Professional Ideologies in Journalism

Professional Ideology	Interventionism	Power Distance	Market Orientation	Objectivism	Empiricism	Relativism	Idealism
Objective journalism	–			+	+	–	+
Advocacy journalism	+			–	–		
Adversarial journalism	+	+	–	–			
Watchdog journalism	+	+	–	+	+		
Investigative journalism		+	–	+	+	+	–
Public/civic journalism	+	+	–	–			
Interpretative journalism			–	–	–		
New journalism				–	–		
Development journalism	+	–	–	+	+		
Peace journalism	+		–	–	+		
Precision journalism	–			+	+		
Qualitative method journalism				–	+		
Service journalism			+				
Popular journalism		–	+			+	–
Existential journalism	+			–	–		

international communication research has become the subject of various publications (e.g., Lauf, 2005) and occasionally leads to fierce debates among scholars from different national backgrounds, and many academic cultures—notably in France and in some parts of Latin America—remain relatively self-contained. This is why the systematic analysis of journalism culture ultimately requires a collaborative effort that involves researchers with very diverse cultural experience and knowledge. Such an attempt is currently undertaken by a multinational network of journalism researchers from a wide array of cultural contexts (see www.worldsofjournalisms.org).

References

Alvesson, M. (2002). *Understanding organizational culture.* London: Sage.

Anderson, J. A., & Baym, G. (2004). Philosophies and philosophic issues in communication, 1995–2004. *Journal of Communication,* **54,** 589–615.

Archer, M. S. (1996). *Culture and agency: The place of culture in social theory, revised edition.* Cambridge, UK: Cambridge University Press.

Berkowitz, D., Limor, Y., & Singer, J. (2004). A cross-cultural look at serving the public interest: American and Israeli journalists consider ethical scenarios. *Journalism,* **5**(2), 159–181.

Bourdieu, P. (1998). *On television and journalism.* London: Pluto.

Campbell, V. (2004). *Information age journalism: Journalism in an international context.* London: Arnold.

Cheng, C.-Y. (1987). Chinese philosophy and contemporary human communication theory. In D. L. Kincaid (Ed.), *Communication theory: Eastern and Western perspectives* (pp. 23–43). San Diego, CA: Academic Press.

Cohen, B. C. (1963). *The press and foreign policy.* Princeton, NJ: Princeton University Press.

Commission on Freedom of the Press. (1947). *A free and responsible press. A general report on mass communication: Newspapers, radio, motion pictures, magazines, and books.* Chicago: University of Chicago Press.

Dancy, J. (1985). *An introduction to contemporary epistemology.* Malden, MA: Blackwell.

Deuze, M. (2002). National news cultures: A comparison of Dutch, German, British, Australian, and U.S. journalists. *Journalism & Mass Communication Quarterly,* **79**(1), 134–149.

Deuze, M. (2005). What is journalism? Professional identity and ideology of journalists reconsidered. *Journalism,* **6,** 442–464.

Donsbach, W. (1995). Lapdogs, watchdogs, and junkyard dogs. *Media Studies Journal,* **9**(4), 17–30.

Donsbach, W., & Patterson, T. E. (2004). Political news journalists: Partisanship, professionalism, and political roles in five countries. In F. Esser & B. Pfetsch (Eds.), *Comparing political communication: Theories, cases, and challenges* (pp. 251–270). New York: Cambridge University Press.

Eide, M., & Knight, G. (1999). Public-private service: Service journalism and the problems of everyday life. *European Journal of Communication,* **14,** 525–547.

Ekström, M. (2002). Epistemologies of TV journalism: A theoretical framework. *Journalism,* **3,** 259–282.

Elliott, D. (1988). All is not relative: Essential shared values and the press. *Journal of Mass Media Ethics,* **3**(1), 28–32.

Esser, F. (1998). Editorial structures and work principles in British and German newsrooms. *European Journal of Communication,* **13,** 375–405.

Forsyth, D. R. (1980). A taxonomy of ethical ideologies. *Journal of Personality and Social Psychology,* **39**(1), 175–184.

Forsyth, D. R. (1981). Moral judgment: The influence of ethical ideology. *Personality and Social Psychology Bulletin,* **7,** 218–223.

Fuller, J. (1996). *News values: Ideas for an information age.* Chicago: University of Chicago Press.

Gans, H. J. (1979). *Deciding what's news: A study of CBS Evening News, NBC Nightly News, Newsweek, and Time.* New York: Pantheon Books.

Golding, P. (1977). Media professionalism in the Third World: The transfer of an ideology. In J. Curran, M. Gurevitch, & J. Woollacott (Eds.), *Mass communication and society* (pp. 291–308). London: Arnold.

Golding, P., & Elliott, P. (1979). *Making the news.* London: Longman.

Gunaratne, S. A. (2006). Democracy, journalism, and systems: Perspectives from East and West. In H. Xiaoming & S. K. Datta-Ray (Eds.), *Issues and challenges in Asian journalism* (pp. 1–24). Singapore: Marshall Cavendish.

Gurevitch, M., & Blumler, J. G. (2004). State of the art of comparative political communication research: Poised for maturity? In F. Esser & B. Pfetsch (Eds.), *Comparing political communication: Theories, cases, and challenges* (pp. 325–343). New York: Cambridge University Press.

Hall, E. T. (1959). *The silent language.* New York: Doubleday.

Hallin, D. C. (2000). Media, political power, and democratization in Mexico. In J. Curran & M.-J. Park (Eds.), *De-Westernizing media studies* (pp. 97–110). London: Routledge.

Hallin, D. C., & Mancini, P. (2004). *Comparing media systems: Three models of media and politics.* New York: Cambridge University Press.

Hanitzsch, T. (2005). Journalists in Indonesia: Educated but timid watchdogs. *Journalism Studies,* **6,** 493–508.

Herrscher, R. (2002). A universal code of journalism ethics: Problems, limitations, and proposals. *Journal of Mass Media Ethics,* **17,** 277–289.

Herscovitz, H. G. (2004). Brazilian journalists' perceptions of media roles, ethics, and foreign influences on Brazilian journalism. *Journalism Studies,* **5**(1), 71–86.

Himelboim, I., & Limor, Y. (2005, May). *The journalistic societal role: An international comparative study of 242 codes of ethics.* 55th Annual Conference of the International Communication Association, New York.

Hofstede, G. (1980). *Culture's consequences: International differences in work-related values.* Beverley Hills, CA: Sage.

Hollifield, A. C., Kosicki, G. M., & Becker, L. B. (2001). Organizational versus professional culture in the newsroom: Television news directors' and newspaper editors' hiring decisions. *Journal of Broadcasting & Electronic Media,* **45**(1), 92–117.

Janowitz, M. (1975). Professional models in journalism: The gatekeeper and the advocate. *Journalism Quarterly,* **52,** 618–626, 662.

Jensen, K. B. (1998). Local empiricism, global theory: Problems and potentials of comparative research on news reception. *Communications,* **23,** 427–445.

Josephi, B. (2006). Journalism in the global age: Between normative and empirical. *Gazette,* **67,** 575–590.

Keeble, R. (2005). Journalism ethics: Towards an Orwellian critique? In S. Allan (Ed.), *Journalism: Critical issues* (pp. 54–66). Maidenhead, UK: Open University Press.

Kovach, B., & Rosenstiel, T. (2001). *The elements of journalism.* London: Atlantic Books.

Köcher, R. (1986). Bloodhounds or missionaries: Role definitions of German and British journalists. *European Journal of Communication,* **1**(1), 43–64.

Knott, D. L., Carroll, V., & Meyer, P. (2002). Social responsibility wins when CEO has been editor. *Newspaper Research Journal,* **23**(1), 25–37.

Lauf, E. (2005). National diversity of major international journals in the field of communication. *Journal of Communication,* **55**(1), 139–151.

Lee, C.-C. (2001). Servants of the state or the market? Media and journalists in China. In J. Tunstall (Ed.), *Media occupations and professions: A reader* (pp. 240–252). New York: Oxford University Press.

Lull, J. (1995). *Media, communication, culture: A global approach.* New York: Columbia University Press.

Ma, E. K. (2000). Rethinking media studies. The case of China. In J. Curran & M.-J. Park (Eds.), *De-Westernizing media studies* (pp. 21–34). London: Routledge.

Marr, M., Wyss, V., Blum, R., & Bonfadelli, H. (2001). *Journalisten in der Schweiz. Eigenschaften, Einstellungen, Einflüsse.* [Journalists in Switzerland. Characteristics, attitudes, influences]. Konstanz, Germany: UVK.

Masterton, M. (Ed.). (1996). *Asian values in journalism.* Singapore: *AMIC.*

McNair, B. (2000). Power, profit, corruption, and lies. *The Russian media in the 1990s.* In J. Curran & M.-J. Park (Eds.). *De-Westernizing media studies* (pp. 79–94). London: Routledge.

McQuail, D. (2000). *McQuail's mass communication theory.* London: Sage.

Merill, J. C., & Odell, J. S. (1983). *Philosophy and journalism.* New York: Longman.

Mwesige, P. G. (2004). Disseminators, advocates, and watchdogs: A profile of Ugandan journalists in the new millennium. *Journalism,* **5**(1), 69–96.

Nasution, Z. (1996). Social and cultural influences on journalism values in Asia. In M. Masterton (Ed.), *Asian values in journalism* (pp. 52–55). Singapore: AMIC.

Pasti, S. (2005). Two generations of contemporary Russian journalists. *European Journal of Communication,* **20**(1), 89–115.

Perkins, M. (2002). International law and the search for universal principles in journalism ethics. *Journal of Mass Media Ethics,* **17,** 193–208.

Plaisance, P. L. (2005, May). *An assessment of media ethics education: Course content and the values and ethical ideologies of media ethics students.* 55th Annual Conference of the International Communication Association, New York.

Plaisance, P. L., & Skewes, E. A. (2003). Personal and professional dimensions of news work: Exploring the link between journalists' values and roles. *Journalism & Mass Communication Quarterly,* **80,** 833–848.

Ramaprasad, J. (2001). A profile of journalists in post-independence Tanzania. *Gazette,* **63,** 539–556.

Ramaprasad, J., & Hamdy, N. N. (2006). Functions of Egyptian journalists: Perceived importance and actual performance. *International Communication Gazette,* **68**(2), 167–185.

Ramaprasad, J., & Kelly, J. D. (2003). Reporting the news from the world's rooftop: A survey of Nepalese journalists. *Gazette,* **65,** 291–315.

Ramaprasad, J., & Rahman, S. (2006). Tradition with a twist: A survey of Bangladeshi journalists. *International Communication Gazette,* **68**(2), 148–165.

Reese, S. D. (2001). Understanding the global journalist: A hierarchy-of-influences approach. *Journalism Studies,* **2**(2), 173–187.

Rosen, J. (2000). Questions and answers about public journalism. *Journalism Studies,* **1,** 679–683.

Sanders, K. (2003). *Ethics & journalism.* London: Sage.

Scholl, A., & Weischenberg, S. (1998). *Journalismus in der Gesellschaft. Theorie, Methodologie und Empirie* [Journalism in society. Theory, methodology and findings]. Opladen, Germany: Westdeutscher Verlag.

Schramm, W. (1964). *Mass media and national development: The role of information in developing countries.* Stanford, CA: Stanford University Press.

Schudson, M. (1990). *Origins of the ideal of objectivity in the professions: Studies in the history of American journalism and American law, 1830–1940.* New York: Garland.

Schudson, M. (2003). *The sociology of news.* New York: W. W. Norton.

Shoemaker, P. J., & Cohen, A. A. (2006). *News around the world: Content, practitioners, and the public.* New York: Routledge.

Shoemaker, P. J., & Reese, S. D. (1996). *Mediating the message: Theories of influence on mass media content.* White Plains, NY: Longman.

Smith, P. B., & Schwartz, S. H. (1997). Values. In J. W. Berry, M. H. Segall, & C. Kagitxibasi (Eds.), *Handbook of cross-cultural psychology: Social behavior and applications* (Vol. 3, pp. 77–118). Boston: Allyn and Bacon.

Splichal, S., & Sparks, C. (1994). *Journalists for the 21st century. Tendencies of professionalization among first-year students in 22 countries.* Norwood, NJ: Ablex.

Underwood, D. (2001). Reporting and the push for market-oriented journalism: Media organizations as business. In W. L. Bennett & R. M. Entman (Eds.), *Mediated politics: Communication in the future of democracy* (pp. 99–116). Cambridge, UK: Cambridge University Press.

van de Vijver, F. J. R., & Leung, K. (1997). *Methods and data analysis for cross-cultural research.* Thousand Oaks, CA: Sage.

Viall, E. K. (1992). Measuring journalistic values: A cosmopolitan-community continuum. *Journal of Mass Media Ethics,* **7**(1), 41–53. Waisbord, S. (2000). *Watchdog journalism in South America: News, accountability, and democracy.* New York: Columbia University Press.

Wallerstein, I. (1991). *Geopolitics and deoculture: Essays on the changing world-system.* Cambridge, MA: Cambridge University Press.

Weaver, D. H. (1998a). *The global journalist: News people around the world.* Cresskill, NJ: Hampton.

Weaver, D. H. (1998b). Journalists around the world: Commonalities and differences. In D. H. Weaver (Ed.), *The global journalist: News people around the world* (pp. 455–480). Cresskill, NJ: Hampton.

Weaver, D. H., Randall, A. B., Brownlee, B. J., Voakes, P., & Wilhoit, G. C. (2007). *The American journalist in the 21st century: U.S. news people at the dawn of a new millennium.* Mahwah, NJ: Lawrence Erlbaum.

Weaver, D. H., & G. C. Wilhoit. (1991). *The American journalist* (2nd. ed.). Bloomington: Indiana University Press.

Weischenberg, S., Scholl, A., & Malik, M. (2006). *Die Souffleure der Mediengesellschaft. Report über die Journalisten in Deutschland* [Prompters of the media society. A report on journalists in Germany]. Konstanz: UVK.

Williams, R. (1958). *Culture and society, 1780–1950.* London: Columbia University Press.

Wirth, W., & S. Kolb. (2004). Designs and methods of comparative political communication research. In F. Esser & B. Pfetsch (Eds), *Comparing political communication: Theories, cases, and challenges* (pp. 87–111). New York: Cambridge University Press.

Wu, W., Weaver, D., & Johnson, O. V. (1996). Professional roles of Russian and U.S. journalists: A omparative study. *Journalism & Mass Communication Quarterly,* **73**, 534–548.

Xiaoge, X. (2005). *Demystifying Asian values in journalism.* Singapore: Marshall Cavendish.

Source: From "Deconstructing Journalism Culture: Toward a Universal Theory," 2007, by T. Hanitzsch, *Communication Theory, 17,* 367–385. Reprinted by permission of Wiley-Blackwell/ICA.

PART II

Cultural Practice of Journalism

Although people who practice journalism consider it to be a profession or paraprofession, journalism can equally be viewed as the activity of a specific cultural group—news represents the tangible outcome of that group's activities. The readings in this part build on the Introduction and Part I to emphasize and exemplify cultural meanings of news, helping the reader to make a transition of vantage points. The sociological vantage point considers how practice within a news organization can be interpreted as a set of rules and processes that reside in the relations among journalists and in the interface between journalists and their organizations. A shift to the cultural vantage point moves the central concern to the way meanings reside in news practice and how those meanings transfer back and forth between journalists and society.

Some of the analytic tools of Part I become helpful here. Regarding levels of analysis, research from the cultural vantage point tends toward the midrange and more macro levels. In other words, the questions are not about the individual or even about a particular media organization but instead journalists as members of a collective field of work and media organizations as one of society's many institutions. Another important consideration for cultural exploration is how journalism becomes a global phenomenon, with both localized characteristics and characteristics that transcend the national to become something larger that is adapted and shared. As Hanitzsch argued, the practice of journalism can be partly linked to professional ideology, but it also represents a struggle for the roles and meanings of journalism in society.

The four readings in Part II do not speak with a unified voice in their emphasis on journalism as a cultural form, but they nonetheless share a common vision for transforming their answers into the cultural vantage point that asks this question: What does news tell us about the professional culture and the society that produces it?

"The Socially Responsible Existentialist: A Normative Emphasis for Journalists in a New Media Environment" by Jane B. Singer suggests that with the challenge to conventional journalism brought about by the open opinion environment of the blog, historical practices—and their related professional norms—are no longer a sufficient way of understanding what constitutes a professional journalist. Online technology, Singer argues, has brought about a fundamental change in the culture of journalism so that defining professionalism through accepted process cannot effectively discriminate between journalists and bloggers, who dwell in a murkier realm somewhere between fact and opinion. Singer suggests that journalists can better be defined as *existentialists,* whose meaning making rests on the twin pillars of freedom of choice and personal responsibility. This socially responsible autonomy becomes a key in separating journalists as neutral information carriers from opinion-oriented bloggers. Tied to the journalist–blogger dichotomy is the notion of gatekeeper: For the journalist, the gates for information are opened judiciously, while the blogger's gates move much more freely. Ultimately, this article concludes that a more open media environment represents a large cultural shift in the meaning of journalistic work.

"Blasphemy as Sacred Rite/Right: 'The Mohammed Cartoons Affair' and Maintenance of Journalistic Ideology" examines how the national contexts of two different journalisms shaped their responses toward the same challenge to their professional ideologies. In this case, Dan Berkowitz and Lyombe Eko invoke two meanings of "cultural"—one being the global context and the other the vantage point for considering journalistic practice as cultural phenomenon. More specifically, this piece looks at how two flagship national newspapers (in France and the United States) reported on the Danish newspaper *Jyllands-Posten*'s publication of 12 satirical cartoons depicting the Muslim prophet Mohammed. The authors argue that each newspaper's coverage represented the epitome of that journalism's professional paradigm—its belief system—within the deeper roots of a national cultural foundation. In each case, the relationship between religion and the state shaped coverage, as did the culturally bound self-conception of journalists. In the French case, for example, the journalistic paradigm advocates journalists not as neutral conveyors of information but as intellectual interpreters of issues and events. In contrast, American journalists pride themselves on the ability to remain neutral bystanders while informing their audiences. For each of these cultures, the publication of the Mohammed cartoons in the Danish newspaper represented different conflicts with their core professional tenets. From the sociological perspective, paradigm repair (see Part IV) represents a functional activity undertaken by its keepers—a way of restoring faith in its professional belief system. Translated to a cultural perspective, paradigm repair becomes a means of "re-presentation," where professional ideals are stated anew as a reminder to society about which dimensions of journalism are most valued. Ultimately, although both can be considered "Western," the journalistic paradigms of France and the United States offer clear contrasts in their basic beliefs.

"The Journalistic Gut Feeling: Journalistic Doxa, News Habitus, and Orthodox News Values" explicitly takes on the challenge of translating journalistic and sociological answers about journalism and news into the cultural perspective. Rather than dealing with journalism at the national level, Ida Schultz aims for a midrange level of analysis viewed through the concepts developed by Bourdieu's field theory. A *field* can be seen as a system of social positions structured by interacting power relationships, a struggle over ownership of social capital. This cultural vantage point adds a helpful nuance by taking the discussion of news away from the debate of professionalism, considering it more generically in terms of its working arrangements. From this position, *habitus* becomes a means of distinguishing between the players of the "news game." An editor, for example, occupies a different social position from that of a new intern and becomes a more respected, knowledgeable player during newsroom interactions; the editor has more "game." An experienced player in the news game owns more "editorial capital"—a form of social capital—which helps evaluate that player's perceived habitus. Just as the discussion of field, habitus, and capital translate newsroom interaction from the social to the cultural, the concept of *doxa* refers to the unspoken elements of journalistic practice that seem natural. Thus, some news values can be considered doxic, something that journalists do not enumerate but nonetheless share within their field. In contrast, the set of news values listed by journalism textbooks—timeliness, proximity, impact, for example—could be called "orthodox" news values because they are formally acknowledged. Most notable among doxic news values is the idea of *exclusivity,* where news items are considered within the context of potential news stories of the day. Schultz depicts this take on news selection as a matter of *positioning,* so that a news story is never newsworthy on its own but through its position in relation to other stories. What journalists experience as their "journalistic gut feeling" thus represents a mix of doxic and orthodox news judgments, which are further shaped by the habitus and social capital of players in the journalistic field.

As with the other selections in this part of the book, Frank Durham's "Media Ritual in Catastrophic Time: The Populist Turn in Television Coverage of Hurricane Katrina" shifts from the lens of sociology to the cultural vantage point. The context of this piece is a case study of television reporters' efforts to cover the aftermath of Hurricane Katrina—at a time when the usual relationship between journalists and their official news sources in government is absent. Here, the work of journalists is depicted as a cultural performance of ritual, and the key to what becomes news is how news resonates culturally with media audiences. Ritual does not represent a fixed routine but instead a fluid working context for making news. Mainstream newspapers and network television work within the domain of "the center," while tabloid media can be considered "off center." In a typical crisis situation, news content results from ritual within mainstream news media, which helps smooth public fears by moving toward a consensus mode with government efforts and aligning the news closer to society's center. Because government actions were initially disconnected from the emergency created by Katrina's destruction, though, the media lacked a center to move toward. Uncharacteristic of their usual actions, network television reporters were left to provide their own interpretations of what had happened—in essence, moving off-center like tabloid news to provide *interpretive* rather than *objective* reporting. In doing so, news ritual was transformed from its usual maintenance role to a kind of journalistic action that could actually draw in a government response.

Taken together, the four selections in Part II begin to contextualize and apply the concepts that have been offered so far. By doing so, these selections demonstrate how thinking about journalists and the news they create is part of both a professional culture and a culture of the society within which they work. The vantage point may still be a bit fuzzy so far, but through some mental "squinting," it should be possible to start seeing news (and the journalistic work that creates it) in a new, cultural light.

4

The Socially Responsible Existentialist

A Normative Emphasis for Journalists in a New Media Environment

Jane B. Singer

Introduction

Changes in the media over the past decade have created many pressures for journalists. New forms of news, a global 24/7 online and cable news environment, an increasing bottom-line emphasis and the resulting squeeze on resources have repositioned news as one of many corporate product lines and far from the most profitable one at that (Bennett, 2005). Amid these and other changes, it has become increasingly difficult to define who is, and is not, a journalist.

Historically, journalists have been defined mainly by professional practices and associated norms, and those in turn have been tied to the media environments in which journalists work. The journalist was the person who wrote that first rough draft of history. The journalist was a community's "gatekeeper," deciding what information was worth knowing (White, 1950). The journalist reconstituted the everyday world by filtering it through a set of institutional routines and structures (Tuchman, 1973), got information to the public quickly, investigated government claims (Weaver and Wilhoit, 1996), and offered society a current, reasoned reflection on the day's events, values and needs (Ranly, 1995). In short, the journalist was someone who engaged in a particular process of gathering, organizing and disseminating timely information in a way that drew its credibility from such ethical precepts as balance and fairness (Gup, 1999).

Yet in our networked world, millions of people gather, organize and disseminate timely information every hour of every day. There is no "gate," and the idea that anyone guard one becomes absurd (Williams and Delli Carpini, 2000); virtually any bit of information, misinformation or disinformation is just a Google search away for the online user. Institutional routines and structures are in a state of flux as news organizations reorganize beats, experiment with convergence and revisit notions of what constitutes news in a scramble to keep audiences from shrinking further. Anyone with a weblog can get information to the public quickly—often, as coverage of both the South Asian tsunami and the New Orleans hurricane demonstrated, much more quickly and efficiently than traditional journalists can. And claims made by officials anywhere in the world are immediately subject to scrutiny by a horde of self-appointed online fact checkers. Surely, in this environment, while all journalists still publish information, not all publishers of information are journalists.

If definitions grounded in process are no longer valid, we must look for other grounds. This article suggests the answer to "who is a journalist" in a democratic society today is a normative one, and its purpose is to explore the nature of contemporary journalism at this fundamental level. To do so, it builds on the notion of "mutualism" (Merrill, 1997), drawing primarily on the seemingly contradictory ethical precepts of independence and accountability. It suggests that journalistic independence is a necessary but not sufficient condition for journalism in the current media environment and is contingent on the notion of individual commitment to social responsibility. The emphasis thus is on a journalist's personal choice to uphold the public trust. Such a definition connects and updates two broader conceptualizations based on earlier competing claims about the central norms of journalism: the existential journalist (Merrill, 1996) and the socially responsible journalist (Commission on Freedom of the Press, 1947).

This article calls renewed attention to the need for a dialectical approach not only to the practice of journalism (Merrill, 1989) but also to the core definition of the journalist. Such a definition avoids attempts to get a handle on the current state of journalism by delineating what processes do or do not constitute journalism, what content is or is not journalistic in nature, what media entities do or do not produce news, and what evolving technologies are or are not platforms for journalism. Instead, it connects production to the individual producer, an existential approach appropriate in a media environment open to all contributors and all sorts of ways to provide information. At the same time, it connects that producer to the erstwhile audience, a socially responsible approach essential in a media environment that also is both interactive and information-rich. In doing so, it draws on constructs of professionalism, which sociologists define as involving both autonomy and public service. Such a definition may be important to the journalist who has an individual need to preserve his or her occupational identity, but it is even more important to members of the public who have a compelling social need to differentiate between information that can be trusted and information that cannot.

Philosophical Grounds: Existentialism and Social Responsibility Theory

The relationship between autonomy and accountability, or between freedom and responsibility, is a long-standing subject of debate within the field of journalism studies. Most theorists seek ways to reconcile the two, claiming that both are vital to the proper functioning of media in a democratic society (Gordon and Kittross, 1999) and that synthesis is needed to avoid an "either–or way of thinking" that leads to anarchy on the one hand and authoritarianism on the other (Merrill, 1997, p. 214). Nonetheless, different observers have tended to lean toward one or the other. Their ethical arguments have been associated with potential polarities contained in two core ideas, existentialism and social responsibility theory (SRT). Although it is simplistic to say that existentialism is concerned with the individual and SRT with the larger public, it nonetheless is true that the two approaches bring to the fore different aspects of the journalist's dual responsibilities to the self and to the audience. An overview of each philosophy in the context of journalism studies may be helpful.

Existentialism

Although its incorporation of a range of diverse positions makes existentialism difficult to define precisely, its central emphasis is on concrete individual existence and, by extension, the ideas of moral individualism, subjectivity, personal choice and commitment (Dreyfus, 2004). Expression of this philosophy dates to 19th-century Danish philosopher Søren Kierkegaard, but it was 20th-century Frenchman Jean-Paul Sartre who emphasized the individual's freedom to choose and the need to take personal responsibility for those choices. "Man is nothing else but what he makes of himself," and the "full responsibility of his existence" rests on him, Sartre wrote (2001, p. 36). Existentialists maintain that because there is no predefined or predestined human nature, people are defined and, ultimately, evaluated solely by their own freely taken choices and actions (*Wikipedia:The Free Encyclopedia,* 2004). However, although existentialism emphasizes individual autonomy, it differs from egoism in the weight it puts on how personal choices may affect others; many noted existentialists, including Kierkegaard, have been Christian thinkers, and others, including Sartre (1973), have stressed the humanism in their philosophy.

Sartre said a journalist should choose to use freedom to disclose social patterns and weaknesses, thus actively promoting change; his colleague, Albert Camus, thought journalists can change society only indirectly through changes within themselves (Bree, 1972; Merrill, 1996). But although Sartre was a sometime-political editor and Camus was a magazine and newspaper reporter, neither existentialist focused primarily on the journalist. [Kierkegaard, for his part, was extremely critical of the press of his day and arguably would have hated the Internet even more, seeing it as combining the worst features of a newspaper and a coffeehouse (Dreyfus, 2001).]

Within journalism studies, the leading advocate of an existentialist approach has been U.S. scholar John C. Merrill. In *The Imperative of Freedom* (1974) and *Existential Journalism* (1996), among other works, Merrill argues that journalistic autonomy is a paramount concept, integral to a commitment to seeking truth. He emphasizes that existentialism incorporates the idea of responsibility but that such responsibility is personal rather than social: a journalist is responsible for a choice or action rather than to others in making that choice or taking that action. Freedom implies self-determination of what is right and good (Merrill, 1989), and the existential journalist would seek autonomy not just from control by outside forces but also from internal controls imposed by employers, ethics codes or traditional newsroom practices (Breed, 1955). In his more recent writings, Merrill has moderated his views, stressing the need for a more Aristotelian ethical approach that combines respect for both the individual and for society, though he continues to distinguish between personal and social responsibility (Merrill, 1997).

Social Responsibility Theory

While existentialism evolved primarily on the European continent, SRT is an AngloAmerican concept (Siebert et al., 1956), and unlike existentialism, it has always had journalism specifically in mind. In the United States, it was first clearly articulated in the post-war 1940s by the Commission on Freedom of the Press, popularly known as the Hutchins Commission, in its report titled *A Free and Responsible Press.* The commission provided five performance standards for journalism, charging it with the responsibility of being, among other things, truthful, comprehensive and fair (Commission on Freedom of the Press, 1947). Moreover, the commission urged journalists to move beyond their interpretation of independence as requiring strict objectivity and to instead seek to provide "the truth about the fact," accepting responsibility for helping readers evaluate the trustworthiness of conflicting sources and gain perspective about complex issues (Siebert et al., 1956, p. 88). Although the commission chose the term "responsible" rather than "accountable," apparently believing it was reasonable to expect responsible behavior but not to demand it, its members clearly stressed the importance of the public's "moral right" to be served by its press (Hocking, 1947, p. 168):

> Since the citizen's *political duty* is at stake, the right to have an adequate service of news becomes a *public responsibility* as well. The phrase freedom of the press" must now cover two sets of rights and not one only. With the rights of editors and publishers to express themselves there must be associated a right of the public to be served with a substantial and honest basis of fact for its judgments of public affairs. Of these two, it is the latter which today tends to take precedence in importance. (Hocking, 1947, p. 169, emphasis in original)

Contemporary scholars have extended these ideas in various ways. For example, the notion of stewardship proposes that journalists "manage their resources of communication with due regard for the rights of others, the rights of the public and the moral health of their own occupation" (Lambeth, 1992, p. 32). The communitarian movement within journalism studies, which has had a professional iteration through civic journalism projects, has gone further. Communitarians see the notion of individual autonomy as inherently problematic. They instead posit a "master norm of universal solidarity" and say journalists should actively work to bring about nothing less than civic transformation through personal and professional commitment to "justice, covenant and empowerment" (Christians et al., 1993, pp. 14–5).

These two quite different approaches to identifying a core journalistic norm have left journalists seeking ways to resolve the apparent conflict between freedom and responsibility. One approach has been to emphasize the ethical decision to use freedom in responsible ways. That is, constraints on freedom must stem from within the individual. That individual will choose to exercise freedom in a way that benefits not just himself or herself but also the larger society; those seeking complete autonomy should not engage in the socially oriented activity of journalism at all (Merrill, 1989). Another approach has been to qualify the notion of freedom as independence from political or social faction rather than from a commitment to the public at large (Kovach and Rosenstiel, 2001). Yet problems remain in determining precisely whom the journalist should be responsible to; once any individual or entity, even one as nebulous as "the public," is defined, the scale tips away from journalistic freedom. Journalists as an occupational group have turned toward ideas about professionalism, particularly professional norms, to help resolve this conflict.

Professional Grounds: Autonomy and Accountability

Aside from a few dictatorships, most nations now possess at least one code of press ethics, delineating the nature of journalists' accountability both to themselves and to a range of others, including peers, sources, subjects and audience members (Bertrand, 2000). In Europe, more than 30 national journalism codes of ethics stress, among other things, press accountability and protection of professional integrity from external influence (Laitila, 1995).

In the United States, although numerous media organizations and outlets have their own codes, the Society of Professional Journalists (SPJ) offers a set of overarching guidelines. In 1996, SPJ, the nation's largest journalist organization, revised its code of ethics, which had been drafted in the post-Watergate 1970s and amended several times since then. The 1996 version, two years in the making, initially was based on three guiding principles: to seek truth, to minimize harm, and to remain independent. But following myriad discussions about journalists' responsibilities to the public, a controversial fourth principle was added: to be accountable (Black et al., 1999). Journalists, the code's authors said, "are accountable to their readers, listeners, viewers and each other." Among their responsibilities under this principle are clarifying and explaining news coverage; inviting dialogue with the public about journalistic conduct; encouraging the public to voice grievances about the news media; and admitting and promptly correcting mistakes (Society of Professional Journalists, 1996).

The addition was controversial for a variety of reasons, not least its apparent conflict with the notion of independence. As Dutch scholars Bardoel and d'Haenens (2004) point out, despite a desire to work for "the people," journalists tend to see accountability to the public and to society as no less threatening than the forces of the state or market. Freedom from faction is a premise to which U.S. journalists have clung fiercely since the demise of the penny press in the 19th century, when the virtues of independence were used simultaneously by newspaper owners as a marketing ploy and by editors as the basis of a claim of professionalism (Kovach and Rosenstiel, 2001). Indeed, autonomy is a central concept in the sociological definition of professionalism. The professional community itself—not any institution, group, or individual external to it—defines what its members do and how they do it. A key mechanism for the community to do so comes by establishing standards of adequate professional practice—for instance, by creating ethics codes. For journalists worldwide, codes have been especially useful as a weapon in demonstrating a willingness to engage in self-reform and thus in fending off the threat of state intervention in the media (Bertrand, 2000).

And yet every profession also has an ideology explaining that autonomy is desired not because it serves the professional's own interests but because it serves the public interest (Daniels, 1973). Moreover, public service is itself another central concept of professionalism. A professional is someone who provides some service to "individuals, groups of people or the public at large" (Hughes, 1965, p. 1), and professional codes often explicitly outline the responsibilities of those inside the occupational group to those outside it (MacIver, 1966). The notions of independence and accountability, then, are not mutually exclusive to any professional community, and journalists are no exception. "It is perfectly reasonable," the authors of the revised SPJ code say, "for journalists to maintain enough independence to remain free from external and internal pressures that dilute the truthtelling enterprise, while simultaneously recognizing that as professionals we are accountable" to the public as well as other journalists (Black et al., 1999, p. 29).

Much of the impetus for the addition of external accountability to the profession's definition of its own core ethical precepts (as well as the controversy surrounding that addition) stemmed from the civic or public journalism movement of the early 1990s, briefly mentioned above in connection with communitarianism. Some journalists loved it; many hated it, or at least thought they did (Rosen, 2001; Voakes, 1999). But the principle arguably has become central to the definition of journalism itself for another reason entirely. The addition of accountability to the U.S. code also coincided with the early phases of a decade of exponential growth in the Internet, with a corresponding growth in use by both media and non-media contributors.

Challenges and Demands of the Current Media Environment

The new online medium inherently changes the notion of an information provider's responsibility to the audience in two potentially opposite ways, one accommodating an absence of accountability and the other accommodating much greater accountability than ever before. On one hand, anyone can publish anything on the Internet, the ultimate free speech zone, with virtual impunity; moreover, the publisher can choose to remain anonymous (Singer, 1996), to ignore challenge or criticism, and to never acknowledge error or inaccuracy. On the other hand, the two-way nature of the medium encourages those reading online content to respond to it, making information production an iterative and readily accessible process in democratic societies.

Journalists and media organizations have responded to this fundamental change in access to the means of disseminating information by drawing on notions of both independence and accountability, often framing their own role in terms of responsibility to try to convince audiences of their trustworthiness and credibility. First, journalists have sought to distinguish themselves from other information sources by emphasizing their commitment to fairness and balance. This emphasis sometimes translates into a too-rigid notion of objectivity that has come under attack for allowing even-handedness to get in the way of communicating the merits of competing claims (Cunningham, 2003). Nonetheless, independence or at least nonpartisanship has been a useful concept in distinguishing most mainstream journalists from blatantly biased sources of information, particularly in an environment in which argument threatens to overwhelm reporting and in which cable programming billed as "news" is increasingly built around the chatter of partisan pundits (Kovach and Rosenstiel, 1999).

Second, commitments to accountability have become more visible. For example, following revelations in 2003 about reporters fabricating stories, top editors at major U.S. newspapers including *USA Today* and *The New York Times* resigned; the *Times* also hired its first "public editor," or ombudsman, and charged him with "publicly evaluating, criticizing and otherwise commenting on the paper's integrity" (Okrent, 2003, p. 2). In fall 2004, when CBS News failed to adequately verify documents relating to President George W. Bush's service in the National Guard, the network (eventually) apologized and set up an independent panel to investigate its own journalism, in an explicit attempt to address charges of partisan motivation in its reporting (cbsnews.com, 2004). Several months later, four CBS News employees, including a senior vice president, were fired for what the panel called "myopic zeal" to break a story that failed to meet "the organization's internal standards" for news (cbsnews.com, 2005). Other media outlets have become more proactive about using their websites for a variety of functions related to accountability, including detailed explanations and dialogue with audience members. For instance, in response to the controversy over its publication and subsequent retraction of a brief item about Guantanamo Bay guards flushing the Koran down a toilet, *Newsweek*'s site offered explanations and apologies by two top editors, an online forum for reader comments, and a podcast of journalists discussing the magazine's actions (Smith, 2005).

Journalists and media organizations also have begun to use the Internet as a vehicle for establishing accountability and distinguishing themselves from non-journalists in this open media environment. One of the hallmarks of online credibility, for example, has become the provision of information about who is behind a website and how to contact that person (Barker, 2005; Reddick and King, 2001). More individual journalists are providing e-mail addresses in a staff list, with their stories or both; indeed, journalists now consider e-mail their most important online tool, particularly for communication with sources (Garrison, 2004).

Evidence abounds that the U.S. public is dubious, at best, about journalistic professions of independence, accountability and trustworthiness, online or off. More than half of Americans say they do not trust journalists to tell the truth (Taylor, 2002); almost as many believe the press has too much freedom to do whatever it likes (McMasters, 2004). A clear majority says news organizations are politically biased, more than a third see them as outright immoral (Project for Excellence, 2005a), and nearly three-quarters think they are influenced by those in power rather than "pretty independent" (Pew Research Center, 2005). Despite such major misgivings, in a media environment packed full of options, Americans still turn to traditional news providers and known "brands" for credible information on the Internet (Project for Excellence, 2005b).

The profusion of information, the resulting search for trustworthy news and the two-way nature of the Internet are just a few of the attributes supporting the central premise of this article: that the current media environment—one in which anyone can publish anything, instantly and to a potentially global audience—demands a rethinking of who might be considered a journalist and what expectations of such a person might be reasonable. Journalists no longer have special access to the mechanisms of widespread production or distribution of information. Nor do they have special access to information itself or to the sources of that information. These and other practical notions of what defined a journalist in the past no longer apply. Instead, the contemporary media environment demonstrates the need to emphasize normative constructs for journalists seeking to delineate themselves from other online information providers. Specifically, a revised consideration of just who is and is not a journalist must include the notion of taking personal responsibility for safeguarding the public trust as a distinguishing characteristic.

Blogs, Partisan Media and the Bottomless News Hole

This section offers a closer look at three changes that are hallmarks of the new media environment and that demonstrate the need for this normative definition of journalism as an enterprise engaged in by existentially responsible practitioners. The changes are the explosion in popularity of weblogs or "blogs"; the partisan fragmentation among both information providers and audiences; and the dissolution of the traditional journalistic roles of gatekeeping and agenda-setting in a media environment marked by unlimited information.

The "Blogosphere"

Although it has been relatively simple to create a functional website for years, the blog may be the most foolproof format yet invented. With start-up software and hosting services available online at little or no cost, it also is the cheapest. The appeal, in addition to the ego trip of seeing one's words glowing from a computer screen, may be the autonomy the format affords. "What I backed into, in doing this blog, was freedom. And not having to write things I didn't believe, and not having to write ways I didn't want to write," said Joshua Micah Marshall (Klam, 2004, p. 49), a sometime magazine writer with a PhD in history whose Talking Points Memo blog has made him a "rock star" of political blogging. Indeed, many bloggers have publicly reveled in this sense of personal empowerment; in the words of Daily Kos blogger Markos Moulitsas, "I can write about whatever I want without somebody telling me I can't" (Smolkin, 2004).

If there is one thing the blogger has, then, it is independence, particularly in the existential sense of being capable of defining oneself solely through one's actions—or words. The notion of accountability in relation to the blogger is more nuanced. Many bloggers claim it is precisely the openness and interactivity of their format that is its greatest attribute—and what separates what they call participatory journalism from traditional forms. If contemporary American journalism is a lecture, blogging is a combination of conversation and seminar, says blogger and former newspaper columnist Dan Gillmor (2004). Bloggers see themselves as engaging in an ongoing dialogue to which readers contribute comments, corrections and critiques, "opening up boring, corporatemindset punditry to a vast range of more interesting competition" (Reynolds, 2003, p. 82). Over time, they say, bloggers gain a following, or not, based on how accurate and relevant they have been, a market-based process (usually minus any actual monetary exchange, though some blogs do attract advertisers) that helps "weed out the charlatans and the credibility-impaired" (Lasica, 2003, p. 73).

Perhaps. Yet ultimately, a blogger need not be accountable precisely because ultimately, he or she serves the self, not the public. Although some argue that once any work is made public—is published—the public becomes a stakeholder in that work (Mitchell and Steele, 2005), it seems clear that autonomy, rather than the sort of responsibility inherent in the notion of stakeholding, is the blogger's defining characteristic. The blog is, again, a purely existential form of self-expression: the blogger can choose either responsibility or irresponsibility, and neither choice need curtail or even influence subsequent decisions or actions.

The core professional concept of public service need not apply at all because the blogger is, proudly, engaging in "amateur journalism" (Lasica, 2002).

An ironic side note: although bloggers may be unaccountable themselves, many are pushing journalists toward more explicit social responsibility by, essentially, shaming them "into doing their jobs better" (Smolkin, 2004). Bloggers are forcing accountability on journalists through close fact-checking and by decrying the journalistic tendency toward arrogance and aloofness (Mitchell and Steele, 2005). Media "watchblogs" ideally serve as a corrective mechanism for sloppy, erroneous or lazy reporting (Andrews, 2003). Examples abound. When former U.S. Senate Majority Leader Trent Lott made a racist comment at a party for a prominent segregationist, bloggers kept the subject alive until professional journalists paid attention. When CBS News reported on Bush's disputed National Guard service without adequate verification of supporting documents, bloggers held journalists' feet to the fire until CBS apologized and launched its investigation. The *Newsweek* controversy cited above was ardently pursued in the blogosphere, as were statements by CNN News executive Eason Jordan in early 2005 about the actions of U.S. forces in Iraq; Jordan subsequently resigned.

Partisan Media and Audience Fragmentation

In addition to being plentiful and prolific, bloggers also tend to be partisan—often adamantly so, expressing their opinions loudly and fervently. While some journalists are beginning to question the primacy of objectivity as a norm, bloggers are untroubled by doubt; in the blogosphere, objectivity is plain verboten (Smolkin, 2004). But the bloggers are only one visible component of the ongoing trend toward overtly partisan media. As the time and space available for news has gone from severely limited to virtually unlimited, media executives have realized that commenting on old or recycled information is much cheaper than gathering new information (Kovach and Rosenstiel, 1999). The more conflict and drama that can be generated in the process, the better (Bennett, 2005).

There certainly is no shortage of commentators. In the realm of political journalism, arguably the most directly relevant to the notion of the journalist as central to a functioning democracy, the amount of partisan spin has become overwhelming. Dueling e-mail, faxes, website gimmicks and more threaten to drown journalists unprepared to deal effectively with the speed, volume and deceptiveness of modern campaigning (Keefer, 2004). In the United States, the "spin room" is now a presidential post-debate staple, creating an absurd spectacle of dozens of high-profile supporters for each side dashing madly about in search of someone to interview them, each bearing a giant sign "announcing their superstars like gladiators entering the Coliseum" (Marinucci, 2004). More insidiously, public relations messages of all sorts are routinely offered as news; video news releases, in particular, are replacing more costly and time-consuming independent reports in cash-strapped television newsrooms (Bennett, 2005).

Journalists are complicit in some of these changes and directly implicated in others that clearly serve their own self-interests and those of their employers, particularly in their participation on cable television talk shows that pit a "liberal" journalist against a "conservative" one. Talk shows cast journalists specifically to fill particular niches in an ideological spectrum, and journalists acknowledge that they often cross lines on such shows that they would never approach in their regular reporting (Kovach and Rosenstiel, 1999). The public can hardly be blamed for seeing the media as biased when the same people deliver both partisan "commentary" and non-partisan "news."

Nor can the public be blamed for gravitating toward outlets, and individual journalists, expressing views that jibe with their own. Although studies suggest that in an information-rich environment, at least some people will seek out a range of views (Horrigan et al., 2004; Iyengar et al., 2001), conservatives and liberals can and do choose sides in radio and television news preferences, especially cable news, and people who say they pay close attention to hard news seem particularly likely to express a preference for news that suits their point of view (Pew Research Center, 2004).

If the explosion of the blogosphere calls for an increased emphasis on accountability as a defining characteristic of journalists, the rise of partisanship calls for a renewed commitment by individual journalists to their own existential independence. Journalism is ultimately an act of character that requires assuming personal responsibility for one's own actions. External pressures created by market forces show no signs of diminishing. Corporate strategies have resulted in ever-narrower targeting of niche audiences; the result has been a press less and less able to serve as a force of social cohesion, and the economic trend is not likely to change. Journalists find themselves in a difficult ethical position if media executives are not committed to putting citizens first—and many clearly are not (Kovach and Rosenstiel, 1999, 2001).

Sometimes a commitment to existential responsibility can even force journalists to put their jobs on the line, as witness the Sinclair Broadcasting bureau chief fired for criticizing his company's plans to air a blatantly partisan political documentary within two weeks of the U.S. election (CNN.com, 2004). Nonetheless, the best approach proposed to date to these difficult and economically driven challenges is an existentially grounded one calling on journalists to exhibit "a tough self-confidence" that involves deciding what they stand for, then articulating it and finally practicing it. "Whether serious journalism survives," observers warn, "is up to those who aspire to call themselves serious journalists" (Kovach and Rosenstiel, 1999, p. 98).

As described above, existentialism involves an individual commitment to, and subsequent responsibility for, a freely made choice. Leading existentialists have emphasized the humanistic, other-oriented nature of choices that are defensible on ethical grounds. For professional journalists, as we have seen, that orientation is connected with the idea of public service. Today, the notion of a "public" is splintering, as the audiences for what once were a relatively few national news outlets fragment into groups able to exist in completely separate media universes. Journalists who choose to appeal to particular niches make a choice that serves increasing fragmentation. Those who seek ways to appeal to a more broadly defined audience—one with a chance to work toward the compromise and resulting consensus on which democracy in enormous and enormously diverse societies depends—can do so only by maintaining a relatively nonpartisan perspective and working to regain the public trust their colleagues are forfeiting. This is the essence of existential responsibility for the journalist, and it is vital if the journalist is to be able to serve the public as his or her professional role shifts from a gatekeeper of information to a trustworthy interpreter of it.

Gatekeeping and Agenda-Setting Roles

Google cheerfully informs users that it will search more than eight billion pages upon request—and much that exists somewhere in the online universe is invisible even to a powerful search engine. In such an environment, the notion of the journalist as gatekeeper seems quaint. In its original journalistic configuration, the term described a newspaper wire editor—"Mr. Gates"—who selected a relatively small number of stories for publication from the options provided by the Associated Press and other wire services (White, 1950). The process was complex, involving a range of social, psychological and professional factors (Shoemaker, 1997); however, it did give the selection and dissemination of information a central place in the definition of what a journalist does. Indeed, this conceptualization of the journalist as the person who decides what others need to know has become deeply ingrained over the years, particularly in connection with the idea of serving the information needs of a democratic society (Gans, 2003; Janowitz, 1975).

Related to gatekeeping is the concept that through their choices about what stories should be allowed to pass through the metaphorical gate, journalists actively shape political reality. Citizens learn what issues and ideas are important to think about because of this agenda-setting function of the media (McCombs and Shaw, 1972). Moreover, journalists generate consensus among an audience through the way they frame particular issues and the prominence those issues are given; thus their agenda-setting role is itself a significant ethical responsibility (McCombs, 1997). Of course, a key question then becomes who or what shapes the journalists' agenda, and that has proven an extremely complex question to address. Influence comes from both inside and outside the journalists' environment, through everything from interpersonal communication, to work routines and norms, to the efforts of newsmakers to attract attention, and more (Shoemaker and Reese, 1991). The latter, in particular, has become an enormous factor, as newsmakers have become increasingly proficient at manipulating images, increasingly proactive in using the Internet to focus attention on particular issues (Ku et al., 2003) and, as mentioned above, increasingly prolific in bombarding journalists with spin (Bennett, 2005; Keefer 2004).

In fact, in an environment in which interactions among participants in the communication process are virtually non-stop and come in myriad forms, an exploration of agenda-setting quickly becomes a journey through a hall of mirrors in which the number of sources, audiences and information providers becomes infinite, and their roles and effects blend and merge together. The traditional idea of a gatekeeper vanishes. The journalist no longer has much if any control over what citizens will see, read or hear, nor what items they will decide are important to think about. In such an open, frenetic and overcrowded media environment, the conceptualization of what a journalist does must turn from an emphasis on process—selecting and disseminating information, framing particular items in particular ways—to an emphasis on ethics.

Gatekeeping is not a matter of keeping an item out of circulation; it is a matter of vetting items for their veracity and of placing them within the broader context that is easily lost under the daily tidal wave of new "information." Agenda-setting is not a matter of identifying what information to think about; it is a matter of identifying what information to trust. Journalists in this anything-goes environment need an existential understanding of the importance of individual, autonomous choices among the virtually unlimited possibilities—and the consequences of those choices. And in making their decisions, they need a sense of their relationship to a public constituted of citizens in a democracy (Kovach and Rosenstiel, 2001) rather than consumers in a giant content-candy store. In short, journalists in such an environment become not gatekeepers but sensemakers, not agenda-setters but interpreters of what it is both credible and valuable—with the notion of independence keeping those interpretations from becoming compromised by partisan loyalties.

A decade ago, when the Web was on the verge of becoming a part of so many people's lives, media historian Michael Schudson invited us to imagine a world in which "governments, businesses, lobbyists, candidates, churches and social movements deliver information directly to citizens." As each person becomes his or her own gatekeeper and goes about setting his or her own information agenda, journalism is abolished. But not for long. People quite quickly realize that they need help in understanding events, in identifying what is most important, most relevant, most interesting. A professional press corps soon reappears (Schudson, 1995, pp. 1–2).

This article has suggested that although journalists have never disappeared, their traditional roles and functions—the traditional definitions that have identified what they do—have been profoundly challenged over the past decade by changes in the media environment, to the point where earlier concepts no longer hold much value. In their place, a new definition—or, more important, a new self-conceptualization by journalists themselves—is called for, one that emphasizes the notion of an existential journalist with a social responsibility to citizens.

The Socially Responsible Existentialist

If ever a medium cried for a combination of the notions of existentialism and social responsibility theory as applied to journalists and journalism, it is the Internet. The Internet affords every individual user complete autonomy over personal communication, along with the power to disseminate that communication globally with a single click. But no inherent social responsibility is connected to that action; an online user need have no obligations to any other user. That is precisely why the journalist must choose to accept those responsibilities. It is their explicit acknowledgment, as well as the ways in which such responsibilities are enacted, that sets him or her apart from those who decline to do so. The heart of the notion of a socially responsible existentialist lies in a combination of freely choosing to be responsible in order to fulfill a social role based on trust. The role has been previously identified (Merrill, 1997) but is more necessary than ever in a media environment marked by an unprecedented range of options and number of communicators. Public service has always been the underpinning of professional journalism, but the nature of that service must adapt to an environment substantially different from the old print and broadcast media world. More information means a greater need for trustworthy sources of, and guides through, that information.

As discussed above, in today's media environment, virtually all the notions of journalism based on past practice are gone. Access to sources of information is open to anyone. Anyone can disseminate his or her views instantly and globally with a few keystrokes. Again, that makes everyone a publisher, but it does not make every publisher a journalist. Professional journalists increasingly will be defined by the degree to which they choose to adhere to the normative goals of their professional culture. Particularly important will be a commitment to helping the public make sense of a world in which an abundance of "facts" creates a greater need for someone who can be trusted to provide the truth about those facts (Commission on Freedom of the Press, 1947).

This article has suggested that a combination of existential freedom with a commitment to trust and responsibility—encompassed by philosophical as well as professional ways of thinking about who journalists are and what they do—provides the most useful conceptual framework for moving the profession forward. It has paired the notions of personal autonomy, action and responsibility, embodied in existentialism, with the explicit public-mindedness of social responsibility theory. The distinctiveness of the journalistic role thus lies in a normative definition that emphasizes responsibilities to the public as a whole but incorporates existential ideas of individual integrity and autonomy, particularly in the sense of freedom from faction.

Such a combination of freedom and responsibility has been articulated before. Kovach and Rosenstiel, who head the Committee of Concerned Journalists and the Project for Excellence in Journalism, respectively, repeatedly have stressed the need for journalists to combine independence from faction with an overarching allegiance to citizens (2001). Scholar John Merrill, in one of his pre-Internet books, put it this way: "Only when the journalist recognizes both self-directed responsibility and other-directed responsibility will journalism stand on a truly moral base" that combines existentialist and humanist strains, among others (1989, p. 243). However, this article goes further. It suggests that ethical commitment to these normative goals is quickly becoming the *only* thing that distinguishes the journalist from other information providers who are independent but not responsible, such as bloggers, or responsible but not independent, such as spin doctors of all stripes. A notion of journalism as an embodiment of existential social responsibility becomes not merely descriptive but definitive.

It is not enough simply to draw up a conceptual definition, of course. The definition must be enacted and, given many citizens' low regard for the media, it must be clearly, consistently, and credibly communicated outside the profession. Survey after survey shows that the public feels ill-served by journalists and media outlets that are none of the things they profess to be—neither ethical nor non-partisan nor even accurate. The majority of Americans no longer trust journalists to tell the truth (Taylor, 2002), let alone to interpret competing versions of "truth." Moreover, news organizations seem either unable, primarily because of their lost role as gatekeepers and agenda-setters, or unwilling, primarily because of economic pressures, to serve as the forces of social cohesion that they once were. While the splintering media environment is only one factor among many, democratic systems that rest on the ability of both citizens and elected representatives to compromise and reach consensus are in jeopardy as more and more people are able to retreat into a world informed solely by their own perspectives and prejudices.

Political, social and economic problems are beyond the power of any individual journalist to resolve. But not being entirely to blame is not the same as being blameless. One key value of existentialism is its reminder that we all have choices to make, and those choices carry with them an inherent responsibility both to ourselves and, ultimately, to others. Journalists as individuals must renew their attention to a moral center in which personal integrity informs professional decisions, difficult though those decisions may be. And journalists as members of a profession with a broader responsibility to society at large must refocus on what will serve a public comprised of citizens in need of trustworthy information rather than consumers in need of yet another media product in a world full of other options (Kovach and Rosenstiel, 2001).

In the end, it is this notion of trust that resolves the question of why it even matters who is defined as a journalist. Aside from the journalist's self-serving need to maintain his or her means of livelihood and role in a changing society, why should anyone else care? The answer lies in the centrality of information as a public good in a democratic society and in the shifting nature of that civic resource. The free flow of information is fundamental to a functioning democracy, and in a traditional media environment, the primary concern of journalists has been to make information available. But today, information—along with misinformation and disinformation—is in overwhelmingly abundant supply. The public needs some means of differentiating between what is valuable to society as a whole and what is less so; otherwise, the notion of a coherent "public" falls apart as each individual seeks out whatever seems most personally appealing at the moment.

Journalism, in various forms over the years, has historically provided such a means of identifying what is socially relevant and important. The need has become even more urgent today. As the nature of the media environment changes, the definition and selfconceptualization of the journalist must shift from one rooted in procedure—the professional process of making information available—to one rooted in ethics—the professional norms guiding determinations about which information has true societal value. This article has suggested that what gains such value is information that people can trust, and that trust is best established and nurtured by those with an existential commitment to social responsibility.

References

Andrews, Paul (2003) "Is Blogging Journalism?," *Nieman Reports* 57(Fall), pp. 63–4.

Bardoel, Jo And D'haenens, Leen (2004) "Media Meet the Citizen: beyond market mechanisms and government regulations," *Communications* 19, pp. 165–94.

Barker, Joe (2005), "Evaluating Web Pages: techniques to apply and questions to ask," University of California Berkeley, Teaching Library Internet Workshops, http://www.lib.berkeley.edu/TeachingLib/Guides/Internet/Evaluate.html.

Bennett, W. Lance (2005) *News: the politics of illusion,* 6th edn, New York: Pearson Education.

Bertrand, Claude-Jean (2000) *Media Ethics and Accountability Systems,* New Brunswick, NJ: Transaction Publishers.

Black, Jay, Steele, Bob and Barney, Ralph (1999) *Doing Ethics in Journalism: a handbook with case studies,* 3rd edn, Needham Heights, MA: Allyn and Bacon.

Bree, Germaine (1972) *Camus and Sartre: crisis and commitment,* New York: Dell.

Breed, Warren (1955) "Social Control in the Newsroom: a functional analysis," *Social Forces* 33, pp. 326–35.

Cbsnews.Com (2004) "CBS Names Memo Probe Panel", 22 September, http://www.cbsnews.com/stories/2004/09/06/politics/main641 481.shtml.

Cbsnews.Com (2005) "CBS Ousts 4 for Bush Guard Story", 10 January, http://www.cbsnews.com/stories/2005/01/10/national/main665727.shtml.

Christians, Clifford G., Ferre, John P. and Fackler, P. Mark (1993) *Good News: social ethics and the press,* New York: Oxford University Press.

Cnn.Com (2004) "Sinclair: stations won't run entire anti-Kerry film," 30 October, *http://*www.cnn.com/2004/ALLPOLITICS/10/20/sinclair.kerry.

Commission On Freedom Of The Press (1947) *A Free and Responsible Press,* Chicago: University of Chicago Press.

Cunningham, Brent (2003) "Re-thinking Objectivity," *Columbia Journalism Review,* July/August, http://www.cjr.org/issues/2003/4/objective-cunningham.asp.

Daniels, Arlene Kaplan (1973) "How Free Should Professions Be?," in: Eliot Friedson (Ed.), *The Professions and Their Prospects,* Beverly Hills, CA: Sage, pp. 39–57.

Dreyfus, Hubert L. (2001) *On the Internet,* London: Routledge.

Dreyfus, Hubert L. (2004) "Existentialism: major themes," *Microsoft Encarta Online Encyclopedia,* http://encarta.msn.com/encyclopedia_761555530/Existentialism.html.

Gans, Herbert J. (2003) *Democracy and the News,* Oxford: Oxford University Press.

Jane B. Singer Garrison, Bruce (2004) "Newspaper Journalists Use E-mail to Gather News," *Newspaper Research Journal* 25(Spring), pp. 58–69.

Gillmor, Dan (2004) *We the Media: grassroots journalism by the people, for the people,* Sebastapol, CA: O'Reilly Media.

Gordon, A. David And Kittross, John Michael (1999) *Controversies in Media Ethics,* 2nd edn, New York: Longman.

Gup, Ted (1999) "Who's a Journalist?," *Media Studies Journal* 13(Spring/Summer), pp. 34–7.

Hocking, William Ernest (1947) *Freedom of the Press: a framework of principle,* Chicago: University of Chicago Press.

Horrigan, John, Garrett, Kelly And Resnick, Paul (2004) "The Internet and Democratic Debate," Pew Internet & American Life Project, 27 October, http://www.pewinternet.org/PPF/r/141/report display.asp.

Hughes, Everett C. (1965) "Professions," in: Kenneth Schuyler Lynn and editors of *Daedalus* (Eds), *The Professions in America,* Boston: Houghton Mifflin, pp. 1–14.

Iyengar, Shanto, Hahn, Kyu And Prior, Marcus (2001) "Has Technology Made Attention to Political Campaigns More Selective? An experimental study of the 2000 presidential campaign," paper presented to the American Political Science Association, San Francisco, 2 September.

Janowitz, Morris (1975) "Professional Models in Journalism: the gatekeeper and the advocate," *Journalism Quarterly* 52, pp. 618–26, 662.

Keefer, Bryan (2004) "Tsunami," *Columbia Journalism Review,* July/August, http://cjr.org/issues/ 2004/4/keefer-tsunami.asp.

Klam, Matthew (2004) "Fear and Laptops on the Campaign Trail," *The New York Times Magazine,* 26 September, pp. 43–9, 115–6, 123.

Kovach, Bill and Rosenstiel, Tom (1999) *Warp Speed: America in the age of mixed media,* New York: Century Foundation Press.

Kovach, Bill and Rosenstiel, Tom (2001) *The Elements of Journalism: what newspeople should know and the public should expect,* New York: Crown Publishers.

Ku, Gyotae, Kaid, Lynda Lee and Pfau, Michael (2003) The Impact of Web Site Campaigning on Traditional News Media and Public Information Processing," *Journalism & Mass Communication Quarterly* 80, pp. 528–47.

Laitila, Tiina (1995) "Journalistic Codes of Ethics in Europe," *European Journal of Communication* 10, pp. 527–44.

Lambeth, Edmund B. (1992) *Committed Journalism: an ethic for the profession,* 2nd edn, Bloomington: Indiana University Press.

Lasica, J. D. (2002) "Blogging as a Form of Journalism," *Online Journalism Review,* 29 April, http://www.ojr.org/ojr/lasica/1019166956.php.

Lasica, J. D. (2003) "Blogs and Journalism Need Each Other," *Nieman Reports* 57(Fall), pp. 70–4.

MacIver, Robert (1966) "Professional Groups and Cultural Norms (General)," in: Howard M. Vollmer and Donald L. Mills (Eds), *Professionalization,* Englewood Cliffs, NJ: Prentice Hall, pp. 50–5.

Marinucci, Carla (2004) "Lies and Half-truths Are Currency of the Realm in Surreal Spin Room," *San Francisco Chronicle,* 14 October, http://www.sfgate.com/cgi-bin/article.cgi?f=/c/a/2004/10/1 4/MNGBU99G3M1 .DTL.

McCombs, Maxwell (1997) "Building Consensus: the news media's agenda-setting roles," *Political Communication* 14, pp. 433–43.

McCombs, Maxwell E. and Shaw, Donald l. (1972) "The Agenda-setting Function of Mass Media," *Public Opinion Quarterly* 36, pp. 176–87.

McMasters, Paul (2004) "Low Marks," *American Journalism Review,* August/September, http:// ajr.org/article.asp?id=3731.

Merrill, John C. (1974) *The Imperative of Freedom: a philosophy of journalistic autonomy,* New York: Hastings House.

Merrill, John C. (1989) *The Dialectic in Journalism: toward a responsible use of press freedom,* Baton Rouge: Louisiana State University Press.

Merrill, John C. (1996) *Existential Journalism,* Ames: Iowa State University Press.

Merrill, John C. (1997) *Journalism Ethics: philosophical foundations for news media,* New York: St. Martin's Press.

Mitchell, Bill and Steele, Bob (2005) "Earn Your Own Trust, Roll Your Own Ethics: transparency and beyond," paper presented to the Blogging, Journalism and Credibility Conference, Harvard University, Cambridge, MA, 17 January, http://cyber.law.harvard.edu/webcred.

Okrent, Daniel (2003) "An Advocate for *Times* Readers Introduces Himself," *The New York Times,* 7 December, p. 2, section 4.

Pew Research Center for the People and the Press (2004) "News Audiences Increasingly Politicized," 8 June, http://people-press.org/reports/display.php3?PageID= 834, http://people-press.org/reports/display.php3?PageID= 837.

Pew Research Center for the People and the Press (2005) "Public More Critical of Press, but Goodwill Persists," 26 June, http://people-press.org/reports/display.php3? ReportID=248.

Project for Excellence in Journalism (2005a) "Overview: public attitudes," in: *The State of the News Media 2005: an annual report on American journalism,* http:// www.stateofthemedia. org/2005/narrative_overview_ publicattitudes.asp?cat=7andmedia=1.

Project for Excellence in Journalism (2005b) "Online: economics," in: *The State of the News Media 2005: an annual report on American journalism,* http://www.stateofthemedia.org/2005/narrative_online_economics.asp?cat =4and media =3.

Ranly, Don (1995) "Journalism: the what and the why," in: Don Ranly (Ed.), *Principles of American Journalism,* Dubuque, IA: Kendall/Hunt Publishing, pp. 3–8.

Reddick, Randy and King, Elliot (2001) *The Online Journ@list: using the Internet and other electronic resources,* 3rd edn, Fort Worth, TX: Harcourt College.

Reynolds, Glenn Harlan (2003) "Weblogs and Journalism: back to the future?," *Nieman Reports* 57(Fall), pp. 81–2.

Rosen, Jay (2001) *What Are Journalists For?* New Haven, CT: Yale University Press.

Sartre, Jean-Paul (1973 [1946]) *Existentialism and Humanism,* P. Mairet (Trans.), London: Eyre Methuen.

Sartre, Jean-Paul (2001) *Essays in Existentialism,* New York: Citadel.

Schudson, Michael (1995) *The Power of News,* Cambridge, MA: Harvard University Press.

Shoemaker, Pamela J. (1997) "A New Gatekeeping Model," in: Dan Berkowitz (Ed.), *Social Meanings of News,* Thousand Oaks, CA: Sage, pp. 57–62.

Shoemaker, Pamela J. and Reese, Stephen D. (1991) *Mediating the Message: Theories of Influence on Mass Media Content,* New York: Longman.

Siebert, Fred S., Peterson, Theodore and Schramm, Wilbur (1956) *Four Theories of the Press,* Chicago: University of Illinois Press.

Singer, Jane B. (1996) "Virtual Anonymity: online accountability and the virtuous virtual journalist," *Journal of Mass Media Ethics* 11(2), pp. 95–106.

Smith, Richard M. (2005) "A Letter to our Readers," *Newsweek* 30 May, http://www.msnbc.msn.com/id/7952950/site/newsweek.

Smolkin, Rachel (2004) "The Expanding Blogosphere," *American Journalism Review,* June/July, http://ajr.org/Article.asp?id=3682.

Society of Professional Journalists (1996) "Code of Ethics," http://spj.org/ethicscode.asp.

Taylor, Humphrey (2002) "Trust in Priests and Clergy Falls 26 Points in Twelve Months," Harris Poll: Harris Interactive, 27 November, http://www.harrisinteractive .com/harris_poll/index.asp?PID = 342.

Tuchman, Gaye (1973) "Making News by Doing Work: routinizing the unexpected," *American Journal of Sociology* 79, pp. 110–31.

Voakes, Paul S. (1999) "Civic Duties: newspaper journalists' views on public journalism," *Journalism & Mass Communication Quarterly* 76, pp. 756–74.

Weaver, David H. and Wilhoit, G. Cleveland (1996) *The American Journalist in the 1990s: U.S. news people at the end of an era,* Mahwah, NJ: Lawrence Erlbaum Associates.

White, David Manning (1950) "The 'Gate Keeper': a case study in the selection of news," *Journalism Quarterly* 27, pp. 383–90.

Wikipedia: The Free Encyclopedia (2004) "Existentialism," http://en.wikipedia.org/wiki/ Existentialism.

Williams, Bruce A. and Delli Carpini, Michael X. (2000) "Unchained Reaction: the collapse of media gatekeeping and the Clinton Lewinsky scandal," *Journalism: Theory, Practice and Criticism* 1, pp. 61–85.

Source: From "The Socially Responsible Existentialist: A Normative Emphasis for Journalists in a New Media Environment," 2006, by J. B. Singer, *Journalism Studies,* 7(1), 2–18. Reprinted by permission of Taylor & Francis/Routledge.

5

Blasphemy as Sacred Rite/Right

"The Mohammed Cartoons Affair" and Maintenance of Journalistic Ideology

Dan Berkowitz

Lyombe Eko

Introduction

On September 30, 2005, Denmark's largest newspaper, *Jyllands-Posten,* published 12 satirical drawings depicting the Muslim prophet Mohammed. The newspaper saw this act as a way of spurring debate about self-censorship in the media at a time when freedom of expression seemed threatened. Although controversial in Denmark, the act of publishing these dozen cartoons drew little attention from the press of other nations.

But the controversy did not go away. More than three months later, an article appeared in *The New York Times* reporting on a "global furor" the cartoons were causing, a clash of Islam and the West in which Denmark had become an unlikely participant (Bilefsky, 2006a). Still, the issue remained mostly quiet in the world news media as boycotts and protests began to boil across the Muslim world. Then, on February 1, 2006, several European newspapers joined the fray, publishing the cartoons once again (Cowell, 2006b). On the face of it, this controversy and the cartoon republications simply represent a form of journalistic solidarity, a broad-based support for freedom of the press. At a deeper level, though, engagement in the issue by other news media represents something larger: the maintenance of a journalistic paradigm and a sacred right to exercise it in the national culture in which it resides. This case explores how two national flagship newspapers—*The New York Times* and France's *Le Monde*—undertook this maintenance work through their coverage. Despite differences in journalistic paradigms, national cultures, and the respective countries' relationships to Islam and terrorism, both newspapers' coverage was aimed at the same basic goal and carried the same significance to the particular journalistic cultures. In addition, this case demonstrates that there is not a paradigm for Western journalism, but instead multiple paradigms that grow from the national cultures in which they are embedded. This study begins with an overview of the issue and how it connects to the national and journalistic cultures of France and the United States. This is followed by conceptual discussions of journalistic paradigm repair, the terrorism news frame, and freedom of the press. Data come from a textual analysis of articles published by the two newspapers during the heat of the controversy in 2006.

Context of the Study

The Danish newspaper *Jyllands-Posten* will go down in history as the newspaper whose cartoons of Prophet Mohammad shook the global village and precipitated what some writers call an unprecedented clash of Western and Arabo-Islamic worldviews (Kauffmann, 2006; Tincq, 2006a). Founded in 1871, *Morgenavisen Jyllands-Posten* is Denmark's largest circulation daily. It is a self-described "liberal newspaper independent of political, financial, organisational, religious and commercial interests" (*Jyllands-Posten,* 2006b).

The global furor over the Mohammad cartoons started with the inability of a Danish author to find an illustrator for a children's book about Prophet Mohammad. *Jyllands-Posten* wrote several articles on the situation and concluded that it was a case of self-censorship, "untenable for non-Muslims to be bound by Muslim scripture" (2006a). In order to find out the extent of self-censorship in Denmark over Islamic issues, the newspaper asked Danish illustrators to "submit their personal interpretations on how the prophet might appear" (2006a). Twelve illustrators sent in cartoons, which were published in September 2005.

However, the newspaper underestimated the emotional reaction of Danish Muslims—and the power of the media in this age of globalization. The imams of Denmark compiled a 43-page dossier that included the 12 cartoons published by *Jyllands-Posten* plus other *fake,* highly inflammatory, anti-Muslim cartoons. In November 2005, a delegation of imams from Denmark traveled to the Middle East to gather support for protests against the Danish cartoons. In Saudi Arabia, the imams distributed the 43-page cartoons dossier in the sidelines of the meeting of the 57-member Islamic Conference Organization. They passed off their cartoon dossier, including the fake, unpublished inflammatory ones, as *Jyllands-Posten* cartoons. This is what triggered the world-wide demonstrations (Howden et al., 2006). The Arabo-Islamic world experienced an unprecedented outpouring of anger at *Jyllands-Posten,* and Denmark.

On January 29, 2006, the Islamic Conference Organization and the Arab League called on the United Nations to pass a resolution "banning attacks on religious beliefs" (Islam Online, 2006). Amid the world-wide riots and calls for punishment of the Danish newspaper and journalists, the leading newspapers of continental Europe republished the cartoons in solidarity with *Jyllands-Posten.* Muslim mobs from Palestine to Libya promptly added the European Union countries to their list of targets.

The Cultural Context for French and American Journalism

Though French and American journalism are part of the "Western" journalistic paradigm, the cultural specificities of the two countries lead to marked contrasts in their journalistic styles, their roles as "cultural institutions," their respective attitudes towards the government, and their conceptualizations of the place of the sacred and the secular in public affairs. French journalism is a literary journalism that has always placed the "exposé of ideas" on a higher plane than the "recitation of events" (Albert, 1977). For the French journalist, being the judge of the event and the guide of the opinions of the readers is more important than being a witness to the event. Thus, to ask French journalists to separate fact from commentary or opinion is to ask for the impossible (Albert, 1977; Gaunt, 1990; Gaunt and Pritchard, 1990; Salinger, 1980).

Most crucially, contemporary French journalists resent being considered "news specialists" because the real form of journalism in France has always been and still is largely news analysis rather than news reporting (Albert, 1977). This is because French journalism has always been more a journalism of expression than a journalism of observation (Gaunt, 1990). It is historically more rooted in a "tradition of literary style, intellectual elegance, and Gallic 'logic' than in the terse exposition of facts" (Gaunt and Pritchard, 1990, p. 185). Indeed, up to the 19th century, French journalists rejected the idea that they could also be reporters. The reasons for this attitude are historic: for centuries, as a result of strict control of information by the authorities under the "Ancien Regime," French journalists got used to receiving information only from the authorities: Their job was to comment on that information (Bellanger et al., 1975).

In a comparative analysis of "Anglo-American" and "Continental" European journalistic styles, Rice and Cooney (1982) observed that the fundamental difference between the two journalistic styles is their treatment of fact and opinion. American newspapers take great pains to separate fact from opinion and to be generally "objective" in their reporting. At French and other continental European newspapers, reporters are *expected* to pass judgment; the real news is a reporter's *assessment* of what happened (Rice and Cooney, 1982). American "worship of facts"—complete with fact checkers—is the aspect of American journalism that "shocks" French readers of American newspapers (Albert, 1977).

The French posture towards religion is also markedly different from the American attitude towards religion. As a Catholic kingdom, France banned the publication of all material critical of the Roman Catholic Church. The Revolution of 1789 led to the suppression of the Catholic religion, "de-Christianization" and secularization of France. The French state set itself up as a "counterchurch" whose creed was secular republicanism (Césari, 2005). Anti-clericalism has always been a feature of French secularism. The Mohammad cartoons controversy—and its ramifications in France—therefore touched a raw political and cultural nerve.

In contrast, it has been argued that American political, cultural and social ideals expressed in the statement the "American way of life" are founded on Puritan values and principles emphasizing discipline and strict moral standards (Bennett, 1998; Emerson, 1968). The Declaration of Independence contains references to God, as well as to a "Supreme Being." Though the First Amendment proscribes the establishment of a national religion, the American national anthem proclaims "In God is our trust," an idea that also appears on American currency. Richard McBrien (1987) describes contemporary American society as a society with a "public religion"—shared religious values like belief in God and good behavior towards others—found in all denominations. Public religion has become part of the national culture, and is the foundation of the "American way of life."

Furthermore, in the United States, unlike France, there is suspicion of government. The threat to American liberties is seen to come from the government, not religion, not the church, not multiculturalism as is the case in France. Indeed, free speech is framed negatively in the United States. The First Amendment expressly bars Congress from interfering with the freedom of speech of Americans.

This cultural context of the French and American press helps put *Le Monde* (the most prestigious newspaper in France) and *The New York Times* (America's newspaper of record) into perspective. Though *Le Monde* expresses several points of view, the newspaper is generally Gaullist (nationalistic) in tone. It is noted for the excellence of its news coverage and the vigor of its editorial analysis (Hachten, 1992; Schramm, 1959). *Le Monde* is widely circulated and read by intellectuals and the international elite, the undisputed symbol of what the French call, *"La Presse d'Opinion"* [the editorial press] (Freiberg, 1981; Jeanneney, 1996). Hostert (1973) found that from its founding in 1944, *Le Monde* was "favorably prejudiced" toward the Soviet Union; in the 1970s the newspaper exhibited what Jeanneney (1996) calls an "unbridled sinophilia." Indeed, *Le Monde* has been accused of having a leftist, anti-American bias (Aron, 1983; Sévillia, 2000), explained in part by the Gallic desire to be independent of perceived American hegemony, and in part by the fact *Le Monde* (and the *Agence France Presse,* from which it got many of its stories) had been infiltrated by the KGB (Andrew and Mitrokhin, 1999).

Maintaining the Journalistic Paradigm Through Sacred Rite

Although the two countries' national cultures and journalistic paradigms are distinct, it would be expected that both would be protected and maintained with equal fervor. In essence, journalism operates through a professional paradigm, a way of seeing and interpreting the world that is taken for granted as *the way* by those who practice it. Because engaging in the journalistic paradigm becomes a lived experience, journalists and the journalistic institution need to find ways of dealing with anomalies that arise over time (Bennett et al., 1985; Berkowitz, 2000; Hindman, 2005; Reese, 1990).

When application of a journalistic paradigm appears faulty, journalists work to assert the boundaries of acceptable practice (Bishop, 2004). This process becomes *ritual,* a meaningful process recognized and enacted by journalists during times of crisis (Couldry, 2005; Ehrlich, 1996). This ritual is not taken lightly, but represents a near-religious performative for the profession, essentially, a sacred rite (Lardellier, 2005). Most crucially, paradigm repair becomes a way of sustaining an intellectual position about authority of knowledge and freedom of speech. Without those elements, the news institution would degenerate into chaos and the very legitimacy of news organizations might be threatened.

Thus, to work within a specific journalistic paradigm becomes a sacred *right;* the process of protecting it becomes a sacred *rite.* This assertion becomes clearer by shifting from a sociological vision of paradigm repair to one based more in a cultural perspective. One of the most common techniques for maintaining specific journalistic paradigms is, to borrow the expression of Derrida (1967), "re-presentation," the act of presenting existing ideas and abstract concepts anew. In times of crises when journalistic paradigms are challenged, abused or misused, journalists re-present these paradigms anew to readers and audiences, in an attempt to re-acquaint these news consumers with what journalism really is and what role it plays in society. This is done by drawing express or implied boundaries between acceptable and unacceptable, legal and illegal, ethical and unethical journalistic practice.

Within the framework of Derrida's (1967) concept of re-presentation, we can assert that when journalists write or speak to their audiences about journalistic paradigms or concepts such as free speech, they also speak to themselves. Doing so reifies these ideals, socializing new members of the profession to the importance of the journalistic paradigm, and reiterating their *right* to work within this paradigm, as well as their sacred *rite* to protect the paradigm. Legrand (2003) viewed re-presentation as the studied re-enactment of political, social and cultural dramas within a context of unequal power relations between a *re-presenter* and the *re-presented.* As an act of power, journalists have the ability to choose content and sources that help perform the task of paradigm maintenance. In short, journalists have the power to "give the last word" to sources that will do the ideological heavy-lifting for them. Foucault concurs that communication is an act of power because to communicate is "to act on the other or on others" (1994, p. 233). Thus, part of the power of journalism is its ability to assume a didactic posture when journalistic ideologies and paradigms come under attack. Every attack on free speech becomes for journalists, a "teachable moment," an opportunity to educate audiences on journalistic values. Thus, the so-called "Mohammad cartoon affair" presents an opportunity to re-examine journalistic paradigm repair from a comparative cultural perspective.

This discussion prompts two research questions. First, how did paradigm work surface in news coverage by *Le Monde* and *The New York Times* about the Mohammad cartoons? Second, what role did national culture play in the nature of paradigm maintenance?

Method

Because this study focuses on the nuances of a news discourse and the contrasts between two newspapers drawn from different languages and cultures, a qualitative approach seemed appropriate. The research team included members knowledgeable in both French and U.S. news media and culture. Preliminary online searches found that many European newspapers, especially French, covered the issue extensively and that the realm of newspapers analyzed needed to be narrow in order to achieve adequate depth of analysis. Ultimately, the researchers decided to draw on the flagship newspaper in each country, *Le Monde* and *The New York Times.* These two newspapers could be considered as representatives of both their cultures and their distinct journalistic paradigms.

Searches were then conducted within the two newspapers to identify news items about the Mohammad cartoons controversy. This was broad-based, using only "Jyllands Posten," with Lexis-Nexis searched for *The New York Times* and the *Le Monde* online archives searched to locate news items there. Because *Le Monde's* editorial style includes cartoons, lively headlines and other visual elements, articles from that newspaper were examined from photocopies of original editions. Inspecting *The New York Times,* in contrast, found it to be relatively staid: visual elements did not contribute additional meaning to the news items. In that case, articles were drawn from a Lexis-Nexis search and printouts were examined. Articles were then read from both newspapers, and those where *Jyllands-Posten* and the cartoon controversy were only peripheral were eliminated from the data set. Overall, 19 of the 21 articles were included from *The New York Times* and 31 of the 40 articles were included from *Le Monde.*

Before analysis took place, the conceptual framework for this study was developed to clarify the interpretive lens. Researchers discussed the framework and considered examples from a preliminary reading of articles that would illustrate the various dimensions of *paradigm work* and *boundary maintenance.* Both agreed that ample evidence was available in these articles. One researcher then read articles from *The New York Times* and one read (in French) articles from *Le Monde,* each seeking basic themes that represented paradigm work strategies in the content. After discussion of the themes, researchers again read the articles to gather material that exemplified the themes.

This type of grounded textual analysis (Lindlof and Taylor, 2002) allows themes to emerge from the content through multiple readings and discussions of the texts. Detailed notes were written on copies of the news items and then re-read as the analysis was written. This process formed the analytic process for the discussions that follow.

Reiterating the Sacred Right to Blaspheme: *Le Monde*'s Discursive Coverage

Virtually all French newspapers and magazines republished some or all of the controversial cartoons in solidarity with *Jyllands-Posten. Le Monde* was in the thick of the fight. It published two of the cartoons, drew one of its own on the front page, and created an online portfolio of the cartoons as they had appeared in *Jyllands-Posten.* This provided an unprecedented opportunity for *Le Monde*—France's newspaper of record—to engage in five key realms of paradigm work, including (1) paradigmatic and ideological maintenance and restatement; (2) differentiating Western and Arabo-Islamic free speech values; (3) differentiating Western and Arabo-Islamic journalistic contexts and values; (4) repairing the European journalistic paradigm battered by *Jyllands-Posten*'s amalgamation of Islam and terrorism; and (5) examining the "border within the border," that is, the distinction between the United States, Britain, and the rest of the West towards the controversial cartoons.

The first *theme—paradigmatic and ideological maintenance*—was accomplished through *Le Monde's* coverage about the clash between freedom of speech and respect for religion. It also used the controversy to represent or restate Western free speech ideologies, particularly France's brand of secular republicanism. On February 2, 2006, a day after newspapers across Europe had republished the controversial Mohammad cartoons, demonstrations had broken out in most of the member countries of the Islamic Conference Organization. *Le Monde* published an editorial ("Caricatures Libres") that day representing French free speech in a rather didactic fashion, concluding:[1]

> Commandments and religious proscriptions cannot therefore be placed above republican laws, without risking dangerous deviations and inquisitions . . . A Muslim may be shocked by an especially spiteful cartoon of Mohammad. But a democracy cannot install an opinion police, without violating human rights. (2006a, p. 2)

This editorial essentially used the cartoon controversy as a teachable opportunity, restating the country's Voltairian, anti-clerical free speech ideology: the French constitution protects freedom of religion, but that does not trump freedom of the press (Kauffmann, 2006).

Le Monde used other tactics beside its own editorials to accomplish this goal. One way was to invite writers (Bechnir et al., 2006), editorial cartoonists and caricaturists from around the world, as well as Arab and Muslim readers of the newspaper to express their opinions on the Mohammad cartoon affair (Sole, 2006). Most of them analyzed the controversy within the framework of France's system of secular republicanism. Though these intellectuals and readers had a wide range of opinions, nearly all supported freedom of expression.

A lawyer, writing in *Le Monde* (Borrillo, 2006), summarized the views of the majority of the contributors invited by *Le Monde,* shoring up the secular republican ideological stance of the newspaper. In "Blasphemy, a Sacred Right," he wrote that in France, blasphemy had been abolished by the Revolution of 1789:

> French laws against religious discrimination were enacted to protect persons belonging to minority groups against acts and pronouncements that incited hatred . . . The law is clearly aimed at protecting persons, not metaphysical [religious] systems. These systems are cultural constructions that can and must be subject to criticism and even derision. (Borrillo, 2006, p. 18)

Le Monde concluded its ideological representation, opining that under France's secular republican system, "the limits of the freedom of expression guaranteed by the Constitution cannot be set by believers, no matter who they are" (D'Arcais, 2006). *Le Monde* also taught these principles by example, republishing two of the controversial cartoons, two of their own, including and adding an ironic front page cartoon of a bearded figure being formed out the words, "I must not draw Mohammad . . . I must not draw Mohammad" repeated as if in punishment.

A second theme involved *mapping out and differentiating Western and Arabo-Islamic human rights values.* In an article entitled "Caricatures: The Geopolitics of Indignations," Roy (2006) contrasted the violent, convulsive demonstrations in the Middle East with the moderate, reasoned reactions in Europe. That article argued that the "map of the riots show that the countries affected by the violence are those in which the regimes and certain political forces have scores to settle with Europeans" (2006, p. 17).

The Mohammed cartoons controversy gave *Le Monde* an opportunity to survey the geopolitical landscape. Tincq mapped out the border areas in which Islam and the West parted company, stating:

> [T]wo systems of mutual exclusion founded on ignorance. Ignorance of the interior motives of the Muslim faith, on the

> one hand; [and] on the other, ignorance of freedom of creation in an Arabo-Islamic world deprived of rights and of democracy . . . The freedom of the artist and the writer is sacred in the West, but Muslims challenge this application of the superiority of a Western ideal that cannot be changed. (2006a, p. 7)

When the 57 member countries of the Islamic Conference Organization submitted a draft resolution to the United Nations that would have declared "the defamation of religions and prophets incompatible with the right of free expression," *Le Monde* saw it as an attempt to diminish the geography of freedom: "How many of these countries respect freedom of expression? How many journalists are imprisoned in these countries? What is the value of [human] rights to Western countries represented at the United Nations?" (Kauffmann, 2006, p. 2).

The newspaper additionally urged Western countries not to succumb to attempts by Muslim countries to extend their "frontiers of the sacred" to the rest of the world.

The third theme dealt with *journalistic realities* in much the same way that *Le Monde* had done with the cultural ones. Here, *Le Monde* did "frontier duty" by contrasting the different political, cultural and social contexts of the Western and Arabo-Islamic press. For example, *Le Monde* reported that when *Jyllands-Posten* published the controversial cartoons, interior ministers of the League of Arab States asked the Danish government to "severely punish" the authors of the controversial cartoons *(Le Monde,* 2006a; Tincq, 2006b). The newspaper also reported that Arab journalists and newspapers that called for calm, and made appeals to reason paid a heavy price, such as the editors-in-chief of two Jordanian newspapers arrested for publishing some of the cartoons. In Yemen, the newspaper *Al-Houriya* was suspended and its editor prosecuted, while in Morocco, the editor and a journalist of *Al-Nahar Al Maghribi* were charged with publishing the cartoons *(Le Monde,* 2006b).

In order to complete its border work, *Le Monde* highlighted the lack of freedom of speech and of the press in the Arabo-Islamic world, contrasting this with the religious neutrality and freedoms enjoyed by the Western press under secular democratic governments. To this end, *Le Monde* published a list of continental European newspapers that had chosen to republish the cartoons in solidarity with *Jyllands-Posten,* including virtually all major French newspapers (Santi, 2006a). However, this picture of journalistic freedom, courage and solidarity was tarnished when the owner of *France Soir,* Raymond Lakah, whom *Le Monde* described as a "Franco-Egyptian businessman," fired his editor, Jacques Lefranc, for republishing the cartoons (Santi, 2006a). *Le Monde*'s coverage implied that the villain of the *France Soir* story was a hyphenated Frenchman, probably more at ease with Arab-style repression than with French secular republicanism.

Le Monde also wrote extensively about *Charlie Hebdo,* a satirical newspaper that rekindled Muslim anger by republishing the controversial Danish cartoons one week after the rest of the European newspapers, and adding a cartoon of its own (Santi, 2006b). Again to show the gulf between the Western press and Muslims, *Le Monde* reported that several Muslim groups sought injunctions against republication of the Mohammad cartoons by *Charlie Hebdo,* or any other newspaper, claiming that the cartoons were racist and xenophobic. These applications, however, were dismissed by French courts (Santi, 2006b). In all, the boundary work by *Le Monde* left the impression of a big contrast between Western free speech values and Arabo-Islamic oppression.

A fourth theme in *Le Monde's* coverage involved *actual journalistic paradigm repair.* Though the newspaper defended *Jyllands-Posten's* right to publish the cartoons, and even republished two of them to defend freedom of speech, *Le Monde* indicated that *Jyllands-Posten* had not lived up to certain journalistic values, pointing out where the Danish newspaper had gone astray. In its first editorial supporting the right of the press to publish the Mohammad cartoons, *Le Monde* stated that *Jyllands-Posten* had made an unjust and hurtful amalgamation of Islam, terrorism, and suicide in some of the cartoons

(Le Monde, 2006a). By implying that Islam was a religion of violence, terrorism and suicide, *Jyllands-Posten* indulged in what Amirou (2006, p. 18) called a "simplistic syllogism: Islamic extremists plant bombs, Mohammad is a Muslim, so Mohammad is a terrorist?"

Indeed, most of the cartoonists invited by *Le Monde* to comment on the controversy thought that the Danish newspaper had gone too far when it directly connected, in some of the cartoons, Islam and terrorism (Herzberg et al., 2006). Kotek (2006), for example, suggested that by connecting Islam and terrorism, *Jyllands-Posten* betrayed its journalistic mission of drawing cartoons that reflect an exaggeration of the truth—rather than falsehood—in order to make the news easier to understand. However, these attempts at journalistic paradigm repair did not mean that *Le Monde* did not support the Danish newspaper's right to publish.

The second sin of *Jyllands-Posten* evident in *Le Monde's* reporting was that the Danish newspaper—like most of the European press—indulged in double standards. *Le Monde* reported that *Jyllands-Posten* had refused to publish some cartoons critical of Christianity because it feared the reactions of Christians. Some Muslim commentators noted that Europe is very sensitive about anything that touches on the Jewish religion as well. Roy summarized the ethical shortcomings and double standards of *Jyllands-Posten* and by extension, the European press:

> No respectable newspaper can publish an anti-Semitic interview. No mainstream newspaper would publish cartoons mocking blind people, midgets, homosexuals or Gypsies. But poor taste works with Islam, because public opinion is permeable to Islamophobia. What shocks the average Muslim is not the representation of the Prophet, but the existence of double standards. (2006, p. 18)

By highlighting the theme of the ethical lapses of *Jyllands-Posten* in most of its coverage of the Mohammad cartoons affair, *Le Monde* actively engaged in repairing the image of journalism. The newspaper clearly insinuated that *Jyllands-Posten*'s ethical lapses and the troubles they ignited were avoidable, a result of journalistic insularity and lack of sophistication.

A fifth and final theme concentrated on the *"border within the border." Le Monde*'s aim was to separate true believers in the Universal Declaration of Human Rights from the rest, and the act of republication of the Mohammad cartoons became the litmus test. *Le Monde* reported that one of the ironies of the controversy was that it divided the West. The United States and Great Britain sided with Muslims, it claimed, while continental European countries had a more ambiguous attitude towards Muslims but came out clearly in support of freedom of speech and of the press *(Le Monde,* 2006c). *Le Monde* described a deep rift between European newspapers—many of which published the cartoons—and the so-called "Anglo-Saxon" press, which generally did not (Kauffmann, 2006; Lesnes, 2006; Roche, 2006; Santi, 2006a).

Le Monde explained this difference in terms of special political and social situations that pertain to Great Britain and the United States, but not to continental Europe. The "extreme reticence and caution" of the highly competitive, fire-eating British press, it claimed, was due to commercial and socio-political reasons:

> Commercial considerations play a decisive role. Popular newspapers like *The Sun* and *The Daily Mail* have a non-negligible Muslim readership . . . the Muslim bourgeois classes read the serious press . . . Furthermore, this affair reflects the fragility of a multicultural society inally, the United Kingdom is a country that is still deeply influenced by religion . . . to the British, the greatest threat to the Anglican church . . . is not Islam, it is secularism. (Roche, 2006, p. 18)

Le Monde also built a boundary between Europeans and Americans, reporting that the United States showed political and journalistic ambivalence. In an article entitled, "Washington Sides with Muslims," the newspaper reported that the cartoons had not been published in the United States for strategic and political reasons rather than for reasons of principle:

> Coming from the country of the First Amendment, under which one can say and write almost anything one wishes, more so than in Europe, this reaction is surprising. But it comes from a country [the United States] where religious expression is increasingly part of public discourse and where the Fourth Estate role of the media has, in the last five years, been curtailed. (Kauffmann, 2006, p. 2)

In all, through these five journalistic strategies, the coverage in *Le Monde* was able to state principles and delineate boundaries of both culture and journalistic practice, while also separating true believers in free speech from those newspapers that supported free speech more in principle than in actual journalistic deed.

Paradigm Work at Arm's Length: Coverage in *The New York Times*

At first thought, coverage of the Mohammed cartoon controversy by *The New York Times* seems an ideal situation for maintaining the journalistic paradigm, because the *Times* is the U.S. standard bearer. News and opinion coverage in the *Times* did not turn out that way, though. In part, this was because the issue was foreign news, with a minimal connection to American media or media values. The issue had a low degree of cultural proximity given Europe's more opinionated media and social climates. Geographically, it was also somewhat distant. The issue's connection to the Middle East and a terrorism frame, though, kept it salient. Overall, the newspaper's coverage appeared as a disinterested spectator: it was *their* news, not *ours.*

Six themes stood out in the coverage, most reflecting only a veiled effort at paradigm maintenance: (1) Danish immigration policy in relation to Muslim protests; (2) the sanctity of Danish (and European) freedom of speech; (3) separating Western media from Middle Eastern media; (4) the terrorism frame, with Middle Eastern people as an "other"; (5) Middle Eastern journalists who served as examples by challenging their dominant news paradigm; and (6) offering mild criticism that separated the Danish journalists from other European and U.S. journalists. Except for the last theme, none raised *Jyllands-Posten* or journalistic freedom as a central part of the discussion.

By pointing out tensions from Middle Eastern immigrants in Denmark and other countries—the *first theme*—the *Times* coverage was able to create a boundary between a journalistic issue and a cultural issue. The suggestion of news coverage here was that even though the media were central to the conflict, it really just served to highlight the growing cultural conflict. By doing this, the news judgment of *Jyllands-Posten* was moved to the background. As the first *Times* story contextualized on January 8,

> The cartoons were published amid the growth of an anti-immigrant sentiment in Denmark, reflected in the rise of the far-right Danish People's Party. The party, which holds 13 percent of the seats in the Danish parliament, has helped to push through the toughest anti-immigration rules on the Continent, including a rule preventing Danish citizens age 24 or younger from bringing in spouses from outside. (Bilefsky, 2006a)

Arguing that it was a "far bigger story" than one about cartoons, another article described the situation as a "'clash of civilizations' between secular Western democracies and Islamic societies," a statement that provided an ideological definition of the West as *democratic* while Islam was built on age-old *societal traditions* that refuse change or challenge from the outside (Cowell, 2006b). At risk, the article pointed out, is the degree that a "receiving culture" needs to "compromise" in order to incorporate these new immigrants. Two days later, that same reporter quoted a high-profile Danish Muslim woman, whose concerns were "pitting faith against newer, secular loyalties" (Cowell, 2006c). In sum, as long as the controversy could be focused on cultural strains, journalistic discretion would not be part of the question, but instead an act that exemplified a society's woes. In terms of the journalistic paradigm, no repair work was needed because a boundary had been built that kept it separate.

The *second theme* follows from the first, posing freedom of speech against dogmatic beliefs. The Danish editor who approved publication of the cartoons spoke strongly about free speech rights, regardless of perspective:

> "Muslims should be allowed to burn the Danish flag in a public square if that's within the boundaries of the law," he said. "Though I think it would be a strange signal to the Danish people who have hosted them." (Bilefsky, 2006a)

An editorial written by a Florida International University professor made explicit that this issue was directed toward maintaining Denmark as a tolerant and open-minded society. The reason for publication of the cartoons, he argued, was to move free speech to a public forum, not to make a statement about Islam:

> This is what it means today to put self-censorship "on the agenda": the particular object of that censorship is a matter of indifference. What is important is not the content of what is expressed but that it be expressed. (Fish, 2006)

Casting the issue this way suggests that the intent was to test free speech and self-censorship through a controversial topic, with no real interest in the issue of Islam and integration on its own. That is, the writer explained that it was problematic for a person not of a certain religion to be held to that religion's taboos: in this case, to refrain from publishing cartoons of Mohammed. Surprisingly, the issue of free speech by the Danish (or European) media was not connected to free speech in the United States.

For this second theme, then, placing philosophies about free speech against Muslim sensitivities about a specific issue once again removed the discussion from the journalistic paradigm. As with the first theme, a boundary was created between media and society, so that the journalistic paradigm remained above question.

The *third theme* involved creation of a boundary between the principled, democratic media of the West and the dogmatic, government-controlled media of the Middle East. This theme was only minimally developed, interfaced with the theme about exemplary journalists, but viewed from the opposite position. Thus, a Syrian announcement about withdrawing its ambassador to Denmark was attributed to SANA, the "Syrian state news agency" (Cowell, 2006b). Another article told of how a Yemeni journalist had become a fugitive after escaping arrest and explained that the king of Jordan felt compelled to jail journalists printing "blasphemous cartoons" because his family is directly descended from Mohammed (Slackman and Fattah, 2006):

> "If freedom of the press affects national unity in a tribal system with high levels of illiteracy, one has to consider how far it can go," said Yemen's foreign minister, Dr. Abu Bakr al Qirbi. "All societies have red lines."

Iranian president Mahmoud Ahmadinejad criticized the European newspapers' freedom of speech, offering an example that highlighted the explicit ideology of his thinking:

> "If your newspapers are free, why do they not publish anything about the innocence of the Palestinians and protest against the crimes committed by the Zionists?" the semi official Mehr news agency quoted him as saying. (Gall and Smith, 2006)

Later in that same article, it was mentioned that a newspaper editor "affiliated with the Iranian Basiji militia, which organized the protest" had arrived to calm protestors it had initially encouraged, asking them to "stop throwing firebombs." An editorial piece in the *Times'* arts section mentioned that an Iranian daily newspaper had launched a contest for the "best cartoon about the Holocaust" (Kimmelman, 2006). And following a meeting of leaders of 57 Muslim nations in Mecca, a news item explained that the event "drew minimal international press coverage," a sharp contrast with the media from within those countries:

> In some countries, like Syria and Iran, that meant heavy press coverage in official news media and virtual government approval of demonstrations that ended with Danish embassies in flames. (Fattah, 2006a)

Overall, then, this theme highlighted the state control of Middle East media, with journalists needing to either report the official position or risk jail. By emphasizing that Middle East media are simply government mouthpieces, these stories imply that Western media are different journalistically, following the "correct" paradigm. Again, a boundary was built that maintained the journalistic paradigm through the act of not questioning it.

The *fourth theme* shows how the terrorism frame was used along with portraying Middle Eastern people as an "other" to place blame their way while removing *Jyllands-Posten's* actions from question. One element of this theme centered on assaults on Danish and European buildings in Gaza. On January 30, an article reported that "about a dozen gunmen demanded an apology from the Danish government and fired automatic rifles in the air in front of the European Union office" (Fattah, 2006a). A few days later, the situation had escalated, as the *Times* described gunmen "firing automatic weapons and spray-painting a warning on the outside gate" (Smith and Fisher, 2006). These warnings soon turned to violence:

> In Gaza, Palestinians marched through the streets, storming European buildings and burning German and Danish flags. Protestors smashed the windows of the German cultural center and threw stones at the European Commission building, the police said. (Associated Press, 2006)

Meanwhile, in the West Bank, a German man was accidentally kidnapped by "two masked gunmen" after mistakenly being thought to be French or Danish. In all, these articles portrayed Palestinians as fanatic, violent, and not too bright.

A second element of this theme suggested that protests and violence were not truly motivated by principle but by the opportunity for a Middle Eastern country to appear oppressed and unite its people behind that oppression. Essentially, articles drawing on this theme suggested that the protests—highly unusual for some countries—were calculated to "undercut the appeal of the West" while also competing politically with citizens beginning to align politically with Islamic-linked movements. One article quoted an Egyptian political scientist:

> "The Saudis did this because they have to score against Islamic fundamentalists," said Mr. Said, the Cairo political scientist. "Syria made an even worse miscalculation," he added, alluding to the sense that the protest had gotten out of hand. The issue of the cartoons came at a critical time in the Muslim world because of Muslim anger over the occupation of Iraq and a sense that Muslims were under siege. (Fattah, 2006b)

Similar ideas came from an article about spreading protests that explained "Iran, for example, is facing international pressure to halt its nuclear program, and Syria has been isolated internationally since the assassination of Lebanon's former prime minister" (Gall and Smith, 2006). An editorial addressed the calculated nature of the uprising directly, characterizing it as "an almost-forgotten incident [that] has been dredged up to score points with the public during politically sensitive times" (Editorial Desk, 2006).

Regarding depiction of violence and terrorism, quite a few examples appeared that helped portray the Middle East as a chaotic region. One common element involved death threats (Bilefsky, 2006a), bomb threats (Cowell, 2006a) and execution (Slackman and Fattah, 2006), at times presented in juxtaposition with the cartoon with Mohammed wearing a bomb/turban (Associated Press, 2006) or mention of a Dutch film producer killed after making a movie critical of Islamic society. Yet other articles interfaced mention of Islam and terrorism (Bilefsky, 2006c; Cowell, 2006d; Smith and Fisher, 2006). Put together, the effect was to make Islam and the Middle East appear unreasonable and reactionary in their responses to the cartoons. Again, *Jyllands-Posten's* publication of the cartoons was not questioned, with blame placed on people from an unreasonable Other world.

A *fifth theme* supported Western journalism while also condemning Middle Eastern journalism by examples of a few Middle Eastern journalists who dared to disagree with the dominant Islamic position. This theme was highlighted in an article about the plight of several journalists (Slackman and Fattah, 2006). It pointed out how 11 journalists in five countries were facing prosecution for printing the cartoons. One writer commented on the chill to free speech:

> "I keep hearing, 'Why are liberals silent?" said Said al Ashmawy, an Egyptian judge and author of books on political Islam. "How can we write? Who is going to protect me? Who is going to publish for me in the first place? With the Islamization of the society, the list of taboos has been increasing daily. You should not write about religion. You should not write about politics or women. Then what is left?"

Another example told of two journalists with an Egyptian weekly that published the cartoons and a criticism in October, shortly after the controversy began to boil. By showing the contrast between these journalists and the rest, the article suggested that Western freedom of speech was an ideal hung onto by a rare few willing to suffer for their principles. Once again, the Western journalistic paradigm was valorized and separated from that of the Middle East.

Finally, a *sixth theme* offered a glimpse of the usual paradigm repair process, where either an *individual* or a media *organization* was separated from the media *institution*. Even then, the scolding and vilifying were relatively weak: the situation was depicted as just a minor infraction. One editorial—the usual forum for paradigm repair—described *Jyllands-Posten*'s publication of the cartoons as "juvenile" yet still within speech protected by the First Amendment (Editorial Desk, 2006). The piece then describe a more appropriate action:

> *The New York Times* and much of the rest of the nation's news media have reported on the cartoons but refrained from showing them. That seems a reasonable choice for news organizations that usually refrain from gratuitous assaults on religious symbols, especially since the cartoons are so easy to describe in words.

This excerpt built a clear division between borderline journalistic behavior and behavior considered exemplary. It demonstrated how a mature media organization would deal with the delicate situation. Similarly, the *Times'* arts desk called the cartoons "callous and feeble," something designed only to "score cheap points" regarding free speech (Kimmelman, 2006). Another news item also subtly separated *Jyllands-Posten*'s act from the principle involved, leading with a reference to the Danish prime minister's support of the ideal that was "distanced from the newspaper's decision" to publish the cartoons (Cowell, 2006a). At the same time, these gentle criticisms were tempered with the point from European commentators that regardless of the tastelessness involved, "conservative Muslims must learn to accept Western standards of free speech" (Smith and Fisher, 2006).

A few articles also gave Flemming Rose, the *Jyllands-Posten* editor, a mild scolding. One discussed several mistakes about possibly publishing Holocaust cartoons and satirical cartoons about Christians and Jews drawn by Muslim cartoonists (Bilefsky, 2006b). Another article mentioned Rose's announced "indefinite leave of absence" from the paper, suggesting he had erred, yet drawing on his shock that Danes had become "objects of hate" (Bilefsky, 2006c). An opinion piece the next day reminded that "Rose may think of himself . . . as being neutral with respect to religion," casting him as a member of "the religion we call liberalism" (Fish, 2006).

Despite these criticisms of the Danish newspaper and its editor, real paradigm repair did not take place. Instead, they were simply moved a little farther away from the mainstream press, retaining their basic legitimacy and a standing invitation to return to the fold of the mainstream. Overall, the thrust of coverage by the *Times* was to re-affirm and re-present the paradigm when a clear opportunity became available.

Conclusion

The Mohammad cartoon affair was perceived in continental Europe as a challenge to journalism, journalistic paradigms and Western free speech ideologies. In the United States and Great Britain, it was viewed at worst as a naïve and as a sophomoric breach of journalistic ethics at best. The first research question asked how paradigm work surfaced in *Le Monde* and *The New York Times.* Surprisingly, *The New York Times* and *Le Monde* covered many of the same issues, but used their coverage to communicate different journalistic and cultural messages. In *The New York Times,* coverage was relatively tangential because the controversy was reported as a distant international incident. This was not "our" news, but "their" news and just the facts would suffice. *Le Monde,* in contrast, reported the controversy as an affair in which it had a stake. As such, *Le Monde* used its coverage of the global controversy to represent and re-state fundamental universal human rights, and French secular republican principles. Additionally, *Le Monde* triangulated an ideological boundary between the West and the Arabo-Islamic countries on matters of freedom of speech and of the press. Finally, *Le Monde* delineated a frontier between continental Europe and the Anglo-Saxon democracies of Britain and the United States.

Re-presentation of journalistic principles and triangulation of boundaries was not prominent in *The New York Times* coverage. Most of these boundaries were clear enough because of differences in geography, language and culture with both Europe and the Middle East. Even journalistic positions and cultural values stood apart clearly between America and the others. Much of the coverage thus focused on disturbances either in or from the Muslim world, a world that had caused problems for the United States through the September 11 attacks and the Iraq war. Although maintenance of the journalistic paradigm was a subtext to most of this coverage, the effect was subtle. The American press system—centered more on freedom of information than on freedom of expression—was not threatened by the Mohammed cartoon controversy, either. As much as anything, the cartoons offered a chance to re-present U.S. ideology toward terrorism and the Middle East.

The second research question asked how differences in national culture played a role in the paradigm work that appeared in the two newspapers. *Le Monde* was clearly in the thick of the fight. It was a *"journal engage"* (an engaged newspaper) facing an issue central to French society: the drive for a unified culture free from the dictates of religion. In doing so, *Le Monde* republished two of the cartoons and added one of its own. Republication of the cartoons by French newspapers made the country a side-show in the huge drama that started in Denmark. Proximity—both geographic and cultural—was clearly a factor here. Additionally, the controversy seized the public imagination because of the large Muslim population in France and the cultural tensions that tend to arise. In contrast, the United States has a relatively smaller and more low-key Muslim population. Ideologically, values of religion have been more in the forefront of American public discourse, while freedom of expression has seen a degree of repression in the dawn of the 21st century.

Although journalistic paradigms are the center of this discussion, national culture cannot be separated from the American and French paradigms. In this case, national difference is key to understanding the journalistic paradigm differences that surfaced in each newspaper's coverage. Particularly, contrasting cultural beliefs about religion and multiculturalism interacted with ideals about freedom of expression and public debate, and created a clear difference in the way that the ritual of paradigm repair unfolded.

Thus, one of the main contributions of this article is to demonstrate the importance of national/cultural differences in journalism, highlighting the utility of this vantage point for understanding why the same event can be covered differently in different countries. Examining the French case alone would detect a visible paradigm process at work, but one that could not be clearly understood by American readers unfamiliar with the nuances of French culture. The American case, if studied on its own, might not reveal paradigm work taking place at all. By analyzing both cases together, the relationship between journalism and the culture in which it is enmeshed becomes clear: there is no single journalistic paradigm, nor even a dominant Western journalistic paradigm. As is demonstrated, the long-standing richness of culture is hard at work. Although the sacred *right* of freedom of speech surfaced in both cases, the concerns underlying that right grow from different roots as does the *rite* designed to maintain its existence.

Note

1. Excerpts from *Le Monde* were originally published in French and translated by one of the authors.

References

Albert, Pierre (1977) *La France, les français et leurs presses [France, the French and Their Press],* Paris: Centre National d'Art et de Culture George Pompidou.

Amirou, Rachid (2006) "Le simplisme comme prophétie" ["Oversimplification as Prophecy"], *Le Monde, 9* February, p. 18.

Andrew, Christopher and Mitrokhin, Vasili (1999) *The Sword and the Shield: the Mitrokhin archive and the secret history of the KGB,* London: Allen Lane and Penguin Press.

Aron, Raymond (1983) *Memoires: 50 ans de reflexions politiques [Memoires: 50 years of political reflections],* Paris: Julliard.

Associated Press (2006) "Outcry Over Prophet Cartoons Grows Louder and More Violent," *The New York Times,* 5 February, p. Al0.

Bechnir, Salim, Cendrey, Jean-Yves, Daeninckx, Didier, Jacques, Paula, Laclavetine, Jean-Marie, Leroy, Gilles, Ndiaye, Marie, Pennac, Daniel, Raynal, Patrick and Boualem, Sansal (2006) "Des écrivains face a la caricature" ["Writers and Caricature"], *Le Monde,* 14 February, p. 21.

Bellanger, Claude, Godechot, Jacques, Guiral, Pierre and Terrou, Fernand (Eds) (1975) *Histoire gènèrale de la presse française [General History of the French Press],* Vol. 4, Paris: Presses Universitaires de France.

Bennett, William (1998) *The Death of Outrage—Bill Clinton and the assault on American ideals,* New York: Free Press.

Bennett W., Lance, Gressett, Lynne and Haltom, William (1985) "Repairing the News: a case study of the news paradigm," *Journal of Communication* 35(3), pp. 50–68.

Berkowitz, Dan (2000) "Doing Double Duty: paradigm repair and the Princess Diana what-a-story," *Journalism: Theory, Practice & Criticism* 1 (2), pp. 125–43.

Bilefsky, Dan (2006a) "Denmark Is Unlikely Front in Islam West Culture War," *The New York Times,* 8 January, p. A3.

Bilefsky, Dan (2006b) "Danish Cartoon Editor on lndefnite Leave," *The New York Times,* 11 February, p. AS.

Bilefsky, Dan (2006c) "Cartoon Dispute Prompts Identity Crisis for Liberal Denmark," *The New York Times,* 12 February, p. A22.

Bishop, Ronald (2004) "The Accidental Journalist: shifting professional boundaries in the wake of Leonardo DiCaprio's interview with former President Clinton," *Journalism Studies* 5(1) pp. 31–43.

Borrillo, Daniel (2006) "Le blaspheme, un droit sacré" ["Blasphemy, a Sacred Right"], *Le Monde,* 9 February, p. 18.

Cesari, Jocelyne (2005) "Islam, Secularism and Multiculturalism After 9/11: a transatlantic comparison," in: Jocelyne Césari and Sean McLoughlin (Eds), *European Muslims and the Secular State,* Aldershot: Ashgate, pp. 39–54.

Couldry, Nick (2005) "Media Rituals: beyond functionalism," in: Eric Rothenbuhler and Mihai Coman (Eds), *Media Anthropology,* Thousand Oaks, CA: Sage, pp. 59–69.

Cowell, Alan (2006a) "Dane Defends Press Freedom as Muslims Protest Cartoons," *The New York Times,* 1 February, p. A 10.

Cowell, Alan (2006b) "More European Papers Print Cartoons of Muhammad, Fueling Dispute with Muslims," *The New York Times,* 2 February, p. A12.

Cowell, Alan (2006c) "Cartoons Force Danish Muslims to Examine Loyalties," *The New York Times,* 4 February, p. A3.

Cowell, Alan (2006d) "West Coming to Grasp Wide Islamic Protests as Sign of Deep Gulf," *The New York Times,* 8 February, p. Al0.

D'arcais, Paolo (2006) "Ma liberté, ta susciptibilité" (My Freedom, Your Sensitiveness"), *Le Monde,* 25 February, p. 4.

Derrida, Jacques (1967) *Voix et le phenomene [Speech and Phenomena],* Paris: Presses Universitaires de France.

Editorial Desk (2006) "Those Danish Cartoons," *The New York Times,* 7 February, p. A20.

Ehrlich, Matthew (1996) "Using 'Ritual' to Study Journalism," *Journal of Communication Inquiry* 20(2), pp. 3–17.

Emerson, Everett (1968) *English Puritanism from John Hooper to John Milton,* Durham, NC: Duke University Press.

Fattah, Hassan (2006a) "Caricature of Muhammad Leads to Boycott of Danish Goods," *The New York Times,* 31 January, p. A3.

Fattah, Hassan (2006b) "At Mecca Meeting, Cartoon Outrage Crystallized," *The New York Times,* 9 February, p. Al.

Fish, Stanley (2006) "Our Faith in Letting it All Hang Out," *The New York Times,* 12 February, p.A15.

Foucault, Michel (1994) *Dits et ecrits [Sayings and Writings],* Vol. IV, Paris: Editions Gallimard.

Freiberg, J. W. (1981) *The French Press: class, state and ideology,* New York: Praeger.

Gall, Carlotta and Smith, Craig (2006) "Muslim Protests Against Cartoons Spread," *The New York Times,* 7 February, p. A8.

Gaunt, Philip (1990) *Choosing the News,* New York: Greenwood Press.

Gaunt, Philip and Pritchard, David (1990) "Outside Over National News Agencies? A study of preferences in the French regional press," *Journalism Quarterly* 67, pp. 184–9.

Hachten, William (1992) *The World News Prism,* Ames: Iowa State University Press.

Herzberg, Nathaniel, Labe, Yves-Marie and Naim, Mouna (2006) "Dieu, Mahomet et les dessinateurs" ["God, Mohammad and Cartoonists"], *Le Monde,* 3 February, p. 3.

Hindman, Elizabeth Blanks (2005) "Jayson Blair, *The New York Times,* and Paradigm Repair," *Journal of Communication* 55(2), pp. 225–41.

Hostert, Guy (1973) *Le journal Le Monde et le Marxisme,* Paris: La Pensée Universelle.

Howden, Daniel, Hardaker, David and Castle, Stephen (2006) "How a Meeting of Leaders in Mecca Set Off the Cartoon Wars Around the World," *The Independent* (online edition), 8 November, http://news.independent .co.uk/world/middleeast/artic1e344482.ece.

Islam Online (2006) "Muslims Seek UN Sanctions Over Danish Cartoons," http://www.islamonline.net/English/News/2006-01/30/articleOl.shtml.

Jeanneney, Jean-Noel (1996) *"Le Monde,"* in: Jacques Julliard and Michel Winock (Eds), *Dictionnaire des intellectuels français [Dictionary of French Intellectuals],* Paris: Editions du Seuil, pp. 794–6.

Jyllands-Posten (2006a) "The Story Behind the Drawings", Internetavisen *Jyllands-Posten (Jyllands-Posten* Internet edition), http://www.jp.dk/udland/artikel:aid =3544932:fid=11328/, last updated 17 February 2006.

Jyllands-Posten (2006b) "What Lies Behind the Name Morgenavisen Jyllands-Posten?", Internetavisen *Jyllands-Posten (Jyllands-Posten* Internet edition), http://www.jp.dk/udland/artikel:aid=3564748:fid =11328/, last updated 17 February 2006.

Kauffmann, Sylvie (2006) "Les fractures de l'affaire Mahomet" ["The Rifts of the Mohammad Affair"], *Le Monde,* 21 February, p. 2.

Kimmelman, Michael (2006) "A Startling New Lesson in the Power of Imagery," *The New York Times,* 8 February, E1.

Kotek, Joel (2006) "Pas de censure, mais des limites pour tous" ["No Censorship But Limits on All"], *Le Monde,* 7 February, p. 19.

Lardellier, Pascal (2005) "Ritual Media: historical perspectives and social functions," in: E. Rothenbuhler and M. Coman (Eds), *Media Anthropology,* Thousand Oaks, CA: Sage, pp. 70–8.

Legrand, Pierre (2003) "The Same and the Different," in: Pierre Legrand and Roderick Munday (Eds), *Comparative Legal Studies: traditions and transitions,* Cambridge: Cambridge University Press, pp. 240–311.

Le Monde (2006a) *Caricatures libres [Free Caricatures],* 3 February.

Le Monde (2006b) "La fèvre gagne le monde musulman" ["Fever Grips the Muslim World"], 8 February, p. 4.

Le Monde (2006c) "La polémique sur les caricature de Mahomet divise l'occident" ["Polemics Over the Caricatures of Mohammad Divide the West"], 21 February, p. 1.

Lesnes, Corine (2006) "Londres et Washington solidaire des Musulmans" ["London and Washington Side with Muslims"], *Le Monde,* 6 February, p. 4.

Lindlof, Thomas and Taylor, Bryan (2002) *Qualitative Communication Research Methods,* 2nd edn, Thousand Oaks, CA: Sage.

Mcbrien, Richard (1987) *Caesar's Coin: religion and politics in America,* New York: Macmillan.

Reese, Stephen (1990) "The News Paradigm and the Ideology of Objectivity: a socialist at the *Wall Street Journal," Critical Studies in Mass Communication* 7(4), pp. 390–409.

Rice, Michael and Cooney, James (Eds) (1982) *Reporting U.S. European Relations,* New York: Pergamon Press.

Roche, Marc (2006) "Au Royaume-Uni, seul un journal d'étudiants a publié les caricatures" [In the United Kingdom, Only One Student Newspaper Published the Caricatures], *Le Monde,* 12 February, p. 18.

Roy, Olivier (2006) "Caricatures: géopolitique de l'indignation" ["Caricatures: the geopolitics of indignation"], *Le Monde,* 9 February, p. 17.

Salinger, Pierre (1980) "*Le Monde:* De Gaulle's only legitimate heir," in: Michael Rice and James Cooney (Eds), *Reporting U.S. European Relations,* New York: Pergamon, pp. 82–113.

Santi, Pascale (2006a) "Le choix des journaux européens" ["The Choice of European Newspapers"], 3 February, *Le Monde,* p. 5.

Santi, Pascale (2006b) "Retour sur la 'une' controversée de 'France Soir'' ["Controversial Return of 'France Soir' to the Front Page"], 7 February, *Le Monde,* p. 1.

Schramm, Wilbur (1959) *One Day in the World's Press,* Stanford, CA: Stanford University.

Sevillia, Jean (2000) *Le terrorisme intellectuel [Intellectual Terrorism],* Paris: Perrin.

Slackman, Michael and Fattah, Hassan (2006) "Furor Over Cartoons Pits Muslim Against Muslim," 22 February, *The New York Times,* p. Al.

Smith, Craig and Fisher, Ian (2006) "Temperatures Rise Over Cartoons Mocking Muhammad," 3 February, *The New York Times,* p. A3.

Sole, Robert (2006) "Sensibilités Musulmanes" ["Muslim Sensibilities"], 12 February, *Le Monde,* p. 17.

Tincq, Henri (2006a) "La colere du monde musulman s'étand contre les caricatures de Mahomet" ["The Anger of the Muslim World Against the Cartoons of Mohammad Spreads"], 2 February, *Le Monde,* p. 7.

Tincq, Henri (2006b) "Mahomet; Le choc des ignorances" ["Mohammad; The clash of ignorance"], *Le Monde,* 11 February, p. 2.

Source: From "Blasphemy as Sacred Rite/Right: 'The Mohammed Cartoons Affair' and Maintenance of Journalistic Ideology," 2007, by D. Berkowitz and L. Eko, *Journalism Studies, 8*(5), 779–797. Reprinted by permission of Taylor & Francis/Routledge.

6

THE JOURNALISTIC GUT FEELING

Journalistic Doxa, News Habitus and Orthodox News Values

IDA SCHULTZ

JOURNALISTIC PRACTICE IN A FIELD PERSPECTIVE

Every day, news editors all over the world have access to endless numbers of events available in press releases, in telegrams, in newspapers, Internet services, etc. All of these events could potentially become news stories but only a few end up in the newspaper, on the Web page, or in the news broadcast. How do journalists make news judgements and why are some events considered newsworthy while others are not?

> For me it has to do with a feeling. Can I picture the story? Can I see the headline? Then I'll believe in the story. (Danish editor, 2003)

The quote above illustrates how journalistic practice involves a seemingly self-evident and self-explaining sense of newsworthiness, the journalistic gut feeling. This article uses the sociology of Pierre Bourdieu to explore everyday constructions of newsworthiness in journalistic practice and argues that the field perspective contributes a promising analytical framework to re-invigorate the genre of news ethnography. The next section introduces the analytical framework of the article and the key concepts: field, journalistic doxa, news habitus, editorial capitals, and the distinction between implicit doxic news values, on the one hand, and the explicit orthodox/heterodox news values, on the other hand. The third and fourth section are ethnographic case studies of news values in Danish journalistic practice based on in-depth interviews, observations and document analyses gathered between 2003 and 2005.[1] The third section discusses the five dominant news values in the Danish journalistic field: timeliness, relevance, identification, conflict, and sensation, and argues that newsworthiness cannot solely be explained by these five orthodox/heterodox news values. The fourth section is an investigation of the news judgements at an editorial conference, showing how the daily routine of press review and the ongoing positioning of news stories point towards a sixth dominant, doxic news value in the Danish journalistic field: exclusivity. The final discussion argues that an important task for media sociology is to investigate the seemingly self-evident orthodox/heterodox news values as well as making visible the doxic news values imbedded in journalistic practice. The remainder of this section will place the study within the tradition of news ethnography and media sociology.

In an international context, the tradition of newsroom studies where ethnographers have studied journalistic practices in news organisations and on newsbeats have provided media and communication research with important insights on the inner workings of media newsrooms (for a review of this literature, see Cottle, 2003; Schudson, 1989; Tuchman, 2002). Previous newsroom studies have given us important knowledge of the individual gate-keeping mechanisms (White, 1950), social control in editorial environments (Breed, 1955; Warner, 1971), the competitor colleague relationship among journalists from different news organisations working the same beat (Tunstall, 1971), and the complex relations betweens news journalists and their sources (for instance, Ericson et al., 1989; Gieber, 1961). Other studies have highlighted the organisational requirements and influence of news policy and budgets on news output (for instance Epstein, 2000 [1973]), the relativity of news production (Altheide, 1976), the constructs imbedded in routine procedures for news work (for instance Fishman, 1980; Tuchman, 1978), and the professional norms guiding journalistic news judgement (for instance Gans, 1979; Schlesinger, 1978). Evidently, news ethnography is a key method for studying the processes and norms guiding the producers and the production, but as most of the studies are Anglo-American and were conducted around the 1970s, we need more research on the everyday processes of news work in different cultural settings in order to understand the diverse, globalised journalistic cultures of the 21st century (Clausen, 2004; Hannerz, 2004). In the words of Simon Cottle (2000), we need a "second wave" of news ethnographies. Naturally, a re-invigoration of the newsroom genre means complementing the previous findings as well as trying to improve the analytical frameworks used in the past. Previous studies within the sociology of news production have either been approached as a question of "political-economy," of "social organisation of news" or of "cultural practices" (Schudson, 1989). In an article addressing the methodological challenges of newsroom studies, Gaye Tuchman (2002) argues that the three approaches should rather be seen as different moments or aspects of news production, approachable from different angles using different methodologies. "News is both a permanent social structure and a means of social reflexivity and contestation; a product as well as a productive process" (Tuchman, 2002, p. 90). Simon Cottle (2003) addresses the same methodological issue when arguing that the reflexive sociology of Bourdieu might bridge the different approaches by investigating *news ecology* of fields instead of news production in particular organisations.[2] For Rodney Benson, the reflexive sociology of Bourdieu is a promising new paradigm for media and journalism studies aimed at analysing the meso-level of journalism using the concept of field (Benson and Neveu, 2005). An analytical strategy which "offers both a theoretical and empirical bridge between the traditionally separated macro-societal' level models of the news-media . . . and microorganisational' approaches" (Benson, 1998, p. 463). Where previous newsroom studies had an explanatory weakness in their focus on particular organisations and internal dynamics, field theory has its strength in taking into consideration the relations between the newsroom and the journalistic field and between the journalistic field and the field of power. In this way, field theory contributes to "explaining how external forces are translated into the semi-autonomous logic of the journalistic field" (Benson, 1998, p. 479). The next section uses empirical excerpts to illustrate the key concepts of reflexive sociology in order to illustrate the analytical framework.

Using Bourdieu to Analyse Journalistic Practice and News Values

In the self-understanding of journalists, the news game begins over and over again with each new day. Journalistic practice is experienced as a daily challenge with very little routine work embedded and every day completely different from the day before. For most journalists, the news agenda is experienced as a blackboard wiped blank every morning: there are no typical days in news work and you just never know what the day is going to be like. An experienced Danish editor describes news work this way:

> It's just completely unpredictable. It changes from one minute to the next and it wears you down, but that's also what's so good about it. (Danish news editor, 2003)

For the ethnographer observing news work, however, this is not so. News work is highly routinised and follows recognisable patterns from day to day. Even though the news stories that are processed are about different events, and even though events and themes will change over time, the daily structuring of journalistic practice is very much the same from day to day.

Journalistic Field, News Habitus, and Editorial Capitals

The core of Bourdieu's analytical framework is the concept of field. Methodologically speaking, "the concept of field is a research tool, the main function of which is to enable the scientific construction of social objects" (Bourdieu, 2005, p. 30). In other words, fields are always empirical questions and the existence of a possible media or journalistic field cannot be answered without empirical investigations. However, a few assumptions can be made about the journalistic field as a research object. Firstly, that the journalistic field is part of the field of *cultural production* together with the arts and sciences, a field that is occupied with producing cultural, "symbolic goods" (Bourdieu, 1993, p. 115). Furthermore, the journalistic field is part of the field of *power,* not least because the constant cultural production of social discourse not only implies production of categories for "vision" of the social world, but at the same time, categories also of "division" (Bourdieu, 2005, p. 37), or more simply put: to give a name, is also to place within a hierarchical, symbolic space.

In contrast to the classic newsroom studies, Bourdieu does not focus on the particular organisation when looking at news values or journalistic practice. Rather, the analytical frame for re-investigating the traditional questions asked by newsroom studies is that of a professional field. This shift of analytical frame looks at journalism in light of cultural production and power, and means that theoretically we can assume that the newsroom is a hierarchical social space, a micro-cosmos reflecting a position in the journalistic field as well as a position in the field of cultural production, the field of power and in the overall social space.

As for the editors and journalists who were the research object of the classical newsroom studies, the sociology of Pierre Bourdieu speaks of agents. In reflexive sociology, what is individual is always (and at the same time) social, or rather, that which might be experienced as subjective will always correspond to a relational position in a field, or to a somewhat objectified position. This is expressed in the concept of *habitus* which works as a "structuring structure" (Bourdieu and Wacquant, 1992, p. 126).

> The habitus is not only a structuring structure, which organizes practices and the perception of practices, but also a structured structure: the principle of division into logical classes which organizes the perception of the social world is itself the product of internalization of the division into social classes. (Bourdieu, 2003 [1979], p. 179)

We can all experience the feeling of being "free," "independent," or "autonomous," but as all social agents are products of a specific social, economic and cultural history, "freedom" is a relative and relational thing—for social practice in general as well as for journalistic practice. Journalists will be able to position themselves to a certain extent but always within the structures of the social space which surrounds him (Bourdieu, 2003 [1979]; Bourdieu and Wacquant, 1992). The quote above, speaking of journalism as "completely unpredictable" can be interpreted as an expression of the freedom an agent will experience. But if news journalism is so "unpredictable" how can journalists process the hundreds of potential news stories before deadline? One of the answers to these questions lies in the concept of habitus which we can understand as a practical mastering of the news game involving a strong, bodily sense of newsworthiness. Generally speaking of the habitus, Bourdieu uses the metaphor of having a feel for the game: "Having a feel for the game is having the game under the skin; it is to master in a practical way the future of the game; it is to have a sense of the history of the game" (1998, p. 81).

Habitus is a conceptual tool for analysing how social agents have different positions in the social space, and how these serve as different dispositions for social action. Using the concept of habitus in analysing news work, it might be appropriate to speak of a "professional habitus," a mastering of a specific, professional game in a specific professional field.[3] We can assume that an editor will have a symbolic position in the social space of the newsroom which will be quite different from the position of a young intern, and that this can be understood as different dispositions in daily news work. For instance, an experienced editor saying "Now, that's a good news story" during an editorial conference, will be quite a different argument to the young intern on his first day at work who claims: "Now, that's a good news story" (see also Bourdieu, 1998 [1996], p. 26). The argument might be exactly the same, just as the news story in question would, but the position from where the argument is uttered is very different—the dispositions of the editor and of the intern are not the same. In fact, the dispositions are so different that even without first-hand knowledge of editorial conferences, the mere thought of a new, young intern defining the core conceptions of the news business seems unlikely.

Journalistic habitus thus implies understanding the journalistic game, and being able to master the rules of that same game. But the game can be played from different positions, and different dispositions point to different forms of mastering the game. In this way we can assume that there will be different positions in the field and that journalistic autonomy will depend on this (Bourdieu, 2005; Marchetti, 2005). It is thus possible to imagine that there will be more specific forms of journalisitic habitus within journalistic fields, such as "editorial habitus," a "reporter habitus," or an "intern habitus," but also forms of journalistic habitus differentiated according to journalistic genres such as a "foreign correspondent habitus," an "investigative reporter habitus," forms of habitus according to media "magazine habitus," "newspaper habitus," "television habitus," etc.[4] Different forms of capital are the key to understanding the distribution of agents in the social space. Bourdieu point to economic capital as one of the two most dominant forms of capital, the other being cultural capital which will be different from field to field (Bourdieu, 1998). Journalistic capital can be understood as the specific, cultural capital of the journalistic field. Fredrik Hovden (2001) has investigated the educational capital of Norwegian journalism students but it is also possible to speak of other forms of what could be termed *editorial capitals* which serve as important capitals in regard to editorial prestige and symbolic capital in the newsroom (Schultz, 2005, 2006). These editorial capitals are, for instance, professional experience (years of work experience, kind of experience, etc.), "formal" organisational position (reporter or editor, general reporter or specialist reporter, etc.), news beat (political news or human-interest news, etc.), journalistic prizes, etc. (Schultz, 2005). The type and amount of editorial capital of the individual agent and the total distribution of capital in a field will constitute the habitus. Returning to the quote about news work being "completely unpredictable" we can acknowledge this as an expression of a journalistic self-image, an important part of this being experiencing "freedom." However, an important assumption in Bourdieu's sociology is the fact that social practice is never completely "free" but will always and at the same time be structured. What journalists experience as "freedom" and "unpredictability" in news work must be conceptualised as freedom within certain frames and structures according to the distribution of capital.

Journalistic Doxa and News Values

Doxa describes the common experience that the world seems self-explaining and self-evident to us (Bourdieu, 2002 [1977], p. 164). Doxa is the taken-for-granted of social practice, the seemingly natural, which we rarely make explicit and which we rarely question (Bourdieu, 1998, p. 57). The general doxa of social practice can be described as "the universe of the tacit presuppositions that we accept as the natives of a certain society" (Bourdieu, 2005, p. 37).

Journalistic doxa is a set of professional beliefs which tend to appear as evident, natural and self-explaining norms of journalistic practice. The journalistic doxa is a "specific doxa, a system of presuppositions inherent in membership in a field" (Bourdieu, 2005, p. 37). Speaking of the journalistic doxa is naming a set of implicit, tacit presuppositions in the journalistic field, not least the practical schemes that editors and reporters take for granted (Bourdieu, 1998 [1996], p. 25). As many news ethnographies have shown, what constitutes a good news story is often very evident for journalists, while a new intern or a visiting ethnographer will need some time and experience before the good news story becomes evident or even recognisable. "With the concept of doxa, we can understand these practicial schemes as principles of both 'vision and division" (Bourdieu, 2005, p. 37). "Doxa is a particular point of view, the point of view of the dominant, which presents and imposes itself as a universal point of view" (Bourdieu, 1998, p. 57).

News ethnographers have previously paid attention to the practical schemes of news work (for instance, Lester, 1980; Molotch and Lester, 1974; Tuchman, 1973). In a widely cited article Gaye Tuchman shows how everyday news work can be seen as a question of "routinizing the unexpected" (Tuchman, 1973). As part of the process of routinisation journalists make use of different news categories and typifications in order to reduce the contingency of news work. News stories, Tuchman shows, are recognised and processed according to different categories such as "hard news" and "soft news." Whereas the analytical framework of Tuchman drawing on the sociology of knowledge and of organisation only makes room for seeing these practical schemes as part and parcel of the process of social construction, for Bourdieu it is also—or even first and foremost—a question of power. "Hard news," we can assume, is not a neutral category, but a practical scheme partly defined by its relation to the category of "soft news" and symbolising a certain position in the journalistic universe. Simply put, for Tuchman the different news classifications such as "hard" and "soft" news serve as principles of vision, whereas Bourdieu urges us also to take into account that typifications are always principles of division. In a field perspective "hard news" and "soft news" will not only be a question of organisational practices or journalistic routines, but categories which value different types of news stories and place them differently in journalistic hierarchies. This theoretical assumption is evident in ethnographic observations as well as in news products: first, looking at what become the top stories in television news or make the headlines in newspapers clearly reflects the dominance of the hard news genre. Second, there are notable differences in who does what which are evident from observations: hard news stories are most often made by men, as the traditional hard (prestigious and well-paying) genres like foreign news, political journalism, economy and business journalism will most often be male territory in the newsroom. Likewise, the traditional soft genres such as (the less prestigious, not so well-paid) genres of human interest, family, and lifestyle are typical female territory. Another observation—which can also be seen in the following analytical section—is that it is the hard news stories which are given most time and consideration at editorial conferences. Quite contrary, the soft news stories are rarely discussed in detail and very often the soft stories are simply allocated. An editor will for instance say, "I assume you will do the interview with the nominated author . . ." or a reporter might say, "I will do a story about the new furniture trend . . ." with no comments from colleagues or editors.

The model in Figure 1 is an illustration of how part of our practical understanding of the everyday world can be talked about and discussed as part of a discursive universe. When it comes to journalistic practice, this can be understood as a sphere of Journalistic Judgement where, for instance, news values (but also professional norms, routines, etc.) are explicit and arguable. At the same time, part of our practical understanding of the everyday world belongs to the universe of the undisputed and taken for granted. For studies of journalistic practice, this can be understood as the sphere of Journalistic Doxa where, for instance, news values are silent and undisputed.

In relation to news ethnography, the model can be used to make an analytical distinction between three forms of news values imbedded in journalistic practice and everyday news work:

- *Doxic news values:* unspoken, taken for granted, self-explaining, undisputed; for instance, the notion of "newsworthiness."
- *Orthodox news values:* outspoken, recognised, agreed upon, dominant; for instance, "hard news."
- *Heterodox news values:* outspoken, misrecognised, disagreed upon, dominated; for instance, "soft news."

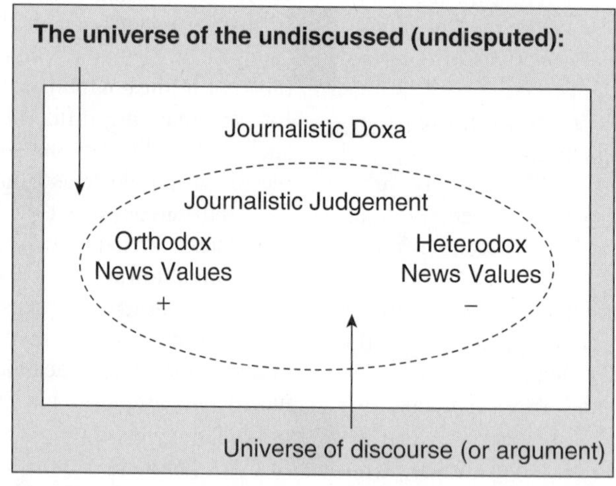

Figure 1 Journalistic doxa. Model based on Bourdieu (2000 [1977], p. 168) and Schultz (1995).

The broken line between the universe of the un-discussed (Journalistic Doxa) and the universe of discourse (Journalistic Judgement) illustrates that it is first and foremost an analytical distinction which should be investigated empirically: the implicitness of "newsworthiness" will, for instance, become an orthodox/heterodox news value if and when it is explicated and reflected upon. The critical sociology of Bourdieu stresses that one of the most important tasks for the social sciences is lay forward investigations of the social and of social practice which gives practitioners the opportunity to become more reflective about their practice (Bourdieu and Wacquant, 1992). For journalism studies and media sociology, it is important to investigate the seemingly self-evident orthodox news values as well as making visible the doxic news values imbedded in journalistic practice.

Orthodox News Values: The Five Danish News Criteria

The case of Danish news journalism illustrates the utility of concepts from Bourdieu to explore the general dynamics of journalistic practice relevant to most western democratic societies. Even though Denmark is part of the North European model of media systems and therefore quite different from the Anglo-American and Southern-European media systems (Hallin and Mancini, 2004), analysing the editorial practices, news judgement, and everyday construction of newsworthiness of Danish newsrooms sheds light on general features of everyday news work.

Timeliness, Relevance, Identification, Conflict and Sensation

In Danish news journalism five *news criteria* are highly institutionalised in the self-understanding of the journalistic field. The five news criteria are reproduced in different journalism readers, taught at journalism schools and discussed in the professional magazines. Wake up any Danish journalist in the middle of the night, and they would repeat these criteria of newsworthiness at the drop of a hat. Other countries will most certainly have other institutionalised news criteria or news criteria that are formulated in different ways,[5] but for Denmark it is these five criteria that are the backbone of journalistic professional training: Timeliness, Relevance, Identification, Sensation, and Conflict. In a journalism reader used in teaching, the criteria are described this way: "The news criteria define certain characteristics which traditionally, by experience, make a story a 'good' story. The criteria, which have been developed over the years in a dialectical relationship between media, sources, public and audience, express the editorial sense of what catches the interest of the audience and 'sells the story', and what makes a story more relevant than another" (Kramhøft, quoted in Schultz, 2005).

Timeliness is most often described as current affairs, as new information. The closer to the media deadline the story is, the more timely it is, which is why the criteria of timeliness will be different from print to electronic media. Printed media have fairly fixed deadlines and need time to get the newspaper printed and distributed to the public whereas electronic media have the possibility of broadcasting live. In this way, the television live report is one of the most timely types of news stories as they are being reported just after they happened, "I am standing in front of the Court House where the defendant has just received his sentence," or reported just before or as they are happening, "I am standing in front of the Court House where we can expect a sentence any second now . . ."

Relevance is a news criterion which in journalism readers is described in terms of the expected importance to the public as a whole or to the specific audience of a given media. As an observer of journalistic practice, relevance is one of the most difficult criteria to understand. Whereas timeliness is closely connected to the temporality of news work and deadlines, relevance seems—at least in the outset—to be more qualitative in nature. Prompted to explain how they understand this news criterion most reporters speak of importance: a relevant story is a story that is either moderately important to a lot of people or very important to a smaller group of people. It also goes without saying that a story that is very important to a large group of people is a very relevant story. When the news criterion of *conflict* is used in the daily construction of newsworthiness, this means selecting stories and angles accentuating conflicts of interest between people, between causes, organisations, etc. Many news stories are being selected and sculptured in the shape of a conflict, for instance political news: "Government says A, opposition says B"; "Minister says A, critics within the party says B"; etc. *Identification* is a news criterion described as a question of closeness between public/audience and events. The closer an event is—socially, geographically, culturally etc.—the more newsworthy the story is (see also Galtung and Ruge, 1965). The devastating environmental disasters of 2004 and 2005 can serve as an example—as evident in the difference in Danish and European newspapers' media coverage of the Tsunami, the New Orleans hurricane and the earthquakes in Kashmir. Naturally, there will be numerous explanations as to the different constructions of newsworthiness in the three cases, but certainly one of them has to do with identification. Scandinavia and Europe is culturally and socially closer to the Western, industrialised city of New Orleans, than to the poor, rural districts on the border between Pakistan and India. Even thought the Tsunami took place in Asian countries far away from Scandinavia, Danish and other European citizens were on holiday in Thailand and Indonesia, and this meant we could easily identify with the disaster, "It could have been me on that holiday resort . . ." —something which is less likely in the case of the Kashmiri earthquakes.

Sensation is the fifth news criterion discussed and reproduced in Danish journalism readers. Sensation is the unusual, the spectacular, the extra-ordinary and the more sensational, the more newsworthy, and very used example of the criterion from the AngloAmerican literature, is "man-bite-dog." It is not unusual when a dog bites a man, but a man biting a dog quite clearly constitutes a sensation.

That the five news criteria are highly institutionalised in Danish news journalism is, as mentioned above, evidenced by the fact that they appear in almost the same form in different journalism readers. Also, they are often referred to in the professional trade magazines of the press. Most significant for the ethnographer though, is the institutionalisation that is observable in talk and in informal conversations. However approached, in whatever context and in print as well as electronic media, it seems that Danish news reporters and editors are totally in sync when it comes to the five news criteria which they know by heart. Even prompted for concrete examples, it is often the same descriptions and examples of stories that serve as shared memory in the field. Another significant observation is that at the same time news criteria are rarely mentioned in everyday news work. The news criteria may be on the tip of any news journalist's tongue when a persistent ethnographer keeps addressing the question of newsworthiness, but in the everyday interactions of the newsroom and editorial conferences, this is not so. In fact, the news criteria are rarely mentioned. In the interview quote below, an editor answers the question about what he thinks the news criteria mean to everyday practice:

> They are somehow part of your spinal cord, part of how you assess and form an opinion about news stories. But it's not as if it's a checklist you pull out, asking yourself, 'Ok, how many criteria does this story apply to?" No. It's more like something being there in the back of your head … It's more something like a feeling, whether you think this is a news story or not. For me, it has something to do with feeling . . . can I picture the story, can I see the headline? . . . then I'll believe in the story. (Danish editor, 2003)

The news criteria are experienced by the editor as something very physical, i.e., "part of your spinal cord," "in the back of your head," "something like a feeling" as if newsworthiness is an integral part of the editor himself. Another observation is that the news criteria are only rarely discussed or explicated in editorial conferences. Even so, asked what the news criteria mean to everyday news work, a reporter explains:

> The news criteria are important when you need to discuss what stories you would like to do—the discussion you need to do have with the editor at the editorial conference. Why are we even doing this story? That's when the criteria become useful, I think. (Danish reporter, 2002)

When the reporter describes the news criteria as something which are important when negotiating stories with the editor, this seems to indicate that the news criteria can serve as a discursive resource or even as legitimisation strategies.

Summing up, this section has placed the five Danish news criteria in the sphere of journalistic judgement where news values are explicit and debatable. The next section will discuss news values in the sphere of journalistic doxa.

Doxic News Values: Exclusivity and . . .

Press review is the practice of constantly being updated on the news flow, of reading news, hearing news, watching news, and following stories and themes, following by-lines of colleagues and competitors, following the performance of one's own media and of the competing media and media outlets (Bourdieu, 1998 [1996]). Bourdieu has described the practice of press review as a "game of mirrors reflecting one another," and criticised how the press review "renders journalistic products so similar" (Bourdieu, 2005, p. 24). Patrick Champagne (1999 [1993] describes the press review as an important tool.

> The "press review" is a professional necessity: it suggests what subjects to treat because "the others" are talking about them, it may give them ideas for stories or at least allow them to situate themselves and to define a perspective that will distinguish them from their competitors. (Champagne, 1999 [1993], p. 47)

In relation to the everyday construction of newsworthiness we must understand the press review as a daily update of the positions in a symbolic news field: in order to decide what is newsworthy, it is necessary to understand relations in the field. The following empirical analysis is from a Danish television newsroom.

It is just after 8 a.m. at the newsroom of the Danish national public service broadcaster DR [Denmarks Radio].[6] The two editors are sitting by their desks with the morning newspapers in front of them. But their working day began hours earlier. Before coming to work the editors have read two, three or more newspapers at home, they have listened to one or two radio news programmes from DR, and probably also a news programme from one of the commercial radio broadcasters. In fact, you might even say that today's news flow began last night when the editors tuned into the late evening news programmes. The editors have probably also opened their home computers at some point during the evening to check out the stories of the Internet news sites, the national news agency Ritzau or of one of international news agencies such as Reuters or AP. Another important source of information is the list of events prepared by the researchers based on a general list of events from Ritzau. The last source of possible news stories that the editors review in the morning is the diary from yesterday. Here the editors note which stories might have been produced without being aired (for instance if an interview with a live guest in the studio took longer than planned), the stories "on the shelf." Most likely these stories are still timely the day after (or several days after) and can thus be part of the planning of the day. The stories "on the shelf" are not prestigious though, as most editors prefer to make their own stories, but for example during absences of key personnel at work, or on days when plans for stories fall apart to a degree where it might be too late to produce new stories in time for the broadcast, it is nice to have stories on the shelf.

Just after 9 a.m. the two editors go upstairs to the meeting room on the first floor. The oval meeting table is placed in a large, open office where the two researchers on duty have desks close by and where several workstations for reporters are placed in the other half of the space. The wall close to the meeting table is covered with magazine racks storing the large regional Danish newspapers and a wide range of journals and magazines. The biggest morning papers, tabloids, and one or two niche newspapers in several copies are spread around the meeting table together with several copies of the list of events prepared by the researchers. On the wall at the narrow end of the meeting table, furthest away from the researchers' desks, hangs a large whiteboard. One of the editors begins to list the potential news stories of the day while the reporters enters the room and places themselves by the table. Figure 2 shows what the whiteboard looked like today.

At a first glance, the stories on the whiteboard might appear to be written in a secret code. However, for the editors and journalists, these few words both signal what the news story is about and what kind of a story it is. Journalists will, for instance, immediately know that when it simply says "IRAQ" under the LATE NEWS, this is because the events in Iraq are a natural part of the agenda at this point in time. Reporters will also know that DANISH ASTRONAUT is not a hard news story, but a soft, human-interest story because it is about people, because it is not about politics, economy, foreign affairs but about the possibility for Danish citizens to participate in the competition at the EEC space program. Also, the reporters are well aware that for some time now a DEFENCE-AGREEMENT has been on its way, even though there is great uncertainty about when it will come or what it will entail. When it says CHECK: ADVISORY BOARDS this indicates that the editors wants a check-up on a big news theme some months before, stories about the new government abolishing most governmental advisory boards while establishing news ones. The headlines written on the whiteboard are a clear mark of the unspoken practices surrounding everyday news journalism. In order to understand what the whiteboard says, you need to be updated on the news flow, the current and previous news stories as well as previous news themes.

These were the other stories on the whiteboard that day: CHURCHES CRITICISE MINISTER OF INTEGRATION [integrations minister] is a story about a handful of religious communities outside the Danish state church, criticising the minister of integration for his political plan to tighten up regulation concerning what is demanded of foreign priests. GOOD CONVICTS is the story about the MINISTER OF JUSTICE and her plan to release well- behaved "good convicts" from prison early on grounds of good behaviour in order to resolve the problem of crowded prisons. MANSOUR-CONVICTION is an event taking place today, the conviction in the case against the Danish Moroccan Said Mansour, who has been under suspicion for being connected to the al-Qaida network. FYNEN: EXERCISE, MENTOR, ID CARDS are three stories proposed by DR's regional television station at the island of Fynen. EXERCISE is about a group of children who exercise as part of a research project on obesity. MENTOR tells the story of a new mentor project for immigrants, and ID CARD is a story showing how minors cheat their way into discos using false identification. GAS STATIONS CLOSING tells how more and more small independent gas stations are closing in Denmark. PUBLIC SERVANT ASSAULTED [socialchef] happened yesterday, when the official of the social security department in the local government of the second largest city in Denmark, Aarhus, was assaulted. SAS-NEGOTIATIONS refers to the ongoing, biannual trade union negotiations in the Scandinavian Airline System where there have been threats of strikes but no result in the negotiation for a couple of days now. For the LATE NEWS, BAAM-REPORTAGE tells the reporters present at the editorial conference that one of the star correspondents has gone to BAAM to make a follow-up story on the devastating earthquake some months before. SITCOM SOLD TO USA: the American TV station ABC has bought the rights to remaking the Danish director Lars Von Triers television series. FOCUS is a three-story format used to present a chosen news story indepth usually consisting of a regular news story, a background story and a live studio interview. Today the FOCUS is the OPENING OF SHOPPING CENTRE in a recently developed part of greater Copenhagen. CAR THEFT is a story from one of the morning papers about an increase in car thefts.

EARLY NEWS	LATE NEWS
CHURCHES CRITICIZE	BAAM-REPORTAGE
MINISTER OF INTEGRATION	SIT-COM SOLD TO USA
GOOD CONVICTS	FOCUS: OPENING OF SHOPPING
MANSOUR-SENTENCE	CENTRE
DANISH ASTRONAUT?	IRAQ
FYNEN: EXERCISE, MENTOR, ID	CAR THEFTS
CARDS	
GAS STATIONS CLOSING	CHECK: ADVISORY BOARDS
PUBLIC SERVANT ASSAULTED	
SAS-NEGOTIATIONS	
DEFENCE-AGREEMENT	

Figure 2 List of potential news stories on the whiteboard.

Exclusivity—The Sixth News Criterion

But how is the knowledge from the press review used in order to decide the newsworthiness of a story? The following sections dig deeper into the practices at the editorial conference showing how different positioning strategies are used.

By 9:10 a.m., all journalists have arrived and found chairs around the table. Many people are present today: all of the domestic reporters assigned to the EARLY NEWS and to the LATE NEWS today, but also editors from DR's other news programme are present, not only to discuss todays news stories but also to co-ordinate stories and resources between the news at noon, the two evening programmes and next day's morning news programme. Present are the two editors for the EARLY NEWS and the LATE NEWS. The foreign news editor, the economic news editor, the planning editor, the morning/noon/afternoon editor including the host, two domestic reporters, two investigative reporters also from domestic news, a political news reporter (from the Parliament beat), an economy reporter, and two interns. Also, the two researchers partake in the editorial meeting but from the side, as they are seated by their desks, and do not always have an active role in the editorial conference. One of the two editors (or both) will be directing the editorial conference which usually begins with the editor presenting the stories on the whiteboard with a few words, for instance ideas for angles or sources. The style and organisation of the meeting will vary from editor to editor, but when the meeting ends, all the stories on the whiteboard have been brainstormed and discussed, new story suggestions have been brainstormed, just as possible angles, pictures, and sources have been discussed across the table. When the editorial conferences end, the first selection of news stories has been made, and the reporters will return to their desks with an assignment.

One of the editors begins the meeting by reading aloud the different stories on the whiteboard and presenting them with a few words: "We need to look at the DEFENCE-AGREEMENT, GOOD

CONVICTS and CHURCHES CRITICISE MINISTER OF INTEGRATION. As you have all heard and read, this is an initiative from the Minister of Justice suggesting that well-behaved convicts should be let out sooner in order to make more room in the prisons. But how much is there in the initiative? [MANSOUR-CONVICTION] The sentence is today. We have been covering that story intensely and now it is time to tie the knot. [EXERCISE] We need a follow-up on the story about obesity from yesterday. [MENTOR] The mentor programme for female immigrants: a positive story. [ID CARDS] Minors cheating their way into discos with false ID CARDs. [GAS STATIONS CLOSING] From yesterday. Gas stations closing in small towns. The news story is all done and ready for broadcast. Maybe we should leave it for the weekend? PUBLIC SERVANT in Aarhus assaulted. Increasing problem with civil servants and politicians being victims of violence. SAS-NEGOTIATIONS: the union walks out in protest. [DEFENCE-AGREEMENT] From Borsen [niche newspaper aimed at a business segment]. The Ministry of Defence has said that there is no story. Nothing new yet, just "drips." When is the actual suggestion for an agreement here?" The editor then points to LATE NEWS at the whiteboard: [BAAM-REPORTAGE] Reportage from Mette Fugl [high-profile female correspondent]. [SIT-COM SOLD TO USA]. Kim Bildsøe's reportage on ABC having bought 11 episodes of Riget to be instructed by Stephen King [Kim Bildsøe is a high-profile male correspondent in Washington, DC]. More and more car thefts happen because the thief has stolen the car key in advance. A reporter asks: isn't that an old story? Another answers: new cars have starter-blocks, that is why there is an increase in thefts using stolen keys. [CAR THEFTS] A third reporter says: car thefts are generally decreasing, but at the same time increasing locally. There are big regional differences. The editor goes on: [OPENING OF SHOPPING CENTRE] The shopping centre in Fields opens on 9 March. The angle could be the story about the Danish supermarket chains feeling under pressure? Could we broaden the story? A Danish franchise chain has called the editor this morning to suggest that there is a war on service, not on prices, on its way. Apparently, this was also the message in their last press release, the editor says. A reporter mentions that a German franchise chain has chosen to open a store in another part of Denmark but not in Fields—could the angle on the news story be wars between chains? A competing shopping centre closer to the heart of Copenhagen is not afraid of the competition. Everybody will make money. Another reporter suggests a lifestyle angle on the story, that people use shopping centers for field trips. A third reporter suggests that the angle could be where all the new customers are supposed to come from? The editor breaks off the brainstorming on the Fields shopping centre and says: we know that the newspapers are going to write about it at the weekend, so we might just as well be ahead of the game.

Positioning the News

By analysing the editorial conference through the perspective of Bourdieu, journalism studies are offered a promising analytical framework for re-invigorating and improving the tradition of newsroom studies. Where most of the classical newsroom studies used titles such as "making," "creating," "manufacturing," or "constructing" the news, the best title verb describing journalistic practice within the analytical framework of reflexive sociology would be *positioning* the news.

The first aspect is that of professional journalistic habitus, or news habitus, a bodily knowledge and feel for the daily news game which can be seen in the journalistic practices surrounding qualification and legitimisation of newsworthiness which almost takes place without words. The speed of news work is just as fast as the case study has attempted to illustrate. Journalistic practice is not the place for thorough detailed discussions of every little news story. Rather, news habitus implies a fast decision-making processes. There is no single recipe for "the good news story" or a single recipe for "newsworthiness" even though editors and reporters alike have a distinct gut feeling of what a good news story is and what newsworthiness is about.

Very little time is spent arguing for or against a specific story just as explicit discussions on which angle or source to choose is only the case for some stories.

The second aspect of journalistic practice, visible through the lenses of Bourdieu, is the differentiation of professional habitus, or in this case news habitus. This is visible in the fact that it is not without importance which reporter or editor comes up with which ideas. For instance, we saw how the IRAQ story and the BAAM story almost were not discussed at all which can be explained by differences in news habitus and editorial capitals: IRAQ and BAAM are stories allocated to and initiated by correspondents with high internal prestige.

Thirdly, reflexive sociology offers an analytical framework which distinguishes between explicit, orthodox values and silent, doxic values. The qualification of stories is very implicit, very embedded, very implied. One example from the case study is the fact that the editors did not explicitly evaluate all the stories or ideas during brainstorming by being blunt and saying: "That is not a good idea." For instance, the story about FEMALE STRESS suggested at the editorial conference was received with a silence from reporters as well as editors, sending a mute signal as an indication of low or no news value. In the Danish professional journalistic field the five orthodox news values are Timeliness, Relevance, Identification, Conflict, and Sensation. These criteria can be understood as the institutionalised, practical schemes of Danish news reporters but very importantly, the criteria are relative when used to construct newsworthiness. For instance, the story about the MANSOUR-CONVICTION takes place later in the afternoon and is considered highly timely, whereas the story about GAS STATIONS CLOSING was made yesterday, but is still considered timely. CAR THEFT can be read in the morning papers and is chosen, whereas OPENING OF SHOPPING CENTRE is chosen exactly because it has not been in the newspapers. When having observed editorial practices for more than a single morning, these paradoxes of journalistic practice can be explained by the existence of a sixth criterion: exclusivity. The story about gas stations has not yet been aired or printed in other media, and therefore, the story is likely to be exclusive. In the same way, the story of Fields might be more timely if printed at the weekend of the opening, but by then the story will be all over the newspapers and in this case not exclusive. In both cases, the outspoken, orthodox/heterodox news values are not sufficient in order to explain the newsworthiness of the stories. In order to explain the newsworthiness of the two stories, we need to consider the silent, doxic value of exclusivity.

Finally, and very importantly, the analytical framework of Bourdieu conceptualises the journalistic field and the newsroom as hierarchical social spaces. This might be the most important theoretical lesson from Bourdieu, and the most substantive improvement in relation to classic newsroom studies, that a news story is never newsworthy in itself or newsworthy only in the eyes of the beholder—rather, the newsworthiness of a story is always a question of positioning. How is the story positioned in relation to other stories in circulation that day? How is the journalist proposing or writing the story positioned in relation to other journalists? How is the media positioned in relation to other media? and so on. A key indication of positioning being key to the construction of newsworthiness is the process of press review. As the case study showed, everyone present at the editorial conference knows the news stories which have been aired on radio, which are on the front pages of the leading newspapers and in the wires from national and international news agencies, but no one really talks about it: there's no need. Knowing the news picture and reading off the positions in the daily news game is all part of journalistic practice. In this way, newsworthiness is constructed by reading the positions in the field: Which stories are on the agenda? Which media has which stories?

Conclusion

This article has used the theoretical framework of Pierre Bourdieu's reflexive sociology to investigate journalistic practices drawing inspiration from the analytical concept of the media field, journalistic doxa, news habitus and editorial capitals. Using the field approach the article draws a distinction between two types of news value in journalistic practice: doxic news values, for instance "newsworthiness," which are silent and belong to the universe of the undisputed, and orthodox/heterodox news values, which are explicit and debatable and belong to the sphere of journalistic judgement. It is argued that what journalists experience as their "journalistic gut feeling" entails both explicit news values—dominant (orthodox) and dominated (heterodox)—as well as silent, taken-for-granted (doxic) news values. Ethnographic analysis of journalistic practices in Danish newsrooms identifies five explicit news values: Timeliness, Relevance, Identification, Conflict, and Sensation, but also a sixth doxic news value: Exclusivity. Following the tradition of Pierre Bourrdieu's sociology, further research is important in order to identify other doxic news values, thus increasing the reflexivity of journalists and journalism—nationally as well as in a comparative perspective.

Acknowledgments

I would like to express sincere gratitude for valuable comments and constructive suggestions from Rodney D. Benson, Department of Culture & Communication, New York University, to Klaus Bruhn Jensen, Department of Film- and Media Studies, Copenhagen University, and to Dorte Caswell, AKF/Institute of Local Government Studies, Copenhagen. Also, I am deeply grateful for the critical, loyal and most insightful reading offered by the two reviewers commissioned by *Journalism Practice.* The article is based upon material from a PhD dissertation (Schultz, 2005) funded by a grant from the research project MODINET (www.modinet.dk).

Notes

1. The primary empirical material for this article is three months of observations of editorial practices at the two Danish national broadcasters DR 1 and TV 2, over 30 taped interviews with editors and reporters, and non-taped informal interviews with over 70 reporters (Schultz, 2005, 2006). The article is based on a Danish PhD dissertation combining reflexive sociology and newsroom ethnography in a methodological design including studies of everyday journalistic practice, a historical analysis of changing journalistic ideals using journalistic prize awards as empirical material, as well as an analysis of the recruitment to the Danish journalistic field (Schultz, 2005).

2. "The term 'news ecology' helps to signal (a) the under-theorised, and ethnographically under-explored, dimension of news differentiation, and (b) how this is constituted in important respects by a system of internally defined relations of difference—differences that are consciously monitored and reproduced by practising journalists both as a means of managing personal career moves within and across the field, but also as a professional means of reproducing specifk forms of news as required" (Cottle, 2003, p. 19).

3. Habitus is a dynamic, relational concept meant for empirical investigation just as the other analytical concepts in Bourdieu's theoretical toolkit. As such, the question of habitus is first and foremost an empirical question. This particular case study of news work has not investigated the social and statistical history and trajectory of the journalists and editors involved (for instance, family background, school, higher education, professional training, etc.) and thus not the primary habitus of the agents. Rather, the theoretical discussions on the possible different habitus' of the newsroom might be understood as a Habitus 2" (Bourdieu 2003 [1979], p. 171) or might even be termed a professional" habitus.

4. As a primary, secondary or even a third habitus is thinkable at the same time, habitus is not necessarily coherent or without complexity. The professional habitus, or secondary habitus, can theoretically be more or less in harmony with the primary habitus and the habitus might thus be more or less integrated, conflictual, or destabilised (Boudieu 2000 [1997], p. 159ff).

5. As an example, Herbert J. Gans' outstanding ethnography, *Deciding What's News,* identifies eight clusters of *enduring vaules* which are Ethnocentrism, Altruistic Democracy, Responsible Capitalism, Small-town Pastoralism, Individualism and Moderatism, Social Order and National Leadership (Gans, 1979, p. 42ff). "Values which can be found in many different types of news stories over a long period of time; Often, they affect what events become news, for some are part and parcel of the definition of news. Enduring values are not timeless, and they may change somewhat over the years; moreover, they also help to shape

opinions, and many times, opinions are only specifications of enduring values" (Gans, 1979, p. 41).

6. Denmark has two public broadcasters showing national news, TV 2 and DR 1, both regulated within the frame of "Public Service Broadcasting" (similar to the structure in the other Scandinavian countries, the United Kingdom and Germany) which means an obligation to meet certain declared standards ("public utility," meaning for instance that broadcasting should be "balanced," etc.), political regulation (laws, declarations, etc.) and "political supervision" (for instance an obligation to deliver annual public service reports" and political representation in the board of directors, etc.). DR is funded primarily by government support (tax revenues) and the income from a household fee whereas TV 2 is funded by advertising revenues, and to a lesser degree, by government support (tax revenues) to the regional affiliates of TV 2.

References

Altheide, David L. (1976) *Creating Reality. How TV news distorts events,* Beverly Hills, CA: Sage Publications.

Benson, Rodney (1998) "Field Theory in a Comparative Context: a new paradigm for media studies," *Theory and Society* 28, pp. 463–98.

Benson, Rodney and Neveu, Erik (2005) "Introduction: field theory as a work in progress," in: R. Benson and E. Neveu (Eds), *Bourdieu and the Journalistic Field,* Cambridge: Polity Press, pp. 1–25.

Bourdieu, Pierre (1993) *The Field of Cultural Production. Essays on art and literature,* Cambridge: Polity Press.

Bourdieu, Pierre (1998) *Practical Reason. On the theory of action,* Cambridge: Polity Press.

Bourdieu, Pierre (1998 [1996]) *On Television,* New York: The New Free Press.

Bourdieu, Pierre (2000 [1997]) *Pascalian Meditations,* Cambridge: Polity Press.

Bourdieu, Pierre (2002 [1977]) *Outline of a Theory of Practice,* Cambridge: Cambridge University Press.

Bourdieu, Pierre (2003 [1979]) *Distinction. A social critique of the judgement of taste,* London: Routledge.

Bourdieu, Pierre (2005) "The Political Field, the Social Science Field, and Journalistic Field," in: R. Benson and E. Neveu (Eds), *Bourdieu and the Journalistic Field,* Cambridge: Polity Press, pp. 29–47.

Bourdieu, Pierre and Wacquant, Loic J. D. (1992) *An Invitation to Reflexive Sociology,* Chicago: University of Chicago Press.

Breed, Warren (1955) "Social Control in the Newsroom: a functional analysis," *Social Forces* 33, pp. 326–35.

Champagne, Patrick (1999 [1993]) "The View from the Media," in: Pierre Bourdieu, Alain Accardo, Garbrielle Balazs, Stéphane Beaud, Francois Bonvin, Emmanuel Bourdieu, Phillipe Bourgois, Sylvain Broccolichi, Patrick Champagne, Rosine Christin, Jean-Pierre Faguer, Sandrine Garcia, Remi Lenoir, Francoise Evrard, Michel Pialoux, Lois Pinto, Denis Podalydès, Abdelmalek Sayed, Charles Soulié and LoIc J. D. Wacquant (Eds), *The Weight of the World. Social suffering in contemporary society,* P. P. Ferguson, S. Emanuel, J. Johnson and S. T. Waryn (Trans.), Cambridge: Polity Press.

Clausen, Lisbeth (2004) "Localizing the Global: 'domestication' processes in international news production," *Media, Culture & Society* 26, pp. 25–44.

Cottle, Simon (2000) "New(s) Times: towards a 'second wave' of news ethnography," *European Journal of Communication Research* 25, pp. 19–41.

Cottle, Simon (2003) "Media Organisation and Production: mapping the field," in: S. Cottle (Ed.), *Media Organisation and Production,* London: Sage Publications.

Epstein, Edward Jay (2000 [1973]) *News from Nowhere. Television and the news,* Chicago: Ivan R. Dee.

Ericson, Richard V., Baranek, Patricia M. and Chan, Janet B. L. (1989) *Negotiating Control. A study of news sources,* Toronto: University of Toronto Press.

Fishman, Mark (1980) *Manufacturing the News,* Austin: University of Texas Press.

Galtung, Johan and Ruge, Marl Holmboe (1965) "The Structure of Foreign News," *Journal of Peace Research* 2, pp. 64–91.

Gans, Herbert J. (1979) *Deciding What's News: a study of CBS Evening News, NBC Nightly News,* Newsweek *and* Time, New York: Pantheon Books.

Gieber, Walter (1961) "Two Communications of the News: a study of the roles of sources and reporters," *Social Forces* 39, pp. 76–83.

Hallin, Daniel C. and Mancini, Paolo (2004) *Comparing Media Systems. Three models of media and politics,* Cambridge: Cambridge University Press.

Hannerz, Ulf (2004) *Foreign News: exploring the world of foreign correspondents.* Chicago: University of Chicago Press.

Hovden, Jan Frederik (2001) "The Norwegian Journalistic Field. Issues and problems in an ongoing research project," paper presented to the 15th Nordic Conference on Media and Communication Research, Reykjavik, 11–13 August.

Lester, Marilyn (1980) "Generating Newsworthiness: the interpretive construction of public events," *American Sociological Review* 45, pp. 984–94.

Marchetti, Dominique (2005) "Subfelds of Specialized Journalism," in: R. Benson and E. Neveu (Eds), *Bourdieu and the Journalistic Field,* Cambridge: Polity Press.

Molotch, Harvey and Lester, Marilyn (1974) "News as Purposive Behavior: on the strategic use of routine events, accidents and scandals," *American Sociological Review* 39, pp. 101–12.

Schlesinger, Philip (1978) *Putting "Reality" Together. BBC News,* J. Tunstall (Ed.), London: Constable.

Schudson, Michael (1989) "The Sociology of News Production," *Media, Culture & Society* 11, pp. 263–82.

Schultz, Ida (2005) "Bag nyhedsværdierne. En etnografsk feltanalyse af nyhedsværdier i journalistisk praksis" ["Positioning the News. An ethnographic field analysis of news values in journalistic practice"], PhD dissertation, Department of Journalism, Roskilde University.

Schultz, Ida (2006) *Bag Nyhederne. Værdier, idealer og praksis [Behind the News. Values, ideals, practice],* Copenhagen: Samfundslitteratur.

Tuchman, Gaye (1973) "Making News by Doing Work: routinizing the unexpected," *American Journal of Sociology* 79, pp. 110–31.

Tuchman, Gaye (1978) *Making News. A study in the construction of reality,* New York: The Free Press.

Tuchman, Gaye (2002) "The Production of News," in: K. B. Jensen (Ed.), *A Handbook of Media and Communication Research. Qualitative and quantitative methodologies,* London: Routledge.

Tunstall, Jeremy (Ed.) (1971) *Journalists at Work. Specialist correspondents: their news organizations, news sources, and competitor colleagues,* London: Constable.

Warner, Malcolm (1971) "Organizational Context and Control of Policy in the Television Newsroom: a participant oberservation study," *British Journal of Sociology* 22, pp. 283–94.

White, David Manning (1950) "The 'Gate Keeper': a case study in the selection of news," *Journalism Quarterly* 27, pp. 383–96.

Source: From "The Journalistic Gut Feeling: Journalistic Doxa, News Habitus and Orthodox News Values," 2007, by I. Schultz, *Journalism Practice, 1*(2), 190–207. Reprinted by permission of Taylor & Francis/Routledge.

7

Media Ritual in Catastrophic Time

The Populist Turn in Television Coverage of Hurricane Katrina

Frank Durham

When Hurricane Katrina ripped through the Gulf Coast of the United States on 29 August, 2005, she destroyed lives and livelihoods, homes and hopes for thousands of people. In her path more than 1,500 people lay dead amid 90,000 square miles of destruction. The storm caused an estimated $200 billion in damage, most of it in coastal Mississippi and New Orleans (One Year After, 2006). At every point on the ground, the ways in which she wreaked havoc were made worse by poorly planned and incompetent relief efforts.

As the news of the destruction appeared on television screens around the nation during the six days after 29 August 2005, cable and network journalists presented viewers with another unexpected sight: reporters often alone on the scene or with official sources who could offer no solutions. Within the ritual context of the media, which might have been expected to present an orderly view of society (Carey, 1975), the media's early coverage of the government's failure—and its own loss in the face of it—became the 'meta-narrative' of this event. Thus, the coverage, itself, transformed the events surrounding Hurricane Katrina into a 'historical turning point', which further undermined an administration weakened by war and shifted the ritual dynamic within which the media worked (Becker, 1995: 632).

This is characterized by National Public Radio's John Burnett's description of his arrival in New Orleans. As he recorded the 'general atmosphere' of the scene (Becker, 1995: 639), he said,

> In many cases, we were first responders. We were there as people were coming out of those flooded neighborhoods. We were the first people they saw. We didn't have

> food. We didn't have water. We didn't have medical care. All we could do was to take their testimony and promise to get the word out. (Burnett, 2006)

But with government relief running almost a week late—the National Guard arrived at the New Orleans Convention Center on 3 September—being left to 'get the word out' stood in stark contrast to previous media responses to national crises, including the JFK assassination, the early Vietnam War, and 11 September 2001 (Whitfield et al., 2005). In those cases, the national press showed a unity with the federal government that Hallin has described as a 'sphere of consensus' (1986).

By contrast, media coverage of Hurricane Katrina produced no such 'consensus' (Hallin, 1986; Schudson, 2002). Instead, viewers watched reporters, who were working 'live', adapt to working without the benefit of 'consensus' and often without significant access to government sources. By examining how the media performed outside of its normal relationship to government, this preliminary textual analysis of network and cable television news transcripts from the week following the hurricane's arrival provides the tools to argue that 11 September created a traditional 'media ritual', fostering unity between people, media, and government, while Katrina led to a de-centered media ritual of critique.

Media Ritual as Routine(s)

Media ritual is fluid (Ettema, 1990). But understanding how, how much, and why depends on conceptualizing the media's ritual relationship to institutional structure. To that end, two paradigmatically different approaches are presented here to define a comprehensive theoretical range for understanding the external boundaries and internal processes of media ritual. The first and more traditional perspective reflects a Durkheimian concept of a structurally centered media (Elliott, 1982; Ettema, 1990). The second presents Couldry's (2003) 'neoDurkheimian' theory of media ritual, which advocates against a central role for the media in favor of a more de-centered and populist form of media. Rather than an exclusive and exhaustive definition of 'media ritual', these theoretical concepts are presented as points of analytical reference within and between which the media covering Hurricane Katrina may have operated.

To extend this theoretical description of media ritual to the level of concept criteria for application in the text analysis, I then present concepts of professionalism and objectivity as normative characteristics of 'centered', or structurally fixed, media ritual described by Ettema (1990), on the one hand, and of tabloidism as indicative of a 'de-centered', or less structurally oriented form of media ritual, on the other hand (Couldry, 2003). Further, by treating the concept of 'media ritual' as a holistic but varying 'cultural performance', it is possible to avoid the traditional production-consumption dichotomy in favor of a theoretical focus on the ways in which journalists resonate culturally with their audiences through their media routines (Ettema, 2005; Langer, 1998). In this sense, this theoretical framework can support the analysis of the ways in which television journalists contributed to 'the *internal structure* of media ritual through recognizable patterns of activities involved in selecting and recording particular aspects of the events' as they covered Hurricane Katrina (Becker, 1995: 629, emphasis added).

'Centered' Media Ritual

The normative concept of 'media ritual' has traditionally been defined in terms of the media's shifting positions within the context of events and, centrally, around the fixed structure of government (Elliot, 1982; Ettema, 1990; Hallin, 1986; Hallin and Gitlin, 1993; Schudson, 2002). Ettema (1990) explains the media–structure relationship as a nexus of 'both stability and change' for journalistic routines. Thus, this dominant, interpretive concept of 'media ritual' suggests a fluid, working context within which reporters and their institutional sources interact to make the 'news' (Ettema, 1990: 310–2).

Elliott has shown that media rituals present an 'interactional approach' that depends on the media's working 'in concert with political and social institutions'. In this important sense, he has recast the traditional functionalism of the 'Durkheimian paradigm of ritual as the instrument and expression of social solidarity' as a more interpretive site of social reproduction. In this way, he rendered the concept of power produced within this process as mutable and 'pluralistic' (1982: 584, 606, 614). By describing the internal corrections that reproduce media ritual as a meta-context for journalism, this flexibility accounts for the way the media can adapt to the realignment of ritual relationships and to their ideological role in producing meaning as social power within them (Thompson, 1990).

As Becker explains,

> Through their actions, media signal when and where the performative character of the event begins and ends, and contribute to the ways the internal structure of the events is defined and sequenced. Yet their most critical role remains the ways their presence continually shifts the focus of the event into reflexivity, pushing the performance into meta-narrative. (1995: 640–1)

Perhaps the most prominent form of 'meta-narrative' recently produced by media ritual was reported in Schudson's (2002) analysis of 'spheres' of news coverage of 11 September. There he compared Hallin's concepts of the 'sphere of legitimate controversy' where normal political coverage takes place to its reflexive complement, the totalizing 'sphere of consensus' (Hallin, 1986: 116–7). In his analysis of *The New York Times'* coverage in the aftermath of the terrorists' attacks, Schudson described the nearly complete ideological closure that occurred between reporters and their official sources, as well as between reporters and their audiences. As the meta-narrative shifted between 'legitimate controversy' of the Fourth Estate to the media's complicity in 'consensus', media ritual can be seen as engaging in an internal self-correction to maintain the media's relationship to a structural 'center' (Ettema, 1990).

By conceptualizing how *The New York Times'* coverage was changed in that moment in New York, Schudson showed how norms of objectivity collapsed in favor of addressing 'the media audience as part of a large national family that had suffered a grievous blow'. He further explained that in such crises, '[J]ournalists feel free to invoke a generalized "we" and to take for granted shared values' (2002: 40). After the September 2001 attacks, Hutcheson and his colleagues (2004) also found that government and military officials consistently emphasized themes based on normative American values of strength and power. Moreover, journalists closely replicated those themes in their own language, as Edelman (1993) has previously suggested. Similarly, following Bird's (2002) description of how the tabloid press and the traditional press converged to present news that addressed the more personalized themes of tabloidism, the question posed here is not whether both news genres converged, but what this re-ordered relationship between journalism and the government looked like and what it meant.

In major national crises prior to Katrina, the norm has been for the press to unify with the government—and for the government to reciprocate (Elliott, 1982). In this reflexive routine, the national media has traditionally shown an unwillingness to criticize the president or the federal government, or to engage in any other normal oppositions. As a matter of 'consensus' in these cases, America has become 'one' and the press has covered it with a nationalistic eye (Schudson, 2002: 40).

Within this closed system, news stories about such crises have become 'meta-narratives', signaling a profound moment of 'catastrophic time' (Becker, 1995: 633). Also known as 'press rites', such 'stories reflect the stability of the social system by showing it under threat, overcoming threat or working in a united consensual way. There is also a general agreement within the press on the way they should be handled and developed' (Elliott, 1982: 584–5). Within this form of media ritual, the 'consensual' element of the ritual of national media coverage presumes that 'the press and media do not act alone in the performance of press ritual but in concert with other political social institutions' (1982: 606). That reporters 'must not only *portray* powerful individuals and institutions, but must *interact* with them', underscores the importance of having access to sources and, especially, sources whose frames for events resonate with the 'meta-narrative' (Ettema, 1990: 311, italics in original).

'Ritual Space' and De-Centered Power: A Populist Paradigm

To consider what happens when the meta-narrative deviates in a way that undermines normative, or 'centered', media ritual, this theoretical framework extends the conceptual range to include Couldry's contradictory concept of media ritual. He argues for a 'radicalized Durkheimian' approach to more popular, 'de-centered' media (2003: 6–9). In his reaction to traditional concepts of media ritual, Couldry has challenged the centrality of the media in the construction of social reality. Instead, he has elaborated a concept that critiques the quality of social organization produced by media, including 'television, radio, and the press, and increasingly the Internet'. Specifically, his concept challenges the 'myth of the mediated centre: the belief, or assumption, that there is a centre to the social world and that, in some sense, the media speaks "for" that centre.' As he has explained, '[T]he myth I am attacking can be expressed another way: as the belief that the concentration of symbolic power in media institutions is legitimate' (2003: 2). By advocating a 'de-centered' media, he argues for a 'radicalized' Durkheimian concept of ritual that can serve as a more localized, and even populist, source of social power for the individual (Couldry, 2000, 2003: 2). He bases this idea on the premise that 'we can only grasp how media-related actions make sense *as* ritual actions, if we analyze a wider space which I call *the ritual space of 'the media'* (Couldry, 2003: 13, italics in original).

As it allows for a radical re-orientation of viewers to media by calling for the media to address themselves through their ritual performances more to their audience and less to a central social structure, Couldry's broadened metaphor of ritual 'space' provides a way to contrast the more conventional, or 'centered', definitions of 'media ritual' with the 'radicalized' Durkheimian concept that Couldry has offered. Heuristically, his distinction between 'centered' and 'decentered' media provides a more fluid way to interpret the possible relationships between the government and the media as they appeared to have changed during the early days of the Katrina crisis within and across television news genres. It also makes it possible to see how social power could be created and applied outside of a centered media ritual context.

Objectivity as a Professional Norm

As it has become a central professional norm, 'objectivity' describes the routinized process of gathering and reporting the news, which has traditionally defined such ritual space (Soloski, 1989). It 'undergirds the basic cultural role that the news media take as theirs: That of neutral or "unbiased" reporting', according to Schiller (1981: 2). As a 'cultural performance', journalists see the ability to construct news narratives that rely on norms of neutrality and facticity as a central professional skill (Tuchman, 1978). Based on these professional values, 'objectivity' constitutes an institutionally defined attempt to help the individual journalist overcome his or her human subjectivities, or what Lippmann (1922) termed the pictures in our heads, to accurately determine and depict an observable, knowable reality (Carey, 1975, 1992).

In this sense, traditional, or 'quality', journalism associated with network journalism adheres to more institutionally bound conventions of professionalism and objectivity, often due to a professional effort that Bishop (1999, 2004) describes as 'boundary maintenance' in a defense of serious journalism against tabloidism. But given the fluidity of media ritual, this boundary should be seen as permeable. Thus, as routines of objectivity serve to reproduce normative media rituals, they also remain subject to external cultural definitions and constraints. This means that the practice of objectivity, both as an ideal and as a routine, should be as subject to change as any other form of media ritual, depending on the constancy of the media-structure relation (Elliott 1982; Ettema 1990; Turner, 1980–1). And because professional norms and values are reflexively related to the structural contexts of their production in this way, it is important to ask how these aspects of media ritual might change when their structural contexts of reproduction change.

In terms that apply to the routines by which reporters reproduce traditional media-structure ritual, Tuchman (1972) describes reporters' adjusting to 'routinely non-routine' news. In this way, she shows the internal reflexivity of the relationship of the media to structure by conceptualizing the shifts between them to accommodate both normal and crisis modes of coverage and, more generally, to maintain the premise of media ritual (Ettema, 1990).

Indeed, where crisis news coverage patterns produce externally observable 'spheres of consensus', they also provide a key example of the way that the structural context of media ritual is maintained internally by adapting to exceptional circumstances (Hallin, 1986). In that context, journalists have long been free to drop their routines of objectivity and professionalism during crises, including during 'moments of tragedy', 'moments of public danger' and 'during threats to national security', according to Schudson (2002: 41). This is supported by a growing body of work based on coverage of the terrorist attacks of 11 September, which suggests a shift in news routines and in journalists' adherence to traditional norms, particularly those of objectivity and detachment, during times of crisis (Anker, 2005; Cho et al., 2003; Reynolds and Barnett, 2003; Zandberg and Motti, 2005; Zelizer and Allan, 2002).

Such a shift offers a contrast to earlier research that suggests an adherence to norms and routines regardless of the story (Berkowitz, 1992; Mindich, 1998; Kovach and Rosenstiel, 2001; Solomon, 1995). For instance, in their examination of national television news coverage of the attacks as a breaking news story, Reynolds and Barnett found that journalists assumed multiple roles, including that of expert and social commentator.

They also found that within such crisis coverage, journalists have commonly reported rumors and frequently included personal references in their reporting. The researchers also suggested that the speed required in covering the story, as well as the endless hours of air time to fill, may allow for 'lapses in the traditional, objective approach to gathering news' (2003: 699). But lapses are not complete deviations and such routines are normally recovered.

Populist Routines of Tabloidism

Because tabloid journalism reflects a professional ideology based on cultural resonance with the audience, rather than on the orthodox structural orientation associated with 'objectivity', it presents a useful theoretical point of reference for the analysis of the coverage of Katrina (Ettema, 1990, 2005). In Sparks' (1992) assessment of differences between the straight press and the tabloids in Britain, he pointed out that tabloid journalism does not present a normative or institutionally legitimated objectivity to support its construction of reality. Rather, it constructs a cultural consensus with viewers based on four core characteristics: highlighting personal narrative, privileging the visual over analysis, referring to the human interest story more than to sourced news, and focusing on 'the immediate issues of daily life' (p. 39). More generally, in a discussion that refers to tabloid journalism in non-crisis circumstances, Langer points out that through this consensus established between journalists and audiences, news viewers are 'referred implicitly to the background assumptions already underpinning cultural knowledge' (Langer, 1998: 19–20; cf. Ettema, 2005).[1]

As a set of production routines which indicate how journalists approach the goal of resonating with their audiences, the emphasis in cable coverage reflects a populist bent that complements the de-centered relationship of media ritual that Couldry (2003) proposes. In contrast to traditional forms of network news, the tabloids also refer to more popular, and therefore less elite, sources, thus representing the 'voice of the people'. This view of reality serves a practical purpose as well, given the vast number of hours that cable news channels must fill compared to their network counterparts (Sparks, 1992). In this comparison, shared assumptions about the meaning of 'hard' news, as well as the news-production routines used to create it, generally differ epistemologically in network and cable news. As a result, viewers tacitly identify the processes used to create traditional news formats with the generation of legitimate news (Langer, 1998).

In this sense, both audiences and journalists may perceive cable-news-gathering routines as falling below normative standards of professionalism and objectivity more than network routines. Instead of viewing well-researched, well-written news stories, viewers often see 'newsgathering in the raw': live interviewing illustrated by unedited videotape and extemporaneous reporting with little time to write or consult sources. The traditional staple of television news—the produced, written, edited and taped package—has been sidelined. What was once the raw ingredient of journalism is now the product (Project for Excellence, 2004).

In supporting this populist approach to news, tabloid-style journalism also includes a reliance on a storytelling style that focuses on personal narratives about individuals rather than on elite sources (Connell, 1998). The personal takes the place of the sourced construction of reality that normally signals 'quality' news. Structure recedes as the public sphere becomes less visible; instead of discursive analysis or even objective description, visual imagery gains prominence, sometimes extending to the re-enactment of events and the use of visual aids such as computer-enhanced photos (Bird, 2000). Although the bulk of the literature on tabloidism refers to British newspapers and the concept owes much to it (Langer, 1998; Sparks, 1992; Sparks and Tulloch, 2000), Bird (2000) makes a more specific reference to the characteristics of American television journalism that applies to the present study. Within the comparison of news coverage of 11 September and Katrina, the importance of these populist dimensions of cable news highlights the obligatory turn away from structural routines and toward a de-centered populism (Couldry, 2003).

With reference to these various concepts of media ritual, this study asks what happened to professional norms as indicators of the structural quality of media ritual in television coverage during the six days following Katrina. More formally, this study asks the following research questions:

RQ 1: How did internal routines of objectivity or tabloidism indicate the quality of media ritual in television news coverage following Hurricane Katrina?

RQ 2: How did power reproduced as media ritual change forms?

RQ 3: What was the role of professional ideology in reporters' adaptation to new forms of media ritual?

Methodology

The cable networks dominated coverage of Katrina and its destruction, with nearly two-thirds of Americans saying they got most of their news about the disaster from CNN, Fox News, MSNBC or CNBC. CNN and Fox alone were the primary sources of news for more than half the nation (Pew Center, 2005). Fox News, in particular, broke its own primetime ratings records in the aftermath of the storm (Donohue, 2005). Although broadcast coverage was limited to fewer hours overall, ABC, CBS, and NBC dominated the television ratings during its regular evening news time slots (Mandese, 2005).

To identify news texts, I conducted an initial close reading of all transcripts of television newscasts by CNN, Fox News, MSNBC, ABC, CBS, and NBC between 29 August and 4 September 2005. Hall has called this method 'a long preliminary soak to select representative examples that can be more intensively analysed' (1975: 15). To ensure the concept validity and comparability of the cases selected, I focused on news transcripts reflecting a traditional, hard news format. This led to the selection of two cable and two network news transcripts for this preliminary study.

All four cases conform to the media ritual concept of 'peak moments', or 'instances that carry particular meaning for the ritual as a whole, serving as symbols that gather and condense the meanings that are dispersed throughout the rest of the event'. They accomplished this quality not because some conclusion or climax had been reached, but because network television cameras were focused on some aspect of the 'general atmosphere'. In this sense, covering Katrina became a 'media event' as much as that coverage transformed the scene into an 'area for performance' (Becker, 1995: 635, 638, 641).

De-Centering Ritual: Television News Coverage of Katrina

This analysis shows how reporters necessarily negotiated the space that was opened following the storm between routines of objectivity and the populist tendencies associated with tabloid journalism. The text analysis shows that journalists changed their relationship to the ideal of government and their relationship within it by challenging the normative belief that government should have been responsible both before and after the storm for the protection of its citizens. Thus, the fundamental relationship of media to 'structure' is shown as it shifted to reflect a more de-centered form of media ritual.

The first newscast studied presents ABC's anchor-reporter team of Charles Gibson and David Kerley. The second example comes from a news report by CBS anchor Bob Schieffer and reporter John Roberts. The third transcript presented shows CNN's Anderson Cooper in an interview with U.S. Senator Mary Landrieu, a Louisiana Democrat and a native of New Orleans. The fourth case shows a typically 'raw' report by Fox network reporter Shepard Smith and his anchor, Sean Hannity.

Charles Gibson and David Kerley of *ABC World News Tonight*

When Charles Gibson opened the ABC nightly newscast, 'World News Tonight' on 30 August 2005, he said,

> Well, sometimes numbers can't fully convey the story. Numbers of dead, or numbers of homeless, or numbers of dollars in damage. Sometimes you have to focus on individual stories. And so, we asked ABC's David Kerley to focus on one block, on Howard Street, in the devastated City of Biloxi, Mississippi. David . . . (Direct Hit, 2005)

As in the previous cases discussed here, this decision by the network to personalize the news also reflected the populist technique of establishing a cultural 'consensus' with viewers by referring to common cultural assumptions (Ettema, 2005; Langer, 1998).

Where Ettema (1990) defines journalism as working within a structurally defined context, the decision by Kerley to focus on the particular was born of necessity: because he had no official sources to interview, his evening news report was forced away from its traditionally objective news routine to engage in a 'non-routine' populist style (Tuchman, 1972).

As they shifted away from source-driven objectivity to a populist news style, Kerley and

Gibson engaged their audience with personal narratives and visuals as narrative devices that were more likely to convey the meaning of the overall social situation (Sparks, 1992). In this report, Kerley found a family from Possum Hollow, Mississippi, a neighborhood near the beach on the Gulf Coast:

(Voice Over): Parts of this neighborhood, Possum Hollow, are a quarter-mile from the beach, but felt the full force of the 20-foot wave surge. As the water engulfed a small apartment building that Herbert Elsea manages, he had a plan, which some residents were afraid to follow.

Herbert Elsea, local resident: And I pulled myself across on the roof. And I couldn't get the other people to go. I think there's about six of us survived out of 14, I think.

Kerley (Voice Over): Yellow tape now marks the spot of eight bodies, tenants who were crushed when the building finally gave way. Across the street, seven other bodies were found today.

Louise Ross, local resident: My house is out in that pile back there.

The personal details continued, as Kerley said: Those who heeded the warnings and evacuated did return today. Louise Ross found clothes in her dryer, but little else.

Louise Ross: It doesn't matter the whole house is gone. Finding that little crystal basketball that belonged to my grandson just meant so much. My pet rock meant so much. 'Cause you cannot ever replace that kind of stuff.

Elizabeth Duvall: Come on. Come with your mama. Let's put that American flag up. We're, we're down, but we're not out. (Direct Hit, 2005)

The patriotic reference after such devastation signaled Duvall's nationalistic bravado, but within the television story it could only reflect a vestige of a different crisis. But unlike 11 September, the trope of national symbolism could not frame this story.

Instead, in this moment, the available populist consensus came not from prior experiences shared with the audience but from the immediate shock of this overwhelming moment: no one had ever seen the government default in the face of a natural disaster like this before. Although the 'meta-narrative' constructed collectively by their reports approximated the shared temporality of Carey's (1975) ideal of communication as ritual, it did so within the collective shock of 'catastrophic time' and, thus, without reference to the commonality of an otherwise routine 'structure' (Becker, 1995: 633).

As the newscast continued, the 'meta-narrative' of the government's abandonment was reinforced. When Gibson closed the segment, he focused on the most likely culprit of the moment (Turner, 1980–1). He said:

> The White House says President Bush will cut short his vacation at his Texas ranch to deal with the storm. The president will head back to the White House tomorrow to oversee the government's response to the hurricane. When we come back, convoys from around the country head to the disaster zone, bringing food, medical supplies, and teams of volunteers. How long will it take to get them to those in need? (Direct Hit, 2005)

In the time that it would take for a substantial federal response—five more days until 5 September—the news would continue to emphasize the cultural consensus of the administration's dereliction in ways that viewers could see and believe.

Bob Schieffer and John Roberts of the *CBS Evening News*

On 31 August 2005, the nightly 30-minute report by CBS Evening News focused on the destruction of the city of New Orleans. From his desk in New York, anchor Bob Schieffer introduced this segment as reporter John Roberts waited to report live from the city:

> In the history of this country, there's never been anything quite like this. Here is the latest: The federal government has declared a public health emergency for the Gulf Coast and launched one of the largest search-and-rescue operations in history. The Pentagon has ordered 10,000 more National Guard troops to Louisiana and Mississippi. In New Orleans, the mayor says the final death toll will likely be in the thousands. They have already counted more than 100 dead in Mississippi. (New Orleans, 2005)

As is nearly unavoidable in crisis situations, this opening summary reported rumors based on poor sources. In New Orleans, the estimates of the eventual death count by the mayor and police chief of New Orleans turned out to be only guesses (Baum, 2006; McFadden and Blumenthal, 2005; Thevenot and Russell, 2005). Reports by these same officials of rape, murder, and widespread looting by roving gangs, particularly by 'Blacks', also proved exaggerated or false (Lewis, 2005). Although the health crisis had been noted by the federal government, the announcement of 'one of the largest search and rescue missions' ever was also wrong: It would be four days after this report before any significant effort by the National Guard, the Red Cross, and—most noticeably—FEMA would begin. And even then, the effort would remain chaotic (Baum, 2006). If the concept of 'structure' needed a more concrete counterpoint, this chaos that followed the storm demonstrated the total loss of social organization that the media were faced with making sense of.

The contrast within the 'meta-narrative' of the crisis was equally telling. As Schieffer continued his report, he showed video of the president looking down from his window seat on Air Force One as it flew over on the way to the White House three days after the storm had hit. Schieffer made it clear that the president had stayed on vacation in Texas and in California for several days to make a speech backing the failing Iraqi war, rather than visiting the disaster area (New Orleans, 2005). Coupled with this voice-over, the video image stepped away from the network's traditionally objective news routines to show viewers an image they could identify with culturally: the president's figurative and literal distance from events on the ground.

After describing the post-Katrina flood in New Orleans during this newscast, Roberts interviewed individual victims. As his narratives showed the everyday context of the storm victims' lives and exemplified their abandonment by officials at all levels, Roberts' report also reflected the populist tactics of tabloidism (Anker, 2005):

Gwendolyn Bryant (Hurricane Survivor): We trying to be honest citizens, but if we die up here, it's because of the State of Louisiana just let us die up here and that's not fair. And I want the whole United States to know this.

Roberts: Barbara Pratt's husband of 53 years died at her feet last night as she frantically tried to flag down police cars.

Barbara Pratt (Wife of Hurricane Victim): Not one of them stopped. One of them police cars could have turned around here and see what was going on.

Roberts: Still marooned on the interstate this afternoon, the only advice police gave her, she says? 'Move the body further away so it wouldn't smell.'

Roberts explained: Emergency response here has been stretched well beyond the breaking point. In the flooded downtown hospitals, officials said today dozens of patients are at risk of dying if they can't be evacuated. (New Orleans, 2005).

Because no routines existed for reporting crises of this scale without formal sources, Roberts adapted his news reporting routines to the circumstances.

Anderson Cooper of CNN: 'Do You Get the Anger?'

CNN's Anderson Cooper interviewed Louisiana Senator Mary Landrieu on 1 September 2005, using satellite technology that allowed him to report from Mississippi while the senator was in Baton Rouge (Cooper, 2005). The television visual opened with a daylight shot of the Superdome and the city of New Orleans, which remained flooded beneath a sunny sky. Cooper appeared on the screen above a banner reading, 'FEDERAL RESPONSE'. After he introduced the senator, he played the objective role of 'watchdog', challenging and even attacking her for the federal government's failings (Carlyle, 1908; Hulteng and Nelson, 1971):

Cooper: Does the federal government bear responsibility for what is happening now? Should they apologize for what is happening now?

Landrieu: Anderson, there will be plenty of time to discuss all of those issues, about why, and how, and what, and if. Let me just say a few things. Thank President Clinton and former President Bush for their strong statements of support and comfort today. I want to thank Senator Frist and Senator Reid for their extraordinary efforts.

Anderson: Tonight, I don't know if you've heard—maybe you all have announced it—but Congress is going to an unprecedented session to pass a $10 billion supplemental bill tonight to keep FEMA and the Red Cross up and operating. (Cooper, 2005)

When presented with an official source, who was offering a factual discussion of the situation, Cooper initially demanded that the social order be restored. But he shifted away from the 'centered-ness' of objectivity to a populist stance to reject the frame offered by Landrieu in favor of his own personal narrative of the tragedy.

Becker (1995) calls this kind of transition from a ritual role a 'liminal moment', which records the boundaries of the event for the viewer. She explains that '[S]uch records are also useful for constructing a *narrative* of the event'. Because they happen when 'individuals are either not yet actively participating (during the transition into performance) or have dropped their performance role , these states are seen as authentic, revealing the essential significance of the event' (1995: 639–40, italics in original). As it framed his coverage, it was important that he shifted to attack the senator from outside of his designated role as a reporter.

Cooper: I haven't heard that, because, for the last four days, I've been seeing dead bodies in the streets here in Mississippi. And to listen to politicians thanking each other and complimenting each other, you know, I got to tell you, there are a lot of people here who are very upset, and very angry, and very frustrated. And when they hear politicians slap—you know, thanking one another, it just, you know, it kind of cuts them the wrong way right now. Because literally there was a body on the streets of this town yesterday being

> eaten by rats, because this woman had been laying in the street for 48 hours. And there's not enough facilities to take her up. Do you get the anger that is out here? (Cooper, 2005)

As his report reflects the shifts common to news routines during crises within objectivity, it also shows how Cooper approached and crossed the boundary between objective and tabloid journalism (Bishop, 1999, 2004).

In this way, Cooper's call for Landrieu to acknowledge the pain and anger of the dispossessed, and his demand for her to acknowledge the horror that was continuing because the government had abandoned its citizens, could be seen as a populist appeal to the cultural sensibilities of his viewing audience (Bird, 2000). When Landrieu insisted on her role within the dominant, but failed, media ritual of objective newsmaking as an antidote to the crisis, Cooper's position was only strengthened. Where the broader 'meta-narrative' of the story showed the government's withdrawal from the people (and the press), Cooper's watchdog response had placed him in opposition to his source in a way that resonated culturally with viewers. But in contradicting her, Cooper shifted the nature of this media ritual by identifying culturally with the storm's victims.

Because of this heated exchange, which produced a nationwide sensation, the senator's detachment from events was highlighted in a way that left her to represent an absent and derelict government. As Cooper's personal narrative characterized the story, the frame became one of anger at the absent government, demonstrating that the 'sphere of legitimate controversy' was not in play and that a 'sphere of consensus' was even less likely. This media ritual had become 'de-centered' (Couldry, 2003).

Shepard Smith and Sean Hannity of Fox News Channel: 'People Don't Know Where to Go'

On 3 September 2005, five days after Katrina, Fox News anchor Sean Hannity interviewed Shepard Smith live from New Orleans for a news report branded 'America's Challenge'. In addition to this banner, the Fox screen was ornamented with waving American flags as Smith stood wearily in the night, dressed in an open-collared shirt and holding his microphone for the stand-up report from the street. His image appeared on a split screen that also showed the flooded streets of the city (CrooksandLiars.com, 2005). As he opened the report with a description of early successes by volunteer workers, his focus was on the government's failure to direct survivors to relief sites:

> [I]t's a catastrophe beyond belief. Bodies outside the New Orleans Convention Center lying on the ground, chaos inside, gunfire against police. A fire burning in the distance now that's been going for better than three hours and no way to fight the thing.

While Smith described people stranded on the Interstate 10 bridge, Hannity asked about the National Guard convoys that were then showing on the network's split screen. He asked, '[Y]ou see the supplies going in. Why are they not getting to that specific location?' Smith's fatigue was apparent as he said, 'I don't know'.

Hannity: But we know for a fact there's—and how many people specifically are there?

Smith: Hundreds, and hundreds, and hundreds, and hundreds of them. See, the thing is, people don't know where to go now. They're not being told where to go. Two days ago, I was on that same bridge at Exit 235 saying there were thousands of people there then who didn't know where to go. (CrooksandLiars.com, 2005)

As Smith described the scene, neither he nor Hannity knew how many people were involved or why authorities were not directing them to safety, because neither had access to any official sources for verification.

Unlike Cooper's interview, Smith's circumstance was typical: he was forced out of the routines of objectivity normally associated with his news show's style of hard news presentation and into a world where government did not present sources and where journalism could not occupy a central mediating role between structure and 'common humanity' (Ettema, 1990: 312). Instead, Smith was left to dramatize, even to embody, the plights of citizens who had been abandoned by their government (Langer, 1998). As a result, the visual of Smith's personal narrative became the news. And objective, or 'hard', news became impossible for lack of the information available from the normal elite sources (Bird, 2000; Edelman, 1993; Schiller, 1981; Soloski, 1989).

This ritual shift did not represent a choice by Smith. Instead, as his report continued, we saw him work with what and who was left as he speculated about the reasons for the lack of leadership on the ground and his own inability to get answers from officials about the disaster:

> It may be because they were worried about chaos in other places if too many people were gathered. There's just no answer to that question. It's one of the first stories I've ever covered where questions as simple as, 'Why do the people on the easily accessible bridge not get food and water, and don't even get instructions of where to go to get food, and water, and medical attention?' It's the first time I've ever not known the answer to that. And I'm not sure there is an answer. (CrooksandLiars.com, 2005)

As dramatized by Smith's solitude on the scene, the immediacy of his narrative and visuals showed an unscripted exchange between reporter and anchor, offering viewers a sense of reality, actuality and immediacy (Montgomery, 2006). Sparks has explained the populism of tabloid news routines: '[T]he personal becomes the explanatory framework within which the social order is presented as transparent' (1992: 39). Rather than presenting more information from sources, this report hinged on Smith's declaration of how much he did *not* know. The break with the dominant structure of the federal government structure meant that media ritual had shifted beyond the centered bounds of normative media ritual (Ettema, 1990).

Conclusion

Prior to Katrina, the concept of 'media ritual' was normatively understood to provide a cohesive and 'centered' context within which journalism could variously mediate the resources of structure as a way to organize daily life. Taken critically as 'expressions of power in society, rather than as expressions of consensus', such rituals have become central to 'the Durkheimian paradigm of ritual as the instrument and expression of social solidarity', according to Elliott (1982: 584). In the case of 11 September, 'media ritual' maintained its structural integrity by following a ritual routine into a closer orbit of the government referred to as 'consensus' (Hallin, 1986; Schudson, 2002; Tuchman, 1972). But by comparison, the media's behavior following Hurricane Katrina presented an anomaly. The ways in which news routines differed present evidence of the changed relationship of the media to the state in this crisis moment. In sum, in the present case the relationship was inverted: where the national media leapt reflexively to form a 'sphere of consensus' with the government at 11 September, the government's post-Katrina default left journalists outside of the traditional meta-routine of a centered media ritual.

Because the traditional press–government media ritual was undermined, broadcast journalists from both cable outlets and networks were forced to vary from their routines of objectivity, producing, instead, a more populist form of coverage that resonated powerfully with their audience's cultural experience of the storm (Ettema, 2005; Langer, 1998). In the end, the power of that resonance may be what finally got the attention of a dissolute administration.

In this way, their reporting borrowed from the more populist routines of American tabloid television journalism in order to reproduce a populist form of power (Bird, 2000). The paradigm shift was not complete, however. By treating the theoretical paradigms of media ritual continuously, this interpretive analysis has shown that the reporters' struggle to regain the footing afforded by traditional, centered media ritual persisted. This may be explainable in terms of professional ideals: where normative concepts of media ritual associated here with objectivity have traditionally been associated with professional ideology (Elliott, 1982), the populist turn of news coverage of Katrina demonstrated reporters' strong adherence to the ideals of professionalism apart from those norms (Kovach and Rosensteil, 2001; Society of Professional Journalists, 1996).

More generally, Couldry suggests that 'While particular rituals will lapse, and while practice itself may be disrupted at times when social experience is profoundly disturbed, the *urge* to create ritual forms is, according to Durkheim, universal'. Given the combination here of the administration's disuse of the media coupled with the storm's effects, the populism practiced by the media clearly represented that professional 'urge' to reconnect to the structural resources represented by the notion of ritual. It is notable that the present comparison to Couldry's (2003) populist concept of media ritual arises here from a structural anomaly, rather than from a popular or more democratic impulse (p. 15: italics in original).

Even when considered apart from its functionalist implications, the structural role of media ritual has long caused scholars to question the role of journalism in American society. In his 1994 critique of the 'emptiness of the American public sphere', Hallin argued that 'it might be time for journalists to rejoin civil society, and to start talking to their readers and viewers as one citizen to another, rather than as experts claiming to be above politics' (p. 176). For nearly a week following Hurricane Katrina, these television reporters and anchors did that, raising important questions about the integrity of American 'civil society' on behalf of individual Americans (Couldry, 2003). In that moment, they found a newly de-centered form of media ritual as they appealed directly to the people in the voice of the people, but in a way that was also intended to get the attention of the absentee government.

On the seventh day following Katrina, 5 September 2005, as the recovery effort began, local, state, and federal government officials resurfaced in the news in more significant numbers than during the week. But as before, they came as the subjects of news, not as sources representing material relief. In particular, Mayor Ray Nagin of New Orleans, Governor Kathleen Blanco of Louisiana, and others pursued rounds of public back-biting with the Bush administration and each other that became known as the 'blame-game'. As the local and state officials fought with Director of Homeland Security Michael Chertoff about how and why the federal government's response had failed, *The New York Times* reported that 'perhaps the only consensus among local, state and federal officials was that the system had failed' (Shane et al., 2005: 1A).

Schudson's (2002) analysis of 11 September suggests that the duration of shifts in media ritual is limited. In his study of 11 September coverage, he observed a span of 17 days before he saw *The New York Times* coverage return to normal. Turner's 'repertoire of motifs' projects a series of stages for such shifts. In this presentation and analysis, this case has demonstrated the first two—the figurative and literal 'breach' that happened to 'challenge authority', and the resulting 'crisis' reflected in the media's loss of its ritual place near the government and as an upholder of dominant social norms. What is not apparent in this 'social drama' is how it will be resolved through a process of 'redress'. And, most importantly, it remains to be seen whether such efforts will lead to 'reintegration' or 'separation' (1980–1: 149). These questions remain for future analyses of the return to a more 'centered' media ritual along the Gulf Coast and in New Orleans, which would need to consider a broader period of time than the moment of crisis considered here.

Acknowledgments

The author wishes to gratefully acknowledge Jane Singer for initially proposing this project following a talk I gave on the topic and for co-authoring an earlier draft that was presented at the 2006 meeting of the International Communication Association. He also wishes to thank Gigi Durham for her constant support. And a wish: perhaps one day when we are not waging false wars abroad, the memory of the tragedy of New Orleans will awaken the political conscience and action at all levels that remain so miserably beyond our reach at this writing.

Note

1. It is appropriate to this study that neither of these scholars refers to 'sensationalism' as a hallmark of tabloidism, because the scale and ferocity of the Katrina disaster surpassed its use.

References

Anker, Elisabeth (2005) 'Villains, Victims and Heroes: Melodrama, Media, and September 11', *Journal of Communication* 55(1): 22–37.

Baum, Dan (2006) 'Deluged: When Katrina Hit, Where Were the Police?', *The New Yorker, 9* January (consulted April 2006): http://www.newyorker.com/archive

Becker, Karin (1995) 'Media and the Ritual Process', *Media, Culture & Society* 17: 629–46.

Berkowitz, Dan (1992) 'Non-Routine News and Newswork: Exploring a What-a-Story', *Journal of Communication* 42(1): 82–94.

Bird, Elizabeth S. (2000) 'Audience Demands in a Murderous Market: Tabloidization in U.S. Television News', in Colin Sparks and John Tulloch (eds) *Global Debates over Media Standards,* pp. 213–28. New York: Rowman & Littlefield.

Bird, Elizabeth S. (2002) 'Taking it Personally: Supermarket Tabloids after September 11', in Barbie Zelizer and Stuart Allan (eds) *Journalism after September 11,* pp. 141–59. New York: Routledge.

Bishop, Ronald (1999) 'From Behind the walls: Boundary Work by News Organizations in their Coverage of Princess Diana's Death', *Journal of Communication Inquiry* 23: 90–112.

Bishop, Ronald (2004) 'The Accidental Journalist: Shifting Professional Boundaries in the Wake of Leonardo DiCaprio's Interview with Former President Clinton', *Journalism Studies* 5(1): 31–43.

Burnett, John (2006) 'Reporter Tells Stories of "Uncivilized Beasts"', NPR audio file, 11 October, (consulted October 2006): http://www.npr.org/templates/story/story.php?storyld=6246211

Carey, James W. (1975) 'A Cultural Approach to Communication', *Communication* 2: 1–22.

Carey, James W. (1992) *Communication as Culture: Essays on Media and Society.* New York: Routledge.

Carlyle, Thomas (1908) *Sartor Resartus: On Heroes, Hero-Worship and the Heroic in History.* New York: E. P. Dutton.

Cho, Jaeho, Michael P. Boyle, Heejo Keum, Mark D. Shevy, Douglas M. McLeod, Dhavan V. Shah and Zhongdang Pan (2003) 'Media, Terrorism, and Emotionality: Emotional Differences in Media Content and Public Reactions to the September 11th Terrorist Attacks', *Journal of Broadcasting & Electronic Media 47:* 309–27.

Connell, I. (1998) 'Mistaken Identities: Tabloid and Broadsheet News Discourse', *Javnost* 5(3): 11–32.

Cooper, Anderson (2005) 'Special Edition: Hurricane Katrina', CNN.com Transcripts: Anderson Cooper 360 Degrees, 1 September, URL (consulted December 2005): http://transcripts.cnn.com/TRANSCRIPTS/0S09/01/acd.01.html

Couldry, Nick (2000) *The Place of Media Power: Pilgrims and Witnesses of the Media Age.* New York: Routledge.

Couldry, Nick (2003) *Media Rituals: A Critical Approach.* New York: Routledge.

CrooksandLiars.com (2005) 'Horror Show', 2 September, URL (consulted October 2005): http://www.crooksandliars.com/2005/09/02.html

'Direct Hit Howard Street Stories' (2005) World News Tonight ABC News Transcripts, 30 August, viewed 15 April 2006 at Lexis-Nexis.

Donohue, Steve (2005) 'Fox News Leads Katrina Ratings', MultichannelNews.com, URL (consulted December 2005): http://www.multichannel.com/article/CA6253483.html?display=Breaking-t-News&referral=SUPP

Edelman, Murray (1993) 'Contestable Categories and Public Opinion', *Political Communication* 10(3): 231–42.

Elliot, Philip (1982) 'Press Performance as Political Ritual', in D. Charles Whitney, Ellen Wartella and Sven Windhall (eds) *Mass Communication Review Yearbook* 3: 583–619.

Ettema, James S. (1990) 'Press Rites and Race Relations: A Study of Mass-Mediated Ritual', *Critical Studies in Mass Communication* 7(4): 309–31.

Ettema, James S. (2005) 'Crafting Cultural Resonance: Imaginative Power in Everyday Journalism', *Journalism* 6(2): 131–52.

Hall, Stuart (1975) 'Introduction', in A. C. H. Smith, E. Immirzi and T. Blackwell (eds) *Paper Voices: The Popular Press and Social Change, 1935–1965,* pp. 9–24. London: Chatto & Windus.

Hallin, Daniel (1986) *'The Uncensored War': The Media and Vietnam.* New York: Oxford University Press.

Hallin, Daniel (1994) *We Keep America on Top of the World.* New York: Routledge.

Hallin, Daniel and Todd Gitlin (1993) 'Agon and Ritual: The Gull War as Popular Culture and as Television Drama', *Political Communication* 10: 411–24.

Hulteng, John L. and Roy P. Nelson (1971) *The Fourth Estate: An Informal Appraisal of the News and Opinion Media.* New York: Harper and Row.

Hutcheson, John, David Domke, Andre Billeaudeaux and Philip Garland (2004) 'US National Identity, Political Elites, and a Patriotic Press Following September 11', *Political Communication* 21(1): 27–50.

Kovach, Bill and Tom Rosenstiel (2001) *The Elements of Journalism: What Newspeople Should Know and the Public Should Expect.* New York: Crown.

Langer, John (1998) *Tabloid Television.* New York: Routledge.

Lewis, Michael (2005) Wading Toward Home', *The New York Times, 9* October, URL (consulted November 2006): http://www.nytimes.com/2005/10/09/Imagazine/O9neworleans.html?ex=1286510400&en=cf2lddfeSc3O733c& ei= 5090&partner= rssuserland&emc=rss

Lippmann, Walter (1922) *Public Opinion.* New York: Macmillan.

McFadden, Robert D. and Ralph Blumenthal (2005) 'Bush Sees Long Recovery for New Orleans; 30,000 Troops in Largest U.S. Relief Effort', *The New York Times,* 1 September, Al.

Mandese, Joe (2005) 'Late-Summer Shakeups: Katrina Wreaks Mayhem, Publicist Plots Strategy', *Broadcasting & Cable,* 5 September, URL (consulted February 2006): http://www.broadcastingcable.com

Mindich, David T. Z. (1998) *Just the Facts: How 'Objectivity' Came to Define American Journalism.* New York: New York University Press.

Montgomery, Martin (2006) 'Broadcast News, the Live "Two-Way" and the Case of Andrew Gilligan', *Media, Culture & Society* 28(2): 233–59.

'New Orleans Suffering through the Aftermath of Hurricane Katrina', (2005) CBS News Transcripts, 31 August, viewed 15 April 2006 at Lexis-Nexis.

'One Year After Katrina: The State of New Orleans and the Gulf Coast' (2006) *Southern Exposure: Special Report* (34)2. Durham, NC: Institute for Southern Studies.

Pew Center for the People and the Press (2005) 'Two-in-Three Critical of Bush's Relief Efforts', 8 September, URL (consulted October 2005): http://people-press.org/reports/display.php3?ReportlD=255%20-%2021k

Project for Excellence in Journalism (2004) 'State of the News Media: Cable TV', URL (consulted October, 2005): http://www.stateofthenewsmedia.Org/narrative_cabletv_intro.asp?media=5

Reynolds, Amy and Brooke Barnett (2003) 'This Just In: How National TV News Handled the Brealdng "Live" Coverage of September 11', *Journalism & Mass Communication Quarterly* 80(3): 689–703.

Schiller, Dan (1981) *Objectivity and the News: The Public and the Rise of Commercial Journalism.* Philadelphia: University of Pennsylvania Press.

Schudson, Michael (2002) 'What's Unusual about Covering Politics as Usual', in Barbie Zelizer and Stuart Allan (eds) *Journalism after September 11,* pp. 36–47. New York: Routledge.

Shane, Scott, Eric, Lipton and Christopher Drew (2005) 'After Failures, Officials Play Blame Game', *The New York Times,* 5 September, 1A.

Society of Professional Journalists (1996) 'Code of Ethics', URL (consulted October 2005): http://spj.org/ethics_code.asp

Solomon, William S. (1995) 'The Site of Newsroom Labor: The Division of Editorial Practices', in Hanno Hardt and Bonnie Brennen (eds) *Newsworkers: Toward a History of the Rank and File,* pp. 110–34. Minneapolis: University of Minnesota Press.

Soloski, John (1989) 'News Reporting and Professionalism: Some Constraints on the Reporting of News', *Media, Culture & Society* 11(1): 207–28.

Sparks, Colin (1992) 'Popular Journalism: Theories and Practice', in Peter Dahlgren and Colin Sparks (eds) *Journalism and Popular Culture,* pp. 1–40. Newbury Park, CA: Sage.

Sparks, Colin and John Tulloch (eds) (2000) *Tabloid Tales: Global Debates Over Media Standards.* New York: Rowman & Littlefield.

Thevenot, Brian and Brian Russell (2005) 'Rape. Murder. Gunfights: For Three Anguished Days the World's Headlines Blared that the Superdome and Convention Center had Descended into Anarchy. But the Truth is that While Conditions Were Squalid for the Thousands Stuck There, Much of the Violence NEVER HAPPENED', *The Times-Picayune,* 26 September, A01.

Thompson, J. B. (1990) *Ideology and Modern Culture: Critical Social Theory in the Era of Mass Communication.* Stanford, CA: Stanford University Press.

Tuchman, Gaye (1972) 'Making News by Doing Work: Routinizing the Unexpected', *American Joumal of Sociology* (79)1: 110–31.

Tuchman, Gaye (1978) Making News: A Study in the Construction of Reality. New York: Free Press.

Turner, Victor W. (1980–1) 'Social Drama and Stories about them', in J. T. Mitchell (ed.) *On Narrative,* pp. 137–67. Chicago, IL: University of Chicago Press.

Whitfield, Fredericka, Tony Harris, Nic Robertson, Ed Lavendra, Carol Lin, Barbara Starr, Elizabeth Cohen and Daniel Sieberg (2005) 'CNN Live Saturday 12:00 PM EST', 3 September, URL (consulted November 2006): Lexis-Nexis.

Zandberg, Eyal and Motti Neiger (2005) 'Between the Nation and the Profession: Journalists as Members of Contradicting Communities', *Media, Culture & Society* 27(1): 131–41.

Zelizer, Barbie and Stuart Allan (2002) 'Introduction: When Trauma Shapes the News', in Barbie Zelizer and Stuart Allan (eds) *Journalism after September11,* pp. 1–24. New York: Routledge.

Source: From "Media Ritual in Catastrophic Time: The Populist Turn in Television Coverage of Hurricane Katrina," 2008, by F. Durham, *Journalism, 9*(1), 95–116. Reprinted by permission of Sage Publications, Ltd.

PART III

Making Meaning in the Journalistic Interpretive Community

Like other fields, journalists work in an environment that shares cultural meanings about doing work and interpreting events as they occur. They could be considered an *interpretive community,* where cultural meanings of the community are learned through belonging and performing the journalistic identity. This meaning system is self-correcting, so that challenges to accepted meanings are kept in check if they begin to stray. Typically, members' historical perspectives of their interpretive community are used to fit the meanings of new occurrences into the frameworks of old ones, although old meanings are sometimes adjusted toward the new ones instead.

The concept of "interpretive community" traces its development to fields outside of journalism and mass communication[1]; yet as people who are interpreters at their core, journalists are an excellent fit to the concept. Likewise news represents the interpretive efforts of journalists' culture—an interpretive community is not defined only by its interpretive actions but also through a sense of belonging to a group with a shared worldview. The selections in this part of the book all follow from this basic sense of interpretive community, even though some authors do not use the term explicitly. This overview teases out that sense of interpretive community, however, guiding the reader into seeing the concept in other parts of the book as well.

"War Journalism and the 'KIA Journalist': The Cases of David Bloom and Michael Kelly" offers an example of a dimension of journalism's interpretive community—news about journalists who have died while covering a war—where meanings are shared and news is adjusted to fit the interpretive community's meanings. From within this community, reporting on war stands out as a form of high ritual, with a sort of historical reverence for past war correspondents and the symbolic meaning of their legacies. Narratives grow from these homages that state and restate the role of a journalist in society, which in turn asserts professional authority and certifies journalists' social role. In the case of two

[1]See, for example, Barbie Zelizer, "Journalists as Interpretive Communities," *Critical Studies in Mass Communication* 10, September 1993, 219–237.

American journalists who died in wartime Iraq—NBC reporter David Bloom and *Washington Post* columnist Michael Kelly—neither journalist actually died from combat injuries, but news about their deaths nonetheless maintained a narrative consistence with wartime heroism. Matt Carlson shows how news stories from the journalistic interpretive community developed a group of themes about the deaths of these reporters that resonated with the community's key values: bravery, volunteerism, sacrifice, and witnessing. Thus, the KIA (killed in action) journalist serves as a valuable moment when the interpretive community can capitalize on a newsworthy event to restate its cultural values both within and outside of its cultural settings.

"The Importance of Ritual in Crisis Journalism" once again contrasts the journalistic vantage point with the cultural perspective. In doing so, Kristina Riegert and Eva-Karin Olsson shift concerns about meaning to journalistic ritual during crisis; it is the significance of the culture's work that is shared by the journalistic interpretive community rather than how the journalistic community interprets events into news content. Much like Durham's piece in Part II, the authors argue that media rituals help society view news media as part of society's center. This ritual maintains journalists' sense of belonging to an interpretive community through the language and meanings shared across media organization. To illustrate their argument, Riegert and Olsson present case studies from the newsrooms of two Swedish television networks, interviewing journalists about their coverage of the September 11, 2001, attacks in the United States and the 2003 murder of Swedish Foreign Minister Anna Lindh. Using Schultz's term in Part II, these television journalists gave priority to their *doxic* news value of social responsibility over the networks' short-term concerns for either technical quality or economic gain. In addition, the ritual of "marathon" crisis coverage within the interpretive community became a means of helping audience members cope with what had happened. In sum, performing ritual crisis news carries meaning for journalists that enhances their sense of belonging to an interpretive group. At the same time, the interpretive group passes along its meanings of events to a society for which they work.

"'Someone's Gotta Be in Control Here': The Institutionalization of Online News and the Creation of a Shared Journalistic Authority" takes the concept of interpretive community to the world of online media, where the shift in ownership and content poses a threat to the traditional locus of control that journalists maintain for their interpretive authority. The argument is similar to Singer's in Part II, but it goes a step beyond to the community building that occurs in a news organization with both print and online forms. Through interviews with 35 journalists at 24 news organizations, Sue Robinson develops a sense of core beliefs that the traditional journalistic interpretive community carries over to its online form. In a way, this selection is about an interpretive community *reinterpreting itself* as its forms and technologies undergo fundamental change—journalists negotiate the place of online blogs and columns as they bring their audience into the folds of their interpretive community. In doing so, control of content becomes an important issue as the news audience comes on board as a co-communicator. One editor referred to this shift in journalism as the work of building a "community of communities." Ultimately, as the notion of journalistic authority shifts, journalists face a challenge that keeps some members in the fold while losing others who do not embrace the community's new meanings.

Finally, "Broader and Deeper: A Study of Newsroom Culture in a Time of Change" explores an unfolding news industry crisis through a scenario where journalists' own organization tells them to change their interpretive community's self-conception. In an effort to hold its audience, this newspaper's new editor mandated change in the newsgathering process, most notably abandoning the government beat reporting system, a mainstay of local journalism. This change created an identity crisis within the interpretive community's membership, escalating to the point where some journalists left their jobs. David Ryfe argues that journalists belong to a "community of practice" that shares an understanding about the forms and processes representing a community ideal. When their community norms are overturned, they experience three stages of change: practicality, identity, and morality. At the core of these journalists' interpretive community belief system is the notion of a "good story," not formally defined yet mutually agreed upon by community members. The change in reporting expectations prevented them from reporting on these good stories. In essence, the interpretive community was required to change its system of interpretation by management rather than being allowed to adapt meanings more organically. Dissonance within the interpretive community was the result.

All in all, this part's focus on a journalistic interpretive community has read between the lines to tease out the concept, helping understand how journalists envision themselves and the work that they do. By living and working in a shared framework for interpretation of meanings—both in their work and in the stories they report—journalists maintain interpretive continuity that accommodates subtle change over time but fails at making quick changes necessitated in their workplace settings.

8

War Journalism and the "KIA Journalist"

The Cases of David Bloom and Michael Kelly

Matt Carlson

Introduction

In war coverage, journalistic norms that govern news gathering and reporting are strained by an absence of routines for finding information, technological challenges, constraints on information access, contestation over the appropriateness of what can be conveyed, and tensions between journalistic norms of detachment and impartiality and patriotic norms of citizenship (Allan & Zelizer, 2004). War correspondents face

> pressure to be selective with the facts, to be more circumspect in comment and analysis, to censor themselves, to accept restrictions on their movements, to submit to the tyranny of the satellite uplink and the demands of the 24-hour "real-time" news agenda. (McLaughlin, 2002, p. 23)

Yet the concerns of journalists go beyond what is normative. They face challenges to their physical safety, including the potential unwillingness of the enemy to recognize their autonomy, "friendly fire" incidents, kidnappings and assassinations by enemy forces, and a generally grueling environment prone to accidents. Put bluntly, the reality of war reporting is that reporters get killed.

This article examines one particular context through which journalists interpret their roles in providing war coverage: discourse surrounding the death of journalists in war—the "KIA journalist": How are these discourses constructed? What attributes of the Killed In Action journalist are celebrated? How do these discourses extend to the role of the journalist in war or in culture more generally? These questions are ways to study how journalists make sense of the risks of war reporting, and on a deeper level how they construct and maintain the authority of the journalistic function in war

Discourse surrounding the first two embedded U.S. journalists to die in the 2003 Iraq War will be examined: Michael Kelly, a columnist for the *Washington Post* and editor-at-large for the *Atlantic Monthly*, and David Bloom, co-anchor of NBC's *Weekend Today Show* and a former White House correspondent.[1] While Bloom and Kelly were not the only journalists killed in the opening weeks of the war, the focus on them here stems from the attention their deaths received in the U.S. news media.

Kelly and Bloom died within two days of each other, on April 4 and April 6, 2003, respectively—in the early stages of the conflict. Three key differences separate Kelly and Bloom. First, they worked in different media. Second, Kelly worked primarily as an opinion columnist whereas Bloom operated as a reporter. Third, Kelly died after coming under fire—although the incident was often misreported as an accident—in contrast to Bloom who died from a pulmonary embolism. Despite the often murky association of Kelly's death with combat and the definitive lack of combat as a cause in Bloom's death, their presence at the war front allows them to be incorporated into narratives that make sense of journalistic risk in combat situations by representing their deaths—and war reporting in general—as meaningful to the larger group rather than as individualized and unnecessary losses.

Online article databases were used to locate discussions of the death of the two journalists in various news media, including newspapers, magazines, and network and cable television news transcripts, as well as the journalism trade press. This discourse analysis follows Fiske (1994), who urges "analyzing what statements were made and therefore what were not, who made them, who did not, and . . . the role of the technological media by which they were circulated" (p. 3). The resulting analysis shows the trends in stories journalists tell about their role in war both to other journalists and to the public.

News From the Front: Journalism and War

The history of war reporting is not a coherent, progressive narrative; it is an erratic practice, marked by differences in newsgathering and reporting technology, access to combat spaces, and the degree of freedom to report. As modes of news gathering and relay change from war to war, the tension for journalists between dispassionate observation and patriotic responsibility—and the concomitant issue of internal and external censorship—has remained a central issue in war reporting (Hudson & Stanier, 1998). Such issues bear on the shape of the reporting, ultimately impacting public opinion (Hallin, 1986). Within the academy, journalists are criticized for a "heady mix of patriotism and fascination with war" (Glasgow University Media Group, 1985, p. 21). Hallin and Gitlin (1994) compare war reporters to "priests": "they are not expected to stand back from consensus, to be objective, but to celebrate" (p. 160). War creates a challenge for journalists to create distance from whom or what they cover. As Morrison and Tumber (1988) note, during the Falklands War, "journalists not merely observed their subjects, but lived their lives and shared their experiences," which created "a door for partiality irrespective of any desire to remain the detached professional outsider" (p. 96). This tension resurfaced in the second Iraq war with the embedding process set out by the U.S. military (Tumber & Palmer, 2004). The assigning of reporters (embeds, as they came to be known) to individual military units was praised for granting news outlets access to the front lines. However, journalists and others questioned whether the arrangement would lead journalists to abdicate their independence by becoming too attached to soldiers whom they depended on for protection (see Ricchiardi, 2003).

The changing technology of news means that war is increasingly represented to audiences visually, situating "twentieth-century civilians as spectators to wars' on-screen representation" (Carruthers, 2000, p. 2). Moreover, even with improvements in news relay from reporters on the front, war coverage is shaped by variability in access and censorship. This was apparent in the first Gulf War, where journalists numbered over a thousand and the transmission of live video via satellite was implemented and widely discussed as a marked improvement in wartime news relay (Zelizer, 1992b). However, military restrictions on war images resulted in uniformity across the reportage of the numerous news outlets operating in the region. Taylor (1998) described this effect as "monopoly in the guise of pluralism" (p. 268). While the management of the press by the military in the first Gulf War kept journalists away from the combat, four journalists were killed when they eschewed military protection to pursue the story independently.

The motivations for journalists to take risks in conflict zones vary. These include being a witness to history, psychological reasons, and "the competitive and individualistic culture of the journalistic profession" (Tumber, 2003, p. 255). There is a desire to be in the action and to tell the story of war to a public that cannot be there first hand. War journalists "know the risks but they shrug them off with fatalistic acceptance and sometimes they become media stories themselves" (McLaughlin, 2002, p. 201). This paper focuses on what it means when a KIA journalist becomes a media story.

The collective memory of war, central to national identity, is mediated through journalists who act as "key figures in creating war narratives; not only reporting from the battlefields, but also collecting and shaping the recollections of soldiers, producing histories, and fictionalizing accounts of war" (Bromley, 2004, p. 236). Additionally, war provides journalism with its own highlights and the mythologizing of past war correspondents, including Edward R. Murrow, Ernie Pyle, and George Orwell. Aside from the symbolic, the collective memory of war journalism also provides working journalists with models of war reportage. Without set routines to turn to, "Images of past wars offer a fertile repository from which journalists can seek cues on how to do their work . . ." (Zelizer, 2004, p. 124).

Connecting Sacrifice With Journalistic Authority

The construction of journalistic sacrifice, nowhere more explicit than with the KIA journalist, connects with narratives of journalistic authority and meaning for the journalistic community as well as for the public. This discourse takes on a symbolic function in creating narratives of what a journalist does and how what she does serves the larger culture. The symbolic dimension takes on extra importance given the lack of standardized qualifications, widespread membership in professional organizations, accreditation, or licensing. Without clear and stable boundaries between journalist/non-journalist, journalism does not correspond easily with professionalism (Jonestone, Slawski, & Bowman, 1976; Singer, 2003; Tunstall, 1971). Journalists must rely on less formal tactics of journalistic affiliation, including self-identification as journalists, working norms, and a collective sense of what being a journalist entails. This can include an orientation toward public service (Gardner, Csikszentmihalyi, & Damon, 2001) and the strategic use of objectivity (Schudson, 1978; Tuchman, 1972).

Given the problematic nature of establishing boundaries around who qualifies as a journalist, it is not surprising to find contestation over the role of journalism more broadly in U.S. culture. In order to perform their function of delivering ostensibly veridical stories to society, journalists must maintain a degree of cultural authority that grants them the ability to tell stories *about* the larger group to the group. Journalistic authority, then, is "the ability of journalists to promote themselves as authoritative and credible spokespersons of 'real-life' events" (Zelizer, 1992a, p. 12). However, how and where this authority exists is an underconceptualized notion.

Weber's typology of authority helps make sense of journalistic authority. Weber delineates authority along three interdependent legitimating dimensions:

1. Rational grounds—resting on a belief in the "legality" of patterns of normative rules and the right of those elevated to authority under such rules to issue commands (legal authority).

2. Traditional grounds—resting on an established belief in the sanctity of immemorial

> traditions and the legitimacy of the status of those exercising authority under them (traditional authority); or finally,
>
> 3. Charismatic grounds—resting on devotion to the specific and exceptional sanctity, heroism or exemplary character of an individual person, and of the normative patterns or order revealed or ordained by him (charismatic authority). (Weber, 1947, p. 328)

While Weber was addressing the requirements for the coordination of groups generally, these categories provide a useful framework for conceptualizing journalistic authority. First, regarding rational grounds, we can identify journalists' championing of normative tropes of journalism, including objectivity, neutrality, and impartiality. Zelizer (1992a) locates authority as "a source of codified knowledge, guiding individuals in appropriate standards of action" (p. 2). The rules extend beyond the journalist; the journalist adheres to them as part of a normative compact regarding what journalism should be. Second, traditional grounds can be located in historical-cultural narratives about journalism that imbricate it with basic democratic functioning (see Gans, 2003). More specifically, journalism finds authority through the collective memory of journalistic success, which has been examined in relation to journalists' autobiographies (Schudson, 1988), the Kennedy assassination (Zelizer, 1992a), and Watergate (Schudson, 1992). Again, a cultural narrative outside of working journalists aids in informing their authority as part of a continued heritage.

The KIA journalist narrative supports charismatic authority by granting war journalists hero status. One of the characteristics of charismatic authority as identified by Weber is that its practitioners are set apart from ordinary people and "treated as endowed with supernatural, superhuman, or at least specifically exceptional powers or qualities" (Weber, 1947, p. 358). As such, they are to be venerated. But this alone does not inform the legitimacy of their authority. Action is required such that "it is the *duty* of those who have been called to a charismatic mission to recognize its quality and act accordingly" (p. 359, original emphasis). Charismatic authority as realized in journalism requires that journalists act on this authority by putting themselves in the position of heroes. We shall see below how the discourse on Bloom and Kelly treats these narratives.

While narratives about the KIA journalist overlap with both history/tradition (by connecting the newly deceased to past KIA journalists) and rationality/norms (witnessing adheres to forms commensurate with journalistic conventions), they make a more tactile and immediate case for continued journalistic authority through heroic narratives of bodily sacrifice in service to the wider culture. The KIA journalist narrative becomes a narrative of virtue, which assigns a moral authority to war journalists. In this view, journalists risk death in order to monitor the exercise of state power manifested in war.

As Eason (1988) notes, journalistic authority is a dynamic and contested concept, and one prone to ruptures. Maintaining authority is a complicated, multifaceted, and ongoing process. This view emphasizes journalism as a cultural practice, "part of a double reality" (Manoff & Schudson, 1986, p. 4) that reports on, yet is inseparable from, the context of the culture in which it operates. The implication is that journalists are neither invisible nor independent observers, but produce meaning in a cultural system marked with its own demands and constraints.

A narrative about the deaths of Kelly and Bloom must be created by others—journalists as well as non-journalists—since Bloom and Kelly are no longer able to construct narratives about themselves. Instead, their deaths are interpreted in frameworks of meaning that move beyond the individual to speak about the role of journalism and the normative attributes of journalists more generally. The discourse described below immediately followed the deaths of Bloom and Kelly, when attention was at its peak, yet the significance of their deaths had not been established.

Kelly, Bloom, and the Narrative(s) of the KIA Journalist

Both Kelly and Bloom participated in the Pentagon's embedding program and traveled with the 3rd Infantry Division near the front of the U.S. advance toward Baghdad. Their placement in the forward portion of the attack garnered them news attention from their own outlets and others. This was more true for Bloom as a television journalist and through a technological advantage gained from a customized vehicle he built for broadcasting from the field. Kelly's death occurred on Thursday, April 4, 2003, when the Humvee in which he was riding swerved to avoid mortar fire and crashed into a canal. Two soldiers escaped, but Kelly and another soldier drowned. Two days later on the morning (Iraq time) of Sunday, April 6, Bloom fell unconscious and died while packing his equipment. His death was quickly attributed to a pulmonary embolism.

Their deaths were widely covered, both individually and, in many cases, jointly. The home outlets for Bloom and Kelly each covered the story extensively. The *Washington Post* ran four stories on Kelly the day after he was killed: a 1,700-word story by media critic Howard Kurtz in the front section, a 1,100-word obituary in the style section, an editorial, and a previously printed (and apolitical) column by Kelly on the op-ed page—along with several letters to the editor. On NBC, the Bloom story dominated the April 6 *Sunday Today Show,* which Bloom had co-anchored before going to Iraq. The coverage featured interviews with former colleagues, reminiscences from NBC journalists, and old clips of Bloom. Throughout the NBC coverage, journalists made familial references. For example, on the *Today Show* of April 7, 2003, Katie Couric said: "We have lost a member of the family today": Bloom's death was also featured on MSNBC and CNBC, as well as on the MSNBC.com Web site.

Even as the deaths received attention across many news outlets, it is important to contextualize Kelly and Bloom in the consuming, multifaceted, ongoing media story of the less-than-three-week-old Iraq War. Thus, coverage of their deaths competes with other stories coming out of the war. At the same time, the deaths of Bloom and Kelly are a reminder to journalists and the public of ongoing dangers to journalists in war.

The Situation of Death: Accidental Versus Combat

Before turning to the specific narratives that developed around Kelly and Bloom, the reporting of each journalist's death needs to be clarified. The initial reporting around Kelly, which persisted even weeks later, was that he was killed in an accident—with no mention of the accident occurring while under fire. Instead, his death was reported as a random incident—a mere accident in a dangerous place. This was true throughout the initial television coverage on April 4. Ted Koppel, who was also embedded in the 3rd Infantry Division, was the first to attribute Kelly's death to combat during ABC's *Nightline* on the evening of Thursday, April 4, 2003 (early Friday in Iraq):

> Yesterday, approaching the airport here outside Baghdad, Michael's humvee, driven by a sergeant, was ambushed. Trying to take evasive action, the driver flipped the vehicle into an irrigation ditch. Two of the soldiers in the humvee made it out. Michael and the sergeant did not.

In the newspaper stories the next morning, the *Washington Post* noted that he was killed in an accident without any mention of combat. In contrast, *The New York Times* related his death to combat with an unnamed military source: "His humvee came under Iraqi fire, and the driver's evasive action caused the vehicle to roll into the water, trapping both men for about 25 minutes, the Army said" (Carr, 2003b, p. Al0). A few days later (April 7) on ABC's *Good Morning America* Charles Gibson combined the accident/combat frames: "Under fire, he was killed last week in a humvee accident:" As time passed, reports continued to oscillate between accident and combat. Even a *New York Post* article on May 8—more than a month after Kelly's death—described it as an accident, without mentioning combat (K. Kelly, 2003). Thus, Kelly is remembered both as a journalist unfortunately killed in a random accident and as a journalist killed after coming under fire.

The continual reporting of Kelly's death as an accident, even as competing sources (*The New York Times* and *Nightline* notably) labeled it as combat-related, is significant. A reluctance to take the combat-death view, which would have been the first question asked by a journalist reporting Kelly's death, indicates an insistence to only report what could be factually verified. The level of evidence needed to promote the cause of death from the default of accident to the level of combat-related was often not met. Had the combat component of his death been widely recognized, the narratives below would have been bolstered in their attempts to promote Kelly as bravely sacrificing himself. In the confused, distant space of war, a greater desire for accuracy as codified in norms of objectivity prevailed over a desire to promote a combat aspect of Kelly's death. Even the *Washington Post*, Kelly's employer, championed his bravery without mentioning combat as a cause in his death.

Bloom's death was quickly and definitively attributed to a pulmonary embolism. This was made explicit in the reportage. For example, the second paragraph of *The New York Times* stated: "NBC said yesterday that the cause was apparently a blood clot, and that the death was not combat-related" (Walsh, 2003, p. A7). While the direct role of combat is excluded from Bloom's death, the degree to which Bloom's pulmonary embolism could be credited to the physical stress of covering the war was subject to speculation. For example, on the *Today Show*, Matt Lauer and Katie Couric pondered the impact of Bloom's working conditions:

Lauer: Also, as you already know, we're mourning the loss of one of our own this morning. David Bloom passed away suddenly on Sunday morning after suffering from a pulmonary embolism or PE while on assignment in Iraq. In just a couple of minutes, we're going to find out what PE is and what could cause one.

Couric: A lot of speculation about being cramped up in one of those tanks for days on end might have . . .

Lauer: Blood clot in the extremities that can then move into the heart and lungs.

Later in the program, in a discussion with a doctor:

Lauer: So when we remember the images of David perched on that vehicle as it moved through the desert hour after hour after hour, and sleeping, as he described to us, in cramped conditions, that could lead to the creation of a clot.

Dr. Halperin: Absolutely, and not only that, add to it the dehydrating effects of being in the desert. (April 7, 2003)

Such speculation peppers the discourse around Bloom. However, the explicitness of the non-combat nature of his death is accepted across the coverage.

When deaths result from combat, the KIA journalist slides easily into narratives of heroism—the archetype being the widely read Scripps-Howard war correspondent Ernie Pyle's death by sniper fire in World War II. Yet the fact that death is not directly and causally related to combat, but one step removed, does not prevent the development of the KIA journalist narrative. The lack of a clear-cut combat causation and attendant narratives of heroism resulting from a violent death means more work by journalists and others to connect the non-combat death with the narratives that give war reporting its specific meaning.

The following sections analyze various themes emerging from the coverage as journalists make meaning out of the deaths of two fellow journalists in a combat zone. These narratives are interrelated. They function together as a field of discourse that makes sense of the deaths of journalists during war by ultimately interpreting their deaths as meaningful sacrifice.

The Brave Journalist

A prevalent narrative in the Bloom and Kelly discourse represents the war journalist as embodying bravery. Risk is recognized as both extraordinary and as a reality of the profession. Dan Rather emphasized reporters' consciousness of this risk: "In war, journalists who take the risks know what the risks are, and they know what they're getting into" (*Larry King Live*, CNN, April 14, 2003). That journalists possess knowledge of risk and continue to put newsgathering above safety translates into bravery. A *New York Post* columnist made this connection explicit: "But let me tell you, these war correspondents bringing the news to a free society have got gold for guts. Millionaires in the currency of bravery" (Dunleavy, 2003, p. 11). The concepts of risk and bravery become concrete in the deaths of Kelly and Bloom, as well as other journalists killed in Iraq. Howard Kurtz captured this explicitness of risk in a *Washington Post* article on war coverage:

> It's been the best of times and the worst of times for journalists. The best because so many of them braved enemy fire and showed the world that they could cover a war honestly and aggressively from the front lines. The worst because some of them died in the process. (Kurtz, 2003b, p. Cl)

Kurtz establishes a dichotomy between the good of the coverage and the bad of death in the name of that coverage, so that the latter informs the value of the former. Risk only has value when the reward outweighs the potential downsides—including death.

At the level of the reporter, the contrast between the duty towards newsgathering and the risk of gathering that news is borne out through discussions of vocational commitment. CNN's Jamie McIntyre reflected on Kelly's death on *Larry King Live*:

> I have to say that when I heard about [Kelly's death], my heart stopped a little bit because, as we've been watching all of these amazing reports that have been coming in from the battlefield, we've certainly been—it's been clear that all of the journalists are in the same danger as the soldiers and the Marines on the ground. It's a very, very serious and sometimes deadly business. (April 4, 2003)

Two days later, following the death of Bloom, King queried fellow CNN journalists Walter Rodgers (also in the embedded 3rd infantry Division), Wolf Blitzer, Christiane Amanpour, and Nic Robertson on how they account for the risk component of their work in light of Kelly and Bloom:

> Walter Rodgers: [Bloom] was a supremely confident journalist. He knew this was going to be his war. He was determined that he was going to be the war correspondent of this war. And he was going to leave his mark.
>
> . . .
>
> Wolf Blitzer: You know, it's just in our blood, you know, Larry. It's our career. And that's what we do. You go into a dangerous assignment before you leave. You say to yourself, well, maybe I shouldn't do this, but then you do it because there's a certain momentum that pushes you to do it. And then while you're doing it, it's great because your adrenaline is pumping. And you're really moving with the story. And

> you're exhilarated. And you just love every second of it.
>
> . . .
>
> Nic Robertson: This is our vocation. And we do believe in bringing the news, the stories, the understanding to the audience.
>
> . . .
>
> Christiane Amanpour: Those of us who have the privilege to go to these places and work in this profession have a responsibility. (April 6, 2003)

In the three quotations above, the journalists invoke the motivational forces of individual determination, excitement, and vocational dedication as reasons for enduring the risk of war reporting.

Both Bloom and Kelly came to speak in the discourse through previous statements confronting and dispensing with the risks of embedded reporting. After reporting Bloom's death, Tom Brokaw made a point of this: "When I recently told David, off air, to take care of himself and not to do anything dumb, he laughed and replied, 'You mean anything dumber?' And then he laughed again" (*NBC Nightly News*, April 6, 2003). A quote by Kelly from Nightline also showed him dismissing risk by rationalizing the situation:

> My own gut feeling is that there's some degree of danger, but if I was going to, sort of, rank danger in things that reporters do, . . . it would be . . . a lot more dangerous to be wandering around Chechnya than doing this, or wandering around Sierra Leone. I mean, here there is some element of danger, but you're surrounded by an army, literally, who is going to try very hard to keep you out of dange. (quoted in Kurtz, 2003a, p. A19)

A sense of irony pervades these quotes as Kelly and Bloom come to embody risk as realized in their deaths.

Volunteerism

Bravery is closely linked with a narrative of volunteerism that foregrounds the conscious decision of a journalist to enter into the risky space of war when it is not required. The fact that Bloom and Kelly volunteered for their Iraq assignments adds another dimension to the narratives that emerge following their deaths: The war correspondent is there as a matter of choice.

After identifying Kelly's death as combat-related, an editorial in *The New York Times* highlighted the courage of war journalists in their willingness to enter into conflict situations in order to fulfill their journalistic mission:

> Reporters enter combat zones aware of the dangers they face. They sign up *voluntarily* because they believe that readers deserve a view from the battlefield, and they judge themselves capable of *accepting* the risks. Unlike soldiers, though, they haven't trained for years to defend themselves. However well integrated with the troops—and Mr. Kelly's columns from Iraq revealed an uncommon rapport with the fighting men and women—reporters are never truly embedded. *Even the steeliest are, in the end, innocents.* ("Michael Kelly," 2003, p. A12, emphasis added)

Thus, while journalists openly accept risk, they are still innocent, in the *Times*' view, in that they are not part of the combat. This holds with the concept of the journalist as detached observer even in the situation of embedding where the reporter is connected to a side and, as a result, in constant close contact with those he (as is usually the case) is covering.

On CNN, Wolf Blitzer connected the risk Kelly undertook with volunteerism: "In recent weeks, [Kelly] was one of those embedded journalists who decided to risk their lives to cover this war for all of us. Michael didn't have to do it, but he wanted to do it" (*Wolf Blitzer Reports*, April 4, 2003). This assertion that Kelly did not need to go is often predicated on his coverage of the first Gulf War. Kelly's reporting and subsequent book (1993) earned him the reputation of a fearless reporter and propelled him to national recognition. Between the Iraq wars Kelly migrated away from reporting toward the editor role and started a family. His involvement in the 2003 war was attributed to a tenacious journalistic spirit. Martin Beiser, former managing editor of *GQ*, said: "I was so mad at him for going back a second time. He had a good war—he didn't need another one" (quoted in Frost, 2003). In another article, Beiser made a similar statement: "He didn't need to do this. He's just a born newsman. He wanted to be where the action was. The courage he showed in the last war put his career on a whole new trajectory and he didn't need to prove anything" (quoted in Kurtz, 2003a, p. A19). David Brooks attributed his involvement to an internalized vocational duty: "It would have been hard to imagine the war with him not wanting to do it. He's one of those people who went into journalism because he wanted to see stuff happen" (quoted in Mnookin, 2003). A newspaper editorial also expressed this idea: "At 46, his career was made, and there was nobody to tell him to go anyplace. But, old reporter that he was, *he had to go* where the big story was, especially because he had the background for it" ("Kelly didn't," 2003, p. B6, emphasis added). Volunteering connects to a sense of duty, even against the barriers of age and familial status.

With Bloom, the ease, in journalistic terms, of his work as morning show anchor was contrasted with the challenge of war reporting. Howard Kurtz described Bloom as "just an irrepressible guy who gave up his cushy *Weekend Today* anchor job. He told his bosses he wanted a piece of this war" (*Reliable Sources*, CNN, April 6, 2003). Bloom's *Weekend Today* co-anchor, Soledad O'Brien, used the language of military recruitment when she recalled, "When the Pentagon first announced its embed program for this war, there was no reporter more gung-ho about joining up than David Bloom" (*Sunday Today*, April 6, 2003). Bloom's volunteerism is marked by enthusiasm for taking the lead in covering a big story, no matter how risky.

Even though Kelly and Bloom were married and had young children, discussion of their familial role was largely absent. Don Browne, a former colleague of Bloom, provided an exception on the *Sunday Today* Show: "[Bloom] was madly in love with journalism, but first and foremost, he was absolutely madly in love with his family" (April 6, 2003). *Newsweek*'s Howard Fineman referred to Kelly as "always a great family man" (*Hardball*, MSNBC, April 4, 2003). But for the most part, the existence of their wives and children were relegated to a single line deep in the stories. For example, *The New York Times* mentioned Kelly's family in the seventeenth paragraph of a nineteen-paragraph story: "In addition to his parents, Mr. Kelly, who lived in Swampscott, Mass., is survived by his wife, Madelyn, and their sons, Tom and Jack" (Carr, 2003b, p. A10). Thus, Kelly and Bloom's responsibility to journalism was featured throughout the discourse while their familial responsibility was avoided.

Sacrifice

Sacrifice—both generally and in the name of witnessing—is a broader narrative that lies at the core of producing interpretations of the deaths of Kelly and Bloom that promote the authority and value of war journalists. Sacrifice is constructed by moving the focus from the reporter as individual to the collective value gained from journalists' presence in the perilous space of war.

NPR's Scott Simon, after mischaracterizing Kelly's death as an accident, noted, "He died doing work that he believed stood for something and could make a difference in [his family's] lives" (*Weekend Edition*, April 5, 2003). This statement connects Kelly's duty toward his vocation with the duty toward his family, with the former serving the latter. Maureen Dowd connects sacrifice to journalism more generally when she said of Kelly: "He had had the best possible life for a journalist and died well, better than full of tubes in a hospital somewhere" (Dowd, 2003, p. A13). The "well" here indicates dying in the act of doing journalism, which serves as a model of the journalistic vocation. This is echoed by the assertion of heroism in the *National Journal*: "[I]n his death, a hero's death, we are all seeing again the virtue and the possibilities of our calling" (Powers, 2003, p. 1170). Kelly's death was used to prompt reinvigoration of the journalistic mission.

Bob Wright, chairman and CEO of NBC, specifically evoked sacrifice in a statement reported on NBC and in many newspaper stories: "In times like these, a journalist's contribution to his country is measured in terms of illustrious commitment and sacrifice. There was no one more devoted to his calling than David Bloom and for that we are both grateful and humbled" (quoted in LeSure, 2003). Respect for Bloom is predicated on the interpretation of his death as a bodily sacrifice—the mark of ultimate devotion—even as his death did not come from combat.

As mentioned above, Ernie Pyle represents the archetype for journalistic sacrifice during war after being killed by sniper fire on a Pacific island in the final days of World War II. Both Bloom and Kelly are problematic fits for the Pyle narrative: the role of combat in Kelly's death was initially foggy and largely omitted. Bloom's pulmonary embolism can be tied only speculatively to conditions of war reporting. Regardless, the fact of their deaths did draw Pyle comparisons. At Bloom's funeral, broadcast on the cable networks and written about the following day in many newspapers, Tom Brokaw said that "David was the Ernie Pyle of his generation." On MSNBC, Chris Matthews said: "[Bloom] took this story and turned it into, not an Edward R. Murrow story but into an Ernie Pyle story. The guy was the G.I.'s reporter. . . . [I]n the war, in the van, in the assault, going into harm's way and filling us in the whole time" (*Hardball*, April 7, 2003). Here, the connection with Pyle is drawn from Bloom's closeness with the soldiers. In the *Christian Science Monitor*, Bloom's use of technology invited the label of "an Ernie Pyle in real time" (Nelson, 2003, p. 11). A newspaper columnist stated: "The war in Iraq has claimed one of its Ernie Pyles" (McGuire, 2003, p. Dl). By mentioning Pyle with little or no accompanying information on who he was, journalists indicate an assumption that their great heroes are universally recognized and revered, even 58 years later.

Kelly also received comparisons with Pyle, but to a lesser degree. A Richmond *Times-Dispatch* editorial compared Kelly to both Pyle and George Orwell:

> Orwell, Pyle, and Kelly make this an honorable trade and humble those who futilely strive to emulate them. Michael Kelly was a patriot. He went into that good night doing what he wanted to do, sharing his final moments with the quiet heroes he admired. ("Michael Kelly," 2003, p. A10)

Again, like Bloom, the closeness of Kelly with the troops was celebrated, even though it was orchestrated by the military. Elsewhere, the *Cincinnati Post* drew a tangential connection between Kelly and Pyle: "Kelly shared a Scripps Howard link with Ernie Pyle. While Pyle was a Scripps Howard columnist, Kelly once worked as a reporter for *The Cincinnati Post*" ("Journalists make," 2003, p. B1). This comment came without any discussion of common virtues, but the juxtaposition suggests a commonality between the two that positions Kelly as worthy of similar veneration.

Witnessing

While Kelly and Bloom were revered for their bravery, voluntary commitment, and sacrifice, these narratives ultimately coincide around the journalist as witness. In the context of the KIA journalist, witnessing serves not merely as the central function of the war journalist, but as a sacred activity at the heart of the journalistic mission. Witnessing becomes the reason for the sacrifice; it establishes value in the loss of life. It provides a firm connection between the collective value of reportage and the deceased individual journalist.

Witnessing connects to the broader journalistic normative function of the press as watchdog, holding power accountable through its vigilance. As a norm, it is meant to extend across journalism from the safe corridors of City Hall to the precarious space of war. CBS's Bob Schieffer notes that for Kelly and Bloom:

> It was not the glamour of the job that drew them to the battlefield, but a passion to be where the story was, which is what reporters are supposed to do. Because *they* and the rest of the reporters covering the war have been there, the rest of *us* are getting a new appreciation of the job the American military has been doing. And because of those reporters, the propaganda from Saddam Hussein's people is put to the lie daily. (*Face the Nation*, April 6, 2003, emphasis added)

Brokaw made the same point during his eulogy at Bloom's funeral in a comparison of soldiers and reporters: "Moreover, warriors and journalists are irreplaceable components in the structure of a constitutional republic, ensuring national security and the right of the people to know what their government is doing in their name and in their interests" (*Buchanan and Press*, MSNBC, April 16, 2003). In this construction, the soldier represents an action of power while the mutually essential reporter provides a check on that power on behalf of the citizen. If the reporter is absent, then power cannot be accounted for by the citizen. Pete Hamill wrote in the *New York Daily News*,

> [Bloom and Kelly] died while working for all of us. They were members of that brave band of reporters who go to bad places to send bulletins to the safe. . . . But in the much larger sense, Kelly and Bloom were witnesses, and as such, they died for all of us. (Hamill, 2003, p. 8)

In the context of war, witnessing requires risk—embodied by the KIA journalist. In an editorial, *USA Today* ("Eyes and ears," 2003, p. A14) used the importance of reporters as witnesses as an explanation for why their deaths garner more attention than soldiers: "Comparing non-combat deaths of reporters to combat losses might seem insensitive. But much of what the public knows about the war came because journalists were willing to travel with the U.S. military." This claim also evokes the narrative of volunteerism—soldiers do not have freedom in choosing risky assignments the way journalists do.

Discourse on witnessing could also be found in the journalism trade press, which often sought to protect the reputation of war journalists. Robert Leger, president of the Society of Professional Journalists, issued a statement following Kelly's death that juxtaposed his sacrifice with the controversies surrounding Peter Arnett and Geraldo Rivera:[2]

> [Kelly] was like the vast majority of reporters covering the war in Iraq, *risking their lives to let Americans* see how this war is being fought so they can *measure the performance* of our leaders. In a week when the antics of two high-profile television journalists have grabbed headlines and cast a cloud over our profession, it is good to remember that most journalists in Iraq are responsibly doing their jobs in extraordinary circumstances. They have *sacrificed* the comforts of home to place themselves in harm's way and serve the public. Michael Kelly's death is a somber reminder of what journalists put on the line. (Society of Professional Journalists, 2003, emphasis added)

This statement encapsulates many of the narratives examined above—bravery, volunteerism, sacrifice, and witnessing—in order to implant Kelly's death with a particular and explicit meaning tied to the professionalism of journalism and its wider cultural role. The editor of the *American Journalism Review* highlights the voluntary commitment of journalists in a discussion of embedding: "These highly successful journalists hardly needed to punch this ticket. But they had to be there because that's where the story was" (Rieder, 2003, p. 6). The *Columbia Journalism Review* defended the witness role of journalism by invoking the sacrifices of Bloom and other journalists killed in the war:

> Some people want to see the war they want to see, and now, the same people want to project their politics onto the events that flow out of the war. The journalist's job is to present the world as it is. Digitized American flags don't cut it. Real reporting and analysis do. ("The world," 2003, p. 2)

The article reiterated the objectivity of journalists and situated on-the-ground reporting as essential to what journalism does while criticizing disparagements of embedded reporters. *Editor and Publisher* collected remembrances of Kelly from fellow journalists and columnists, many of them saluting Kelly's decision to eschew safety in order to witness the war first-hand (Astor, 2003).

Bloom as Detached Witness and Attached Subject

Bloom was praised for being a witness amidst the dangers of war. *US News and World Report* referred to Bloom as "a seeker of truth and eyewitness to history" (Simon & Cannon, 2003, p. 41). The discourse also recognizes Bloom's presence as a subject within the story he was witnessing. As a television reporter, his image is inseparable from the stories he covers—his figure becomes enmeshed with the image of Iraq appearing on television. He cannot remain visually detached from his reportage. Instead, he remains a focal point. The story becomes as much about Bloom moving through Iraq as about the U.S. military. His experiences are witnessed by viewers through Bloom's continual, and mostly live, reporting. Howard Kurtz made note of the melding of Bloom's image and war itself: "But someone like Bloom reporting from the desert around the clock on little sleep becomes, in a sense, the *face of the war*, the narrator of the war, bringing the soldiers' stories, good and bad, into our homes" (*Wolf Blitzer Reports*, April 6, 2003, emphasis added). Elsewhere, Kurtz connected Bloom's image in the war to the sense of loss following his death:

> But the fact is that, because of the technology, these people are coming into our living room in real time, telling us about the weather, what the troops are doing. . . . And so I think all of us perhaps feel touched when a journalist goes down, only because they've become our eyes and ears on this battlefield in a way that I've never seen before in wartime. (*Late Edition*, CNN, April 6, 2003)

With television, a reporter is not only the "eyes" of the viewer, but also the watched. A *Richmond Times-Dispatch* columnist wrote: "David Bloom gave us a face to follow across the Iraqi desert," and then, "[S]adly, now Bloom has given us a face that represents everyone who has died in the war" (Malone, 2003, p. Dl). Bloom comes to stand in for loss in the war; he personalizes the tragedies of war, not only as reporter, but as victim.

Kelly as Reporter, Not Columnist

Many of the articles about Kelly's death used a quote from Kelly that appeared in *The New York Times* less than a week before he was killed on the importance of bearing witness:

> There was a real sense after the last gulf war that witness had been lost. The people in the military care about that history a great deal, because it is their history. I think that it was the primal motivating impulse [in having embedded reporters], and they decided to take a gamble. (quoted in Carr, 2003a, p. A2)

Witnessing was central to many accounts of Kelly's death, especially in editorials. For example, the *New York Post* ("Michael Kelly: 1957–2003," 2003, p. 22) spoke of the importance of bearing witness as a means of understanding: "He made the world a little easier to understand—which, after all, is the point—and he did it with grace. Michael Kelly is dead at 46, in pursuit of the truth, and he is irreplaceable."

Much of the discourse celebrating Kelly's capacity as a witness situates him in the role of reporter, bound up with allegiance to the journalistic norms of objectivity and detachment. For example, the *Portland Oregonian* used Kelly's death to herald the role of the reporter:

> The highest calling in journalism is that of reporter. The world is full of people who can write well, or edit or organize other people. The world is not full of people who are willing to endure pain, hardship and derision simply to see or learn something, write down what they see and learn, and offer those observations to others. ("Death of a reporter," 2003, p. C4)

The journalistic model proposed in this editorial reduces the journalistic role to relay (a "gatekeeper" for Janowitz, 1975), distinguished only through the willingness to sacrifice safety to perform this relay. However, Kelly was not an objective reporter, but a columnist who had been writing columns in favor of the Iraq invasion in the *Washington Post* well in advance of the war.[3] His columns regularly berated the antiwar movement as he based his support on both moral grounds and ensuring national security. In February 2003, Kelly wrote:

> To choose perpetuation of tyranny over rescue from tyranny, where rescue may be achieved, is immoral. . . .To march against the war is not to give peace a chance. It is to give tyranny a chance. It is to give the Iraqi nuke a chance. It is to give the next terrorist mass murder a chance. It is to march for the furtherance of evil instead of the vanquishing of evil. (M. Kelly, 2003, p. A29)

Such statements would seem to disqualify Kelly's stance as a reporter and instead cast him in the realm of opinion. Even as an embed, Kelly's reportage appeared in the oped section of the *Washington Post*.

Kelly's role as a columnist was not completely absent in the discourse. On ABC's *Good Morning America*, Charles Gibson captured Kelly's partisan commitment when he asserted that he "was determined to bear witness to the end of Saddam's regime" (April 7, 2003). The *Boston Globe* quoted a colleague of Kelly's: "I think his going over there—and now his death—represent an act of principle. . . . He believed in the moral necessity of this war" (quoted in Jurkowitz, 2003, p. Al). For the most part, however, the discourse around Kelly was that of a reporter, without distinction for his role as an advocate. This elision makes the journalist-as-witness narrative less problematic. As a self-interested advocate of the war, Kelly was both witness and promoter; he committed the normative journalistic sin of not being detached and impartial. In the witnessing narrative established above, the value of journalists in observing and relaying information is that they do so without preconditioned interpretations. Normatively, the war reporter is charged with risking life and limb to give facts to a distant public who can use these ostensibly neutral facts to form rational opinions on the war. What is highlighted, ultimately, is not the form of Kelly's journalism, but his proximity to the event occurring. "By promoting their proximity, journalists can both claim authorship and establish authority for their stories" (Zelizer, 1990, p. 38). Here, authority emanates from others choosing to privilege location over form.

Criticisms of Kelly and Bloom Coverage

The discourse around Kelly and Bloom was not monolithic. Even some journalists criticized the volume of coverage the two reporters' deaths received, compared with soldiers who had been killed. For example, the *Tacoma News Tribune* ("Michael Kelly, KIA," 2003, p. B5) editorialized: "The life of a well-known journalist is ultimately of no greater value than that of an obscure private whose death may not be grieved far beyond his hometown." This was echoed in another newspaper column: "And when one of these journalists does not come back, the networks and newspapers treat their deaths as if they are as important, or even more important, than the deaths of the 50-plus soldiers who have been killed" (Bothum, 2003, p. Dl). A *USA Today* story (Kasindorf, 2003, p. A5) noted that journalist deaths were reported much more quickly than soldiers who were killed. Specifically, Kelly's death was reported more than a day in advance of the soldier with whom he was riding. A column in the *Chicago Sun-Times* dismissed claims that Bloom was a hero by highlighting the distinction between the cause of his death and the hazards of combat:

> Many lives have been lost in Iraq during the two-and-a-half weeks of fighting for regime change. This was just one of them, and it was only tangentially connected with the war, which will continue to claim many more lives for some time to come. (Rosenthal, 2003, p. 45)

Each of these criticisms offers a counter-narrative to the popular narratives of bravery, volunteerism, and sacrifice in the name of witnessing that other outlets expressed in various forms. This criticism underscores the contestation occurring around discursive production. Interpretations are promoted against competing interpretations. What occurs is an active construction of meaning and not a natural or automatic accumulation of heroic narratives.

Conclusion: From Reporter to Reported

The deaths of journalists Michael Kelly and David Bloom during the early weeks of the Iraq War in 2003 were accompanied by a reflexive wave of discourse from journalists (and others) that dealt with the place of the journalist in war. Within this discourse, a number of narratives related to bravery, volunteerism, sacrifice, and witnessing were used to make sense of Kelly and Bloom's deaths, although not in a monolithic or completely uncontested manner.

For journalists covering wars, the defining aspect of combat is omnipresent risk. They are not detached from this risk, but located inextricably in the field of risk that is the war zone. There is no delineation between working and not-working. Instead, the journalist in the space of war is always working by being there and consequently always a potential casualty as a journalist. In this way, the deaths of Kelly (from combat, yet widely reported as an accident) and Bloom (credited to a pulmonary embolism) are granted significance within a narrative I have termed the "KIA journalist"—the journalist who has been killed while covering a story in the dangerous place of war, even if the death did not occur directly from combat. As such, "killed in action" grants breadth to a notion of "action," connecting it with the professional role of the war journalist rather than the specific cause of death. The importance of this distinction arises from the assignment of the tropes of bravery and sacrifice to journalists who were not killed in combat. The discourse around Bloom (and often Kelly when his death was misidentified as an accident) demonstrates that narratives of sacrifice—including comparisons with Ernie Pyle—are not precluded by a non-combat-related cause of death. Instead of the individualized memorializing that would be expected to follow the unexpected death of a prominent journalist, Kelly and Bloom's deaths were widely interpreted as war reporters bravely risking—and losing—their lives in order to act as witness to the war and hold the government accountable for its actions on the battlefield. Meanwhile, charges of overt careerism or of failing in parental duties are absent in the discourse. At the same time, breadth is also granted to the notion of "reporter" as Kelly's position as a pro-war opinion columnist was often omitted in order to fit his death with narratives of sacrifice and witnessing linked closely with narratives of journalistic objectivity.

The discursive constructions pursued by journalists create meaning around the deaths of Kelly and Bloom by putting the collective value of the reportage ahead of the individual value of their lives. This is the essence of sacrifice in general, but the specificity of the journalistic sacrifice lies in the value of witnessing. Journalists endure and succumb to risk, the KIA journalist narratives tell us, in order to report on power that cannot be held accountable in any other way. The journalist acts as a stand-in and as a relay of information to give citizens, from places they cannot go, the information they desire to monitor power. In this way, it is a moral narrative of sacrifice; the KIA journalist voluntarily places himself in danger for the benefit of a greater good that is defined through the discourse.

Ultimately, the KIA journalist provides a symbol of individual risk for collective good. The narratives that emerged around Kelly and Bloom and gave their deaths meaning had the twin impact of signaling to other journalists and to the public the importance of the KIA journalist while at the same time bolstering the heroics of working journalists still in the space of combat. Most of the discourse examined in this paper occurred directly after the early-April deaths of Kelly and Bloom, three weeks into the war, when hundreds of embedded reporters still occupied the risky space of war journalism (newly signified by Kelly and Bloom, as well as other KIA journalists). In this sense, the heroic, self-sacrificing KIA journalist invokes Weber's notion of charismatic authority, which, along with normative and historical dimensions, serves to reinforce journalists' cultural authority and position through these frameworks of significance. Consequently, the narratives of the war journalist inform the importance of journalism more generally. The KIA journalist is constructed to invite reverence, thus becoming an example of what journalism does well and why it remains important.

War possesses a key place in the collective memory of a nation, which makes it a prime site for journalists to locate the importance of their own work. Journalists can be seen as belonging to an "imagined community," to borrow from Benedict Anderson's conception of the nation. The use of this term in regard to journalism conjures an image of a symbolic collective connected by common normative ideals and a shared history that positions it within the larger cultural framework. "Communities are to be distinguished, not by their falsity/genuineness, but by the style in which they are imagined" (Anderson, 1983, p. 6). The narratives of the war journalist reflect this style, as he or she becomes a normative model for all of journalism. Examples of sacrifice and witness provide evidence for journalism's continued and historical importance. Thus, Kelly and Bloom, as understood in the narratives of the KIA journalist, come to serve as models for journalists and of journalism, a reminder of the cultural place occupied by journalists to tell stories to and about society, especially in the places we cannot go.

Notes

1. Three other U.S. journalists had died covering the war in Iraq as of November 1, 2005. Boston Globe reporter Elizabeth Neuffer died in a car accident on May 8, 2003. Los Angeles Times reporter Mark Fineman died of a heart attack on September 23, 2003. Freelance journalist Steven Vincent was killed after being kidnapped by gunmen on August, 2, 2005. For a list of journalists who have died in Iraq, see http://icasualties.org/oif/journalist.aspx (accessed on November 1, 2005). Overall, the Committee to Protect Journalists reports that 58 journalists have been killed as a result of hostile action (David Bloom is not included) as of November 1, 2005. For details, see http://www.cpj.org/briefings/iraq/iraq_danger.html (accessed on November 1, 2005).

2. Arnett was fired from NBC and National Geographic for criticizing the U.S. military on Iraqi television. Rivera voluntarily left Iraq after upsetting the U.S. military for revealing operational details of the unit in which he was embedded for the Fox News Channel.

3. Kelly's career included stints as a reporter (with the *Cincinnati Post, Baltimore Sun,* and *New York Times*), editor (with *The New Yorker, New Republic, National Journal,* and *Atlantic Monthly*) and columnist (with the *National Journal* and *Washington Post*).

REFERENCES

Allan, S., & Zelizer, B. (2004). Rules of engagement. In S. Allan & B. Zelizer (Eds.), *Reporting war: Journalism in wartime* (pp. 3–21). London: Routledge.

Anderson, B. (1983). *Imagined communities*. London: Verso.

Astor, D. (2003, May 5). Kelly and Friedman get wartime kudos. *Editor & Publisher*, p. 29.

Buthum, P. (2003, April 8). Reporters became part of the war story. *York Daily Record*, p. Dl.

Bromley, M. (2004). The battlefield is the media: War reporting and the formation of national identity in Australia—from Belmont to Baghdad. In S. Allan & B. Zelizer (Eds.), *Reporting war: Journalism in wartime* (pp. 224–244). London: Routledge.

Carr, D. (2003a, March 31). Reporters' new battlefield access has its risks as well as its rewards. *The New York Times*, p. A2.

Carr, D. (2003b, April 5). Michael Kelly, 46, editor and columnist, dies in Iraq. *The New York Times*, p. A10.

Carruthers, S. (2000). *The media at war*. New York: St. Martin's Press.

Death of a reporter. (2003, April 5). *Portland Oregonian*, p. C4.

Dowd, M. (2003, April 6). The best possible life. *The New York Times*, p. A13.

Dunleavy, S. (2003, April 7). Pen may be sword, but it's no shield. *New York Post*, p. 11.

Eason, D. (1988). On journalistic authority: The Janet Cooke scandal. In J. Carey (Ed.), *Media, myths, and narratives: Television and the press* (pp. 205–227). Newbury Park, CA: Sage.

"Eyes and ears" of war also give casualties human face. (2003, April 7). *USA Today*, p. A14.

Fiske, J. (1994). *Media matters*. Minneapolis, MN: University of Minnesota Press.

Frost, G. (2003, April 4). US journalist Michael Kelly killed in Iraq. *Reuters*.

Gans, H. (2003). *Democracy and the news*. Oxford, UK: Oxford University Press.

Gardner, H., Csikszentmihalyi, M., & Damon, W. (2001). *Good work: When excellence and ethics meet*. New York: Basic Books.

Glasgow University Media Group. (1985). *War and peace news*. Milton Keynes, UK: Open University Press.

Hallin, D. (1986). *The "uncensored war": The media and Vietnam*. Berkeley, CA: University of California Press.

Hallin, D., & Gitlin, T. (1994). The Gulf War as popular culture and television drama. In L. Bennett & D. Paletz (Eds.), *Taken by storm: The media, public opinion, and US foreign policy in the Gulf War* (pp. 149–166). Chicago: University of Chicago Press.

Hamill, P. (2003, April 7). Two who fell so we could see. *New York Daily News*, p. 8.

Hudson, M., & Stanier, J. (1998). *War and the media: A random searchlight*. New York: New York University Press.

Janowitz, M. (1975). Professional models in journalism: The gatekeeper and the advocate. *Journalism Quarterly, 52*, 618–626, 662.

Johnstone, J., Slawski, E., & Bowman, W. (1976). *The news people: A sociological portrait of American journalists and their work*. Urbana: University of Illinois Press.

Journalists make ultimate sacrifice in war with Iraq. (2003, April 15). *Cincinnati Post*, p. Bl.

Jurkowitz, M. (2003, April 5). Atlantic editor dies in Iraq. *Boston Globe*, p. Al.

Kasindorf, M. (2003, April 18). At times, military system lagged media; Live battlefield reports pressured Pentagon to get information to families faster. *USA Today*, p. A5.

Kelly didn t have to be in Iraq. (2003, April 6). *Dayton Daily News*, p. B6.

Kelly, K. (2003, May 8). Atlantic hits jackpot with mag honors. *New York Post*, p. 32.

Kelly, M. (1993). *Martyrs' day: Chronicle of a small war*. New York: Random House.

Kelly, M. (2003, February 19). Immorality on the march. *Washington Post*, p. A29.

Kurtz, H. (2003a, April 5). Post columnist dies in wreck near Baghdad; Michael Kelly is first U.S. journalist killed. *Washington Post*, p. A19.

Kurtz, H. (2003b, April 14). Down in the trenches, up in the public's opinion. *The Washington Post*, p. Cl.

LeSure, E. (2003, April 6). Former Miami NBC reporter dies while covering war in Iraq. *Associated Press*.

Malone, J. (2003, April 8). Bloom put face on war. *Richmond Times-Dispatch*, p. Dl.

Manoff, R., & Schudson, M. (Eds.). (1986). *Reading the news*. New York: Pantheon.

McGuire, M. (2003, April 8). Bloom kept the focus on the troops. *Albany Times Union*, p. Dl.

McLaughlin, G. (2002). *The war correspondent*. London: Pluto Press.

Michael Kelly. (2003, April 5). *New York Times*, p. A12.

Michael Kelly. (2003, April 5). *Richmond Times-Dispatch*, p. Al0.

Michael Kelly: 1957 2003. (2003, April 5). *New York Post*, p. 22.

Michael Kelly, KIA. (2003, April 5). *Tacoma News Tribune*, p. B5.

Mnookin, S. (2003, April 4). Michael Kelly, 1957–2003; The longtime war reporter and magazine editor 'loved to fight'. *Newsweek Online*.

Morrison, D., & Tumber, H. (1998). *Journalists at war*. London: Sage.

Nelson, T. (2003, April 9). Embedded in the world: No excuses. *Christian Science Monitor*, p. 11.

Powers, W. (2003, April 12). The subversions of Mr. Kelly. *National Journal*, p. 1170.

Ricchiardi, S. (2003, May). Close to the action. *American Journalism Review*, pp. 28–36.

Rieder, R. (2003, May). The Pentagon's embedding plan was a winner for journalists and their audiences. *American Journalism Review*, p. 6.

Rosenthal, P. (2003, April 7). Another death in the desert; NBC newsman David Bloom's name is added to casualties. *Chicago Sun-Times*, p. 45.

Schudson, M. (1978). *Discovering the news*. New York: Basic Books.

Schudson, M. (1988). What is a reporter? In J. Carey (Ed.), *Media, myths, and narratives: Television and the press* (pp. 228–245). Newbury Park, CA: Sage.

Schudson, M. (1992). *Watergate in American memory*. New York: Basic Books.

Simon, R., & Cannon, A. (2003, April 14). Death of an embed. *US News and World Report*, p. 41.

Singer, J. (2003). 'Who are these guys? The online challenge to the notion of journalistic professionalism. *Journalism, 4*, 139–163.

Society of Professional Journalists (2003, April 4). First American journalist dies in Iraq. Press release. Retrieved April 14, 2006 from http://www.spj.org/news.asp?ref=318.

Taylor, P. (1998). *War and the media: Propaganda and persuasion in the Gulf War* (2nd ed.). Manchester, UK: Manchester University Press.

The world as it is. (2003, May). *Columbia Journalism Review*, p. 2.

Tuchman, G. (1972). Objectivity as strategic ritual: An examination of newsmen's notions of objectivity. *American Journal of Sociology*, 77, 660–679.

Tumber, H. (2003). Reporting under fire: The physical safety and emotional welfare of journalists. In B. Zelizer & S. Allan (Eds.), *Journalism after September 11* (pp. 247–262). London: Routledge.

Tumber, H., & Palmer, J. (2004). *Media at war: The Iraq crisis*. London: Sage.

Tunstall, J. (1971). *Journalists at work*. Beverly Hills, CA: Sage.

Walsh, M. (2003, April 7). David Bloom, 39, dies in Iraq; Reporter was with troops. *New York Times*, p. A7.

Weber, M. (1947). *The theory of social and economic organization* (T. Parsons, Trans. & Ed.). New York: Free Press.

Zelizer, B. (1990). Where is the author in American TV news? On the construction and presentation of proximity, authorship, and journalistic authority. *Semiotica, 80* (1/2), 37–48.

Zelizer, B. (1992a). *Covering the body: The Kennedy assassination, the media and the shaping of collective memory*. Chicago: University of Chicago Press.

Zelizer, B. (1992b). CNN, the Gulf War, and journalistic practice. *Journal of Communication, 42*, 66–81.

Zelizer, B. (2004). When war is reduced to a photograph. In S. Allan & B. Zelizer (Eds.), *Reporting war: Journalism in wartime* (pp. 115–135). London: Routledge.

Source: From "War Journalism and the 'KIA Journalist': The Cases of David Bloom and Michael Kelly," 2006, by M. Carlson, *Critical Studies in Media Communication, 23*(2), 91–111. Reprinted by permission of Taylor & Francis/Routledge.

9

The Importance of Ritual in Crisis Journalism

Kristina Riegert

Eva-Karin Olsson

Introduction

Media research on crises, disasters and extraordinary events has traditionally centred on the interaction between the media, the state authorities and citizens. The focus has commonly been on how citizens perceive and experience disasters, crises or armed conflict through the media, how government authorities deal with the crisis in relation to the media, and whether the media have fulfilled their tasks of "informing, scrutinising and explaining" the causes and consequences of crises. This research is predominantly concerned with issues related to the informational flow of the media. The questions posed are often reminiscent of those in early journalism research in which news content is either held to some standard of "good" reporting, or compared to the government's or some other "factual" versions of events, where the media's task is to mirror them correctly (Hedman et al., 1996; Leth and Thurén, 2002; Nohrstedt, 2000; Tierney et al., 200, p. 141). As Gunilla Jarlbro sums up in her review of crisis journalism, scholars describe the sources and content of crisis coverage, but we are still left with the question as to *why* this coverage looks as it does (Jarlbro, 2004, p. 64).

In an age when crises are reported as "disaster marathons," i.e., in long live broadcasts, traditional crisis communication approaches do not help us answer the "why" question. For example, if information dissemination is paramount in extreme crisis, why does television news continue live for hour after hour, with no new information forthcoming? In this article, we are inspired by James Carey's (1975) "ritual" view in which the purpose of communication is not so much the transmission of useful, intelligible information, but the creation of meaning, and the expression of commonality (or ostracism) among members of a community. The media's role has to do with the maintenance of society through time, representing shared beliefs, understandings, and emotions, whether in celebration or in mourning. Scholars in this "culturalist" tradition emphasise the ritual and communal functions of journalism, of news in terms of its meaning-making functions rather than its informational functions (Carey, 1989; Rothenbuhler and Coman, 2005; Zelizer, 1997). Here, journalism creates spaces for remembering, sharing, celebrating and mourning among members of a community, and genres of journalism are seen as forms of story-telling inherited from the culture in which they work (Schudson, 2002).

We think that communication as ritual should also be studied from within the newsroom, especially through journalists' perceptions of their work (Cottle, 2000). So with this "culturalist" approach as a theoretical lens, we have analysed the results of interviews with senior news editors and media managers from the Swedish public service channel SVT and the hybrid commercial broadcaster TV4 about their decisions and actions during two cases: after the terrorist attacks of September 11th and the murder of the Swedish Foreign Minister Anna Lindh in a department store in 2003. The semi-structured interviews, which were conducted within a year of the crisis events, were part of a larger project on crisis management at SVT and TV4. The interviewees consisted of the senior management group at each news organisation—i.e., those responsible for the overarching programme planning decisions on how to cover the two extraordinary events.[1] The interviews focused on the decisions of the management groups and their motivations for doing so.

We were struck by how these motivations went beyond traditional journalistic role conceptions, i.e., beyond being interpreters, disseminators and adversaries (Shoemaker and Reese, 1991; Weaver and Wilhoit, 1996). Even Melin-Higgins' (1996) characterisation of Swedish journalists' roles as "teachers and bloodhounds" does not quite apply to the cases examined here (cf. Köcher, 1986). The news managers understood their decisions during these crises in terms of "being there," reassuring audiences and helping to "work through" events. Secondly, they clearly wanted their channel, rather than the competition, to be the channel audiences turn to in a crisis. In this way, beating the competition becomes a motivator for the media rituals. Both reinforce the notion that through the media we gain access to what is important in society during crisis.

Journalists' Definitions of Extreme Crisis Events

The attacks of September 11th and the murder of Foreign Minister Anna Lindh may seem to be quite different and it is fair to ask whether they can be compared analytically. We are interested in stories the media themselves define as "big stories," "holy shit" stories or "what-a-story" (Berkowitz, 1997; Ehrlich, 1996; Tuchman, 1978), i.e., stories in which the media break from their normal routines and practices, which require extra resources, continuous coverage and quick decisions by media management.

The attacks of September 11th and the murder of the Swedish Foreign Minister were both defined by the news managers as "big" stories, which needed to be dealt with in ways that deviate from everyday news events. Interestingly enough, there was pretty much of a consensus in the management groups of the two news organisations about what kind of big story requires breaking away from the normal television schedule. Both of the events under study here were put in a distinct category and related to other extreme crisis events, such as the murder of the Prime Minister Olof Palme 1986, the *Estonia* ferry catastrophe 1994, and the Gothenburg fire 1998, where 63 young people died and 200 were injured (other news events mentioned were the death of Princess Diana and Gulf War I).

Although the managers placed the events in a category of news that required nonroutine action, pinpointing exactly what distinguished these kinds of events was harder for them to describe. When talking about how to categorise these kinds of stories, references were made to what can be referred to as "journalistic intuition." As one manager from TV4 said, "It is in your body. You act naturally. You know the pattern, the reflexes and how to handle the process." Or another manager at SVT: "It is the radar that takes over, you *feel* the impact of the event."

One of the characteristics common to "what-a-story" events was the element of surprise. For example, one manager thought that the terror attacks were comparable to the *Estonia* shipwreck since both were surprising, and initially very hard to grasp due to their unlikely nature. According to one of the members of the SVT management group, the terror attacks were similar to the murder of the Swedish Prime Minister Olof Palme who was shot dead on a busy street in Stockholm in 1986. "I think that both the Palme murder and 9/11 were events that no one would expect to happen, where reality beat fiction. Not even a group of journalists could make up such a story—they were simply just too much." According to this logic, the sudden knife attack on Foreign Minister Anna Lindh in a department store in broad daylight did not have the same shock effect because the murder of a Swedish politician had happened once before. The same reasoning can be seen at TV4 where one of the managers said that Anna Lindh cannot be compared to 9/ 11 since the latter was a totally *new* kind of event. Thus, while there are differences between these two events, the media managers at Swedish television news stations put them in the same category of events.

The Culturalist Tradition Regarding Extraordinary Events

If one wants to study extreme crisis events through a ritual perspective, it is hard to ignore Dayan and Katz's (1992) well-known notion of "media events," which denotes preplanned "conquests, coronations and contests" transmitted live to millions of people, breaking with the everyday routines of the media. These large-scale events like the state funerals of dignitaries, the Olympic Games, the Pope's visits or historic summit meetings, connect multiple locations and millions of viewers. The significance of media events is not simply the re-constitution of older forms of ritual, but new mediated ones gained through the shared experience of watching live in millions of homes across nations and peoples. These "high holidays" of mass communication differ from experiencing events on site, they turn private homes into public spaces, and create new collective memories which integrate and consolidate people into society (Dayan and Katz, 1992, pp. 94–5). Media events share with media coverage of large-scale crises the ritual function of bringing people and institutions together in a common space and place, a common "here and now."

Due to new communications technology and the increasing availability of real-time events on 24-hour news channels, the notion of media events has been applied to other types of events than those originally envisioned by Dayan and Katz, such as large-scale crises. Bouvier (2005) appropriates the notion for her analysis of the BBC coverage of the terrorist attacks of September 11th. These were media events, she argues, because of their historical significance, their interruption of normal media routines, the mass international viewership and live, round-the-clock character. Tamar Liebes (1998) also appropriates the notion of media events for an analysis of breaking news, like large-scale disasters and crises, so called "disaster marathons." These "disaster marathons" are quite a recent phenomenon, she says, up until the 1990s routine schedules were seldom interrupted by unplanned events. Despite the difference regarding whether the events are unplanned or pre-planned, whether they are brought about by the establishment or by some outside power, they share the same feature of bringing large parts of society together around a ritual of watching television.

> Like traditional media events, these major disruptive events, paradoxically, also unite the collective, albeit through shared fear and shared mourning. Both types of events shower society with symbolic meaning, some of which cross societal boundaries to become universal symbols. As in the case of prearranged media events, the impact of catastrophes such as the explosion of the Challenger on takeoff and the Columbia on

> landing, the Kennedy and Rabin assassinations, the near disaster at Three Mile Island, and the real one in downtown New York on September 11, 2001, cannot be separated from the manner of their meditation and the ways in which they are experienced by the public at large. (Liebes and Blondheim, 2005, pp. 188–9)

Nick Couldry (2003) describes rituals as habitual (recurring patterns) and formalised actions (not ideas) involving "transcendent" values, i.e. societal values that transcend the actions performed. Like other definitions of ritual, this refers to recurring actions that are not necessarily intended or articulated by the performers (Rappaport, 1999), but which contain a broader significance than the manifest formal actions performed. Thus, media rituals are

> the whole range of situations where media themselves "stand-in," or appear to "stand-in," for something wider, something linked to the fundamental organisational level on which we are, or imagine ourselves to be connected as members of a society. (Couldry, 2003, p. 4)

In other words, it is through media rituals that we act out or "naturalise" the idea that through the media we gain access to "reality" at society's social centre.[2] What media rituals do is to reinforce and legitimise the status of media institutions as being at the centre of society. Through these rituals, says Couldry (2003), we come to accept the symbolic power of media institutions, that they "speak for us all," that being "in" the media is more important than being "outside" the media, or that what is happening "now" (live) is more important than what happened several weeks ago.

Coman (2005) says "ritualisation" is the method through which journalism gains control over the processes of sense-making and various realities surrounding particular events; its ultimate purpose—to reinforce journalism's authority as a central institution in society. How is this achieved? He cites Zelizer's study of the John F. Kennedy murder, where journalists gained authority by taking on roles as eyewitnesses, representatives, investigators and interpreters, "journalists promoted, legitimized, and secured their authority to control the process of reporting and retelling events; that is, to dominate the process of constructing variants of reality according to the audience's expectations" (Coman, 2005, p. 51). They do this by presenting sequences of facts and their meaning as if they had a pre-established order, setting them into the context of "generally acknowledged truths" and by assuming a role in which they speak for society as a whole. Interestingly, he notes that in a crisis, these ritual performances are particularly evident when journalists break from their normal working procedures and their usual objectivistic language. Instead of being viewed as a transgression of journalistic norms, their engagement with the event reinforces the legitimacy of journalists as central actors in the mediation of truth.

So, media rituals can be said to function as a way for media organisations, television in this case, to establish authority by playing a key part in society's healing process. The television station with the authority to interpret what is going on for the majority of the public also has definitional power over how the event will be perceived in historical terms. Whether or not we want to call our cases media events, they were extraordinary events, whether they bring together the community in a shared sense of celebration, shame, sorrow, horror or trauma, or whether they contribute to a division or fissure within society, as Liebes (1998) claims they also do, being in the media means being at the centre of the "reality" of a crisis event. Being outside the media, finding out about it days after the event, is to have missed something "important" or so says the ritual act of watching.

But what is the view from inside the newsroom? How do journalists themselves perceive their roles in the midst of this crisis? Are they aware of the media's ritual functions in crisis and does this play into their decision-making? As noted previously, the literature on journalistic role conceptions seldom discuss the possibility that journalists purposely take on the roles of comforter, psychologist, and co-mourner in times of crisis.

How the Changing Media Landscape Affects Swedish Crisis Coverage

In order to understand newsroom practices in conditions of extreme crisis, the news organisations need to be placed in their proper context. The last two decades have witnessed a tremendous transformation in the global media infrastructure due to technological development and de-regulation on both the national and international levels. These changes have led many media organisations more clearly towards what McManus (1994) calls "market-driven journalism." The increased competition from satellite and cable channels has also put heavy pressure on public service broadcasting organisations to justify their existence, while technological developments translate into increased pressure to broadcast the latest—in real time.

However, we do not see competition solely in economic terms, the social and cultural imperatives of competition are also part and parcel of journalistic culture. For example, what it means to be a television journalist involves knowing how to produce a story with powerful visuals, knowing how to monitor and interpret audience ratings, making decisions about what kinds of stories are worth more or less resources. According to Matthew Ehrlich, there is a "competitive ethos" enacted by television newsworkers and organisations whereby

> News is competition. This competition is enacted via "a race that determines who's the best" a race against *deadlines* in which newsworkers try to beat the clock, a race for *news* in which newsworkers compete for stories (and, as in the examples cited above, try to make each other "cry"), and of course, a race for *ratings* and *shares* in which newsworkers and organisations attempt to curry audience favour. The race is run "every day"; it is built into regular organisational rituals and routines. And it never ends. (Ehrlich, 1997, p. 304)

He goes on to argue that, on a larger scale, this competitive ethos is part of journalism as an interpretive community, i.e., a community that defines itself through a common set of discourses that follow journalists from one organisation to another.

Even though deregulation and technology have had a profound impact on media development in the last two decades, the impact of competition on news organisations varies depending on the political culture, media regulation and, consequently, on the way the media landscape in a particular country is drawn. Riegert (2004) found, for instance, that the existence of a strong public service tradition played a decisive role in the way commercial television news journalists viewed news content and how they tried to compete. In Sweden, the media landscape profoundly changed when the monopoly position of the public service organisation (SVT) was shaken by the entry of commercial television on to the market in the late 1980s and the establishment of TV4 as a terrestrial broadcaster in 1991 (Hadenius and Weibull, 1999)[3] One of the effects of the entry of TV4 on to the market was that it forced a structural reorganisation of its rival public service broadcaster.

The news desk at TV4 is tiny compared to SVT, and TV4 started in a kind of rebellious spirit against SVT with the explicit aim to compete (Asp, 1995). For its part, SVT tries to retain its status through marketing independent and serious journalism as a quality standard. Another organisational response of SVT during the 1990s has been to merge two previously competing news desks, to increase the amount of news bulletins and to launch a 24-hour digital channel (Jönsson, 2004, p. 83). Another result of the new "duopoly" was the growing importance of audience ratings on the consciousness of journalists (Djerf-Pierre and Weibull, 2001). After the introduction of TV4, SVT instituted as one of its goals that its two channels should have at least a 50 percent audience share on an ordinary day. This is a policy indication that SVT would compete for viewers, although the organisation itself is a public service, something that has sparked some debate. This debate misses the point that audience ratings are not simply financial indicators, they have psychological implications for journalists, such as the need to evaluate one's own organisation and its performance.

Competition, in this sense, is about how to increase the prestige of the channel in order to attract programme rights and personnel. Declining or low viewing figures threaten the licence financing of public service, and therefore broadcasters' credibility as an alternative to commercial channels. The notion of public service as a central authoritative institution in society, achieved by high viewing figures, reveals the cultural and social contingency of this view of public service, if compared to countries where public service broadcasting is weak. The stronger position a public service channel has, the more it can appear to be independent from politicians, something which increases its authority and centrality in society (Syvertsen, 1997). In Sweden, where the landscape of television news is determined mainly by public service and a hybrid commercial organisation, competition for prestige and authority are just as important as purely financial considerations. What we will argue therefore is that the social and cultural aspects of competition become motivators for media rituals during great crisis.

SVT and TV4 During September 11th and the Murder of Anna Lindh

This section describes the organisation of the newsroom and their immediate reactions to the crisis events in terms of i.e. *when and how much* to broadcast. The two Swedish television organisations were structured in different ways at the time of September 11, 2001 and the murder of Foreign Minister Lindh (2003). While TV4 had only one news desk and one channel, SVT had three news programmes airing on two analogue channels and one digital channel. These issued from two news desks, one of which was the common news desk for the two main news bulletins, *Aktuellt* and *Rapport,* whereas the new digital 24-hour news programme SVT24 had its own desk. The common news desk was the result of a (then) recent merger between *Aktuellt* and *Rapport*'s news desks, which meant that it was the new SVT24 that had the responsibility for extra broadcasting of the September 11th terror attacks. During the murder of Anna Lindh, there was one common news desk and the responsibility for extra broadcasting had been transferred back to the main news bulletin, *Rapport.* TV4 retained its organisation with one news desk during the latter crisis.

The two TV stations chose different strategies during both extraordinary events. We will briefly recount how the two news organisations perceived events at the time. The first plane, which crashed into the first tower of the World Trade Center at 2:45 p.m. Swedish time, was generally perceived as an accident caused by a smaller sports plane. After the second plane, which crashed at 3:03 p.m., the perception changed from an accident to a planned attack. That impression was further strengthened when a plane crashed into the Pentagon at 3:40 p.m. and the collapse of the World Trade Center south tower at 4:00 p.m. Until the tower collapsed, the management group at TV4 thought the event could be handled by putting in extra bulletins, but when the management group saw the tower collapsing, they decided to clear the channel of all other programming and go live with continuous news from the United States. All commercials were cancelled and a studio programme was inserted to alternate with news updates. CNN was re-broadcast as a backup when TV4 ran out of its own material.

At SVT there was no similar turning point in perception of the event, the strategy of SVT was to switch *ad hoc* between its two terrestrial channels when spots could be found for extra newscasts. SVT did not clear any one channel to broadcast exclusively or continuously on the terror attacks. Their main focus was on editorially worked through material airing on the ordinary (but prolonged) news programmes at their established time, together with extra updates. Aside from an extra talk show airing between 8 and 9 p.m., there was no studio programme, and between 6:40 and 7:00 p.m. there was no information on the terror attacks. Thus, SVT's viewers were offered a variety of cultural and regional news, Finnish news, sign language and sports news in addition to the breaking news of the crisis in the United States.

At 4:14 p.m. on the afternoon of 10 September 2003 the Swedish Foreign Minister was stabbed by an unknown man while shopping at a big department store in Stockholm. The minister had taken a break from her hectic schedule, as the referendum concerning Swedish EMU-membership was set for 14 September. The Swedish news agency TT's first flash at 4:42 p.m. confirmed that Anna Lindh had been stabbed. Initially, the rumour in the newsrooms was that she had a scratch on her arm. Not long after, however, about 5:00 p.m., she went into emergency surgery, which implied that the situation was much more serious than previously thought. SVT put in two extra news broadcasts between 5:00 and 6:00 p.m., but by SVT's regular early evening broadcast of *Aktuellt,* the decision had been taken to put in a live studio programme, which continued until past midnight. According to one of the managers, at the time no one thought the minister was going to die, but due to the impending Euro-referendum it was assumed to be a politically motivated attack. At TV4 the management group talked about whether to go live on the event that evening. The managers of both the news and current affairs desks wanted an extra studio programme put in, but were blocked by the Programme Director's argument that with so little available information the programme would be based on speculation and TV4 had done too much of that kind of reporting lately. TV4 chose therefore to put in extra newscasts throughout the evening. A total of three press conferences were held that evening, the last of which was at 3:00 a.m. by the medical team where the Foreign Minister was described as critical but stable. However, due to complications after the surgery, Anna Lindh died at 5:29 a.m. The Prime Minister announced her death at a press conference at 9:00 p.m. Upon receiving the information both the management groups at TV4 and SVT cancelled all other programming that day.

Media Rituals in Scheduling and Format

How do the ritual aspects of coverage play into media managers' decisions in terms of scheduling in the two crisis events analysed here? We found several types of argument for massive rescheduling and going live to the event. These had to do with anticipation of what audiences expected and therefore to retain one's role as the channel audiences turn to in times of extreme crisis. In spite of the trade-offs involving quality and economic loss, "being there" was judged to be important.

How Big Is the Story?

According to Liebes and Blondheim (2005), the relationship between television and its audience becomes more important during historic moments and extreme crisis since the way the media performs will be part of the way audiences will remember the event itself. The ability to determine an adequate response to the "what-a-story" is thus a crucial aspect of the media's role during a crisis situation.

> TV is, during occasions like this, expected to be continuously present and it is no longer enough to only do news programmes, you must also be constantly present, because otherwise you are not showing enough respect

> for the event even though it will be covered better on *Aktuellt* and *Rapport* . . . And it is not a lesson learned from 9/11, so much as with the entrance of channels such as CNN or SVT24 on to the market. There is a feeling that if something big is happening it should be broadcast continuously. (interview about Anna Lindh, SVT)[4]

Being continuously present is, according to this media manager, important as a way of dignifying the event, of demonstrating one's respect for the impact of the event. Notice that this overrides the journalistically superior news programmes, due to the competition from rolling news channels.

A member of the management group at SVT said scheduling issues are among the most stressful situations, "since this is when the organisation is put to the test, when you are trying to understand and judge the power or the impact of the event in relation to an ordinary Swede's judgement of the event" (interview about 9/11, SVT). This illustrates the preoccupation with mirroring audience perceptions of events during times of crisis. One of the biggest mistakes according to members of the SVT management group was that there was no coverage at all of the September 11th attacks between 6:40 and 7:00 p.m. It was not the case that the public missed vital information during these 20 minutes, and if new information had come in, there was a preparedness to go on the air. The problem was rather the symbolic dimension of this "miss." In hindsight, "If we would have understood what we thereafter started to understand, it is clear that we would have sent whatever the hell we had" (interview about 9/11, SVT). This can be compared to the insight TV4 had when the first tower fell, that the magnitude of the event demanded that the ordinary schedule be suspended immediately, even if it meant re-broadcasting CNN live. Indeed, the importance of meeting audience expectations in what amounts to a collective process of trying to digest this catastrophe is illustrated by heavy criticism of SVT in the public debate following the events of September 11th (Hadenius, 2001). Interestingly, the debate did not charge SVT with mismanaging its informational duties, but was directed at the lack of correspondence between scheduling and the magnitude of the event.

Choosing the Right Format

The format chosen at TV4 during the terror attacks was considered to be a great success. This consisted of a live studio programme interspliced with news updates and rebroadcasting CNN. At SVT, on the other hand, there was a lot of self-criticism after 9/11. One of the obstacles was that audiences were made to surf between three different channels, SVT24 and the news programmes *Rapport* and *Aktuellt,* to find news about the attacks. In the aftermath, a reorganisation took place in which the responsibility for broadcasting extraordinary crisis was moved from SVT24 back to *Aktuellt* and *Rapport* because these are established, focused formats familiar to audiences.

Another aspect of the news format has to do with the choice of anchorperson. According to the interviews, there is a general desire to keep the same anchorperson throughout a crisis, which ultimately should be the person with highest credibility among viewers.

> I understand that it was quite tough for the people who were working, since they had to work for many hours. But from an audience perspective, and from a publicist's perspective, I think it is a good idea to keep the same people. My conviction is that you, as an anchor, form a kind of symbiotic relationship with the viewers. You are the one who mediates the sad news and it is you who comes back on a regular basis. (interview about Anna Lindh, SVT)

The importance of the anchoring function is based on the idea that a personal relationship is built up between the anchor and the audience. According to the media managers at SVT this was one aspect of that lost battle during September 11th. One of the SVT interviewees said that aside from forcing the audience to change channels, they also forced audiences to "jump between anchors." In hindsight what should had been done, and what was done during the Anna Lindh murder, was to use the most reliable and trustworthy anchor the station had (interview about 9/11, SVT). The choice of anchorperson is thus an important part of a larger scheduling strategy.

According to TV4, it is important to "think at the level of the big picture. It is also important who sits there, who is the one that mediates the news to the public" (interview about 9/11, TV4). Retaining the same face throughout a crisis provides the audience with a sense of continuity and security; i.e., it fulfills a psychological function. Further, it underlines the bond the TV stations perceive they need to have with audiences in situations like this.

Value Re-Orientation

Even if re-scheduling is seen as a desirable option it is not always a straightforward decision to make, even in the midst of a crisis. In fact, the decision to wipe the evening schedule and go live involves a trade-off between what was already scheduled and crisis coverage. Due to their nature, being a commercial and a public service station, respectively, the two television organisations confronted different dilemmas. For TV4, September 11th was a trade-off between economic values—in terms of commercials—and the greater public good.

> Immediately there was pressure about whether we could afford to lose all that money. On the other hand, there was the other pressure, how can we journalistically show that this is such an important event that we have to do it in a special way. (interview about 9/ 11, TV4)

In this case, it was deemed more important to increase the news organisation's image of taking social responsibility than incur the economic losses associated with removing commercials. This short-term monetary loss was quickly replaced by a realisation that TV4 increased its status and credibility through its coverage, according to the TV4 news executives.

For SVT, the trade-off did not involve financial cost, but values such as quality in terms of professionally edited news packages as well as fulfilling its other public service obligations. SVT chose to take its other public service values into consideration and continued with its regularly scheduled programmes.

> Our starting point was to air continuously, to do it quickly and with diversity. And it was the focus on diversity that made us use our old method of cruising between the channels, and to broadcast other programmes on the other channel. (interview about 9/11, SVT)

In other words, SVT chose to focus on "diversity" rather than "consistency." Again, it is the relationship with the audience that is in focus. There is also a competitive aspect in this, since the audience preferred to turn somewhere else if consistency is lacking. Still, there is a trade-off even for SVT. A quote from one of the SVT managers reveals the conflict behind the decision, "It was an obvious decision from a public service perspective, but from an audience perspective it was a difficult one" (interview about 9/11, SVT).

Just Being There . . . to Explain, Comfort and Reassure

Long before the current capability for continuous live television, television pictures have claimed to represent a reality, "out there," "right now, as we speak." The claim of live news coverage represents a claim to an unmediated access to the real, an impossibility, of course, because we can never have unmediated access to the real. Nonetheless this promise exerts a powerful force on viewers and producers alike. Liveness gives the impression that we are closer to the centre where things are happening, closer to the "truth," i.e., when a journalist is standing on the spot telling us, apparently *ad lib,* what is happening at this very moment. This is why, according to Bourdon, "live television, to a certain extent, likes unexpected events to occur; as this is the best way to demonstrate that it fulfils its commitments" (Bourdon, 2000, p. 536). According to Couldry (2003), the power of the media ritual of liveness has to do with its potential to connect us in our homes to "real" events happening in the social world out there. We watch because we know other people are watching at the same time.

From a journalistic standpoint, long live broadcasts are not entirely compatible with one of journalism's cornerstones—that news coverage is about providing information. The idea of broadcasting despite the fact that nothing new is happening goes against traditional editorial values and opens up for speculation, rumour mongering and repetition. Furthermore, liveness as a format places high demands on the reporters and editors of the news programmes. As expressed by one TV4 manager, it is "hard to talk about something when you don't know what to say." Yet, live broadcasting was the preferred scheduling by both SVT and TV4 upon the news that the Foreign Minister Anna Lindh was murdered in 2003. But what were the journalists' motivations for going live? This section focuses on the justifications journalists made for going live, despite these problems. When the Foreign Minister was stabbed on 10 September, the management group at SVT thought that the limited information available made going live problematic. The decision to do so was taken in order "to be on the safe side" (interview about Anna Lindh, SVT). The dilemma is explained by one of the SVT managers.

> It is a troublesome situation since you have to comment on something when you don't know what is really going on. And then there is the need to just be present for the audience. Some co-workers argue that it is better to keep a strict line and only to broadcast when something big has happened. Me, and the rest of the management group, do not agree. We think that when there is an event of this character [September 11th], there is an intrinsic value in broadcasting that nothing new has happened. And if something new happens, the public will feel much better knowing that we are there broadcasting. (interview about Anna Lindh, SVT)

According to the reasoning above (for both cases), going live has to do with providing the public with a sense of security by simply "being there," reporting as if from the fireside. We interpret this as SVT aspiring to perform a therapeutic role in helping the audience to understand and process the two events. This is also clear from the reasoning at TV4 (who had waited to set up a live studio until it was announced she had died): "We have discussed it in evaluations afterwards, that we should have [broadcast more] at an earlier stage. In hindsight, [we should] have put more pressure into producing an extra news programme, since presence is always better than non-presence" (interview about Anna Lindh, TV4).

As expressed by another one of the SVT management group, "Our presence is important even if nothing new has happened" or, put another way, "nothing new has happened—and that should not be underestimated as news" (interview about Anna Lindh, SVT). The management group at SVT also refer to presence in terms of preparedness: if new information becomes available, the audience should feel certain that they would find out about it right away. "On a psychological level we think that it is important to know that if something new should happen in the coming hours, it will be enough to have SVT and to switch it on" (interview about Anna Lindh, SVT).

Another motivation for long live broadcasts seems to be the idea of helping the audience process the event. According to SVT, broadcasting during September 11th was partly done in order to help people digest the event and contribute to some kind of comprehension about what had happened. "We tried to take some kind of responsibility since the event was terribly frightening for many people and it demanded reflection, explanation and a lot of talk" (interview about 9/11, SVT). One of the managers at TV4 explains that from the very beginning they understood that newscasts would not be enough but that a studio programme with another pace was needed in order to meet the audience need to come down from the shock and try to understand the situation. Continuous live broadcasting was here seen as a way of supporting the public in its search for what these attacks meant.

If the attacks of September 11th were frightening and hard to grasp and liveness was needed for providing a feeling of safety and understanding, then the murder of Anna Lindh was more about the news organisations participating in an emotional process of national grieving. SVT was broadcasting the whole day with various studio guests, so "after a while there isn't so much new information coming in, but there is value in the processing that goes on" in these situations (interview about Anna Lindh, SVT). The managers at TV4 also talked about the value of processing the event as a reason for providing continuous coverage the day after the murder. From the interviews it is clear that the journalists aspired to fulfill emotional needs, by providing understanding and taking part in a collective grieving process.

According to the managers at SVT, both crises illustrate a dynamic process, but the Anna Lindh case was more predictable, journalistically speaking, since Sweden had gone through a similar experience with the murder of its Prime Minister Olof Palme in 1986. Having already experienced this, the Anna Lindh case was easier to deal with, since the different angles were readily available from the organisation's common "memory" of experience. Indeed, the Anna Lindh murder was reported from different angles, one of which was the "police angle," searching for the perpetrator. But when she died, "things moved into another phase because then it was a matter of grief—the emotional perspective. And with that you have to start thinking about the memory perspective" (interview about Anna Lindh, SVT).

Finally, in the same way that television broadcasters attempt to provide comfort and understanding when a crisis happens, they also feel an obligation to provide the audience with a sense that life continues. One of the most important questions is thus when to stop broadcasting since, "There is also a need to return to normal, since people have a need for routines" (interview about 9/11, TV4). Journalists try to do this by providing people a sense of hope and of moving on. To sum up, there seems to be a clear ambition from the management groups in times of crisis of fulfilling a therapeutic role in relation to society.

Conclusion

This article has analysed the motivations and decisions by media managers during two extraordinary, tragic events. Instead of the usual focus on whether the "right" information was conveyed and whether the media distorted the crisis, we found the culturalist approach of the emphasis on ritual and meaning-making to be more appropriate in explaining why the coverage looked as it did.

Ritual reporting during crisis might be understood in light of a movement from detached professionalism to a greater sensitivity for the audience perspective (Carey, 2002). News organisations face dilemmas regarding economic trade-offs, quality considerations and competition when radical re-scheduling comes into play. As one of the SVT managers observed, these kinds of situations are when the organisation is really put to the test. If the TV schedule does not reflect audience perceptions of the magnitude of the crisis, the audience could turn elsewhere, thus both the TV stations want to dignify the event by long live broadcasts. In this way, competition is an important motivator for ritual performance.

The public service SVT changed its scheduling policy after the September 11th attacks, because its "mistake" cost it its privileged position as a central institution in Swedish society during crisis. If one fails to provide that common space for audiences during crisis, then the media organisation loses its role in the historical drama. We connected this to Couldry's notion of media rituals as actions whereby the media demonstrate that they are at the very centre of what is important to society.

From the two cases, it seems like "disaster" marathons were the preferable format. This means that the media organisations have to deal with a situation in which normal editorial standards do not apply. As we saw, the media managers made a case for "presence" as a value in itself. Staying live in order to "be there" is a balancing act between repetition and speculation, on the one hand, and providing a sense of security and understanding, on the other. In the balance between the two, the ritual functions of the latter outweigh the worries of the former. In times of crisis, fulfilling psychological needs such as comfort and "working through" seem to be important journalistic objectives. It is worth investigating further, within the scholarship of journalistic role conceptions, the finding that journalists saw themselves as taking on the roles of psychologist, comforter and co-mourner. Indeed, with the increasing use of live coverage by news organisations, it is possible that this therapeutic role becomes more important than previously for television news organisations. Indeed, in the U.S. news coverage of Hurricane Katrina reporters were seen crying on camera.

We conclude that it is important to broaden the perspective of crisis reporting away from narrow informational aspects if we want to understand the way journalists think and act during extraordinary events. In order to do so, aspects like a sense of belonging, competition and comfort must be taken into account.

Acknowledgments

This research was supported by a grant from SEMA (the Swedish Emergency Management Agency).

Notes

1. The interviews from 9/11 include six members of the management group of the Swedish Broadcasting Organisation, SVT (the Planning Director, the News Division Manager, the News and Factual Programming Director, the Editors of the evening news programmes, *Rapport* and *Aktuellt)* and six members of the Management group at TV4 (the Management Director, the Programme Director, the Broadcasting Director, the News Editor, the Planning Director and the Current Affairs Director). The empirical material in the Anna Lindh case was more limited and consisted of four interviews with SVT management group members (Section Head for News and Factual Programming, the Head of the News Division, the Head of *Rapport,* the Planning Director) and one at TV4 with the Head of Current Affairs programmes. The interviews were structured around questions concerning organizational processes and decisions during the first two days of each crisis. Decision making is in general difficult to observe live, which makes retrospective interviews an established way to collect empirical material. This does not mean that interviews are unproblematic, since there is always a risk that the interviewees are biased in some way. One must keep in mind that the informant might not recall all the details in the decision-making process, or that they reconstruct the event to appear more logical than it was, since they might not be aware of the factors affecting their decision making. In order to try to minimise biases in the material, firstly, the described reasons have been set against the actual decision taken and the reasoning behind them. Secondly, the management groups consist of several persons and their statements have been controlled against one another.

2. Couldry seems to argue that there is no societal centre and therefore calls it the "myth of the mediated centre." Whether or not the media actually constitute society's centre and whether this is a "myth" is irrelevant to our argument. It is enough to argue that media organisations market themselves as being at society's centre.

3. TV4 is considered a hybrid between commercial and public service television, since it is contractually obligated to follow certain public service quality conditions. For example, there are specific standards on news and current affairs, children's, regional and cultural programmes. These standards are similar to the ones SVT are bound to, with the difference that TV4 has no obligation to cater to minorities.

4. This denotes which station the interviewee worked at and which case they were interviewed about. In order to ensure full co-operation anonymity was granted to the interviewees. The quotes are translated from Swedish by the authors.

References

Asp, Kent (1995) *Kommersialiserade nyheter på gott och ont. En jam jämförande undersökning av Rapport TV2 och nyheterna TV4,* Arbetsrapport nr 50, Kungälv: Institutionen för Journalistik och Masskomm unikation, Göteborgs Universitet.

Berkowitz, Dan (1997) "Non-routine News and Newswork: exploring a what-a-story," in: Dan Berkowitz (Ed.), *Social Meanings of News: a text-reader,* London: Sage, pp. 362–75.

Bourdon, Jerome (2000) "Live Television Is Still Alive: on television as an unfulfilled promise," *Media, Culture & Society* 22, pp. 531–56.

Bouvier, Gwen (2005) "'Breaking' News: the first hours of the BBC coverage of 9/11 as a media event," *Journal for Crime, Conflict and the Media* 1(4), pp. 19–43.

Carey, James W. (1975) "A Cultural Approach to Communication," *Communication* 2, pp. 1–22.

Carey, James W. (1989) *Communication as Culture: essays on media and society,* Boston: Unwin Hyman.

Carey, James W. (2002) "Globalization Isn't New; Anti-globalization Isn't Either: September 11 and the history of nations," *Prometheus* 20(3), pp. 289–94.

Coman, Mihai (2005) "Cultural Anthropology and Mass Media: a processual approach," in: Eric Rothenbuhier and Mihai Coman (Eds), *Media Anthropology,* London: Sage.

Cottle, Simon (2000) "New(s) Times: Towards a 'Second Wave' of News Ethnography," *Communications* 25(1), pp. 19–41.

Couldry, Nick (2003) *Media Rituals: a critical approach,* London: Routledge.

Dayan, Daniel and Katz, Elihu (1992) *Media Events: the live broadcasting of history,* Cambridge, MA: Harvard University Press.

Djerf-Pierre, Monika and Weibull, Lennart (2001) *Spegla, granska, tolka,* Stockholm: Prisma.

Ehrlich, Matthew (1996) "Using Ritual to Study Journalism," *Journal of Communication Inquiry* 20(2), pp. 3–17.

Ehrlich, Matthew (1997) "The Competitive Ethos in Television Newswork," in: Dan Berkowitz (Ed.), *The Social Meanings of News: a text-reader,* London: Sage.

Hadenius, Stig (2001) "Stig Hadenius synar terrorns dag i medierna: TV 4 gjorde sitt jobb bättre än SVT," *Dagens Nyheter,* 14 September.

Hadenius, Stig and Weibull, Lennart (1999) *Massmedier,* 7th edn, Stockholm: Bonnier Alba.

Hedman, Love, Nowak, Kjell and Hadenius, Stig (1996) *Estonia i nyheterna,* Rapport 168: del 3, Stockholm: Styrelsen för Psykologiskt försvar.

Jarlbro, Gunilla (2004) *Krisjournalistik eller journalistik i kris? En forskningsöversikt om medier, risker och kriser,* Vol. 1, Stockholm: KBM:s Temaserie.

Jönsson, Anna Maria (2004) "Public Service som ideologi och praktik," in: Lars Nord and Jesper Strömbäck (Eds), *Medierna och demokratin,* Lund: Studentlitteratur.

Köcher, Renate (1986) "Bloodhounds or Missionaries: role definitions of Germanand British journalists," *European Journal of Communication* 1(1), pp. 43–64.

Leth, Göran and Thurén, Torsten (2002) *11 September. Mediernas bevakning av terrorattackerna,* Rapport nr 6, Stockholm: Stiftelsen Institutet för Mediestudier.

Liebes, Tamar (1998) "Television's Disaster Marathons," in: Tamar Liebes and James Curran (Eds), *Media, Ritual and Identity,* London: Routledge, pp. 3–22.

Liebes, Tamar and Blondheim, Menahem (2005) "Myths to the Rescue: how live television intervenes in history," in: Eric W. Rothenbuhler and Mihai Coman (Eds), *Media Anthropology,* London: Sage, pp. 188–98.

McManus, John H. (1994) *Market-driven Journalism: let the citizen beware,* Thousand Oaks, CA: Sage.

Melin-Higgins, Margareta (1996) *Pedagoger och spårhundar: en studie av svenska journalisters yrkesideal,* Kungälv: Institutionen för Journalistik och Masskommunikation, Göteborgs Universitet.

Nohrstedt, Stig-Arne (2000) "Communication Challenges in Connection with Catastrophes and States of Emergency: a review of the literature," *Nordicom Review* 2 (Special issue: The 14th Nordic Conference on Media and Communication Research), pp. 137–156.

Rappaport, Roy A. (1999) *Ritual and Religion in the Making of Humanity,* Cambridge: Cambridge University Press.

Riegert, Kristina (2004) "The Cultures of the Foreign News Desk: comparative U.S. and European national perspectives," paper presented to the Fifth International Crossroads in Cultural Studies Conference, University of Illinois, Urbana-Champaign.

Röhl, Willhelm (1979) *Centralredaktionen 1972 78. Några dokumentariska anteckningar,* Stockholm: Sveriges Radio.

Rothenbuhler, Eric and Coman, Mihai (Eds) (2005) *Media Anthropology,* Thousand Oaks, CA: Sage.

Schudson, Michael (2002) "What's Unusual About Covering Politics as Usual," in: Barbie Zelizer and Stuart Allan

(Eds), *Journalism After September 11,* London: Routledge.

Shoemaker, Pamela and Reese, Stephen (1991) *Mediating the Message: theories of influences on mass media content,* White Plains, NY: Longman.

Syvertsen, Trine (1997) *Den store Tv-krigen. Norsk allmenfjersyn 1988–96,* Sandviken, Bergen: Fag bokforlaget.

Tierney, Kathleen, Lindell, Michael K. and Perry, Ronald W. (2001) *Facing the Unexpected,* Washington, DC: National Academy Press.

Tuchman, Gaye (1978) *Making News: a study in the construction of reality,* New York: The Free Press.

Weaver, David and Wilhoit, Cleveland G. (1996) *The American Journalist in the 1990s: US news people at the end of an era,* Mahwah, NJ: Lawrence Erlbaum.

Zelizer, Barbie (1997) "Has Communication Explained Journalism," in: Dan Berkowitz (Ed.), *Social Meanings of News: a text-reader,* Thousand Oaks, CA: Sage, pp. 23–30.

Source: From "The Importance of Ritual in Crisis Journalism," 2007, by K. Riegert and E.-K. Olsson, *Journalism Practice, 1*(2), 143–158. Reprinted by permission of Taylor & Francis/Routledge.

10

"Someone's Gotta Be in Control Here"

The Institutionalization of Online News and the Creation of a Shared Journalistic Authority

Sue Robinson

Introduction

Journalists explain daily happenings according to a uniform mission, agreed-upon routines, and established societal relationships. Their product—American newspaper stories in this case—helps shape the social order by controlling information dissemination in a fairly structured environment. As a result, the press enjoys the status of a political institution that operates with some authority. The characteristics of an institution include "taken-for-granted social patterns of behavior valued in and of themselves [that] encompass procedures, routines, assumptions, which extend over space and endure over time, in order to preside over a societal sector" (Cook, 1998, p. 84). The Web has provided the institution of the news media with a new portal for the dissemination of information. The diffusion of new multimedia and interactive technologies has allowed audiences to take over some of this control. This leads to the question: If the press as an institution helps create our political, economic, cultural, and social reality through a constructed product, and online news is moving toward depicting that reality minus the construction, then doesn't such technology undermine the press as an institution in some ways? This is a broad question that can be pared down into more manageable research questions: How do print and online journalists conceive of their mission for the newspapers' websites? How have routines such as story writing, formatting, and editing changed because of the technology available? What role is the audience meant to play upon this new platform?

Transformations in journalists' mission, routines, and relationships with audiences would have significant ramifications for the state of the press as an institution (Cook, 2006). But scholars have disagreed whether these transformations will truly be revolutionary, or something merely evolutionary. Resnik (1998), in the *Politics of Cyberspace,* argued that the Web is becoming "normalized" and hinted that a commoditization of information is occurring. In this same book, Kellner (1998) contended that cyberspace is becoming "decommoditized;" its potential is not so much utopian as limitless. Society has only to educate itself and train in the technology to improve democratic public spheres. Which version of the Internet's power is accurate in regards to the press? Informed by the literature about journalism as a political institution and as an evolving Fourth Estate, this paper scrutinizes the stated missions, practices, and societal relationships of journalists to consider whether the Internet is becoming normalized (and thus, institutionalized), or whether it has remained something more nebulous, more alternative, or even more democratically perfect.

Offering the words of 35 journalists from in-depth interviews as evidence, this study suggests that news considerations center on personal experience for journalists and their audiences. A number of sub-themes emerged over and over again in these interviews. For these journalists, the newspaper websites represent an opportunity for community building, broadcast thinking, brand and competition channeling, immediate reporting, limitless content producing, customizing, personalizing, dialoguing, experiencing, and transparent information sharing. Most startlingly, the evidence indicates that journalists are sharing their ability to tell the day's news with people outside of the institution. Journalists hope cyberspace's particular attributes will save their industry and preserve the press's authority by building communities on the virtual pages of their newspapers. Eventually, such dramatic changes in news production will have implications for the press's ultimate authority as a societal institution.

News as an Authoritative Political Institution

Media are not a series of organizations, but a singular institution that has reenforced the dominant ideology and political power structure, wielded authoritarian influence and operated as a place of collective guidance for people's thoughts, principles and actions (Cook, 1998). To be considered institutional, an entity must have the ability to control communication messages and contribute to the social order, according to Giddens (1979). Institutions establish that social order's environment by discarding some messages in favor of other more politically palpable ones (March and Olsen, 1989). "Political institutions not only respond to their environments but create those environments at the same time" (March and Olsen, 1989, p. 162). Such a structure also stems from the developments of media that carry those messages, noted Giddens (1979), who tracked the birth of writing as the impetus for our current linear way of thinking and acting.

Putting aside that not everyone believes the press is an institution in and of itself (see Lippmann, 1922, who contended that the press is no substitute for our institutions or Gans, 1998, who described the press as a tool rather than a guide), this paper takes up those scholars from Cater (1959) to Cook (1998) who have insisted that the press is a Fourth Estate of democracy with an entrenched organizational system. Its stated missions have traditionally included its desire to monitor government and those in power, tell stories that inform people, lead public discussions, and generally provide a truthful, accurate, relevant, and interesting accounting of the day's news (Kovach and Rosenstiel, 2001). There lies power in news (Schudson, 1995), which constructs the picture of reality in our heads (Lippmann, 1922), tells us what we think about (Cohen, 1963), and provides a structure for our communication rituals (Carey, 1992 [1989]).

Routines form the basis of the longevity inherent in press's institutional power. The meaning of life is inextricably intertwined with the centrality of rules and the construction of a constructed ordered society (March and Olson, 1989). News production tends to be hierarchal (in other words, a top-down approach from officials to reporters to the audience, but also from media owner to publisher to editor to reporter). It is also often both multivocal and conventional.

News scholars have documented newspaper journalists' professional norms and routines such as their methods of verification (Kovach and Rosenstiel, 2001), their careful selection of story topics and facts (Altheide, 1976; Tuchman, 1978), and their reliance on other media as a check for news value (Zelizer, 1992). Such methods "have an important impact on the production of symbolic content" (Shoemaker and Reese, 1996, p. 137). By certain "strategic rituals," they determine the "who, what, when, where, and why of our lives" (Tuchman, 1972, p. 667), and in doing so, solidify their own importance in the community.

In addition, journalists "construct and reconstruct social reality by establishing the context in which social phenomenon are perceived and defined" (Tuchman, 1997 [1973], p. 188). Molotch and Lester (1997 [1974]) saw "media as reflecting not a world out there, but the practices of those having the power to determine the experience of others" (1997 [1974], p. 206). Indeed, "what the news means depends on how the news gets made" (Sigal, 1973, p. 1). "Routine is closely linked to tradition in the sense that tradition underwrites the continuity of practice in the elapsing of time. Any influences which corrode or place in question traditional practices carry with them the likelihood of accelerated change" (p. 220). But Giddens cautioned that typical institutions are of an *evolutionary* nature; traditional practices tend to be replaced by other practices that also soon become traditional. Such changes are rarely *revolutionary* in nature.

Finally, the institution believes itself to exude authority and has convinced everyone else that it does (see Cater, 1959; Schudson, 1995; Zelizer, 1992). Media have achieved this power to tell news stories in part through their way of weaving a specific narrative described by Zelizer (1992), their strategic rituals of objectivity described by Tuchman (1972), and their standard of formatting described by Schudson (1995). The communicative form matters to the nature of the press society relationship, as does sourcing, content and framing. Audiences look to the news to set their political and economical agenda and to explain the news. But the press also serves as an integral component to people's social lives. Journalistic communication offers a "sacred ceremony which draws persons together in fellowship and commonality" (Carey, 1992 [1989], p. 18). Journalists have nurtured this relationship with their publics by providing familiar, often standardized stories, and then helping to prioritize the news for people. The nature of these relationships reflects a certain hierarchy of influence, according to Shoemaker and Reese (1996).

Institutions, News, and New Technology

In the past, new media have played a part in altering the press's missions, routines, and relationships. Medium theorists study how new channels create new environments and thus necessarily alter social interactions (Meyrowitz, 1985). Democracy is substantially changed by new technology, noted Friedland as he in 1996 heralded the savior potential of the Internet even from within the conglomerated matrix of media that exists. Abramson et al. (1988) argued that it was new technology that shaped the current news institution as national, private, centralized and weak. Television, video and computers shepherded in "unmediated news" (Abramson et al., 1988, pp. 292–3) and the demise of gatekeeping, at least as we have traditionally understood it. Many scholars tout the Internet's abilities to save democracy by ridding journalism of the bias and topdown hierarchy that are said to result from the industry's learned routines. Newhagen and Levy (1998) described multimedia (that is, the ability of the technology to relay different kinds of media from within one channel, such as both text and video) as a catalyst for information metamorphosis, one that reverses the sender receiver nodes. The Internet's information capacity is diffuse and parallel, not condensed as in traditional media. Interactivity levels (Downes and McMillan, 2000) and hyperlinks (Pavlik, 2001) also involve the audience in the construction of the message, even of data collection, and create a more layered journalism.

The relationship between media and their audiences has been rearticulated because of the interactivity and multimedia (Matheson, 2004). "New media are bringing about a realignment between and among news organizations, journalists and their many publics, including audiences, sources, competition, advertisers and the government" (Pavlik, 2001, p. 1). Even the scholar who wrote the book advocating the press as a singular political institution in 1998 was rethinking that position by 2006, in part because of the Internet: "I argue here that we need to approach the news media with attention to the institutional walls surrounding them *and* the ways the news-making process includes actors on both sides of that wall" (Cook, 2006, p. 161)—now more than ever, Cook suggested.

It should be noted that many scholars downplay the Internet's democratizing abilities in a world entrenched in institutional media controlled by various powers-that-be. What good is hyperlinking if no editor allows it to flow off the site of the institution? Instead journalists are merely folding the technology into existing routines, according to some of these scholars. Golding called this the "mediatization" of new technologies "as they follow past scenarios of commercialization, differentiated access, exclusion of the poor, privatization, deregulation, and globalization" (2000, p. 814). Resnick (1998) thought of it as the "normalization" of the Web as being divided into traditional concepts of labor mirrored in the non-virtual capitalistic world; Singer (2005) showed that journalists' political weblogs tend to link to other mainstream news sites, creating "in some ways an enhancement of traditional journalistic norms."

In-depth interviews with news producers would offer a chance to explore the nature of the press as an institution in the latest emergent media environment. The research questions arose from this understanding of the press as an institutional body whose particular missions, practices, and relationships with its audiences have given journalists the power to tell the news. These questions are, once again: How do print and online journalists conceive of their mission for the newspapers' websites? How have routines such as story writing, formatting, and editing changed because of the technology available? What role is the audience meant to play upon this new platform?

Method: Journalist Interviews

Interviewing the creators of news products has provided other researchers essential insight into journalistic norms and practices. White (1950), Gans (1979), Tuchman (1997 [1973]), and many others have used the words of reporters and editors to develop news communication models and value systems that describe the industry and its operations. Deuze (2005) queried reporters and editors on the differences between working for tabloids and mainstream papers in order to understand professional identity. Interviewing in newsrooms, Lowrey (2003) revealed journalists' motivations and detailed their professional norms in determining when and to what extent news photos were manipulated. Gieber (1999 [1964]) decided that news was, in fact, what "newspapermen make it," as a result of his discussions with editors. Talking to journalists allowed Gieber to know not only what news is, but also how it is determined.

This article reports the evidence gleaned from 35 in-depth interviews with print and online editors, reporters, multimedia producers, and photographers from 24 publications. I employed purposive sampling because I wanted a targeted population of journalists. I chose each newspaper based on its presence on the Web, as well as its geography and size. I wanted a fairly equitable sampling of large, medium, and small newspapers. Each interview request was customized according to the organizations' specific features or projects, though the basic interview template was always the same to provide consistency. I chose the journalists similarly. Several print-only reporters were included in the sample of 35 to give me a breadth of perspective. The response rate was about 50 percent. I found the journalists by contacting the top 10 and bottom 10 of the largest 100 newspapers by circulation, as determined by Audit Bureau Circulation (2006). Most of the nation's largest publications, including *USA Today, The New York Times, The*

Washington Post, Chicago Tribune, Dallas Morning News, and *The Los Angeles Times,* are represented in my sample. I selected 40 others in the same list, choosing every other publication going down the list. I found smaller papers (those under 100,000 circulation) through the online news trade organizations Online News Association and Cyberjournalist.net, which recognize newspapers for their online coverage. I contacted my own former newsroom, the *Burlington Free Press* in Vermont, a Gannett paper of about 65,000 circulation. I was able to interview three very different sources there—the managing editor, a traditional print reporter-turned-blogger, and a photographer/videographer. I received approval from my university's Institutional Review Board to interview these subjects. The interviewed sources gave permission to use their name and company affiliation. Each had an opportunity to review and edit his or her comments.

I conducted the interviews via e-mail, on the phone, or in person at conferences during 2005 and 2006. Each interview lasted about an hour. I asked the journalists to compare their print and online missions, routines, and relationships with the public. The interview questions were chosen according to the definition of the press as an institution that controls information. I textually analyzed the journalists' words. My unit of analysis was the journalists' words. I transcribed each interview, reading through each twice. I compared their words to my understanding of the traditional newspaper press as an enduring institution whose enduring routines help it preside over a societal sector (Cook, 1998). Thus, these pages are organized according to journalists' perceptions of their online missions, their news craft, and their relationships with sources and readers.

Journalistic Missions

Same Old Missions, Still an Institution, They Say

An institution must believe itself to be an authority and go about its business with an enduring purpose as such (Cook, 1998). In the beginning of each interview, the editors and reporters reaffirmed that the primary mission of their newspapers' websites is to deliver information and to perpetuate their publication's brand. In doing so, the publications have hoped to expand their authority as their community's news purveyors (Len Apcar, Jon Donley, Ellen Foley, Geoff Gevalt, Steve Smith, Brian Thevenot, Eric Ulken, interviews).

Len Apcar, the (former) NYTimes.com editor in chief, termed the online newsroom an "institution," synonymous with *The New York Times'* brand. He emphasized that "a scoop is a scoop is a scoop no matter what." In other words, *The Times* in any form must dominate both print and online news competitors (Apcar, interview). Indeed, most of these newsroom leaders considered the Web a vehicle to "recapture circulation losses" (Gevalt, interview) by "building bridges to help my industry survive in the new media world" (Donley, interview). Newspaper Web journalism still depends on old, institutional media: "Your success," said Jim Brady, executive editor of the Washingtonpost.com (interview), "is only as good as your relationship with the print paper since they provide 90 percent of your content." To these online editors—mostly former print journalists—the online staff works in a "newsroom" in both name and objective. Old terminology framed much of these conversations: newsroom, editing, sources, gatekeeping, inform, community knowledge, agenda setting.

The press remains an authoritative institution, insisted these journalists. "We encourage people to help us set the agenda" (Ulken, interview). As a blog writer, Mark Memmott of USAToday.com considers himself both a "filter" and a "guide" to help people navigate through the vast stores of information in the world. A NYTimes.com's blog during the 2004 presidential campaign amounted to an updated version of a print product called "Political Points." Len Apcar from the NYTimes.com employed the term "authoritative read" for the blog, called "Times on the Trail," pointing out that the blog was not only produced by "news staff" but also "edited." At the International Symposium for

Online Journalism in Austin, Texas, in April 2005, journalists, bloggers, academics, and even Apcar himself questioned whether such a product could thus be considered a free-flowing blog in the cyberspace sense. But editors said it was important to maintain authorial control, and that blog or not, certain standards had to be met.

Indeed, by mid-2006, most of those newspaper journalists interviewed had limited their reader commentary or explicitly moderated discussions. NYTimes.com was forced to close down many of its online message boards, which "turned out to be sewers of profanity" (Apcar, interview). "We want to keep the discussion focused on the topic at hand, and to allow people to not get to know each other too well and start holding grudges" (Mark Briggs, interview). The print editors and the online department at *The Burlington Free Press* battled over the rules for reader commentary after a mother wrote about the rape of her children by her husband, naming both perpetrator and rape victims. Managing Editor Geoff Gevalt had a hard time getting the online editors to take down the posts. "They said, 'You don't have to worry about slander as much on the Web.' Oh really? You don't?" Gevalt (interview) said. "We have to keep asking, who's in charge? Newspapers must keep the same standards for fairness, accuracy and civility that it follows in the newspaper. Someone has gotta be in control here." The newspapers' journalistic mission has not transformed, regardless of the delivery vessel switch, wrote Suzanne Levinson (interview), the managing editor of the Miamiherald.com.

New Missions Emerge

Nevertheless, once the interview conversations turned to story conception, it became obvious that these traditional journalistic missions have expanded for the new kinds of news products made possible by the Internet technology. "We are in the midst of an evolution" (Briggs, interview). "We are changing the rules" (Gevalt, interview). "We are creating a new form of journalism" (Tom Pellegrene, interview). In the interviews, journalists ticked off the questions they said have been circulating in their newsrooms, including "Would this new journalism be more of a service or a product?" and "What would its relationship be to the old brand?" The editors' words made it clear that a battle over identity was being fought. New terminology entered the conversations: experience, senses, total package, flexibility, personalization, translation, richness, layers, fun, play, platform, and community building (as opposed to community knowledge).

Reporters, photographers, and editors have begun to think about the purpose of their news stories differently online. The print medium limits storytelling, and thus inhibits the basic informative mission of journalism, said Washingtonpost.com's Tom Kennedy (interview). Even though he stated in an e-mail interview that his mission is "to produce content that meshes with stories being received from the *Washington Post* newspaper," he expounded in a question and answer with Cyberiournalist.net:

> I don't want to be bound by those strictures . . . For most print products, there's such a force of institutional history that it's very difficult to allow for new possibilities. [At Washingtonpost.com] virtually everything is new and fresh so there's more of an "aha" moment when you start to see good stuff. (Willis, 2003)

The editors constantly repeated the mantra that people need to *experience* the news. On their websites, journalists said they felt a certain freedom of purpose, a breakaway from formulaic storytelling to "experiment" and "explore." Even a resolutely print reporter from *The Providence Journal* in Rhode Island likened his ability to add audio and video to his stories as creating "richer and enhanced experiences" for his readers (Peter Lord, interview), a sentiment shared by most of the journalists. The online journalist's new job is to give readers "a sense of the journey" of the reporter as he or she discovers the news, said Memmott of *USA Today.* "I take (readers) along in sounds and visuals as well as with my words and give readers a chance to experience what I am experiencing in the field, alongside me" (Memmott, interview). The *Los Angeles Times'* photographer Rick Loomis described how he painstakingly paired audio of the doctors discussing the life or death of a soldier with powerful images of deadly wounds. He recorded one mother talking to her son, who must now eat via a tube and "talk" using a pen and paper. "If you just saw her words on a page, it might move you. But if you hear his mom, hearing her voice catch, her frustration, well, every mother recognizes that anguish. It makes her more real." He suggested that "if you hear something and see the words on the page and view the pictures, you multiple the intensity of the experience" (Loomis, interview). A multimedia producer at NYTimes.com stated the following: "I look at what I do as a whole other thing apart from traditional journalism" (Naka Nathaniel, interview).

By moving the conversation from information-oriented missions to ones incorporating experience, the journalists have opened the process of communication. News dissemination is now incorporating not only multiple actors, as Cook (2006) noted, but also multiple authors, for the technology has made the reader's perspective an integral component of the content production. Any concentration on personal experience—be it the journalist's or the audience member's—through multimedia and interactivity makes the resulting product more fluid and dynamic; this new process seems less like the assembling of a car (a Gans' 1979 analogy of newsmaking) and more like a road trip in that car. Indeed, such shifts in purpose indicate that the individual level for ideological influences on media content can no longer lay at the center of Shoemaker and Reese's hierarchal model from 1996. Rather, newsmakers are thinking about how individuals can help in the driving of that car, the experiencing of news.

The Newsmaking Process

News media have garnered the authority of a political institution in part because of its standardized routines and procedures (Cook, 1998). Today journalists are thinking differently about their online stories and incorporating technological considerations into every aspect of their jobs.

Online, the processes of news production have fundamentally changed the creation of the news narrative, according to these editors. "The whole notion of story is beginning to change," said the online editor at the *Spokesman-Review*. Ben Estes (interview) from the *Chicago Tribune* noted that "what we can do online goes beyond print journalism." Naka Nathaniel, trained as a print journalist, paired the columns of *New York Times'* Nicholas Kristof with video, audio, and interactive graphics. "We have this horrible story that needs to be conveyed, but on the printed page, it sounds a bit flat. Online we can put a face and a voice to those stories . . . and in doing that we can highlight different things than he can in the column" (Nathaniel, interview). As a result, the narrative present in the one-dimensional column grows into something more three-dimensional, he said. "Now we are trying to make more instant coverage and add a component of interactivity, so that you can go backwards or sideways if you want (as a reader)" (Nathaniel, interview).

To do this, the online journalist must develop new "nodes of thinking" that bring the "user to the next level" (Jody Brannon, interview). This has meant that formerly text-only reporters must branch into oral storytelling techniques (Lord, interview). Photographers must consider story chronology and think about sounds and text as much as they have thought about visual storytelling (Peter Huoppi, Loomis, Nhat Meyer, interviews):

> The gathering process is much more complicated for multimedia. Equipment-wise we now have to remember to bring our audio recorder and microphone, make sure those batteries are up and running. You also have to balance shooting and taking audio . . . We also have to shoot a lot more images. (Meyer, interview)

Whereas reporters used to file a story and head home, today "we have asked them to do more, to think about a little different story, one that will give them a broader audience, and it's a bit more extra work" (Nathaniel, interview). "The good reporters are going to be the ones who want to tell a story using all the tools available to them," said George Rodrigue, managing editor of the *Dallas Morning News* (interview).

Gatekeeping—the art of deciding what is newsworthy—has remained a central component of these routines. Information selection is more important than ever. After one trip to Zimbabwe with Kristof, Nathaniel was charged with paring down 10 40-minute videotapes into 2.5 minutes for the website. Similarly, photographer Nhat Meyer at the *San Jose Mercury News* described the lengthy processing of editing audio for slide shows: "One has to limit him/herself to what a reader can handle. Just because we can produce a piece that is 20 minutes long doesn't mean that anyone will watch it or be interested by it" (Meyer, interview).

Editors once concerned only with news value are now considering technology (Pellegrene, interview). The more technological the element, the more technological the process considerations become. There is less content editing and more digital troubleshooting. These journalists identified their "assets in their arsenal," as the software, hardware, and multimedia tools at their disposal (Brannon, interview). For example, Rick Loomis, a photographer for the *Los Angeles Times,* said he had to train his print reporter not to respond to sources during interviews, to just let them talk so as not to disrupt the audio (interview). In some newsrooms, those responsible for the multimedia complained that they were more technicians or computer coders than journalists. Word choices for headlines are made according to Web search engines. Ellen Foley, editor of *The Wisconsin State Journal,* even called the next generation of journalists "technologists."

This has meant learning new-world skills such as multimedia storytelling and computer programming, while remembering old-world standards of accuracy (Brannon, Foley, Loomis, personal comunications). In some cases, the online reporters have been subject to even higher standards: Alberto Cairo from Spain's largest newspaper, *El Mundo,* noted that in a multimedia world of graphics, producers like him need a much more detailed picture of what happened than a print reporter would need. For example, a reporter covering the March 11, 2005, train bombs in Spain could write in the newspaper article that the bombs were placed in a bag or that the terrorists arrived at the station in a vehicle. However, the online producer must know what that bag or vehicle looked like (was it a backpack or a satchel? A truck or a car?) in order to be able to draw it accurately (Cairo, 2005).

Editors said they rely on off-site partners and writers to have completed the vetting process (Brannon, interview). They feed their websites with the Associated Press and other wire service content automatically. Most newspaper blogs are even directing readers to competitor work (Memmott, interview). That NYTimes.com blog "Times on the Trail" mentioned earlier linked to off-site competitors, with Apcar arguing that

> We knew that there is plenty of other very good reporting out there. And we knew that to have credibility with the reader we couldn't just say, well, here's what *The Times* is reporting and ignore everybody else. (Dube, 2004)

This indicates that the "strategic rituals" of the institution to be objective, accurate, and alone (or at least, ahead) in its news coverage are relaxing or expanding. If a newsroom's routines result in "the standardized, recurring patterns of news and entertainment content," ensuring that "a media system will respond in predictable ways" (Shoemaker and Reese, 1996, p. 106), then such drastic changes to traditional practices introduce uncertainty into what was once considered to be a fairly structured, hierarchical, institutional system.

Relationships With Readers, Communities

News media retain authority because they "preside over a societal sector," acting as an institutional guide in establishing community and individual identity, according to Cook (1998). Online, readers have been invited into the institution, according to these interviews. Gatekeeping has diminished as editors let "readers into the door more," said Nathaniel (interview). Another journalist said, "the audience is becoming part of the presentation" (Dube, 2005). Readers have more control over the news (Donley, Foley, Huoppi, Randall Keith, Smith, interviews), and more access to both sources and journalists (Gevalt, Keith, interviews).

The reader comments feed back into the newsroom information loop. Reader feedback caused *Times* columnist Nicholas Kristof to go back into Zimbabwe and Sudan, for example (Nathaniel, interview). During Hurricane Katrina, the New Orleans' Nola.com's extensive reader forums became sources of information for rescuers as loved ones posted news of pleas for help from family and friends still trapped (Donley, interview):

> At times when our forums clogged, rescuers contacted us to plead with us to speed them up—that they were being used to save lives. A news video shot from inside a Coast Guard helicopter showed a rescuer holding a page printout from Nola.com with addresses circled, matched with GPS coordinates. The blog and forums were also used to reunite families. A Chalmette woman wrote to thank us, saying that she was able to locate 200 family members from St. Bernard Parish, by using our forums.

In addition, a popular story often warrants its own discussion topic in the site's forum, said Joe Territo of nj.com (interview). "We follow the users. What they want, we can give them like in no other medium." More than a thousand readers have agreed to serve on an electronic advisory board at the *Greeley Tribune* in Colorado for reporters seeking information, sources, and feedback (Chris Cobler, interview).

Sources can post their own versions of interviews (Ken Sands, interview). Readers can dictate their own experience with the news (Cobler, interview). Readers have turned into authors and narrators, and reporters have become readers (Jamie Gumbrecht, Pellegrene, interviews). Multimedia and interactivity have become a way for people to "explore their personal spaces," said Brannon (interview). "We're a partner with the public now," said Brady (interview). Editors wanted to link audiences to the power elite, said Apcar (interview): "We're a switch connecting both sides."

Journalists and audiences interact on the same level, as co-communicators who together negotiate the meaning of the news. E-mail, blogs, forums, comment boards, chats, and Q&As all open up the "dialogue." These journalists hoped the Web would build community relationships by offering a place for discourse. "I want blog readers to feel as if they are in on a joke. I want them to feel as if we are all part of the same community" (Gumbrecht, interview). One editor even referred to journalists and their audiences as "disjointed families" (Pellegrene, interview).

Journalists have started new dialogues by introducing themselves to readers online. Reporters are making themselves characters in their own news stories. Slide shows and video allow the reader to understand a little bit about what it is like to be a journalist (Memmott, interview). During the Iraq War, USAToday.com's Mark Memmott was embedded with the American troops and wrote a blog utilizing both multimedia and interactivity. His multimedia contained his conversations with troops and photos of himself during his voyages, as well as personal accounts, feelings, and perceptions of the events going on around him. Entertainment columnist Brent Hallenbeck described his foray into blog writing about local music as an informal journaling (interview). Nola.com's Jon Donley shared with readers his own anguish at missing family members during Hurricane

Katrina: "I bared my heart about my own daughter, a Ninth Ward resident who was missing for five days" (Donley, interview).

Some print reporters have taken on celebrity status in their communities as a result of their online activities (Pellegrene, interview). Reporters at the *Journal Gazette* in Fort Wayne, Indiana, created a daily blog about their diets, called Weighty Matters. "People saw them at the gym, came up to them on the street. It turned them into stars for a short period of time" (Pellegrene, interview). No longer are newspaper reporters hiding behind the anonymity of bylines (Patrick Schmidt, interview).

Visitors to online newspaper sites can choose how they want to learn about the news of the day. While one person can listen to an audio feature, another might gravitate toward the interactive graphic. Still another may grasp the significance of the news in the photo galleries available—all on the same topic. Multimedia have allowed readers to hear "the pathos of people mourning. It is a palpable emotive experience with a story that evokes a totally different understanding," Brannon of USAToday.com (interview) said.

Indeed, the ultimate mission of journalism on the Web is to construct communal relationships, to build a "community of communities," said Jon Donley, editor of *The Times-Picayune's* Web partner, Nola.com. These interviews indicated that the public and civic journalism movements of the 1980s were being resurrected online. During that time period, some newspapers sought to involve citizens in their communities by hosting town meetings and forums that connected them with their leaders. Publications took direction for news coverage from reader panels, and journalistic investigations were supposed to perform a public service as much as a watchdog role. The movement lost momentum in the mid-1990s, in part because of media conglomeration and consolidation. Cyberspace has brought it back in full force.

"From the moment I went online, I determined that we would create a place without space limits, in which grassroots people could express themselves. A guided tour of people telling their own stories" (Donley, interview). *The Providence Journal* created a "guest book" for visitors to reporter Peter Lord's multi-part series on "Saving Block Island" (Lord, interview). In this commentary, readers related childhood anecdotes about Block Island. *The Los Angeles Times* hosted a conversation with hundreds of people about the Iraq War project, which photographer Rick Loomis illustrated with audio, photographs, slide shows and other multimedia: "I didn't even know what to say to half of these people, I was just so overwhelmed by what they shared" (Loomis, interview). *The Wisconsin State Journal* prominently displays readers' comments in forums and blogs, even using them to decide what to put on the front page (Foley, interview). "As a community paper, it has always been about trying to get as many people's names into the paper as possible, and the Web allows us to do that in spades," said Chris Cobler, publisher of the 26,000-circulation *Greeley Tribune* in Colorado.

It should be noted that in traditional public journalism, the newspaper's reporters, editors, and publishers remained at the center of the community building. Online, citizens are charged with creating the forums themselves. The official mission for Nola.com, the online partner of *The Times-Picayune,* follows as an example:

> What We Want to Be
>
> Everything local on the Web: the best possible website, with the widest possible appeal, that keeps the audience coming back for more, many times throughout each day.
>
> - The leading 24/7 local source of breaking news, sports, entertainment, business and lifestyle coverage.
> - The most engaging and interactive local site, with multimedia content produced specifically for the Web.
> - A true online community, empowering the audience to collaboratively build and shape the site into the deepest, most diverse resource for all kinds of local information and entertainment.

- The most innovative local Web environment, where the local audience can network, share ideas, entertain themselves and get to know one another.
- The online voice of the audience that we serve. (Donley, interview)

Only the very first point in the above list makes any reference to the print world and its core missions. Nola.com editor Jon Donley further described his mission to establish Nola.com and *The Times-Picayune* as a "place" where "the heart of the community" is kept. Local audiences of Nola.com are meant to "network, share ideas, entertain *themselves*" in this environment. Again, it is the *personal experience* of audience members and their relationship to the raw material of the news (as opposed to the journalism) that matters on these sites, not information. This idea reverberated throughout the interviews (Cobler, Gevalt, Ulken, interviews). Such an approach to journalist–audience relationships brings to mind Gans' desire for multiperspectival news, but in an even more dynamic sense. When sources and readers have greater access to the journalism, the journalists, and the information itself, the symbolic arena expands, becomes more diverse, more complex, more layered, and perhaps more reflective of reality (Gans, 1979).

Conclusion

Journalists said they are seeking to reinforce journalistic authority. To accomplish this, they have aimed to provide transparency and build credibility.

> In terms of transparency, the reader is much more involved in the story process or at least they can be. They can have a say in how we gather the news. They can have a say in how we select the news. They are making decisions about what stories they want to read. They are not respecting our traditions of putting five stories on the front page or the home page and just going with that. (Cobler, interview)

Journalists contended that this "unfiltered look at the news" (Martha Carr, interview) would "fix our credibility problems with the public" (Gevalt, interview). For example, the *Spokesman-Review* posted all its interview transcripts as well as the legal documents associated with its investigation of Spokane Mayor Jim West, accused of pedophilia.

> This was very self-serving, and that was to establish a culture of transparency. We wanted to throw everything we had at everyone, so people would see that we were not making this stuff up. It was an offensive move on our part. (Smith, interviews)

The *USAToday* reporter added that the linking and the extra material provide "a very transparent way to reassure people that what happened was real" (Memmott, interview). The posting of raw data and other reporter materials formerly left on the cutting room floor should make for a more accurate story (Gevalt, Memmott, Smith, interviews). "What goes online is a more accurate and truer representation of reality" (Briggs, interview). Donley at Nola.com described a series of 83 photos that he posted from a local resident who snapped pictures as the water rose outside his living room window. The resident continued shooting as he climbed into his attic, broke through the roof, and sat in hurricane winds. "No professional photographer provided shots of this authenticity," Donley noted.

This discussion about authenticity, transparency, and audience experience echoes that of earlier journalists such as Edward Murrow, who promised to bring viewers the news experience with the radio microphone during the early days of World War II, and then with the television camera. Today the multimedia and interactivity of the Web can make every news event an enhanced "see it now" moment, said the journalists interviewed. Once "there" at the site of the news, users can manipulate the presentation and alter the content on the pages of the virtual newspaper. Hyperlinks—and users' clicking ability—have become the new quotation marks, the new strategy of providing credibility and objectivity. Readers can literally create and change content, advancing Murrow's promise of "seeing it now" to "experiencing" it now. Journalists have allowed readers to peek past the institutional curtain to see the working parts of newsgathering. In that glimpse, readers are supposed to feel as if they participated in the reporting. In this way, journalists hope the newsgathering seems more "real," and the news therefore more authentic.

In providing the raw material, hyperlinks, multimedia, reader-only forums and other Web accompaniments, the press is (knowingly) creating a new form of journalism—one that offers a literal news experience. The new missions push journalists to give customers a personal and communal experience, as much as they strive to be an information transmitter, an agenda setter, and a community leader. Ultimately, these online editors and producers hope that when people are able to *experience* the news in various media and *interact* with it, such informed citizenry will then *participate in* the marketplace of ideas and politics. This new kind of journalism approaches Gans' idea for a multiperspectival newsmaking process, one whose rigid structuring of missions, routines and practices, and relationships has relaxed.

Ironically, in producing the news in this manner, the industry is also (perhaps unwittingly) undermining its own role as a societal institution whose jurisdiction has been over life's facts. These particular changes in content, control, and mission have several implications for the authority of the press to tell its news stories in this new environment. News scholarship holds that the press's authority results from its status as an institution, and that its power comes from the professional norms accepted by audiences. These editors reported that they see their service function in society eventually becoming a "platform"—a much different concept than an "institution." They see their mission as providing a "switch" between individuals, the journalists and the news sources. Their newsroom practices incorporate technological considerations of multimedia and interactivity, ahead of gatekeeping, news value determinations and other traditional professional norms. Their routines include posting the raw material of their reporting, writing the "back-story" of the newsgathering, and creating citizen-submitted journalism sites. Their relationships have changed with the new audience interaction encouraged on their publications' websites.

These notions imply a new sharing of authoritative space on the pages of the electronic newspaper. Journalistic authority in terms of its institutional cache cannot help but become diluted as it makes room for such expansions. With these changes to journalistic missions, routines, and societal relationships, newspapers and their websites are turning into an interactive public sphere that just may be forming a new kind of institution, one whose enduring boundaries are malleable and constructed as much by the content receivers as by the information producers. Such changes must have implications for the press's power to dictate knowledge to society. The institution of the press is still fully functioning, but the news is no longer the sole purview of the press.

Acknowledgments

The author acknowledges Dr. Carolyn Kitch, Dr. Andrew Mendelson, and Dr. Jan Fernback of Temple University as well as the half dozen reviewers who advised her on this paper in its various forms. She also expresses her gratitude to the 35 journalists who participated in this research. A version of this paper won the Top Paper category at the International Symposium for Online Journalism in Texas during April 2006.

Note

1. Those interviewed were Len Apcar, former executive editor of NYTimes.com (1.7 million circulation), 8 April and 7 October 2006; Jan Biles, print

reporter for the *Capital-Journal* (Topika, KS; 64,000 circulation), 22 July and 7 October 2006; Jim Brady, executive editor of Washingtonpost.com (960,684 circulation), 8 April 2005 and 6 October 2006; Jody Brannon, former managing editor of USAToday.com (2.5 million circulation), 6 April 2005 and 5 October 2006; Mark Briggs, online editor for *The News-Tribune* (Tacoma, WA; 138,000 circulation), 28 June and 2 October 2006; Martha Carr, assistant city editor for *The Times-Picayune* (253,000 circulation), 27 July and 5 October 2006; Chris Cobler, publisher and editor for *The Greeley Tribune* (CO; 26,000 circulation), 27 July and 12 October 2006; Jon Donley, editor of Nola.com, Web partner for *The Times-Picayune* (253,000 circulation), 25 July and 1 November 2006; Ben Estes, editor of the Chicagotribune.com (957,212 circulation), 26 June and 3 October 2006; Doug Feaver, former executive editor for the Washingtonpost.com (960,684), 8 March 2005 and 7 October 2006; Ellen Foley, editor of *The Wisconsin State Journal* (Madison; 92,000 circulation), 18 August and 12 October 2006; Geoff Gevalt, managing editor of *The Burlington Free Press* (VT; 65,000 circulation), 27 June and 28 September 2006; Jamie Gumbrecht, print cultural reporter for the *Lexington Herald Reader* (KY; 141,000 circulation), 23 June and 5 October 2006; Brent Hallenbeck, print reporter and blogger for *The Burlington Free Press* (VT; 65,000 circulation), 27 June and 16 October 2006; Peter Huoppi, photographer/videographer for *The Burlington Free Press* (VT; 65,000 circulation), 25 July and 2 October 2006; Randall Keith, online editorial director for *The San Jose Mercury News* (263,000 circulation), 5 August and 5 October 2006; Tom Kennedy, managing editor of Washingtonpost.com (960,684 circulation), 6 and 8 March 2005; Jason Laughlin, print reporter for *The Courier- Post* (Cherry Hill, NJ; 92,000 circulation), 15 August and 1 October 2006; Suzanne Levinson, managing editor of the Miamiherald.com (390,000 circulation), 28 March 2005 and 5 October 2006; Eric Loomis, photographer for *The Los Angeles Times* (1.23 million circulation), 20 August and 4 October 2006; Peter Lord, science reporter for the *Providence Journal* (RI; 230,000), 22 June, 21 July and 3 October 2006; Bill Marvel, print reporter for *The Dallas Morning News* (800,000 circulation), 21 June and 1 October 2006; Mark Memmott, print-turned-Web reporter of *USA Today* (2.5 million circulation), 26 July 2005 and 6 October 2006; Nhat Meyer, photographer for *The San Jose Mercury News* (263,000 circulation), 15 August and 10 October 2006; Bill Morlin, print reporter for *The Spokesman-Review* (Spokane, WA; 119,000 circulation), 21 July and 2 October 2006; Naka Nathaniel, multimedia producer for the NYTimes.com (1.7 million circulation), 24 March 2005 and 7 October 2006; Tom Pellegrene, online technology editor for *The Journal Gazette* (Fort Wayne, IN; 121,000 circulation), 26 June and 9 October 2006; George Rodrigue, managing editor and vice-president of *The Dallas Morning News* (800,000 circulation), 7 April and 6 October 2006; Ken Sands, online editor for *The SpokesmanReview* (Spokane, WA; 119,000 circulation), 20 July and 6 October 2006; Patrick Schmidt, sports writer for the *Casper Star Tribune* in Wyoming (73,000 circulation), 27 July and 4 October 2006; Steven Smith, print editor for *The Spokesman-Review* (Spokane, WA; 119,000 circulation), 28 June and 2 October 2006; Joe Territo, director of content development for Advance Internet, New House Company and nj.com (48,000 circulation), 9 April 2005 and 1 October 2006; Brian Thevenot, city reporter for *The Times-Picayune* (253,000 circulation), 5 August and 3 October 2006; Eric Ulken, night managing editor of *The Los Angeles Times* (1.23 million circulation), 5 August and 6 October 2006; Larry Webb, multimedia developer of USAToday.com (2.5 million circulation), 26 July and 5 October 2006.

References

Abramson, Jeffrey B., Arterton, F. Christopher and Orren, Gary R. (1988) *The Electronic Commonwealth: the impact of new media technologies on democratic politics,* New York: Basic Books Publishers.

Altheide, David. L. (1976) *Creating Reality: how TV news distorts events,* Beverly Hills, CA: Sage.

Audit Bureau Circulation (2006) "Top 100 Newspapers in the United States," http://www.infoplease.com/ipea/A0004420.html, accessed 27 September 2006.

Carey, James (1989 [1992]) *Communication as Culture,* New York: Routledge.

Cairo, Alberto (2005, April 8) Conference Talk, *International Symposium for Online Journalism,* Austin, Texas.

Cater, Douglass (1959) *The Fourth Branch of Government,* Boston: Houghton Mifflin Company.

Cohen, Bernard C. (1963) *The Press and Foreign Policy,* Princeton, NJ: Princeton University Press.

Cook, Timothy (1998) *Governing with the News: the news media as a political institution,* Chicago: University of Chicago Press.

Cook, Timothy (2006) "The News Media as a Political Institution: looking backward and looking forward," *Political Communication* 23, pp. 159–71.

Deuze, Mark (2005) "Popular Journalism and Professional Ideology: tabloid reporters and editors speak out," *Media, Culture & Society* 27, pp. 861–82.

Downes, E. J. and McMillan, Sally (2000) "Interactivity Defined," *New Media & Society* 2, pp. 159–79.

Dube, Jonathon (2004, February 12) "Q&A with NYTimes.com Editor on blogs," *CyberJournalist. net,* March 31, 2005, www.cyberjournalist.net.

Dube, Jonathon (2005, April 8) Conference Talk, *International Symposium for Online Journalism,* Austin, Texas.

Friedland, Lewis (1996) "Electronic Democracy and the New Citizenship," *Media, Culture & Society* 18, pp. 185–212.

Gans, Herbert J. (1979) *Deciding What's News: a study of CBS Evening News, NBC Nightly News, Newsweek and Time,* New York: Vintage Books.

Gans, Herbert J. (1998) "What Can Journalists Actually Do for American Democracy?", *Harvard International Journal of Press/Politics* 3(4), pp. 6 12.

Giddens, Anthony (1979) *Central Problems in Social Theory,* Berkeley: University of California Press.

Gieber, Walter (1999 [1964]) "News Is What Newspapermen Make It," in: Howard Tumber (Ed.), *News: a reader,* Oxford: Oxford University Press, pp. 218–23.

Golding, Peter (2000) "Worldwide Wedge: division and contradiction in the global information infrastructure," in: Paul Morris and Sue Thornham (Eds), *Media Studies: a reader,* New York: NYU Press, pp. 802–14.

Kellner, Douglas (1998) "Intellectuals, the New Public Sphere, and Techno-Publics," in: Chris Toulouse and Timothy Luke (Eds), *Politics of Cyberspace,* New York: Routledge, pp. 167–86.

Kovach, Bill and Rosenstiel, Tom (2001) *The Elements of Journalism,* New York: Three Rivers Press.

Lippmann, Walter (1922) "The World Outside and the Pictures in Our Heads," *Public Opinion,* New York: Harcourt Brace.

Lowrey, Wilson (2003) "Normative Conflict in the Newsroom: the case of digital photo manipulation," *Journal of Mass Media Ethics* 18, pp. 123–42.

March, James G. and Olsen, Johan P. (1989) *Rediscovering Institutions: the organizational basis of politics,* New York: The Free Press.

Matheson, David (2004) "Weblogs and the Epistemology of the News," *New Media & Society* 6, pp. 443–68.

Meyrowitz, Joshua (1985) *No Sense of Place: the impact of electronic media on social behavior,* New York: Oxford University Press.

Molotch, Harvey and Lester, Marilyn (1997 [1974]) "News as Purposive Behavior," in: Dan Berkowitz (Ed.), *Social Meanings of News: a text-reader,* London: Sage Publications, pp. 210–29.

Newhagen, J. E. and Levy, Mark R. (1998) "The Future of Journalism in a Distributed Communication Architecture," in: Diane L. Borden and Kerric Harvey (Eds), *The Electronic Grapevine: rumor, reputation and reporting in the new on-line environment,* London: Lawrence Erlbaum Associates, pp. 9–22.

Pavlik, John (2001) *Journalism and New Media,* New York: Columbia University Press.

Resnik, David (1998) "Politics on the Internet: the normalization of cyberspace," in: Chris Toulouse and Timothy Luke (Eds), *Politics of Cyberspace,* New York: Routledge, pp.48–68.

Schudson, Michael (1995) *The Power of News,* Cambridge, MA: Harvard University Press.

Shoemaker, Pamela J. and Reese, Stephen (1996) *Mediating the Message: theories of influences on mass media content,* New York: Longman Publishers.

Sigal, Leon V. (1973) *Reporters and Officials: the organization and politics of newsmaking,* Lexington, MA: D. C. Heath.

Singer, Jane B. (2005) "The Political J-Blogger: 'normalizing' a new media form to fit old norms and practices," *Journalism: Theory, Practice and Criticism* 6, pp. 173–98.

Tuchman, Gaye (1972) "Objectivity as Strategic Ritual: an examination of newsmen's notions of objectivity," *American Journal of Sociology 77,* pp. *660–79.*

Tuchman, Gaye (1978) *Making News,* New York: The Free Press.

Tuchman, Gaye (1997 [1973]) "Making News by Doing Work: routinizing the unexpected," in Dan Berkowitz (Ed.), *Social Meanings of News: a text-reader,* London: Sage Publications, pp. 173–92.

White, David Manning (1950) "The Gate Keeper: a case study in the selection of news," *Journalism Quarterly* 2, pp. 383–90.

Willis, D. (2003, March 6) "Online storytelling's 'zeitgeist of exploration,'" *CyberJournalist.net,* accessed March 31, 2005, www.cyberjournalist.net.

Zelizer, Barbie (1992) *Covering the Body,* Chicago: University of Chicago Press.

Source: From "'Someone's Gotta Be in Control Here': The Institutionalization of Online News and the Creation of a Shared Journalistic Authority," 2007, by S. Robinson. *Journalism Practice, 1*(3), 305–321. Reprinted by permission of Taylor & Francis/Routledge.

11

Broader and Deeper

A Study of Newsroom Culture in a Time of Change

David M. Ryfe

It is now conventional wisdom that mainstream American journalism must, as one commentator has bluntly put it, 'adapt or die' (Smolkin, 2006). Spurred by this sense, news organizations around the country – from the San Jose *Mercury News* to the Atlanta *Journal Constitution*—are engaging in great experimentation. Yet, researchers know very little about how some journalists are processing these changes. This is so because, since a spate of research in the 1970s (Epstein, 1973; Fishman, 1980; Gans, 1979; Roschco, 1975; Sigal, 1973; Sigelman, 1973; Tuchman, 1972, 1973, 1978), few ethnographic studies of newsrooms have appeared. From media reports, we know that journalists are being laid off in record numbers (for the most recent numbers, see stateofthemedia .org). We also know from survey research that morale in newsrooms is generally very low (Weaver et al., 2006). And, from a few studies partly based on interviews with journalists, we know that economic pressures are keenly felt in newsrooms (cf. Downie and Kaiser, 2002; McManus, 1994; Underwood, 1995). However, little is known about how the routines and practices of news production are changing (if at all), how journalists understand these changes, and what all of this means for the production of news or the self-conception of journalists.

In recent years, a new generation of ethnographic studies has begun to take account of the new environment facing journalism (see collections edited by Boyer and Hannerz, 2006 and Klinenberg and Benzecry, 2005. Also see Benson, 2001; Boczkowski, 2004). The present essay contributes to this literature. It does so in the context of an 18-month ethnographic investigation of *The Daily Times,* a mid-size daily American newspaper, that took place from 2005 to 2006 (see Appendix). As I entered the newsroom in January 2005, a new editor (whom I will call 'Calvin Thomas') had just taken control of the newsroom. In an interview, Thomas described himself as a 'change agent' who was brought in to make whatever changes he deemed necessary to reverse the newspaper's circulation declines. He also saw himself, first and foremost, as a 'journalist'. He appreciated hard news, especially the kind that held government agencies accountable for their actions. In order to compete in the new environment yet preserve traditional journalistic ideals, Thomas felt that his reporters had to change the way that they gathered and reported the news. Over the next 18 months, four of which I spent interning for the City Desk, I witnessed Thomas' effort to alter his reporters' newsgathering routines, and I watched as reporters struggled to implement the new practices. It is difficult to know the extent to which this single case study mirrors trends within journalism as a whole. However, at the least, it offers an initial effort to understand how print journalists are processing the transformation underway in their industry.

Briefly, I find that the culture of professionalism in the newsroom is remarkably resilient and resistant to change. From the beginning, most reporters—even, or perhaps especially, the most experienced of them—had difficulty adapting to Thomas' new guidelines. They especially chafed at his insistence that they avoid gathering daily news from courthouses, police bureaus, and other bureaucratic agencies. In the midst of trying, many experienced something of an identity crisis. They complained that they felt less and less like 'real' reporters. Out of this unease, a few began to question the legitimacy of the new direction Thomas had taken them. In other words, they moved from feeling that Thomas' new direction was difficult to enact toward a sense that it was the wrong thing to do. Once they came to this judgment, many reporters quit–sending a dramatic message to the rest of the staff. Those who remained, remarkably enough, simply began to ignore the new guidelines in favor of more conventional practices. As I left the newsroom in August 2006, the news columns had changed very little, and the way reporters gathered the news had changed even less.

If the question then is how reporters are processing efforts to transform their industry, my work suggests the beginnings of an answer: they are resistant and even resentful of what they see as encroachments onto their professional turf.[2] The next question, of course, is why? If the alternative is 'death', why are reporters unwilling to adapt? The original ethnographic studies of the 1970s provide a basis for an answer. The work of Gans, Tuchman, Fishman and others shows that journalistic routines speak to functional and symbolic needs of the profession. Perhaps most importantly, reporters need ready and relatively cheap access to information. Without such access, they literally could not fill their papers on a daily basis. The routine of visiting public agencies has become routine precisely because it satisfies a functional need (on this point, see also Cook, 1998; Sparrow, 1999). It also speaks to important symbolic needs of journalists. Reporters do not toil alone, in isolation, but belong—and feel that they belong—to a broader 'community of practice' (on this concept, see Wenger, 1998). Like any such community, the community of journalists contains conceptions of what 'good' journalism is, and what it requires, and who a 'good' journalist is, and how she might be distinguished from a bad one. Such symbolic criteria arise out of the practice of newsgathering (on this conceptual point, see Ryfe, 2006). For example, out of the routine of interacting with officials at public agencies, reporters have developed a sense of themselves as 'watchdogs', and this identity is one symbolic measure by which they identify 'good' journalism. The upshot of this perspective is that resistance to change among reporters is institutional and cultural. Deviations from their basic routines and practices may threaten journalists' ability to find and transform information into news, and may also trouble deep-seated conceptions of identity and value within the profession.

I elaborate this argument below, but begin with a brief description of Calvin Thomas' plan to revive *The Daily Times.*

A Plan to Revive *The Daily Times*

Like other large, urban newspapers, *The Daily Times* has fallen on hard times. At one time, it had been known as a very strong regional newspaper.

Many of its reporters during those years went on to prestigious careers at major news outlets. Today, however, a simple, glaring fact defines the paper: since the mid-1970s, its circulation has been essentially flat.[3] According to the Ayer's Directory of Publications (Ayer, 1974), in 1974 the paper had a daily circulation of 141,957 and a Sunday circulation of 242,834. For 2005, those numbers were about 170,000 and 230,000, respectively. These numbers have remained roughly constant despite the fact that the city has nearly doubled in population since that time, and is now one of the fastest growing cities in the country. Moreover, the newspaper's fixed costs have risen substantially, and it faces significant competition from weekly and local newspapers, and from Internet news outlets. To be sure, the newspaper is still profitable. Exact figures are difficult to obtain, but editors have told me that the paper has yearly profit margins of 25 percent or higher[4]. However, these margins have been bought at the cost of the news staff. The numbers fluctuate, but the City Desk, which is primarily responsible for filling the front and local sections of the paper, has about 15 reporters. In the 1970s, it had double that number. Some of the older reporters remember a time when the City Desk had a stable of seven general assignment reporters. Today, the paper has no general assignment reporters. Overall, the paper employs more news staff, but these workers are distributed across more sections, like weekly AM sections and a free weekly aimed at teenagers. Nonetheless, given the city's population and economic boom, corporate executives believe that the newspaper ought to be growing in both circulation and advertising revenue.

At the end of 2004, they installed Thomas as Executive Vice President and Editor of News to make this happen. Thomas had a plan for growing circulation. He believed that growth in circulation required making the front section stronger, and to do this, he needed to change the way that reporters gathered and reported the news. To his way of thinking, *The Daily Times* simply could not compete with television and Internet news outlets on daily or breaking news. Rather, the paper's competitive advantage lay in the fact that no other news organization in the community had its resources to produce quality, in-depth journalism. Thomas' idea was to leverage these resources to get beyond daily events: provide context, identify trends, and investigate issues. One of his favorite phrases was that his reporters should 'break the news' rather than 'cover breaking news'. In this distinction, Thomas meant to convey the idea that his reporters ought to get out in front of events. They ought to cover committee meetings before the meetings occur; they ought to uncover information that forces other institutions to react (rather than being reactive themselves). Thomas also reasoned that, like every large urban daily, his paper increasingly served suburban readers (on the impact of suburbanization on city newspapers generally, see Kaniss, 1991). Half of *The Daily Times'* circulation came from the suburbs, and the counties that ring the metropolitan area were growing in population at nearly twice the rate of the urban center. For this reason, he wanted to regionalize the news to capture these markets. This meant that if an event happened in the city, he wanted his reporters to find out if similar things were happening in the surrounding counties, and to write that broader story. Finally, from market research, Thomas knew that readers simply were not interested in 'process' news. They did not recognize news of the latest city hall meeting, for instance, or of an agency's planning session, as important or relevant to their lives (this notion has become conventional wisdom in the news business, hence the explosion of 'news you can use' in both print and broadcast journalism). Thomas wanted his reporters to write high-impact stories that would, as he and others were fond of saying, grab readers by the lapels.

What kind of news followed from these ideas? Early on, Thomas expressed his intention to provide each reporter with a guide that laid out the technical details for every beat. However, for reasons that remain unclear, this never happened. Instead, Thomas issued three directives, and these became the guiding rules for news coverage. On the front page of the newspaper (and only on the front page), he did NOT want to see three kinds of stories: government or political process stories; daily, or incremental, stories; or, soft, feature-type stories. Instead, he wanted the front page to be filled with broader and deeper stories, analytic stories that 'took a hard look at', or 'brought the news home about', some issue, event, or trend. He wanted more of what he called 'enterprise' rather than daily reporting. During his tenure, the key buzzwords in the newsroom were 'depth, breadth, and impact'.

Thomas never formally announced these changes. On his arrival in the newsroom, he intended to hold individual meetings with reporters, but only three or four of these took place. Six months into his new job, he had yet to even introduce himself to most of the reporters. He did give a talk before the entire staff at which he briefly alluded to his new plan. For the most part, however, he relied on his top-line editors—especially the managing editor and the city editor—to work with reporters on the new vision. Over time, editors and reporters worked together to figure out how to do broader, deeper, and high-impact daily stories in the context of daily newsgathering.

As I watched this process unfold, I witnessed reporters moving through three distinctive stages, which I will call concerns for practicality, identity, and, finally, morality. These stages did not always occur in order, and not every reporter experienced all three. Generally, however, they describe a process in which reporters moved from grappling with the practicality of the new vision toward making normative judgments about its value.

How Do I Do This?

Just weeks into Thomas' tenure, word of the changes began to trickle down to reporters. John Robbie, *The Daily Times* Federal Courts reporter, was told flatly not to visit the courthouse any longer: Thomas was not interested in legal process stories. Maria Lopes, the paper's lone statehouse beat reporter, was told that Thomas did not want stories on legislative meetings. Sandy Hickel, the new transportation reporter, was told not to report on, or attend, public meetings held by the Department of Transportation. Anna Short, a long-time education reporter, was told not to cover education hearings. As an example, during the city's negotiations with the teacher's union, the two sides met once a week. Short was told not to cover these meetings, but to wait until negotiations had concluded: 'Editors,' she told me, 'don't want to publish anything that doesn't have a conclusion.'[5] Cops reporter Sebastian Bottom was told not to do 'murder of the day' stories. City hall reporters Kate Landers and Tom Campbell were told not to cover City Council meetings.

In these early days, reporters were simply puzzled by the new directives. How were they to produce news without closely attending to the institutions that comprised their beats? Their puzzlement is not surprising. After all, reporters have been relying on centralized agencies to find newsworthy information since the days of the town crier (Mott, 1952; Schudson, 1978; Tuchman, 1978). In some ways, it is a simple matter of efficiency. By definition, the news is 'new'. This means that reporters must have reliable, steady (read: daily) access to new information that they can place in their papers. Government agencies that constitute the core of most journalistic beats are perfectly placed to provide such information. Indeed, as Cook (1998: 44) notes, by the early 20th century, government had created an entire publicity infrastructure to support the newsgathering efforts of reporters—effectively subsidizing the news business with free information. Daily interaction with agents of these institutions, therefore, is a staple routine of modern newsgathering (cf. Fishman, 1980; Gans, 1979; Sigal, 1973). Interactions with these agencies also serve other journalistic needs. For example, by virtue of routine contact with institutions on their beats, reporters gain something that no one else in the newsroom possesses, namely, access to information. They use this access to their advantage in negotiations with editors over which stories to write in what order. Moreover, the more autonomy they have in making such decisions, the more status journalists gain in the eyes of other reporters. For this reason, reporters often compete for access to the best sources of information. Those with the best sources of information not only enjoy more autonomy within their newsrooms, they also gain more esteem within the community of journalists.

It is, perhaps, a measure of their recognition that *something* must change that reporters at *The Daily Times* initially embraced Thomas' new edict. Most welcomed his arrival in the newsroom, and many appreciated his aggressive, hard news style. As one might expect, however, it turns out that covering a beat without routine visits to public institutions is very hard. Without these visits, reporters lost access to the steadiest diet of information at their disposal. In the absence of this access, they struggled mightily to find other ways to routinely capture useful information. No one struggled more than Sandy Hickel, the new transportation beat reporter. Hickel had been a reporter before her stint at *The Daily Times,* but her most recent job (which she held for five years) had been as a public information officer for a university. Moreover, she had never covered this beat before and was thrown in with little guidance, other than to do enterprise reporting and avoid public meetings. But where, she kept asking, was she supposed to get information for these stories if she didn't attend the department's meetings (5 March 2005)? She told me that there was no place even to meet the right people except at these meetings. Unable to solve this puzzle, she often failed to meet her quota of stories per week.

Perhaps because she was new to the newsroom, Hickel never shared her anxiety with editors. Other reporters were not so reticent. Several months in to Thomas' regime, the newsroom was abuzz with confusion about the new directive. 'How am I supposed to cover my beat if I'm not down there?' John Robbie (the Federal Courts reporter) asked (28 March 2005). To Sebastian Bottom, the cops reporter, covering the murder of the day was less important than the opportunity to establish relationships with detectives. How was he supposed to establish these relationships when he couldn't go down to crime scenes?

Thomas was rarely in the newsroom to explain how this might be done. Without this instruction, reporters began to chafe at their loss of autonomy in making news judgments. A meeting in mid-March 2005 between the managing editor, Zeb Campbell, and a group of reporters illuminates the growing tension. At this meeting, Anna Short sat on the edge of her seat furrowing her brow while Campbell talked (17 March 2005). Seeing her mounting frustration, Campbell asked if she wanted to say something. This prompt led Short to launch into a minutes-long complaint. She understood that Thomas wanted broader and deeper stories. 'But how much?' she asked. And did this mean that she was never to cover an education meeting again? I don't 'feel that [I can] go on my beat and determine on my own what meetings to attend and which not,' she told Campbell. 'This,' she concluded, as if to confirm Campbell's assessment, 'is very frustrating.' Campbell offered some rough guidelines to assist her and the others in making these decisions. Later, Short dismissed them as 'speaking in generalities.' Roy Olden, the city editor, tried to offer more specific suggestions. He said that Short and the other reporters ought to get ahead of meetings by receiving and writing about their agendas beforehand. The idea, he said, is to explain so well what is about to happen that the newspaper sets the public agenda—it makes the news and becomes a player in town—without having to cover meetings themselves. Later, as the 'specialties team' met in their area to decompress, Short remained confused. 'I didn't learn anything new,' she said, as others nodded their heads.[6]

Reporters had difficulty not only with the logistics of covering beats in the new way. They also had difficulty gleaning 'broader and deeper' stories on the basis of the information they were able to gather. An example from my own experience illustrates the dilemma (16 March 2006). Like other interns, I was not assigned a specific beat. Instead, on days when I was not pursuing my own story ideas, the city editor gave me assignments. One day he asked me to attend a press conference at which the Department of Transportation was to announce that it had added new consumer-friendly features to its website. As I wrote down the requisite who, what, when, where information for my eight-inch story, the public information officer happened to mention that half of the people who take the state's driver's license test fail on the first attempt, and that half of those who take the test a second time fail again. So, 25 percent of people who take the state's driver's license test fail their first two attempts. That number seemed high to me, but in the midst of getting the basic information correct, I didn't make much of it. Later that afternoon, however, after I had filed the story, I happened to mention the factoid to Thomas. His eyes got wide as he exclaimed, 'You missed the real story!' According to him, the 'deeper' story was why so many people were failing the state's test. Who was failing? Teenagers? Immigrants? Why were they failing? Where were they failing? In rural counties? Suburbs? What did this mean for the safety of state roads? Local television, he said, would run the press conference story four times before the paper came out tomorrow. No one would have this broader story. Patting me on the back as he walked away, he said: you should have run with that story.

All of this made me frustrated. I felt like I had done something wrong. But how was I to know that this factoid was the beginning of a broader story? As a reporter, I had been trained to get basic facts—the 5-Ws, as they call them. I relied on my sources to point out important facts and relevant trends. Outside of interaction with sources, I had no routine way of quickly and efficiently gleaning broader stories from these facts. Though more experienced than me, many other reporters expressed similar distress at this situation. Months into the new regime, Clark Brown, line editor for the 'cops 'n courts' team, pulled Sebastian Bottom aside for a conversation about his recent lack of productivity. Apparently, he had been struggling to produce two stories per week, and often failed to file the required 'weekender' story. After the meeting, Bottom angrily told me, 'they (meaning, his editors) haven't given me any techniques to make this happen. Meanwhile, they don't want me to go down to crime scenes . . .' (24 August 2005).

One day, I asked Jeremy Schmidt, the assistant managing editor for Visuals, about these issues (3 August 2005). Thomas hired Schmidt because he was known in the news business as a forward thinker. I asked him how reporters were supposed to accomplish the new goals. He said: 'Reporters have to step back and reflect on what they can add to a story—what kind of questions need to be addressed to broaden a story, to take a hard look at the issue.' Yes, I said, pressing him, but what are these questions? Can they be distilled into a new set of 5-Ws? Schmidt leaned into me and said, 'This question is crucial for newspapers because they have to sell . . . the value-added they give . . . is precisely their ability to go broader and deeper . . .' Yes, I pressed, but how do you do this? He didn't know, but said that an article on the 'new 5-Ws' would be an excellent contribution to the profession. Later that day, I asked the city editor if there was a new set of 5-Ws to do broader, deeper reporting. He stopped his multi-tasking (at that moment, he had been writing an e-mail, looking over copy, and drinking coffee) and gave me a hard look. 'That is an excellent question. Let me think about it.' A few minutes later he passed by my desk on his way to his next meeting and said 'Breadth, Context, and Impact.' I wrote the words down quickly and turned my head up to say, 'These are not specific questions . . . ' but it was too late. He had disappeared into the conference room.

'This Feels Weird'

If you ask a journalist what a reporter is, she will often describe what a reporter does: a reporter is someone who writes factual stories of the day's events . . . etc. (Tuchman, 1973). She answers in this way because the identity of a journalist is tightly bound to its practice. This means, in part, that journalism will always be at best a 'quasi-profession' (on this point, see Benson and Neveu, 2005), or better yet, a craft (Adam and Clark, 2006). It also means that a change in practice may implicate a change in identity. That such a change was at hand in *The Daily Times* newsroom is suggested by Short's complaint that she did not 'feel that [she could] go on [her] beat and determine on [her] own what meetings to attend and which not.' Prevented from routinely visiting sources and events on her education beat, Short felt less and less like a 'real' reporter.

By the sixth month of the new regime, many reporters shared Short's sense that the new way of producing news did not feel right. For example, I stopped by Maria Lopes' desk to ask how things were going. In reply, she described a recent scene in which she and other statehouse reporters had been hanging out in the statehouse pressroom. Though Lopes was working on an enterprise project, most of the others were, as usual, hanging out while they waited for news to happen. Then word came of an interesting development in a committee meeting down the hall. All of the other reporters immediately fled the pressroom and ran down the hallway. Lopes, however, stayed put. Her enterprise story had to be filed the next day, and anyway she had been told not to cover legislative meetings. 'That made me feel really weird,' she said. She felt like she was writing for a magazine rather than a daily newspaper. Some months later, Chad Lowe was put on the same beat and expressed a similar feeling. A few weeks into his new beat, he told me that other reporters were accusing the paper of 'abandoning' the statehouse. He defended the paper's new direction, but admitted that he didn't feel much like a daily reporter (8 September 2005).

Other reporters expressed similar feelings. Maureen Holly said that she 'felt weird' about going to state education board meetings and not reporting on the meetings themselves. Sebastian Bottom, the cops reporter, experienced a particularly telling moment (20 July 2005). The year before, Bottom had won a company investigative journalism award for a series on state trooper chases on the region's interstate highways. Apparently, such chases often cause accidents. During the early morning budget meeting one day, Bottom popped his head into the conference room and announced, 'There's been another [trooper] crash today.' After Roy Olden told him to follow up on it, Bottom rushed back to his desk to call his editor, Clark Brown (who was driving to the office). While he cradled the phone to his ear, he busily gathered his things and began to walk down the hallway. He abruptly stopped when Brown asked him about the enterprise story he was supposed to work on that morning. Bottom said, 'It's basically done,' but Brown told him to wait. This annoyed Bottom to no end. Roughly half a century ago, Joseph and Stuart Alsop (1958: 5) wrote that a reporter's legs were more important than his brains. Translated: rushing to accidents is just what reporters do (and are). After Brown arrived and listened to Bottom's appeal, he decided that Bottom ought to finish his enterprise story. It was more important than spending the morning at an accident that may or may not produce news. He then handed the trooper story to an intern and asked her to follow-up by phone. Later, Bottom seethed, calling Brown's decision 'idiotic' and saying that the newspaper had reverted to 'desktop journalism'. Under the new regime, Bottom didn't feel like he was doing journalism any more. Anna Short put the matter this way: 'I just want to feel like a professional . . . [like I] can make a professional news judgment [about what to report].' Like other reporters, Short wanted to feel like a reporter ought to feel, which entailed, at the very least, control over basic decisions as to how to cover her beat.

Reporters were not alone in feeling some distress under the new guidelines. Editors also expressed a sense that the new practices left them feeling strange. One morning in early May 2005, editors found themselves scrambling to cover a scandal that had hit the statehouse (26 May 2005). By midmorning, several of them huddled in an office to determine who was covering what. As they discussed options, someone asked if the legislature was doing anything else that day. 'Yes, they're passing the budget,' someone else immediately said, prompting this quick reply from the statehouse editor: 'Oh, we're not covering that anyway.' The group burst into laughter at the idea that they weren't covering the budget signing. 'Well,' she continued, somewhat defensively, 'we're not doing committee stuff, honestly.' This prompted more laughter. Prior to Thomas' arrival, a story about the legislature passing the budget not only would have been done, it would have appeared on the front page. In the context of a highly stressful day, the laughter can be seen as a way of deflating tension. But it is also a register of a broader unease. In this moment, editors contemplated exactly how far they had come from conventional journalistic practices: they weren't even covering the budget signing any more! As if reading the collective mind, the managing editor said, 'But we considered some of these budget stories as front page stories this week.' He meant to imply that the paper was not too far removed from old habits—at least editors had considered these stories. However, at that moment the governor began a televised press conference on the scandal and the issue was dropped. Though it largely remained unspoken, for editors and reporters alike unease about whether the news they produced was 'good' or 'serious' or 'professional' remained.

'If This Isn't a Story, I Don't Know What Is'

Because journalists have, in a sense, made a virtue of necessity, the distance between feeling weird and feeling moral indignation about a change to one of their practices is not that far. From the outside, for instance, it may seem that reporting on government agencies is merely a necessity for reporters. After all, where else are they going to acquire a steady, not to mention free, stream of information? As many observers have noted, however, for reporters patrolling these agencies (as 'watchdogs') it has become a sort of moral imperative (cf. Bennett and Serrin, 2005). At *The Daily Times,* reporters often expressed this imperative in the form of a challenge. On many occasions, reporters asked me for my opinion about what was happening in the newsroom. Did I think that avoiding daily contact with public agencies was a good thing? Were they crazy for feeling frustrated? Not wanting to lead them too much, typically I hedged my responses. Almost always this caused them to proclaim, in remarkably similar terms (the same language, the same flat, declarative tone), this sentiment: if I don't watch these agencies closely, then who will? The sense of the statement is that public agencies need to be patrolled, and that, in fulfilling this role, reporters performed an important, if not always valued (apparently, even by their own news organizations), public service.

From the point of view of the organization, of course, covering public agencies is as much, if not more, a business decision as a public service. If, in the past, news executives sent their reporters to these agencies, it was because these were places where information could be found cheaply and efficiently. This fact implies that the interests of news organizations and those of journalists are not quite aligned. Journalists participate in a professional culture that is more or less autonomous from the business organizations for which they toil (on this issue, see Benson and Neveu, 2005). I say 'more or less' because the specific degree of autonomy journalists enjoy is locally negotiated. This is to say, it depends on the interactions between news executives, editors, and reporters in specific newsrooms. In this light, many reporters at *The Daily Times* interpreted Thomas' new rules as an encroachment on their autonomy.

Reporters did not express their frustration in terms of power. To do so would have been too confrontational, too highly charged, and also too nakedly self-interested. Rather, they expressed it in moral terms. Their turn to the idea of a 'good story'—a concept that seemed almost sacred to them—was a common manifestation of this transition. About six months into my time at the paper, Stan Henson, the last general assignment reporter on the City Desk, used this concept to explain his discontent with the new rules. In his 20-year career, Henson had worked for four newspapers. At every one of them, he told me, executives had a plan for reviving the newspaper. And at every stop, Henson ignored the plans (2 May 2005). To him, doing journalism was simple: he went out in the world and found 'good stories'. If he knew his craft well enough, the stories would come through and the audience would follow. After all, everyone likes a good story. To Henson, this basic fact had been true since the beginning of newspapers. It was true when newspapers were doing well, and it was true today. As a journalist paid to find these stories, Henson believed that news executives should simply get out of the way. Let their reporters do what they do best: find good stories that people will be interested in reading. Henson's reference to 'good stories' is a way of justifying reporters' need for autonomy in moral terms: autonomy is not an end in itself, but a way of serving a larger purpose, namely, of finding 'good stories'.

Consider the following anecdote. In the early days of my time at the paper, a thief began to steal purses out of homes in an affluent part of town. Under the policy of not covering daily crime, the 'cops 'n courts' reporters ignored the story. But the thief continued to steal purses. After he had stolen about 10 purses, local television news dubbed him the 'Hillwood Mugger' and began to give his exploits more prominent coverage. In turn, the police department held more press conferences to manage the increased news attention, which only increased the amount of television coverage. As this happened, *The Daily Times* continued to ignore the story. In the first three weeks of the crime spree, *The Daily Times* did not publish one story on the mugger. At this point, chatter in the newsroom grew. Reporters who lived in that part of town told anyone who would listen that these crimes were all anyone in the community talked about. Finally, after about 20 purses had been snatched (and police helicopters had begun circling around the neighborhood on nightly patrols), a group of women reporters met with the managing editor to ask why the paper wasn't covering the story. They argued that it 'must be' because the 'cops 'n courts' reporters were men, and so didn't understand how important purses are to women, and how violated they feel when purses are stolen. The managing editor had not even heard of the story, but assured the women that he would look into it. Clark Brown, the line editor for 'cops 'n courts', explained that his team was working on a 'broader and deeper' look at crime in the area, but that otherwise they were simply following the 'no daily crime' rule. When they heard this excuse, other reporters shook their heads in amazement. 'If this isn't a story', one of them told me, 'I don't know what is. We should be leading with this story and we're not even covering it' (10 March 2005). To this reporter, as to many others, editors had hamstrung their reporters to such an extent that even obviously good stories were being missed.

Over time, more and more reporters expressed similar views. Referring to the murder-of-the day stories that he had done his entire 10-year career, Bottom said that they 'are just too good to pass up' (10 March 2005). One day, Jan Markel—one of the paper's line editors—heard that a reporter had passed on two events that occurred the night before: a man had been stabbed with a sword and a high school valedictorian had been ushered from the stage after uttering some off-color comments. Markel sent the reporter to cover these stories. I stepped over and reminded her that, as daily stories, they were neither 'broad' nor 'deep'. She shot back: 'There are some stories that are just interesting. We got beat on these stories last night so we're going to do something here . . . the first part of "newspaper" is news', she concluded, 'and that's what we publish' (25 May 2005). I once asked Nelly Putnam, a line editor, about whether the paper should cover stories that had already been broadcast on television news. She immediately said, 'Yes . . . People read the paper differently than they watch television . . . they have time to meditate on the details . . . they expect to be able to do that' (4 August 2005).

Motivated by a sense that the newspaper was no longer producing 'good journalism', many senior reporters simply quit. Shelly Warren left in February 2005. That April, John Robbie quit in a huff, taking a job as a public information officer for a state government agency. Stan

Henson left the next month to take a job with another newspaper. Liam Nelson took a job at a weekly publication. Fed up with being micro-managed on her beat, Anna Short retired. Two business reporters left. Word in the newsroom had it that these reporters felt that they could not do 'good' stories any longer. Sandy Hickel was fired for underproduction. Nelly Putnam asked to be transferred to the Living Section so that, she told me, she could edit the kind of stories she liked to read.

It is difficult to know if this level of turnover—11 reporters in two years—was high. At the end of the exodus, Bottom remarked that more people had left in the past year than had taken early retirement a few years before. And, he observed, most of them were taking jobs at inferior newspapers or quitting the business altogether. Historically however, news organizations have always experienced high turnover rates. Today, that is truer than ever before. In this newsroom, however, reporters strongly felt these losses, and most attributed them to the changes Thomas had implemented.

Of those who remained behind, the most common response, remarkably enough, was to simply ignore the new rules. Like Stan Henson, some of the more experienced reporters never bought into Thomas' new approach, and therefore never adapted their routines. About a year into Thomas' tenure, this response became more prevalent across the newsroom. Though I never witnessed them vocalize their intention, more and more reporters began to revert to their traditional practices. For example, one evening a typical murder-of-the-day came over the police scanner. As directed, the night cops reporter ignored the news and continued to work on his enterprise story. The next morning Sebastian Bottom learned more details about the murder from local television news. Apparently, a man had been murdered in his bathtub by the illegal immigrant boyfriend of his spouse—who had been living undetected in the man's walk-in closet for months! Without consulting anyone, Bottom went down to the scene and talked with neighbors. When I later asked him why, he said, 'I didn't even think about it. It's just a good story and I had to cover it'. In the process, he learned new details that had not been reported on local television news, and on that basis got the story in the paper (in newsroom jargon, by getting new information, he had 'spun the story forward').

On another occasion, the FBI announced that it had asked the Mexican government to extradite a local man whose wife had been killed a decade earlier. At the time, the man had been a prime suspect, but had never been charged with the crime. Apparently, the FBI now felt that it had enough evidence to charge the man with her murder. Editors assigned several reporters to cover various angles of the case, going so far as to send one down to Mexico to talk with the man's neighbors. When I asked why they were devoting so much attention to a story that clearly violated the new directive (it was not even a recent murder and had no direct relevance to readers), the enterprise editor told me, 'it has all the elements of a good story. It's a who-dun-it, a romance, and a local story all rolled into one'.

At the end of Thomas' tenure, reporters and editors still used the new language he had introduced. They spoke of broadening stories and focusing on impact. But they used this language largely to justify stories that they had always done. Crime reporters covered 'murders of the day'. City hall and statehouse reporters covered the political process. A team specially organized to cover state healthcare wrote many daily stories about government committee meetings. Government officials remained the most prominent sources in most stories. Reporters were still not happy, of course. Too many had left and not been replaced, and after a bruising two years morale in the newsroom was very low. However, their news practices proved resilient in the face of Thomas' changes, and flexible enough to make it seem like they were going along. As I left the newsroom in August 2006, the front page looked pretty much the same as it had the day that Thomas stepped foot in the newsroom. Six months later, the company reassigned him to a smaller newspaper in another part of the country.

Conclusion

For reporters, the practice of journalism is tightly bound to its purpose: they see how they gather and report the news as how they *ought* to gather and report the news. One way of distilling the story I have told here is to say that Thomas pulled a single thread from this amalgamation of purpose and practice. He did not wish to change everything about the way his reporters gathered and reported the news. For instance, he did not tell his reporters to stop serving the public. He did not tell them to stop seeking the truth, to hold the powerful accountable, or to put aside techniques of verification. He merely asked them to stop attending so closely to the public agencies they covered: stop writing daily 'process' stories on city and state politics; stop filling the paper with coverage of daily crime; focus less on city happenings and more on regional trends. To his mind, Thomas had good reasons to ask for these changes. To be sure, not all of his reasons were journalistic. Many of them were market-driven. Still, of the many changes Thomas might have implemented in his newsroom, he asked for relatively few.

His reporters, as I have shown, ultimately rejected these changes. In thinking about how and why they made this judgment, three observations stand out. First, it is difficult to exaggerate the role of public agencies in providing reporters with timely and steady access to information. Following reporters on their daily beats, the original ethnographers of newsrooms were all struck by the intimacy of reporters' relationships with these agencies. Given that the number of reporters producing the news has shrunk dramatically in the last 30 years, if anything one would expect this relationship to be even more intimate today. This was certainly true at *The Daily Times,* where interaction with public agencies comprised a good bit of what reporters did on a daily basis.

Second, because their professional identity is tightly bound to practice, reporters can quickly feel at sea when one of their key practices (like routine interactions with officials at public agencies) is disrupted. What, after all, is a reporter if not someone who rushes down to a murder scene, asks the tough question at a statehouse press conference, or wheedles information out of administrative assistants at city hall? These are all practices associated with the broader routine of covering public agencies. Reporters' relationships with officials who inhabit these agencies fulfill important symbolic needs. They grant them a sense of professional independence; bring a measure of authority to their coverage; and serve as an important benchmark for what counts as good journalism, and a good reporter. As this routine was disrupted, reporters and editors at *The Daily Times* began to feel less and less like 'real' reporters. They chafed at the sudden loss of independence and worried about whether the news they produced was 'good' or 'serious'.

Finally, journalists use a moral vocabulary to express their frustration with what they see as encroachments on their professional turf. To them, there is 'good' journalism and 'bad' journalism, and while criteria for distinguishing the two are not always clear, a 'good' journalist can tell the difference. Perhaps another way of saying this is that *only* a journalist can tell the difference. These notions, after all, of 'good' and 'bad' separate insiders from outsiders, and set the terms on which journalists struggle for status within their field. This observation encourages us to recognize that the disruptions roiling news organizations today are exogenous to the culture of journalism. There is little pressure to change from within the culture of journalism. Like Stan Henson, most of the reporters at *The Daily Times* believe that the purpose and practice of journalism are and ought to remain constant. To them, it is a truism that people want to read good, fact-based, truthful stories told in an engaging way. Given this sensibility, it should not be surprising that reporters react with moral indignation when they perceive restrictions on their freedom to produce such journalism.

As I said at the outset, the specifics of the situation at *The Daily Times* may not apply to other news organizations. I suspect, however, that the cascade effect I witnessed—from confusion to frustration to moral indignation—is common. The field of journalism studies needs more ethnographic work to discover if this is true, and if true, what it means for the ways that news organizations will respond to their rapidly changing environment.

Appendix

Data for this study were collected during 18 months of fieldwork at *The Daily Times*. From January 2005 to August 2006, I spent an average of two days per week (and sometimes three) in the newsroom of the *Times*. Over this period, I attended budget meetings and other news meetings, observed reporters and editors interacting with one another, conducted formal interviews with every reporter and editor working on the City Desk, held many more impromptu discussions as events occurred, and followed reporters around on their beats. I also conducted four formal interviews with Calvin Thomas.

From May to July 2006, I also worked as a faculty intern for the paper. For two days per week over 12 weeks I reported on and wrote 27 stories for the City Desk on topics ranging from government press conferences, to the release of academic studies, to events at the state legislature.

By agreement with Thomas, I did not audio-record any conversation or interview. Instead, I compiled my observations and conversations into four ringed binders of fieldnotes. These fieldnotes form the core of data on which I have drawn in this paper. All observations mentioned in the paper come from these fieldnotes. At times, I have had to paraphrase language used by individuals. However, any text placed in quotation marks is a direct quote from one of my sources.

Notes

1. In the writing of this article, I have changed all proper names, including that of the newspaper, Thomas, editors and reporters, to protect their anonymity.

2. This finding is consistent with other research. For instance, Boczkowski (2004: 48) finds that the response of print reporters to the introduction of new technology has been 'reactive, defensive, and pragmatic'. And Klinenberg (2005: 53) observes that, in the face of management efforts to create a 'converged newsroom', reporters at 'Metro News' sought to 'defend their status' by 'making use of the language of the professions . . .'

3. The story I tell here mirrors broader national trends. On those trends, see Klinenberg (2007). For how these trends are playing out in newsrooms elsewhere around the world, see the collection edited by Boyer and Hannerz (2006).

4. Such high profit margins have been driven in part by the shift from privately owned to publicly traded newspaper companies. Cranberg et al. (2001) ably tell the story of this shift. Interestingly, the recent sale of the Tribune Company to a private owner (which also involved journalists and other employees sharing ownership) may signal a slow-down of this trend. In this connection, I should note that many journalists point to the public trading of newspapers as perhaps the greatest threat facing American journalism (cf. Fallows, 1996; Merritt, 2005; Squires, 1993). In many ways, they may be right. However, even within economic constraints, journalists have choices to make with regard to the kind of news they produce. One way of describing my analysis of *The Daily Times* is that it is a story of an editor seeking to work within economic constraints—and the response of reporters to his efforts.

5. Fieldnotes interview, 6 February 2005. Hereafter material from my ethnographic work will be designated in the text by date of entry in my notebook.

6. Short's conclusion is supported by Claire Persons, line editor for another team. After her meeting with Campbell and Olden, she said 'things weren't necessarily clarified . . . people left with more questions than answers. The theme was more enterprise, but [how reporters were to accomplish this without doing much daily news] neither Campbell nor Olden said,' Fieldnotes, 2 June 2005.

References

Adam, G. S. and R. P. Clark (2006) *Journalism: The Democratic Craft*. New York: Oxford.

Alsop, J. and S. Alsop (1958) *The Reporters Trade*. New York: Reynal.

Ayer (1974) *Directory of Publications, Vol. 106*. Philadelphia: Ayer Press.

Bennett, W. L. and W. Serrin (2005) 'The Watchdog Role', in Geneva Overholser and Kathleen Hall Jamieson (eds) *The Press*, pp. 169–88. Oxford: Oxford University Press.

Benson, R. (2001) 'Tearing down the "Wall" in American Journalism', *International Journal of the Humanities* 1: 102–13.

Benson, R. and E. Neveu (eds) (2005) *Bourdieu and the Journalistic Field*. London: Blackwell.

Boczkowski, P. (2004) *Digitizing the News: Innovation in Online Newspapers*. Cambridge: MIT Press.

Boyer, D. and U. Hannerz (2006) 'Introduction: Worlds of Journalism', *Ethnography* 7: 5–17.

Cook, T. E. (1998) *Governing with the News: The News Media as a Political Institution*. Chicago, IL: The University of Chicago Press.

Cranberg, G., R. Bezanson and J. Soloski (2001) *Taking Stock: Journalism and the Publicly Traded Newspaper Company*. Ames: Iowa State University Press.

Downie, L. and R. G. Kaiser (2002) *The News About the News: American Journalism in Peril*. New York: Random House.

Epstein, E. J. (1973) *News from Nowhere: Television and the News*. New York: Vintage Books.

Fallows, J. (1996) *Breaking the News: How the Media Undermine American Democracy*. New York: Pantheon.

Fishman, M. (1980) *Manufacturing the News*. Austin: University of Texas Press.

Gans, H. (1979) *Deciding What's News: A Study of CBS Evening News, NBC Nightly News, Newsweek, and Time*. New York: Pantheon.

Kaniss, P. (1991) *Making Local News*. Chicago, IL: The University of Chicago Press.

Klinenberg, E. (2005) 'Convergence: News Production in a Digital Age', *American Academy of Political and Social Science* 597: 48–63.

Klinenberg, E. (2007) *Fighting for Air: The Battle to Control America's Media*. New York: Metropolitan Books.

Klinenberg E. and C. Benzecry (2005) 'Introduction: Cultural Production in a Digital Age', *Annals of the American Academy of Political and Social Science* 597: 6–18.

McManus, J. H. (1994) *Market-Driven Journalism: Let the Citizen Beware?* Thousand Oaks, CA: SAGE.

Merritt, D. (2005) *Knightfall: Knight Ridder and How the Erosion of Newspaper Journalism Is Putting Democracy at Risk*. New York: American Management Association.

Mott, F. L. (1952) *The News in America*. Cambridge, MA: Harvard University Press.

Roschco, B. (1975 *Newsmaking*. Chicago, IL: The University of Chicago Press.

Ryfe, D. (2006) 'The Nature of News Rules', *Political Communication* 23: 1–12.

Schudson, M. (1978) *Discovering the News: A Social History of American Newspapers*. New York: Basic Books.

Sigal, L. (1973) *Reporters and Officials: The Organization and Politics of Newsmaking*. Lexington, MA: D.C. Heath.

Sigelman, L. (1973) 'Reporting the News: An Organizational Analysis', *The American Journal of Sociology 79:* 132–51.

Smolkin, R. (2006) 'Adapt or Die', *American Journalism Review* (June/July), URL (consulted December 2007): http://www.ajr.org/Article.asp?id=4111

Sparrow, B. (1999) *Uncertain Guardians: The News Media* as a *Political Institution*. Baltimore, MD: The Johns Hopkins University Press.

Squires, J. (1993) *Read All About It! The Corporate Takeover of America's Newspapers*. New York: Times Books.

Tuchman, G. (1972) 'Objectivity as Strategic Ritual: An Examination of Newsmen's Notions of Objectivity', *American Journal of Sociology 77:* 660–79.

Tuchman, G. (1973) 'Making News by Doing Work: Routinizing the Unexpected', *American Journal of Sociology* 79: 110–31.

Tuchman, G. (1978) *Making News: A Study in the Construction of Reality*. New York: The Free Press.

Underwood, D. (1995) *When MBAs Rule the Newsroom: How* the *Marketers and Managers Are Reshaping Today's Media*. New York: Columbia University Press.

Weaver, D. H., R. A. Beam, B. J. Brownlee, P. S. Voakes and G. Cleveland Wilhoit (2006) *The American Journalism in the Twenty-First Century: U.S. News People at the Dawn of a New Millennium*. New York: Routledge.

Wenger, E. (1998) *Communities of Practice: Learning, Meaning, and Identity*. Cambridge: Cambridge University Press.

Source: From "Broader and Deeper: A Study of Newsroom Culture in a Time of Change," 2009, by D. Ryfe, *Journalism, 10*(2), 197–216. Reprinted by permission of Sage Publications, Ltd.

PART IV

REPAIRING THE JOURNALISTIC PARADIGM

Embedded in the culture of journalism is what can be called its "professional paradigm." That paradigm includes both a worldview of what is considered an acceptable journalistic product and a faith in the specific set of procedures that should be used to make that product. Much as sociologists of the earlier research about news production explained that journalists learned the rules of working in a news organization "by osmosis," a cultural answer says that the professional paradigm is learned through immersion in the journalistic culture. This culture is experienced and learned in newsrooms, propagated in journalism classrooms, and ultimately expected by news media audiences.

The paradigm that shapes the production of news centers on objectivity and impartiality but also incorporates an ethical mandate for boundaries of acceptable practice and quality control. Because the paradigm represents a belief system, its believers also feel compelled to protect the system from outside threats and to defend it when situations violate the paradigm's expectations. The news paradigm contains some common expectations across national cultures yet is also adapted to fit its particular cultural settings. The readings in this part of the book begin by introducing the conceptual elements of paradigm repair and then explore variations on the basic concept. Each piece challenges conventional thinking about paradigm repair, suggesting alternative ways that it can be understood and applied.

"The Princess and the Paparazzi: Blame, Responsibility, and the Media's Role in the Death of Diana" places repair of the professional news paradigm within the context of news coverage of Princess Diana's death in an automobile crash after being chased by photographers on motorcycles. Elizabeth Blanks Hindman defines the concept of a paradigm as "a culturally shared vision of 'the way things are' that mightily resists challenge, either from external or internal sources." This article's aim is to explain how the news media reconciled their involvement in Diana's death—a clear paradigmatic dilemma because tenets of the paradigm compel journalists to remain bystanders to news events, rather than playing a role that causes an outcome to the event. Drawing on attribution theory, Hindman shows how the mainstream news media isolated themselves from the paparazzi and supermarket tabloid papers while separating themselves from the poor decisions made by Diana and the tabloid newspaper audience. In essence, individual level attribution theory is applied to the institutional level of analysis. This approach differs from the earlier use of the concept, distancing the news institution from paradigm violators rather than working to show how the violators' actions were clear anomalies. In addition, social actors outside of journalism—the victims and the audience—were equally blamed for the outcome.

"'These Crowded Circumstances': When Pack Journalists Bash Pack Journalism" applies paradigm repair to understanding pack journalism as another kind of paradigm violation. Pack journalism appears as a paradigm violation because its roaming band of reporters ultimately becomes part of the story itself through the public attention it receives. This is especially so for "what-a-story" coverage, a really big story handled through "emergency-routine" work. Russell Frank argues that the "objectivity violation" aspect of paradigm repair research gets replaced in the journalistic lore by new concerns for "minimizing harm" and "accountability." In contrast to previous studies, Frank suggests that pack journalism paradigm repair separates a single news organization from the pack by writing critically about the pack's actions (but nonetheless running with the pack in its coverage). The notion of "boundary-work rhetoric" explains how reporting on pack journalism becomes a means of creating these separations. Drawing again on the case of Princess Diana's death, Frank presents boundary work as an element of "distanced reflexivity," where a journalist writes about the work of journalists as if he or she were not part of the pack. Through a textual analysis of 14 news situations, Frank shows how paradigm repair turns into criticism of the journalistic pack while also separating the "higher" form of print journalism from the more visible, technology-driven broadcast journalists.

"Israeli Image Repair: Recasting the Deviant Actor to Retell the Story" offers an extension of paradigm repair, demonstrating how journalists engage in "culture repair" when an occurrence departs from the expected narrative of the cultural norm. Specifically, this study examines what happens when a terrorist is also a member of the culture that he attacks, drawing on case studies of Arab and Jewish terrorists within Israel. From a starting position of "objectivity repair," Robert L. Handley turns to the concept of "cultural repair work" by the media, which he argues is a hegemonic effort to "reinforce a society's prevailing ideology." Unlike objectivity repair through the editorial pages, culture repair appears in the news pages, recasting deviating actors into their proper roles and overlooking conflicting details so that the stereotypical character rings true. Through a textual analysis of nine news stories, Handley shows how journalistic narratives relocated an Israeli Arab as a West Bank Palestinian. Within this process, national ties of the journalist and ties of the journalist's country to the site of terrorism (in this case, Israel) may lead to different forms of image repair, demonstrating how it is politically and culturally bound.

"A Paradigm in Process: What the Scapegoating of Vusi Mona Signalled About South African Journalism" serves as a reminder of the differences among press systems and their political contexts. Here, Guy Berger presents a case where the journalistic paradigm is unsettled and uncertain, in relation to a South African journalist who violated conventional ethical boundaries. As the author explains, the paradigm was not damaged but instead "imagined collective subscription" to the paradigm required confirmation. Like authors who have coined news terms such as paradigm boosterism and paradigm adjustment, Berger suggests that this case study represents "paradigm status reinforcement." The journalism paradigm in South Africa is portrayed as in flux, without a stable model of journalism that can be repaired or maintained by consensus, so that paradigm management becomes difficult. Through this conceptual framework, Berger offers three "Paradigm Challenges" that illustrate the framework's utility for understanding the specific South

African context and—more broadly—other press systems that are undergoing fundamental change.

In all, the readings in Part IV suggest that journalism tends toward norms for professional behavior and content. Occasionally situations arise where journalists' actions and expectations do not coincide, calling the culture of the profession and the society into question. When this happens, journalists, media organizations, the media institution, and even the media audience work to reconfirm what becomes accepted as a conventional norm. This phenomenon has been envisioned as a professional paradigm—a shared way of seeing and interpreting the meanings of journalism and news.

12

The Princess and the Paparazzi

Blame, Responsibility, and the Media's Role in the Death of Diana

Elizabeth Blanks Hindman

Late in the evening of 30 August 1997, Diana, Princess of Wales, and her new boyfriend, Dodi Fayed, left a Paris hotel. As their car drove through the Paris streets it was chased by about six photographers on motorcycles.[1] Driver Henri Paul lost control and the car crashed in a tunnel, killing Paul and Fayed instantly and leaving Diana and her bodyguard severely injured.[2] Diana was taken to a hospital, where she died several hours later, early on 31 August. Within hours people on both sides of the Atlantic were blaming the photographers—called "paparazzi"—and the media as a whole for the crash and for the culture of celebrity coverage that led to it. Diana's brother, Earl Spencer, was widely quoted on 31 August as saying, "I always believed the press would kill her in the end. But not even I could imagine that they would take such a direct hand in her death as seems to be the case. . . . It would appear that every proprietor and editor of every publication that has paid for intrusive and exploitative photographs of her, encouraging greedy and ruthless individuals to risk everything in pursuit of Diana's image, has blood on his hands today."[3]

Within a few days it became clear that Paul had been drunk and speeding at up to 120 miles per hour. Nevertheless, the role of the media in the crash, both directly and indirectly, provoked significant discussion of media responsibility.[4] Criticism centered on the actual crash and role of the chasing photographers as well as on the role of the media as an institution in providing, or maintaining, a culture of celebrity. The case provides a rare opportunity for examining what the news media said about media responsibility. While much commentary came in bylined columns or from identifiable individuals on broadcast media, this research focuses on institutional "views" as demonstrated in unsigned newspaper editorials. The purpose here is to explore how, in the face of enormous criticism, mainstream media explained the media's role in and responsibility for the death of Princess Diana. Specifically, this case study applies literature on attribution theory and paradigm repair in a qualitative analysis of newspaper editorials. It concludes that mainstream newspapers attempted to restore the news paradigm in two key ways. First, they isolated themselves from the paparazzi and supermarket-style tabloids, rhetorically distancing themselves from "those" media, then attributing responsibility for the crash to characteristics of the tabloids that the mainstream did not share. Second, having brought Diana and the audience into the news process by suggesting that both were active participants in defining news, they separated themselves from the "poor" decisions made by Diana and the audience. In these ways the newspapers were able to absolve themselves of responsibility for the crash and act as agents of paradigm repair. Conversely, a few acknowledged fundamental flaws in the routines of journalism, and through attribution of responsibility contradicted the concept of paradigm repair.

This case study uses attribution theory both to expand and counter the growing body of work on the repair of the news paradigm. Research on paradigm repair provides the underpinnings and a rationale for why mainstream newspapers felt the need to distance themselves from supermarket tabloids and paparazzi following Diana's death.

Paradigm Repair

Bennett, Gressett, and Haltorn[5] used the term "paradigm repair" to explain how journalists distance themselves from other journalists or media organizations who fail to uphold journalistic routines and values—like objectivity—and consequently call into question the very foundations of those values. Drawing on Kuhn's ideas,[6] Bennett, Gressett, and Haltom define paradigm as "a set of broadly shared assumptions about how to gather and interpret information relevant to a particular sphere of activity. . . . When a group acquires near universal faith in the validity of a system representing and applying information, that system attains paradigmatic status."[7] In simpler terms, then, a paradigm is a culturally shared vision of "the way things are" that mightily resists challenge, either from external or internal sources.

A number of writers have applied the paradigm concept to journalism, using the rich literature on journalistic routines.[8] The "routines" studies differ in their purposes and approaches, but offer similar descriptions of methods journalists use to gather and formulate news, methods that present certain sources and information as factual and unbiased while limiting discussion of public issues. For example, Breed explores how news organizations socialize new reporters and teach them the unwritten rules of news definition and writing through a system of reward and punishment. Tuchman notes that journalists create the semblance of objectivity through a "strategic ritual" of presenting opposing points of view and using direct quotations; Gans observes that definitions of news focus primarily on the perspectives of public officials and what they see as important; Gitlin explains how mainstream media eliminate political perspectives beyond those of established political parties; and both Eliasoph and Hindman found that journalists for alternative, or oppositional, media follow routines similar to those of mainstream journalists.[9] The ultimate result of these studies is a description of the news paradigm, in which discussion of public issues is limited to mainstream topics and points of view, information from public officials is presented as authoritative, and the presentation and definition of news itself is seen as biased neither by the individual journalist nor by the very system of news creation. Journalists, and indeed most of American society, are trained to understand what constitutes news, both in topic and format, and to dismiss attempts to challenge those definitions.

Nonetheless, challenges do emerge, and when that occurs, the news media face a dilemma. When a "problem" story or situation arises—a man sets himself on fire only after the television news crew arrives,[10] for example, or a former writer for the *Wall Street Journal* announces he is a socialist and that while employed by the *Journal* he also wrote for radical publications[11]—journalists must either redefine the paradigm or explain the problem as inconsistent with the paradigm (an "anomaly"). Evidence shows they choose the latter. In the first case, the particular news crew was faulted for "making" the news rather than reporting it (the man would not have immolated himself without the crew's presence); in the second case the *Wall Street Journal* and others quickly explained how the socialist reporter and his newspaper followed "proper" conventions of reporting and editing, regardless of the reporter's political beliefs. What was not acknowledged in media responses to either case, because it would have challenged the paradigm, is that many events ("pseudo-events," to use Boorstin's term[12]) exist only because of journalists' presence, and that all journalists have some kind of ideological bias; indeed, the entire structure of news creation is biased on an ideological level. Nevertheless, these very public variances from the perceived norms of journalism must be confronted, dissociated, and dismissed through the process of paradigm repair, which Berkowitz explains as an effort "to restore faith in the paradigm of objectivity by isolating the people or organizations that stray from the rest of the news media institution."[13]

Paradigm repair is effected in a number of ways, each of which ultimately involves excluding the errant individual or organization. One way, Hackett explains, is for the media to reassert their objectivity: "It is as if television states that 'we' (the nation, the public, consumers, television journalists) are nonideological; 'we' represent good, sound common sense. The problem is with 'them' out there . . . who are ideologically motivated, or who have allowed their narrow interests to override the public welfare."[14] Reese suggests that repair can follow a number of strategies, including "(a) disengaging and distancing these threatening values from the wayward reporter's work, (b) reasserting the ability of journalistic routines to prevent threatening values from 'distorting' the news, and (c) marginalizing the man and his message, making both appear ineffectual."[15] As both Berkowitz and Bennett, Gressett, and Haltom note, repair often comes in the form of post-hoc clarification: "Editorial commentary will be devoted to those stories that have been flagged as examples of bad journalism. The standard repair work at this level will be to point out that the offending story would not have developed if proper reporting methods had been observed. . . ."[16]

The death of the Princess of Wales after her car was chased by media representatives provides a clear example of the journalistic paradigm in need of redefinition or repair. Certainly her death would not have come that evening had the paparazzi not been present. The paparazzi at least indirectly violated one of the unwritten rules of the news paradigm: journalists don't kill people or have a direct hand in their deaths. Applying the concepts of paradigm repair and what-a-story to coverage of Diana's death, Berkowitz suggests that the mainstream media engaged in "paradigm boosterism"—in which the mainstream concluded that they, unlike the supermarket tabloids, did not make the news; instead they "mirror[ed] the world's occurrences."[17] Bishop, who examined broadcast and print news coverage of the first week after the incident, found that the mainstream media concluded that "the paparazzi were responsible for Princess Diana's death" and "mainstream journalists do not engage in the kind of behavior engaged in by the paparazzi and by tabloid newspapers."[18] The paparazzi shook—but did not dislodge—the paradigm through their active, harmful involvement in an event that would not have occurred without their presence. Mainstream media sustained the paradigm throughout the next few weeks by attempting to distance themselves from the paparazzi and supermarket tabloids.

Attribution Theory

While the concepts of paradigm, paradigm repair, and paradigm boosterism are cultural in origin and give a reason for *why* the mainstream reacted the way they did, attribution theory, an individual-level theory first used in psychology, offers insight into *how* the mainstream media went about the job of repair. Attribution theory is concerned primarily with how individuals assess causality for actions, how they "understand, predict, and control the world around them."[19] It is useful here, as a way of analyzing mainstream newspapers, because individual editorials—the "voice" of the newspaper—are the unit of analysis.

Attribution theory "describes the principles people follow in making judgments about the causes of events, others' behavior, and their own behavior."[20] Weiner notes that people are likely to explain why some thing happened "when an outcome is unexpected . . . and when desires have not been fulfilled."[21] Oskamp, summarizing basic assumptions of attribution theory, maintains that individuals use attribution both to explain why something occurred and to make inferences about the characteristics of the person or group acting. Specifically, "people first observe another person's actions and the effects of those actions, then use that information to infer the person's intentions, and finally make attributions about the person's traits or dispositions on the basis of the inferred intentions. This is called the theory of correspondent inferences because the perceiver is trying to form an inference that the person's behavior and the intentions that led to it correspond to an underlying, stable personality characteristic."[22]

One key element of attribution theory particularly relevant here is the concept of internal versus external attribution. First described by Heider in the late 1950s, internal attribution occurs when people attribute the causes of actions to internal, controllable, characteristics of the actor, while external attribution involves attributing the causes of actions to situations external to—and likely uncontrollable by—the actor.[23] These hold true whether the attributor is observing his or her own actions or those of others. Several researchers have found that individuals tend to attribute their own actions to external factors and the actions of others to internal characteristics, a phenomenon known as "the fundamental attribution error."[24] In situations in which an observer sees undesirable behavior or outcomes, fundamental attribution error leads to blaming the victim or the actor for negative consequences of the action.[25] Ross and DiTecco suggest that "an observer wants to assign blame to the innocent victim of an accident . . . because a chance (external) attribution would imply that a misfortune of similar magnitude could occur to anyone, including the observer."[26] Similarly, blaming the actor's internal characteristics for negative consequences enables observers to distance them selves from the situation.

Others, however, suggest that this applies primarily in situations in which the attributor is an observer witnessing the actions of others; when a negative behavior or an outcome is caused by (or happening to) the attributor, he or she will usually attribute the cause to external forces.[27] Finally, when observers are attempting to assign causality for a negative outcome, the degree of similarity the observers see between themselves and the actor also influences the attribution. Specifically, "identification or perceived similarity with the harmdoer reduces blaming responses by observers."[28] The more the observer sees him- or herself as like the actor/harmdoer, the less likely he or she is to attribute the harm to characteristics internal to the actor.

Attribution theory has been used to explain rape victim blame,[29] people's images of Arabs during the Gulf War,[30] opinions of people with voluntary versus involuntary disabilities,[31] and various publics' reactions to the O.J. Simpson murder case.[32] Like the coverage of the O.J. Simpson trial, the death of the Princess of Wales led to a significant amount of editorializing on the responsibility—and negative role—of the media in the situation. Attribution theory is applied here as a framework for analysis of mainstream newspaper editorials' discussion of the media's possible role as a cause of Diana's death, with focus on the following key concepts:

- Actors (those directly involved in a situation) tend to attribute negative outcomes or behavior to external, and therefore uncontrollable, characteristics or situations.
- Actors (those directly involved in a situation) tend to attribute positive outcomes or behavior to internal, controllable characteristics.
- When observers (those not directly involved in a situation) perceive themselves as similar to an actor, they are more

likely to attribute negative outcomes or behavior to external, and therefore uncontrollable, characteristics or situations.

- When observers (those not directly involved in a situation) perceive themselves as different from an actor, they are more likely to attribute negative outcomes or behavior to internal characteristics or actors or situations controllable by actors.

Attribution theory provides a means of exploring how the mainstream media approached the task of repairing the news paradigm. Beginning with the assumption that Diana's death was a negative outcome—a tragedy—this study considers this question: How did mainstream newspapers explain the news media's role in and responsibility for the death of Diana, Princess of Wales?

Method

Mainstream newspapers' unsigned editorials provide the official viewpoint of an individual newspaper, and it can be argued that those editorials get as close as is possible to being an institutional voice of each newspaper. Additionally, as the "individual" voice of a newspaper,[33] editorials provide a logical means of applying the individual-oriented attribution theory described above. Most organizations at one time or another publicly present their organizational or corporate view on an issue or event. For newspapers, this appears in an unsigned editorial. Hynds notes that by the middle of the twentieth century newspaper editorials had become "institutionalized"[34] and that most daily newspapers devote at least one page each day to editorials and related items.[35] His survey found that editors largely agreed that the editorial page "should provide a forum for the exchange of information and opinion and should provide community leadership through institutional stands on issues."[36] Editorials are also often a source of paradigm repair, as Berkowitz[37] and Bennett, Gressett, and Haltom[38] explain. Unsigned mainstream newspaper editorials, then, were determined to be a good source for institutional views of the mainstream press.

A search was conducted of the Lexis-Nexis database for editorials on the Princess of Wales published between 31 August 1997, when she died, and 30 September 1997, when consensus was that the driver's drunkenness—and not the pursuit by photographers—was the primary cause of the accident. Though not every U.S. newspaper is included in the database, the vast majority of daily, general audience newspapers are available. Initially, four searches were conducted, each using one of Lexis-Nexis' regional listings of newspapers (Northeast, Southeast, Midwest, and Western) and involving 366 total titles, most of which are general interest dailies. Obvious "niche publications" (Texas Construction, for example, or New Mexico Jewish Link) were excluded. Then, searches of each regional listing were conducted using the terms "Princess" and "Diana." Those searches yielded well over 3,000 total articles (many were duplicate wire service stories and columns), which were examined individually to determine which were unsigned editorials from general interest daily newspapers. Ultimately, the search yielded 77 editorials in mainstream newspapers, 62 of which discussed the media's role in either Diana's death itself or coverage of her death. The majority—35—of the editorials were published within three days of the accident, with nine on Monday, 1 September, four on 2 September, and 22 on 3 September.[39] Clearly, the weight of the discussion of the media's role in Diana's death came within a week of the accident, which is not-surprising, given that by 3 September it had become clear that driver Henri Paul was legally drunk and speeding.

Once appropriate editorials were determined, they were analyzed using what Altheide[40] calls "ethnographic content analysis," which involves approaching texts (in this case the editorials) systematically, but with an openness to themes that might surface from the analysis. This inductive method contrasts with deductive content analysis, which organizes texts into previously determined categories. The advantage to using the inductive method here is that, as Patton explains, "core meanings" can be found in the emerging patterns and themes.[41] Themes, Altheide writes, are "the recurring typical theses that run through"[42] the texts under study. Themes, however, are dependent in part on the way in which the topic is framed, the "parameter . . . [that focuses] on what will be discussed, how it will be discussed, and above all, how it will not be discussed."[43] Editorials gave the newspapers "permission" to state their opinions, and the concepts of paradigm repair and attribution theory provided a starting point for examination of themes; the themes came from the discussion within the editorials.

The 62 editorials first were read for a sense of the overall tone and an understanding of the issues involved. Then they were read again as specific themes, keywords, and concepts began to emerge; those early themes were placed into general categories related to attribution theory, specifically those concepts related to actor, outsider, internal attribution, and external attribution. Unusual arguments were noted, even when they did not fit overall emerging themes. Finally, once the themes were determined, a final reading allowed fine-tuning and ultimate placement of statements into the various thematic categories.

Results

Discussion surrounding the media's role in Diana's death fell into three categories. In the first two—attributing blame to photographers and supermarket tabloids[44] and to nonmedia outsiders—the mainstream newspapers generally represented themselves as observers in no way connected with the photographers' actions. Here, the mainstream distanced themselves and attributed blame to "those other" participants as anomalies in the news process. In the third—justification of or acknowledgment of mainstream actions and coverage—the newspapers saw themselves as part of the controversy, but offered mixed explanations for how it could have occurred. This third category indicates a desire both to repair the paradigm and to acknowledge its shortcomings.

The Paparazzi. On 1 September, the day after Diana's death, the *Ft. Lauderdale Sun-Sentinel*[45] defined "paparazzi" for a potentially confused public: "That Italian word," the *Sun-Sentinel* wrote, "means a swarm of stinging, biting insects or of freelance photographers aggressively pursuing celebrities." Other descriptions of the paparazzi and their actions included "outrageous,"[46] "relentless,"[47] obnoxious,"[48] and "cruel."[49] A number of newspapers used wildlife metaphors to describe the photographers, including "hounding,"[50] "jackals,"[51] "birds of prey,"[52] "bottom-feeders,"[53] "reptilian,"[54] and "wolf pack.[55] "According to the *St. Louis Post-Dispatch,*[56] the "feeding frenzy" had worsened as Diana's relationship to Fayed became public. Two newspapers used yet another wildlife image to separate themselves from the paparazzi: The *Hartford Courant*[57] argued that the paparazzi were "vultures troll[ing] on the fringes of journalism," while the *New York Daily News*[58] suggested that they "confirm the worst stereotypes of the media: vultures who will do anything to make money." What remained unsaid—but implied—was that the vultures differed dramatically from the mainstream.

In addition, the mainstream newspapers offered specific criticisms of the photographers' actions the night of the crash. One week after Diana's death, despite evidence of drunken driving and excessive speed, the Chapel Hill *Herald* refused to absolve the paparazzi. The driver was drunk, the *Herald* admitted, "but the plain fact remains that the chase would not have occurred without the pursuing flock of photographers seeking a jackpot of a snapshot."[59] Three days later, the *New York Daily News* agreed: [A] pack of slavering stalkarazzi were at the center of the fatal chase."[60] Others were slightly more charitable, acknowledging other factors in the crash. As early as 1 September, the *Denver Post* suggested that "it is too easy to blame . . . the predatory paparazzi."[61] The next day more newspapers agreed, one saying, "The role of the paparazzi is still unclear."[62] Others wrote that there was "ample blame to go around"[63] and that it was "premature to draw any cosmic conclusions."[61] These statements were typical, as many newspapers used internal attribution to lay fault with the paparazzi while acknowledging that the paparazzi could not have controlled the reckless driving that contributed to the crash. Clearly, though, the mainstream presented the paparazzi as unlike themselves, and possessing negative characteristics that had at a minimum contributed to—if they did not outright cause—Diana's death.

The Tabloids. Similarly, the mainstream distanced themselves from the supermarket tabloid-style newspapers, through general condemnation—"checkbook journalism . . . tabloid sleaze"[65]—and by a call for tabloids to repudiate the paparazzi—"It is time for those tabloid editors to disavow 'stalker-razzi' bounty hunters who go beyond the bounds of decency."[66] In an accidental irony, one newspaper wrote, "Editors can simply refuse to buy or relay material that goes beyond the bounds of decent intrusion,"[67] apparently distinguishing tabloid intrusion from the "decent" intrusion by the mainstream. Other newspapers used the language of ethics to call for change. The "senseless, needless Diana tragedy," one wrote, "will shame" the tabloids and their readers.[68] And the Greensboro *News & Record* clearly placed the discussion into the realm of ethics, when it wrote, "Punishing the paparazzi may make others think twice. But until the publishers develop some moral fiber, it will be open season on celebrities."[69] This statement in particular demonstrated the mainstream's belief that the tabloids' internal characteristic (lack of moral fiber) led indirectly to the chase.

Several editorials singled out certain tabloids for condemnation, especially the *National Enquirer,* which refused to buy death-scene photos, but had bought paparazzi photos before and thus contributed to the crash itself by providing a market for the photos. In condemning the tabloids, none of the mainstream newspapers admitted to publishing celebrity photos. Instead, their focus was on the tabloids' "unorthodox" newsgathering techniques and news definitions. One highly unusual editorial, however, broke with the rest of the mainstream's attempt to separate themselves from the tabloids. On 3 September, CBS Evening News anchor Dan Rather and two reporters had discussed the role of the supermarket tabloids, and concluded that Rupert Murdoch—"media mogul of tabloid sleaze"[70]—was ultimately responsible for Diana's death. The *Augusta Chronicle* was outraged. "Let's get this straight," it wrote. "The CBS gang is fingering Murdoch as the personification of evil in tabloid journalism." The *Chronicle* then observed that Murdoch's Fox TV network was in fact competing for network television audiences. "Might that have anything to do with CBS' ridiculous slam?" asked the *Chronicle*, which then equated CBS with Murdoch himself: "They call that 'news'? It's the ugliest kind of tabloid journalism." The *Chronicle* was not taking blame itself or for the mainstream in general, and therefore its attribution here can still be seen as that of an observer. Nonetheless, this provides a rare example of mainstream criticism of another mainstream media organization. With that one exception, however, the mainstream editorials focused on paparazzi and supermarket tabloids, making it clear that "they" were anomalies, responsible for the crash.

"Two-Way Exploitation"—Blaming Outsiders. The newspapers also condemned Diana herself, celebrities in general, and Henri Paul. While earlier research on paradigm repair focuses on media responses to errant media organizations or individuals, evidence here suggests that paradigm repair extends to all parties in the news process, in this case the subjects and the audience. Recall that paradigm repair is the process journalists use to distance themselves from failures of journalistic routines and to re-establish the supposedly immutable nature of those routines. In this case, the mainstream newspapers used attribution to perform a delicate dance, claiming outsiders (subjects and audiences) were part of the newsmaking process while simultaneously distancing themselves from those outsiders when they failed to uphold the news paradigm.

The newspapers articulated mixed feelings about Diana and her relationship with the press. Her public life had begun with her engagement and marriage to Prince Charles in 1981, described then as a fairy tale come true. A number of the newspapers recalled that image at her death, but added that the fairy tale had "imploded."[71] Hers was a "Cinderella's story in reverse"[72] that "didn't end with 'And she lived happily ever after.'"[73] To others she was a tragic figure[74] about whom "the ancient Greeks could not have written a sadder script."[75] Yet she was blamed because she was a Cinderella who used media for her own purposes. She used the "double-edged sword of media attention"[76] to outmaneuver her husband in the court of public opinion.[77] She was a "master of manipulating the media to her advantage."[78] She begged for privacy, some editorials noted, while feeding tidbits to the press. "Her pleas for privacy, for herself and her two young sons were heart-rending," wrote the *Commercial Appeal*. "But they were sometimes difficult to square with her frequent appearances on the covers of such magazines as People and Vanity Fair—coverage with which she often cooperated."[79] The *Wisconsin State Journal* more forcefully suggested that "Diana herself shared some responsibility for her untimely death" because she had given the paparazzi and other media what they needed in a "two parts parasitic, one part symbiotic" relationship.[80] The blame continued in the *Chicago Tribune,* which also suggested that Diana had a role in her own death: "No one understood the uses of the press better than Diana herself. . . . her celebrity was carefully cultivated and adroitly used."[81] On the other hand, the *Tribune* and others appreciated that she used her celebrity status to gain coverage for AIDS and humanitarian causes in Bosnia and Angola, and to campaign against land mines.[82] In each case she was clearly cast as an active part of the news process, but one who that night failed to uphold "her" part.

Celebrities. The mainstream newspapers were very clear in their assessment of Diana as someone who knew how to use the media to her advantage—an "internal characteristic" they then used to blame her for the paparazzi's presence that night in Paris. Other celebrities were similarly criticized for their love-hate relationship with the media and for using the media to further their careers while complaining about the coverage. The *Columbus Dispatch*, for example, suggested that celebrities often bring ovcr-the-line media coverage on themselves, through "as siduously court[ing] publicity when it suits their purposes."[83] The *Daily News* of Los Angeles asserted that "[celebrities'] status and hunger for fame . . . drive this whole system of frantic photography by pursuing hordes of cameramen."[84] Shortly after the crash, actors George Clooney, Alec Baldwin, and Tom Cruise all held press conferences to complain about tabloids and paparazzi. None of these actors, the *Providence Journal-Bulletin* noted, "as far as we know, has expressed remorse about his professional success or stratospheric wealth."[85] In this editorial, at least, celebrities were most certainly seen as active participants in the news process and held accountable for the actions of the media.

Others gave celebrities a bit more room. Just because they are famous because of media coverage, suggested one, they do not give up their rights not to be stalked or harassed, particularly in private situations.[86] The *Commercial Appeal* neatly summarized this perspective in a clear example of external attribution: "The curse of celebrity is that it finally cannot be controlled by those who achieve it."[87] To these newspapers, then, Diana and other celebrities are not to blame for media coverage.[88]

The Driver. Not surprisingly, driver Henri Paul received heavy criticism. By 3 September, Paris officials had reported Paul's blood alcohol level at .187 percent, almost four times the legal limit in France, and that he had been speeding at at least 100 miles per hour. Most who discussed Paul acknowledged the paparazzi's role in the chase but maintained that Paul's choice to drive drunk and too fast contributed at least equally to the crash. He "showed appalling judgment,"[89] and was "foolish."[90] Some newspapers used external attribution to cast Paul as a key element in the news process, for he was "taunting the media pack,"[91] saying, as the *Asheville Citizen-Times* put it, "catch me if you can."[92] For most, however, the crash resulted from a combination of chasing paparazzi, a drunken driver, and excessive speed, all of which were presented as controllable—and thus internal—characteristics of those involved.

The Public. Though Diana and Henri Paul were the only individuals blamed by name, the newspapers said the public at large also played a significant role in Diana's death. As with descriptions of the paparazzi, metaphors abounded in the descriptions of the public, this time in terms of food: "The public fed its obsession" with Diana through the photographs; readers' "appetite for news" of her led them to "gobble up" stories about her;[93] the Diana phenomenon was "voraciously consumed,"[94] and the public's "hunger"[95] and "unquenchable thirst"[96] for her were "insatiable."[97] Others described the public and culture at large as "celebrity-crazed"[98] and sardonically noted a certain hypocrisy: "[W]ho among us now expressing revulsion at the paparazzi's tactics," editorialized New York *Newsday,* "closed their eyes to the sunnier images of a scantily clad Diana yachting through the Mediterranean with her beau? And who will shun the special 'Diana' editions that will now proliferate as fast as publishers can bring them to market?"[99] Finally, some bluntly laid blame for her death squarely with her fans. The *Atlanta Constitution* said: "This week, many of Diana's loyal fans will be weeping for their tragic heroine, but if they had not purchased the papers that exploited in the first place, she might not be dead."[100] In each of these cases the newspapers concluded that the public bore at least some responsibility for Diana's death, which then lessened the responsibility of the paparazzi, the tabloids, and the media as a whole.

Of course, the public received its information from the media, so in blaming Diana's fans the newspapers created a dilemma for themselves. They solved it primarily by justifying the coverage based on the wishes of the market, and returning blame to the consumers. The audience was a crucial element in the news process, the editorials emphasized, and the audience's taste for nontraditional news led to Diana's death. At least the solution was simple: The audiences should simply stop buying. "The best check on tabloid journalism . . ." wrote the *Commercial Appeal,* "[is] the discipline of the marketplace. . . . If [the] audience were to disappear, if readers worldwide were to show their revulsion by refusing to patronize trash tabloids and their broadcast equivalents, the paparazzi and other scandal-sheet purveyors would be out of work tomorrow."[101] "[C]onsumers can refuse to fuel the frenzy with their dollars," the *Denver Post* agreed.[102] "People . . . should stop supporting the tabloid press and watching tabloid television programs," noted the *Hartford Courant.*[103] The *San Francisco Chronicle* suggested that audiences were responsible for, and could control, content: "The most effective and independent enforcers of taste are readers, who deliver their judgments at the news-stand."[104] A few repudiated this idea and acknowledged the difficulties of expecting audiences and the market to define media behavior. The *Daily News* of Los Angeles described the interconnections between celebrities, freelance photographers, the media, and the audiences as a tragic circle. Once the cycle of publicity and exposure gets started, those who try to benefit from it and to control it may be shocked to discover that it can't be turned off like a switch."[105] This view was not typical, however. The majority of the discussions of the audience's role and the marketplace used those as excuses—distancing the tabloids, and indeed all media—from blame for Diana's death. In these examples, the failure was not the media's but the audience's. Once the audience mended its ways, the news process would be restored.

Discussion of the outsiders—Diana, celebrities, the driver, and the audience—generally offered evidence of the media's attempt at paradigm repair. As explained earlier, the concept of paradigm repair has been applied to journalists distancing themselves from other journalists. Here, the mainstream press performed a two-step procedure: First, the newspapers had to define Diana and the others as key factors in the news process so that they could be blamed for failing to act in the "right" way. If Diana and the others were not seen as part of the process, actively in control, the newspapers would not be able to blame them for the failure of that process. Second, once the group was re-cast as insiders they immediately had to be defined as anomalies, else the very foundations of news routines would be shaken.

"Respectable Journalists" and "We Are All Accountable"—The Role of the Mainstream Media. The third major theme to arise from the editorials concerned the mainstream media themselves. While paparazzi were more directly involved with Diana's death, all news media came under criticism in the days following the crash. In response, some editorials very specifically distanced themselves from the paparazzi and supermarket tabloids; some acknowledged similarities among the various types of media; and a few accepted responsibility themselves.

Most vociferous were the newspapers separating themselves from the paparazzi and tabloids. These newspapers saw a clear difference between mainstream media and those more directly responsible for Diana's death. They distinguished themselves carefully, explaining that "legitimate journalism recognizes and respects the difference between public officials' and famous people's public conduct and their right to privacy";[106] "Respectable journalists don't chase their prey on motor scooters";[107] and "There is a line that a publication of character does not cross."[108] The *Chicago Tribune* attempted to draw that line specifically, in a classic example of paradigm repair: "Serious newspapers and other serious media. . . . are recorders and reporters of events, not manufacturers of them."[109] A few newspapers made specific commitments designed to separate themselves further from the paparazzi. For example, the *Indianapolis Star* wrote, "The Star and Nexus don't trespass, we don't stalk celebrities, and we don't purchase pictures from people who do."[110] The *New York Daily News* took a similar stance, and called on other media to follow: "By refusing to publish unauthorized photos of Diana's children, The News aims to help eliminate the financial incentive for taking them. We do it in the name of decency. But only if the rest of the media does the same will the era of the stalking paparazzi finally be finished."[111] These newspapers, by implication, could control themselves through their inherent decency, unlike the supermarket tabloids. This attribution, describing characteristics that separate the mainstream from tabloid, demonstrates the editorials' attempt to repair the news paradigm through isolating the tabloids.

Some of the newspapers were particularly worried about potential backlash—either through legal means or public opinion—against all news media. The Ft. Lauderdale *Sun-Sentinel,* which perhaps was more sensitive than other mainstream newspapers because of its proximity to the headquarters of the *National Enquirer,* wrote, "First of all, there is no such thing as 'the press.' . . . 'The press' didn't kill Diana, but a few irresponsible, unprofessional and morally bankrupt photographers might have contributed to her death. If illegal acts occurred, then arrest, prosecute and severely punish those responsible."[112] The *Detroit News* agreed, writing, "the paparazzi can be a pretty disgusting lot, [but] they shouldn't become an excuse for muzzling a free press."[113] And they had legitimate cause for concern. By the day after Diana's death there were already calls for legislation to limit press invasions of privacy, and by the middle of the month at least two state legislators (in California[114] and Connecticut[115]) and one member of Congress had introduced, or were considering introducing, legislation to curb media access to celebrities. To the general calls for stricter laws, the newspapers replied, first, that France already had the strictest privacy laws in Europe but that none had been violated,[116] and second, that in the United States existing trespass, stalking, and harassment laws provided enough protection to celebrities and ordinary citizens.[117]

Several made a public's-right-to-know argument, noting that one of the costs of maintaining a free press is a loss of privacy. The *Detroit News,* for example, wrote, "[W]here do you draw the line and still protect the right of the public to have the information necessary to make informed judgments about people and policies that affect their lives, particularly people who so actively court publicity?"[118] And *The New York Times* reacted forcefully to proposals by California State Sen. Tom Hayden (the ex-husband of actress Jane Fonda) and U.S. Rep. Sonny Bono (himself a celebrity) to increase privacy rights at the expense of press freedom. "[I]t would be a grave loss for the United States," editorialized the *Times,* "with its freer and more vital journalism, to mark this sad death with a rush to bad, unnecessary and potentially unconstitutional legislation. . . . [T]here is simply no way to draft a statute to prevent picture-taking in public places without resorting to the language and methods of censorship."[119] The *Chicago Tribune,* too, defended the press against Rep. Bono's "Protection from Personal intrusion Bill," which would have punished "persistently" following someone when that individual had a "reasonable expectation of privacy." This might include, the *Tribune* noted, "an ambush interview on CNN, CBS's '60 Minutes,' NBC's 'Dateline' or ABC's 'Nightline.'"[120] The implication, of course, was that interviews on those mainstream networks are valuable and worth protecting, while perhaps interviews or photos from non-mainstream media were not.

Accepting Responsibility. A few newspapers acknowledged that the line separating mainstream media from the supermarket tabloids was blurry, and consequently set themselves up to share responsibility. Evidence from these editorials counters the claim that when confronted with a failure of news routines media will attempt to rationalize that failure as an anomaly. Here, a small number of mainstream newspapers admitted the paradigm's faults, rather than defending it through attributing blame elsewhere.

When Diana's relationship with Dodi Fayed became public during the summer of 1997, noted the *News & Record,* mainstream media had covered the story, "justif[ying its] 'news value' by reporting that the London tabloids were having a feeding frenzy over Di and Dodi. Either way, readers got the same story and pictures."[121] The same editorial—and others, as well—expressed outrage at video and photos of Diana's sons taken in the days following her death. In particular, video of Prince William and Prince Harry in a car on their way to church the morning after the crash provoked wrath. The paparazzi were there, shooting photos, but "so were mainstream photographers. Pictures of the two boys, their faces pale and drawn, appeared on network television shows and in *The New York Times* and other prominent newspapers." Other newspapers agreed. The *Baltimore Sun* also condemned the day-after photos of William and Harry, and noted that if the crash had not happened, "photos of Di and Dodi in that car would have wound up even in respectable publications."[122] The consensus among a small number of the newspapers was that the difference between "respectable publications" and supermarket tabloids was minimal. The *Wall Street Journal* said: "It is remarkable to see a professional mind-set that studiously reports the sins of the tabloids and paparazzi, even as it shoves its own sump pumps deep into the life of Lady Diana and runs the open hoses onto the nation's living room floors."[123]

Finally, a few newspapers accepted blame, either for the mainstream media at large or for themselves. Typically this was accompanied by a call to action, as when the *New York Daily News* promised not to buy or publish unauthorized photos of Prince William and Prince Harry, and concluded that "the media have an obligation to exercise self-discipline."[124] Similarly, the *Columbus Dispatch* challenged "editors at news papers and magazines and in television to exhibit a conscience."[125] The *Baltimore Sun* wrote simply, "[W]e are all accountable,"[126] and the *Sun-Sentinel* called for "a return to some old-fashioned personal virtues . . . like restraint, professionalism, human decency and adherence to the Golden Rule."[127] But only the *Denver Post* took direct responsibility, saying, "Today we collectively hang our heads and promise to do better. We here at The Post know of our own contribution. . . ."[128] As other newspapers had done with the tabloids, these newspapers saw internal characteristics of the media as contributing to Diana's death. The difference, of course, was here it was their own characteristics, rather than those distinctive to the tabloids, which had led ultimately to the crash. These newspapers saw themselves as not so different from the paparazzi and supermarket tabloids; thus, they admitted the responsibility they felt for the crash and media coverage that contributed to it. From them came the rare acknowledgment that, in fact, the routines of journalism had contributed to the tragedy.

Conclusion

The study of sixty-two newspaper editorials published within a month of Princess Diana's death found three general themes related to paradigm repair. First, the mainstream press distanced themselves from, and then blamed, the paparazzi who chased her car the night of her death, as well as from the supermarket tabloids that typically purchased pictures from those photographers. Second, the mainstream shifted blame to those outside the media, in particular Diana herself, her driver, and the public at large, each of whom was blamed in some way for the crash. Third, some of the mainstream newspapers acknowledged their similarities to the supermarket tabloids and consequently accepted some responsibility for their part in the general culture of celebrity that indirectly led to Diana's death.

Internal attribution appeared frequently in the editorials, and helped explain how the newspapers expedited paradigm repair. As noted earlier, paradigm repair focuses on perceived failures of journalistic routines, failures that are seen as potentially calling into question the very basis for journalistic values like objectivity and definitions of news. When an individual journalist or media organization fails to uphold those routines or values, other journalists must either redefine the worth of those values (which they seldom do) or exorcise the offending party. Internal attribution concludes that people attribute causes of actions to the internal, controllable, characteristics of the actor, at least when there is a negative outcome to the action. In this case, the innate characteristics of the paparazzi (they are vultures) and the supermarket tabloids (they are greedy, and willing to pay huge sums for photos) "caused" the crash. In short, to bring about paradigm repair the mainstream newspapers concluded that because these characteristics are controllable, the paparazzi and tabloids could have prevented Diana's death by acting differently. The editorials used internal attribution in these cases to argue that they—the mainstream—are not like the "bottom-feeders" of journalism.

The editorials also offered an opportunity to expand the concept of paradigm repair, for some newspapers included the failures of the subjects (Diana, celebrities, and the driver) and the public in their attempt to restore credibility to the news process. The newspapers faced a challenge in dealing with the subjects and the public, for they simultaneously claimed them as part of the newsmaking process and as outsiders to that process. Diana and other celebrities are responsible for media coverage of themselves, the explanation went, using internal attribution, because they know how to use the media to their advantage; they are an active part of the news process. In this way the newspapers expanded the realm in which paradigm repair is affected and were able to free themselves of blame. Once Diana was cast as an active newsmaker responsible for definitions of news, in a classic blame-the-victim move the newspapers defined Diana as an anomaly—outside acceptable news processes—when she failed to uphold her part, by inviting publicity and therefore "causing" the paparazzi to follow her. Similarly, the newspapers brought the public into the fold as active participant in creating news, and then used external attribution to distance themselves from the results of the public's demands.

Relatively few editorials accepted blame, even generally. Those that did used internal attribution: they said that characteristics that are shared by all news institutions led at least indirectly to Diana's death. All of the newspapers that did accept blame, either for the media at large or themselves specifically, recognized that journalistic routines had led to terrible consequences and called for a change in the media's method. These newspapers can be seen as acknowledging, at least in a limited way, inherent problems in the news paradigm.

The findings in this case study are similar to an earlier study of the media's views of the media's role in the O.J. Simpson case.[129] That study found that the mainstream press distinguished itself from the supermarket tabloids and then accused them of irresponsible behavior, and that the mainstream shifted blame to Simpson, others involved in his case, and the public at large. Those themes certainly repeated themselves in the present case.

This case study is limited in part because it combines literature from two very different approaches to media research (a cultural concept and a psychological concept), and it is an examination of only one case. In addition, because no newspaper published more than two editorials on the media's role in the crash, patterns within newspaper organizations cannot be determined. Finally, only unsigned editorials were examined here; by excluding signed opinion pieces by editors, ombudsmen, or other news personnel the study may have neglected other sources that would shed light on the ways mainstream news media attempted paradigm repair. Nevertheless, it builds on a large body of literature that has attempted to explain how news routines are maintained and repaired. As this and earlier studies found, in major cases involving challenges to news routines, the mainstream press tends to distance itself as much as possible from blame and to defend its methods of doing business. It does so much as most of us do, by defining negative characteristics of others as responsible for the negative outcome, or by concluding that external forces, out of the media's control, caused the problem.

Notes

1. By 3 September, six photographers and one motorcycle driver had been named as suspects in Diana's death, though at least one of those photographers denied being part of the chase.

2. The bodyguard survived.

3. Quoted in Jacqueline Sharkey, "The Diana Aftermath," *American Journalism Review* 19 (November 1997): 19.

4. For example, in the months following the crash both *American Journalism Review* and *Editor & Publisher* devoted significant space to examination of the media's role in the incident, and a Lexis-Nexis search of newspaper editorial content (not news stories) for the month after her death using the terms "Diana" and "media" or "news" yielded 454 columns, 27 signed editorials, and 77 editorials. Refereed research on the incident has focused on the impact of Diana's death on popular culture as well as on the media. See, for example, Tony Walter, "From Cathedral to Supermarket: Mourning, Silence and Solidarity," *The Sociological Review* 49 (November 2001): 494–511; J. Mallory Wober, "A Feeding Frenzy, or Feeling Friendsy? Events After the Death of Diana, Princess of Wales," *Journal of Popular Culture* 34 (summer 2000):127–34; Dan Berkowitz, "Doing Double Duty: Paradigm Repair and the Princess Diana What-a-story," *Journalism* 1 (August 2000): 125–44.

5. W. Lance Bennett, Lynne A. Gressett, and William Haltom, "Repairing the News: A Case Study of the News Paradigm," *Journal of Communication* 35 (spring 1975): 50–68.

6. Thomas S. Kuhn, *The Structure of Scientific Revolutions* (Chicago: University of Chicago Press, 1962).

7. Bennett, Gressett, and Haltom, "Repairing the News," 54.

8. See, for example, Warren Breed, "Social Control in the News room," *Social Forces* 33 (May 1955): 326–35; Mark Fishman, *Manufacturing the News* (Austin: University of Texas Press, 1980); Herbert Gans, *Deciding What's News* (New York: Pantheon, 1979); Todd Gitlin, *The Whole World is Watching* (Berkeley: University of California Press, 1980); Harvey Molotch and Marilyn Lester, "News as Purposive Behavior: On the Strategic Use of Routine Events, Accidents, and Scandals," *American Sociological Review* 39 (February 1974): 101–112; Michael Schudson, *Discovering the News: A Social History of American Newspapers* (New York: Basic Books, 1978); Michael Schudson, "The Sociology of News Production," in *Social Meanings of News,* ed. Dan Berkowitz (Thousand Oaks, CA: Sage, 1997); Leon V. Sigal, *Reporters and Officials* (Lexington, MA: Lexington Books, 1973); Leon V. Sigal, "Sources Make the News," in *Reading the News,* ed. Robert

Karl Manoff and Michael Schudson (New York: Pantheon, 1987); John Soloski, "News Reporting and Professionalism: Some Constraints on the Reporting of News," *Media, Culture and Society* 11 (1989): 207–228; Gaye Tuchman, "Objectivity as Strategic Ritual: An Examination of Newsmen's Notions of Objectivity, "*American Journal of Sociology 77* (January 1972): 660–79; Gaye Tuchman, *Making News: A Study in the Construction of Reality* (New York: Free Press, 1976).

9. Nina Eliasoph, "Routines and the Making of Oppositional News," *Critical Studies in Mass Communication* 5 (December 1988): 313–34; Eliza beth Blanks Hindman, "'Spectacles of the Poor': Conventions of Alternative News," *Journalism & Mass Communication Quarterly* 75 (spring 1998): 177–93.

10. Bennett, Gressett, and Haltom, "Repairing the News."

11. Stephen D. Reese, "The News Paradigm and the Ideology of Objectivity: A Socialist at The Wall Street Journal," *Critical Studies in Mass Communication 7* (December 1990): 390–409.

12. Daniel J. Boorstin, *The Image* (New York: Atheneum, 1962).

13. Berkowitz, "Doing Double Duty," 126.

14. Robert A. Hackett, "Decline of a Paradigm? Bias and Objectivity in News Media Studies," *Critical Studies in Mass Communication* 1 (September 1984): 249.

15. Reese, "The News Paradigm and the Ideology of Objectivity," 400.

16. Bennett, Gressett, and Haltom, "Repairing the News," 52.

17. Berkowitz, "Doing Double Duty," 133.

18. Ronald Bishop, "From Behind the Walls: Boundary Work by News Organizations in their Coverage of Princess Diana's Death," *Journal of Communication Inquiry* 23 (January 1999): 94.

19. Stuart Oskamp, *Attitudes and Opinions,* 2d ed. (Englewood Cliffs, NJ: Prentice Hall, 1991), 34.

20. Karen Huffman, Mark Vernoy, and Barbara Williams, *Psychology in Action,* 2d ed. (New York: John Wiley and Sons), 549.

21. Bernard Weiner, "The Emotional Consequences of Causal Attributions," in *Affect and Cognition: the Seventeenth Annual Carnegie Symposium on Cognition,* ed. by Margaret Sydnor Clark and Susan T. Fiske. (Hillsdale, NJ: Lawrence Erlbaum, 1982), 185–86.

22. Oskamp, *Attitudes and Opinions,* 35.

23. Oskamp, *Attitudes and Opinions,* 34.

24. Huffman, Vernoy, and Williams, *Psychology in Action,* 551; Oskamp, *Attitudes and Opinions,* 43; Daniel Heradstveit and G. Matthew Bonham, "Attribution Theory and Arab Images of the Gulf War," *Political Psychology* 17 (June 1996): 274.

25. Huffman, Vernoy, and Williams, *Psychology in Action,* 551; Oskamp, *Attitudes and Opinions,* 43.

26. Michael Ross and Don DiTecco, "An Attributional Analysis of Moral Judgments," *Journal of Social Issues* 31 (summer 1975): 95.

27. Heradstveit and Bonham, "Attribution Theory and Arab Images of the Gulf War," 275.

28. Ross and DiTecco, "An Attributional Analysis of Moral Judgments," 97.

29. Norma B. Gray, Gloria J. Palileo, and G. David Johnson, "Explaining Rape Victim Blame: A Test of Attribution Theory," *Sociological Spectrum* 13 (October-December 1993): 378.

30. Heradstveit and Bonham, "Attribution Theory and Arab Images of the Gulf War."

31. Laurie Larwood, "Attributional Effects of Equal Employment Opportunity: Theory Development at the Intersection of EEO Policy and Management Practice," *Group and Organization Management* 20 (December 1995): 391.

32. Sandra Graham, Bernard Weiner, and Gail Sahar Zucker, "An Attributional Analysis of Punishment Goals and Public Reactions to O.J. Simpson," *Personality and Social Psychology Bulletin* 23 (April 1997): 331; Elizabeth Blanks Hindman, "'Lynch-Mob Journalism' vs. 'Compelling Human Drama': Editorial Responses to Coverage of the Pretrial Phase of the O.J. Simpson Case," *Journalism & Mass Communication Quarterly* 76 (autumn 1999): 499–515.

33. One scholar notes that newspapers use their editorials to "[perform] their basic function of maintaining a posture of constructive criticism of the social, political, economic, and sometimes even moral dilemmas of society." Harry W. Stonecipher, *Editorial and Persuasive Writing: Opinion Functions of the News Media,* 2d ed. (Maniaroneck, NY: Hastings House, 1990), 4.

34. Ernest C. Hynds, "Changes in Editorials: A Study of Three Newspapers, 1955–1985," *Journalism Quarterly* 67 (summer 1990): 302–312.

35. Ernest C. Hynds, "Editors at Most U.S. Dailies See Vital Roles for Editorial Page," *Journalism Quarterly* 71 (autumn 1994): 574.

36. Hynds, "Editors at Most U.S. Dailies," 575.

37. Berkowitz, "Doing Double Duty."

38. Bennett, Gressett, and Haltom "Repairing the News."

39. Additionally, three were published on 4 September, and four on 5 September. Six were published on Saturday, 6 September, the day of Diana's funeral, and three were published on Sunday, 7 September. Finally, three were published on 9 September; one each on 10 and 12 September; two on 14 September; and one each on 15, 16, 18, and 29 September.

40. David L. Altheide, *Qualitative Media Analysis* (Thousand Oaks, CA: Sage, 1996), 16.

41. Michael Quinn Patron, *Qualitative Research and Evaluation Methods,* 3d ed. (Thousand Oaks, CA: Sage, 2002), 453.

42. Altheide, *Qualitative Media Analysis,* 31.

43. Altheide, *Qualitative Media Analysis,* 31.

44. Here both "tabloids" and "supermarket tabloids" are used to describe a particular genre of newspaper, which largely focuses on celebrities and sensationalized news. These are distinguished from tabloid-format newspapers like the *Rocky Mountain News,* which are considered "mainstream."

45. "Death of 'People's Princess' Shines Spotlight on Privacy and Paparazzi," *Ft. Lauderdale Sun-Sentinel,* 1 September 1997, sec. A, p. 18.

46. "Circle of Tragedy: There's a Use-me, Use-you Relationship Between Celebrities and Photographers," *Daily News of Los Angeles,* 3 September 1997, sec. N, p. 14.

47. "Mourning a Lost Princess," *Indianapolis News,* 3 September 1997, sec. A, p. 10.

48. "Paparazzi and Freedom of the Press," *Tampa Tribune, 5* September 1997, p. 8.

49. "The People's Princess: Diana's Compassion Made the World Love Her," *San Diego Union-Tribune,* 1 September 1997, sec. B, p. 6.

50. "Princess Diana's Death," *Washington Post,* 1 September 1997, sec. A, p. 20; "A World Without Diana Will be Lean, and Not Only for Tabloids," 3 September 1997, *Greensboro* (*NC*) *News & Record,* sec. A, p. 11.

51. "The Victim of Jackals," *Miami Herald,* 1 September 1997, sec. A, p. 22; "Who is Responsible for Diana's Death?" *San Francisco Chronicle,* 3 September 1997, sec. A, p. 18.

52. "The Blame Game Grows," *Boston Herald,* 3 September 1997, p. 22.

53. "Her Death was Tragic, Her Life Often Inspiring," *Memphis Commercial Appeal,* 3 September 1997, sec. A, p. 8.

54. "Princess Di: Tabloid Stalkers Not Sole Culprits," *Cincinnati Enquirer,* 3 September 1997, sec. A, p. 6.

55. "Diana's Death—Many Causes of Tragedy," *Charleston Gazette,* 3 September 1997, sec. A, p. 4; "Dems Divided—and Conquered," *New York Daily* News, 10 September 1997, p. 32.

56. "Unhappily Ever After," *St. Louis Post-Dispatch,* 3 September 1997, sec. B, p. 6.

57. "A Shock Felt Around the World," *Hartford Courant,* 1 September 1997, sec. A, p. 12.

58. "The Grief and its Lessons," *New York Daily News,* 1 September 1997, sec. Special, p. 8.

59. "Tragedy Should Turn Media to Self-Regulation," *Chapel Hill (NC) Herald, 7* September 1997, p. 4.

60. "Dems Divided—and Conquered," *New York Daily News,* 10 September 1997, p. 32.

61. "Death of a Princess," *Denver Post,* 1 September 1997, sec. B, p. 11.

62. "The Tragedy of Diana; At the Mercy of Strangers," *Greensboro (NC) News & Record,* 2 September 1997, sec. A, p. 6.

63. "Many Share Fault for Diana's Fate," *Wisconsin Slate journal,* 2 September 1997, sec. A, p. 9.

64. "Princess Di: Tabloid Stalkers Not Sole Culprits," *Cincinnati Enquirer,* 3 September 1997, sec. A, p. 6.

65. "The People's Princess: Diana's Compassion Made the World Love Her," *San Diego Union-Tribune,* 1 September 1997, sec. B, p. 6.

66. "She was the Queen of People's Hearts," *Dallas Morning News,* 1 September 1997, sec. A, p. 34.

67. "Death of a Princess," *Denver Post,* 1 September 1997, sec. B, p. 11.

68. "Diana's Death—Many Causes of Tragedy," *Charleston Gazette,* 3 September 1997, sec. A, p. 4.

69. "The Tragedy of Diana; At the Mercy of Strangers," *Greensboro (NC) News & Record,* 2 September 1997, sec. A, p. 6.

70. "CBS Smears Murdoch," *Augusta (GA) Chronicle,* 14 September 1997, sec. A, p. 4, quoting Dan Rather.

71. "Death of a Princess," *Denver Post,* 1 September 1997, sec. B, p. 11.

72. "The Victim of Jackals," *Miami Herald,* 1 September 1997, sec. A, p. 22.

73. "Diana Truly Was Princess of the People," *Albuquerque Journal, 2* September 1997, sec. A, p. 8.

74. "Mourning a Lost Princess," *Indianapolis News,* 3 September 1997, sec. A, p. 10.

75. "Princess Diana," *Augusta (GA) Chronicle,* 3 September 1997, sec. A, p. 4.

76. "Grief for a Princess," *Raleigh (NC) News and Observer,* 3 September 1997, sec. A, p. 12.

77. "She was the Queen of People's Hearts," *Dallas Morning News,* 1 September 1997, sec. A, p. 34.

78. "The Tragedy of Diana; At the Mercy of Strangers," *Greensboro (N.C.) News & Record,* 2 September 1997, sec. A, p. 6.

79. "Her Death was Tragic, Her Life Often Inspiring," *Memphis Commercial Appeal,* 3 September 1997, sec. A, p. 8.

80. "Many Share Fault for Diana's Fate," *Wisconsin State Journal, 2* September 1997, sec. A, p. 9.

81. "The Princess, the Press, the Public," *Chicago Tribune,* 2 September 1997, p. 10.

82. "The Passing of a Princess," *St. Petersburg Times,* 2 September 1997, sec. A, p. 10.

83. "'Paparazzi' Where Should the Media Draw the Line?" *Columbus Dispatch,* 18 September 1997, sec. A, p. 12.

84. "Circle of Tragedy: There's a Use-me, Use-you Relationship Between Celebrities and Photographers," *Daily News of Los Angeles,* 3 September 1997, sec. N, p. 14.

85. "Two-Way Exploitation," *Providence Journal-Bulletin,* 5 September 1997, sec. B, p. 6.

86. "Privacy and the Press: Beyond Tabloids: Princess Diana's Death Gives Mainstream Media Cause for Reflection," *Baltimore Sun,* 6 September 1997, sec. A, p. 10.

87. "Her Death was Tragic, Her Life Often Inspiring," *Memphis Commercial Appeal,* 3 September 1997, sec. A, p. 8.

88. Within this study there was not a way to predict which newspapers would blame Diana and which would exonerate her.

89. "Many Share Fault for Diana's Fate," *Wisconsin State Journal, 2* September 1997, sec. A, p. 9.

90. "Paparazzi and Freedom of the Press," *Tampa Tribune,* 5 September 1997, p. 8.

91. "The Blame Game Grows," *Boston Herald,* 3 September 1997, p. 22.

92. "Our Fascination with Celebrity Sows Seeds of Tragedy," *Asheville (NC) Citizen-Times,* 3 September 1997, sec. A, p. 6.

93. "A World Without Diana Will be Lean, and Not Only for Tabloids," 3 September 1997, *Greensboro (NC) News & Record,* sec. A, p. 11.

94. "Crossing the Line," *Indianapolis Star,* 3 September 1997, sec. A, p. 14.

95. "Circle of Tragedy: There's a Use-me, Use-you Relationship Between Celebrities and Photographers," *Daily News of Los Angeles,* 3 September 1997, sec. N, p. 14.

96. "Deadly Pursuit: Paparazzi and the Public Need to Reexamine the Obsession with Celebrity Journalism," *New York Newsday,* 3 September 1997, sec. A, p. 38.

97. "Death of 'People's Princess' Shines Spotlight on Privacy and Paparazzi," *Ft. Lauderdale Sun-Sentinel,* 1 September 1997, sec. A, p. 18; "Unhappily Ever After," *St. Louis Post-Dispatch,* 3 September 1997, sec. B, p. 6.

98. "Circle of Tragedy: There's a Use-me, Use-you Relationship Between Celebrities and Photographers," *Daily News of Los Angeles,* 3 September 1997, sec. N, p. 14.

99. "Deadly Pursuit: Paparazzi and the Public Need to Reexamine the Obsession with Celebrity Journalism," *New York Newsday,* 3 September 1997, sec. A, p. 38.

100. "A Princess Loved to Death," *Atlanta Journal and Constitution,* 1 September 1997, sec. A, p. 18.

101. "Her Death was Tragic, Her Life Often Inspiring," *Memphis Commercial Appeal,* 3 September 1997, sec. A, p. 8.

102. "Death of a Princess," *Denver Post,* 1 September 1997, sec. B, p. 11.

103. "A Shock Felt Around the World," *Hartford Courant,* 1 September 1997, sec. A, p. 12.

104. "Who is Responsible for Diana's Death?" *San Francisco Chronicle,* 3 September 1997, sec. A, p. 18.

105. "Circle of Tragedy: There's a Use-me, Use-you Relationship Between Celebrities and Photographers," *Daily News of Los Angeles,* 3 September 1997, sec. N, p. 14.

106. "The Victim of Jackals," *Miami Herald,* 1 September 1997, sec. A, p. 22.

107. "Diana's Death—Many Causes of Tragedy," *Charleston Gazette,* 3 September 1997, sec. A, p. 4, quoting *The New York Times*' Walter Goodman.

108. "Crossing the Line," *Indianapolis Star,* 3 September 1997, sec. A, p. 14.

109. "The Princess, the Press, the Public," *Chicago Tribune,* 2 September 1997, p. 10.

110. "Crossing the Line," *Indianapolis Star,* 3 September 1997, sec. A, p. 14.

111. "Dems Divided—and Conquered," *New York Daily News,* 10 September 1997, p. 32.

112. "Death of 'People's Princess' Shines Spotlight on Privacy and Paparazzi," *Ft. Lauderdale Sun-Sentinel,* 1 September 1997, sec. A, p. 18.

113. "Princess Diana and the Press," *Detroit News,* 3 September 1997, sec. A, p. 10.

114. "Circle of Tragedy: There's a Use-me, Use-you Relationship Between Celebrities and Photographers," *Daily News of Los Angeles,* 3 September 1997, sec. N, p. 14.

115. "Stalking Laws: Leave Tough Enough Alone," *Hartford Courant,* 12 September 1997, sec. A, p. 20.

116. "The Passing of a Princess," *St. Petersburg Times, 2* September 1997, sec. A, p. 10.

117. "Princess Diana and the Press," *Detroit News,* 3 September 1997, sec. A, p. 10; "Crossing the Line," *Indianapolis Star,* 3 September 1997, sec. A, p. 14; "Privacy and the Press: Beyond Tabloids: Princess Diana's Death Gives Mainstream Media Cause for Reflection," *Baltimore Sun,* 6 September 1997, sec. A, p. 10.

118. "Princess Diana and the Press," *Detroit News,* 3 September 1997, sec. A, p. 10.

119. "A Sad Death, a Bad Law," *New York Times,* 15 September 1997, sec. A, p. 22.

120. "A Tangled Leash on Paparazzi," *Chicago Tribune,* 29 September 1997, p. 10.

121. "A World Without Diana Will be Lean, and Not Only for Tabloids," 3 September 1997, *Greensboro (NC) News & Record,* sec. A, p. 11.

122. "Privacy and the Press: Beyond Tabloids: Princess Diana's Death Gives Mainstream Media Cause for Reflection," *Baltimore Sun,* 6 September 1997, sec. A, p. 10.

123. "From O.J. to Diana," *Wall Street Journal,* 3 September 1997, sec. A, p. 20.

124. "Dems Divided—and Conquered," *New York Daily News,* 10 September 1997, p. 32.

125. "'Paparazzi' Where Should the Media Draw the Line?" *Columbus Dispatch,* 18 September 1997, sec. A, p. 12.

126. "Privacy and the Press: Beyond Tabloids: Princess Diana's Death Gives Mainstream Media Cause for Reflection," *Baltimore Sun,* 6 September 1997, sec. A, p. 10.

127. "Death of 'People's Princess' Shines Spotlight on Privacy and Paparazzi," *Ft. Lauderdale Sun-Sentinel,* 1 September 1997, sec. A, p. 18.

128. "Death of a Princess," *Denver Post,* 1 September 1997, sec. B, p. 11.

129. Hindman, "Lynch-Mob Journalism."

Source: From "The Princess and the Paparazzi: Blame, Responsibility, and the Media's Role in the Death of Diana," 2003, by E. Blanks Hindman, *Journalism & Mass Communication Quarterly, 80*(3), 666–688. Reprinted by permission of AEJMC.

13

"These Crowded Circumstances"

When Pack Journalists Bash Pack Journalism

Russell Frank

Nobody likes pack journalism—not the reporters who are members of the pack, not the objects of the pack's attention and not the readers who deplore the pack's intrusiveness and obtrusiveness even as they stay with the coverage. To distance themselves from the pack, reporters have hit upon the curious rhetorical strategy of writing about it as if they were not a part of it. A sampling of the headlines on some of the stories to be analyzed in this article will give some idea of the kind of media bashing that has become a routine component of the coverage of any occurrence that draws a crowd of journalists:

- Jasper, Texas, on the eve of the trial of the men accused in the 1998 dragging death of James Byrd, Jr:

  'Circus' Has Come Back to Town; Media Invasion Boosts Jasper Business, But Many Residents Eager for Horde to Go (Stewart, 1999)

- Pendleton, New York, a month after the Oklahoma City bombing:

  'Sick of Being Interviewed'; Notoriety, Media Invasion Unite McVeigh's Hometown (Brady, 1995)

- Charlottesville, Virginia, after babies switched at birth had been restored to their biological parents:

  Families Struggle with Private Matter—and Glare of Media Spotlight (Shear, 1998).

- Valmeyer, Illinois, the day after a gunman killed two police officers at the U.S. Capitol:

  Hometown of a Shooting Suspect Copes with a Media Frenzy (Arterburn, 1998)

- Carlisle, Iowa, awaiting the birth of the McCaughey septuplets:

  The Talk of this Small Town is Privacy; Carlisle Fends off Media Frenzy to Protect a Family Expecting Septuplets (Von Sternberg, 1997)

- Springfield, Oregon, a day after the shooting spree at Thurston High School: Backlash to Media Mob:

  'You Have No Sympathy' (Postman, 1998)
- Washington, D.C., as Paula Jones arrives at President Clinton's deposition:

  Media Circus in Full Roar as the 'Lion' Faces 'Lamb' *(Boston Herald,* 1998)

This study excerpts these and several other newspaper stories in which the news media's presence is highlighted, and analyzes them as 'strategic rituals' (Tuchman, 1972) aimed at maintaining the culture of journalism in the face of public disaffection with intrusive reporting and excessive coverage. Following Schudson's (2001) discussion of the emergence of objectivity as a moral norm of American journalism, the analysis treats what will be referred to as reflexive media criticism as a manifestation of two other moral norms articulated in the 1996 iteration of the Code of Ethics of the Society of Professional Journalists: 'Minimize Harm' and 'Be Accountable'. Whether pejorative depictions of pack journalism should be regarded as a genuine move toward greater accountability or mere lip service is debatable. Either way, reflexive media criticism constitutes significant evidence that an occupational culture with a reputation for ignoring external criticism has begun to recognize that its image is in need of repair.

This article builds on recent studies of paradigm repair and boundary-work rhetoric but parts company with them in one important respect: instead of treating reflexive media criticism as a form of objectivity paradigm repair, it proposes that reporters who write about the depredations of the pack are straying from the objectivity paradigm altogether. Objectivity demands that reporters stay out of the story. Reflexive media criticism implicitly acknowledges that journalists' comportment and, indeed, their very presence affects both the people they write about and the way their audiences experience and assess the magnitude of an event. It suggests that they have become at least as worried about their perceived lack of sensitivity as they have been about their perceived lack of objectivity.

Reflexive media criticism differs from past journalistic practice in three significant ways. First, observations and quotes about press behavior are being included in the 'scene pieces' that have become a standard component of the what-a-story package (Wizda, 1997), instead of in sidebars specifically devoted to media performance or in 'post mortem' commentary. Second, instead of quoting other journalists or journalists-turned-scholars, the reporters are furnishing critiques of press behavior obtained from the subjects of the news coverage and from the neighbors and townspeople who are watching the journalists go about their business. Third, instead of distancing themselves from tabloid journalists or other pseudo-journalists whose work is intended more to entertain than inform, print reporters are distancing themselves from fellow journalists who work in television.

The first section of this article will be a review of terms: what-a-story, pack journalism, paradigm repair, boundary-work rhetoric and reflexivity. The second section outlines the data-gathering strategy. The third offers a rhetorical analysis of two sets of examples of stories that call attention to the intrusive presence of journalists at the scene of a what-a-story—one that criticizes journalists in general and the other that singles out the television journalists for special opprobrium. The conclusion suggests that these self-critiques are signs that journalists are struggling, perhaps clumsily, to address public disapproval of the way they operate.

Background

The What-a-Story

Tuchman coined the term 'what-a-story' in 1973 to signify an event so consequential, dramatic or unusual that news organizations practically drop everything to cover it. Tuchman was interested in one of the fundamental paradoxes of newswork: the routinization of extraordinary events. Though inelegant, the term 'what-a-story' has gained currency among scholars interested in the sociology of newswork (see, for example,

Bennett et al., 1985; Vincent et al., 1997; Berkowitz, 1997, 2000; Bishop, 1999), in part, one suspects, because of its emic origins in the newsroom itself. Reporters and editors are apt to exclaim, 'What a story!' when the enormity of the event in question hits them. (They have not, however, adopted Tuchman's clunky compound noun.) A dizzying number of events have been accorded the what-a-story treatment in recent years but, as Berkowitz (1997) notes, communications scholars have been slow to analyze them: scholars (unlike the journalists they study) are more interested in the typical than in the anomalous.

Tuchman's (1978) initial study of the what-a-story phenomenon focuses on how an individual news organization responds to a big, breaking news event. 'For newspapers', Berkowitz (1997: 364) writes, 'the organizational level of analysis seems adequate, because most cities have only one major newspaper'. Competitive pressures come into play when the subject of study is television news, says Berkowitz, but he too is mostly concerned with how one television station manages the coverage of a what-a-story. The what-a-story is not, by nature, a local story, however. When the big story breaks, print and broadcast editors throughout the region, if not the state and country, shift into what-a-story mode. Indeed, in a later study of the coverage of the death of Princess Diana, Berkowitz (2000) notes that reporters highlighted the magnitude of the story by specifically mentioning the amount of time, space or personnel other media were devoting to it. The what-a-story, in short, goes hand in hand with pack journalism.

Pack Journalism

It is an article of faith that the public is better served by a multitude of journalistic versions of events than by one. The competition is supposed to keep everyone on their toes in a way that pool reporting might not. Yet, the term 'pack journalism' is pejorative. 'Everybody denounces pack journalism, including the men who form the pack', Timothy Crouse (1972: 8) pointed out in *The Boys on the Bus*. 'Any self-respecting journalist would sooner endorse incest than come out in favor of pack journalism.'

Crouse's focus, of course, is on 'the men who form the pack' of reporters who trailed after the presidential candidates in the 1972 election. In fact, though, the members of the press corps see themselves more as members of a docile herd than a slavering pack. The herd is the enemy of the scoop. What one member of the herd has, all will have. 'There were three thousand reporters in Washington' (for President Kennedy's funeral), Jimmy Breslin (1997: 466) recalled. 'I knew I could not perform the simplest act of reporting if I had to do it in these crowded circumstances.' Separate yourself from the herd, as Breslin did in writing his famous story about the man who dug the fallen president's grave, and you risk missing what everyone else has. Editors become nervous about printing what the other papers do not have and about not printing what the other papers do have.

The term 'pack journalism' better fits the public perception of journalists when they descend en masse to cover a big story. In the story excerpts to be examined in this article, news-workers come across less as docile sheep than as aggressive wolves or dogs, running over anyone or anything that gets in their way, ready, seemingly, to tear their quarry to pieces.

One solution to the dilemma of herd journalism that also addresses public distaste for pack journalism is for reporters to distance themselves from the crowd journalistically rather than physically; that is to write about the pack or herd as if they were not a part of it. Such a strategy, nicely facilitated by the third-person rhetoric of objectivity, enables them to acknowledge that the news media have become part of the story without violating professional taboos against becoming part of the story themselves. Instead of protesting their involvement directly, they use exasperated sources as mouthpieces to condemn, and, therefore, distance themselves from, the boorish behavior of their colleagues. Instead of demonstrating that 'while individuals might have strayed, the institution itself has remained intact', as Berkowitz (2000: 129) would have it, the message is that the institution might have strayed but *this* newspaper or, at least, this individual has remained intact (ethically speaking).

Paradigm Repair

Cecil (2002: 47) defines paradigm repair as 'the process of reasserting objectivity as the core of journalists' ideology when that ideology itself has been challenged by the critics of "unobjective" journalists'. Cecil's discussion of objectivity, like those of Hackett (1984) and Berkowitz (2000), is predicated on a narrow view of objectivity as absence of bias or opinion. Repairing the objectivity paradigm is a matter of reassuring the public that a given breach of the norms of unbiased, neutral reporting was an aberration and that the norms remain intact.

In his case study of news coverage of the death of Princess Diana, Berkowitz (2000) argues that the role of the paparazzi in the crash made the press part of the story, thus compromising press objectivity (how do you write objectively about yourself?)—unless the mainstream press took pains to distance itself from the paparazzi and the tabloids. That, of course, is what the mainstream press did: those were not 'our' photographers who chased Diana and Dodi Fayed through the streets of Paris.

Berkowitz's argument is reasonable as far as it goes but the reason the objectivity paradigm repair was not altogether successful is that it did not address a larger critique of press behavior. The photographers on motorcycles may have been paparazzi that rainy night but the mainstream press could scarcely claim to be innocent of an insatiable appetite for news of the 'fairytale princess'. That demand intensified competition, which only fueled the paparazzi's zeal. The real problem confronting the mainstream press in the aftermath of Diana's death was not damage to its reputation for objectivity but heightened public concern about press insensitivity and invasion of privacy.

In this regard, it is worth looking at the differences between the 1987 and 1996 versions of the Code of Ethics of the Society of Professional Journalists (SPJ): the section on 'Fair Play' has been replaced by expanded sections on 'minimizing harm' and accountability in the latest version of the code. The words 'compassion' and 'sensitivity' appear for the first time. The section on 'Accuracy and Objectivity' has been renamed 'Seek Truth and Report It'. The word 'objectivity' no longer appears.

'Too often', then-SPJ president Steve Geimann (1996) wrote in accounting for the 'Minimize Harm' section, 'we've seen colleagues abuse the privacy of innocent people who find themselves in the center of a media storm through no fault of their own. We have to remember that individuals who don't seek the limelight retain their rights'. Geimann did not explain why the concept of objectivity was dropped from the code.

Knowlton (1997; see also Mindich, 1998) suggests that the change reflects how hopelessly problematized the concept of objectivity became under the onslaught of postmodern critiques of what Streckfuss (1990) refers to as 'scientific naturalism'. By the time the new code of ethics was written, sociological studies of journalism had made strong cases for the 'constructedness' of the news: each story is a product of a set of decisions about what to cover and how to cover it that reflects the values and work routines of the people making the decisions. Similarities among multiple accounts of the same occurrence say more about the shared culture of journalism than about the 'objectivity' of the accounts themselves.

The objectivity paradigm may also have created some image problems for journalism. Reporters' detachment can come across as disengagement or indifference. Proponents of public or civic journalism said that instead of just writing about a community's problems, journalists needed to help find solutions. Instead of just covering the sound bites and the photo opportunities and contrasting the image presented by a politician with past actions, statements and voting records—'gotcha' journalism—they should be finding out what the public thinks the issues are and then making the politicians address those issues. As stakeholders in the communities they serve, journalists should convene forums, set the agenda, serve as the liaison between the citizens and the politicians. The movement toward civic or public journalism is a move away from the objectivity paradigm and toward a more activist role for the press (see Fallows, 1996: 260–7).

The other image problem arising from the objectivity paradigm is the perception that reporters and photographers care more about their stories and photos than they do about the people who appear in those stories and photos. The 'just-the-facts' orientation of the objectivity paradigm makes journalists appear to lack compassion or to be oblivious to the potential harm caused by making the facts public.

In short, it is more than coincidence that the word 'objectivity' dropped out of the Code of Ethics at the same time provisions were added that call on journalists to show greater sensitivity toward and compassion for people who become embroiled in the news. This is not to suggest that the practice of journalism in the United States has shifted away from the objectivity paradigm. To the extent that objectivity encompasses the journalism community's 'conceptual . . . and methodological commitments' (Kuhn, 1962: 42), it remains the dominant model for reporting and writing the news. But if, in addition to a set of practices, objectivity is a norm—a set of 'morally potent prescriptions about what should be prevalent behavior' (Schudson, 2001: 151)—it seems reasonable to suggest, in light of mounting criticism of sensationalistic and intrusive coverage of tragedy and crime, that the injunctions to 'minimize harm' and 'be accountable' have also become journalistic norms.

The death of Princess Diana brought the crisis of press insensitivity and excess to a head. If we look at the what-a-stories mentioned by Bishop (1999) in his study of damage control in the wake of Diana's death—the O. J. Simpson trial, Richard Jewell and the Olympics bombing, the Oklahoma City bombing—and add a few more to the list—the Columbine High School massacre, the JonBenet Ramsey case, the dragging death of James Byrd Jr in Jasper, Texas, the Susan Smith story in South Carolina, TWA Flight 800, the death of John F. Kennedy Jr—we find that most of them involve violent crime, disaster or tragedy and, therefore, victims and survivors. Coverage of these stories will thus raise privacy issues, in particular, and sensitivity issues, in general (Steele and Scanlan, 1996).

Doubtless many reporters show compassion and sensitivity when they work alone. But put enough reporters in the same place at the same time and the sheer number of people asking questions, taking pictures and occupying physical space can overwhelm even the most accommodating sources (Kurtz, 1998). In a column about his paper's coverage of the school shooting in Springfield, Oregon, *Seattle Times* editor Michael Fancher (1998) discusses the decision to send columnist Jerry Large to Springfield to 'help readers connect to the experience of parents in Springfield'. Fancher describes Large as a writer 'with a "wise parental voice"'. But when he got to Springfield, Large wrote, 'I quickly realized. . . that I was just part of a horde'.

Boundary-Work Rhetoric

Winch (1997: 3) defines the term 'boundary-work rhetoric', which he borrows from the sociology of science, as 'the rhetorical strategy of one group wishing to distinguish itself from another'. Journalists engage in boundary-work rhetoric, according to Winch, when their 'cultural authority' has been undermined by a blurring of distinctions between what they do and the work of other mass communicators, including tabloid journalists. To the extent that paradigm repair entails journalists' making distinctions between work done according to professional norms and work that violates those norms, it becomes indistinguishable from boundary work. Indeed, the defenses of mainstream journalism following Princess Diana's death that Berkowitz (2000) calls paradigm repair, Bishop (1999) separates into a two-part process that began with boundary work and then shifted into paradigm repair. The boundary work entailed blaming the paparazzi and the tabloids for Diana's death.

Paradigm repair entailed acknowledging that the mainstream, too, had gone too far in its coverage of celebrities.

The focus of the two Diana studies on the mainstream's attempts to distinguish itself from the tabloids and the paparazzi can be seen as part of a larger effort to maintain clear distinctions between news and entertainment (Winch, 1997). But the what-a-stories collected for this article suggest that reporters are also trying to make distinctions between sensitive and insensitive journalists. In some of the stories, as we shall see, print reporters try to distance themselves from their colleagues in television (Berkowitz, 1997).

Reflexivity

Anthropologists Barbara Myerhoff and Jay Ruby (1982: 2) define reflexivity as 'the capacity of any system of signification to turn back upon itself, to make itself its own object by referring to itself . . . Reflexive knowledge, then, contains not only messages, but also information as to how it came into being, the process by which it was obtained'. Such 'navel-gazing' seems to run counter to journalistic norms of functioning as fly-on-the-wall observers who strive not to influence what they observe or become 'part of the story'.

In fact, though, the 'Be Accountable' section of the SPJ Code of Ethics calls on journalists to 'clarify and explain news coverage' to their audiences and 'expose' the 'unethical practices' of their colleagues. Clarifications and explanations may appear in corrections, ombudsman columns, editors' notes, editorials or even in the copy itself, as when a story about a sexual assault includes a boilerplate statement that the newspaper does not print the names of the victims of such crimes. Exposés of the unethical behavior of other journalists tend to appear in trade magazines, in academic journals and occasionally in newspapers, either in columns or stories by in-house media beat writers like Howard Kurtz at *The Washington Post,* Jacques Steinberg at *The New York Times* or David Shaw at the *Los Angeles Times* (Berkowitz, 2000). What-a-story coverage frequently includes a story that evaluates the news coverage as it unfolds. At *The New York Times,* for example, the what-a-story package typically includes a story-about-the-story or meta-story labeled 'The Media', which examines both print and broadcast coverage, or 'Critic's Notebook', which narrows the focus to television news. Where once journalists discussed press performance 'backstage' among themselves (Zelizer, 1993), now, says Bishop (1999), such introspective discussions are taking place publicly, as part of the news coverage itself.

These writings, though distanced in the sense that the writers are not drawing attention to their own behavior, might also be considered reflexive to the degree that they make explicit the ethical norms of the profession and make the profession of journalism itself the subject of inquiry (Winch, 1997: 23). This study is concerned with the sort of reflexivity practiced by reporters whose scene-setting coverage of a big, non-routine news story includes mention of the intrusive presence of their fellow news-workers. This kind of reporting might also be considered distanced in the sense that it does not explicitly examine the reporter's own role or presence: it refers to the media 'horde' or 'frenzy' or 'circus' as if the reporter were not part of it. It differs from other kinds of media criticism and 'self-examination narratives' (Bishop, 1999) in one striking way: the sources of press criticism are not other professional journalists or academics but the people whose lives are affected by the news media presence—including the reporters themselves. Zelizer (1997) and Bishop (2001) have observed that most news media criticism comes from members or former members of the news media. The stories to be examined here suggest that reporters have begun to allow critical voices outside the profession to be heard.

The Stories

Search Strategy

The following discussion rests on two sets of LEXIS-NEXIS searches. The first set of searches was for the terms 'media horde', 'media frenzy', 'media invasion', 'media onslaught', 'media assault', 'media circus', 'media swarm' and 'media mob'. The presence of any of these terms in a story would indicate that (a) we have entered the realm of the what-a-story and (b) the media presence has reached a critical mass that has made it 'part of the story'.

Not surprisingly, each search returned hundreds of documents for the five-year period beginning in January 1995 and ending in December 1999. The searches for 'media frenzy' and 'media circus' each returned more than 1000 stories for the same period. Narrowing the search to one year's worth of stories (1999) got the numbers down to a more manageable data set (457 'media frenzy' stories and 438 'media circus' stories). But some of these stories had more to do with the phenomenon of what Kurtz (1998) calls the 'mediathon'—saturation coverage of, say, the Clinton–Lewinsky scandal—than with the concentration of news-workers at a location where a what-a-story has taken place.

Totals for the other searches ranged from 110 stories with 'media invasion' to 139 with 'media swarm', 201 with 'media assault', 352 with 'media onslaught', 402 with 'media mob', on up to 925 with 'media horde'. Many more of these stories specifically addressed the news media presence at a what-a-story site. The recurrence of the terms 'television trucks' or 'TV trucks' in these stories led me to look for them specifically. This search turned up 366 stories over the same five-year period.

The use of LEXIS-NEXIS searches requires several cautionary notes. First, the raw numbers were compromised by the inclusion of stories that were entertainment- or sports-related: the Super Bowl also draws a media horde. Second, searches for stories from American newspapers about events in American places are problematized by the inclusion of international English-language newspapers and the gathering of news media personnel in foreign lands. Third, no search for a given theme can be exhaustive because there can be endless linguistic variation on the theme. A search for 'media horde', for example, will not retrieve a story with the phrase 'a horde of media types'. Fourth, even if the search results were exhaustive, they could not tell us what percentage of the total number of what-a-stories include commentary about the media presence and there is no simple or accurate way to obtain that total. And fifth, when a motif recurs across a range of stories, any set of temporal parameters is going to be arbitrary: why five years? Why those five years?

Despite all these limitations, the searches accomplished two purposes. First, the raw numbers appear to be large enough to confirm, at least to this researcher's satisfaction, the preliminary impression that reflexive media criticism has become a recurrent theme in what-a-story coverage. Second, they generated a body of specific instances of the phenomenon upon which to base the rest of this discussion. Ultimately, the discussion was narrowed to 14 stories in which the media presence is discussed at some length, often with quotes from sources.

All 14 are scene pieces, that is stories that give readers a sense of how residents of a suddenly newsworthy place are reacting to the news. All but three are crime-related. The ones that are not concern unusual births: octuplets in Houston, septuplets in Iowa and switched babies in Virginia. Of the crime stories, two are about the hometowns of suspected criminals—Oklahoma City bomber Timothy McVeigh and Russell 'Rusty' Weston Jr, accused of killing two police officers at the U.S. Capitol in 1998. Two are connected to trials of notorious cases—the dragging death of James Byrd Jr in Jasper, Texas and Unabomber Ted Kaczynski in Lincoln, Montana. Four are the scenes of school shootings: two in Springfield, Oregon, one in Jonesboro, Arkansas, and one in Littleton, Colorado. One is on the occasion of the razing of O. J. Simpson's house in Los Angeles and one is from continuing coverage of the JonBenet Ramsey case in Boulder, Colorado.

'We're All So Sick of Being Interviewed'

In this first set of examples of distanced reflexivity, reporters are fairly evenhanded in calling attention to the intrusive presence of print and broadcast news-workers. Typically, the reporters quote people who express their weariness of the media spotlight: 'We're all so sick of being interviewed,' a resident of Oklahoma City bomber Timothy McVeigh's hometown of Pendleton, New York, told a *USA TODAY* reporter. 'You can't go to church or the country store without having a microphone shoved in your face' (Brady, 1995).

In Carlisle, Iowa, a *Minneapolis Star Tribune* reporter interviewed a waitress about the

> gabbling horde of journalists awaiting the birth of the McCaughey septuplets. The waitress angrily swiped the laminated counter and explained why the media invasion wasn't going over well. 'This is something new for us—Carlisle is just not used to this kind of attention,' she said. 'Never has been'. No, she had absolutely no interest in seeing her name in print. (Von Sternberg, 1997)

In a story on the JonBenet Ramsey case, the *Atlanta Journal Constitution* quotes a Boulder, Colorado, resident:

> Standing across from more than 100 reporters and a cluster of TV satellite trucks Thursday, Phil Robertson expressed his disgust that the case remains such a draw. 'I think it's absurd,' said the 65-year-old Boulder resident. 'I wonder how many journalists are over in Pakistan. That's a real story.' (Croft and Schneider, 1999)

A *Baltimore Sun* reporter was among the journalists who converged on Lincoln, Montana, on the eve of the trial of Unabomber suspect Ted Kaczynski: 'With Kaczynski's arrest came an onslaught of reporters, television trucks and photographers. "I must say, it was very annoying," said Dyan Walker, manager of the Lost Woodsman Gallery and Café' (Banisky, 1997).

One common strategy for conveying public disdain for the media presence is to quote people expressing their wish that the media people depart. Reporting on the crowd of onlookers and newsworkers who had gathered to watch the demolition of O. J. Simpson's house, a *Los Angeles Times* reporter quoted an angry neighbor: 'I think the news crews should get away from here and go report on Lewinsky' (Martin, 1998).

In Charlottesville, Virginia, a *Washington Post* reporter wrote about a switched baby story that had made national headlines:

> Despite the new 'No Trespassing' sign in her front yard, reporters still camp out on Johnson's lawn, and photographers still pester her for 'just one more picture' of daughter Callie Marie Johnson. . . .
>
> 'My life, they feel like it's public property,' Johnson said of the journalists, agents and even her neighbors. 'Everything I do. Everything I say. I am sick of this. I want my life back.' (Shear, 1998)

Needless to say, there is something rather odd about interviewing someone who says she is sick of being interviewed. Eventually, of course, the news crews do take their leave—a sure sign that the what-a-story coverage is winding down. Reporting from Jonesboro, Arkansas, in the wake of a school shooting, *New York Times* reporter Rick Bragg (1998) wrote: 'Many of the television crews and print reporters made plans to leave tonight, and the glare of attention, while it will throb in this city of 50,000 for some time, finally began to ease. People here were grateful for that.'

A *Seattle Times* reporter seems to make himself the brunt of Springfield, Oregon's, disgust with the 'media mob that was interfering with the grieving' following the shootings at Thurston High School. The story quotes a city councilman:

> 'You have no compassion, no sympathy,' he lectured a reporter. 'This is our community. We'll deal with it. You're not here to help with the problem. You don't offer anything.' (Postman, 1998)

Usually 'a reporter' is newspaper code for the reporter whose byline is on the story.

The story goes on to note that 'people are sick of the repetitive and sometimes inexplicable questions' and that reporters had resorted to 'deceit and trickery' to get into local hospitals that were caring for shooting victims. It quotes a sign on the school fence blaming the media for making school shooters famous and tells of adults shielding students from 'aggressive' reporters and of students pushing through the TV crews. In what appears to be an indirect quote from a grief counselor, the reporter declares that the healing process 'has been perverted by the media crush'. Perhaps what we are seeing here is what Bishop (2001: 23) calls a 'ritual sacrifice, performed in the hope that it persuades the audience to regain its faith in journalism'. In the end, though, a defender of the media is given the last word. '"To me, this was everyone saying let's not blame it on Kip," said Mandee Axtell, 15, who helped rip down the anti-media sign on the fence. "But it is his fault"' (Postman, 1998).

Tom R. Arterburn (1998) of the *Christian Science Monitor* takes a different approach in reporting on the town of Valmeyer, Illinois, home of Russell 'Rusty' Weston Jr, who killed two police officers at the U.S. Capitol in 1998. Arterburn distances himself from the 'herd of reporters' by letting them do his work for him. They ask the questions. He hangs in the background as if he were an observer of reporters rather than a reporter himself:

> 'How does the fact that this suspect hails from your hometown make you feel?' asks a correspondent for *The Miami Herald,* one of the first reporters to trace Mr. Weston to Valmeyer. . . .
>
> 'What did you think when you heard it was one of your neighbors who did this?' asks a *Los Angeles Times* reporter. . . .
>
> And so it went throughout the day: Citizens of Anytown, USA, cutting their lawns, cleaning their garages and watching big-city strangers wearing designer shades and beepers emerge from satellite trucks, news vans, and rental cars, looking for information on one of the town's own—one who kept to himself and never caused any obvious trouble, they say.

In distancing themselves from the pack and adopting the point of view of the intruded-upon rather than of the intruder, the reporters are assuming that readers' sympathies are with the 'Citizens of Anytown USA'. The assumption is warranted by recent surveys of public attitudes toward the news media. The American Society of Newspaper Editors' (ASNE) 1998 Journalism Credibility Project (Urban, 1998), for example, concluded that 'the public is demanding a serious re-examination of the energy and space spent on sensational national news'. While far fewer journalists agreed with the statement that 'journalists chase sensational stories because they think it will sell papers, not because they think it's important news'—46 percent of those surveyed compared to 85 percent of the public surveyed—ASNE concluded that many journalists agreed with their critics.

At the same time, as Kurtz (1998) noted about the public's response to stories like the O. J. Simpson case and the Monica Lewinsky scandal, 'the same public that complains about saturation coverage is devouring it in record numbers.' It may be that reporters who are ashamed to be part of the pack call attention to media intrusion to try to forge a bond with readers who are ashamed to be part of the audience. Alternatively, they may be hoping that if they goad readers into voicing their own complaints about what-a-story coverage their editors will see the light and back off.

'Meanwhile the Hungry Television Cameras Roam the Square'

Images of television trucks and jostling camera operators dominate television coverage of a what-a-story. At the end of President Clinton's impeachment saga, the *Atlanta Journal Constitution* (1999) ran a 'by-the-numbers' summary that included this statistic: 'Satellite television trucks parked at the federal courthouse for Lewinsky's first appearance before the grand jury: 22'. Such images present both a problem and an opportunity to print journalists. The problem is that all journalists tend to get lumped together, whether they work for the *National Enquirer* or the *Cincinnati Enquirer,* whether for a television station or a newspaper, so any negative attention further damages all journalists' already-tarnished reputations (Winch, 1997; Berkowitz, 2000). The opportunity is that the images lend themselves to image repair and boundary work. By calling attention to their colleagues' worst excesses, reporters can implicitly disapprove of and distance themselves from those excesses. By calling attention to the television trucks, print reporters can draw a boundary separating the intrusive TV people, with their trucks and cables and cameras, from the more discrete print reporters with their slim stenographers' notebooks and pocket tape recorders.

In a story headlined 'Terror in Littleton: The Media', a *New York Times* reporter notes that 'teary-eyed students had to step over tangles of cables that provided the power for television camera lights' to get to a makeshift memorial for classmates killed in the Columbine High School massacre (Sink, 1999).

Reporting from Jonesboro, Arkansas, in the aftermath of that school shooting, Rick Bragg (1998) writes:

> The first mass invasion of news media here has been an ugly one for so many people. Two television camera people cursed each other outside the county jail because one had gotten in the way of the other's shot.
>
> Today, Sheriff Haas told reporters, some from around the world, that his switchboard was flooded with complaints from people here. Television trucks block driveways and access roads. Some reporters have refused to leave doorsteps when people asked them to, or have been trespassing or offering money for stories.

On the eve of the trial of one of the men accused in the dragging death of James Byrd, a *Houston Chronicle* reporter described the scene in Jasper, Texas:

> Meanwhile the hungry television cameras roam the square, looking for someone important to photograph. . .
>
> 'The circus has come to town', mused local real estate agent John Matthews, who stepped from his office on the square with his old dog, Domino, to survey the hubbub . . .
>
> 'We'll just be glad when it's over and you can all go home', Matthews said. (Stewart, 1999)

Another *Houston Chronicle* reporter went so far as to interview local television reporters about a hospital's efforts to keep them at bay following the birth of octuplets:

> Television trucks lined Bates Street outside the hospital entrance, where many reporters were grumbling about the security situation.
>
> 'We're not doing anybody any harm', KHOU-TV, Channel 11, reporter Ron Trevino said, 'but I can understand people's need for privacy'.
>
> His co-worker at KHOU-TV, Carolyn Campbell, was outright aggravated.
>
> 'We couldn't go across the street', she said. 'It's crazy. It makes it difficult to do our jobs on deadline'.
>
> One television reporter said a man wearing a Texas Children's Hospital badge kept moving around the area, taking pictures of reporters and photographers.
>
> 'You get the feeling they wish we weren't here', said KTRK-TV, Channel 13 reporter Jim Bergamo. (Makeig, 1998)

Conclusion

As Bishop (1999) has shown, journalists have begun to recognize that public disaffection demands that they give an account of themselves when they appear to be 'going too far' in their pursuit of news. This study of boundary-work rhetoric in what-a-stories suggests that print reporters are specifically addressing themselves to concerns about their insensitivity or lack of compassion, either by acknowledging the obtrusiveness of, and implicitly distancing themselves from, 'the pack' or by suggesting that television news-workers, with their cameras and cables and microphones, are the real problem (and not print journalists). This kind of reflexive discourse may be seen as an attempt to build boundaries between the individual reporter and the pack on one hand, and between print reporters and television journalists on the other. It certainly goes beyond the work of objectivity paradigm repair that is the focus of other studies.

Zelizer (1993) wrote about the kinds of maintenance work that takes place in journalists' backstage conversations. Bishop (1999: 92) noted that the self-criticism had gone public in the meta-stories that accompany what-a-story coverage and was 'fast becoming a journalistic routine'. Zelizer (1997) called for less self-criticism and more external criticism. Wherever the challenges come from, Overholser (2000) thought journalists needed to be as willing to listen to criticism as they were to criticize.

The what-a-story, by drawing a pack of reporters, strains the fiction of the fly-on-the-wall journalist to the breaking point: jam enough journalists into the same location and the 'locals', especially in a place where a large media presence is unusual, will react as much to the crush of reporters as to the event itself. The journalists thus become, willy-nilly, part of the event. Objectivity then demands, paradoxically, that the reporters abandon objectivity and write themselves into the story.

Distanced reflexivity offers a way out. By adhering to the third-person rhetoric of objectivity, the writer can make 'the media' an Other. 'The media' have become part of the story; this reporter has not. Such a strategy enables reporters to separate themselves from the pack and align themselves with the pack's critics.

In the 14 examples cited here, reporters either encourage sources to vent their disgust, anger, weariness or annoyance with news-workers' aggressiveness and lack of respect for privacy or they offer their own overtly negative descriptions of 'the media', 'reporters' or 'journalists' as an 'invasion', an 'onslaught', a 'mob', a 'crush', a 'herd' or as 'big-city strangers wearing designer shades and beepers'.

The question that remains is what readers should make of all this built-in press criticism? Do they have a right to expect a newspaper that gives voice to public disgust with journalistic excess to curtail its own excesses? Or should they read it as further evidence of journalistic arrogance: the reporters may *feel* like they do not deserve to be lumped in with their loutish colleagues or that they have managed to convey their regret or contrition to the people they interviewed. But what may come across to readers is that the reporters are exemplars of the very phenomenon that their sources decry—either so self-absorbed that they do not even realize when they are being insulted or so cynical that they think they can absolve themselves of guilt merely by confessing their sins (see Bishop, 2001: 36).

References

Atlanta Journal Constitution (1999) 'The End of Impeachment: By the Numbers', (13 Feb.): 12A.

Arterburn, T. R. (1998) 'Hometown of a Shooting Suspect Copes with a Media Frenzy', *Christian Science Monitor* (28 Jul.): 5.

Banisky, S. (1997) 'Unabomber Saga Frustrates Town', *Baltimore Sun* (5 Nov.): 1A.

Bennett, W. L., L. A. Gressett and W. Haltom (1985) 'Repairing the News: A Case Study of the News Paradigm', *Journal of Communication* 35: 50–68.

Berkowitz, D. (1997) 'Non-routine News and Newswork: Exploring a What-a-Story', in D. Berkowitz (ed.) *Social Meanings of News*, pp. 362–75. Thousand Oaks, CA: Sage.

Berkowitz, D. (2000) 'Doing Double Duty: Paradigm Repair and the Princess Diana What-a-Story', *Journalism* 1: 125–43.

Bishop, R. (1999) 'From Behind the Walls: Boundary Work by News Organizations in Their Coverage of Princess Diana's Death', *Journal of Communication Inquiry* 23: 91–113.

Bishop, R. (2001) 'News Media, Heal Thyselves: Sourcing Patterns in News Stories about News Media Performance', *Journal of Communication Inquiry* 25: 22–37.

Boston Herald (1998) 'Media Circus in Full Roar as the "Lion" Faces "Lamb" (18 Jan.): 4.

Brady, E. (1995) '"Sick of Being Interviewed": Notoriety, Media Invasion Unite McVeigh's Hometown', *USA TODAY* (22 May): 6A.

Bragg, R. (1998) 'Funerals End for Jonesboro, But Not Questions', *The New York Times* (29 Mar.): 30.

Breslin, J. (1997) 'It's an Honor', in K. Kerrane and B. Yagoda (eds) *The Art of Fact*, pp. 466–8. New York: Simon and Schuster.

Cecil, M. (2002) 'Bad Apples: Paradigm Overhaul and the CNN/Time "Tailwind" Story', *Journal of Communication Inquiry* 26: 46–58.

Croft, J. and C. Schneider (1999) 'Why This Slaying Rivets America', *Atlanta Journal and Constitution* (15 Oct.): 1A.

Crouse, T. (1972 [1984]) *The Boys on the Bus.* New York: Ballantine.

Fallows, J. (1996) *Breaking the News.* New York: Pantheon Books.

Fancher, M. (1998) 'In Springfield, We Tried to Find Answers without Intruding on City's Grief', *Seattle Times* (31 May): A19.

Geimann, S. (1996) 'Journalism Ethics on Front Burner for Coming Year', *Quill* (Nov.): 84: 13.

Hackett, R. A. (1984) 'Decline of a Paradigm? Bias and Objectivity in News Media Studies', *Critical Studies in Mass Communication* 1: 91–114.

Knowlton, S. (1997) *Moral Reasoning for Journalists.* Westport, CT and London: Praeger.

Kuhn, T. (1962) *The Structure of Scientific Revolutions.* Chicago and London: University of Chicago Press.

Kurtz, H. (1998) 'Though Fed up with Media, Public Maintains an Appetite for the Story', *The Washington Post* (12 Feb.): A1.

Makeig, J. (1998) 'Hospital Cracks Down on News Media; Security Tight after Birth of Octuplets', *Houston Chronicle* (22 Dec.): A28.

Martin, H. (1998) 'Former Simpson Home Razed by New Owners', *Los Angeles Times* (30 Jul.): B1.

Mindich, D. T. Z. (1998) *How 'Objectivity' Came to Define American Journalism.* New York: New York University Press.

Myerhoff, B. and J. Ruby (1982) 'Introduction', in J. Ruby (ed.) *A Crack in the Mirror,* pp. 1–35. Philadelphia: University of Pennsylvania Press.

Overholser, G. (2000) 'It's Time for Newspapers to Do Real Self-Criticism', *Columbia Journalism* Review (Jan.–Feb.): 64–5.

Postman, D. (1998) 'Backlash to Media Mob: "You Have No Sympathy", *Seattle Times* (23 May): A1.

Reese, S. D. (1990) 'The News Paradigm and the Ideology of Objectivity: A Socialist at *The Wall Street Journal', Critical Studies in Mass Communication* 7: 390–409.

Schudson, M. (2001) 'The Objectivity Norm in American Journalism', *Journalism* 2: 149–70.

Shear, M. D. (1998) 'Families Struggle with Private Matter – and Glare of Media Spotlight', *The Washington Post* (16 Aug.): B1.

Sink, M. (1999) 'Terror in Littleton: The Media', *The New York Times* (25 Apr.): 30.

Steele, B. and C. Scanlan (1996) 'The Bummer Beat', URL (consulted September 2001): http://www. poynter.org/research/me/et index_htm

Stewart, R. (1999) '"Circus" Has Come Back to Town', *Houston Chronicle* (21 Feb.): A1.

Streckfuss, R. (1990) 'Objectivity in Journalism: A Search and Reassessment', *Journalism Quarterly* 67: 973–83.

Tuchman, G. (1972) 'Objectivity as Strategic Ritual: An Examination of Newsmen's Notions of Objectivity', *American Journal of Sociology* 77(4): 660–79.

Tuchman, G. (1973) 'Making News by Doing Work: Routinizing the Unexpected', *American Journal of Sociology* 79(1): 110–31.

Tuchman, G. (1978) *Making News: A Study in the Construction of Reality.* New York: Free Press.

Urban, C. (1998) 'Examining Our Credibility', American Society of Newspaper Editors, URL (consulted September 2001): http://www.asne.org/kiosk/reports/99reports/1999examiningourcredibility/

Vincent, R. C., B. K. Crow and D. K. Davis (1997) 'When Technology Fails: The Drama of Airline Crashes in Network Television News', in D. Berkowitz (ed.) *Social Meanings of News,* pp. 351–61. Thousand Oaks, CA: Sage.

Von Sternberg, B. (1997) 'The Talk of This Small Iowa Town Is Privacy', *Minneapolis Star Tribune* (5 Nov.): 1A.

Winch, S. (1997) *Mapping the Cultural Space of Journalism.* Westport, CT: Praeger.

Wizda, S. (1997) 'Parachute Journalism', *American Journalism Review* (Jul./Aug.): 19: 40–4.

Zelizer, B. (1993) 'Journalists As Interpretive Communities', *Critical Studies in Mass Communication* 10: 219–37.

Zelizer, B. (1997) 'Journalism in the Mirror', *The Nation* (17 Feb.): 10.

Source: From "'These Crowded Circumstances': When Pack Journalists Bash Pack Journalism," 2003, by R. Frank, *Journalism, 4*(4), 441–458. Reprinted by permission of Sage Publications, Ltd.

14

Israeli Image Repair

Recasting the Deviant Actor to Retell the Story

Robert L. Handley

Two days before the 9/11 terror attacks, a suicide bomber killed several Israelis. Two years earlier, suicide car bombers exploded their vehicles inside Israel. In August 2005, a terrorist boarded an Israeli bus and proceeded to shoot and kill fellow passengers. These attacks were unique in that all were carried out by Israeli citizens rather than Palestinians from the Occupied Territories.

Terror attacks perpetrated by Israeli citizens pose a problem for journalists who are accustomed to covering terror attacks committed by Palestinians. When the citizen becomes a terrorist, journalists may feel the need to reconcile the conflicting image the citizen-terrorist creates, "repairing" the image boundaries that the citizen-terrorist wrecked. The dominant Western narrative about terror in Israel is that Palestinians kill Israelis and Israelis respond (Philo & Berry, 2004), but this narrative is challenged when Israeli citizens commit terror acts against other Israeli citizens. The ethnicity of the citizen-terrorist also complicated journalists' repair work. Two of the attacks were carried out by Arab citizens of Israel, while one attack was perpetrated by a Jewish citizen. The Arab citizen-terrorists, long having constituted the role of "Other," violated their roles as citizens by committing terror but fulfilled their role as violent aggressor. The Jewish citizen-terrorist violated both his roles as citizen and victim of terror.

Below, I argue that coverage in two elite U.S. newspapers "repaired" the citizen-terrorist image boundaries in these three Israeli cases. This repair work was mediated by the ethnicity of the citizen-terrorist and done to recast the Arab-as-aggressor and Jew-as-victim so that the dominant story could again be told. Analysis supports critical theorists' claim that foreign news coverage tends to support the foreign policy of the nation-state to which foreign correspondents belong (Herman & Chomsky, 2002). Generalizations of specific findings are qualified by the fact that these terrorist attacks are foreign news for the country whose foreign policy interests are threatened by the material challenge these attacks pose to the dominant narrative. The Israeli press or other foreign presses whose countries of residences do not show allegiance to Israel might repair the Israeli citizen-terrorist images differently or not at all, depending on their countries' national interests and how culturally and geographically proximate terror attacks are to their nation-state (Nossek, 2004; Nossek & Berkowitz, 2006). In general, when facts threaten the narratives on which reporters rely to construct the news, reporters should try to construct meaning about those facts in a way that restores the original narrative, particularly when the facts threaten basic cultural values and the foreign policy interests of the country in which reporters reside.

Journalism Literature

In response to paradigm violations, journalists perform repair work. News media repair the objectivity paradigm when rogue journalists and new media threaten it. In response to rogue journalists, the press can distance itself from the individual's work, marginalize the individual, and reassert journalistic norms (Reese, 1990). Gary Webb was castigated for "theorizing" instead of providing the "smoking gun" that would become journalistic fact (McCoy, 2001), and in response to Jayson Blair, who was caught plagiarizing, *The New York Times* distanced itself from Blair and pointed to its history, awards, and status to defend the paper (Hindman, 2005). Journalists reasserted the status of journalism by citing critics who blamed a local television station for creating instead of reporting the news after the station had filmed a man lighting himself on fire (W. W. Bennett, Gressett, & Haltom, 1985). In response to the role the press played in Princess Diana's death, the mainstream press blamed the audience and even Princess Diana for her death (Hindman, 2003) and participated in "paradigm boosterism" (Berkowitz, 2000) to distance itself from the paparazzi and tabloid press.

Whereas objectivity repair occurs in the editorial pages, journalists perform what Berkowitz and Burke-Odland (2004) call "cultural repair work" when faced with the conflicting image the citizen-terrorist has created. By repairing culture, journalists reestablish familiar stories and identities that real events have damaged. Unlike objectivity repair work, which views journalism as an information-gathering activity, cultural repair work sees journalism as performing a mythological function. According to this view, journalists rely on archetypes to understand that which they report and in doing so repeatedly reinforce a society's prevailing ideology (Lule, 2001). Although faced with infinite particularities, journalists essentially tell the same story over and over again (Bird & Dardenne, 1988). By relying on these established narratives, journalists can fill in the blanks with facts relevant to the current situation, forcing what is new to fit the old story (Berkowitz, 2000). The archetypal narrative allows reporters to "typify" news stories in order to reduce infinite news variability within finite time constraints (Tuchman, 1973).

Because cultural repair work repairs culture, but not objectivity, it can occur in the news pages (Berkowitz & Burke-Odland, 2004). In the case of the Israeli citizen-terrorist, journalists may repair the integrity of terrorist and citizen images that was damaged by the citizen-terrorist reality. The citizen-terrorist is a conflicting image, or the product of two formerly incompatible images whose boundaries have overlapped to create a new image. Because the conflicting image violates the boundaries of the two images that compose it, meaning makers are faced with resolving the image in order to repair the old images that have converged to form it. Essentially, the conflicting image is created when actors violate the roles that the archetypal narrative imposes on them. Journalists are tasked with recasting the deviating actors, thus preserving the familiar narrative in the process.

The conflicting image may also be the result of a stereotype violation. Whereas we may classify persons according to their complex individuality, the roles that they play when we encounter them, the type of person that they are and choose to be, or their membership in a class, we may also condemn people to stereotypes (Dyer, 1984). Stereotypes reduce a group of people to a perceived essential character, erect fixed boundaries, and occur when there are gross inequalities of power, whether that power functions through representation or coercion (Hall, 1997). These stereotypes, or representations, are imposed on particular actors in part because they appear natural to those who construct them (Dyer, 1984). Those who cast actors in roles, however, do not present typecasts as constructions, but as natural. Naturalized stereotypes are seen as unmodifiable, justifying the maintenance of the social relationships on which the representations are based and which they serve (Hall, 1997). Naturalized, the roles become "common sense": achieving hegemony by being experienced as if they were real (Williams, 1980).

The conflicting image, because it is a visible violation of those naturalized type-casts, is, in a sense, counterhegemonic. Yet the process by which they are repaired and therefore preserved is hegemonic. Indeed, Gramsci argued that hegemony is a "moving equilibrium" that "liquidates" its challengers. In the same way that the dominant culture is alert to emergent cultures (Williams, 1980), the producers of the eternally recurring narrative and roles are alert to emergent narratives and behavioral, or casting, deviations. When faced with the conflicting image, journalists should resurrect the boundaries eroded by it.

Previous research has identified several repair strategies. When journalists could not rely on the Good Mother archetype (Lule, 2001) after Palestinian women participated in suicide attacks, journalists sought a new Woman Warrior archetype (Berkowitz, 2005). The U.S. military pulled the woman out of a soldier to remove the woman from a violent agent (Meyer, 1992), and prosecutors have pulled the gender out of violent women in order to more easily convict a female defendant (Farr, 2000). Journalists used illness to explain away a Texas mother's murder of her children (Barnett, 2005), and they sought explanations for women's involvement in suicide bombings even though they took male martyr videos at face value (Patkin, 2004). A local television producer in New Mexico asserted that journalists try to understand why murder occurs in White neighborhoods but spend little time covering murders in minority neighborhoods (Heider, 2000).

In sum, journalists may "solve" the image by understanding what led to its creation (explaining why the two images converged), may seek alternative frameworks through which to understand the conflicting image (alternative archetypes), or may pull the images apart.

Faced with the reality of the Israeli citizen-terrorist, U.S. foreign reporters should seek to resolve that conflicting image to maintain the narrative that Israel responds to Arab or Palestinian terror. Reportorial work is not only mediated by ideal expectations about real individuals and perceived groups of people but professional routines and national identity. U.S. reporters organize themselves around elite institutions to subsidize their daily information needs (Tuchman, 1978) and rely heavily on elite sources to frame foreign news (Herman & Chomsky, 2002). Foreign reporters "wear a pair of domestic glasses." When foreign events relate in some way to the national interest of the nation-state in which foreign reporters reside, reporters will subordinate professional norms to their national identity. As a result, news coverage becomes less "open" and more "closed," that is, less "objective" and more "interpretive" in a way that favors the foreign policy of the country in which the reporter resides (Nossek, 2004).

Events related to Israel are often newsworthy in the United States because of U.S. national interests in the Middle East and its allegiance to Israel. Although the U.S.-Israel relationship is complex and contradictory, the United States has historically backed Israel. The United States has major interests in Middle Eastern energy and was an ally with Israel against the former Soviet Union (Chomsky, 1999). At times critical of Israel, the United States has nevertheless generally rejected Palestinian self-determination and talks with Palestinian leaders, and has seen the Israeli-Palestinian conflict as originating from Palestinian violence against Israel (Smith, 2004). After the September 11, 2001, attacks against the United States, Israel aligned itself with the United States in its "war on terror" and shared a mutual interest in Iraqi regime change (Smith, 2004). The common view that the Israeli-Palestinian conflict exists because of Palestinian violence and terrorism means that U.S. foreign reporters ought to repair the image of the citizen-terrorist when Israelis commit terror attacks and do so in a way that restores the dominant narrative that terror comes from the Occupied Territories, not Israel.

The Israeli-Arab Context

For the West, Arabs and Muslims have long played the role of the Other. For Said (2003), this meant that the Arab-Muslim world, or the Orient, is the direct contrast of the West, "its contrasting image, idea, personality, experience" (p. 2). In Said's view, the Orient is the binary opposite of the Occident, but the Other can also be constructed through dialogue, classification, and the creation of the self. However the Arab-Muslim Other is constructed, the construction of it as a difference to the West is essential to the creation of meaning in the West (Hall, 1997).

The Orient represented as the Other is used to express Western superiority to Oriental inferiority. Subsequently, terror acts carried out by individuals from the Arab-Muslim world are explained by reducing the attacks to the eventual outcome of perceived Arab and Muslim innately violent behavior (Daniel, 1997; Said, 1997). Although images of Middle Eastern peoples have generally improved in Western media, scholars list a long history in which they have been shown as aggressors, violent and irrational, and determined to destroy Israel (see Kamalipour, 1997).

The Israeli Arabs, Palestinians who remained inside Israel and were granted citizenship after 1948, constitute approximately 20% of Israel's population and are seen as an Other inside the state. The ongoing Arab-Israeli conflict has meant that Israel's Arab citizens have been subject to what Lustick (1980) has called an elaborate system of control whereby they are fragmented, co-opted, and made economically dependent on the Jewish sector. They are seen as a security threat by both the state (Peleg, 1988) and most of the Jewish Israeli citizenry (Rudge, 2004). They are seen as a potential fifth column or Trojan Horse who would show allegiance to the Arab states should an Arab-Israeli war occur (Jabareen, 2006), and the threat discourse justified imposed military rule on the Arab population between 1948–1966. Because of their large numbers, they are also seen as a demographic threat to the Jewish state (Yonah, 2004), and the state has rejected legal language that would eradicate the institutionalized view that Israel is a state that belongs to its Jewish citizens only (Ghanem & Rouhana, 2001).

The general Jewish population also discriminates against the Arab population. The vast majority of Jewish immigrants from the former Soviet Union reported that they would refuse to have relations with Arabs, even at work, joining "the national consensus that prevails among the Jewish majority" (Al-Haj, 2004, p. 692). Other surveys have shown that nearly 64% of Israeli Jews want the Arabs to leave Israel, and slightly less than half want the state to limit Arab political rights (Rudge, 2004).

When journalists are faced with the task of resolving the citizen-terrorist image, that task is complicated by the ethnicity of the citizen who becomes a terrorist. I argue that although journalists repaired the citizen-terrorist image when it was played by either an Israeli Arab or Israeli Jew, journalists also had to restore the narrative that Arabs attack Israel and Israel responds. In doing so, journalists recast the Jew-as-victim and maintained the Arab-as-aggressor role even when the Arab was a victim.

Method

Through multiple readings and detailed note taking of two U.S. elite newspapers, *The New York*

Times and *The Washington Post,* articles about Jewish and Arab terrorists were analyzed with an eye toward image resolution. These papers are important to analyze because they are two of the most powerful and important papers in the United States. Each is an important international news gatekeeper and sets the standard for reporting in the United States and elsewhere. *The New York Times,* for example, has been called a role model for journalism worldwide (Tunstall, 1977). Foreign news in the United States is mediated by a few gatekeepers (Nosek, 2004), and *Times* and *Post* foreign reporters represent a large portion of these gatekeepers among U.S. news media. Each paper helps set the agenda and frame for other U.S. news outlets, and both are an important means through which U.S. policy makers receive their information about events in other parts of the world. Thus, they are central to the opinion-formation processes among U.S. policy makers and help determine how other U.S. reporters cover foreign news.

If an image is conflicting, there should be evidence that journalists have tried to resolve the image in order to repair original images. When an image is conflicting, it initiates an ideological struggle over the meaning of the new image and how it is to be resolved. Therefore, ideological analysis following Foss (1996) is appropriate. According to this model, the researcher should ask (1) What is or are the preferred reading(s) of the text? (2) Whose interests are represented in the text? and (3) What are the rhetorical features that promote some ideologies over others? More specific to this analysis, I ask (1) To what extent are these images repaired? (2) Which sources are legitimized in the process of repair? and (3) How are these images repaired?

Three attacks were chosen for analysis. The first occurred on September 5, 1999, and was the first car bombing carried out by Israeli Arabs: Jad Azayzeh, Amir Masalha, and Nazal Kraim. The second attack was carried out by Muhammad Saker Habashi, who became the first Israeli Arab suicide bomber on September 9, 2001. The third attack occurred on August 4, 2005, by Jewish Israeli Natan Zada.

These attacks share four characteristics. First, Israel declared each an act of terror. Second, the attackers all targeted members of the competing ethnic community. Third, the attacks were carried out by individuals, although there was some suspicion that the Arab attackers were recruited by Palestinians. Fourth, all the attacks took place within Israel's borders by Israeli citizens against Israeli citizens.

Stories were gathered from Nexis. Attackers were identified by outside scholarly and popular reading as well as broad Nexis terms such as *Israeli Arab* and *attack.* Stories were collected by identifying keywords in initial articles, such as the town in which the attacks took place, the method of violence, and the attackers' names, including alternative spellings. Only stories that identified the attackers or their citizenship and ethnicity and were centrally about the attacks were included for analysis.

In all, nine stories were analyzed (four about Zada, three about the car bombing, and two about the suicide bombing). The analysis of these stories, though a small number, is important because it illustrates how repair work can be subtly done in a limited amount of space. This case study is important for readers in the United States and other countries because it shows how reporters in one country can construct meaning in a way that diffuses the threat that material realities pose to ideal representations. Repair work can be done to protect the foreign interests of the nation-state in which the reporter resides, and therefore has international implications.

Solving the Arab Citizen-Terrorist, Restoring the Narrative

The press made it manifestly clear that each Israeli Arab attacker represented a departure from the normal attacker. The 1999 car bombings were departures from the usual suicide attacks "carried out by Palestinians from the militant Islamic groups Hamas and Islamic Holy War" (Greenberg, 1999b, p. A10), and they unsettled Israelis "who have come to believe that

Palestinian extremist groups are the only ones waging terrorist campaigns against the Jewish state" (O'Connor, 1999, p. A10). The 2001 suicide bomber "hardly fit the profile of a suicide bomber" because he had not come from the West Bank, was middle-aged, was married, and had six children (Hockstader, 2001, p. A1).

In defining the aberration, journalists had to define the norm from which the new terrorists were deviating. According to this norm, the typical terrorist enters Israel from the Occupied Territories, is young, has no familial commitments, and is Muslim. Although the 2001 suicide bomber "hardly fit the profile," there was one characteristic he shared: "However, Israeli authorities said he was active in Israel's Islamic Movement and that security agents had been on his trail for a week, pursuing rumors that he intended to carry out some sort of attack" (Hockstader, 2001, p. Al). Although the attacks were new, Said (1997) would argue that journalists found a familiar narrative element in Islam, and this would help journalists resolve the conflicting citizen-terrorist image by blaming terror on Islam, not on a citizen.

In seeking to understand the newness of the attacks, journalists sought various sources: Israeli Arab citizens and leaders, Muslim leaders, and the Israeli state. Predictably, the Arab and Muslim community distanced itself from the attackers. The 1999 car bombings sent "shock waves through Israeli Arab communities after the identities of the men were made public by the police" (Greenberg, 1999a, p. A3). An Arab member of the Knesset (MK) asserted that "Whoever carried out such an act is enemy number one of the Arab community," and a leader in the Islamic Movement stated that "These are acts from the fringe" (Greenberg, 1999b, p. A10). Following the 2001 attack, "Israeli Arabs and their political leaders insisted that no underground terrorist movement had taken root in their community" (Hockstader, 2001, p. A1). A community leader from the attacker's hometown stated that the attacker "hurt everyone in the village," and the journalist wrote that the town "is not known as a hotbed of militance," implying that the towns' citizens were reasonably integrated into Israel because the town had "recently produced a general in the army" (J. Bennett, 2001, p. A3).

One of the attacker's family

> argued that he was an unlikely candidate for a suicide attack, suggesting that he had been duped into driving the car laden with explosives to Tiberias. He had recently refurbished a home and gotten married, they said, and his wife was three months' pregnant. He drove to Tiberias with Mr. Azaizeh; suicide bombers usually travel alone. (Greenberg, 1999a, p. A3)

But journalists did not exclusively rely on the Arab view to explain the newness. The Arabs argued that the attackers were duped by Palestinians: "But details emerging from an investigation painted a different picture, indicating possible links between the men and Islamic militants in the West Bank" (Greenberg, 1999a, p. A3). The alternative explanation, which came from the state, did not see the bombers as people who were duped but as people who were consciously linked to West Bank Muslims. The state supported the Arab view that the attackers were not representative of the Israeli Arab community and asserted that "it is more likely that Palestinian extremist groups used Israeli Arabs to transport the bombs to their intended targets": exploiting Israeli Arab alienation with the state, and arrests made in relation to the crime "seemed to substantiate" this (O'Connor, 1999, p. A16). After the 2001 attacks as well, Israel blamed Arafat and the Palestinian Authority for "inciting Arab citizens of Israel to violence" (Hockstader, 2001, p. A1). The attacks were not born in the Arab community, but in the West Bank.

Legitimizing the state's view that the Arabs were not "dupes" but had made a conscious choice to commit terror acts, journalists could fit the new facts to the old story. That the Israeli Arab attackers were exploited by West Bank Palestinians meant that journalists could graft the old narrative—Palestinian terrorists attack

Israel and Israel responds—onto the new facts. This was particularly true after the 2001 suicide bombing because the Arab citizen-terrorist was more familiar by that point. The suicide bombing, although presented as a "first," was also represented as only one in a series of attacks. Three attacks occurred that day, two by Palestinians and one by an Israeli Arab, and they "came one after another in what seemed rolling waves of bad news" (Hockstader, 2001, p. A1). The Israeli Arab attack was another in "a jackhammer series of terrorist blows" that day (J. Bennett, 2001, p. A3). After the Israeli Arab suicide bombing, for which Israel stated that the Palestinian Authority was to blame and for which Hamas claimed responsibility, journalists stated that Israel "responded" to the attacks by attacking the West Bank (J. Bennett, 2001, p. A3; Hockstader, 2001, p. A1).

Thus, the old narrative was grafted onto new facts and was consequently restored. That restoration was made possible because journalists pushed the Arab citizen-terrorist into the West Bank. In effect, the journalists had pulled the terrorist out of the citizen-terrorist and simultaneously pushed the Arab suicide bomber into the West Bank. With the Arab and his terror coming from the West Bank, the image of the citizen-as-victim was restored and so was the image of Arab/Muslim-as-terrorist. By resolving the Arab citizen-terrorist image, journalists could tell the same story they are accustomed to: Arabs attack Israel and Israel responds.

If Israeli Arabs were not dupes of West Bank Palestinians, then they chose to commit terror, and their loyalty to Israel was consequently questioned. In 1999, journalists seemed to position the Arabs as loyal citizens: "Although doubts about the loyalty of one million Arab citizens of Israel linger among Jewish Israelis, and although the Israeli Arabs sympathize with the national aspirations of their Palestinian brothers, few Israeli Arabs have been involved in anti-Jewish attacks" (Greenberg, 1999a, p. A3). In fact, Arabs had shown "decades of civic loyalty" (Greenberg, 1999b, p. A10), and a subhead declared "Most of Minority Group Said to Be Loyal Citizens" (O'Connor, 1999, p. A16). Yet by 2001, once the new facts were more closely molded to fit the old story, journalists more strongly questioned Arab loyalty to Israel. Wrote one journalist,

> One of today's attacks, the bombing here, for which the group Hamas claimed responsibility, is likely to have the greatest reverberation, since it demonstrated that not even the most formidable boundary along the West Bank would be a bulwark against all threats. (J. Bennett, 2001, p. A3)

The headlines the day of the attack read "Israel Attacked From Within" (Hockstader, 2001) and "Israeli Arab's Suicide Bomb Points to Enemy Within" (J. Bennett, 2001). The Israeli Arabs had become an "enemy within," the outcome of Palestinian terror infecting Israel proper. The old narrative, that foreign Arabs attack Israel, was restored, and the image of the Arab-as-aggressor was maintained.

Solving the Jewish Citizen-Terrorist, Restoring Jewish-Arab Roles

As they had with the Israeli Arab citizen-terrorists, journalists made it clear that Zada's terror had violated the norm of Jewish attacks. "Jewish militants have carried out a number of attacks against Arabs in the past, but most were directed against Palestinians in the West Bank rather than Arabs who are Israeli citizens" (Myre, 2005b, p. A4). Already, then, journalists had some framework within which to report Zada's attack.

By itself, this framework did not resolve the conflicting citizen-terrorist image. To do so, journalists sought a variety of voices to help them understand the attacks, including Arab citizens and leaders, Jewish town leaders, Jewish settlers in the Territories, and the military. Arab sources tried to locate the attack in a larger context, as the result of Israeli discrimination against and discourse about Arab citizens. One journalist wrote that

> many of the Israeli Arabs who came to bury friends and family held the government complicit in the crime. Some said Israel's security services, never slow to move against militant Palestinians accused of plotting against Israel, should have done the same against extremist groups such as the one Zada belonged to. (Wilson, 2005b, p. A11)

An Arab MK asserted, "Israeli politicians are always talking about Israeli Arabs as the enemy and as security threats. This is the fruit of that kind of talk" (Myre, 2005a, p. A3).

Jewish sources received more attention than Arab sources, therefore assuming more legitimacy than Arab sources, and seemed to locate the cause of the attack either within Zada himself or in Kach, a Jewish terrorist organization located in the West Bank. When the attack occurred, Zada was wearing his military uniform, and this made it important for the Israeli military to distance itself from him. For the military, the attack was not the result of racist discourse or discrimination, as the Arabs had claimed, but of the Zada individual: "the military said in a statement that he had been a 'problematic' soldier before he went absent without leave" in protest against settler pullouts in Gaza (Myre, 2005a, p. A3).

All other Jewish leaders denied that Zada represented anything about them, denigrating Zada to distance themselves from him. Prime Minister Ariel Sharon called his attack "a reprehensible act by a bloodthirsty Jewish terrorist" (Wilson, 2005a, p. A1), and the leader of the Yesha Council, an organization of Jewish settlements in the Occupied Territories, said that Zada "is a terrorist, a lunatic and immoral. He had no connection to my values" (Wilson, 2005b, p. A1). From this point of view, Zada was not the "fruit" of racist discourse, as the Arab MK had put it, but an individual working on his own.

The military, Zada's hometown of Rishon Letzion, and the Tapuah settlement he relocated to after his desertion from the army all refused him burial under their land. Tapuah leaders refused to admit that Zada had become a resident there, and like the military and Rishon Letzion in Israel proper, they wanted to distance themselves from him. Yet the press, by pointing to Zada's Israeli identification card, which stated he had indeed become a Tapuah settler, located his terror as originating from there. Having placed Zada in the West Bank, the press focused on Zada's transformation, noting how he had been born the son of secular parents and was then transformed into a "religiously observant Jew" in "a stronghold of religious extremists" (Wilson, 2005a, p. A1).

In sum, journalists resolved the conflicting Jewish citizen-terrorist image the same way they resolved the conflicting Arab citizen-terrorist image: They pulled the terrorist out of the citizen-terrorist and pushed him into the West Bank. In this way, the narrative that terrorists kill citizens was restored and each image repaired.

In the process of resolving the citizen-terrorist image, journalists also repaired the Jewish component of that image by focusing much of their attention on potential Arab reaction. Wrote one journalist,

> Arabs have been viewed by successive Israeli governments as a potential threat to security. The Israeli Arab population is growing quickly, especially in the south, and Israeli security services have expressed fear, particularly during times of strife, that its loyalties might lie with fellow Arabs in the territories Israel has occupied since the 1967 Middle East war. (Wilson, 2005b, p. A11)

Unlike in 2001, the press seemed to take the position that Arabs are loyal to the state:

> Israeli authorities braced for possible unrest on Friday [after the attack], fearing that Israeli Arabs, who account for more

> than one million of Israel's 6.8 million citizens, might riot. But as of Friday night, no trouble was reported in Arab communities inside Israel. (Myre, 2005a, p. A3)

Since 2000, journalists inaccurately reported, Israeli Arabs had only been implicated in helping Palestinian attackers from the West Bank. Journalists might have affirmed Arab loyalty in their coverage, but the act of questioning it at all deflected attention away from Jewish terror. Zada's terror raised no questions about Jewish loyalty to the state. Thus, the focus on potential Arab violence restored the image of Arab-as- aggressor and Israel-as-victim.

Discussion

This study contributes to repair and mythology literature by introducing the conflicting images concept. According to this concept, real world events lead individuals to violate the behavioral boundaries imposed on them by the producers of eternal stories. When people violate their roles, meaning makers must determine the reason for that violation in order to recast the individual into her or his expected role. If the actor deviates from her or his character, the story is destroyed. When journalists are faced with a conflicting image, then, they also face a possible breach in the recurring stories they tell. To save the eternal story, they must recast the actors into their typecast parts.

When the citizen becomes a terrorist, and when an Israeli Jew becomes aggressor, actual behavior deviates from predicted behavior scripted by dominant stories that U.S. journalists tell. Journalists must recast these actors in order to tell the "right" story. To understand how journalists solved the citizen-terrorist image when it is played by an Israeli Arab or Israeli Jew, I asked about (1) the extent to which the image was repaired, (2) which sources were given legitimacy during repair work, and (3) how the image was repaired.

Whether the citizen-terrorist was played by an Israeli Jew or Arab, journalists pulled the terrorist out of the citizen-terrorist and pushed him into the West Bank. Doing so meant that the terrorist was a foreigner and that journalists repaired the citizen and terrorist images/roles. Whereas other research has shown that meaning makers can solve a conflicting image by seeking alternative archetypes (Berkowitz, 2005), pulling apart the images (Farr, 2000), or by explaining away the behavioral deviation (Barnett, 2005), this study also shows that journalists can push an image component into another, more compatible image.

In trying to resolve the citizen-terrorist image, journalists sought out various sources to help them do so. Whether the citizen-terrorist was Jewish or Arab, journalists sought both Arab and Jewish voices. In all cases, journalists legitimized the Israeli state explanation for the newness of the attacks. However, the implications for this varied with the ethnicity of the citizen-terrorist. When the citizen-terrorist was played by an Arab, both the Arabs and the Israeli state explained that the attacks had originated in the West Bank, even as they differed about whether Arab attackers were dupes or consciously exploited. The attacks, therefore, were not representative of the Arab community, and this served the Arab interest. When the citizen-terrorist was played by an Israeli Jew, on the other hand, the explanation provided by the Israeli Arabs and the state differed. Whereas the Arab population wanted to blame Israeli racist discourse and anti-Arab discrimination for the attacks, the press legitimized the state position that the problem was actually located in extremist settlers. In this way, state interests were served, because the state could deflect attention away from what Israeli Arabs argued was the state's complicity in Zada's terror.

Whether the citizen-terrorist is played by an Arab or Jew, U.S. foreign reporters solved the conflicting image by pulling the terrorist from Israel and pushing him into the West Bank. However, journalists treated the ethnic component of the citizen-terrorist differently. When an individual Arab attacked, the press questioned the loyalty of the entire Arab population to Israel.

When a Jewish Israeli attacked, the press did not question the loyalty of Israeli Jews in general. Instead, it focused attention on potential Arab violence. Doing so helped restore the Arab-as-aggressor and Jew-as-victim, therefore rescuing the dominant narrative that Arabs attack Israel and Israel responds (Philo & Berry, 2004).

When foreign events threaten the national interests of a country, foreign reporters in those countries should subordinate professional norms to their national identities (Nossek, 2004). Repair work is not only mediated by violations of ideal expectations or dominant narratives and professional routines but by the national identities of reporters. When U.S. reporters repaired the narrative that Israel responds to terrorism that originates in the Occupied Territories, they served U.S. foreign policy and Israeli domestic policy. To legitimize both U.S. and Israeli regional interests, the Israeli-Palestinian conflict must be perceived as being caused by Palestinian terrorism, particularly now that Israel is an ally in the "war on terror."

Because national interests, national identities, and reliance on official sources mediate press coverage, the specific findings here are most generalizable to the foreign press in those nation-states who have strong allegiances to Israel and therefore subscribe to the narrative that Israel is a victim of Palestinian and Arab terrorism and violence. Foreign reporters in nation-states not aligned with Israel may not see the Israeli citizen-terrorist as a conflicting image if they do not subscribe to the narrative that Israeli responds to Arab and Palestinian aggression. Or, reporters who reside in nation-states opposed to Israeli policies might repair the citizen-terrorist in different ways. They may, for example, fix the "Arabness" of an Arab Israeli citizen terrorist and construct meaning about a Jewish Israeli citizen terrorist in a way that serves their own country's foreign policy. The Israeli press may repair the images differently from the U.S. press as well, particularly because the attacks are culturally and geographically closer for them than other reporters (Nossek & Berkowitz, 2006).

Therefore, findings here should not be taken to mean that reporters everywhere repair the specific Israeli citizen-terrorist in the same way, or at all. More generally, though, reporters everywhere may feel the need to repair ideal narratives when they are threatened by actors' real deviations from imposed roles, especially among foreign reporters who face new facts that threaten their country's national interests. All reporters, to make their work easier, tend to subscribe to certain narratives. To maintain those narratives and the cultural assumptions they represent, reporters need to repair conflicting images when they appear. Future research might look further into this.

Future research might also look further into Israel-Arab or Israel-Palestine questions by looking at other instances in which the dominant Israel-Arab story is challenged by real occurrences, to determine the extent to which journalists resuscitate that story. For example, Baruch Goldstein, a Jewish settler in the West Bank, killed several Palestinians and received much press attention in 1994. Scholars may take a more sociological approach and examine the extent to which journalists devote more or fewer resources to events that they perceive as the norm, and those they do not. For example, researchers may wish to see if journalists devote more or less time and resources to White crime, perceiving it as rare and therefore newsworthy, or Black crime, perceiving it as common and deserving only of fleeting attention.

References

Al-Haj, M. (2004). The political culture of the 1990s immigrants from the former Soviet Union in Israel and their views toward an indigenous Arab minority: A case of ethnocratic multiculturalism. *Journal of Ethnic and Migration Studies, 30*(4), 681–696.

Barnett, B. (2005). Perfect mother or artist of obscenity? Narrative and myth in a qualitative analysis of press coverage of the Andrea Yates murders. *Journal of Communication Inquiry, 29,* 9–29.

Bennett, J. (2001, September 10). Israel's Arab suicide bomb points to enemy within. *The New York Times,* p. A3.

Bennett, W. L., Gresset, L. A., & Haltom, W. (1985). Repairing the news: A case study of the news par adigm. *Journal of Communication, 35*(2), 50–68.

Berkowitz, D. (2000). Doing double duty: Paradigm repair and the Princess Diana what-a-story. *Journalism, 1*(2), 125–143.

Berkowitz, D. (2005). Suicide bombers as women warriors: Making news through mythical archetypes. *Journalism and Mass Communication Quarterly, 82*(3), 607–622.

Berkowitz, D., & Burke-Odland, S. (2004, August). *"My mum's a suicide bomber": Motherhood, terrorism, news, and ideological repair.* Paper presented at the annual Association for Education in Journalism & Mass Communication, Toronto, Canada.

Bird, S. E., & Dardenne, R. W. (1988). Myth, chronicle and story: Exploring the narrative qualities of news. In J. W. Carey (Ed.) *Media, myths, and narratives: Television and the press* (pp. 67–86). Beverly Hills, CA: Sage.

Chomsky, N. (1999). *Fateful triangle: The United States, Israel, and the Palestinians* (Updated ed.). Cambridge, MA: South End Press.

Daniel, A. (1997). U.S. media coverage of the *Intifada* and American public opinion. In Y. R. Kamalipour (Ed.), *The U.S. media and the Middle East: Image and perception* (pp. 62–71). Westport, CT: Praeger.

Dyer, R. (1984). *Gays and film.* New York: Zoetrope.

Farr, K. A. (2000). Defeminizing and dehumanizing female murderers: Depictions of lesbians on death row. *Women & Criminal Justice, 11*(1), 49–66.

Foss, S. K. (1996). *Rhetorical criticism: Exploration & practice* (2nd ed.). Prospect Heights, IL: Waveland.

Ghanem, A., & Rouhana, N. N. (2001). Citizenship and the parliamentary politics of minorities in ethnic states: The Palestinian citizens of Israel. *Nationalism & Ethnic Politics, 47*(4), 66–86.

Greenberg, J. (1999a, September 8). Of bombs and Israeli Arabs, and years of loyalty. *The New York Times,* p. A3.

Greenberg, J. (1999b, September 7). Israeli Arabs suspected in car blasts, police hint. *The New York Times,* p. A10.

Hall, S. (Ed.). (1997). *Representation: Cultural representations and signifying practices.* Thousand Oaks, CA: Sage.

Heider, D. (2000). *White news: Why local news programs don't cover people of color.* Mahwah, NJ: Lawrence Erlbaum.

Herman, E. S., & Chomsky, N. (2002). *Manufacturing consent: The political economy of the mass media.* New York: Pantheon.

Hindman, E. B. (2003). The princess and the paparazzi: Blame, responsibility, and the media's role in the death of Diana. *Journalism and Mass Communication Quarterly, 80*(3), 666–688.

Hindman, E. B. (2005). Jayson Blair, *The New York Times,* and paradigm repair. *Journal of Communication, 55*(2), 225–241.

Hockstader, L. (2001, September 10). Israel attacked from within: Suicide bombing is first by Arab citizen. *The Washington Post,* p. Al.

Jabareen, Y. T. (2006). Law and education: Critical perspectives on Arab Palestinian education in Israel. *American Behavioral Scientist, 49*(8), 1052–1074.

Kamalipour, Y. R. (Ed.). (1997). *The U.S. media and the Middle East: Image and perception.* Westport, CT: Praeger.

Lule, J. (2001). *Daily news, eternal stories: The mythological role of journalism.* New York: Guilford.

Lustick, I. (1980). *Arabs in the Jewish state: Israel's control of a national minority.* Austin: University of Texas Press.

McCoy, M. E. (2001). Dark alliance: News repair and institutional authority in the age of the Internet. *Journal of Communication, 51*(1), 164–193.

Meyer, L. D. (1992). Creating G. I. Jane: The regulation of sexuality and sexual behavior in the Women's Army Corps during World War II. *Feminist Studies, 18*(3), 581–602.

Myre, G. (2005a, August 6). Israeli Arab town mourns 4 victims of Jewish gunman. *The New York Times,* p. A3.

Myre, G. (2005b, August 5). Jewish militant opens fire on bus of Israeli Arabs, killing 4. *The New York Times,* p. A4.

Nossek, H. (2004). Our news and their news: The role of national identity in the coverage of foreign news. *Journalism, 5*(3), 343–368.

Nossek, H., & Berkowitz, D. (2006). Telling "our" story through news of terrorism: Mythical newswork as journalistic practice in crisis. *Journalism Studies, 7*(5), 691–707.

O'Connor, M. (1999, September 7). 5 Israeli Arabs arrested in car bomb blasts: Most of minority group said to be loyal citizens. *The Washington Post,* p. A16.

Patkin, T. T. (2004). Explosive baggage: Female Palestinian suicide bombers and the rhetoric of emotion. *Women and Language, 27*(2), 79–88.

Peleg, I. (1988). Israel's constitutional order and *Kulturkampf* The role of Ben-Gurion. *Israel Studies, 3*(1), 230–250.

Philo, G., & Berry, M. (2004). *Bad news from Israel.* Ann Arbor, MI: Pluto Press.

Reese, S. D. (1990). The news paradigm and the ideology *of* objectivity: A socialist at *The Wall Street Journal. Critical Studies in Mass Communication, 7,* 390–409.

Rudge, D. (2004, June 23). 64% of Jewish Israelis want Israeli Arabs to leave Survey. *The Jerusalem Post,* p. 6.

Said, E. W. (1997). *Covering Islam: How the media and the experts determine how we see the rest of the world* (Rev. ed.). New York: Vintage.

Said, E. W. (2003). *Orientalism* (25th anniversary ed.). New York: Vintage.

Smith, C. D. (2004). *Palestine and the Arab-Israeli conflict: A history with documents* (5th ed.). New York: St. Martin's.

Tuchman, G. (1973). Making news by doing work: Routinizing the unexpected. *American Journal of Sociology, 79*(1), 110–131.

Tuchman, G. (1978). *Making news: A study in the construction of reality.* New York: Free Press.

Tunstall, J. (1977). *The media are American: Anglo-American media in the world.* London: Constable.

Williams, R. (1980). *Problems in materialism and culture: Selected essays.* London: Verso.

Wilson, S. (2005a, August 5). Jewish settler kills four Israeli Arabs in attack on bus.he *Washington Post,* p. A1.

Wilson, S. (2005b, August 6). With prayers, tears, Israeli Arabs bury dead: Killings intensify resentment, fear. *The Washington Post,* p. A1.

Yonah, Y. (2004). Israel's immigration policies: The twofold face of the "demographic threat." *Social Identities, 10(2)* 195–218.

Source: From "Israeli Image Repair: Recasting the Deviant Actor to Retell the Story," 2008, by R. L. Handley, *Journal of Communication Inquiry, 32*(2), 140–154. Reprinted by permission of Sage Publications, Inc.

15

A Paradigm in Process

What the Scapegoating of Vusi Mona Signalled About South African Journalism

Guy Berger

Introduction

In the decade emerging from apartheid's polarisation of media roles into partisan ones, and a discrediting of 'neutrality' (see TRC 1997), the many journalists who supported a democratic dispensation faced a conundrum. Should they continue with a hostile stand against the state, when the leading liberation movement, the ANC, had assumed political office? And even if muddling through this challenge was complex, what complicated things even more were the growing rifts within the ruling party. Thus, those press people sympathetic to the agenda of transforming and rebuilding South Africa were confronted with the question as to which ANC faction really stood for democracy, while those journalists wanting to retain some independence from politics, faced the reality of different political forces seeking to manipulate the media for factional purposes.

Within this evolving context, South Africa's media during 2003 encountered evidence of very diverse interpretations of journalism as a recognisable paradigm, including some that contained clear violations of conventional journalistic ethics. This was highlighted most graphically during the cross-questioning of Vusi Mona at a judicial enquiry, dubbed the 'Hefer Commission'. The event prompted unprecedented condemnation of an individual South African journalist by his peers—who also exonerated themselves of similar ethical problems and avoided deeper analysis of the saga.[1]

To a large extent, the case lends itself to being analysed in terms of 'paradigm repair' (see Berkowitz 2000; Cecil 2002). In terms of this, it would be yet another instance of the media closing ranks against a threat by scapegoating a problematic individual in order to restore its credibility. The image then would be one of a community operating collectively, and in an intuitively functionalist way, to marginalise a lone renegade in order to contain the damage. This reading would accord with what Zelizer (2004: 5, 17), in her review of research into journalists as 'a group with systematic relations', describes as 'the forces that help maintain a social group's solidarity'. There was indeed evidence in this case of normative boundary-setting over an imagined singular journalism, with references to apparently clear and agreed professional values and processes. The experience further indicates a 'classic' case of journalists portraying themselves and their industry as an idealised reference group capable of being damaged as a whole by the behaviour of a single deviant.

At the same time, this is also not quite a typical 'paradigm repair' case (akin to those discussed by Ettema & Whitney 1987; Soloski 1989; Windhal & Rosengren 1978). As will be shown, the representations carried in the media did not unify all noticeable differences within the ranks or claim a homogeneity of community on all issues that emerged. Further, as will be shown in this article, the Mona case highlights some limiting assumptions within the conventional rendition of the 'paradigm repair' framework, and the need for modifications when applying the perspective to a transitional society such as South Africa's.

The term 'repair' is often used loosely in the literature, even when it is not in fact an instance where the dominant paradigm of journalism is actually damaged and in need of fixing. Rather, it is the *imagined collective subscription* to the paradigm (by the wider journalistic community) that is the subject of repair, not the paradigm as such (which typically remains intact). Accordingly, there is a form of reassertion and bolstering of the paradigm, and the phrase 'paradigm repair' in these instances should rather be understood as referring to 'paradigm status reinforcement'. Where a paradigm per se really does get damaged, in the sense of losing the credibility of its explanation and rationales, two possible responses have been identified by Hindman (2005: 238). One is to actually change the paradigm; the other is to acknowledge that there are flaws in it, but to carry on regardless. Both of these, as will be shown, can be seen in certain elements of the Mona case.

However, the 'classic' response recorded in journalism studies literature is neither change nor troubled persistence. It is, instead, 'reinforcement' (as noted above) in the sense of upholding the paradigm as a paragon of orthodox practice, contrasting this with anomalous action by discrediting the particular deviationist/s.[2] This 'classic' practice is also part of the Mona case study, following many of the strategies typically taken to restore the faith that a given paradigm remains in mainstream place. These strategies have been cited as: denial of damage, evading responsibility by shifting blame onto a 'renegade', and reducing the offence by contextualising it and highlighting good intentions (ibid: 228). The overall 'paradigm repair' framework in this article therefore encapsulates a mix of three elements: 'paradigm status reinforcement', persistence of damage, and part real repair.

What also makes the Mona case interesting is the way in which it highlights three limiting assumptions usually implicit in the 'paradigm repair' perspective on acute ethical violations (such as noted in, for example, Bennett et al. 1985; Berkowitz 1997; Lewis 2007; Ruggerio 2004), and which need re-thinking in regard to the Mona case.

The first is that the perspective usually operates in instances where there is a clear 'culprit' (e.g., Janet Cooke, Jayson Blair—see Larsosa & Dai 2007) who unambiguously violates obvious paradigmatic norms and places him- or herself outside the bounds of journalism. In this case, by contrast, Mona and fellow journalist Ranjeni Munusamy each often claimed to have been loyal to certain journalism precepts. This point of view of a 'deviant' denying that there has been deviation has not been evident in much of the literature. A second limit is that the 'paradigm repair' framework tends to focus on controversy around 'objectivity' (without, incidentally, always adequately explicating the notion), whereas the Mona case went beyond this into deeper issues of motivations, interpretations of confidentiality, and relations with authority (in this case, specifically a judicial enquiry). The third constraint within the perspective of 'paradigm repair' is that it usually assumes the existence of a coherent and stable model of journalism, capable of 'paradigm maintenance' (Livio 2006): in other words, a body of conventional wisdom that can organically reproduce its singularity in the face of a temporary disruption or challenge, and also accommodate gradual changes in hegemony. This was not the case in this South African instance, as will be shown below.[3]

What the Mona case suggests is that 'paradigm repair' in the sense of a 'community of believers' (Eason 1988) that successfully shrugs off a challenge and continues with business as usual, is not necessarily evident in transitional societies in which a journalism paradigm may already be variegated and uncertain in certain respects. While there was unison in some matters against Mona, this was not the case across the board. Thus while overcoming a 'bad apple' experience (Cecil 2002) may occur in cases of flagrant violation of a norm like 'objectivity' (such as fabrication), it is not so 'easy' to move on when it comes to broader issues implicating journalists' orientations to power and politics, and at a time when journalistic roles are in flux.

Mona's downfall stemmed from his decision to publish as fact damaging allegations about a senior public official, Bulelani Ngcuka, who at the time was the head of the Directorate of Public Prosecutions and its investigative unit known as the 'Scorpions'. The published allegations were that the director was a former apartheid spy who was abusing his anti-corruption powers to settle old scores with the then deputy president and would-be president, Jacob Zuma, who—it was claimed—had learnt of Ngcuka's hidden history many years earlier. Numerous journalistic problems surfaced as the story unfolded, although Mona's were the ones most focused on by the media.

The allegations became a major public issue with their publication on 7 September 2003 in Mona's *City Press* of a front page 'splash'. This led President Thabo Mbeki to appoint the Hefer Commission of Inquiry, which in turn gave insight into an imbroglio which deeply implicated and profoundly affected many media practitioners.

It is the case that Munusamy, the reporter who secured the actual story, featured very frequently over the period, but it was Mona as editor who drew the most press attention and condemnation. By contrast, most other journalists escaped criticism. Yet in three major areas of ethical concern that can be abstracted from the experience, the conduct by media people other than Mona show that the paradigm of South African journalism itself was neither clear cut, nor adhered to universally. These areas are firstly, the motives of the media players; secondly, their stance in regard to confidential briefings; and thirdly, their position in regard to giving testimony in judicial hearings.

Paradigm Challenge 1: Media Actors and Non-Journalistic Motivations

Mona provoked public questions after he authorised publication of Munusamy's story, while at least two other editors (at the *Sunday Times* and e.tv) with the information had refrained. The story had enormous repercussions because it seemed to deal a fatal political blow to Ngcuka's expressed claim that there was a prima facie case of corruption against Zuma. Breaking the spy story prompted speculation as to whether a pro-Zuma political agenda was being played out in *City Press*. It also begged the question whether Mona was either letting this happen without knowing it, or doing it for deliberate 'non-journalistic' reasons. Ngcuka himself raised the question of motives in regard to the *City Press* article. 'I do believe that the story was published . . . to divert the public's attention from the investigation by my office of Deputy President Jacob Zuma, former Minister of Transport Mac Maharaj and Schabir Shaik,' he said in an affadavit to the Hefer Commission *(Pretoria News,* 31 October 2003). To assess Mona's record in this regard, it is worth comparing it to that of other players.

Ranjeni Munusamy and 'Non-Journalistic' Agendas

The main source of the spy story was former ANC intelligence official, Mo Shaik (brother of Schabir, mentioned above), who had worked closely with Maharaj (also a former ANC underground operative and subsequent minister of transport). Like Zuma, Maharaj was also being investigated for corruption by the Scorpions. As emerged during the Hefer Commission, Shaik reconstructed a report he had done for the ANC in 1989 after an investigation into Ngcuka. The reconstructed report strongly implied that Ngcuka had indeed been an apartheid agent. Shaik gave a copy of the document to, amongst others, Ranjeni Munusamy, who at the time was a senior political writer on the *Sunday Times.*

Shaik, who was a strong supporter of Zuma, later told Hefer that he believed the reason for Ngcuka probing the deputy president was due to a personal-cum-political agenda flowing from the (alleged) spy history of the director of public prosecutions. The question why Shaik worked with Munusamy elicited speculation that she was part of his and Maharaj's pro-Zuma political camp. Munusamy herself has denied this, and argued that she was drawn in as a journalist, rather than by any political alignment (Interview, 17 June 2004; *Cape Argus,* 17 September 2003; *Sowetan,* 6 October 2003; *Witness,* 20 September 2003; www.journalism.co.za, accessed 5 January 2005). She said that her motivation was solely to shed light on the tensions between Ngcuka and Zuma *(Cape Argus,* 17 September 2003) and told the *Witness* (20 September 2003) that as the *Sunday Times* 'had pursued with ferocity the allegations against Zuma, it was ethically questionable not to run those against Ngcuka'. The story, she said, 'was not to prove that he was a spy' and that her 'only interest was that he had been investigated' *(Sowetan,* 6 October 2003). These reasons in her defence were not inherently at odds with many of the norms of mainstream journalism in South Africa. Where questions could be asked, however, was in regard to her extraordinary pushing for publication (and more, of a story whose key claim lacked clear proof), whether she had taken any precautions against being used, and whether her story was in the public interest and not only in the interests of the Zuma camp. All this also had ramifications for whether she would later count as a *bona fide* journalist when seeking to make a legitimate professional case in relation to compulsory testimony (see below).

Notwithstanding Munusamy's claims there was much condemnation of her in the media. Representative of this was the following in *Fair Lady* magazine (April 2004)—'Principled journalist or handmaiden of the pro-Zuma faction of the ANC? Will the real Ranjeni Munusamy please stand up?' In the ensuing article, her professional integrity was further questioned for actions on an earlier occasion in which she had revealed the identity of a confidential source (named Bheki Jacobs). It also claimed that her career had been built through 'a number of strategically used affairs'. The suggestion was that her Ngcuka smear was therefore the latest manifestation of a standing character flaw incompatible with the precepts ofjournalistic ethics and independence. 'Paradigm repair' insight would read this thrust as suggesting that it was, by nature, inherently incompatible with the character of a journalist. It can be noted that journalism itself does not definitively deify deontological ethics and personal conduct, and indeed at least sometimes condones teleological ethics. Regardless, however, Munusamy was painted as being beyond the pale of journalistic identity.

Despite such negative publicity, Munusamy was employed at *Business Day* within months of leaving the *Sunday Times,* and was later appointed as a regular reporter at *THISDAY.* Thus, even in as much as some of her conduct was questionable, it did not stop her from continuing as a journalist in the mainstream media. After *THISDAY* collapsed in 2005, Munusamy emerged as a media spokesperson within the pro-Zuma camp. Mona, however, was a 'permanent' casualty in terms of practising as a journalist, later emerging as a spokesperson for the Rhema church.

Questioning the *Sunday Times'* Own Agenda

While Munusamy denied being politically partisan, she accused her editor on the *Sunday Times,* Mathatha Tsedu, of blocking the story for political motives. She alleged that he was too close to Ngcuka and the Scorpions (Henk Rossouw, 22 September, www.journalism.co.za). It is indeed the case that Tsedu had attended a confidential briefing (see below) at which Ngcuka had strongly rebutted the spy charges. His paper had also featured an editorial favourable towards Ngcuka directly after this. But Tsedu rejects claims of non-journalistic motives: according to him, he would have published the spy story had Munusamy been able to verify that indeed (a) there had been an investigation in 1989, (b) that the reconstructed report was an accurate representation of the original one, and (c) that the claim—that Ngcuka had been an agent—could be proved (Interview, 27 May 2004).

However, a case can be made for publishing a story that Zuma's allies were trying to damage Ngcuka with unverified allegations that he had been a spy. That there were suspicions about the political motives of the *Sunday Times* was evident not only in the fact that Munusamy could consider it plausible to dispute Tsedu's integrity, but also that her view was echoed in degrees by other journalists (see Eric Naki, *Daily Dispatch,* 17 October 2003; Kevin Davie, *THISDAY,* 12 November 2003). Tsedu's position, in short, was not unambiguously legitimated in terms of a journalistic paradigm. Left unresolved, therefore, was the grey area whether the *Sunday Times* and in equal fashion e.tv were wholly without blemish in their initial decisions to withhold publication in any form, and if so, whether sympathy towards Ngcuka (or antipathy towards Zuma) accounted for this stance. Instead, Mona became a lightning rod for media outrage concerning his betrayal of what was presented as an unambiguous paradigm of 'professionalism'—one touted implicitly as being without political alignments. In other words, he was judged within a paradigm more aligned to a U.S. (rather than a U.K. or European) ideal type—and one that is certainly not incontestably hegemonic in South African journalism and its history.

The Concerns Around Mona

Mona prompted a degree of journalistic condemnation in immediate reaction to his decision to put the spy claims as fact into the public domain. *Business Day* editorialised against the decision, and media columnist Anton Harber also attacked it strongly. Responding to Harber, who is a founding editor of the *Weekly Mail,* Mona wrote on 14 September about a *Weekly Mail* article in 1991 which had suggested that contemporary ANC leader, Peter Mokaba, was a spy. Mona went on to add:

> Wasn't there a possibility that the rumour—on which the *Weekly Mail's* story was based—was planted by military intelligence in a bid to portray Mokaba as a traitor? Or better still, couldn't there have been a possibility that the 'disinformation' originated from people . . . who did not see eye to eye with Mokaba? Wasn't the *Weekly Mail* being used?

The title of Mona's column, in reference to Harber, was 'Pot calling kettle black'. It enabled Mona to represent himself as fending off hypocrisy, and as holding the moral high ground for having vented the story about Ngcuka's (alleged) history.

Wider journalistic condemnation of the *City Press* editor was slow to emerge. One reason may be respect in the profession for the previous stances that Mona had taken as an editor. For example (and in what must count as famous last words), early in 2003 Mona had written (in relation to a *City Press* story about rotten chickens being sold in South Africa): '. . . we have a responsibility to inform, and to do so accurately and fairly, especially when we are subjecting someone or an institution to serious allegations' (cited in *Witness,* 22 March 2003). This conventional journalistic principle does not seem to have operated with regard to his publishing the spy story as fact. However, in the immediate aftermath of his publishing the spy story, it seemed most of the media community gave him the benefit of the doubt and overlooked the ethical problems involved.

A delay in expressing outrage at Mona's conduct was also possibly a function of the fact that he had actually showed himself (a few months earlier) to be cautious about publishing negative information about Ngcuka. As he wrote in his column on 27 July 2003: 'For some time now the media has heard all sorts of damaging rumours about Ngcuka. That we have not published these proves a level of maturity by the SA media'. A month later, he wrote: 'We were recently treated to very damaging rumours, through an anonymous e-mail, about the head of the National Prosecuting Authority, Bulelani Ngcuka'. In the same column, Mona continued: 'I have been exposed to the most vitriolic foul-mouthing against black leaders. . . . Almost every week I have to make serious decisions about such stories, their credibility and the motives of the sources who bring them to our attention.' The slander 'destroyed reputations and assassinated characters' *(City Press,* 17 August 2003). It does not subsequently seem to have occurred to Mona (when publishing the spy story just three weeks later with the sub-heading presenting the claim as fact) that he was himself guilty of perpetrating a major character assassination.

Thus, although there were good reasons why Mona could have been roundly condemned by the media early on in the saga, it is also evident why it took some time for a united and forceful condemnation to emerge. In the meantime, there was no call to engage in paradigm status repair.

Mona's Motivation—Journalistic, Personal or Political?

What helped unleash media people's hostility towards their erstwhile colleague was the emerging story of what had motivated Mona in deciding to publish Munusamy's story. Mona told the Hefer Commission that he was neutral in the conflict between Zuma and Ngcuka (*Volksblad,* 2 December 2003). Instead, he said he was driven by directly personal—rather than journalistic—reasons. This was in regard to him claiming to have experienced growing ethical unhappiness about the defamatory character of a confidential briefing given by Ngcuka.

This claim was strongly challenged at the hearings. Mona was reminded that directly following the briefing he had published a favourable editorial comment on Ngcuka (see next section below). His change of mind in later damning the man was reported as being the consequence of a more self-serving personal motive, viz that he had subsequently come to believe that he too was being probed for corruption by Ngcuka's Scorpions. Although Mona tried to deny this, many in the media gave credence to the allegation (see, for example, *The Sunday Independent,* 30 November; *Die Volksblad,* 2 December 2003). According to the then *City Press* deputy editor, Wally Mbhele (Interview, 15 October 2004), Mona told him he had heard on the Saturday prior to publication that he was being investigated. The imputation is that personal anger against Ngcuka would have been a factor prompting Mona to rush into publication.[4]

For his part, Mona only acknowledged that he had been 'reckless' in publishing. Meanwhile, what was clear from his testimony, however, was that he seemed to believe that a personal motivation of moral outrage (even if manufactured retrospectively) would be compatible with a journalistic identity in post-apartheid South Africa. Arguably, if he had been convincing this position might have 'played' within his peer community, given the historical specificity of the South African journalism paradigm, where taking sides on major issues of principle is not deemed out of the question. On the other hand, hostility may still have emanated because his cavalier damaging of Ngcuka in the interests of Zuma would not necessarily have been shared by many journalists who believed that the deputy president was indeed implicated in corruption. Accordingly, an unacknowledged factor in the demonising of Mona was that not only did he flout a particular journalistic ethic of impartiality sometimes upheld (but not always practised) in the South African media, but that he did so in a direction that allied him to the interests of a political faction not in favour with the mainstream media.

It may be noted that at the commission Mona claimed that his senior staff had been party to the decision to publish. The point arising from this is that to the extent that a number of people (i.e., including his deputy Mbhele—interview 15 October 2004) ultimately agreed to publication, it was only Mona who, to put it colloquially, 'carried the can'. His colleagues did not elicit the same media condemnation as was meted out to him. Soon after the whole episode, Mbhele was appointed to a senior position on the *Sunday Times*.[5]

When Mona went on to present himself as the epitome of journalistic virtue at the commission, and then crumpled under cross-questioning, his ostracisation by his alienated fraternity was both inevitable and irreversible. This outcome was abetted by the man himself being quick to ascribe ulterior motives to those who had publicised damaging information against him. Thus, he argued that *The Star*'s reports on a conflict of interests in regard to his being an editor as well as being active in a public relations company, had been brought up to discredit his publishing the spy claims (*Sowetan,* 29 September 2003; *City Press,* 28 September 2003).

Although Mona was publicised as having a dubious grip on media ethics, it is also far from being an unassailable fact that Munusamy, Tsedu and the *Sunday Times,* possibly e.tv, Mona's senior colleagues at *City Press,* and even *The Star* (with the conflict of interests story) were all operating exclusively within the canons of a U.S.-style paradigm of politically impartial journalism. It may be that none of these other players promoted extra-journalistic agendas, or had leanings for or against Ngcuka and Zuma. What is at least certain is that their actions—in the context of an intense and underhand political conflict outside the ambit of the media could not easily be neutral. The result was that, as is reflected in letters to the press and in many broadcast programmes, many in the public began to ask whether journalists in general were indeed independent professionals. The media as a trustworthy source of information came under question in the face of concerns about shenanigans behind journalistic output. Yet far from discussing and debating the complexities about a detached versus a partisan paradigm, the response of much of the media—as is evident below—was to scapegoat Mona in a classic paradigm repair manner.

Paradigm Challenge 2: Vusi Mona's Responses to Ngcuka's Confidential Briefing

That Mona became a substitute for wider problems is also evident in him receiving almost exclusive blame for breaking confidentiality in the case of the Ngcuka briefing when other senior media people also behaved in journalistically questionable ways on this matter.[6]

The controversy in this case arose from a meeting convened on 24 July 2003, by Ngcuka as National Director of Public Prosecutions. In attendance besides Mona were Jimmy Seepe of *City Press,* John Dludlu of *Sowetan,* Mathatha Tsedu of the *Sunday Times,* Mondli Makhanya of *Mail & Guardian,* Jovial Rantao of *The Star* and *Sunday Independent,* and Phalane Motale of *Sunday Sun* (*Sowetan,* 27 November). In the course of the extensive briefing the editors heard (as was later alleged by Mona) that the director had made racist remarks about Indians and denigrated the reputations of several figures in the Zuma camp. Ngcuka had intended the occasion to be confidential—notwithstanding ambiguities about what this meant. The responses by the editors to this signal the grey ethical areas around confidentiality. Yet much of the coverage was artificially framed as paradigm black-and-white issues within journalism.

Editorial Independence in Regard to Briefings

Mona's questionable behaviour with regard to the briefing was not limited to the generally held belief that he leaked its contents (see below), nor even that he did so for an agenda seemingly based on pure self-interest. It also emerged that he appeared to have lapsed in terms of maintaining journalistic independence in his immediate assessment and response to the briefing. The danger of a confidential briefing is where the institution sways the judgement of journalists, undermining paradigmatic principles of autonomy and editorial judgement which are supposed to be based only on news values, institutional editorial policies, and an aspiration for balance and fairness. Even if a political–interventionist role is often accepted in the practice of South African journalism (and sometimes in theory), the issue of independently taking up such a partisan position is still a privileged ethic.

Shortly after the briefing Mona published a column in which he came out strongly in favour of Ngcuka, in regard to attacks on this public official. He wrote: 'If some of us don't like his decisions, tough luck'. He also said: 'Until it can be proven that he (Ngcuka) is prone to poor judgement in the execution of his work or that he is using his office to pursue personal agendas, Ngcuka should be left alone' (*THISDAY,* 27 November 2003). Plausibly, one can therefore suggest that Mona was probably positively reinforced or influenced by the briefing, even though it did not take long for him to change and unleash hostile information about Ngcuka.

The *Mail & Guardian* attempted to deal with the issue of the briefing co-opting editors, by arguing that confidential meetings brought in sources who if they were to be identified would prefer to remain silent, and that editors were not automatically influenced by the spin they received on such occasions. But Mona was not alone in taking a position favourable to Ngcuka consequent upon the secret meeting—as noted earlier, Tsedu also followed up with a pro-Ngcuka editorial. Yet neither case was especially singled out in the media for questionable stances emerging from what was patently a spin-doctoring occasion. Broader media defensiveness about the institution of confidential briefings took the place of debate and self-scrutiny about participation in the practice. The impression of editors being flattered by being brought into proximity with power and being influenced by such, while being bound to keep their involvement secret, was not challenged. In other words, editors turned a blind eye to repairing damage to the paradigm by changing it, preferring instead just to restate it.

Editors Colluding in 'Divide-and-Rule'?

A different dimension to confidential briefings which failed to elicit broad self-scrutiny in the media itself was raised by Eric Naki of the *Daily Dispatch.* Naki criticised the failure of all the editors at the meeting to question why only African editors had been invited. He asked whether 'the editors, including Mona, approved of the approach by the National Prosecutions Authority to discriminate against certain editors', and argued: 'It is always unacceptable and a bad practice to discriminate against certain sectors of the media—never mind racial discrimination' *(Daily Dispatch,* 28 November 2003.)

The Star's Jovial Rantao hit back angrily in a column in his paper on 26 September. He argued that no one had complained about all-white briefings during the apartheid era. Although this position hardly justified the post-apartheid mirror opposite, it was Mona, however, who remained in the adverse spotlight. This was probably in part because he later attacked his fellow attendees for failing to criticise the briefing (although uncontested evidence at Hefer was that he himself had at the time actually called for more such briefings). It was primarily, however, Mona's violation of the secrecy of the briefing that led to him being attacked by his peers. The wider problematic and substantive issue of being hand-picked for participation in secret briefings was not addressed by the media in any way that went deeper than Rantao's racial counterpunch. Damage to this aspect of the paradigm was thus left to stand.

Breaking Confidences and Breaking Ranks

The key condemnation of Mona came from his link to the original leakage of the apparent contents of the briefing. He told the Hefer probe that after various media had published a version of the briefing, he had sent a (near identical) version to the Public Protector, the Human Rights Commission, and the Chief Justice (in one report, the head of the Constitutional Court is also named) *(The Star,* 2 December 2003; *Sowetan,* 28 November 2003). Not only that, he also admitted to having discussed the briefing with a public relations associate, Dominic Ntsele, shortly after the actual event. In addition he conceded that the similarities between his notes and those published in *Business Day* by David Gleason (22 September 2003) could have come from him via Ntsele. Mona further said he had sent his version to *City Press* at a later point when he had left the paper, although he rather thinly denied that what was published in *City Press* on 28 September 2003 (by the acting editor Mbhele) and emanating from 'Concerned Citizen', was also his. According to Mbhele, however, Mona wrote the 'Concerned Citizen' document (Interview, 15 October 2004). Compounding all this, Mona also admitted under questioning at Hefer that he had left out in his circulated version that Ngucka had expressly rebutted the spy allegation during the session.

In addition, Mona also initially tried to claim to Hefer there that the event had not in fact been off the record. This further discredited him as a professional journalist. However, before testifying at the commission he also told *THISDAY* that he would be testifying as an ordinary citizen, not as a journalist (26 November 2003). And, in addressing the commission, he followed up with: 'In my view, it was not an off-the-record briefing as understood in journalism. It was a character assassination session . . . ' *(THISDAY,* 27 November 2003). The problem, as Tsedu later pointed out, was that Mona had attended the original briefing as a journalist *(The Star,* 27 November 2003). He was therefore guilty of violating a paradigm principle of respecting confidentiality, and thus in this regard the paradigm as an ideal type remained untouched. There was no questioning about Mbhele's decision to publish the 'Concerned Citizen' version of the briefing although this paper had had two senior staffers (Mona and Seepe) at the infamous occasion, and was therefore supposedly bound by the confidentiality assumed to have been agreed to by these staff representatives.

When Press Ethics Meet Public Interest Rationales

In justifying his leaks, Mona said he sought to give priority to the constitution (which specified rights to dignity which were, he said, violated at the briefing), over the professional journalistic ethic of respecting confidentiality. Journalist Eric Naki pursued this angle, saying that Mona had juxtaposed the sanctity of the constitution (i.e., the right of individuals such as Zuma and Maharaj to dignity), with the sanctity of the 'off-the-record' principle, and in so doing had put the media on the spot *(Daily Dispatch,* 28 November 2003). Another journalist, Dries van Heerden, wrote in *Rapport:* 'What do the other editors say about whether Ngcuka misused his position during the briefing? Are the principles of justice and truth more important than confidentiality?' (7 December 2003).

However, the debate did not go much further in the media. This silence was an interesting omission, given that a similar principle (of journalistic ethical standards versus the constitution—as representing public interest) was at the centre of a storm about whether or not journalists should give evidence in legal proceedings (see section below). It meant, at the end, that the questions about the self-privileged status of journalism were largely ignored in the media.

The Paradigm's 'Confidentiality' Clarity Unravels

Mona's breaking of confidentiality raised ire, rather than any deeper issues. Yet, his actions were not completely distant from the way several other journalists dealt with the Ngcuka briefing in regard to what 'confidentiality' actually meant. Mona himself was inconsistent on this issue. In his column cited earlier, he said he would not disclose information about the briefing because it was 'off the record'. Later, he told the Hefer Commission he believed he was professionally entitled to use the information in the briefing, as long as he did not identify the source. Finally, he admitted to the commission that he had indeed broken the terms of the occasion.

Naki wrote: 'For me, "off the record" means that absolutely nothing must be written or recorded about the issue. I do not agree with Mona's assertion that you can simply use the information as long as you do not attribute it to the source' *(Daily Dispatch,* 28 November 2003). However, one journalist who appears to have taken this latter interpretation of the event was *The Star's* Rantao. In the view of *Business Day:* 'The first to break the [confidentiality] rule was Rantao, who called Mac Maharaj—subject of an investigation by the Scorpions—and informed the former transport minister that his wife would be charged for tax evasion' (Xolani Xundu, 26 November 2003; see also Hopewell Radebe, 10 October 2003). Another journalist with an expedient interpretation of the confidentiality of the briefing was Tsedu. According to him, the *Sunday Times* had followed up a titbit from Ngcuka about questions having been sent to Jacob Zuma by the Scorpions. The paper, Tsedu elaborated, then obtained the list independently of the Scorpions (Interview, 27 May 2004).

Columnist Wyndham Hartley tried to clarify the distinctions between 'off the record', 'not for attribution', and 'background'. He said that when a source did not understand the difference, the journalist had a responsibility to inform the person of the options *(Weekend Post,* 29 November 2003). Clearly, not just Mona, but all the editors at the briefing, had failed to appraise Ngcuka of these distinctions.

In some respects the media discourse in the press left the paradigm in disarray. Off the pages, the South African National Editors Forum (Sanef) later engaged in what could be called 'paradigm clarification' by adopting a set of guidelines for confidential briefings (see Sanef 2004).[7]

Summing Up

The confidential briefing controversy as a whole thus raised a number of ambiguities in South African journalism, which were not limited to Mona. These were whether editors let themselves be influenced by a confidential briefing; whether they should take a stand as to who is invited to such an event; whether they feel confidentiality is more important than constitutional rights and public interest considerations; whether they clarify confidentiality; and, overall, how they understand and respect a commitment to confidentiality.

What was mainly underlined in this case was the paradigm principle that once a journalist gives a source a commitment to confidentiality, huge opprobrium is incurred by default certainly to the extent exhibited by Mona. But other journalists, including Mbhele, who as acting editor still published a version of the briefing, and Rantao and Tsedu who followed up in various ways that are contentious, remained leaders in the industry.[8] The instance as a whole showed 'classic' attempts at repairing the status of the paradigm by defending confidential briefings, avoiding fundamental problems in the paradigm, and heaping blame on Mona. But in an exception to the general response of paradigm status repair, there was an effort to change some of the paradigm's inadequacies by adopting a set of guidelines.

Paradigm Challenge 3: Testifying and Confidentiality of Sources

Internationally, many journalists have concerns about being drawn into judicial process. For decades, South African journalists have resisted testifying in criminal courts, and even in civil cases. It can be said that prior to this case it was a paradigmatic principle to keep members of the Fourth Estate separate and distinct from the policing and judicial arms of the state.

The ethic of not testifying implies that testifying per se deters sources from speaking freely to the media and that this limits the public interest in a free flow of information. The paradigm logic here would apply whether testimony is given on a voluntary or compulsory basis. The position then has the kernel in it of total non-participation in legal proceedings. If this is taken to represent at least one strand of 'correct' professional ethics, it was sorely tested and not only by Mona in person, but by a large number of journalists who argued in favour of testifying. Thus on this issue, any notion of a single hegemonic approach within the overall paradigm was irrevocably overturned.

The Complexities Emerge

In much of the media at the time of the commission, a far-from-hardline position developed in relation to journalists who were required (and refused) to testify. The commission itself showed sensitivity to journalists' concerns about coercion, and began by issuing invitations, rather than subpoenas, to several journalists. What this meant, then, was not only the issue of giving testimony per se at the commission, but the extent to which this would be mandatory if the invitees declined the requests. There seemed to be a sense that the inquiry was not quite the same as a court of law. But this stance of lesser antipathy towards testifying at the commission did not apply to Vusi Mona's voluntarily giving of evidence. His appearance was anathema to many journalists (see *THISDAY,* 26 November 2003). Yet, tellingly, there was no condemnation of another editor Phalane Motale (also an attendee at the Ngcuka briefing) who was reported as having voluntarily handed in an affidavit to the commission.

As it turned out, none of those invited (even those who declined) were called upon further, and only Munusamy received a subpoena when she declined to appear voluntarily. Despite questions about her political motivations, many journalists did accept that she was being subpoenaed in relation to work done in the name (if not perhaps the spirit) of journalism. However, while many of them evinced widespread hostility to Mona's testimony, they were not averse to questioning the sacrosanct ethical principle against testifying in regard to Munusamy, whether voluntarily or not.

What especially complicated the principle of 'no testifying' was the commission's decision to make a distinction in regard to Munusamy specifically naming sources and her rendering of other testimony. Various media highlighted the difference and commended Hefer for suggesting he would not necessarily require the former aspect in her evidence (see *Witness, 6* November 2003; *Sunday Times,* 19 October 2003; *Business Day,* 14 October 2003; *Business Day,* 20 October 2003; *The Citizen,* 12 November 2003). *The Star*'s columnist Max du Preez said Munusamy should give evidence, and simply stop when it came to keeping sources confidential. At that point, if she were forced to continue (said Du Preez) it would call for protest (*The Star,* 27 November 2003). Significantly, no journalist gave Mona the benefit of the same distinction, even though in his testimony he refused to disclose the identity of what he claimed were some of his sources. However, Hefer's nuance failed to win support across the board. For example, the *Sowetan* leaned against testifying (see 1 December 2003), while Sanef took a position to support Munusamy in her refusal to give evidence.

What emerges from all this is that Mona was thoroughly criticised for giving testimony (although it is also the case that much criticism was also driven in large part over the contents—and not wholly the principle—of his testimony). Meanwhile, there were many in the media who had relinquished the previously inflexible 'line' that journalists ought never to have truck with judicial proceedings. There was no paradigm 'repair' as such in this instance.

Defining Whether a Person Counts as a Journalist

The definition and building of boundaries is a well-described practice for how journalists differentiate themselves from others and protect the authority of the group (see Bishop 1999). Mona was condemned in the media for having brought journalism into disrepute, and despite his problems he was judged by standards pertaining to journalists. This contrasted with Munusamy—of whom it was asked whether she had abused her position as a reporter to the extent that she did not count as a journalist (at least in regard to this particular story).

It was the eyebrows being raised about Munusamy's original motivation in punting the spy story so strongly (by openly giving it to a rival paper) that challenged the journalistic community about whether or not she should be supported in her refusal to give evidence at the commission. Yet her former employer, the *Sunday Times,* agreed to pay her costs, saying that it was 'in support of the principle that journalists must not be obliged to reveal their sources' (*Fair Lady,* April 2004). Four media organisations also came together as an *amicus curae,* arguing that there were professional ethical and constitutional reasons for exempting journalists. They were Sanef, the Freedom of Expression Institute, Media Workers Association of South Africa, and Media Institute of Southern Africa (South Africa chapter), and their decision was based on the paradigm's long-held principle, rather than the person of Munusamy. However, this was far from being unanimously supported in the media—precisely because of the particularities of the reporter concerned. In Sanef, numerous journalists argued that in the specifics of this case, and in contradistinction to the general principle, Munusamy ought to give evidence (information from author's personal experience).

The debate was also made public in the media where various voices queried whether, if exemption were conceded to journalists, Munusamy should count as a journalist. Wrote one commentator: 'Was she as independent of her sources as she now wants to be from the judiciary, or was she misused in a smear campaign? Did she thoroughly enough try to verify the facts that were given to her by anonymous sources?' (Herman Wasserman, *Rapport,* 2 November 2003). A stronger letter in *Mail & Guardian* (30 October), by Mark Lowe, an opposition MP, was carried under the headline: 'Journalism? PR more likely'. He argued: 'Munusamy didn't deserve the label "journalist" . . . "Public relations officer for Zuma" would suit her better'.

The media reported others making a similar point. During the commission, Ngcuka said Munusamy should testify because '(s)he was playing a role much greater than that of a journalist' *(Pretoria News,* 31 October 2003). His lawyer said Munusamy had not acted simply as a journalist, but had actively promoted the story. 'She put herself outside the normal protection of a journalist' *(Mail & Guardian,* 23 October 2003).

Managing editor of the *Sunday Times,* Ray Hartley, asked whether Munusamy counted as a journalist, as distinct from being a source of a story. He concluded that she had obtained the information while working as a journalist, and in regard to this point, the case for her exemption was what would apply to all journalists. However, he said her spy story was not an impartial news report, but a political intervention. For him, in effect, while Munusamy counted as a journalist, her work in this instance did not constitute journalism. The inference then was that there was no case for her to be exempted from testifying (19 October 2003).

In the end Munusamy's appeal against giving evidence fell away when Hefer concluded the inquiry without her input. But an enduring result of the saga was that the inquiry challenged the media community's general understanding about involvement in legal proceedings. Mona was judged as a journalist and condemned, while at the same time distinctions were made to legitimate and encourage Munusamy to testify. She was urged to violate a time-honoured stand in South African journalism; he was disowned when he did. Not forthcoming in the media was deeper discussion about the broader public interest implications and precedents had Munusamy (or other media persons) ended up giving evidence, or about the longer-term significance of the different views on the matter for the paradigm position going forward.

Conclusion

The biggest casualty of the period was Mona, and the extent of his paradigmatic transgressions demonstrates why he came to this fate. These led to sweeping—but uninterrogated—declarations by the media about the damage to the institution more broadly. 'Journalism has had a disastrous month', said an article in *The Star* (29 September 2003). The commission could be said in part to be about journalism's failure, was the verdict of journalist Andrew Donaldson *(Sunday Times,* 30 November). The *Sunday Tribune* said that the revelations about Mona's moonlighting in public relations 'again called into question the lack of integrity among this country's media'. The *Sunday Times* opined: 'Journalism will count the costs of this shameful performance' (30 November 2003). 'Journalism goes on trial, and emerges looking shabby as abuse claim falters' was a headline in *Business Day* (28 November 2003). *Sowetan* said of Mona: 'No one could justifiably deny that his evidence has done considerable damage to our profession' (Editorial comment, 1 December 2003). *The Citizen* editorialised: '. . . because of him, journalists will have to strive harder to regain an (*sic*) retain public trust' (29 November 2003).

In the face of these generalisations condemning Mona, *THISDAY* editorialised in a way that explicitly exonerated the media qua institution: '(A) wide range of commentators have suggested that Mona's apparently unethical journalistic behaviour has landed the profession in a crisis.' However: 'His behaviour seems like an exception to the rule'. Thus, said the paper, Tsedu and other editors had not published the spy story, because the sources could confirm it satisfactorily; also, it argued, most editors did follow the dictum of protecting sources (Editorial comment, 4 December 2003.)

The other side of the coin of such pontificating was a lack of serious self-criticism. In 'classic' paradigm repair style, the finger was pointed solely at one individual. Mona's problem was that he was well suited to fulfilling the role of the mythological malicious trickster who deserves to be made into an equally mythological scapegoat (see Lule 2001). The point, however, is not easy condemnation of Mona for clear-cut infringements of a broader dominant paradigm of media ethics, but the fact that his case was represented in a way that eclipsed wider culpabilities, divergences and ethical uncertainties, as well as the need for in-depth discussion thereof.

In particular, in all this the relation of the media to external political battles, and the decision whether or not to publish within this fray was left aside. The extent of analysis of the period went only as far as the wider arms deal background in regard to which Ngcuka was investigating Zuma—it did not touch on the media's role in regard to the succession politics, nor did it raise questions about the president's possible background involvement in regard to Ngcuka's original investigation of Zuma, or his convening of a commission that he would probably have known would expose the Zuma camp as lacking proof against Ngcuka. There was little analysis of how the media was treated as a political battleground or of how best to respond to this challenge.[9] The operating U.S.-style tenet that journalists should report, and not become actors in, the news (Berkowitz 2000: 128) was not explicitly surfaced or contextualised in terms of the realities of the media as susceptible to functional briefings and leaks. Neither was the paradigm of the role of South African journalism in post-apartheid conditions the subject of contextual discussion.

It is true that Sanef went on to produce a set of guidelines on confidential briefings as a result of the controversies, suggesting that the issue went wider than Mona's violation. There was some debate also around testifying issues. But on the whole it can be argued that the media's response was mainly myopic—concentrating on Mona (and to a lesser extent, Munusamy) to the exclusion of deeper self-questioning.

The case served a dual purpose, akin to that described by Berkowitz (2000), of re-affirming identity and confidence among professional journalists themselves, and reclaiming the value of their work for the wider society. However, unlike cases of 'paradigm repair' in more settled societies, this one did not claim to bind journalists together in defence of one particular take on all issues, but also saw a diversity of positions emerging in regard to motivations, confidentiality issues and testifying. There was little appreciation for the fact that aside from some obvious parameters, aspects of the post-apartheid journalism paradigm itself were fragile, inchoate and uncertain. The assumed 'consensus' character of the paradigm on the whole was reinforced, even while simultaneously and ironically revealing that it did not apply when it came to the many issues, not least the principle of not testifying. For these reasons of flux, this was not a case where the professional community could simply 'continue operating as before, because they have isolated and dismissed the anomaly' (Hindman 2005: 227).

The Mona case showed that South Africa's paradigm of journalism is in transition, and suggests that the unresolved issues therein, such as political alignment versus impartiality, relations to political battles, and stances on testifying, are likely to generate controversies for some time to come. It also demonstrates that the media 'paradigm repair' framework, in a young democracy at least, is operational but not comprehensive, and far from being a comprehensively successful process. Aside from the 'classic' repair and reinforcement responses to challenges, there are also manifestations of paradigm flux and paradigm change and of greater concern the persistence of paradigm problems as well. The significance of this complexity may have a bearing on future studies using the paradigm repair framework.

Endnotes

1. A description of the case can be found in Berger (2004). Some of the insights in that work are theorised in this article.

2. Wall (2007), however, describes a case where 'paradigm repair' did not lead to boundary closure among professional journalists.

3. Wasserman (2005) has applied the framework of 'paradigm repair' to relations between mainstream and tabloid newspapers in South Africa, but without going so far as to comment on how the country's context complicates application of the approach.

4. The same personal motives—anger at being investigated—may have been at work not only in regard to running Munusamy's spy story, but also in Mona's decision to break the briefing's confidentiality. It has not been possible to establish this.

5. In unrelated musical chairs Tsedu was also fired from that paper, and went on to take up the *City Press* top job when it was later vacated by Mona.

6. The belief that Mona operated with an extra-journalistic agenda in disclosing the contents of the confidential briefing was probably the major factor in triggering the ultimate attacks on the man by his peers, as indicated by the tone of reports in *THISDAY* (28 November 2003) and *Sowetan* (28 November 2003), and the express condemnation of him by the National Editors' Forum.

7. Disclosure: this author was the initiator of these guidelines.

8. It should be noted, however, that Mbhele later wrote an apology in *City Press* for what happened when he was acting editor at the publication.

9. One exception was an article by Xolani Xundu who argued: 'SA's Fourth Estate is on trial for taking sides in the arms deal investigation and of finding Deputy President Jacob Zuma guilty of corruption. This was particularly noticeable after the media began reporting on issues raised in an off-the-record briefing with Scorpions chief Bulelani Ngcuka, and then allowed itself to be used by warring factions in the saga that evolved' (*Business Day,* 26 November 2003).

Postscript: The publication by Vusi Mona of the spy claims against the Director of Public Prosecutions, Bulelani Ngcuka, failed to stop the investigation into alleged corruption by Jacob Zuma. The probe continued, in fits and starts, through the years until charges were dropped in 2009. At the same time, Zuma emerged politically triumphant by winning leadership of the ANC in December 2007, and going on to become the South African president after April 2009. Vusi Mona reappeared during the ANC's 2009 electoral campaign, when Zuma was afforded a platform to speak to the influential Rhema Church congregation. Mona had become spokesperson for the church. After the election, Mona was rewarded with an appointment as Deputy Director of Communications in Zuma's presidential office. While Judge Hefer had concluded that the ex-editor of City Press was unlikely to ever find employment in the media again, this individual was evidently not discredited from the point of view of Zuma camp. His official appointment as a political spokesperson served to confirm the earlier paradigm repair activity which had seen him ostracized by editors. Yet, his status also obscured differences within the press itself in that it reinforced the classic metanarrative of a divide between government and a homogeneous and politically independent media.

References

Bennett, W.L., L.A. Gressett and W. Halton. 1985. Repairing the news: A case study of the news paradigm. *Journal of Communication 35: 50–68.*

Berger, G. 2004. Media ethics and the Hefer Commission. In N. Levy (ed), *Balancing secrecy and transparency in a democracy: Hefer Commission–the case study.* Pretoria: South African National Academy of Intelligence.

Berkowitz, D. 1997. *Social meanings of news: A text-reader.* London: Sage.

——. 2000. Doing double duty: Paradigm repair and the Princess Diana what-a-story. *Journalism* 1: 125–141.

Bishop, R. 1999. From behind the walls: Boundary work by news organizations in their coverage of Princess Diana's death. *Journal of Communication Inquiry* 23(1): 91–113.

Cecil, M. 2002. Bad apples: Paradigm overhaul and the CNN/Time 'Tailwind' story. *Journal of Communication Inquiry* 26 (1): 46–58.

Eason, D.L. 1988. On journalistic authority: The Janet Cooke scandal. In J.W. Carey (ed), *Media, myths, and narratives. Television and the press,* 205–227. Newbury Park: Sage.

Ettema, J. and D.C. Whitney. 1987. Professional mass communicators. In C.H. Berger and S.H. Chaffee (eds), *Handbook of communication science,* 747–780. Newbury Park: Sage.

Haas, T. 2006. Mainstream news media self-criticism: A proposal for future research. *Critical Studies in Media Communication* 23 (4): 350–355.

Hindman, E.B. 2005. Jayson Blair, *The New York Times,* and paradigm repair. *Journal of Communication* 55: 225–355.

Lasorsa, D. L. and J. Dai. 2007. Newsroom's normal accident? *Journalism Practice* 1(2): 159–174.

Lewis, N. P. 2007. Paradigm disguise: Systemic influences on newspaper plagiarism. https://drum.umd.edu/dspace/bitstream/1903/6803/1/umi-umd-4289.pdf (accessed on 5 January 2008).

Livio, O. 2006. Routinizing the unaccepted: Maintaining the journalistic paradigm through media discourse in Israel. Paper presented at the annual meeting of the International Communication Association, Sheraton New York, New York City, NY. 2006-10-05 <http://www.allacademic.com/meta/p14057_index.html> (accessed on 5 November 2007).

Lule, J. 2000. *Daily news, eternal stories. The mythological role of journalism.* New York: Guilford.

Ruggerio, T.E. 2004. Paradigm repair and changing journalistic perceptions of the Internet as an objective news source. *Convergence: The International Journal of Research into New Media Technologies* 10(4): 92–106.

Sanef. 2004. *Sanef guidelines on 'confidential briefings and sources'.* Adopted at Sanef Council, 30 May 2004, Durban. http://www.sanef.org.za/ethics_codes/sanef/ (accessed 5 November 2007).

Soloski, J. 1989. News reporting and professionalism: Some constraints on the reporting of the news. *Media, Culture and Society* 11(4): 204–228.

TRC. 1997. Report of the Truth and Reconciliation Commission: Vol. 4, Ch. 6: Institutional hearing: The media. http://www.struth.org.za./index-pl?&file=repnrt/4chapo6.htm (accessed 6 February 2001). http://www.truth.org.za/

Wall, M. 2007. Mainstream news media and blogger criticism: Expanding the boundaries of journalism's 'interpretive community'. Paper delivered at World Journalism Education Congress, June 25–27, Singapore.

Wasserman, H. 2005. A 'danger to journalism'. *Rhodes Journalism Review* (25 November): 34.

Windhal, S. and K. Rosengren. 1978. Newsman's professionalization: Some methodological problems. *Journalism Quarterly* 55(3): 466–473.

Zelizer, B. 2004. *Taking journalism seriously: News and the Academy.* London: Sage.

Source: From "A Paradigm in Process: What the Scapegoating of Vusi Mona Signalled About South African Journalism," 2008, by G. Berger, *Communication, 34*(1), 1–20. Reprinted by permission of Taylor & Francis/Routledge.

PART V

News Narratives as Cultural Text

News can be considered a form of cultural story that corresponds to larger, well-known narratives. The readings in Part V show ways that news draws upon familiar narrative forms to report on events that resonate with cultural values. In essence, connecting news to a culture's mythical narratives induces sacred elements of that culture. This outcome is not done through conscious intent but instead as a by-product of living in a culture—for journalists to report through myth seems natural, the appropriate story to tell.

One of the downsides to casting news as myth is that few occurrences present a perfect fit to how a mythical narrative "is supposed to go." In these cases, journalists face two options. One option is to write a narrative that does not resonate with a culture and its values; a second option is to selectively choose or adjust story elements to create a better fit between mythical narrative and reality; the latter scenario becomes more likely. Myth takes an assortment of facts that a journalist encounters and helps retell a story that feels comfortable and natural. Thus, for journalists, mythical narratives become a convenient way to streamline the work of reporting the news; once an appropriate narrative emerges, the story plot and its requisite actors become self-evident.

One drawback to telling news through mythical narrative is its lack of tangible context—it is the enduring values of news that matters most. This presents a challenge to the tenet of journalism's professional ideology that says each occurrence should be interpreted on its own terms, devoid of any frame of reference for choosing story elements or story actors. To use myth for storytelling devices implies that a journalist is simply rehashing an old story. But without those narrative aids, news cannot resonate with its audience and can seem "wrong." "Why Peace Journalism Isn't News" takes the position that events are not naturally comical, tragic, or farcical but take on those characteristics as journalists cast them into specific story forms. Liz Fawcett argues that once a story form has been cast, a journalist "feels compelled to meet certain expectations" for how the "drama" will unfold as news. Key among these expectations are the cultural values of the news audience. Fawcett demonstrates this through two Irish newspapers' reporting on national political violence in the 1990s. Because news narratives reflect specific cultural positions, once those positions are chosen, they need to be followed and maintained; some narrative options then get closed off. Although specific narratives frame news in a particular way, it is not the frames that are important but the social and cultural values that they represent.

"'Lost Boys' and the Promised Land: U.S. Newspaper Coverage of Sudanese Refugees" picks up on the idea of news as a framed narrative that expresses a society's dominant values. Many of these narratives are enduring and well established; by going back to familiar narrative forms, journalists are able to maintain audience interest in their work. At the same time, these narratives contain commonsense values and reinforce the status quo. Much like Fawcett's argument about the need to stick with a narrative form's basic structure once it has been chosen, Melinda B. Robins asserts that these standardized formats constrain journalists into "representations of reality akin to stereotypes." Thus, for coverage of news about American efforts to rescue war orphans from Sudan, the nation is portrayed as a backward people from a dark continent, which simultaneously reinforces America's cherished beliefs about itself. Within this narrative, a positive outcome for a "lost boy" is to quickly make the transition from jungle life and crocodiles into American consumer culture—electric appliances, junk food snacks, and minimum-wage jobs. In all, the narratives contained in this story are replete with dichotomies such as primitive/civilized or hell/paradise that allow little questioning of the values embedded within. Ultimately, the case study that Robins presents is yet another example of how familiar narratives help to create resonant but constructed news stories.

"Crafting Cultural Resonance: Imaginative Power in Everyday Journalism" picks up on this last point to argue that news built upon common narrative frameworks is most likely to seem accurate and authentic to media audiences. James S. Ettema defines resonance as "a public and cultural relation among object, tradition, and audience." Narrative fidelity thus speaks to the goodness-of-fit between issue frames and public perceptions. Journalistic processes such as assigning, reporting, writing, and editing are the means of crafting cultural resonance. Resonance, Ettema argues, "elevates news to myth and deepens it into ritual." The case he presents about a Japanese exchange student shot to death on Halloween by a homeowner mistaking him for an intruder becomes an ironic forum for exploring resonance in news. Through several ironic twists—such as the boy lacking cultural understanding to "freeze" or be shot—the audience is able to anticipate what will happen next and then watch it unfold just as expected. In a strange way, *awareness* of the boy's *unawareness* is exactly what makes the story resonant, as does American coverage of Japanese news about the shooting that criticizes America's propensity to guns and violence. In a reverse of the "Lost Boys" narrative, America becomes the backward nation and the Japanese Other turns into the morally righteous. When the homeowner was acquitted of wrongdoing, this plot reversal became stronger yet, and oddly, America's rough-and-tough individualistic character becomes all the more resonant.

"*Medea* in the Media: Narrative and Myth in the Newspaper Coverage of Women Who Kill Their Children" goes beyond a single case to see how a recurring narrative folded into news coverage of 10 women who murdered their own children—much like the mythical Medea. This narrative becomes prime terrain for building familiar cultural scripts into news, frequently focusing on the good mother/bad mother archetypes and also more broadly restating the media's role in reinforcing myths about motherhood, femininity, and women's social roles. After identifying four dominant motherhood narratives, Barbara Barnett takes on the story of the flawed mother, which in turn becomes either the *good mother* who became mentally ill from the stress of her work or the *inept caretaker* who lacked commonsense parenting skills all along. In the first case, irony once again becomes an element because testimonials to a mother's dedication and caring stand in stark contrast to the evil deed she undertook—again, the sense of irony creates a foreboding that the audience can move back and forth to interpret a self-fulfilling prophecy. News based on the inept mother, in contrast, becomes a moral play, with women ironically killing their children to save their own honor or simply because their children interfered with romantic interests. Throughout, the similarity in story elements becomes a striking means of demonstrating the larger power of mythical narrative informing the news.

From these four readings, it becomes clear that the values inherent in cultural narratives inform news in a predictable way so that news ultimately reproduces cultural values and contributes to their longevity. News as a familiar narrative becomes a helpful way of seeing news for what it is and helps account for the easy connection between the journalist and the media audience. It should also be clear from these readings that narratives pervade the news much more deeply than the specific case studies the authors introduce—challenging the reader to go beyond simple identification of a narrative and move outward toward an understanding of news as a part of the culture it serves.

16

Why Peace Journalism Isn't News

Liz Fawcett

Introduction

During the late 1990s, two Northern Ireland newspapers attempted a historic exercise in what has been called "peace journalism" (Conflict and Peace Courses, 1997). The newspapers, one nationalist and the other unionist, published joint editorials urging compromise in a dispute that has played a central symbolic role within the Northern Ireland conflict. The subject of the controversy was an annual Orange Order parade from the parish church of Drumcree in County Armagh.

The joint editorials of these two newspapers, the *Irish News* and the *News Letter,* were examples of a model of conflict reporting advocated by Johan Galtung (Conflict and Peace Courses, 1997, p. 44). At an international gathering of journalists and academics, he characterised the reporting of conflict as reactive and conducted along "us–them," "win–lose" lines. This mode of journalism saw peace as something that could be achieved only through victory and/or a ceasefire. By contrast, the model of peace journalism which he proposed was proactive, "win–win" oriented and saw peace as being realised through non-violence and creativity. While the traditional mode of conflict journalism focused on the visible effects of violence and on tangible outcomes and institutions, peace journalism adopted a more analytical approach, examining the role of social structures and cultures.

Most academic analysis of the reporting of conflict has concentrated on two factors that influence the way conflict is covered; firstly, the relationship of the media with governments and military authorities during a conflict (for example, Aulich, 1992; Herman and Chomsky, 1994; Kellner, 1992; Liebes, 1992; 1997; Philo and McLaughlin, 1995) and, secondly, the influence of journalistic routines and practices (Conflict and Peace Courses, 1997; Williams, 1992; Wolfsfeld, 1997b). This paper focuses on *textual* and *discursive* constraints on the coverage of conflict. It presents a case study in which those constraints privileged conflict frames over the development of the type of conciliation frame that would be favoured by advocates of peace journalism. The paper also illustrates how those discursive structures can actually position newspapers to behave like politicians and storytellers, using conflict frames in a strategic way.

Discursive Patterns in News Media Coverage

This paper focuses on the constraints placed on journalists reporting conflict on two regional newspapers in Northern Ireland. The U.K.'s regional and local press is rarely highbrow but aims instead to appear reflective about the concerns of "ordinary people" in the local community. It is fond of reaffirming a sense of community and "normality" by highlighting negative stories about those labelled as deviants in a manner that could fairly be described as "institutionalized intolerance" (Critcher et al., 1977, p. 166). It is the type of journalism which presents its audience as sharing a set of common virtues such as "common sense, caring, decency and responsibility" (Knight, 1989, p. 124).[1]

The superficial "common sense" morality that underpins much popular journalism at both national and local level helps to explain the prevalence of certain discursive frames that journalists tend to adopt when they report conflict. Wolfsfeld (1997a) and Wolfsfeld et al. (2000) identify two key frames used by protagonists in conflicts and rebellions: the *law and order* frame and the *injustice and defiance* frame. The *law and order* frame is used to portray one side of a conflict as a threat to "law and order," while the *injustice and defiance* frame focuses on constructing one party as being the victim of injustice and determined to stand up for its rights.

Part of the reason for the appeal for the media of popular frames of conflict is that they can be developed into rhetorical packages of argument and image, similar to those used by politicians. Each frame is underpinned by a series of rhetorical elements that fit together to form what Wolfsfeld (1997a), drawing on Gamson and Lasch (1983), terms an "interpretative package." In a conflict, each set of protagonists will have its interpretative package organised around what it sees as the central issues in that conflict.

These frames can also be developed into "stories" through certain of the narrative forms used by novelists and dramatists. Indeed, all news reporting is a form of narrative (Ettema and Glasser, 1988; Lipari, 1994; Olson, 1995). As Altheide and Snow (1979, p. 89) observe, the journalistic worldview holds that "any event can be summarily covered and presented as a narrative account with a beginning, middle and end." Thus, although journalists do not necessarily want to be storytellers and politicians, the discursive and rhetorical structures that they use can lead them to take on these roles when reporting conflict, as this case study illustrates.

Unionist and Nationalist Discourses in Northern Ireland

The newspapers that form the focus of this case study, the *Irish News* and the *News Letter,* are the only two regional daily morning papers in Northern Ireland.[2] The *Irish News* is nationalist in outlook, in 1998, 92 per cent of its readers were Catholic.[3] The *News Letter* was staunchly unionist, but has moderated its tone since the prospect of political change in Northern Ireland looked imminent. Eighty-five percent of its readers were Protestant in 1998.[4]

The reporting of both newspapers has reflected the interests and concerns of the ethnic group with which each identifies (Elliott, 1977; Kelly, 1986; Rolston, 1991).[5] An analysis of the coverage of a number of violent incidents in early 1992 shows that both newspapers employed variations of the frames identified by Wolfsfeld. The *News Letter* used a *law and order* frame that focused on fighting "terrorism." The *Irish News,* on the other hand, focused on ordinary people as the victims of violence and, where the security forces had carried out attacks, on concerns over the injustice of such behaviour.[6]

The *law and order* frame is reflected in the constant calls from unionist politicians throughout the Troubles for tougher security measures to be used against paramilitaries as the first, essential step in bringing about peace. Conversely, the concern of the *Irish News* for the victims of injustice reflects a wider discourse within the nationalist community which attaches great significance to the concept of martyrdom (Kearney, 1980; 1997; Ruane and Todd, 1996) and values patience, piety and suffering (Loftus, 1986; O'Connor, 1993). However, the image of martyrdom does not form part of loyalist culture.[7] As Kearney notes (1980, p. 68), "Suffering for them [loyalists] is not transformed into sacrifice and martyrdom but feared rather as a threat to their very existence as a distinct people." This leads loyalists to identify strongly with "the triumphalist symbols of their historical victories: the Apprentice Boys parade and the Orange Day [*sic*] celebrations commemorate political and military success not failure."

Drumcree: Framing the Conflict

This case study focuses on the way in which these two newspapers reported what has become known as the "Siege of Drumcree": an annual and often violent conflict over an Orange Order parade which attracted international attention in the four-year period covered by this study, from 1995 to 1998. The Orange Order parade takes place on a Sunday early in July each year, shortly before the Twelfth parades.[8] The Orangemen's stated purpose is to parade to and from a service at the parish church of Drumcree. Their traditional route back from the church had taken in the Garvaghy Road, which runs alongside a nationalist estate. The residents of this estate were fiercely opposed to the use of this route by the Orangemen.

Not surprisingly, the *Irish News* and the *News Letter* framed the Drumcree conflict in sharply contrasting manners. In many ways, they acted like politicians in their forceful and colourful use of rhetoric, and in the strategic use they made of particular frames or arguments. This section of the article identifies the frames used by each newspaper in its coverage of Drumcree. It examines the way in which these frames were linked to cultural and political discourses.

In July 1995, the Royal Ulster Constabulary (RUC) told the marchers to take another route because there was judged to be a serious risk of a violent clash between local residents and the Orangemen if the marchers went down the Garvaghy Road. The Orangemen refused and loyalists responded by blocking major routes around the port of Larne. Two days later, the RUC allowed the Orangemen through after an apparent compromise between marchers and residents. However, in 1996, a much more ugly scenario unfolded when the RUC again rerouted the parade away from the Garvaghy Road. There were fierce clashes at Drumcree and in many other parts of Northern Ireland. Again, much of the violence was initiated by loyalists. Eventually, the RUC allowed the marchers through, to the fury of nationalists.

The controversy was framed predominantly in terms of a "win–lose" frame by both the *Irish News* and the *News Letter;* the underlying assumption was that one side would lose while the other would win. The *Irish News* did carry editorials that urged compromise as the disputes began in both 1995 and 1996. However, it adopted a much less conciliatory line as events unfolded. It is worth exploring in more detail how each newspaper covered the conflict. The analysis that follows includes headlines, news reports, news features, photographs, captions and editorials, since these all played a part in the way each newspaper framed the dispute.

The *News Letter*

In 1995, the *News Letter* employed an *injustice and defiance* frame, treating the dispute like an honourable war. One photograph, headlined "Kitchen Teams Show Blitz Spirit," showed women making sandwiches for the Orange Order protesters *(News Letter,* 11 July 1995). The accompanying article featured one of the protesters who was a Dunkirk veteran. The following day, after the Orangemen had been allowed down the Garvaghy Road as a result of an apparent compromise, the *News Letter* (12 July 1995) carried a double-page colour spread headlined "A Hero's Welcome" and subheaded "Sound sleep in soft bed marks happy ending."

The following year, however, the frame that shaped the *News Letter*'s coverage changed as the scale of loyalist violence intensified. The day after the Orangemen were prevented from going down Garvaghy Road, the *News Letter*'s front page (8 July 1996) showed protesters standing around at Drumcree with a large white on black headline "DEFIANCE!" Page three was topped by another large headline "Loyalist Solidarity." Thus, the predominant frame was one of *injustice and defiance.* However, the newspaper's editorial was situated within a *law and order* frame, arguing that the RUC could have allowed the parade through and handled the resulting situation with "firmness." The *law and order* frame predominated in the newspaper the following day as the focus of its coverage switched to the escalating loyalist violence. When the Orangemen were eventually allowed down the road, the *News Letter* (12 July 1996) greeted the decision with an editorial headlined "Common Sense Wins the Day." The core issue, as far as the newspaper was concerned, was how to enable order to prevail.

In 1997, when the parade was allowed through without a stand-off, the paper's main focus was on what it saw as the vicious response of republicans to a reasonable decision with regard to the parade; again, its concern was the rule of law and order, and the "disorderly" behaviour of republican protesters. However, the following year, the predominant frame switched back to *injustice and defiance.* On Monday, 7 July 1998, for example, the *News Letter* ran an editorial headlined "Bouquet of Barbed Wire" and illustrated it with a large half-page photo of elderly Orangemen halted by a security-force barrier of steel and barbed wire. The editorial began,

> It is not difficult to understand why Orangemen felt stripped of their dignity at Drumcree yesterday. Before their walk along the Garvaghy Road became so contentious, few of the members of Portadown LOL [Loyal Orange Lodge] could have imagined that they would one day be faced by the might of the British Army ranged against them with weapons, heavy-duty armour and barricades of steel and barbed wire.

The *Irish News*

The *Irish News* framed the dispute in less pugnacious terms than the *News Letter,* portraying the Garvaghy Road residents as passive victims of aggression. We might term this frame *injustice and martyrdom.* When the Orangemen went down the Garvaghy Road in 1995, the *Irish News* (12 July 1995) commented in its editorial:

> Yesterday in Portadown the Orange Order had its day. The decision to allow its members to walk down the Garvaghy Road was a victory for mob rule. Once more unionism used brute force to get its way.

This line was echoed in 1996 when the newspaper argued that the decision to allow the Orangemen along the Garvaghy Road was caving in to "mob rule." The newspaper ran a large banner headline "BETRAYED" together with a picture of two tearful Catholic girls *(Irish News,* 12 July 1996). The girls were staying in a hostel after being driven out of their home by loyalists. Once again, the newspaper's coverage fitted within an *injustice and martyrdom* frame. This theme was continued during the following two years. In 1997, when the parade was allowed through by police, the *Irish News (7* July 1997) carried a large front-page picture of a Garvaghy Road resident in tears with blood pouring from her head. The headline caption read, "Blood and Tears as Orangemen Take Garvaghy Road." The overall image was of the Garvaghy Road residents as "innocent victims." In 1998, the most prominent images reiterated this theme; there were photographs of children fleeing from loyalist protesters close to the Garvaghy Road, violence in loyalist areas, and Orangemen protesting at Hillsborough with a caption that read, "We won't be going away you know" *(Irish News,* 8 July 1998).

The Joint Editorials

Despite the very different picture of the conflict painted by each newspaper, the two papers actually linked up to produce joint editorials on Drumcree in 1997 and 1998. About a month before the 1997 Drumcree parade was due to take place, the two papers published a joint editorial that proposed a simple compromise; both sides would honour an interim two-year agreement that would allow the Orangemen to march down the Garvaghy Road one year and to follow a different route the other year *(Irish News* and *News Letter,* 12 June 1997).

The proposal was not taken up by either side.[9] Nevertheless, the editorial did represent a major step for both newspapers, particularly the *News Letter.* While the *Irish News* received very few complaints about the editorial, the *News Letter* had many telephone calls from Orangemen who said they felt betrayed and that they were not buying the newspaper again.[10] However, as we have seen, when the Orangeman were allowed down the Garvaghy Road without a stand-off, the newspapers reverted to their respective sides in their framing of the conflict.

This level of dissensus did not, however, prevent the two newspapers from producing a second joint editorial on Drumcree the following year, 1998. This editorial *(Irish News* and *News Letter,* 4 July 1998) urged both sides to talk to each other and proposed that

> this year—as a gesture of good faith by both sides—the residents should lift their objections to the parade returning to Portadown by Garvaghy Road, and the Orangemen should voluntarily decide to return to Portadown by the uncontentious outward route.

In this case, the editorial was published just a few days before the Drumcree parade was due to take place. This time, the parade followed in the wake of a referendum that had supported the Good Friday Agreement, the political solution that had finally been drawn up by unionist and nationalist politicians. The first election to that Assembly had followed swiftly with the result that the Ulster Unionist leader, David Trimble, was now Northern Ireland's First Minister, with Seamus Mallon of the nationalist Social and Democratic Labour Party (SDLP) as his deputy. Moreover, the remit to rule on controversial Orange parades had passed to the government-appointed Parades Commission, which both the Commission and the government insisted was an independent body. The Commission had already ruled that the 1998 parade could not pass down the Garvaghy Road. It was clear that the government was determined to stand by the Commission's decision.

The *News Letter* had wholeheartedly supported the Good Friday Agreement, despite the fact that a significant minority of unionists was implacably opposed to it.[11] This decision represented an important milestone in a gradual shift that the newspaper had been making away from a fairly hardline unionist position (Brown, 1998; Mullin, 1999). The joint editorial on Drumcree was in keeping with the newspaper's support for the Agreement and with the spirit of optimism engendered by the referendum However, that "feel good factor" evaporated as a new stand-off between the Orangemen and the security forces began over the Drumcree parade. The dissolution of that optimism was reflected in the coverage by both the *News Letter* and the *Irish News,* which was shaped largely by the familiar *injustice and defiance* and *injustice and martyrdom* frames, respectively.

Yet, despite the fact that these were the predominant frames during Drumcree 1998, they diverged from the central editorial line taken by each newspaper. In their editorials, both newspapers continued to call for compromise. This meant both newspapers had a decidedly schizophrenic tone. For example, while the first part of the *News Letter*'s "Bouquet of Barbed Wire" editorial, cited above, was shaped by an *injustice and defiance* frame, the article went on to urge David Trimble and Seamus Mallon to work for a compromise and called on both sides in the dispute to find a resolution. The conciliatory message was not what the reader might have expected from the decidedly uncompromising photograph and headline.

The Strategic Use of Media Frames

The most significant feature of the coverage of both newspapers was the use they made of variations of the *law and order* and *injustice and defiance* frames. The basic case put by both the Garvaghy Road residents and the Orangemen fitted within a broader version of the *injustice and defiance* frame identified by Wolfsfeld; both sides portrayed their demand to have their way as an absolute right, and any infringement of that right as injustice. However, the frame adopted by the residents and the *Irish News* portrayed the residents as passive oppressed victims; it was a frame best summed up as *injustice and martyrdom* rather than *injustice and defiance.*[12]

This is not surprising in view of our discussion of the very different types of symbolism within unionist and nationalist discourses. Both the Garvaghy Road residents and the Portadown Orangemen were prepared to resist *passively* any attempt by the authorities to enforce a solution to the conflict which they did not agree with. Thus, the Garvaghy Road residents and their supporters were as "defiant" as the Orangemen, and yet this was not the image portrayed by the residents or the *Irish News.* Both the residents and the newspaper framed the residents as passive victims, focusing on images of oppression rather than on the fact that the residents were taking a stand against this injustice. This framing is consistent with the framing of violent conflict identified in previous coverage of the *Irish News* and resonates with the cultural significance that nationalists attach to martyrdom.

As noted above, loyalist culture is coloured by a sense of pride which at times becomes triumphalist. it is perhaps no surprise then that the *News Letter*'s coverage was frequently underpinned by an *injustice and defiance* rather than *injustice and martyrdom* frame. The *injustice and defiance* frame shaped all the *News Letter's* coverage in 1995, some of its coverage in 1996 and much of its reporting in 1998. However, in both 1996 and 1997 a *law and order* frame was predominant. The main issue for the newspaper in 1996 was how to enable order to prevail. This may well have been because loyalist violence quickly escalated to a much greater level than the previous year. It was doubtless also influenced by the fact that a number of leading unionist politicians used the "restoration of order" argument. Both these politicians and the *News Letter* believed order would be restored if the police permitted the parade to go ahead without the agreement of residents. In 1997, the decision to allow the Portadown Orangemen down the Garvaghy Road without a stand-off prompted widespread violence in nationalist areas; hence, the *law and order* frame was the obvious one for the *News Letter* to adopt.

The shifting frames of the *News Letter*'s coverage were consistent in one sense, however; each time, they supported the aim of the Orangemen in their bid to march down the road. Like unionist politicians, the newspaper deployed different frames in a strategic way; the *law and order* and *injustice and defiance* frames could be substituted for each other as best fitted the circumstances. By contrast, the joint editorials that urged compromise in 1997 and 1998 were proactive attempts by the two newspapers to set a conciliatory agenda before conflict broke out. The problem with the compromise frame of the joint editorials was that most of the events that occurred during the four Drumcree Parades could be fitted much more easily into a *law and order* or an *injustice* narrative, it is also important to note that the *News Letter*'s *law and order* frame was consistent with the *law and order* frame it had adopted in earlier years with regard to violent attack by paramilitary groups and members of the security forces.

Political Rhetoric

However, it was not just the *content* of political discourse which was mirrored in the *News Letter*'s coverage. What is also evident in the coverage of both newspapers is the employment of the same discursive *strategies* used by politicians in their speeches and debates. The most fully developed of these centred on a frame of *injustice and defiance* in the *News Letter* and *injustice and martyrdom* in the *Irish News.* Figure 1 illustrates the extent to which a newspaper is able to use elements of the type of rhetorical interpretative package identified by Gamson and Lasch (1983). The elements of the package are to be found in headlines, news articles, captions, editorials and prominent quotes.

The Newspaper as Storyteller

Equally important, however, are the elements of narrative form which shape news accounts. News is a form of narrative (Ettema and Glasser, 1988; Lipari, 1994; Olson, 1995). As White (1984) has pointed out, any set of events can be plotted in different ways. No set of events is *intrinsically* comical, tragic or farcical; they have to be constructed by the storyteller *within* a particular story form. This is a process undertaken by the journalist just as much as by the novelist or dramatist. It has been argued quite rightly that this is not a *conscious* process; journalists do not intentionally use particular narrative forms (Olson, 1995). Rather, narrative form functions in an *intrinsic* way to shape audience expectations and reactions. However, like the elements of political rhetoric, narrative form positions journalists to act strategically—this time as storytellers. In other words, once a particular "drama" has begun, the journalist feels compelled to meet certain expectations.

Olson (1995) highlights the use of progressive narrative forms in news reporting; these advance a story in a predictable way that taps into the expectations and cultural values of the audience or readers. This includes ensuring that the reactions of key actors are seen as appropriate emotional responses to the story's events. As Olson notes, the presence of these forms in news journalism may help to explain journalists' predilection for "moving the story on" rather than offering explanation and analysis.

In the coverage of Drumcree, the reporting of both newspapers was structured by progressive narrative forms. Both newspapers told the story in a manner that allowed it to progress from one stage to the next in a way that would be recognisable and acceptable to their readers. However, the use of these progressive forms firmly excluded the possibility of developing alternative narratives. Thus, while both newspapers could call for compromise before the annual conflict over Drumcree actually began, the repetition of the compromise theme was not made meaningful by the narrative framing within which it was placed. That narrative form conveyed a sense of injustice for which anger and bitterness, rather than conciliation, were the appropriate responses.

However, in 1998, there was a twist in the plot which led both newspapers to converge in the way in which they framed the Drumcree story. In this instance, the logic of progressive form worked to bring the two newspapers towards a common narrative. In the early hours of Sunday, 12 July, three young brothers were murdered in an arson attack in Ballymoney, County Antrim. Richard, Mark and Jason Quinn had a Catholic mother and the police said the killings were undoubtedly sectarian in motive. The murders so moved the Orange Order's Grand Chaplain for County Armagh, Revd William Bingham, that he invited television cameras into his Sunday service so that he could publicly call on the Orangemen to abandon their protest. Church leaders and politicians swiftly followed with similar pleas.

Yet, the Orange Order refused to call off its protest. Two days later, the *News Letter* (14 July 1998) attributed to the Order some responsibility for the murders, and criticised the Order's subsequent response:

> Had the Orange Order signalled that it was scaling down the protest to a token level because of the orgy of violence and intimidation which accompanied it, and as a mark of respect to the three brothers, it would have earned widespread respect.
>
> Instead the Order continued to wash its hands of any responsibility for events at Drumcree or anywhere else, giving the impression that it regards human life and peace on our streets as less important than its right to march through a Catholic area.

The *Irish News* (18 July 1998) took up the same theme in an editorial a few days later, in which it described Orangeism as being "stuck in

	News Letter	*Irish News*
Meta-frame (14)	Injustice and defiance	Injustice and martyrdom
Core frame (15)	The issue is whether the Orangemen should be prevented from marching because of republican threats of violence	The issue is whether the Orangemen should get their way through loyalist violence
Core position	Orangemen should not be prevented from marching by a republican-orchestrated campaign of protest	Orangemen should not be able to get their way because of loyalist brute force
Metaphors		Time bomb/long hot summer
Historical exemplars	The Blitz (Second World War), Ulster Workers' Council strike	West Bank (i.e., Israelis versus Palestinians)
Catchphrases	"Traditional Orange march"/"Sinn Fein thugs and bully boys"	"Brute force"
Depictions	Orangemen as decent and honourable/nationalist protest as orchestrated by republican "bully boys"	Loyalists and Orangemen as using "brute force" to get their way/ nationalist residents as decent and honourable
Visual images/captions	Police blocking the way of Orangemen/Orangemen and Ian Paisley as heroes (after the march was allowed through)	Police enforcing law and order/ nationalists staging peaceful protest
Causes	Republican orchestration	Dishonourable victory through the use of brute force
Outcome (16)	Honourable victory	Dishonourable victory through the use of brute force
Appeals to principle	Right to march *traditional* route/don't give in to republican blackmail	"Tradition" must evolve/we mustn't give in to "mob rule" by loyalists

Figure 1 Drumcree 1995: competing interpretative packages.[13]

its own rut" and declared "last weekend's tragedy gave it the opportunity to retire with dignity. It did not take it."

Thus, it took a tragedy to bring the two newspapers towards a common frame with regard to Drumcree. When the 1998 Drumcree conflict began, each newspaper treated its respective side in the dispute as the victims of injustice (the *Irish News* referring to past treatment of the Garvaghy Road residents). In these circumstances, the *injustice and defiance* and the *injustice and martyrdom* frames acted as the obvious frames around which journalists from each newspaper respectively could shape their coverage. The deaths of the Quinn brothers did not alter the *injustice and defiance* frame of the Orange Order protesters. Part of the reason for this was that they questioned the link that the police had made with loyalists. However, the murders did raise a chorus of protest from leading Protestant clergymen and moderate unionist politicians. This new injustice outweighed the grievances of the Orangemen in the minds of those who spoke out. Given the strong reaction from these èlite sections of unionism, the emergence of these young and innocent victims of violence was not a story a progressive unionist newspaper could downplay. These victims fitted into the narrative of compromise and reconciliation; they were "worthy victims" by the estimation of both nationalists and moderate unionists. A frame that might best be labelled *injustice and innocent victims* was employed both by politicians representing these political viewpoints, and by the two newspapers that form the focus of this case study.

Conclusion

Ozgunes and Terzis (2000) found a desire among Greek and Turkish journalists to step beyond their normal routine practices and to report the Greek–Turkish conflict in a more constructive way. Doubtless, an attitudes survey of journalists on the *Irish News* and the *News Letter* would reveal similar expressed sentiments. The fact that journalists working for a news outlet identified with one side of a conflict rarely do become peacemakers can be traced, in large part, to the constraining nature of the news text.

In other words, the rhetorical and narrative forms used by the news media facilitate certain frames or discourses, while closing off the development of alternative ways of viewing a set of events. We have seen how the *Irish News* and *News Letter* employed discursive strategies similar to those of politicians, and each presented a rhetorical package of arguments and symbols. We have also seen how both newspapers unconsciously allowed their reporting to be structured by narrative forms that excluded arguments aimed at finding a compromise solution to the Drumcree dispute. This helps to explain why neither newspaper really developed the conciliatory arguments they put forward in their joint editorials, until the Quinn murders altered the "narrative."

Thus, rhetorical and narrative structures *shape* and *constrain* the manner in which newspapers report conflict. At the same time, this paper has argued that those very structures can *position* newspapers as both politicians and storytellers in their coverage of conflict; this, in turn, means newspapers are likely to act strategically, finding the frame that best suits their purpose as politician and storyteller. In attempting to find ways of encouraging newspapers to promote "win–win" as opposed to "win–lose" frames of conflict (Conflict and Peace Courses, 1997), it will be necessary to address the power of these discursive structures, as well as the power of the political and professional cultures within which journalists operate.

Acknowledgments

The author would like to thank John Hill for his comments on an earlier draft of this article.

Notes

1. Knight saw this approach as a feature of tabloid press and television journalism, but it could equally be applied to broadsheet newspapers that aim to have popular appeal.
2. The other daily regional newspaper, the *Belfast Telegraph,* has a late morning edition but is essentially an evening newspaper.
3. Source: percentage readership figure from the Target Group Index for 1998, courtesy of the *Belfast Telegraph.*
4. Source: as in note 3.
5. In the author's view, both Catholics and Protestants in Northern Ireland can be considered as ethnic groups. See Fawcett (2000, pp. 3–4).
6. The analysis examined coverage of incidents during January and February 1992 in both newspapers.

The relevant incidents with regard to this analysis were: a van bomb explosion in the centre of Belfast in which five security force members were injured *(Irish News* and *News Letter,* 6 January 1992), an IRA bomb attack on a bus in County Tyrone in which seven passengers were killed and six seriously injured *(Irish News* and *News Letter,* 18 January 1992), the killing of three men in a Sinn Fé in office by an off-duty policeman *(Irish News* and *News Letter,* 5 February 1992), a loyalist gun attack at a bookmaker's shop in Belfast in which five people were killed *(Irish News* and *News Letter,* 6 February 1992), and the shooting of four men by soldiers in County Tyrone *(Irish News* and *News Letter,* 17 February 1992).

7. The term "loyalist" rather than "unionist" is used here because the quote by Kearney cited in the text refers specifically to loyalists In Northern Ireland, the term is generally used to refer to those who support, or who would have broad sympathies with, loyalist paramilitary groups and/or political parties and organisations linked to such groups. Therefore, the term does not refer to the whole unionist community. However, it is fair to say that the wider unionist community does not attach great cultural significance to the concept of martyrdom.

8. The main Orange Order parades are held on 12 July each year on what is known as "the Twelfth." The parades commemorate the victory of King William of Orange at the Battle of the Boyne in 1690. While the parades appear archaic to many outsiders, they have been traditionally regarded by unionists as an opportunity' to celebrate their identity. However, many nationalists in Northern Ireland view the parades as triumpha list and offensive. For a much fuller discussion of the significance of the parades, see Jarman and Bryan (1996), Jarman (1997) and Fawcett (2000, pp. 88–102).

9. According to the Editor-in-Chief of the *News Letter,* Geoff Martin, it appears that the editorial did play a part in influencing the Orange Order to make a concession on another parade that year. This view is based on conversations Mr. Martin had at the time with members of the Orange Order.

10. This information was provided by the editors of each newspaper.

11. The available evidence suggests that a significant minority of unionists opposed the Good Friday Agreement, but it is impossible to be sure of the exact proportion. A referendum on the Good Friday Agreement was held in Northern Ireland in May 1998. However, voters were not asked to state whether they were nationalist or unionist supporters, and the turnout for the referendum was very low (56.3 percent). Polls conducted at the time suggested that a narrow majority of those unionists who voted supported the Agreement (see Wilford, 1999).

12. I am using here the *Oxford English Dictionary* (Thompson, 1996, p. 612) definition of a martyr as "a person who suffers for adhering to a principle, cause, etc."

13. Figure 1 is based on the concept of an "interpretative package" first put forward by Gamson and Lasch (1983) and used by Wolfsfeld (1997a). The categorisation analyses the package in terms of the framing and reasoning devices it utilises Framing devices are those which give the set of ideas its coherence and provide a framework within which these ideas can be presented and viewed. These devices comprise metaphors, exemplars, catchphrases, depictions, and visual images. There are also certain reasoning devices; these provide justifications for the stance adopted by the interpretative package. Gamson and Lasch categorise these mechanisms as causes, consequences (see note 16) and appeals to principle All these devices are rhetorical strategies used by politicians in argung a case.

14. The "meta-frame" is the broad frame, linked to wider cultural discourses, within which the interpretative package is situated.

15. Wolfsfeld (1997a) defines the "core frame" in a conflict situation as the frame that encapsulates what each set of protagonists sees as the central issue. The core frame provides the central idea around which the interpretative package is constructed.

16. In this case study, the "consequences" category used by Gamson and Lasch (1983) and Wolfsfeld (1997a) has been adapted to show how the two newspapers portrayed the actual outcome of the events that took place.

References

Altheide, David L. and Snow, Robert P. (1979) *Media Logic,* Beverly Hills: Sage.

Aulich, James (1992) "Wildlife in the South Atlantic: graphic satire, patriotism and the fourth estate," in: James Aulich (Ed.), *Framing the Falklands War: nationhood, culture and identity,* Milton Keynes: Open University Press, pp. 84–116.

Brown, Rob (1998) "In an era of cutthroat competition, here is one UK editor who will risk alienating his core readership," *The Guardian,* 18 May, pp. 10–11.

Conflict and Peace Courses (1997) The *Peace Journalism Option,* Buckinghamshire, UK: Taplow.

Conflict and Peace Courses/TRANSCEND Peace and Development Network.

Critcher, Chas, Parker, Margaret and Sondhi, Ranjit (1977) "Race in the Provincial Press: a case study of five West Midlands newspapers," in: UNESCO, *Ethnicity and* the *Media: an analysis of media reporting in* the *United Kingdom, Canada and Ireland,* Paris, pp. 25–192.

Elliott, Philip (1977) "Reporting Northern Ireland: a study of news in Great Britan, Northern Ireland and the Republic of Ireland," in: UNESCO, *Ethnicity and* the *Media: an analysis of media reporting in the United Kingdom, Canada and Ireland,* Paris, 8 pp. 263–376.

Ettema, James S. and Glasser, Theodore L. (1988) "Narrative Form and Moral Force: the realization of guilt and innocence through investigative journalism," *Journal of Communication* 38(3), pp. 8–26.

Fawcett, Liz (2000) *Religion, Ethnicity and Social Change,* Basingstoke: Macmillan.

Gamson, William A. and Lasch, Kathryn E. 1983. "The Political Culture of Social Welfare Policy," in: Shimon E. Spiro and Ephraim Yuchtmann-Yaar (Eds), *Evaluating the Welfare State: Social and Political Perspectives,* New York: Academic Press, pp. 397–415.

Herman, Edward and Chomsky, Noam (1994) [1988] *Manufacturing Consent: the political economy of the mass media,* London: Vintage.

Jarman, Neil (1997) *Material Conflicts: parades and visual displays in Northern Ireland,* Oxford: Berg.

Jarman, Neil and Bryan, Dominic (1996) *Parade and Protest: a discussion of parading disputes in Northern Ireland,* Coleraine: Centre for the Study of Conflict, University of Ulster.

Kearney, Richard (1980) "The IRA's Strategy of Failure," *Crane Bag* 14(2), pp. 62–70.

Kearney, Richard (1997) *Postnationalist Ireland: politics, culture, philosophy,* London: Routledge.

Kellner, Douglas (1992) The *Persian Gulf TV War,* Boulder: Westview Press.

Kelly, Mary (1986) "Pox er, Control and Media Coverage of the Northern Ireland Conflict," in: Patrick Clancy, Sheelagh Drudy, Kathryn Lynch and Liam O'Dowd (Eds), *Ireland: A Sociological Profile,* Dublin: Institute of Public Administration, pp. 400–23.

Knight, Graham (1989) "The Reality Effects of Tabloid Television News," in: Marc Raboy and Peter A. Bruck (Eds), *Communication for and against Democracy,* Montreal: Black Rose, pp. 111–29.

Liebes, Tamar (1992) "Our War/Their War: comparing the *Intifadeh* and the Gulf War on U.S. and Israeli television," *Critical Studies in Mass Communication* 9, pp. 44–55.

Liebes, Tamar (1997) *Reporting* the *Arab–Israeli Conflict: how hegemony works,* London: Routledge.

Lipari, Lisbeth (1994) "As the Word Turns: drama, rhetoric, and press coverage of the Hill–Thomas hearings," *Political Communication* 11(3), pp. 299–308.

Loftus, Belinda (1986) "Matters of Life and Death: Protestant and Catholic ways of seeing death in Northern Ireland," *Circa* 26, pp. 14–18.

Mullin, John (1999) "Challenging the Union," *The Guardian,* 7 June, p. 10.

O'Connor, Fionnuala (1993) *In Search of a State: Catholics in Northern Ireland,* Belfast: Blackstaff Press.

Olson, Kathryn M. (1995) "The Function of Form in Newspapers' Political Conflict Coverage: *The New York Times'* shaping of expectations in the Bitburg controversy," *Political Communication* 12(1), pp. 43–64.

Ozgunes, Neslihan and Terzis, Georgios (2000) "Constraints and Remedies for Journalists Reporting National Conflict: the case of Greece and Turkey," *Journalism Studies* 1(3), pp. 405–26.

Philo, Greg and McLaughlin, Greg (1995) "The British Media and the Gulf War," in: Greg Philo (Ed.), *Glasgow Media Group* Reader, *Volume 2: industry, economy, war and politics,* London: Routledge, pp. 146–56.

Rolston, Bill (1991) "News Fit to Print: Belfast's daily newspapers," in: Bill Rolston (Ed.), The *Media and Northern Ireland: covering* the *Troubles,* Basingtoke: Macmillan, pp. 152–86.

Ruane, Joseph and Todd, Jennifer (1996) The *Dynamics of Conflict in Northern Ireland: power, conflict and emancipation,* Cambridge: Cambridge University Press.

Thompson, Della (Ed.) (1996) The *Oxford Compact English Dictionary,* Oxford: Oxford University Press.

White, Hayden (1984) "The Question of Narrative in Contemporary Historical Theory," *History and Theory* 23(1), pp. 1–33.

Wilford, Rick (1999) "Epilogue," in: Paul Mitchell and Rick Wilford (Eds), *Politics in Northern Ireland,* Boulder: Westview Press.

Williams, Kevin (1992) "Something More Important than the Truth: ethical issues in war reporting," in: Andrew Belsey and Ruth Chadwick (Eds), *Ethical Issues in Journalism*, London: Routledge, pp. 154–70.

Wolfsfeld, Gadi (1997a) *Media and Political Conflict: news from the Middle East*, Cambridge: Cambridge University Press.

Wolfsfeld, Gadi (1997b) "Promoting Peace through the News Media: some initial lessons from the old peace process," *Press/Politics* 2, pp. 52–70.

Wolfsfeld, Gadi, Avraham, Eli and Aburaiya, Issam (2000) "When Prophecy Always Fails: Israeli press coverage of the Arab minority's Land Day protests," *Political Communication* 17(2), pp. 115–31.

Source: From "Why Peace Journalism Isn't News," 2002, by L. Fawcett, *Journalism Studies, 3*(2), 213–223. Reprinted by permission of Taylor & Francis/Routledge.

17

"Lost Boys" and the Promised Land

U.S. Newspaper Coverage of Sudanese Refugees

Melinda B. Robins

Amazing Grace, how sweet the sound that saved a wretch like me, I once was lost, but now I'm found, was blind but now I see. (U.S. gospel song)

'I don't want ever to be a man', Peter said with passion. 'I want always to be a little boy . . . '. *(Peter and Wendy*, by J. M. Barrie)

Scholars have long described U.S. media coverage of international news, especially that from poor countries, as problematic (e.g., Masmoudi, 1979; Hawk, 1992; Herman and McChesney, 1997). More recently—and especially since the 2001 destruction of the World Trade Center—much concern also has been leveled at Americans' profound ignorance of world affairs during a time of deepening economic and political globalization. Coverage of Africa in particular perhaps has been the least adequate to understanding the complex political, social and economic realities of the continent. Hawk (1992: 3–14) details how the U.S. media construct and perpetuate images of African countries as hopelessly confusing and of their peoples as doggedly 'backward', unwittingly promoting the hackneyed 'dark continent' label that implies an inability to carry out the West's Enlightenment project of rationality and technology.

More than 20 years after the turmoil at UNESCO over charges of unbalanced coverage of the Third World by the western media (e.g., MacBride, 1980), the steamroller of economic and cultural globalization and the proliferation of media outlets in a digital age could have meant an increase in foreign news coverage, but the reverse has been true (Randal, 2000: 35). In the 21st century, coverage in the U.S. media of international news continues to follow the 'coups and earthquakes' approach. Coverage of Africa in particular still is skewed to crisis reporting or U.S. foreign policy concerns. Veteran newsman Peter Arnett (1998) describes how after the Cold War ended, the U.S. broadcasting industry essentially gave up on improved coverage of Africa's 54 nations and territories and more than 800 million people. Today, only the largest newspapers maintain small reporting staffs in Africa, mostly in Cairo and South Africa, skimming over the rest of the continent unless there is conflict or catastrophe. Phillips (1999) discusses how the limitations imposed by higher profit expectations, costs and logistics have become paramount, especially when it comes to foreign news. To make it into the headlines, such stories must be 'clear cut, accessible and cheap' (Phillips, 1999: 132). As Hawk (1992: 2) notes, Americans need contextual information to understand the news. 'The image of Africa in the American mind is worse than incomplete: It is inaccurate.'

From a cultural studies perspective, Brock (1992: 157) describes how media content helps to create the images and promote the paradigms that define Americans' relationship to and expectations of Africa and Africans. Also, because the U.S. media are overwhelmingly profit-driven, their corporate owners are concerned first with marketing the news. Making use of well-established American images such as 'the rugged individual' and 'the American Dream' continues to be a time-tested marketing technique. In turn, a devastated and 'backward' Africa has a comfortable place in the American mind and media. Stories about war and AIDS predominate. Domke (1997: 1–3), following Hall (1995: 18–22), describes how the press helps to shape and reinforce values and attitudes, even as the ideologies embedded in its messages encourage a 'common-sense' and uncontestable acceptance of a status quo. Therefore, the media can serve as an important model for public discourse about foreign affairs, even as they help to establish the range of criteria for defining, debating and resolving social issues.

As Tuchman noted more than 20 years ago (1978), since many Americans aren't interested in foreign news, the media attempt to meet their civic responsibility to inform the electorate by turning complicated foreign stories into local stories and in the process lose the complexities of international political and economic forces. The focus of this study—the resettlement in the USA of the so-called 'Lost Boys' of Sudan—is an excellent example of this phenomenon. In the early 1990s, a stream of some 10,000 orphaned or displaced boys and young men walked 1,000 miles or more to escape a decades-long civil war and sporadic famine in Sudan. Those who didn't die of starvation or violence en route ended up in refugee camps in bordering Kenya and Ethiopia, where they languished for years. In early 2001, 500 of them emigrated to the USA, becoming the largest resettled group of unaccompanied refugee teenagers in history. More than 4000 were to follow, to be resettled in states from Massachusetts to Minnesota. The project was funded by the U.S. government and carried out by social service agencies, especially Lutheran and Catholic organizations (Corbett, 2001; Barry, 2001a).

This article looks at coverage in top U.S. newspapers of this quasi-Biblical tale of exile and long wandering followed by supposed redemption. The 'Lost Boys' stories unintentionally reveal much about the USA even as they introduce a group of strangers in its midst. In analyzing these stories, I foreground the overlapping and intersecting dynamics of longstanding media practices that influence form and content, the continuing struggle over how to cover complex foreign news stories and the efforts to redress inadequate coverage of diverse communities within the USA. First, I detail how top U.S. newspapers covered the political and economic context of contemporary Sudan as an example of the difficulty of, and perhaps lack of interest in, covering Africa in general. I then draw upon Gans' (1980) early interrogations into 'enduring themes' in news content, Carey's (1988) categorization of a ritual versus transmission view of news and Lule's (2001) investigations into news narratives and the mythological role of journalism to help tease out underlying ideological patterns in coverage of this story. I present a textual analysis of U.S. newspaper coverage in early 2001, when the refugees were being relocated across the country, and examine how the U.S. media framed this story based on American national myths and consumer values. I also uncover how racist characterizations of Africans—for example, the use of the word 'boys' to describe young black men—are presented without question because these particular black men have been 'Othered' as foreigners. In sum, the coverage of the 'Lost Boys' provides readers with a feel-good fairy tale about the human spirit and the generosity of the mythical American heartland even as it fails to provide adequate political and economic context and elides the entrenched realities of racism in the USA.

SUDAN IN THE U.S. MEDIA

In spring 2001, U.S. Secretary of State Cohn Powell visited Africa. Journalists followed his seven-day tour of the vast continent and his criticism of various regimes. Powell had especially harsh words for Sudan's President Omar elBashir, whom he condemned for suppressing religious freedom in the southern part of the country, where Christians and animists live in an area rich in oil reserves (see Lacey, 2001). Earlier that year, U.S. President George W. Bush also criticized the Sudanese dictator. Why this intensified interest in Sudan, when more than 20 years of civil war, sporadic famine and the deaths and displacement of millions had received only sporadic attention? Veteran *New York Times* reporter Jane Perlez (2001: 3) offers Sudan as a case example of how 'a curious, even capricious, combination of events can suddenly turn a distant, nearly forgotten conflict into a burning issue'. She details how the Bush administration, and the U.S. media, began to pay increasing attention to Sudan in early 2001 due to two powerful lobbying interests: religion and oil. U.S. oil companies at that time were lobbying hard to overturn a congressional ban on operations in Sudan due to its alleged support of terrorism, even as Canadian, Swedish, Malaysian and Chinese companies had been pumping Sudanese oil since it began to flow in 1998. These revenues had fattened the coffers of the country's government and allowed it to intensify its war against the south (see Reeves, 2001). Simultaneous to these lobbying efforts, both the Roman Catholic Church (which wants the USA to end the war) and the evangelical right (which wants the USA to arm the rebels in southern Sudan) also were exerting much pressure in Washington during the period under study.

Moeller (1999) describes how Sudan's civil war and famine were ignored for years by the U.S. media even as its neighbors in the nearby Horn of Africa (Ethiopia and Somalia in particular) were receiving extensive aid in the 1980s and 1990s. Sudan, a country beset with religious and political factions, had no clear-cut (and easily covered) 'good guys' or 'bad guys' and had not been as much of a focus of U.S. Cold War foreign policy as had the countries of the Horn. Even though the story of famine in Sudan was nearly identical to that occurring simultaneously in Somalia, covering both would have entailed massive expense on the ground and, it was feared, generated what has come to be called 'compassion fatigue' (see Phillips, 1999) at home. As civil war and starvation produced destruction and death in Ethiopia and Somalia, a bloody civil war was raging in Sudan, Africa's largest country geographically. As of mid 2001, some five million southern Sudanese reportedly had been driven from their homes, and another two million had died. In her work on how media overkill on stories that mirror U.S. foreign policy can produce compassion fatigue in Americans, Moeller (1999: 138) notes that there is only ever room for one crisis at a time. With the USA preoccupied in Somalia, Sudan was bypassed.

The concept of compassion fatigue, however, is inadequate to understanding U.S. coverage of African affairs. Also at play in this study are the many organizational and ideological influences on news selection and content. Shoemaker and Reese (1991), for example, note that media content is influenced by journalists' socialization and attitudes, by the various standardized routines for organizing the media and by many forces outside the newsroom. Editors tend to make decisions on news coverage based partly on their perceptions of what their audiences want. Altheide (1985: 14) describes a 'media logic' that helps to define what a given type of content should be like. This results in standardized formats that journalists are constrained to produce, which can present representations of reality akin to stereotypes. In this study, the stories predominantly analyzed are human-interest features, one of the formats useful to journalists and audiences alike because such stories are easily presented and digested. That these formats are ubiquitous also suggests their role in perpetuating simplified versions of 'Africa' and 'Africans' even as they tell the stories of a mythical and multicultural 'America' that resonate with readers.

Myth-Making and the Media

Useful to this study is Gans' (1980: 39–57) classic typology of 'enduring values' in U.S. news, including ethnocentrism (the USA is the best country in the world), a commitment to altruistic democracy (U.S. politics reflect the public interest, with citizens participating in selfless grassroots activity) and responsible capitalism (capitalism creates increased prosperity for all and refrains from unreasonable profits and gross exploitation) together with individualism tempered by moderation (Americans can protect individual freedoms against the encroachments of nation and society, even as they discourage excess or extremism). Following Gans, Carey (1988) describes a 'ritual view' of communication, in contrast to the dominant 'transmission' view that conceptualizes the media primarily as gatherers and disseminators of information. Rather, a ritual view helps to reveal how the media present stories that draw people together in their shared beliefs (p. 18). Even as journalists attempt to present objective facts and information, they also are telling the stories of 'America' (Gans, 1980: 5).

Although Americans profess deep-seated disenchantment with their public institutions, they also cherish a self-image of individual achievement and the notion of a manifest destiny of continuing progress. In his work on the 'seven master myths' of U.S. news coverage, Lule (2001: 29) describes how journalists approach events with stories already in mind that have been borrowed from long-held shared narratives. Thus, news plays a mythological role by drawing upon this universally understood stock of archetypal stories that support and sustain the social order and help people make sense of the world and their place in it (pp. 33–6). The implications of the human-interest story in this conception of news are especially provocative. First, such stories help to affirm a belief that individual action is crucial to society's well-being, even though people may, in fact, be nearly powerless politically. Human-interest stories also tend to ignore history and social context, with less effort made to explore complex situations and more reliance on personalized story frames that make such analysis difficult (Lule 2001: 119–20). In turn, the 'Lost Boys' stories reveal Americans' most-cherished beliefs about themselves and the USA, even as they satisfy the need not only to help the weak but also to tame and civilize. These stories valorize American compassion and willingness to help others less fortunate than themselves around the world. The Sudanese 'Lost Boys' are shown as coming to a mostly color-blind land of opportunity in which they can pull themselves up by their bootstraps by embracing the American way, thus eliding the realities of being a black man in the USA.

Method

Fürsich (2002: 275), after Mander (1999), notes that scholarly investigation of the narrative dimensions of news helps to reveal the ideological underpinnings of journalistic work even though news stories are assumed to be merely a rendition of the facts. I use textual analysis to uncover some of the narrative elements that situate the Sudanese refugees resettled in American cities as blank slates, 'Lost Boys' coming from a situation beyond understanding that is timeless and a historical. The texts covered in this study were identified by doing a search on Lexis-Nexis in June 2001 of major U.S. newspapers, using the key words 'Lost Boys and Sudan', which turned up 56 articles from the previous three years. Of these, corrections, letters to the editor, editorials, photo captions and foreign newspapers were eliminated. This left the 28 stories that comprise my textual set. The majority of these stories were published between December 2000 and June 2001—when the first wave of Sudanese immigrants came to the USA—in the daily newspapers of the major U.S. cities in which they were resettled, including Atlanta, Baltimore, Boston, Columbus, Houston, Minneapolis, Los Angeles, New York, Omaha, Phoenix and Seattle.

Only four of these stories eschewed personalized story frames focusing on one or another 'Lost Boy' in the lead paragraph. This highlights mainstream journalism's commitment to the ideology of individualism, which is an obstacle to a full explanation of the causes of social ills (see Parisi, 1998; Galtung and Ruge, 1973). In the following section, I describe some of the narrative elements employed in these texts to tell the story of U.S. values even as they present a complex foreign news story made palatable to local readers. I identify the portrayal of a Blank Darkness to describe how the media tended to construct the refugees as incomplete, vessels waiting to be filled; the USA as Promised Land to describe how the mythical American heartland has become a place where success is measured by the ability to consume; Power of the Individual to highlight the American obsession with rugged individualism and to reveal an undercurrent of ethnocentrism; and Altruistic Democracy/Responsible Capitalism as a hegemonic discourse.

Blank Darkness

Despite the ubiquity of the phrase 'Lost Boys' in headlines, captions and stories, few reporters explain that the term came from aid workers as they recalled the parentless boys of Neverland who wouldn't grow up in the story of Peter Pan. However, the term is used uncritically by those reporters who do mention its origins; for example, no quote marks are placed around the phrase and the words are lowercased, resulting in a loss of irony. This tends to situate these young men, who have endured brutal political and physical conditions, as child-like. That they indeed *have* chosen to grow up—in fact, their story shows their determination to survive and succeed—is not explicitly explored. Rather, even as the facts of the story show them to be brave young men who have survived terrible hardships, they are constructed as waiting to be filled by American material culture. The result is a striking and unresolved contrast between the presented facts of their journey and the way journalists have tended to frame them. Tellingly, the use of the word 'boys', which one would hope is now unacceptable if applied to African American young men, easily slips into print when referring to African Others.

In these articles, Africa rarely has modern referents and the people who live there are often rendered helpless. One reporter describes Michael Nyak, who is 6 feet tall, as, a *child–man* with glowing dark skin . . . who was clad only in tattered rags' before he arrived in the USA (emphasis added). Using the familiar feature-writer's technique of focusing on an individual to act as proxy for all, this reporter continues:

> Nyak stands in his west Phoenix apartment studying the mysterious chunk of white plastic. He lifts it off the floor, spins it around, raises the lid, tugs at the thin white rope coming out of the bottom. 'One of our friends gave this to us,' Michael says graciously, 'but we don't know the use of it'. . . . The mystery gift is a coffeemaker, but it might as well have dropped from the sky—like the apartment's stove, refrigerator, table lamp and toilet. (Pancrazio, 2001a)

That these young men seem to come from a land outside of time or history is graphically rendered on the cover of *The New York Times Magazine* (Corbett, 2001). A Sudanese teenager wearing a ski hat and a down coat, his skin purplish black, stands alone on an empty field of snow in the Midwest. He frowns into the distance. The desolate emptiness of the setting mystifies the refugee's status, distances him from normal life and displays him as a tabula rasa.

Inside the magazine, another photo continues this representation: three Sudanese teenagers and an adult sit in a sparsely furnished living room. In the background is a small square of a window, outside of which is that same dark, desolate winter afternoon already seen on the magazine's cover. The reporter begins her story by describing them when they arrive in Minneapolis en route to North Dakota. As they exit the plane, the 'three . . . African boys'—this despite the fact that one is 21 years old—[are] 'confronted by a swirling river of white faces and rolling suitcases, blinking television screens and telephones that rang, inexplicably, from the inside of people's pockets'. Their inability to understand the modern, technological world—and U.S. material culture – is also described in the *Los Angeles Times,* as the reporter follows them through Hornbacher's, a Midwestern grocery store that proves to be 'full of wonders':

> The electric doors. The grocery carts. The riotous rows of brightly packed food and the ample-bodied white people who filled their carts with whatever they wished to buy . . . the boys wandered tentatively through the produce section, looking but not touching, until [one] discovered a bin of green mangoes, which triggered a round of excited Dinka chatter. (Corbett, 2001)

In the *Boston Globe,* Paulson (2000) quotes Joseph Doolin, president of Catholic Charities, who describes the Sudanese as very different from other refugees who come from such places as Bosnia (where, it should be remembered, the people are Caucasian). 'They come here with zero English, zero work skills, and most of them will find a doorknob a fascinating technological gadget because they come from a very *primitive* rural milieu' (emphasis added). The use of the word 'primitive', generally unacceptable in contemporary news-writing when referring to human beings, is offered without comment, perhaps because it is in a quote. Meanwhile, a reporter describes the arrival of nine others who have 'a look in their eyes of unimaginable distance'. As they file through the airport terminal, their belongings in plastic bags, they peer around (Barry, 2000)

> like visitors from another planet. Days ago, when they left Nairobi, the Lost Boys were issued socks, but did not seem certain how to put them on. An American aid worker quietly explained flush toilets in a stall at the Nairobi airport. Then he peeled the 'all-cotton' stickers off their chests, one by one, realizing they wouldn't have known to do it themselves.

One journalistic convention is to paraphrase direct quotes when the speaker has difficulty speaking English, unless there is overriding reason to present these verbatim. Most reporters in this study choose the latter route. This provides readers with deeply stilted English and results in an appearance of ignorance by the refugees; e.g., Corbett (2001) quotes one refugee: '"We have learned the cleaning machine," one says of the vacuum cleaner'. Since no translators were employed for those refugees whose English was minimal, the journalists often speak for their sources. In one story, the reporter even thinks for one of them. Pondering the many problems the refugees would encounter in America, she notes: 'I am quite certain that Peter was thinking something similar when he ducked out of the USAir flight that carried his all-male family to Fargo, a city that is 97 percent white' (Corbett, 2001).

Much of the content in these stories focuses on the contrasts between Them and Us. In the *Boston Globe,* Barry (2001b) reports on the teens' progress in U.S. high schools:

> To some who worked with the students, those early days were spellbinding. In math, for instance, where they were initially assessed at an eighth-grade or lower level, the students were picking up new concepts incredibly fast, 'doing something symbolically that I wouldn't have thought possible', said math teacher Richard Thorne. 'It's interesting to watch how a

> mind absorbs something,' he said. 'It's like a tabula rasa'.

The refugees sometimes become objects for anthropomorphizing. In *The New York Times,* Corbett (2001) describes Philip Jok, 'known for springing up from the ground like a grasshopper during tribal dances', and 'famous for writing long, extemporaneous songs about cattle'. He is one of the refugees whose trip to 'the outside world . . . seems a trip not just across continents, but through time'. Barry (2001a) writes, 'Leaving Africa, the departing boys would shake off the rhythms of a thousand years.'

Miller (1985: 16–18) describes how the West has constructed Africa as a 'third part of the world', a dark nullity that barely existed before Westerners turned their gaze upon it. Following Miller, the 'Lost Boys' become fulfilled only when they enter middle-class American life. The Blank Darkness they come from begins to dissipate when they are able to embrace consumerism in the American Promised Land.

Promised Land

Gans (1980) describes how the media construct an ideal American democracy by telling the stories of ordinary people in the mythical heartland. In covering the 'Lost Boys' story, the media also valorize small-town pastoralism (despite the fact that most of the refugees were relocated in large cities such as Boston, Omaha and Minneapolis), simultaneously evoking a Promised Land to be found in the shopping mall. In doing so, the media tell the story of an America whose democracy is defined by material success, a garden where the poor and dispossessed can find succor by working to buy consumer goods. Interestingly, Marshall (2000: 52) describes how the media have often been criticized for ignoring religion because of the American Enlightenment's focus on rationalism and science. However, as democracy and capitalism have become one interwoven concept in the USA, so too have religion and materialistic values. Many of the stories analyzed in this study utilize such phrases as 'The Promised Land', 'amazing grace', 'an almost biblical journey', 'epic story' and 'long wandering in the desert'. In the *Los Angeles Times,* Simmons (1999) writes that *'The horsemen* came by night, thundering from one mud-and-thatch hut to another, shooting and slashing men, women and children' (emphasis added). Thus, the refugees have escaped the apocalypse of darkest Africa.

The New York Times Magazine (Corbett, 2001) headlines its cover story as 'From Hell to Fargo'. The story describes three refugees coming from Africa, arriving at the 'brightly lighted' Minneapolis airport en route to North Dakota. They are confused; they cannot find the gate for their connection. A 'kindly' person rescues them. In the *Boston Globe,* Paulson (2000) notes that 'the trip through the airport brings them to the other side'. Barry (2000) calls their arrival 'the entry into a strange new world'. This hopeful narrative describes a progressive trajectory from darkness into light, 'From Hell to Fargo'.

The refugees are categorized as universally 'devout Christians', although this may not be the case. In the USA, reporters note, they find the freedom to worship as they please. In the *Omaha World-Herald,* Buttry (2001a) tells the story of Mangong Akech, who found a home

> in the embrace of Thanksgiving Lutheran Church in Bellevue. Akech, now 20, carries a piece of shrapnel in his chest from a land mine he stepped on as a boy in Sudan. He struggled with emotion as he tried to express gratitude in a language he is still learning. 'When I arrive here in this apartment with all these *things',* he said, gesturing to the furniture around him in his Bellevue apartment, 'and the people of Thanksgiving Lutheran Church, that is the dream of God coming in my mind, that I need to be baptized—the *things* they give us and the way they welcome us'. (Emphasis added)

Thus, the ministering by the kind church people of Bellevue is presented as coming mostly in the form of material goods, the 'things' filling their new rooms and refrigerators. In the *Atlanta Journal and Constitution,* Bixler (2001a) describes how church volunteer Dee Clement spends hours with Mou Mou, teaching him to cook an egg and make a telephone call.

> She opened a cabinet in Mou Mou's kitchen and found half-empty jars of Knott's Berry Farm strawberry preserves and Prego Mini-Meatball Pasta Sauce. That prompted a lesson on refrigeration. 'You see that?' she said. 'That's mold. If you eat that, it will make you sick.' Mou Mou stared at the jar. Then he turned toward the automatic dishwasher. 'We were shown that if you want to wash, you put soap in there and then you turn the handle,' he said. He could not open a plastic lid for the detergent and looked to Clement for help. She reached over and paused when she spotted a loaf of bread among the dishes. 'What's this?' she says. 'Why is there bread in the dishwasher?' She moved the loaf to the refrigerator. He watched her without saying anything.

The church volunteer, as an expert consumer of American processed food, is presented as the mistress of Mou Mou's fate, saving him from his ignorance of modern industrial life.

In constructing the USA as the Promised Land, the reporters elide the simultaneous realities of a less-pleasant aspect of U.S. history and contemporary life: racism and violence. Simmons (1999), for example, notes that the young men will have trouble 'solving problems without the violence they have been exposed to most of their lives', as if violence wasn't an everyday reality in the USA. Gans (1980: 42) finds that another official norm to which the news pays frequent attention is racial integration. In this study, only Lush (2001) notes that the arrival of 50 Sudanese 'Lost Boys' to northeast Florida increased the black population in the greater Port Richey area by 15 percent:

> Nancy Gray acknowledged that some people haven't been happy with the county's newest residents. 'It bothers me when I hear people say, "Why are you bringing these people over here?"' she said.

Power of the Individual

Even as news everywhere values its own nation above all, this comes through most explicitly in foreign news, which judges other countries by the extent to which they live up to or imitate U.S. practices and values. Gans (1980: 42) describes how the media conceive of the nation in anthropological terms and 'when the news is tragic or traumatic, it becomes the nation-cum-individual whose character and moral strength are tested' (p. 20). The articles in this study are more than human-interest feature stories about refugees coming to the USA. Rather, they construct and reconfirm what Americans believe are their best qualities. Overwhelmingly, media coverage of this evocative story naturalizes and reaffirms a certain version of Americans and American life: that Americans are generous and kind people, and that individuals will prevail—if they have 'the right stuff'.

Traditional symbols of U.S. material success and consumer society abound in these stories—the supermarket, the modern kitchen, the brand-name clothing—as does imagery that epitomizes U.S. society as free and open. That these young men would want to embrace uncritically everything American is rarely challenged. The *Arizona Republic* (Pancrazio, 2001a) describes Gai as 'missing his six bottom front teeth, pulled in a traditional Dinka ritual. Gai said he'd like to have those teeth replaced, "in order to be like you".' A story in the *Minneapolis Star Tribune* (Haga, 2001), quotes the foster parents of several refugees: 'My son, Marty, is 16, and they want to do what he does. If he walks down the left side of the road, they walk down the left side of the road'. Simmons (2000) is one of the few reporters to imply that the refugees might want to go home. 'It's very bad to leave my people behind . . . They are suffering and it pains me',

Martin said. 'Once I get my education, I will come back to help them.'

In another comparison, a *New York Times* reporter (Corbett, 2001) contrasts conditions in the USA to those in East Africa. She notes that schooling there consists of long rows of boys scratching letters in the dirt with sticks, with teachers caning them if they moved. 'So they learned to sit for hours on their knees in the sun, naked or nearly naked . . . Meanwhile, the schools in America were indoors. . . . and no one was being caned.' In another story, Bixler (2001a) asks a group of refugees what they were told about America by camp workers before they left Africa. 'Rugged individualism' seems to have been on the lesson plan: '"They told us that in the United States, life depends on you. It depends on what you want it to be," Mou Mou said.'

Corbett (2001) stresses that the young men are unaware of American cultural products and modern Western history. She employs a common journalistic technique by presenting quotes from her sources to say what she cannot due to the ideal of objectivity. Thus, a tutor says he is unable to grasp the refugees' 'level of innocence . . . They don't know the Earth revolves around the Sun, who Elvis Presley is, who Hitler was, what World War II was . . . You might as well be talking Sanskrit.' At the same time, the tutor is 'amazed' at the refugees' self-discipline and that they could survive without adult supervision, displaying a profound ignorance of the harsh realities of childhood in the developing world.

The stories set up an unquestioned expectation that the Sudanese will change in the USA, to be gauged by how well they embrace its cultural products. *Newsday* reporter Brown (2001) relates the story of a church volunteer taking the young men to a Wal-Mart. '"These are Yankees caps," Palen told Ngong. "Have you heard of the New York Yankees?" "No," he said, trying one on. He will.' Barry (2001b) indicates that one thing is certain: they will change for the better. She quotes an American educator: 'Give them six months. Let America do its work.'

In sum, many of these stories perpetuate an assumption that change can happen only in one direction, from the 'there' of Africa to the 'here' of contemporary America. That the USA could learn from the 'Lost Boys' disappears in the valorizing of American values.

Altruistic Democracy/ Responsible Capitalism

Gans (1980: 46) notes how the media portray an optimistic faith that business people will compete with each other to create increased prosperity for all even as they refrain from unreasonable profits or exploitation of workers or customers. Concurrently, the news media imply that political actions are based on the public interest and public service. Citizens are said to participate in this through grassroots activity. In the 20-plus years since Gans' interrogations, the concept 'democracy' has become even more conflated with 'capitalism' and therefore the freedom to consume. In these articles, U.S. consumer society is naturalized as part of the political structure. Freedom is exemplified by the bountiful choice of products. For the 'Lost Boys', learning about freedom is shown as happening at the shopping mall. In *Newsday,* Brown (2001) describes a shopping trip led by a church volunteer:

> 'There's McDonald's,' she said, indicating a nearby business that is an American icon. 'Have you heard of McDonald's?' 'Nooo,' said a somewhat dazed-looking Emmanuel Ngong, 21, a young man with five inverted triangles cut into his forehead, a sign of reaching manhood in his Dinka ethnic group. 'It's food, fast food,' Palen explained as she directed the four young Sudanese toward the blue jeans section. 'Like hamburgers.'

Every reporter without exception describes how the refugees have never seen a flush toilet, an electric light, a refrigerator, a TV, a computer. Fergus (2001), however, interviews one refugee who seems to be learning fast: 'With an air conditioner humming loudly above him, James talks about the present as he eats a few Oatmeal Creme cookies and sips a Coke . . . "But I prefer Diet Coke," James says of his snack.' James has embraced some of what the reporter terms 'the finer things in life,' including doors with locks. He carries his new apartment keys on a key chain that he has been given which reads: 'Don't Mess with Texas'.

In the USA, everyone can get a job—at minimum wage. Buttry (2001b) notes that the Sudanese refugees in Nebraska are finding work, 'thanks to Omaha's labor shortage.' They work in meatpacking, as janitors or dishwashers—the jobs held by the undocumented worker, the poor and the dispossessed. Meanwhile, the reporter quotes an aid worker speaking about how the Sudanese had become dependent in the refugee camps, used to receiving everything without working for it, going from 'an environment where you've basically been given everything at the camp to an environment where you have to work, you have to produce . . . it's a huge leap.' That both situations can exist simultaneously is not examined.

Several reporters were able to visit the refugee camps in East Africa and could relate how indoctrination about the American way of life began before the teenagers left the continent. In *The New York Times,* Corbett (2001) recounts the English lessons they received: 'The words describing America had piled up without real meaning: freedom, democracy, a safe place, a land with enough food for everyone'—even though an estimated 30 million Americans go to bed hungry every night (Mayer, 2001). Raghavan (2000) tells how reading materials in one camp 'included a Nordstrom's catalog and newspaper ads for Circuit City and other American stores.' These details are offered uncritically by the reporters, showing a common-sense acceptance of consumer society.

Perhaps because these stories are conceived as local human-interest features, none of these articles examines the powerful and often negative effects of economic globalization on the poorest countries in the world. *Christian Science Monitor* reporter Mike Crawley (2000) notices in the Kakuna refugee camp that one of the few decorations on the mud walls is a Coca-Cola contest poster. The name of the contest is 'Win What You Dream'. Barry (2001a) inadvertently shows that the refugees come from a world that might be more nuanced than that rendered elsewhere in her story.

> The elders spoke words of advice into a Sanyo boom box so the young men could carry cassettes of recorded wisdom with them to America. 'Don't go and be attracted by the high life,' one bearded and bony man admonished. 'Beer is a new thing to you. Don't just go and get involved in that. There are many Negroes in America. Don't think you know them just because of their hair'.

This indicates that much has been left out, especially those details that hint at an Africa more complicated than it appears in these feature stories. A commitment to altruistic democracy and responsible capitalism is accepted and represented as a fact of life rather than an omission of critical analysis of global economic change.

Discussion

Hawk (1992) notes that the simplest way to communicate the African story in comprehensible form in limited space is by reductionist colonial metaphors familiar to the reader, especially that of the tribe and collective 'Africa'. The resulting media image is a 'crocodile-infested dark continent where jungle life has perpetually eluded civilization' (p. 9).

> The word 'African', as it is used in the Western press, does not mean anyone who lives on the African continent, but rather people who are black and live on the African continent. It is a colonial label. North Africans and descendants of European settlers are not included in the term. This narrow, racial definition of

> Africa, structured by the language employed to tell the African story, tells readers and viewers that the continent has a simple, homogenous culture. (Hawk, 1992: 8)

Most of the stories analyzed in this study contain the words 'crocodile' or 'crocodile-infested' and have many references to lions. Use of the inaccurate and superficial tribal categories used by the colonial powers also is apparent, with 39 references to 'Dinka', 16 to 'Nuer', 17 to 'tribe' and 11 to 'tribal'. There were 10 references to 'naked' and several to 'primitive' and 'traditional'. What missionary evangelization was to the 19th century—a justification for intervention – economic development is now (Hawk, 1992). Religious conversion—in the case of the 'Lost Boys', conversion to the bounty of U.S. material culture— is an antidote to a lesser way of life. Ironically, the many moments of compassion expressed in these stories, as the refugees struggle to fit into U.S. society, ultimately lend credibility to narrow stereotypes of 'tribe' and the collective 'African', even as they reaffirm American values. The narratives are comprised of clear dichotomies—primitive/civilized, poverty/wealth, ignorance/knowledge, hell/paradise—that leave little room for critical analysis.

Many of the stories contain discrepancies in the details of Sudan's civil war, including the number of years of war, how many miles the boys walked and for how long, how many people have been killed or displaced. Admittedly, accurate information of this kind is difficult to obtain and even harder to verify. However, in these stories, this information tends to be presented as authoritative rather than in obvious dispute by authorities. Information on the Sudanese war also is sometimes presented out of context. Buttry (2001a) notes that 'Bul Mabior Deng was 3 years old when the bombs forced him from his home', with no explanation of where the bombs came from or why. The stories about the 'Lost Boys' analyzed in this study neatly categorize the Sudanese civil war as between 'the Moslem North' and 'the Christian South', while only three mention the crucial factor of the country's massive oil reserves. Journalistic shortcuts also can be found. Pancrazio (2001a) tells readers that 'Last spring, James Machar Geu found his way from the killing fields of Africa to All Saints' Episcopal Church on Central Avenue'. The term used to describe the effects of the murderous Khmer Rouge government of Cambodia is transferred half a world away, even though the situations have little in common. The use of this kind of shorthand is not limited to stories of Others, however; it is a time-tested convention in a business restricted by deadlines and space requirements, and by a reporter's measure of how much detail readers or viewers will tolerate. Following Gans (1980) and Lule (2001), this also highlights the importance of narrative to the human-interest feature: although factual 'evidence' in the form of official statements and statistics is expected in any newspaper story, its importance from a journalistic standpoint is less crucial in a feature than the narrative itself.

As noted earlier in this study, alternative explanations for the shortage of critical analysis in these stories take into account the realities of the U.S. news business, especially the conventions and qualities of the human-interest feature format and editors' perceptions of their audiences' (lack of) interest in both foreign news and complex background information. Local reporters also can be hampered in their attempts to adequately handle stories with difficult historical and political situations with which they have no experience. Still, at least a few of these reporters are veteran journalists who work at major newspapers and have some international experience. It can be assumed that these features were not produced under strict deadline, a situation which could have allowed room for more nuanced information.

There are counter examples—for example, the sanitized mention of possible racial tension in Port Richey, FL, mentioned earlier (Lush 2001)—but their rarity is telling, indicating that the exception reinforces the rule. Analysis of 'Lost Boys' coverage leads us not simply to hegemonic discourse but to the underlying and unquestioned ideological assumptions to be found in human- interest reporting, in this case that of U.S. political and economic dominance. What is reinforced here is the commonsense assumption by Americans that the best answer to the world's problems comes from the USA and its consumer culture. As human-interest features, these are among the best in the business, written by award-winning journalists. Readers most likely can experience an important moment of connection with people very different than themselves. But even as the stories of the 'Lost Boys' bring a long-neglected international news story to the forefront, they also undermine their authors' intention to enlighten readers about the world.

It can be argued that the 'Lost Boys' is less of a story about Africa or foreign news than it is about U.S. ethnic diversity. Pan and Kosicki (1996) cite 'impressive evidence' of dramatic increases in the acceptance by Americans of the principles of racial equality and integration, as represented in media coverage. However, Parisi (1998), in his analysis of U.S. media coverage of urban racism, notes that while today's stories seem to address calls for more compassionate, contextual coverage of black life—and, by extension in this study, of the African Other—rather than providing improved coverage, they extend the phenomenon of modern racism. Sincere moments of compassion inadvertently lend credibility to narrow and reinforced stereotypes. With the 'Lost Boys', the problem is compounded by the fact that Africans constitute only a small minority in U.S. immigrant communities, bringing them onto the radar screen only when a story with this kind of human-interest potential emerges. Even as stories about immigrants from Latin America, Eastern Europe and Southeast Asia have become commonplace in the major media, Africans in the USA, by and large, are still invisible. Despite increasing concern and important efforts to cover diversity, the 'Lost Boys' story represents an attempt that had limited and questionable results. Dines (1998: 291), citing Wiegman (1993), notes that historically, media stereotypes of the black man (the sexual demon alongside the Uncle Tom) have served to define black men as outside the normal realm of (white) masculinity by constructing them as 'Other'.

With international news, the problems of media misrepresentations of Others and insufficient contextual information to help audiences make sense of complex stories are assumed to have been redressed in the 20 years since the rancorous call for a New World Information Order (MacBride, 1980) and, earlier, the Hutchins Commission (1947) critique of U.S. media coverage of race. This study of newspaper coverage of the 'Lost Boys' indicates that, rather than showing an increased sensitivity to international news, many just recycle incomplete images of Africa that fit into American expectations. Lule (1998) notes the movement within the news industry toward a more just and humane framework for international coverage after the Cold War, as the East–West dichotomy that governed U.S. international reporting for nearly four decades collapsed. Even so, U.S. media construction and perpetuation of incomplete images of Africans persists during a time of profound political and economic globalization. More than 20 years ago, Gans (1980: 31–7) found foreign news treated with less detachment, with explicit value judgements not justifiable in domestic news appearing in stories about the rest of the world. The story of the 'Lost Boys' shows that this tendency is still very powerful.

Gronbeck (2001) describes 'suppression by omission' to explain media content. Sometimes the omission includes not just vital details of a story (e.g., adequate explanation of the complex Sudanese situation) but the entire story itself. Stories that might reflect poorly upon 'the powers that be' are not likely to see the light. Stories that might contradict the dominant ideology of U.S. capitalism also rarely surface. In this study, the framing of the USA as the consumer Promised Land excludes other conceptions of capitalism that are not as unregulated as they are in the USA. The commercial media, with its space and time limitations and 24-hour news cycles, forces everything into black and white, sacrificing the shades of gray that allow for 'thinking out of the box' and provide the potential to effect positive change. The localization of the 'Lost Boys' story turns a complex and ever-changing international situation into an emotional issue confined to these some 4,000 refugees. The complexity of international affairs, the churning engine of economic globalization and the role of the USA in world affairs all fade away.

The 'Lost Boys' stories do succeed in easing complicated African history and politics onto the front pages even as the news hole for such coverage continues to shrink. Lule (1998: 170) calls for a new model for the coverage of international news, 'a journalism of social justice that gives overdue attention to the suffering of people who fell unnoted outside the media's former Cold War framework'. He describes how journalists can achieve this by seeking stories of the anonymous and thereby changing the criteria for newsworthiness; giving voice to the silenced and allowing them to express their own experiences in their own words; and moving beyond the surface description of a tragic situation to explore the fundamental structures that helped create it (Lule, 1998: 172–3). Following Lule, the story of the 'Lost Boys' provides a local, human face to far-away tragedy but unsuccessfully moves past easy, surface explanations of complex international situations. Although these stories were excellent examples of human-interest feature writing, this study suggests that an authentic paradigm shift concerning international news coverage by the U.S. media has yet to occur.

References

Altheide, David L. (1985) *Media Power.* Thousand Oaks: Sage Publications.

Arnett, Peter (1998) '"Goodbye, World": State of the American Newspaper Special Report 6', *American Journalism Review* (Nov.). Available at http://ajr.newslink.org/special/part6.html (25 June 2001).

Brock, L. (1992) 'Inkatha: Notions of the "Primitive" and "Tribal" in reporting on South Africa', in Beverly Hawk (ed.) *Africa's Media Image,* pp. 149–61. New York: Praeger.

Carey, James W. (1988) 'A Cultural Approach to Communication', in J. W. Carey, *Communication as Culture: Essays on Media and Society,* pp. 13–35. Boston: Unwin Hyman.

Dines, Gail (1998) 'King Kong and the White Woman', *Violence Against Women* 4(3): 291–307.

Domke, D. (1997) 'Journalists, Framing and Discourse about Race Relations', *Journalism & Mass Communication Monographs* 164 (Dec). Columbia, SC: Association for Education in Journalism and Mass Communication.

Fürsich, Elfriede (2002) 'Nation, Capitalism, Myth: Covering News of Economic Globalization', *Journalism and Mass Communication Quarterly* 79(2): 273–93.

Galtung, J. and M. Ruge (1973) 'Structuring and Selecting News', in S. Cohen and J. Young (eds) *The Manufacture of News: A Reader,* pp. 52–63. Beverly Hills, CA: Sage.

Gans, Herbert (1980) *Deciding What's News: A Study of CBS Evening News, NBC Nightly News, Newsweek and Time.* New York: Vintage Books.

Gronbeck, B. E. (2001) 'Reducing the Scope', Posting to CRTNET News discussion on news frames, 24 May. National Communication Association. Archives available at http://lists.psu.edu/archives/crtnet.html

Hall, Stuart (1995) 'The Whites of Their Eyes: Racial Ideologies and the Media', in G. Dines and J. Humez (eds) *Gender, Race and Class in Media,* pp. 18–22. Thousand Oaks: Sage.

Hawk, Beverly (1992) 'Introduction: Metaphors of African Coverage', in B. Hawk (ed) *Africa's Media Image,* pp. 3–14. New York: Praeger.

Herman, Edward S. and Robert W. McChesney (1997) *The Global Media: The New Missionaries of Corporate Capitalism.* Washington, DC: Cassell.

Hutchins Commission on Freedom of the Press (1947) *A Free and Responsible Press; a General Report on Mass Communication: Newspapers, Radio, Motion Pictures, Magazines, and Books.* Chicago: University of Chicago Press.

Lacey, M. (2001) 'At End of Africa Trip, Powell Urges Sudan to Halt Civil War', *The New York Times* (27 May): A21.

Lule, Jack (1998) 'New Values and Social Justice: US News and the Brazilian Street Children', *Howard Journal of Communications* 9(3): 169–86.

Lule, Jack (2001) *Daily News, Eternal Stories: The Mythological Role of Journalism.* New York: Guilford Press.

MacBride, Sean (1980) *Many Voices, One World: Communication and Society Today and Tomorrow,* Report for the International Commission for the Study of Communication Problems. New York: Unipub.

Mander, M. (ed.) (1999) *Framing Friction: Media and Social Conflict.* Champaign: University of Illinois Press.

Marshall, P. (2000) 'Keeping the Faith: Religion, Freedom, and International Affairs', *USA Today Magazine* 128 (2656): 52–4.

Masmoudi, M. (1979) 'The New World Information Order', *Journal of Communication* (Spring): 172–84.

Mayer, Shannon (2001) 'Hunger in America: Mark of Shame', *The New York Times* (15 Jan.): 14.

Miller, Christopher (1985) *Blank Darkness: Africanist Discourse in French.* Chicago: University of Chicago Press.

Moeller, Susan (1999) *Compassion Fatigue: How the Media Sell Disease, Famine, War and Death.* New York: Routledge.

Pan, Z. and Gerald Kosicki (1996) 'Assessing News Media Influences on the Formation of Whites' Racial Policy Preferences', *Communication Research* 23(2): 147–79.

Parisi, Peter (1998) 'A Sort of Compassion: *The Washington Post* Explains the "Crisis in Urban America" ', *Howard Journal of Communication* 9(3): 187–203.

Perlez, Jane (2001) 'Suddenly in Sudan, A Moment to Care', *The New York Times Week in Review* (17 Jun.): 3.

Phillips, T. (1999) 'Compassion Fatigue and the Media', *Contemporary Review* 275(1604): 129–33.

Randal, J. (2000) *The Decline, But Not Yet Total Fall, of Foreign News in the US Media,* Working Paper Series 2000–2. Cambridge, MA: Joan Shorenstein Center on the Press, Politics and Public Policy, John F. Kennedy School of Government, Harvard.

Reeves, E. (2001) 'America's Sudan Policy'. Testimony, House Committee on International Relations, 28 March. Online at http://www.house.gov/international_relations/reev0328.htm, accessed 28 June 2001.

Shoemaker, F J. and S. D. Reese (1991) *Mediating the Message.* New York: Longman.

Tuchman, Gaye (1978) *Making News: A Study in the Construction of Reality.* New York: The Free Press.

Wiegman, R. (1993) 'Feminism, "The Boyz," and Other Matters Regarding the Male', in S. Cohan and I. R. Hark (eds) *Screening the Male: Exploring Masculinities in Hollywood Cinema,* pp. 173–93. New York: Routledge.

Newspaper Articles Analyzed

Alonzo-Dunsmoor, M. (2001) 'Accident Claims "Lost Boy of Sudan" ', *Arizona Republic* (16th Jun.): 1.

Barry, E. (2000) 'Sudan's Lost Boys Find New Home', *Boston Globe* (3 Dec.): 1.

Barry, E. (2001a) 'Strangers in a Strange Land', *Boston Globe* (17 Jan.): 1.

Barry, E. (2001b) 'Dinka Values, Teenage Rites', *Boston Globe* (18 Mar.): 1.

Barry, E. (2001c) 'One of Sudan's "Lost Boys" is Charged with Rape', *Boston Globe* (28 Aug.): 1.

Barry, E. (2001d) 'African and American', *Boston Globe* (30 Dec.): 1.

Bixler, M. (2001a) 'Some Lost Boys of Sudan Find Haven Here', *Atlanta Journal and Constitution* (18 Apr.): 1.

Brown, F (2001) 'Sudanese Refugees Find a Home in Syracuse', *Newsday* (6 Jun.): 21.

Buttry, S. (2001a) 'Sudanese Find Help in Omaha', *Omaha World-Herald* (15 Jan.): 1.

Buttry, S. (2001b) 'In Omaha, Cousins Escape Endless War', *Omaha World-Herald* (14 Jan.): 1.

Carmen, B. (2001) 'Sixth-graders Find Meaning Reaching Out to Lost Boys', *Colum bus Dispatch* (8 Apr.): 1C.

Corbett, S. (2001) 'The Long, Long Road to Fargo: The Lost Boys of Sudan Land in America', *The New York Times Magazine* (1 Apr.): 48–55.

Crawley, M. (2000) '"Lost Boys" of Sudan Find New Life in America', *Christian Science Monitor* (7 Nov.): 1.

Dunbar, Chrystal (1994) 'War in Sudan Leaves Thousands Homeless', *New York Amsterdam News* (28 May): 26.

Fergus, M. A. (2001) 'Coming to America', *Houston Chronicle* (15 Apr.): L1.

Haga, C. (2001) 'Finding Their Way', *Minneapolis Star Tribune* (22 Apr.): 1.

Jones, C. (2000) 'Sudan's "Lost Boys" Find New Homes, Lives Across the USA', *USA Today* (20 Dec.): 1.

Lush, T. (2001) 'The Lost Boys', *St Petersburg Times* (16 Feb.): B1.

Macdonald, S. (2000) 'Whole New World for Refugee Teens', *Seattle Times* (14 Nov.): 1.

Pancrazio, A. C. (2001a) 'Valley Adopts "Lost Boys" ', *Arizona Republic* (6 May): B1.

Pancrazio, A. C. (2001b) 'Farewell to a "Lost Boy" ', *Arizona Republic* (21 Jun.): 1.

Paulson, M. (2000) 'In US, Chance for Refugees After Years of War', *Boston Globe* (8 Jul.): 1.

Raghavan, S. (2000) 'Sudan's Lost Boys are Coming to America for Christmas', *San Diego Union-Tribune.* (24 Dec.): E3.

Rhor, M. (2000) 'Aiming to Give "Lost Boys" a Home in Philadelphia', *Philadelphia Inquirer* (6 Nov.): 1.

Rivera, J. (2000) 'Finding Safe Homes in US for "Lost Boys" from Sudan', *Baltimore Sun* (10 Nov.): lB.

Satchell, M. (2001) 'The Journey from Hell to Fargo, ND.', *US News & World Report* (12 Feb.): 52.

Scott, D. C. (2000) 'Today's Story Line: The American Dream', *Christian Science Monitor* (7 Nov.): 6.

Simmons, A. (1999) Lost Boys of Sudan Look West', *Los Angeles Times* (3 Feb.): 1.

Simmons, A. (2000) 'US Life is Next Challenge for "Lost Boys" of Sudan', *Los Angeles Times* (4 Nov.): 1.

Source: From "'Lost Boys' and the Promised Land: U.S. Newspaper Coverage of Sudanese Refugees," 2003, by M. B. Robins, *Journalism, 4*(1), 29–49. Reprinted by permission of Sage Publications, Ltd.

18

Crafting Cultural Resonance

Imaginative Power in Everyday Journalism

James S. Ettema

If references to myth and ritual in the study of journalism are to be taken seriously, we may read the truth of news much as that of scripture. Exactly how the texts of either news or scripture—stories of sin and retribution, for example, or sacrifice and redemption—correspond to actual events is always open to scholarly debate. Beyond debate, however, is the understanding that both sorts of text cohere within the system of meanings and values that produced them. Thus we may read, even in the mundane stories of daily journalism, important truths about the cultural constitution of our world.

Reading the news in just this way, Andie Tucher's *Froth & Scum: Truth, Beauty, Goodness, and the Ax Murder in America's First Mass Medium* (1994) recounts an archetypal story of sin and retribution. Writing of the scramble by the penny press in 1836 to exploit the death of a young woman—allegedly the murder of a prostitute at the hand of a client—Tucher argues, 'Coverage of the murder, although it frequently wandered away from objective, verifiable fact never strayed far from Truth'. Indeed the competing penny newspapers offered readers their choice of Truth. 'Large, universal truths concerning death and sex and evil illuminated the penny-press reporting of Helen Jewett's life', Tucher concludes. 'Subterranean, parochial truths involving class, privilege, ambition, and resentment informed the debate over Robinson's guilt' (p. 61).

Tucher's reference to 'Truth' is, of course, intended as irony. But in reading the text for insight into the mentalities that produced and consumed it, she still finds reality reflected in the pages of the penny press. It is, however, less the reality of Jewett's life than the reality of New Yorkers making lives of their own by choosing 'an identity, a community and truth they could understand and accept' from among the cultural resources presented by competing newspapers in that place and time (p. 61). These narratives of a killing and its aftermath reframed truths, both universal and parochial, in the cultural moment of an emergent urban America. More than simply stirring ancient preoccupations, these stories provided new and compelling instances of them.

Therein lay their fascination—their cultural resonance—for their audience.

Toward a Conception of Resonance

This study takes up the question of what exactly we are reading when we claim to be reading communication-as-culture in this way. Specifically, the point of departure is the question of how the news captures and projects cultural resonance. Scholarly conventional wisdom holds news to be realities constructed within frameworks that emphasize certain facts while suppressing others and thereby promote certain political and moral evaluations while hindering others. But if these frames are to construct reality effectively, as Tucher suggested, they must resonate with what writers and readers take to be real and important matters of life.

Michael Schudson (1989: 159) has identified resonance as one of five 'dimensions of cultural power' in his review of 'perspectives from media studies on the efficacy of symbols'. Resonance, he concluded, 'is not a private relation between cultural object and individual, not even a social relation between cultural object and audience, but a public and cultural relation among object, tradition and audience' (p. 170).[1] Even though Schudson grounded his understanding of resonance in media studies, the concept remains relatively undeveloped in that literature, especially so in the cultural analysis of journalism.[2] Not so, however, in the literature on social movements, where resonance has long been part of the conceptual vocabulary for analyzing a movement's effectiveness in mobilizing public support.

Any brief review of that literature must highlight Snow and Benford's essential essay, 'Ideology, Frame Resonance, and Participant Mobilization' (1988). Arguing that an effective movement must frame its issue in a way that 'strikes a responsive chord', these sociologists divided the phenomenological aspect of frames into three components, all of which are variations on the theme of goodness-of-fit between issue frames and public perceptions. One component is *empirical credibility* defined as believability of the evidence for the reality of social problem as captured within the frame. The others are *experiential commensurability,* the harmony of lived experience with the frame, and *narrative fidelity,* the correspondence between 'cultural narrations' and the frame. Tucher's reading seems especially attuned to the third of these when she conceives of both writers and readers as drawing upon a cultural repertoire of themes and stories (cf. Williams and Kubal, 1999).

Because frames are constrained by pre-existing belief systems, social movements must define problems in ways that align useable frames with relevant beliefs (Snow et al., 1986). Addressing the question of the ideological work that effective frames must accomplish, Snow and Benford (1992) outlined three functions that can be characterized as the management of public moral outrage. In performing the *punctuation* function, frames 'underscore and embellish the seriousness and injustice of a social condition' (p. 137). Serving the *attribution* function, frames identify culpable agents (diagnostic attribution) and specify actions necessary to ameliorate the problem (prognostic attribution). And serving the *articulation* function, they 'align a vast array of events and experiences so that they hang together in a relatively unified and meaningful fashion' (p. 138). Snow and Benford concluded, 'what gives a collective action frame its novelty is not so much its innovative ideational elements as the manner in which activities articulate them or tie them together' (p. 138). While pre-existing beliefs constrain frames, coherent and compelling storytelling, among other activities, animates them.

These concepts have influenced journalism studies although the idea of framing has been employed in that literature with far more enthusiasm than consistency. Even so the idea has proven to be less 'a fractured paradigm', as Robert Entman (1993: 51) maintained, than a malleable one. Like many other concepts in the analysis of culture, this one retains its intellectual currency precisely because it can be made to do whatever work needs to be done. Nonetheless, the best claim to a consensus definition of framing lies with Entman. 'To frame', he wrote, 'is to select some aspects of perceived reality and make them more salient in a communicating text in such a way as to promote a particular problem definition, causal interpretation, moral evaluation and/or treatment recommendation' (Entman, 1993: 52). This definition, with its concern for definition and interpretation (punctuation) as well as evaluation and recommendation (attribution), maps well, if incompletely, onto the sociological conception of framing. Thus, the social-movement literature remains valuable in the conceptual vocabulary of journalism studies (e.g., Reese et al., 2001).

At the same time, journalism studies, with its vast literature on 'communicating texts' and the craft by which they are produced, can suggest some useful elaborations on the theory of social movements. By Entman's definition, framing works its ideological effects through the crafting of *salience.* The social-movement literature reminds us, however, that these effects also require the crafting of *resonance.* Paralleling the idea of salience as a textual effect produced by the processes of selection in fact-gathering and emphasis in news-writing, this study develops the idea of resonance as an effect produced by the same professional practices when accomplished with eloquence. Just as the processes of assigning, reporting, writing, and editing the news are all decision-making with regard to salience, so these processes are, or can be, the crafting of cultural resonance. Resonance is not simply there, in the world, to be appropriated from a cultural repertoire. Like salience, it must be enacted in the processes of message production. And like salience, which promotes certain moral evaluations and hinders others, resonance is a key element of journalism as a moralistic, if not always moral craft. Resonance elevates news to myth and deepens it into ritual.

A Case Study: Just a Normal Killing

Understood as the production of a textual effect, the crafting of resonance draws upon narrative structures and rhetorical strategies available to writers of both fact and fiction. This study seeks resonance among the structures and strategies that recurred in the continuing coverage of a specific news event. The method, in other words, is to analyze and appreciate the figurative language that multiple journalists from multiple newspapers on multiple occasions employed to tell and retell the story. Thus, the operational indicator of resonance or, more exactly, the indicator of journalistic effort to *craft* resonance is the recurrence of formal textual features. For example, repeated distillation of the event to the same few iconic elements. How these features project 'cultural power', in Schudson's terms, and thereby help constitute the 'public and cultural relation among object, tradition and audience' is the key question of this study. The question, posed in the vernacular, is simply how such features *make the story work* (Binder, 1993).

Of course, the idea that these features somehow do help make the story work supposes that audiences respond to them. This study offers no evidence of reader response. However, the resonance of the news to be recounted here may still echo faintly in the memory of many readers even though, as one headline writer observed, the event was just a normal killing in late 20th century America. With regard to reader response, then, an operational indicator of resonance might be the ease with which a few iconic elements summon the story from memory. Here are a few elements that serve to test the story's resonance: in suburban Baton Rouge, a Japanese exchange student and his American host search for a Halloween party. They come to a house alluringly decorated for the holiday. It is the wrong house.

For Japanese and Americans who, by 1992, were mature readers of the news, these elements may be enough to summon more of the story: A man pointing a .44 Magnum yells 'Freeze!' The American kid, almost by instinct, halts. The Japanese kid does not comprehend and steps forward. In an instant he lies bleeding to death on the concrete of the carport. The homeowner is tried for manslaughter. Under the terms of Louisiana's 'shoot the burglar' law, he is acquitted. Spectators in the courtroom cheer as the verdict is announced. And all the while Japan looks on in bewildered outrage.

Though these events may linger in living memory, the account that follows of Yoshihiro Hattori's death, like Tucher's account of Helen Jewett's death, is an exercise in the recovery of mass-mediated memory. This account, again paralleling Tucher's, speaks of its particular cultural moment. That moment in the early 1990s was the end of Japan's economic and cultural invincibility *in the American mind* (e.g., Prestowitz, 1988). Just as the tides of national fortune began to turn across the Pacific, the death of one young man fixed America in the withering stare of the one nation that could, at that moment, most effectively evoke self-doubt.

There is one more parallel. Both accounts are memories of an all-too-frequently recurring event in American experience: armed violence. Indeed the paradox of singular poignancy amid eternal recurrence is why these accounts hold lessons for us. The point, however, is that the death of Yoshihiro Hattori yielded the fullness of its public and cultural meaning only because it was framed—articulated, punctuated, and attributed—so as to capture the full measure of resonance through such familiar yet powerful textual effects as irony, gaze, and reflexivity. Thanks to the imaginative potential of mainstream daily journalism, this tragedy was, for a moment, more than just a normal killing.

Articulation of the 'Freeze' Case

Front-page news, with its big-fact-first style, may deny its readers the pleasure of suspense but not that of irony. Within the frame of situational irony (the narrative structure in which the characters are led to expect one thing while the readers know quite another awaits), the last moments in a young life are articulated as a sequence of dramatically poignant reversals. Peaceful scenes — a quiet street with holiday decorations—are juxtaposed with violent ones—blood on the concrete—in a sequence that reaches its climax in the confrontation between the kid who, it turns out, speaks little English and the man with the gun who yells, of all things, 'Freeze!' The story, with its conclusion established from the beginning, moves through each turn with terrible inevitability. It is within and through this artfully ironic telling that this story first acquires its resonance. 'East Brookside is a quiet street', as the *New Orleans Times Picayune* sets the scene for violence on the evening of 17 October 1992. In this account, the sequence of ironic reversals begins with the smallest and most innocent of mistakes:

> Though two weeks before Halloween, there was a costume party on East Brookside that night. The party was in full swing—the two boys were the only guests yet to arrive. Hattori, a Japanese exchange student, was to meet a Japanese girl who he'd never met but had talked with on the telephone several times.
>
> He was eager and gregarious that night, say those who saw him. He was ready to party, but when he and Haymaker pulled up at 10311, they were at the wrong house. (Rose, 1992: E1)

The house at 10311 East Brookside was six doors from the boys' intended destination at 10131 East Brookside. Nonetheless, that house—the tragically wrong house—was invitingly adorned with Halloween decorations. *The New York Times* lead its initial account of the killing with this promise of a party that lured the boys to the wrong door:

> The Halloween decorations, a paper skeleton, a plastic ghost are still in place outside Rodney Peairs's neat brick ranch-style house near here, and a faint reddish stain is still outlined on the floor of the carport.
>
> The decorations are what drew a 16-year-old Japanese exchange student, Yoshihiro Hattori, to the house in the rural suburb of Central, and the stain is the result.

> Saturday night, young Hattori and an American school friend were looking for a Halloween party in the quiet neighborhood. But they knocked on the wrong door . . . *(The New York Times,* 1992: A1)

Bonnie Peairs answered the knock. Perhaps startled by the boys' costumes, she slammed the door and screamed for her husband to get his gun. 'There was no thinking involved,' she later testified about that moment. 'I wish I could have thought. If I could have just thought' *(The New York Times,* 1993b: A11). Then the next ironic turn of events: thinking the woman's reaction had been party fun, the boys headed for a side door under the carport. Rodney Peairs opened that door with a .44 Magnum in his hand as Yoshi stepped forward. That fateful step was most artfully articulated in a profile of the boy published by *The New York Times* just after his death:

> Yoshihiro Hattori was a young man who danced his way through the brief two months he spent in America. Lithe and athletic, the 16-year-old Japanese exchange student danced in the halls of McKinley High and danced in the kitchen of his American host.
>
> 'What Yoshi liked to do was move,' Holly Haymaker remembered sadly this week . . . Not speaking much English, he expressed himself through playful movement. On Saturday, the trusting Yoshihiro Hattori moved fatally toward Rodney Peairs . . . . (Nossiter, 1992: A12)

And still another turn: 'Freeze!' Mr Peairs shouted at the boys. 'To a Japanese the term might have no threatening connotation and might even be mistaken for the word "please," since in spoken Japanese the "l" and the "r" sounds are identical,' explained the *Boston Globe* in an article written after the trial (Nickerson, 1993: 13). 'Hattori would have been taught in his English class here that "freeze" has to do with making ice,' *The Washington Post* observed sardonically (Reid, 1992: A32). And so the American boy began backing slowly away. The Japanese boy, however, continued forward.

In its report of the funeral, the Associated Press captured what happened next in its typically terse style. Nonetheless, two iconic details, the order to freeze and the gun, seemed essential to capturing the moment of Yoshihiro Hattori's death. 'He did not heed the homeowner's order to "freeze"—an English word he did not understand—and was shot in the chest with a .44-caliber Magnum at close range' *(Boston Globe,* 1992: 1A). 'Hattori was pronounced dead at a local hospital,' the *Times Picayune* reported, bringing one of its accounts to conclusion. 'He never met the Japanese girl down the street' (Rose, 1992: E10).

Despite the singularity of the circumstances, the many parallel accounts of these few seconds resonate with a well-crafted universality. Indeed, they provide a textbook case of the poetics by which tragedy is constituted. As Vincent et al. (1989) demonstrated of television news about air crashes, reports framed as irony direct our attention toward the eternal mysteries of fate when, inevitably, technical explanations leave us feeling no less vulnerable. Irony locates and organizes occurrences, for example, the heroic efforts of a pilot to save a plane that is surely doomed, in a way that vastly multiplies both their singular drama and their universal poignancy. The ironic turn gives a sense not merely of tragedy but of watching it approach on a course that we can discern in retrospect even if we could not have predicted. Framed in this way, the account of a specific tragedy transcends the facts to become a meditation on the inevitability, yet uncertainty of death.

While irony may seem to flow naturally from death and disaster, the accounts of Yoshihiro Hattori's death remind us that irony is crafted through selection and juxtaposition of elements. The story line identifies the images and details to be dramatically rendered: the transposed numbers, the Halloween decorations on the wrong house, the inexplicably frightened woman, the man who shouts 'Freeze!', the .44 Magnum. Each of those elements, in turn, marks a fateful step toward death that the reader knows awaits. Thus, we might take this story simply to be a reminder of irony's enduring role in 'cultural narrations' and of journalists' skill in working endless variations. Instead, let's ask this story to tell us something more about why irony, especially irony colored by blood, remains a timeless resource for resonance making.

An answer lies in a particular way that irony can be made to mediate the demands of harsh reality and human desire. 'Characterizations of the world cast in an Ironic mode are often regarded as intrinsically sophisticated and realistic', observed historiographer Hayden White (1973: 37) as a prelude to a warning about the debilitating effects of irony that has decayed into cynicism. Even as the 'Ironic mode' confronts the reality of human folly, it will disable the urge to social action if it admits to the cynic's dark desire. But cynical disengagement is not the only stance that irony allows. Great art 'keeps its distance from things,' observed Thomas Mann (1960: 88), 'it hovers over them and smiles down upon them, regardless of how much, at the same time, it involves the reader or hearer in them by a process of weblike entanglement.' Of this more benign detachment, Mann concluded, 'Objectivity is irony.'

If cynicism is dark, Mann's objectivity promises light. 'The ironist's awareness of himself as the unobserved observer tends to enhance his feeling of freedom,' argued D. C. Muecke (1969: 218) commenting on Mann's assertion. This sort of objective detachment is not devoid of feelings for the victims of the irony, whether contempt for their folly or pity for their plight. Nonetheless, it offers a sense, that is to say it produces an *effect,* of liberating vision. The ironist's 'awareness of the victim's unawareness invites him to see the victim as committed where he feels disengaged; bound or trapped where he feels free', Muecke concluded. The ironic stance offers the 'feeling of being lifted up, unburdened and liberated' (p. 218).

To articulate occurrences as steps toward a fate that the reader knows awaits but the characters do not is to offer the effect of what philosopher Hilary Putnam (1981: 50) characterized as the 'god's eye view'. That would be the only view to yield knowledge unmotivated by human interest or unconstrained by human language. While such a view can never be available to us, we can experience a simulation of it. This is the attraction of irony to those who aim to produce a discourse of the real such as history or journalism. Irony seems to grant their impossible desire: objective knowledge of deep truths. As ironists we smile serenely, though not always joyfully, down on the world because we think that, from here, we can see reality as it is. Irony raises us, wrote Goethe, 'above happiness or unhappiness, good or evil, death or life' (quoted in Muecke, 1969: 219). Borne on powerful wings of ironic imagination, a story like Yoshihiro Hattori's effects our ascent above death itself. It suspends us there, for a moment, to gaze down on that most universal truth.

Punctuation and the International Media Echo

Precisely because it is the most universal truth, death is not news. The parochial truth surrounding a particular death, however, may become news. While the ironic articulation of Yoshihiro Hattori's death made it interesting, another frame made it important. In Japan, the story was immediately evaluated and characterized—that is to say, punctuated—by the news media as an outrageous instance of an American social ill: gun violence. The concern here, however, is not the Japanese coverage of the story. Rather, it is the U.S. coverage of the Japanese coverage—that is to say, the American punctuation of the Japanese punctuation. From the very first, the U.S. press framed the story as an international incident that brought collective shame to America. As an international incident, however, the killing and its aftermath were not so much a diplomatic incident as a media incident, a perfect example of the 'international media echo' (Frederick, 1993: 228). While the Japanese government said little, the Japanese media made a big story of Yoshi's death and Mr. Peairs' trial. In turn, the U.S. media made a big story of the Japanese media making a big story of those events.

Within the international incident frame, the American press portrayed the entire Japanese nation as looking on with both fascination and disgust. *The New York Times* succinctly summarized the frame in a headline: 'Japan Watches Intently as a Slaying Trial Begins' *(The New York Times,* 1993a: A12). The story reported that the killing had 'reinforced a cultural gulf between the United States and Japan', suggesting that Japan was not watching the trial of an individual American so much as the trial of America itself. Sometimes the U.S. coverage characterized the Japanese coverage as stereotypical. 'For many Japanese', continued the *Times* report on the trial, 'the killing strengthened their stereotype of the United States: a violent nation, its finger on a hair-trigger'. Overall, however, American journalism displayed very little defensiveness. The Japanese, it seemed, had a point: something really was wrong in America. Thus, both the U.S. and Japanese coverage punctuated the killing itself within the same gun-violence-as-social-problem frame. At the same time, however, the American press worked to craft the resonance of the ongoing story less from the moral urgency of the problem itself than from Japan's keen awareness of the problem. Resonance arose within the mediated echo of Japan's outrage and contempt.

Among American newspapers, *The Washington Post* made the media echo reverberate most resonantly. Its initial story, written from Tokyo by T. R. Reid, began:

> All of Japan's national TV networks here took time during their national news programs tonight to offer a lesson in English. In tones of amazement and terror, the news anchors explained how the word 'freeze' can be used to mean, 'Don't move or I'll shoot!'. (Reid, 1992: A1)

Next the reporter recounted the shooting; but after a few paragraphs, he returned to his central concern. 'For the American news media, it was just another killing', Reid wrote. 'In Japan, though, the real-life Halloween horror story quickly became a major national concern.' To illustrate the contention that the story confirmed 'all the worst impressions the Japanese hold in their intense love–hate relationship with the colossus across the Pacific', the report went on to quote several Japanese commentators. 'Guns everywhere—it's like a cancer', said one. 'No wonder we Japanese can't understand American society', said another (Reid, 1992: A32).

For the *New Orleans Times Picayune,* the shooting was a local story; but even its earliest reports were framed in terms of an international incident rather than a local accident. A report headlined 'Killing Hurts Nation's Image' led with a statement by Yoshi's father who expressed hope that the 'the incident will neither damage U.S.–Japanese relations nor dissuade Japanese students from studying in America' (Nicholas, 1992: B1). The report went on to note the 'enormous interest in Japan where TV networks have devoted time to explaining the various meanings of the word "freeze" in English'. Then it turned to a local source that could serve as the voice of Japan. 'In Japan, the value of life is very important', said the Japanese consul-general in New Orleans, apparently marking a contrast with the USA. 'That is why people pay attention to this case.'

As legal proceedings got underway, the echo could be heard again. The *Atlanta Constitution* reported on the pretrial hearing with a story headlined 'Culture Clash Plays Out in Louisiana'. It began:

> It has been nearly three months since a Japanese exchange student who revered the United States died in a uniquely American fashion: He was shot in the chest by a homeowner with a .44 Magnum who believed the 16-year-old was an intruder. (Cheakalos, 1993: A3)

With a concise summary of its own frame, the report continued,

> The private tragedy immediately became an international incident that has not

> abated in Japan where the shooting has drawn enormous media attention and public outrage. For the Japanese, Mr. Peairs has become a symbol of an increasingly violent and armed America.

When the jury returned with a verdict, the media echo boomed again across the Pacific. 'Virtually all media reports here took the verdict as confirmation of their worst stereotypes about the United States: a sick country that has lost its greatness amid nagging social problems and constant fear', wrote T. R. Reid (1993a: A14) tuning-in from his post in Tokyo. '[A] recurrent theme in today's Japanese reports was that Mr. Peairs won acquittal because most Americans consider it normal to shoot and kill and unknown visitor at the door.' The next day, Reid reported that the Hattori family might seek 'an American-style remedy for their American loss', a civil suit against Mr. and Mrs. Peairs. The story went on to reiterate the Japanese diagnosis of an American sickness. 'All the national Japanese newspapers ran editorials today on the so-called "freeze case"', Reid reported. 'Nearly all referred to the United States as "The Gun Society," and the consensus view was expressed by the *Yomiuri Shimbun,* Japan's biggest newspaper: "The pathology of life in The Gun Society is horrifying".' (Reid, 1993b: A22).

The *Los Angeles Times* emphasized the offense taken by the Japanese at the behavior of courtroom spectators who whooped and cheered at the verdict. 'Sure, I've got a gun', said a Louisiana resident in what was characterized by Japanese television as a typical comment. 'In this society, you've got to have a gun' (Watanabe, 1993: A4). Like many other stories, this report noted that the case had become 'a symbol of the gulf between Japan and the United States in attitudes toward gun ownership, self-defense and crime'. However, it went on to suggest briefly that an even more fundamental difference between the two countries was the conception of personal responsibility. 'Many Japanese also shook their heads in amazement that an act of killing could produce an innocent verdict, because the system here does not generally offer the same gradations of culpability', the story reported, 'and the act of shooting itself is generally seen to constitute criminal intent'. The fact that in Japan the act of shooting itself implies criminal intent might have prompted a discussion of how, in addition to the mere availability of guns, America's system of justice, its standards of conduct, and its sense of moral responsibility evolved together into a culture so tolerant of violence. The reporter did not pursue the point.

Thus, while the ironic frame for the events leading to Yoshi's death had created the effect of *looking,* the international incident frame for the aftermath created the effect of *being looked at*—'Japan watches'. The news, like other forms of media, enables and directs the gaze of its audience upon others. Through that gaze others are evaluated and differences between self and others are recognized. The gaze of West upon East in this fashion is, of course, an ancient enterprise. As Homi Bhabha (1983: 33) reminds us, however, looking relations are alienating for the object of the gaze and the possibility of confrontation—'the threatened return of the look'—is always present. Exactly this threat was realized when, as Reid noted in his report on the verdict, many Japanese reporters 'allowed a tone of moral superiority to seep into their stories'. The return of the look was explicit: 'Japan has always looked up to America', Reid quoted one television commentator as saying. 'But now, which society is more mature? The idea that you protect people by shooting guns is barbarian.' Another commentator was quoted in response to the Japanese government's statement that the verdict reflected a cultural difference in attitudes toward gun ownership. 'It is said that the ready acceptance of guns in America is just the result of a cultural difference', he said. 'But over there—how can you call it a "culture"?' (Reid, 1993a: A14). Reduced to stereotypical pathologies, America was now the degenerate and dangerous other.

In these journalistic constructions of the Japanese *other* to reflect the American *self,* the moral polarity of the old Orientalist opposition is reversed. Here, the moral superiority of the other puts the self to shame. In so far as authorial intent is admissible into evidence, the *Post's*

T. R. Reid, for one, was quite willing to acknowledge his efforts to construct a Japan that could stand in moral opposition to the United States. 'It's very, very expensive for *The Washington Post* to keep me and my wife and three children in this country', he said in an interview conducted in Tokyo in 1994.[3] 'So damn it, I better teach Americans something to justify this.' Reid claimed the role of social observer but hardly a disinterested one. 'When I first came here, rich Japan and how they got rich and how they became a world super power, that was my story', he said. 'Now I feel that my story is how they became a world *social* power, how they became such a peaceful, free society. We Americans have got to learn this somewhere.'

In sum, the effect of the international media echo was to fix America in the humiliating gaze of the people who, at that moment, could most readily evoke self-doubt, anxiety, and guilt. America, even if stereotyped and misunderstood, stood exposed and ashamed—at least in these carefully crafted news texts. If read as a call for America to learn a lesson, to come to terms with itself, and to begin a project of social renewal, then this effect too is an expression of desire. To suppose that such a thing is possible, after all, is to desire much. But be that as it may, the crafting of America's shame in the sight of the Japanese other is exquisite.

Attribution and Editorial Iconography

From the first mention of blood on concrete, the news accounts of Yoshihiro Hattori's death and Japan's response must be read as moral discourse. On the front page, moral meanings of news are conveyed surreptitiously through selection of stories and sequencing of facts. As the news moves from the front page to the editorial page, however, moral meanings may briefly become the object of reflection. This is the setting in which journalists, to borrow a phrase from anthropologist Victor Turner (1984: 23), may 'talk about what they normally talk'. That is to say, editorialists may write not only reflectively but also reflexively. 'A reflexive act implies an agent's action upon himself, indicating the identity of subject and object', Turner wrote. 'When the subject is plural and human, and hence a cultural entity, the agent's action is motivated by and with reference to cultural definitions of who it is that acts and to whom action is directed'. Such acts of plural reflexivity, whether religious ritual or newspaper editorial, are acts of cultural self-definition. While anthropologists have often celebrated the role of reflexivity in maintaining the bonds of tribal societies, mass-mediated societies also seek a meaningful sense of self. Identity and community, as Tucher noted, are enduring desires.

The New York Times began its comment on Rodney Peairs' acquittal in an editorial headlined 'Gun Crazy' by reducing the ironic reversals of the shooting to their iconic essentials *(The New York Times,* 1993c: A22). 'Last October a 16-year-old Japanese exchange student named Yoshihiro Hattori adopted an old American custom and got all dressed up for Halloween', the editorial began. 'A few hours later he was dead—because of another old American custom.' Other images race by: the boys ringing the wrong doorbell, Mrs. Peairs wishing she 'could have just thought', and Mr. Peairs ordering Yoshi to 'Freeze!'. Next, the editorialist quoted the defense attorney who argued at trial, 'In your house, if you want to do it, you have the right to answer everybody that comes to your door with a gun'. By this logic, the editorialist suggested, anyone who comes to the door, 'the youngster selling Girl Scout cookies . . . the local minister . . . anyone whose lost his way', can expect a bullet. Thus, in a few key phrases, the editorial recalled the story and in a few more it brought to bear the reflexive potential inherent in the justifiably horrified gaze of the Japanese. 'We Japanese don't understand the gun society of America', said a surrogate for the generalized Japanese other. And to this the editorialist responded, 'Just think stupidity, intolerance, a warped interpretation of the right to bear arms'.

If the effect was to create a reflexive moment in which a nation looked into its darkening psyche, that moment was brief and unfocused. What could be seen in the moral gloaming was more than a reckless mistake by a defendant and more than a miscarriage of justice by a jury. What could not be so clearly seen was a coherent and compelling attribution of the problem these events seemed to imply. The notion of 'gun crazy' as the imagined insanity in the imagined American community yielded no real sense of explanation, no allocation of responsibility, no call to action. Most critically it denied to its readers a sense of moral agency. It rejected the identity of the shooter: the one who answers the door with a gun. But it offered the reader only the identity of victim: the one who's lost the way and can only dread what waits behind the door.

The *Chicago Tribune's* editorialist constructed much the same moment of unfocused soul searching in its editorial, 'Just a Normal Baton Rouge Killing' *(Chicago Tribune,* 1993: 18). The *Tribune* denounced the acquittal as 'profoundly poisonous, not so much to the relationship between the United States and Japan or between Americans and Japanese as to the attitudes of decency, trust and neighborliness among Americans'. Quoting the defense attorney's remark about the right to answer the door with a gun, this editorialist also developed the motif of victimization. 'God help all the school kids selling candy . . . political activists seeking signatures . . . and the out-of-towner who dares knock on a door to ask directions.' Noting Yoshi's death was 'one more example of the tragedy that can result from the ready availability of guns in America', the editorialist observed in passing that the prosecutor had 'pointedly avoided making a gun-control argument in presenting his case'. But the editorialist too avoided the argument.

Some newspapers did use the acquittal as an opportunity to editorialize explicitly on behalf of gun control. True to iconic form, the *San Francisco Chronicle* recalled the most essential images of the shooting: the exchange student, the wrong house, and the gun. And of the most essential element of the trial: the affirmation of the right to answer the door with gun-in-hand. In Japan, according to the editorial, 'the verdict was taken as evidence that the United States had lost its greatness and become a sick country' *(San Francisco Chronicle,* 1993: A18). For the *Chronicle,* the verdict was taken as evidence that the U.S. Congress must pass the so-called Brady Bill imposing a waiting period on handgun purchases. With the notion of a 'sick country', the *Chronicle* found its own pathogenic metaphor for American life but, like the metaphors of insanity and poison, the notion of a national illness generated little real insight. The metaphors implied a problem beyond the mere availability of guns but the malady that, presumably, afflicted the American soul went undiagnosed. And in turn, no remedies beyond a small dose of gun control, if even that, could be prescribed. Once again the story was articulated as ironic tragedy and punctuated as shameful problem but not attributed to any clearly specified cause.

For the most part, the editorializing about the acquittal illustrates how icons can be crafted to summarize the story and symbolize the problem but, nonetheless, fail to make a point. However, among the reflections upon the meaning of the verdict, a column by the *Atlanta Constitution*'s Cynthia Tucker perhaps most adeptly talked *about* that which is normally talked. Tucker summoned yet again the deadly sequence of events: the boys looking for a Halloween party, the knock on the wrong door, the screaming woman who later wished that she 'could have thought', and the man with a .44 Magnum who yells 'Freeze!'. For Tucker, these images refuted the 'simple slogans' used by 'the cult of gun ownership'. She subverted the gun lobby's typical frame for gun violence—guns don't kill people, people kill people—by constructing its anti-frame. If the person is not guilty, then the gun did kill. 'What if there had been no gun in the Peairs household?', the columnist demanded. 'When Mrs. Peairs screamed, wouldn't her husband have run to lock the door? Wouldn't they have called the police? Wouldn't Yoshi Hattori be alive?' (Tucker, 1993: D5).[4]

In the brief reflexive moment of Tucker's column, we can begin to theorize a source of resonance for attributional frames around social issues. Drawing upon Umberto Eco, critic Robert Siegle examined the role of reflexivity in critiquing the codes and conventions by which we understand the world. 'By [reflexively] forcing awareness of these codes on readers, texts "train semiosis," as Eco puts it, by compelling them to reconsider the various codes and discover new possibilities within them', Siegle argued. 'To train semiosis is to train revolution' (Siegle, 1986: 10–11). He concluded that 'the final effect of reflexivity is to lead readers to recognize their "world" as an alternative fiction to that in the text, but still nonetheless a fiction constituted by a matrix of conventions' (p. 238). The critic was writing about the novel, of course, but where he referred to 'fiction' we might easily substitute 'truth'. The point is that reflexive texts, whatever their claims to art or truth, make our familiar world strange without making it incomprehensible. And this applies to the plurally reflexive discourse theorized by Turner and practiced in a simple but craftsman-like way by Tucker.

There is one more idea we that can borrow from what Siegle calls the 'constitutive poetics' of reflexivity. It concerns the metaphorical 'reflex motion' that can release enough imaginative power to reconstitute social reality. Reflexivity, configured as merely a turning back on itself, produces a text that 'turns away from what is represented and loses itself in self-contemplation', according to Siegle (1986: 2). Such a 180-degree turn produces a self-absorbed text that cannot affect our view of reality, our core values, or our philosophical assumptions. For Siegle, the reflex motion must be a full turn: 'the reflexive circuit'. Configured as a 360-degree turn, reflexivity produces an outward-looking text that sees the world in new and unfamiliar ways.

Journalism, supposing that it would lose itself in self-contemplation, is characteristically hostile to the mere mention of reflexivity. But contemplation by journalists of their own codes and conventions, a mere 180-degree turn, is not the goal here. Journalism is a discourse composed of many other discourses. Our goal should be a full turn of the reflexive circuit that can enable new readings of journalism's constituent discourses—those of governments, markets, and, in the instance at hand, the gun lobby and its opponents. For strategists of social action, in other words, the question is how they might coax or compel the full turn of reflexive circuit through which publics would come to think *about,* rather than merely *in,* the usual symbols and slogans.[5] Tucker shows us how to see the world differently for a resonant moment.

Conclusion: Poetics of Social Action

Resonant journalism records the 'Truth' of which Tucher wrote, whether universal or parochial. And in such Truth, as this account suggests, we can often read Desire. Beyond goodness-of-fit to a cultural repertoire, resonance invokes and remakes a longing for that which can be glimpsed in imagination—for meaningful identity, perhaps, or fulfilling community—even when beyond reach in reality. In the case at hand, a tragedy and a trial were crafted by daily assignment reporting and editorializing into three familiar yet compelling entries into the vast catalogue of human longings: a story that transcends death, confession that expiates shame, and the possibility—even if inadequately imagined—of redemptive action. These mythic dreams about ultimate knowledge and deliverance from evil may have been anxious and guilty; but they expressed, even if inchoately, an urge to understand and act within a real world of human affairs. That such craft is possible, indeed common, is a central insight of the communication-as-culture perspective on the news.

Journalism, like any but the most elementary uses of language, is simultaneously literal and figurative, grounded in reality and myth, an expression of truth and desire. While the social and cultural longings of the sort recounted here are not the only source of resonance—fear is certainly another (Bird, 2003) and, of course, desire may be intensely private—such longings provide a basis, even if tenuous, for social action. With this in mind, we should ask theorists of media-framing not only to reveal the politics of textual representation but also to adduce a constitutive poetics of social action. While the aesthetics of frame resonance that comes to us from the sociology of social movements underestimates the craft of resonance-making, those rudimentary aesthetic principles hold an important first lesson. Resonance, we learn, is a matter of commensurability to our lived experience—that is to say, goodness of fit to our past. It is also a matter of empirical credibility—goodness of fit to what we know of the current moment. Surely too it must be a matter of goodness of fit to our future—that is to say, the future as we desire it, or as we might learn to desire it from stories that are discerningly chosen and resonantly told. This requires not merely fidelity to familiar narratives but the re-imagining and renewal of those narratives in a way that might transform desire into thoughtful deliberation, sound judgement, and wise action.

Postscript

Whatever the skill by which it is crafted, resonance inevitably fades. Its power is paradoxically evanescent. Listen as the resonance of the Hattori tragedy lingers for an agonizing moment and is then damped:

> Takuma Ito and Go Matsuura were enticed here from Japan by a promise that has lured countless others to Southern California: the prospect of making movies. Now both are going home, victims at age 19 of what increasing numbers of Japanese have come to believe is as American as Hollywood: senseless, deadly violence dispensed with ubiquitous handguns. (Margolick, 1994: B7)

This report from *The New York Times* went on to describe the scene at a supermarket parking lot where the students had been shot during a carjacking. Two parking spaces had become an impromptu shrine delineated by flowers, votive candles, and an empty carton on which someone had written: 'We must have gun control. Who is next? Your child?'

Within the frame of the Japanese gaze, the deaths of these students were consistently linked to Yoshi's. 'The shootings were the latest attacks to draw Japanese outrage against American violence and came as Japan is still reeling after Rodney Peairs of Baton Rouge was acquitted in May 1993 of manslaughter for the 1992 fatal shooting of Japanese exchange student Yoshihiro Hattori, 16', reported *USA Today* (Sanchez, 1994: 6A). The next day's follow-up developed the international incident theme. 'Seven people were murdered here last weekend—a number ordinary enough that none warranted front page stories in major city newspapers', the story began. 'But in Japan, where murder is virtually unknown, two have rocked the country' (Price and Lovitt, 1994: 1A). The report went on to say that the Japanese media had a new English phrase to teach their audience: carjacking. It concluded with several of *USA Today's* signature factoids, among them the rate of violent crimes per 100,000 of population: for the USA, 757.5, and for Japan, 2.1.

The *San Diego Union-Tribune* also returned to rhetoric made familiar the year before. 'Here, it is considered part of a spiral of mind numbing violence', its report began. 'But to visiting Japanese nationals, the killing of two Japanese students during a carjacking has come to symbolize what is wrong with America' (Rofe, 1994: A3). The death of Yoshi Hattori had created a specific categorical frame, gun violence against Japanese students, making the deaths of Takuma and Go far more resonant than it might otherwise have been in both Japan and the United States. But if this story seems to sharpen rather than dull the meaning of what happened to Yoshihiro Hattori, it was not yet complete.

In Southern California, the economic and cultural stakes of gun violence against Japanese visitors were far greater than in Louisiana. Public officials could not afford to stand self-consciously silent in the Japanese gaze. 'As the weekend slayings of two Marymount College students sent shock waves through Japan and Japanese American communities', reported the *Los Angeles Times,* 'US dignitaries rushed Monday to reassure frantic parents and to counter charges in the Japanese media that Southern California is a gun-infested danger zone' (Moffat and Sanchez, 1994: A1). The story went on to cite a State Department spokesman who worried that the murders were creating 'a very distorted and one-sided view of the United States'. It also cited the U.S. President who expressed his condolences to the Japanese Prime Minister; the Governor of California who called for the death penalty for carjackers; the Mayor of Los Angeles who vowed not to rest until the city was safe; and a spokesman for the Convention and Visitors Bureau who insisted the city was already safe. In between the promises and assurances the story worried about the flow of cash brought by foreign students and tourists to the city.

And so officials intervened to begin the process of normalization—bringing events to symbolic closure with apologies or assurances—that follows any major breach of social or natural order. The deaths of Takuma and Go, and Yoshi too, began to lose their poignant singularity as they collided with economic and political interest. Falling back into that 'spiral of mind numbing violence', they were just more instances that spoke to the need for . . . well, if not gun control then maybe the death penalty. If indeed anything need be done at all. Each was, after all, just a normal killing.

Notes

1. Although Schudson (1989) defined resonance in terms of a 'public and cultural relation' between object (text) and audience, his essay invokes the traditional separation between content and effect by associating resonance with audience response and rhetorical force with features of the text. In Schudson's terms then, the argument here is intended to emphasize that cultural *relation* by examining how texts can be crafted to evoke resonance.

2. A classic formulation of media resonance is Tony Schwartz's (1973) *The Responsive Chord.* Among the mentions of resonance in journalism studies is Bird and Dardenne's (1988) essay, 'Myth, Chronicle and Story: Exploring the Narrative Qualities of News', which associates the concept with recurrence of stereotypical story elements. See also Lule (2001) and Bird (2003).

3. Sarah E. Holsen, who wrote on the Hattori tragedy for her senior honors thesis in Communication Studies at Northwestern University, conducted this interview and collected many of the newspaper accounts cited in this article.

4. Webb Haymaker's parents should be credited for first developing this theme in 'Another Magnum, Another Victim', a column appearing in *The New York Times.* 'Had Mr. Peairs not been armed, he might have acted on the human instinct to exchange words, to ask questions,' they wrote. 'But the gun perverted that instinct, substituting its voice for the human one' (Haymaker and Haymaker, 1992: A21).

5. Ryan et al. (2001) provide an example of communication activism in support of this goal.

References

Bhabha, Homi K. (1983) 'The Other Question—Homi K. Bhabha Reconsiders the Stereotype and Colonial Discourse', *Screen* 24(6): 18–36.

Binder, Amy (1993) 'Constructing Racial Rhetoric: Media Depictions of Harm in Heavy Metal and Rap Music', *American Sociological Review* 58(Dec.): 753–67.

Bird, S. Elizabeth (2003) *The Audience in Everyday Life.* New York: Routledge.

Bird, S. Elizabeth and Robert W. Dardenne (1988) 'Myth, Chronicle and Story: Exploring the Narrative Qualities of News', in James W. Carey (ed.) *Media, Myths, and Narratives: Television and the Press.* Newbury Park, CA: Sage.

Boston Globe (1992) 'Japanese Mourners Call for US Gun Ban' (27 Oct.): 1.

Cheakalos, Christina (1993) 'Culture Clash Plays Out in Louisiana', *Atlanta Constitution* (7 Jan.): A3.

Chicago Tribune (1993) 'Just a Normal Baton Rouge Killing' (25 May): A18.

Entman, Robert M. (1993) 'Framing: Toward Clarification of a Fractured Paradigm', *Journal of Communication* 43(4): 51–68.

Frederick, Howard M. (1993) *Global Communication & International Relations.* Belmont, CA: Wadsworth.

Haymaker, Holley G. and Richard Haymaker (1992) 'Another Magnum, Another Victim', *The New York Times* (31 Oct.): A21.

Lule, Jack (2001) *Daily News, Eternal Stories: The Mythological Role of Journalism.* New York: The Guilford Press.

Mann, Thomas (1960) 'The Art of the Novel', in Haskell M. Block and Herman Salinger (eds) *The Creative Vision: Modern European Writers on Their Art.* Grove Press: New York.

Margolick, David (1994) 'Lamenting Lost Lives, Lost Dreams', *The New York Times* (29 Mar.): B7.

Moffat, Susan and Jesus Sanchez (1994) 'U.S. Rushes to Reassure Japan after Carjacking', *Los Angeles Times* (29 Mar.): A1.

Muecke, D. C. (1969) *The Compass of Irony.* London: Methuen.

Nicholas, Peter (1992) 'Killing Hurts Nation's Image', *New Orleans Times Picayune* (21 Oct.): B1, B2.

Nickerson, Colin (1993) 'Japanese Saddened, Not Shocked at US Verdict', *Boston Globe* (25 May): 1, 13.

Nossiter, Adam (1992) 'Student's Trust in People Proved Fatal', *The New York Times* (23 Oct.): A12.

Prestowitz, Clyde (1988) *Trading Places: How We Allowed Japan to Take the Lead.* New York: Basic Books.

Price, Richard and Jonathan T. Lovitt (1994) 'Murder of Two Students Stuns Japan', *USA Today* (29 Mar.): 1A.

Putnam, Hilary (1981) *Reason, Truth and History.* New York: Cambridge University Press.

Reese, Stephen D., Oscar H. Gandy Jr and August E. Grant (2001) *Framing Public Life: Perspectives on Media and Our Understanding of the Social World.* Mahwah, NJ: Lawrence Erlbaum Associates.

Reid, T. R. (1992) 'Japanese Image of U.S. Affirmed in Student's Death', *The Washington Post* (20 Oct.): A1, A32.

Reid, T. R. (1993a) 'Japanese Media Disparage Acquittal in "Freeze Case"', *The Washington Post* (25 May): A14.

Reid, T. R. (1993b) 'Parents of Slain Japanese Student Mulling Civil Suit', *The Washington Post* (26 May): A22.

Rofe, John (1994) 'Japanese Decry Tragedy in L.A.', *San Diego Union-Tribune* (29 Mar.): A3.

Rose, Christopher (1992) 'One Cloudy Night on a Quiet Street', *New Orleans Times Picayune* (20 Oct.): E1, E10

Ryan, Charlotte, Kevin M. Carragee and William Meinhofer (2001) 'Theory into Practice: Framing, the News Media, and Collective Action', *Journal of Broadca sting & Electronic Media* 45: 175–82.

Sanchez, Sandra (1994) 'Violence in USA Again Stuns Japan', *USA Today* (28 Mar.): 6A.

San Francisco Chronicle (1993) 'The Heavy Cost of Guns at Home' (25 May): A18.

Schudson, Michael (1989) 'How Culture Works: Perspectives from Media Studies on the Efficacy of Symbols', *Theory and Society* 18: 153–80.

Schwartz, Tony (1973) *The Responsive Chord.* Garden City: Anchor Press/Doubleday.

Siegle, Robert (1986) *The Politics of Reflexivity: Narrative and the Constitutive Poetics of Culture.* Baltimore, MD: Johns Hopkins University Press.

Snow, David A. and Robert D. Benford (1988) 'Ideology, Frame Resonance, and Participant Mobilization', *International Social Movement Research* 1: 197–217.

Snow, David A. and Robert D. Benford (1992) 'Master Frames and Cycles of Protest', in Aldon D. Morris and Carol McClurg Mueller (eds) *Frontiers in Social Movement Theory,* pp. 133–55. New Haven, CT: Yale University Press.

Snow, David A., E. Burke Rochford Jr, Steven K. Worden and Robert D. Benford (1986) 'Frame Alignment Processes, Micromobilization, Movement and Participation', *American Sociological Review* 51: 464–81.

The New York Times (1992) 'Grief Spans Sea as Gun Ends a Life Mistakenly' (21 Oct.): A1.

The New York Times (1993a) 'Japan Watches Intently as Slaying Trial Begins' (19 May): A12.

The New York Times (1993b) 'Acquittal in Doorstep Killing of Japanese Student' (24 May): A1, A11.

The New York Times (1993c) 'Gun Crazy' (25 May): A22.

Tucher, Andie (1994) *Froth & Scum: Truth, Beauty, Goodness, and the Ax Murder in America's First Mass Medium.* Chapel Hill: University of North Carolina Press.

Tucker, Cynthia (1993) 'A Tragedy Shoots Down Gun Lobby's Myths', *Atlanta Journal and Atlanta Constitution* (30 May): D5.

Turner, Victor (1984) 'Liminality and the Performance Genres', in John J. MacAloon (ed.) Rite, *Drama Festival, Spectacle,* pp. 19–41. Philadelphia: Institute for the Study of Human Issues.

Vincent, Richard C., Bryan K. Crow and Dennis K. Davis (1989) 'When Technology Fails: The Drama of Airline Crashes in Network Television News', *Journalism Monographs* 117.

Watanabe, Teresa (1993) 'Japanese Angered by U.S. Acquittal of Student's Killer', *Los Angeles Times* (25 May): A4.

White, Hayden (1973) *Metahistory: The Historical Imagination in Nineteenth Century Europe.* Baltimore, MD: Johns Hopkins University Press.

Williams, Rhys H. and Timothy J. Kubal (1999) 'Movement Frames and the Cultural Environment: Resonance, Failure, and the Boundaries of the Legitimate', *Research in Social Movements, Conflict and Change* 21: 225–48.

Source: From "Crafting Cultural Resonance: Imaginative Power in Everyday Journalism," 2005, by J. S. Ettema, *Journalism, 6*(2), 131–152. Reprinted by permission of Sage Publications, Ltd.

19

MEDEA IN THE MEDIA

Narrative and Myth in Newspaper Coverage of Women Who Kill Their Children

BARBARA BARNETT

Motherhood has been represented in contemporary society as a supreme calling, a happy achievement, a heavenly blessing, a womanly profession, the consummate feminine achievement (Brockington, 1996; Daily, 1982; De Beauvoir, 1952 [1949]; Diquinzio, 1999; Douglas and Michaels, 2004; Nicolson, 2001; Rich, 1976; Showalter, 1982; Thurer, 1994). Mothers are supposed to be guided by 'natural' feminine instincts that confer an angelic temperament and make them instantly loving toward their infants, clairvoyant about their children's needs, and willing to place their own desires second to those of their families (Ladd-Taylor and Umansky, 1998; Nicolson, 2001). 'Motherhood is expected to come naturally. When the umbilical cord is cut, and the baby passes into the new parents' eager arms, maternal aptitude is expected to flow like breast milk' (Harberger et al., 1992: 43).

Feminist scholars have challenged traditional notions of motherhood, suggesting that it is not a singular experience for all women; that race, class and sexual orientation can affect the circumstances in which women mother; that motherhood is not desired by all women; and that ideals of what motherhood should be often are far different from the day-to-day realities of child care (Chase, 2001; Collins, 1993, 1995; De Beauvoir, 1952 [1949]; Firestone, 1970; Hollway and Featherstone, 1997; Kitzinger, 1995; Kristeva, 1986; Ladd-Taylor and Umansky, 1998; Nicolson, 2001; Oakley, 1979; Rich, 1976; Ruddick, 1995; Thompson, 2002; Thurer, 1994; Trujillo, 1997). Feminists have further suggested that mothers are often objects, not subjects, in the discourse on their experiences (Cixous, 1981; De Beauvoir, 1952 [1949]; Irigaray, 1985 [1977]; Kristeva, 1986; Lazarre, 1976; Oakley, 1979; Rich, 1976; Ruddick, 1995). When women are silent, myth may define stories of motherhood, and such fictions create unrealistic expectations of maternal perfection (Douglas and Michaels, 2004; Ruddick, 1980, 1995; Thurer, 1994; Wolf, 2001).

Professional codes of conduct encourage journalists to respect truth and to report events in ways that emphasize accuracy, fairness, and balance (International Federation of Journalists, 1986 [1954]; Society of Professional Journalists, 1996). However, news and myth are intertwined as journalists rely on familiar cultural scripts to tell their stories (Bird and Dardenne, 1997; Hanson, 2001; Kitch, 2002; Lule, 2001, 2002). One familiar myth in journalists' repertoire of stories is that of the good and bad mother: the good mother is the consummate nurturer; the bad mother, the consummate destroyer (Lule, 2001).

This analysis examines maternal myths and how these myths inform journalistic accounts of infanticide. While scholars have studied journalistic representations of women as victims of violence (see, for example, Meyers, 1997), less research has been conducted on women's roles as perpetrators of violence, particularly violence in the domestic sphere. An analysis of news accounts of women who kill their children can offer insights into how the media challenge or reinforce myths about motherhood, femininity, and women's roles.

Literature Review

Although fictional stories, such as Euripides' *Medea,* have depicted infanticide as an unsavory crime committed by women on the verge of desperation, factual accounts have presented infanticide as an action driven by intricate motives (Brockington, 1996; Kumar and Marks, 1992; Milner, 2000; Rich, 1976). Across time and cultures, parents have murdered their children (Milner, 2000), with deaths framed as a sacrificial killing to appease angry gods, as a means of gender balance, or as a form of birth control when too many children were born too quickly.

> Numberless women have killed children they knew they could not rear, whether economically or emotionally, children forced upon them by rape, ignorance, poverty, marriage, or by the absence of, or sanctions against, birth control and abortion. (Rich, 1976: 258)

In contemporary America, infanticide is a covert practice—but one that occurs nonetheless. The U.S. Department of Justice (2001) reported that more than 13,500 children were murdered in the USA from 1976 through 1999, with the most likely culprit a parent. Thirty-one percent of children were murdered by their fathers, while 30 percent were killed by their mothers. While men typically commit most of the homicides in the industrialized world, women are more likely than men to kill family members (Jensen, 2001), and a unique aspect of child murders is that the perpetrators are as likely to be women as men (Alder and Polk, 2001). Women may kill their children because of economic stress (Gauthier et al., 2003; Jensen, 2001), to avoid the social stigma of an out-of-wedlock pregnancy, because they feel isolated or depressed about a romantic relationship, or, as part of a complex murder-suicide plot, in which the woman hopes she and her children will be reunited in heaven (Alder and Polk, 2001). Additionally, postpartum illness has been cited in medical literature, news accounts, and court documents as a cause of child murders (Grundy, 1859; Hamilton, 1962; Hamilton and Harberger, 1992; Hickman and LeVine, 1992).

Although parents murder their children with disturbing frequency—nearly one child per day in the USA—the news media treat such events as rare and spectacular (Milner, 2000), and infanticide becomes especially newsworthy if the perpetrator is the child's mother (Coward, 1997; Douglas and Michaels, 2004).

> On the face of it, such an action by a mother (infanticide) is a violation not only of broadly maintained understandings of women as non-violent, but also, perhaps more powerfully, of dominant ideologies about the nature and role of motherhood. (Alder and Polk, 2001: 1–2)

Feminists have suggested that factual accounts of motherhood have strong foundations in fiction, that ancient myths of women as all-powerful creators or destroyers and Victorian ideals of female virtue have shaped modern (and unrealistic) stories of motherhood (Ladd-Taylor and Umansky, 1998; Macdonald, 1995; Sanger, 1999; Showalter, 1982). The myth of the perfect mother permeates mass media, yet the 'ridiculous, honey-hued ideals of perfect motherhood in the news media and the reality of mothers' everyday lives' stand in stark contrast (Douglas and Michaels, 2004: 2). Journalists' use of myth, while often unintentional, offers a compass for readers, a way to help them navigate and make sense of complicated events (Fisher, 1987; Hanson, 2001; Kitch, 2002; Koch, 1990; Lule, 2001, 2002; Tuchman, 1978). Myths inform, but they also serve a comforting purpose 'by telling tales that explain baffling or frightening phenomena and provide acceptable answers' (Bird and Dardenne, 1997: 336).

Research Questions

The purpose of this article is to explore journalistic accounts of maternal infanticide. Specifically, this research project asks:

RQ1: How do the media portray women who have murdered their children?

RQ2: What collective narratives (stories) do the media tell about women who have murdered their children?

RQ3: How do news media narratives reflect or challenge myths about motherhood, women, and femininity?

Methodology

To examine the narratives and myths embedded in journalistic accounts of infanticide, I conducted a qualitative textual analysis of newspaper stories published in the USA since the 1990s. Narrative analysis is a logical tool to analyze the meanings of media texts: 'Narrative is the best way to understand the human experience because it is the way humans understand their own lives' (Richardson, 1990: 133). In this phase of the research, I developed a matrix, adapted from a rhetorical framework by Foss (1989), which allowed for the examination of narrative elements—events, characters, setting, narrator, temporal relationships, and causal relationships. The unit of analysis in this research project was the news article. The matrix was used to analyze and deconstruct the text of each news story, to describe narrative content, to analyze narrative substance, and to evaluate narrative meaning. At the end of the process, I developed a list of dominant narratives and myths that emerged. I also conducted a simple content analysis of news articles to determine how journalists and sources described the crime of infanticide and its perpetrators.

I began this project by conducting a Lexis-Nexis search of major U.S. newspapers to retrieve print news articles about women who killed their children, using search terms such as 'infanticide', 'motherhood and violence', and 'motherhood and murder'. After reviewing headlines and lead paragraphs, I selected 10 cases of infanticide for in-depth analysis and again used LexisNexis to retrieve stories about these cases from local newspapers, national newspapers, and national news magazines. The result was a data set of approximately 250 articles. In this study, I analyzed the following cases:

- Bethe Feltman, who tried to kill herself after feeding the anti-psychotic drugs she was taking for postpartum depression to her three-year-old son and three-month-old daughter.
- Andrea Yates, who drowned her five youngsters in the bathtub of her home, then told police she committed the murders because she was a bad mother and wanted to save her children from Satan.
- Melissa Drexler, a teen who gave birth to her baby in a bathroom stall at the prom, then returned to the dance floor.

- Amy Grossberg, a teen who gave birth to her son at a Delaware hotel, then abandoned the baby in a Dumpster.
- Susan Smith, a white woman who told police a black man hijacked her car, taking her two sons hostage; Smith told the story to cover up the fact she had drowned the boys.
- Marie Noe, a homemaker who was arrested at age 69 for the murders of eight of her 10 children—all of whom Noe had said died from Sudden Infant Death Syndrome.
- Awilda Lopez, a mother who beat her six-year-old daughter to death in a case that eventually led to an overhaul of the state's child welfare services.
- Jennie Bain, whose two sons died inside a hot car while she attended an impromptu party inside a hotel.
- Khoua Her, a Hmong refugee in the USA, who strangled her six children, then tried to commit suicide.
- Urbelina Emiliano, a Mexican immigrant to New York, who helped her husband and brother bury her infant daughter alive; Emiliano's husband was not the father of her child, and they murdered the baby to protect the husband's honor.

My reason for selecting these cases is that they provided a breadth of diverse maternal experiences, including women's experiences with postpartum psychosis, unplanned pregnancy, and alcohol and drug abuse.

While qualitative methods are appropriate for discovering meanings, they often rely on a small sample for data analysis. Therefore, the results of this study may not be generalizable. Although I made an effort to retrieve stories that represented women from a broad range of ages, ethnicities, and economic circumstances, I included only articles from mainstream publications. Reports in alternative newspapers and news magazines might have revealed a different perspective; however, the LexisNexis database did not include these publications, and other Internet and library searches failed to provide a sufficient number of articles for analysis. In addition, I limited my sample to U.S. newspapers, in part because many stories about infanticide in developing countries focused on the general topic, not on specific cases. Another limitation was that, while stories mentioned ethnicity, they did not identify women by race, so I was not able to consider that as a factor in analysis.

FINDINGS: THE FLAWED MOTHER

Four dominant narratives emerged from this analysis. In this article, I discuss only one of the narratives—the flawed mother; other narratives are discussed elsewhere (Barnett, 2005, 2006a, b)

The content analysis revealed that journalists typically reported maternal infanticide as a sensational crime story, relying on police officers to supply the facts of the case and relying on attorneys, relatives, and neighbors to explain women's actions. Infanticide was presented as horrific and surprising—even when there were past reports of violence in the home or parental neglect—and both journalists and sources characterized women's actions as unfathomable (see Table 1).

Women who killed their children were most often portrayed as evil, deceptive, and callous. In some articles, however, friends, relatives, and neighbors characterized the women as good mothers who made mistakes that resulted in children's deaths; when women who killed their children were interviewed, they presented themselves as good mothers who made isolated errors in judgment. Journalists and sources typically remarked that only an insane woman would murder her children (see Table 2).

Because content analysis examines frequencies but does not explore meaning (Riffe et al., 1998), the primary focus of this study was a qualitative textual analysis of news articles. This phase of the analysis revealed that journalists told the stories of infanticide as mysteries, but

Table 1 Characterizations of Infanticide in News Stories*

Descriptors	By News Source	By Journalist
Horrible, shocking	13%	16%
Mysterious	17%	11%
Tragic	15%	4%
Rare	6%	6%
Preventable	6%	4%

*Several descriptors may have appeared in a single story. Percentages do not add up to 100.

Table 2 Characterizations of Women Who Killed Their Children*

Descriptors	By News Source	By Journalist
Callous, uncaring	12%	10%
Insane or mentally ill	31%	23%
Good mothers	23%	4%
Deceptive, devious	17%	15%
Unaware actions would cause harm	14%	2%
Abusive, neglectful	22%	16%
Remorseful	10%	5%
Suicidal	10%	6%

*Several descriptors may have appeared in a single story. Percentages do not add up to 100.

not classic 'who dunnits'. Instead, the mystery was 'why did she do it?', and journalists explained women's motives through interviews with police, lawyers, family, and friends. Johnson-Carter (2005) suggested that journalists engage in 'motivational analysis. . . to reveal inner most secrets for an audience' (p. 123), and much of the reporting on infanticide incorporated explanations as reporters tried to answer the question of how a mother could harm her children. In news accounts of infanticide, journalists often played the role of the shocked observer, mirroring Hackett and Zhao's (1998) concept of journalism as 'a kind of Greek chorus' (p. 31). For example, a *Newsweek* subheadline on Melissa Drexler's arrest asked, 'Why did a teenager hide her pregnancy and then deliver and dump her baby between dances?' (Koehl, 1997), while the *Chattanooga (Tennessee) Free Press* began the first story on Jennie Bain's arrest with the lead: 'How a mother could leave her two toddlers to die in an unventilated, sweltering car while she partied for hours with friends at a motel seems incomprehensible. . .' *(Chattanooga Free Press,* 1995a: para. 1). When Andrea Yates killed her five children, *Newsweek* asked, 'How could a mother commit such a crime against nature and all morality, ending the lives she had so recently borne and nurtured?' (Thomas et al., 2001, para. 1).

Journalists and sources answered the question 'why?' by explaining that mothers who killed their children were flawed women who failed at caretaking tasks. News accounts presented two different types of flawed mothers. The first group was characterized as superior caretakers who nurtured not only their own children but other family members, other people's children, the sick, their neighbors, and strangers in the community. The adjective 'perfect' was used frequently to describe them; ironically, the terms 'normal' and 'ordinary' were used as well. This group killed because they were mentally ill. The second group included women who were inept caretakers. These women either performed their mothering tasks poorly or rejected mothering work altogether, putting personal pleasure and convenience above maternal sacrifice.

This dichotomy mirrored Meyer et al.'s characterizations of 'mad' and 'bad' mothers:

> Women portrayed as 'mad' have been characterized as morally 'pure' women who by all accounts have conformed to traditional gender roles and notions of femininity. These women are often viewed as 'good mothers,' and their crimes are considered irrational, uncontrollable acts, usually the direct result of mental illness. In contrast, women characterized as 'bad' are. . . depicted as cold, callous, evil mothers who have often been neglectful of their children or their domestic responsibilities . . . These mothers are often portrayed as sexually promiscuous, non-remorseful, and even non-feminine. (2001: 70)

One of the women who cared too much was Bethe Feltman, diagnosed with postpartum depression at the time she killed her children. The former middle-school teacher, who became a stay-at-home mom after her first child was born, taught Sunday School, participated in the Mothers of Preschoolers support group, brought meals to sick neighbors in her suburban neighborhood, and wrote letters of encouragement to a missionary family in Ecuador (Vaughan and Gutierrez, 1998, para. 2). Former students remembered Feltman as supportive, although five male college professors could not remember her at all, and her college girlfriends said she was the ideal roommate, thoughtful, studious, and deeply religious. 'I guess I remember her as just a very good girl', one said (Meadow, 1998). In interactions with her own children, Feltman appeared loving and tender. Lynne Ford, the custodian at the Feltmans' church, remembered her as gentle with her shy three-year-old son. 'She was so patient, so kind, a perfect mother' (Crowder, 1998).

Community members were horrified when Feltman killed her children, but they also expressed compassion toward a woman whose sickness appeared to transform her from loving to violent. In accounts of the Feltman murders, reporters privileged news sources' remarks that postpartum depression was a form of insanity. 'This is not a made-up disease', said Jeffrey Metzner, a Denver forensic psychiatrist. Dr Doris Gundersen of the University of Colorado Health Sciences Center suggested that 'we must be careful not to punish women who develop this disorder and commit infanticide when their illness goes unrecognized or undertreated' (Lindsay, 1998). News stories cast Feltman as the mad mother—a woman who was a perfect caretaker until illness damaged her.

Unlike Feltman, Andrea Yates was presented as both a mad/bad mother. The young mother of five was the supreme caretaker and achiever, but that changed on 20 June 2001, when she drowned her children in the bathtub of their suburban home. Relatives and friends were stunned, describing Yates as kind, conscientious, and loving. Yates' mother, Jutta Kennedy, told the press: 'She was always trying to be such a good girl . . . She was the most compassionate of my children. Always thinking of other people, never herself. She was always trying to care for everybody' (Thomas et al., 2001, para. 7). Terry Arnold, who owned the home-school bookstore Yates visited weekly, called her 'a totally delightful woman', who spoke lovingly of her husband, was very gentle with her children, and appeared 'very upbeat' (Bardwell et al., 2001, paras 34, 39). Yates' brother Andrew Kennedy said his sister 'was just a good person. She followed the Ten Commandments. . . She loved them [the children] a lot' (Rendon, 2001, para. 17).

The valedictorian of her high school class and a registered nurse, Yates cared for patients in a cancer unit until she resigned to rear and home-school her children. While pregnant and caring for her own young family, she also provided daily care for her father, who suffered from Alzheimer's disease. 'She would change his clothes and wash him and help feed him', Yates' mother recalled (Thomas et al., 2001, para. 7). *The Houston Chronicle* reported that 'Yates has spent her adult life catering to the deepest needs and visions of others, strangers and loved ones alike' (Bernstein and Garcia, 2001, para. 3), and *Newsweek* observed that 'if anything, she cared too much . . . In a horribly twisted way, she may have tried to be too good a mother' (Thomas et al., 2001, para. 6).

Family and friends saw Yates as a diligent caretaker, but they also saw signs that she was suffering from postpartum psychosis. Relatives sought psychiatric help for Yates, yet no one suspected Yates, who had tried twice to kill herself, would become violent with the children. Husband Russell Yates said that neither he nor his mother-in-law, who visited the home daily, 'saw Andrea as dangerous. We didn't know what she was thinking. Neither of us thought it would be a problem leaving her by herself an hour here and there' (Christian, 2002a, para. 6). Russell Yates also explained that his wife hid her moods well. 'She's a very private person. She doesn't say much' (Thomas et al., 2001, para. 14). Like Lazarre's (1976) ideal mother, Yates was quiet, giving, and undemanding.

Prosecuting attorneys presented a different portrait of Yates, one that cast her as selfish and manipulative. Yates exemplified 'an evil mindset beyond what most people can imagine' (Tolson, 2001, para. 28), according to one prosecutor. Some attorneys acknowledged that Yates might be insane, but they argued that mental illness did not excuse her from her maternal responsibilities. One legal consultant made essentialist arguments that Yates deserved harsh punishment because 'all women will reject the idea of destroying their young' (Christian, 2002b, para. 13). Indeed, jurors did not believe mental illness excused Yates, and when they convicted her of murder, prosecutor Kaye Williford deemed the verdict appropriate. 'To find her not guilty by reason of insanity is to say that we no longer have self-accountability in our society' (Christian and Teachey, 2002, para. 38).

Journalists did, in some cases, challenge simplistic representations of Yates as sick or mean by asking why Yates did not receive adequate care for postpartum psychosis. A *Newsweek* writer concluded her article on doctors' failed attempts to treat Yates by asking whether Yates' admission that she heard Satan tell her to kill her children was an 'admission of culpability, or is it a cry of anguish?' (Gesalman, 2002, para. 6). *The Houston Chronicle* published an explanatory article about the illness and noted 'in hindsight, Houstonians can see that Andrea Yates was overburdened, did cry for help and did receive help, although it was inadequate' (Feldman, 2001, para. 33). *The Chronicle* also reported that area residents questioned Russell Yates' failure to protect his children from their sick mother (Snyder, 2002; Teachey, 2001), an issue that was not raised in the Feltman case, even though Bethe Feltman told her husband she fantasized about drowning their children.

While news accounts explored the issue of postpartum psychosis as a cause in the Yates and Feltman murders, articles did not explore the types of services available for women who suffer from the illness. Nor did articles advise family members what steps to take if they suspected a loved one was a threat to children.

What is also remarkable in stories about Yates and Feltman is that so few people acknowledged the women's caregiving work as unusually demanding. In spite of her work as a teacher, church volunteer, and mother, one news reporter described Feltman as having 'lived a life that was stunningly ordinary' (Meadow, 1998). Andrea Yates cared for a sick parent and five children, and her husband viewed his wife's full-time caretaking as stressful but manageable (Bardwell et al., 2001). Women's mothering work is taken for granted because it is considered 'natural' (First, 1994), and newspaper articles about Feltman and Yates reinforced the notion that women who strove to be perfect, worked non-stop, and never complained were just fulfilling a biological destiny.

The ideal of perfection was one of the factors that apparently motivated Amy Grossberg not to tell her parents she was pregnant. Grossberg 'put a premium on being the perfect daughter, and she thought this [pregnancy] would be a disappointment to her family', an attorney explained (Hanley, 1998b, para. 22). John Daley, a friend, observed that in Grossberg's wealthy New Jersey community, 'there's a lot of pressure . . . especially with the girls, to be the perfect princess' (Peyser et al., 1996, para. 12). When Grossberg was arrested after giving birth to her son in a Delaware motel, then throwing his body into a Dumpster, one family friend told *Newsweek* it was 'like Barbie getting busted' (Peyser et al., 1996, para. 9). Friends described Grossberg as obedient and affectionate—terms that might be applied to a cocker spaniel but in this case were used to describe a model adolescent girl.

Kristeva (1986) observed that Marian images portray mothers as quiet, and this expectation of silence allowed Melissa Drexler's pregnancy to go unnoticed among family and friends. In her comings and goings in high school, Drexler lived 'an undistinguished life, she was an ordinary girl' (Goodnough and Weber, 1997, para. 1). The New Jersey teen was so inconspicuous, no one suspected she was pregnant; no one even noticed when her water broke in the car on the way to the prom.

Drexler and Grossberg shared the common bond of an unplanned adolescent pregnancy, and in telling their stories, journalists and sources often characterized the two young mothers as individuals concerned more with protecting a secret than protecting a newborn. A prosecutor in the Grossberg case said the young woman showed 'chilling indifference' toward her child (Hanley, 1998a, para. 11), and when Drexler confessed in court, reporters observed that 'the innocence of her voice seemed misplaced against the remorseless account she gave of killing her newborn' (Zambito, 1998, para. 2). There were, however, some cracks in this flawed mother narrative. News reports on the Drexler case included comments from prosecutors and the judge who suggested the young woman panicked when her baby was born, a *Newsweek* article on Drexler questioned the 'awesome power of denial over a young woman's heart and mind' (Koehl, 1997), and a *New York Times'* article on Grossberg explained infanticide as a centuries-old practice, noting that adolescents may kill their newborns because they fear society's disapproval (Hoffman, 1996). It is worth noting that in news coverage of the Drexler and Grossberg cases, journalists reported that the young women *concealed* their pregnancies. Journalists might also have asked the question: what made these young women so invisible that adults around them did not notice the pregnancies?

Kristeva (1986) theorized that Marian ideals situate mothers as sexually pure and child focused, and this construct transformed Susan Smith from good girl to bad mother in her community's eyes. Smith's mother, Linda Russell, characterized her daughter as an ideal adolescent. 'Susan always minded', Russell said. 'If she was supposed to be home at 10, she was home at 10. I always knew where she was and who she was with and what time she'd be back.

She was dependable and responsible' (Baxley, 1995a, para. 21). A former schoolmate remembered Smith as 'perfect. You've got your bad girls at high school, and you've got your good girls. She was your good girl' (Adler et al., 1994, para. 14). Perhaps the images of perfection and compliance were what led to feelings of betrayal and anger among community members when the sheriff revealed that Smith's children were missing—not because they were in the back seat when a black man carjacked her car—but because the white woman had pushed the car into a lake with the boys strapped inside. *Newsweek* said town residents saw efforts to search for the boys' kidnapper 'mocked by an even greater evil than it imagined' (Adler et al., 1994, para. 4).

At Smith's murder trial, witnesses commented on Smith's love for her children, but it was her love affairs with men that gained the most news interest. Sources portrayed Smith's sexual life as complex, tangled, and squalid, a series of short-lived sexual relationships motivated by lust and greed. Smith's romantic relationship with co-worker Tom Findlay became a centerpiece of trial debate, as prosecutors argued that Findlay did not want the responsibilities of parenting, and Smith murdered her sons to remove the chief obstacle in their relationship.

However, Smith's attorneys suggested that her relationship with another man—her stepfather—also might have played a role in the children's murders: Smith was molested by her stepfather, but when journalists revealed that Smith willingly had sex with her stepfather six months before her sons drowned, news reports characterized Smith as a temptress who invited and enjoyed sexual attention. Smith 'succumbed to her own molestation as a teenager and grew up to become a promiscuous, sexually exploitive young adult', *Newsweek* reported (Morganthau et al., 1995, para. 1). While one psychiatrist testified that Smith's sexual encounters were a reflection of 'her aim to please people and a desire for affection rather than any heightened sexual interest' (Baxley, 1995b, para. 27), *Newsweek* writers suggested that Smith, at age 15, indeed might have been responsible for her stepfather's actions: 'Although Russell clearly initiated sexual contact, the case file suggests Susan may have led him on' (Morganthau et al., 1995, para. 7).

Smith's attorneys argued that she 'tried to cope with a failing life, and she snapped', while prosecutors said 'this is a case of I, I, I, and me, me, me' (Baxley, 1995c, paras 25, 6). In their efforts to adhere to the professional standards of balanced reporting, journalists presented accounts of Smith as victim and victimizer; in so doing, articles reinforced the mad/bad mother dichotomy. Missing from news articles were serious examinations of power in parental relationships, the long-term effects of sexual abuse, and the use of sex as a bargaining tool for women who have few economic options. Feminists have theorized that sexuality and maternity are generally not compatible in Marian constructs of motherhood (De Beauvoir, 1952 [1949]; Kristeva, 1986), and journalists might have considered the relevance of Smith's sexual history in her murder trial by asking whether a man who killed his children would have been subject to questions about his sexual life.

Another flawed mother was Jennie Bain, whose children died in a hot car as she partied inside a motel room with four men. Like Smith, Bain was not homebound or child focused, and her relationships with men were an issue in news coverage of her trial. Bain's mother-in-law, Annette Ducker, said it was Bain's wanton behavior that prompted her son to file for divorce and to ask for custody of the children. 'James knew she had her men, and he didn't think she was taking care of the babies . . . She'd go out and leave him with the kids. He'd have to go hunt her. He found her drunk on several occasions' (*Chattanooga Free Press,* 1995b: paras 24, 27). James Ducker, Bain's estranged husband, noted that his ex-wife was carousing with men the day his children died. 'Any mother who was a good mother wouldn't have her children out at 3:30 in the morning' *(Chattanooga Free Press,* 1995c: para. 6). Yet one article challenged the flawed mother narrative by questioning the role of fathers in child care. At Bain's trial, the judge called attention to the fact that, in spite of his protests that Bain repeatedly abandoned the children, Ducker had not seen his sons in a year (Williams, 1995).

Awilda Lopez, who beat her six-year-old daughter, Alisa Izquierdo, to death, was characterized by journalists and news sources as a violent mother who drifted from man to man and drug to drug. *The New York Times* reported that she 'lived in apartment 20A with six children by four different fathers' (Bruni, 1995, para. 21), and those who came in contact with Lopez described her as an urban savage, who waged an unjust war against her own child. One 22-year veteran of the police force called the Lopez case 'the worst case of child abuse I've ever seen' (Bruni, 1995, para. 3). When Lopez was arrested, *Newsweek* described her as a 'ranting, wild-haired' woman, who screamed her innocence as she was taken away by police (Peyser and Power, 1995, paras 2, 8), and at her sentencing, *Daily News* journalists said the 'crackhead', who had 'previously expressed little remorse' over her child's death (Ross and Gentile, 1996, paras 5, 7), was the most despised woman in New York . . . ' reviled even among criminals' (Daly, 1996, paras 2, 6). In reporting this story, journalists focused primarily on the failure of the New York City social services system to protect Alisa, subsequent bureaucratic changes that led to an overhaul of the social services system, and passage of a state law to open child abuse records to public inspection. Journalists, however, did not explore the availability of services for mothers who admit, as did Lopez, that she needed help in caring for her children. Journalists might have asked what happens when a woman admits she is not a good mother. What resources are available when women admit they do not mother well?

Khoua Her, a Hmong immigrant who killed her six children and tried unsuccessfully to kill herself in a Minnesota public housing project, was presented not only as a flawed mother but a disagreeable human being. Relatives and police told reporters Her was a chronic troublemaker, a malcontent who shunned maternal duties, and a violent woman who threatened her husband with a gun—the antithesis of Lazarre's imaginary good mother. Neighbors said the young woman neglected her children, her husband said she had a bad temper, and her mother-in-law described her as 'an evil daughter-in-law' reluctant to hold or touch her babies (Police piece, 1998, para. 10). However, news reports also presented Her as a woman plagued by violence, poverty, and poor health. Her said she was beaten and threatened by her husband, that she had been raped, and that her daughter was raped.

When police responded to Her's call saying she had murdered her children, the Associated Press reported: 'Police knew the address . . . They'd been called there at least 15 times in the past 18 months' in response to reports of spousal violence (Taus, 1998, para. 1). Reporters might have questioned why, with Her's history as a victim and perpetrator of violence, police did not suspect she might harm her children. Journalists also might have asked how Her's position as a cultural outsider affected her ability to find work in the United States and how young age—Her had six children by the time she was 24—affected her mothering skills.

Journalists also failed to closely examine the role cultural differences may have played in the case of Urbelina Emiliano, who helped her husband kill her two-day-old daughter, fathered by another man. Although journalists reported Emiliano's testimony that she did not want to harm her child, one lawyer scoffed at the idea 'that this young mother would sacrifice the life of her baby to save the pride. . . the machismo [of her husband] . . . that is an absolutely ridiculous concept' (Peterson, 1995, para. 19). Ridiculous or not, honor killings do occur—families kill daughters who are raped so they do not bring shame to the entire clan, husbands and wives kill spouses who are unfaithful. Journalists might have placed Emiliano's claims in a larger cultural context and asked how Emiliano's poverty and lack of education played a role in her decision to obey her husband rather than protect her child.

Because this analysis covered a 12-year-period, questions may be raised about how media coverage changed. There were, in fact, no radical changes over time; an article about the 10-year anniversary of the Susan Smith killings illustrates the point. A reporter observed that Smith left a 'dark and lasting memory' on the town (Caston, 2004, para. 6), and local residents said they continued to resent Smith for lying and harming her children. The attorney who prosecuted the case recalled he had trouble explaining the case to his four-year-old because 'Mama is supposed to be everything safe and protecting. Mama is home' (Caston, 2004, para. 23). There were, however, two changes worth noting in news coverage. First, while most stories portrayed fathers as victims of unpredictable women, news stories about Andrea Yates raised the question of paternal responsibility, not only for the crime of infanticide but in the larger context of children's well-being. Second, a news story prompted police to re-open the investigation into the cause of the deaths of Marie Noe's children. In earlier decades, journalists presented Noe as a sympathetic victim of tragic circumstances and did not openly question her role in the children's deaths.

Discussion and Conclusions: Power and Gender

Gans wrote that 'much news is about the violation of values' (1980: 40), and, as this article illustrates, infanticide represents the violation of deeply held values about right and wrong, childhood innocence, and women's roles, and news articles reflected those deeply ingrained cultural norms. The flawed mother narrative illustrates the underlying assumption that mothers are all-powering, all-knowing, and all-loving, all the time. Cooey (1999) observed that 'the penalty for a mother's failure to meet cultural idealizations of motherhood is demonization' (p. 230), and casting mothers who kill their children as insane or evil was a narrative device that helped journalists simplify their stories. However, demonization allowed reporters to ignore a central paradox in Western culture: we idealize motherhood but offer little social support for women engaged in the day-to-day tasks of child care (Daily, 1982; Kitzinger, 1995).

American society is predicated on the concepts of personal freedom and individual responsibility, and an underlying assumption in this set of articles is that women acted autonomously and in their own self-interests. Journalists might ask how this ideology works in a gendered culture, where women typically are taught that they should defer to others, respect authorities, and consider marriage and children as markers of success and status. Ruddick (1995) observed that women have seemingly tremendous power as mothers; however, they are often powerless in other settings. Journalists might have asked how much autonomy these women had in their relationships, homes, and communities.

Because journalists reported maternal infanticides as local crime stories, reporters tended to rely on attorneys as sources, and this source selection helped perpetuate the idea that infanticide is the isolated act of a flawed individual. Johnson-Carter (2005) theorized that journalists believe that use of official sources provides sufficient facts. In order to help readers better understand the complexities of infanticide, journalists might have looked beyond official legal sources and considered the value of non-official sources, such as mothers themselves, who could speak to the joys and stresses of child care. In addition, journalists might consider whether feminist scholars could add to the understanding of infanticide by offering historical context about the crime.

Finally, journalists might consider the disparity in charges and sentences for women who killed their children. Only one article in this data set called attention to differences in sentencing (Caruso, 2003), and that article mentioned only four cases nationwide. It is interesting to note that, among the 10 cases studied in this research project, the youngest and oldest criminals received the lightest sentences. Prosecutors originally demanded the death penalty for Amy Grossberg, then agreed to accept a manslaughter plea and a 30-month prison sentence. Melissa Drexler pleaded guilty to aggravated manslaughter, a more severe charge than Grossberg's, and received a harsher punishment; yet she served only a few months longer than Grossberg. Marie Noe murdered eight children but did not spend time in prison; instead, she was sentenced to 20 years of probation and placed under house arrest. Bethe Feltman did not spend any time in prison; she was declared legally insane and sent to a state psychiatric hospital, where she spent four years before returning home under continued medical supervision. In contrast, Andrea Yates was pronounced guilty by a jury and sentenced to life in prison for the murders of two of her five children (although she was recently retired and found not guilty by reason of insanity). Khoua Her pleaded guilty to second-degree murder and was sentenced to serve two consecutive 25-year prison terms, plus four concurrent terms. Susan Smith was spared the death penalty but was sentenced to 30 years to life in prison. Urbelina Emiliano received a sentence of 15 years to life, as did Awilda Lopez. Jennie Bain was sentenced to 18 years in prison for the deaths of her two sons. Journalists might have placed sentences in a larger national context, and they also might have explored laws on infanticide in other countries. Journalists' failure to examine discrepancies in sentences represents a missed opportunity to raise the question of whether justice was equally applied.

A larger issue raised by news accounts of maternal infanticide is how to help women who cannot or do not mother well and what role journalists might play in shaping this discourse. Kitzinger (1995) theorized that Western cultures are particularly prone to child abuse because children are treated as possessions, and 'there is little social support for a mother who is in danger of physically abusing her child, and a great deal of depression among new mothers goes unnoticed and neglected' (p. 214). Journalists might look more closely at how the idealization of motherhood discourages women from asking for help—and discourages society from offering services to help them, assuming that maternal instinct will 'right' any troubled situation. Examining community responsibility in infanticide does not mean that women who kill their children should not be accountable for their harmful actions; they should. However, exploring infanticide as a social problem, not just an individual problem, adds another layer of inquiry to reporting, allowing journalists to present a more thorough and accurate account of infanticide.

A shortcoming of this analysis was that I was unable to determine whether there were differences in coverage by female and male reporters. News stories included multiple bylines, bylines with initials not names that might indicate whether a writer was male or female, or no bylines, so I did not analyze articles based on reporters' sex. A future research project would be to interview reporters and editors about their coverage of infanticide, news organizations' policies of reporting and covering child abuse, and journalists' personal attitudes about the stories they wrote. In developing a greater understanding of news coverage of infanticide, it will be important not only to examine the content and framing of these stories of intimate violence but to consider the perspectives of the storytellers themselves. Also, it will be important to examine how the media portray men who have killed their children, to explore myths about fatherhood.

As a former journalist, I recognize that deadlines, source availability, economic resources, and community norms shape news coverage. However, I invite journalists to move beyond simplistic explanations of infanticide as the outburst of one demented individual and to consider this crime as a larger problem affected by romanticized notions of motherhood, gender norms that delegate child care responsibilities primarily to women, lack of recognition of the hard work involved in daily child care, lack of understanding about postpartum depression, and lack of family, community, and institutional support for mothers. The media should not *excuse* women who kill their children; however, the media can *explain* why women come to this violent point in their lives, and journalists can become more aware of how maternal myths shape the news stories they write.

References

Adler, J., G. Carroll, V. Smith and P. Rogers (1994) 'Innocents Lost', *Newsweek,* 14 November (consulted 4 November 2002) LexisNexis.

Alder, C. and K. Polk (2001) *Child Victims of Homicide.* Cambridge: Cambridge University Press.

Associated Press (1998) 'Police Piece Together Clues in Six Children's Deaths', 6 September (consulted 21 October 2002) LexisNexis.

Bardwell, S. K., M. Glenn, R. Rendon, M. Garcia and L. Teachey (2001) 'Mom Details Drownings of 5 Kids; Eldest Fled, Was Dragged back to Tub', *The Houston Chronicle,* 22 June (consulted 15 February 2002) LexisNexis.

Barnett, B. (2005) 'Accountable Mothers, Blameless Fathers: Narratives of Gender and Responsibility in News Articles about Maternal Violence', Paper presented at the annual meeting of the Association for Education in Journalism and Mass Communication, August, San Antonio, TX, USA.

Barnett, B. (2006a) 'Embracing the Imaginary Good Mother: Narratives of Love and Violence from Women who Killed their Children', *Iowa Journal of Communication* 38(1): 5–26.

Barnett, B. (2006b) 'The Wounded Community: Mother-blaming in Journalistic Accounts of Maternal Infanticide', Paper presented at the annual conference of the International Communication Association, June, Dresden, Germany.

Baxley, C. (1995a) 'Mother Stands by Susan Smith, Grieves for Grandsons', *The Post and Courier,* 25 January (consulted 4 November 2002) LexisNexis.

Baxley, C. (1995b) 'Ex-boyfriend Feared Suicide. Smith Trial: About a Week before Her Sons Died, Susan Smith Told Her Boss that She Loved Tom Findlay, but He Didn't Love Her Back', *The Post and Courier,* 20 July (consulted 4 November 2002) LexisNexis.

Baxley, C. (1995c) 'Prosecutor: Smith Sons Were in Way. Bomb Threat: The Union County Courthouse Was Cleared and Court Ended Tuesday Afternoon after a
Bomb Threat Was Made, but Nothing Was Found', *The Post and Courier,* 19 July (consulted 4 November 2002) LexisNexis.

Bernstein, A. and M. Garcia (2001) 'A Life Unraveled; Mother Depicted as Private, Caring, and Burdened by Hidden Problems', *The Houston Chronicle,* 24 June (consulted 15 February 2002) LexisNexis.

Bird, S. E. and R. W. Dardenne (1997) 'Myth, Chronicle and Story: Exploring the Narrative Qualities of News', in D. Berkowitz (ed.) *Social Meanings of News: A Text-reader,* pp. 333–50. Thousand Oaks, CA: Sage.

Brockington, I. (1996) *Motherhood and Mental Health.* Oxford: Oxford University.

Bruni, F. (1995) 'The Case of Alisa: A Child Dies, and the Questions Abound', *The New York Times,* 24 November (consulted 6 November 2002) LexisNexis.

Caruso, D. B. (2003) 'Mother Who Killed 8 Serves Probation while Others Face Prison', Associated Press, 22 May (consulted 1 June 2005) LexisNexis.

Caston, P. (2004) 'A Decade Later, Case Still Haunts AH: Residents of Union Ready to Move Past Susan Smith Drama', *The Post and Courier,* 25 October (consulted 12 May 2005) LexisNexis.

Chase, S. E. (2001) '"Good" Mothers and "Bad Mothers"', in S. E. Chase and M. F. Rogers (eds) *Mothers and Children: Feminist Analyses and Personal Narratives,* pp. 30–59. New Brunswick, NJ: Rutgers University.

Chattanooga Free Press (1995a) '2 Tots in Car 8 Hours Die from Heat', 7 June (consulted 21 October 2002) LexisNexis.

Chattanooga Free Press (1995b) 'Funeral Is Today for Pair of Toddlers Who Died in Car', 8 June (consulted 21 October 2002) LexisNexis.

Chattanooga Free Press (1995c) 'Mother Sits Inside Auto at Funeral of 2 Toddlers', 9 June (consulted 21 October 2002) LexisNexis.

Christian, C. (2002a) 'Yates' Husband Testifies; Didn't See His Wife "as Dangerous"', *The Houston Chronicle,* 28 February (consulted 4 March 2002) LexisNexis.

Christian, C. (2002b) 'Expert: Makeup of Yates Jury May Hint at Defense Strategy', *The Houston Chronicle,* 31 January (consulted 15 July 2004) LexisNexis.

Christian, C. and L. Teachey (2002) 'Yates Found Guilty; Jury Takes 3 1/2 Hours to Convict Mother in Children's Death's, *The Houston Chronicle,* 13 March (consulted 26 March 2002) LexisNexis.

Cixous, H. (1981) 'Castration or Decapitation?', *Signs* 7(1): 41–55.

Collins, P. H. (1993) 'Mammies, Matriarchs, and Other Controlling Images', in M. Pearsall (ed.) *Women and Values: Readings in Recent Feminist Philosophy,* 3rd edn, pp. 174–90. Belmont, CA: Wadsworth.

Collins, P. H. (1995) 'The Meaning of Motherhood in Black Culture: Bloodmothers, Othermothers, and Women-centered Networks', in A. Kesselman, L. D. McNair and N. Schniedewind (eds) *Women: Images and Realities: A Multicultural Anthology,* pp. 201–4. Mountainview, CA: Mayfield.

Cooey, P. M. (1999) '"Ordinary Mother" as Oxymoron: The Collusion of Theology, Theory, and Politics in the Undermining of Mothers', in J. E. Hanigsberg and S. Ruddick (eds) *Mother Troubles: Rethinking Contemporary Maternal Dilemmas,* pp. 229–49. Boston, MA: Beacon.

Coward, R. (1997) 'The Heaven and Hell of Mothering: Mothering and Ambivalence in the Mass Media', in W. Hollway and B. Featherstone (eds) *Mothering and Ambi valence,* pp. 111–18. London: Routledge.

Crowder, C. (1998) 'Deaths of Young Siblings Leave Mourners Puzzled', *The Rocky Mountain News,* 18 April (consulted 8 November 2002) LexisNexis.

Daily, A. (1982) *Inventing Motherhood: The Consequences of the Ideal.* London: Burnett.

Daly, M. (1996) 'A First, Cold Talk with Elisa's Mom', *Daily News,* 10 April (consulted 6 November 2002) LexisNexis.

De Beauvoir, S. (1952 [1949]) *The Second Sex,* trans. H. M. Parshley. New York: Alfred A. Knopf.

Diquinzio, P. (1999) *The Impossibility of Motherhood: Feminism, Individualism and the Problem of Mothering.* New York: Routledge.

Douglas, S. J. and M. W. Michaels (2004) *The Mommy Myth: The Idealization of Motherhood and How It Has Undermined Women.* New York: Free Press.

Feldman, C. (2001) 'Yates' Case Draws Attention to New Moms' Mental Health; Baby Blues', *The Houston Chronicle,* 26 June (consulted 26 June 2006) LexisNexis.

Firestone, S. (1970) *The Dialectic of Sex: The Case for Feminist Revolution.* New York: William Morrow.

First, E. (1994) 'Mothering, Hate and Winnicott', in D. Bassin, M. Honey and M. M. Kaplan (eds) *Representations of Motherhood,* pp. 149–61. New Haven, CT: Yale University.

Fisher, W. R. (1987) *Human Communication as Narration: Toward a Philosophy of Reason, Value, and Action.* Columbia: University of South Carolina.

Foss, S. (1989) *Rhetorical Criticism: Exploration and Practice.* Prospect Heights, IL: Waveland.

Gans, H. J. (1980) *Deciding What's News: A Study* of CBS Evening News, NBC Nightly News, Newsweek *and* Time. New York: Vintage.

Gauthier, D. K., N. K. Chaudoir and C. J. Forsyth (2003) 'A Sociological Analysis of Maternal Infanticide in the United States, 1984–1996', *Deviant Behavior* 24(4): 393–405.

Gesalman, A. B. (2002) 'A Dark State of Mind: Andrea Yates Drowned Her Five Kids. But Is She Culpable for the Crime?', *Newsweek,* 4 March (consulted 25 February 2002) LexisNexis.

Goodnough, A. and B. Weber (1997) 'The Picture of Ordinary: Before Prom Night, a Suspect Was the Girl Next Door', *The New York Times,* 2 July (consulted 4 November 2002) LexisNexis.

Grundy, R. (1859) 'Observations upon Puerperal Insanity', *American Journal of Insanity* 6: 294–320.

Hackett, R. A. and Y. Zhao (1998) *Sustaining Democracy? Journalism and the Politics of Objectivity.* Toronto: Garamond.

Hamilton, J. A. (1962) *Postpartum Psychological Problems.* St. Louis: C. V. Mosby.

Hamilton, J. A. and P. N. Harberger (eds) (1992) *Postpartum Psychiatric Illness: A Picture Puzzle.* Philadelphia: University of Pennsylvania.

Hanley, R. (1998a) 'Teenager Pleads Guilty in Death of Her Newborn, as Boyfriend Did', *The New York Times,* 23 April (consulted 4 November 2002) LexisNexis.

Hanley, R. (1998b) 'Teenagers Get Terms in Prison in Baby's Death', *The New York Times,* 10 July 10, p. Al (consulted 4 November 2002) LexisNexis.

Hanson, C. (2001) 'All the News that Fits the Myth', *Columbia Journalism Review* Jan/Feb: 50–3.

Harberger, P. N., N. G. Berchtold and J. I. Honikman (1992) 'Cries for Help', in J. A. Hamilton and P. N. Harberger (eds) *Postpartum Psychiatric Illness: A Picture Puzzle,* pp. 41–60. Philadelphia: University of Pennsylvania.

Hickman, S. A. and D. L. LeVine (1992) 'Postpartum Disorders and the Law', in J. A. Hamilton and P. N. Harberger (eds) *Postpartum Psychiatric Illness: A Picture Puzzle,* pp. 282–95. Philadelphia: University of Pennsylvania.

Hoffman, J. (1996) 'The Charge Is Murder; an Infant's Death, an Ancient Debate', *The New York Times,* 22 December (consulted 4 November 2002) LexisNexis.

Hollway, W. and B. Featherstone (eds) (1997) *Mothering and Ambivalence.* London: Routledge.

International Federation of Journalists (1986 [1954]) *Journalism Ethics,* URL (consulted April 2005): http://www.ifj.org

Irigaray, L. (1985 [1977]) 'Cosi fan tutti', in *This Sex Which Is Not One,* trans. C. Porter and C. Burke, pp. 86–105. Ithaca, NY: Cornell University.

Jensen, V. (2001) *Why Women Kill: Homicide and Gender Equality.* Boulder, CO: Lynne Rienner.

Johnson-Carter, K. S. (2005) *News Narratives and News Framing: Constructing Political Reality.* Lanham, MD: Rowman and Littlefield.

Kitch, C. (2002) '"A Death in the American Family": Myth, Memory, and National Values in the Media Mourning of John F. Kennedy Jr', *Journalism and Mass Communication Quarterly* 79(2): 294–309.

Kitzinger, S. (1995) *Ourselves as Mothers: The Universal Experience of Motherhood,* 2nd edn. Reading, MA: Addison-Wesley.

Koch, T. (1990) *The News as Myth: Fact and Context in Journalism.* New York: Greenwood.

Koehl, C. (1997) 'Tragedy at the Prom', *Newsweek,* 23 June (consulted 4 November 2002) LexisNexis.

Kristeva, J. (1986) 'Stabat Mater', in T. Moi (ed.) *The Kristeva Reader,* trans. S. Hand and L. S. Roudiez, pp. 160–86. Oxford: Basil Blackwell.

Kumar, R. and M. Marks (1992) 'Infanticide and the Law in England and Wales', in J. A. Hamilton and P. N. Harberger (eds) *Postpartum Psychiatric Illness: A Picture Puzzle,* pp. 257–74. Philadelphia: University of Pennsylvania.

Ladd-Taylor, M. and L. Umansky (1998) 'Introduction', in M. Ladd-Taylor and L. Umansky (eds) *Bad Mothers: The Politics of Blame in Twentieth-century America,* pp. 1–28. New York: New York University.

Lazarre, J. (1976) *The Mother Knot.* New York: McGraw-Hill.

Lindsay, S. (1998) 'Mom Accused of Killing Kids May Attempt Rare Defense; Postpartum Depression Is Central to Legal Claim', *The Rocky Mountain News,* 26 April (consulted 8 November 2002) LexisNexis.

Lule, J. (2001) *Daily News, Eternal Stories: The Mythological Role of Journalism.* New York: Guilford.

Lule, J. (2002) 'Myth and Terror on the Editorial Page: *The New York Times* Responds to September 11, 2001', *Journalism and Mass Communication Quarterly* 79(2): 275–93.

Macdonald, M. (1995) *Representing Women: Myths of Femininity in the Popular Media.* London: Edward Arnold.

Meadow, J. B. (1998) 'A Mother Accused; Longtime Friends Remember Murder Suspect Bethe Feltman as Kind, Deeply Religious', *The Rocky Mountain News,* 11 May (consulted 8 November 2002) LexisNexis.

Meyer, C. L., M. Oberman, K. White, M. Rone, P. Batra and T. C. Proano (2001) *Mothers Who Kill their Children: Understanding the Acts of Moms from Susan Smith to the 'Prom Mom'.* New York: New York University.

Meyers, M. (1997) *News Coverage of Violence against Women: Engendering Blame.* Thousand Oaks, CA: Sage.

Milner, L. H. (2000) *Hardness of Heart, Hardness of Life: The Stain of Human Infanticide.* Lanham, MD: University Press of America.

Morganthau, T., V. Smith, M. O'Shea and G. Carroll (1995) 'Condemned', *Newsweek, 7* August (consulted 4 November 2002) LexisNexis.

Nicolson, P. (2001) *Postnatal Depression: Facing the Paradox of Loss, Happiness and Motherhood.* Chichester, NY: Wiley.

Oakley, A. (1979) *Becoming a Mother.* Oxford: Martin Robertson.

Peterson, H. (1995) 'Killer Mom Sentenced', *Daily News,* 20 July (consulted 6 November 2002) LexisNexis.

Peyser, M. and C. Power (1995) 'The Death of Little Elisa', *Newsweek,* 11 December (consulted 6 November 2002) LexisNexis.

Peyser, M., G. Beals, S. Miller, A. Underwood, A. R. Gajilan and C. Kalb (1996) 'Death in a Dumpster', *Newsweek,* 2 December (consulted 7 January 2002) LexisNexis.

Rendon, R. (2001) 'Brother: Yates Thought Drownings "Best Thing"; He Says Sister Felt She Was a Bad Mom', *The Houston Chronicle,* 14 July (consulted 15 February 2002) LexisNexis.

Rich, A. (1976) *Of Woman Born: Motherhood* as *Experience and Institution.* New York: W. W. Norton.

Richardson, L. (1990) 'Narrative and Sociology', *Journal of Contemporary Ethnography* 19: 116–35.

Riffe, D., S. Lacy and F. G. Fico (1998) *Analyzing Media Messages: Using Quantitative Content Analysis in Research.* Mahwah, NJ: Lawrence Erlbaum.

Ross, B. and D. Gentile (1996) 'Elisa's Mom Gets 15 to Life', *Daily News,* 1 August (consulted 6 November 2002) LexisNexis.

Ruddick, S. (1980) 'Maternal Thinking', *Feminist Studies* 6.342–67.

Ruddick, S. (1995) *Maternal Thinking: Toward a Politics of Peace,* 2nd edn. Boston, MA: Beacon.

Sanger, C. (1999) 'Leaving Children for Work', in J. D. Hanigsberg and S. Ruddick (eds) *Mother Troubles: Rethinking Contemporary Maternal Dilemmas,* pp. 97–116. Boston, MA: Beacon.

Showalter, E. (1982) 'Women Writers and the Double Standard: Victorian Notions of Motherhood', in S. Cahill (ed.) *Motherhood: A Reader for Men and Women,* pp. 67–71. New York: Avon.

Society of Professional Journalists (1996) *Code of Ethics,* URL (consulted April 2005): http://spj.org

Snyder, M. (2002) 'Russell Yates on trial, too, with public's commentary', *The Houston Chronicle,* 13 March (consulted 30 March 2002) LexisNexis.

Taus, M. (1998) 'Minnesota Woman in Custody in Deaths of Her Six Children', Associated Press, 4 September (consulted 21 October 2002) LexisNexis.

Teachey, L. (2001) 'NOW Will Raise Funds for Yates' Legal Defense; Spotlight Placed on Depression Issue', *The Houston Chronicle,* 24 August (consulted 15 February 2002) LexisNexis.

Thomas, E., D. Johnson, A. Gesalman, V. E. Smith, E. Pierce, K. Peraino and A. Murr (2001) 'Motherhood and Murder', *Newsweek,* 2 July (consulted 2 March 2002) LexisNexis.

Thompson, J. (2002) *Mommy Queerest: Contemporary Rhetorics of Lesbian Maternal Identity.* Amherst and Boston: University of Massachusetts.

Thurer, S. L. (1994) *The Myths of Motherhood: How Culture Reinvents the Good Mother.* Boston, MA: Hougton Mifflin.

Tolson, M. (2001) 'What Now for Andrea Yates? The Mother of Five Drowned Children Is Accused of a Horrifying Crime, but Most Such Cases Haven't Led to a Death

Sentence', *The Houston Chronicle,* 1 July (consulted 15 July 2004) LexisNexis.

Trujillo, C. (1997) 'Chicana Lesbians: Fear and Loathing in the Chicana Community', in A. M. Garcia (ed.) *Chicana Feminist Thought: The Basic Historical Writing,* pp. 281–6. New York: Routledge.

Tuchman, G. (1978) *Making News: A Study in the Construction of Reality.* New York: The Free Press.

U.S. Department of Justice (2001) *Homicide trends in the U.S.: Infanticide,* 4 January, URL (consulted 23 September 2002): http//www.ojp.usdoj.gov/bjs/homicide/children.htm

Vaughan, K. and H. Gutierrez (1998) 'Husband Raises Possibility that Woman Killed Children; Deaths Stun Friends; Autopsy Results Awaited', *The Rocky Mountain News,* 12 April (consulted 8 November 2002) LexisNexis.

Williams, M. (1995) 'Mother Gets Prison Term; 2 Sons Perished in Car', *The* Chattanooga *Times,* 10 November (consulted 21 October 2002) LexisNexis.

Wolf, N. (2001) *(misconceptions): Truth, Lies and the Unexpected on the Journey to Motherhood.* New York: Doubleday.

Zambito, T. (1998) 'Prom Mom Admits Slaying; Manslaughter Plea Accepted', *The Record,* 21 August (consulted 4 November 2002) LexisNexis.

Source: From "*Medea* in the Media: Narrative and Myth in the Newspaper Coverage of Women Who Kill Their Children," 2006, by B. Barnett, *Journalism, 7*(4), 411–432. Reprinted by permission of Sage Publications, Ltd.

PART VI

News as Collective Memory

The concept of collective memory—that journalists draw on events from the past to report on occurrences in the present—is a rich but understudied cultural approach for understanding how news comes to be. In a most basic way, the notion of collective memory directly contradicts the professional journalistic paradigm's core tenet of objectivity that calls for new occurrences to be treated independently. Journalism is supposed to be ahistorical and fresh rather than rehashing what has been. Nonetheless, journalism regularly draws on historical memory to add perspective to what is happening *now.* Collective memory, however, goes beyond just remembering the past when it commemorates recent occurrences and provides a comparison between standards of the past and conditions of the present. In a way, collective memory serves journalists and society by offering a prognosis for the future. Going one step further, collective memory lends authority and credibility to both the journalism and the values of society by returning people's minds to recall what once had been.

From a sociological position, a concept similar to collective memory is *typification.* When journalists come upon a new occurrence, they might envision things according to how the story should go "for one of those," such as a bombing, plane crash, scandal, rescue, or even something as mundane as an annual holiday celebration. By typifying an occurrence, journalists can estimate the expected story plot and the social actors who will likely be involved. With a story typification in place, journalists can estimate the kind of work that an occurrence will require and begin to plan how the task can be completed on deadline.

The problem with typification as an analytic concept is its lack of grounding. It is a generic concept in that sense, unconnected to any specific instance. Journalists, however, do think about the meanings of past occurrences for their interpretive community when they come across new instances. Comparisons to past occurrences allow an assessment of the magnitude of a present situation, sensing if it would be a "big story" (sometimes called a "what-a-story") or something of more modest proportions. These comparisons also allow journalists a sense of how an occurrence or issue is likely to turn out, drawing upon historical cues to provide perspective for their audiences. For example, it is one thing to assert that a presidential candidate is a dynamic figure with a strong drive toward social reform, but it is something much more powerful to elicit comparisons between the candidate and American presidents like Abraham Lincoln and John F. Kennedy. That is one of the key values of understanding the construction of news from the perspective of collective memory. Although it is often said that "News is a first draft of history," it is equally plausible that history helps journalists create a first draft of news.

"Reporting Through the Lens of the Past: From Challenger to Columbia" takes on just such an argument in studying news of the Columbia space shuttle disaster as interpreted through collective memory of a similar disaster with the Challenger shuttle 17 years earlier. Going beyond simple matching of one disaster to the other, Jill Edy and Miglena Daradanova argue that collective memory affects the search for information even when the earlier event is not explicitly referenced. The tangible realm of facts about an event that comes from collective memory can lead to a more limited interpretation of a new occurrence than the generic template of typification would allow. In other words, matching the facts of one event to those of an emerging event would be even more cognitively tempting than making a connection between a new event and the way that "one of those" would typically go. What is important, the authors remind us, is not a single person's memory of an event but rather how a reporter shares a "public past" with others.

"Memory in Journalism and the Memory of Journalism: Israeli Journalists and the Constructed Legacy of *Haolam Hazeh*" picks up on the shared sense of collective memory as a community experience by examining how journalists interpret their present professional culture by their collective memory of the profession's past. This application of collective memory contrasts with the more usual linking of present events with the memory of past ones. Further, professional memory links with the context of a society's larger cultural narratives. From this cultural juxtaposition, journalists can be seen as memory agents in three levels: telling the public about events, situating journalistic coverage within larger contexts, and identifying journalists' professional roles in shaping social memories. Oren Meyers accomplishes these ideas through analysis of journalistic discourse about the radical Israeli newspaper *Haolam Hazeh* by other Israeli newspapers over a period of more than 50 years. By avoiding a single amalgamated time point, Meyers allows the professional culture to be depicted in a way that reflects a shifting journalistic consciousness.

"Making Memories Matter: Journalistic Authority and the Memorializing Discourse Around Mary McGrory and David Brinkley" presents the idea that by commemorating the death of legendary, pioneering journalists of national stature, journalists are able to refresh society's minds about what journalism had once been—to an extent restoring journalism's declining cultural authority in the national mind. In effect, Matt Carlson explains, reporting on the death of journalists becomes a form of ritual storytelling that forms a high point of journalistic culture. This kind of reporting can be seen as "collective nostalgia," which can either restore what once had been in the public's mind or conversely, to maintain and expand the separation between practices of the past and visions for the future. Drawing on interview comments from political and celebrity nonjournalists enhances the degree of this effect by expanding the scope of authority. In all, these deceased journalists serve as models for what journalism can be, reminding society of how news can serve its enduring interests.

"'We Were All There': Remembering America in the Anniversary Coverage of Hurricane Katrina" continues this notion of journalism as commemoration work, but rather than harkening back to a distant past, the study considers media coverage of a first anniversary—in this case the anniversary of Hurricane Katrina in New Orleans. While Durham's (Chapter 7) study of news reporting on Katrina as it unfolded showed how the mainstream media departed from their usual reporting mode to cover for the failure of government, Sue Robinson's study depicts a national press at odds with a local one. For the national media, commemoration of the Katrina anniversary represents a chance to highlight government's ongoing failures. Local media, however, avoid pointing out what is wrong with society, instead presenting a narrative about the restoration of community. Taken together, the dual narratives become a dialogue of hope, restating national values (through criticism of governmental failures) while also recalling the community of the past that might one day rise anew.

In all, the concept of collective memory serves as a rich means of showing how the past informs news of the present while also demonstrating how journalism represents the culture on which it reports. The first two selections in Part VI demonstrate applications of the concept for understanding news and journalism; the second two selections show how journalism of commemoration becomes a form of collective memory about both journalism and the culture in which it is embedded.

20

Reporting Through the Lens of the Past

From Challenger to Columbia

Jill A. Edy

Miglena Daradanova

The National Aeronautics and Space Administration refers to 1 February 2003 as a 'bad day'. At about 8:00 am local time on Saturday morning, the space shuttle Columbia broke up in the atmosphere above Dallas, Texas, only 16 minutes shy of its scheduled landing in Florida. All seven astronauts aboard were killed, and pieces of the craft were scattered across at least two states. No spacecraft had ever been destroyed on re-entry. Reporters and NASA officials waiting to welcome home the astronauts now had a very different sort of day ahead of them. The president spoke, memorial services were planned, and late that afternoon, the first formal briefings were held to provide the media with information about the crash. The electronic media, then, had minutes, the print media mere hours, to gather information and recount the story of Columbia's demise. Such extreme deadline pressures are not uncommon in journalism, but they are far from routine reporting.

Previous research has shown how general reporting rules and practices help reporters gather information and tell stories about unexpected events. Tuchman (1972) describes the role of 'typifications', categories reporters use to define what kind of news an event represents, what kinds of resources are needed to cover that event, and whether it is 'hard' or 'soft' news. Berkowitz's (1992) subsequent work on how reporters cover major, unexpected events expands Tuchman's analysis to explore the use of typifications as a means of making decisions about what sort of story to tell about an event. Other researchers have also emphasized the use of story templates or narrative genres to transform events into stories (e.g., Darnton, 1990; Lule 2001). Work in this tradition has emphasized how reporters categorize specific events as members of a class of events-as-news.

This study demonstrates that reporters sometimes rely not on generic categories but on collective memory of specific pasts to structure their reporting on major, unexpected events and that this practice has important implications for the ways reporters inform the public. Almost exactly 17 years before Columbia crashed, on 28 January 1986, the space shuttle Challenger was destroyed shortly after lift-off, and in the chaotic week following Columbia's fiery end, reporters turned repeatedly to their shared memories of this public past, to the 'lessons' of the Challenger accident, as they questioned officials and assembled information into stories.

Earlier research on the role of the past in the news may have underestimated its influence. Studies have shown that journalists use the past frequently (Edy, 2001) and in a variety of ways (Edy, 1999; Lang and Lang, 1989). When using the past as a tool for interpreting more recent events, journalists tend to draw historical analogies that compare the past to the present or make use of the past as a historical context, a part of the environment that gave rise to current circumstances (Edy, 1999). Recent research has demonstrated that reporters are increasingly likely to situate current events in historical contexts (Barnhurst, 2003; Barnhurst and Mutz, 1997). However, in considering only explicit references to past events in finished news stories, these studies may have missed how collective memory structures reporters' search for information and influences the interpretive structure of news without being invoked explicitly in the finished product.

The particular properties of collective memories offer unique opportunities and dangers for journalists in serving their democratic functions. Collective memory can offer reporters storytelling opportunities they would otherwise be hard-pressed to employ. Literature in political communication has described reporters' dependency on public officials for information (e.g., Sigal, 1973) and the consequent dominance of official perspectives and story frames in the news (e.g., Bennett, 1990; Entman, 1991; Gitlin, 1980). Critical scholars have actively wondered how to free the news from its dependence on officials and elites. Lawrence (2000) argues that accidents like the Columbia crash and other forms of what she calls 'event-driven news' offer more possibilities for media independence from elites than does routine (or 'institutionally-driven') news. However, not every accidental event results in a loss of elite control (see for example Entman, 1991), and Lawrence (2000) observes that event-driven news coverage is under-theorized. Collective memory may be an especially important tool for reporters in resisting official stories that are offered up to account for events. It can suggest an alternative interpretation, and its status as a 'real' event certifies the 'objectivity' of the interpretation it suggests.

At the same time, using the past as a reporting tool presents risks. Typification of any kind emphasizes what is 'routine' about even a major, unexpected event rather than what is distinctive about it. Collective memory does the same: it emphasizes similarities between past and present. The result may be that reporters and officials miss important innovations and differences. Indeed, collective memory presents greater risks in this regard than typification. Because of their generic nature, typifications may be more changeable as an event unfolds over time. In contrast, specific memories draw stronger parallels between past and present and are thus difficult to abandon. Of course, in a socially constructed world, what 'really' caused Columbia's crash is unknowable. The official investigation report is another version of the story that may be based on solid science but is also influenced by organizational politics. Still, it is worthwhile thinking about the risks of using collective memory to guide storytelling, particularly in light of the fact that its use is often invisible to audiences.

Unlike typification, collective remembering draws upon a specific, historical past rather than an ahistorical accumulation of like events. However, collective memory may be the wellspring of typifications, for specific pasts may evolve into generalized expectations or social values that eventually come to be dissociated from the pasts that gave rise to them. Evidence of such a connection has remained elusive, although Schudson's (1992) work on Watergate and Novick's (1999) and Zelizer's (1998) on the Holocaust do take important steps in this direction.

This study examines how collective memory shapes reporters' search for information about current events and its impacts on the way news stories about current events are framed, considering explicit references to the past and more indirect references that draw upon nuanced constructions of the similarities between past and present. Understanding how collective memory is invoked in news coverage is important because it helps to explain the choice of sources and of news frames, and because using the past to frame the present, whether explicitly or implicitly, can be a double-edged sword. It can grant reporters some independence from elite representations of events without violating the tenets of objectivity (see Edy, 1999), but it can also lead reporters to ask the wrong questions of officials and fail to hold them accountable (see Schudson, 1992). This study not only presents a richer picture of the ways that collective memory of the past influences news of the present, it also offers some insight into how specific pasts evolve into more generic typifications.

Methods

To trace the presence of Challenger memories in the coverage of Columbia's demise, we began with a reporter's account of the 'lessons' of Challenger. Malcolm McDowell's 'instant' history of the Challenger accident, published in early 1987, is a space reporter's summation of the accident and subsequent investigation. We used it as a guide to how the Challenger accident is remembered in the popular media.

To assess the role of these Challenger memories in the information-gathering process, we examined transcripts of the press briefings held the day Columbia failed to return home safely and in the four days that followed, looking for similarities between reporters' construction of the event as revealed in their questions and the collective memory of Challenger as outlined by McDowell (1987). Although reporters gather information in many ways, briefings are one of the few places that this process is visible and preserved for later analysis. These first few days are likely to be crucial in the overall framing of the event because reporters are searching for 'a handle' on 'the story'. News frames established early in an event's trajectory are influential for reporters, elites, and audiences because altering them requires changing information-gathering patterns and the expectations of news professionals and audiences.

To examine how Challenger memories move from the information-gathering phase to the news itself, we examined the reports produced by some of the journalists credited with asking Challenger-derived questions at the briefings. We chose the reporters partly because their persistent interest in similarities between the two accidents, indicated by their questions at the briefings, suggested they were likely to use the past in their reporting. Two other considerations also played a role: the prominence and influence of the organizations they work for, and the availability of their reports in the Nexis database. In addition to analyzing their storytelling, we considered their selection of interview subjects as an indicator of Challenger's influence.

Finally, we conducted semi-structured telephone interviews with two of the reporters whose coverage we examined in order to validate our assessment that Challenger memories permeate Columbia's coverage. Our interview protocol, which consisted of four questions (available from the authors), was designed to encourage our subjects to describe their own process for covering the Columbia story before we specifically asked about the Challenger accident or revealed the central purpose of our research. In both interviews, our subjects brought up Challenger, often several times, before we did. Despite our brief protocol, interviews lasted approximately one hour as reporters shared at length their experiences in covering the Columbia crash. One might ask whether the memories of experienced space reporters are in fact collective, particularly if, like Kathy Sawyer of the *Washington Post,* they covered the Challenger crash. However, the essence of collective memory is not whether or not one has a personal memory of a public event but rather whether one shares an understanding of the public past with others. Our analysis focuses on commonalities in reporting and storytelling shared by all of these reporters that reveals a shared understanding of the Challenger accident.

'Lessons' of History: Challenger

Scholars and pundits consider the launching of the space shuttle Challenger on 28 January 1986 to be an archetypal example of bad decision-making arising from poor decision-making processes (Esser and Lidoerfer, 1989; Hirokawa et al., 1988) and institutional culture (Vaughan, 1997). The immediate causes of its destruction were cold weather conditions that exacerbated problems with the O-rings, essentially large synthetic rubber washers, used in the solid rocket boosters that should have helped put the shuttle in orbit. Stiff with cold, the O-rings failed to seal, a booster exploded, and the orbiter was destroyed. But the 'lessons of history' from the Challenger disaster have typically focused not on mechanical failure but on the decision-making process and institutional culture that led to the launch decision despite concerns about the weather and the O-rings' performance.

The renowned, iconic event that illustrates processes thought to contribute to the accident was a lengthy teleconference held the night before the launch. NASA representatives and the outside contractor that made the solid rocket boosters, Morton-Thiokol, had known for more than a year that the O-rings often experienced partial failure during a launch and that if they failed, the shuttle would be seriously damaged or destroyed. Yet they believed, or convinced themselves, that the shuttles were safe enough to fly while the O-ring technology was redesigned. On the day before Challenger was to launch, engineers at Morton-Thiokol expressed reservations about O-ring performance during the proposed launch because it was scheduled to occur on a morning when weather forecasters said the Kennedy Space Center would experience record cold, an overnight low of 18F degrees. Previous experience suggested that the O-rings were even more vulnerable in cold weather. A teleconference was scheduled to discuss the issue. As McDowell claims:

> The long Monday night teleconference has acquired mythical proportions Many people have come to view the conference as a tense and acrimonious battle of wills between callous bureaucrats on one side and greedy capitalists on the other, with a virtuous group of engineers forming a Greek chorus of alarm, which the villainous managers on both sides scornfully ignored. (McDowell, 1987: 191)

Somewhere in the decision-making process, a critical line was crossed. Although the flight safety standards set out by NASA demanded that contractors and managers certify the shuttle safe to fly, in the course of the meetings, NASA administrators, managers and contractors began to demand evidence that the shuttle was *not* safe to fly as a prerequisite for delaying the launch. The Morton-Thiokol engineers (and, later, engineers at Rockwell International asked about potential problems that the buildup of ice on the fixed service structure that surrounded the shuttle might produce) could not provide hard data that the shuttle was not safe because launch conditions were outside of known parameters. Managers and corporate representatives therefore certified that it was safe.

Reasons for these failures have been variously placed. Communication chains were flawed. Morton-Thiokol was renegotiating its valuable contract to provide NASA with solid rocket boosters and may have been reluctant to acknowledge the weaknesses of its technology. NASA managers and administrators, seeking to preserve and expand their budget and assure the future of manned spaceflight, had emphasized the reliability and routine nature of shuttle flight, so repeated delays and delicate technology were more than an annoyance. Putting Challenger in space on 28 January could mean a mention in the president's state of the union address that night, an important bump up the federal agenda. And so they launched. Less than a minute later, the shuttle experienced a catastrophic explosion.

McDowell (1987) suggests that reporters had incentive to learn the 'lessons' of Challenger. He argues that prior to the Challenger crash, space reporters were uncritical, typically unaware, of NASA's deficiencies. While he defends his profession by saying that NASA was adept at carefully controlling information, he also notes reporters' failures to question the information they were provided. For reporters, there is no greater sin. Whether or not the next generation of space reporters was motivated by a desire to do better than its forebears, the 'lessons' of Challenger were an important resource for them on a chaotic Saturday morning and in the first few days that followed.

In locating the briefing questions asked during the first five days that drew upon the Challenger accident, we went beyond those that explicitly mentioned the 1986 crash. We also identified those that brought the 'lessons' of Challenger to bear upon the Columbia crash, including those that

- sought to uncover NASA decision-making practices regarding flight safety,
- asked about prior knowledge of troubled systems,
- questioned the performance of outside contractors,
- asked about weather conditions and ice.

Briefings

Knowing how a specific event was reported without being in position to observe the process unfolding is difficult. Even post hoc interviews with the reporters themselves, which we use here to corroborate our assessment of Columbia's coverage, are subject to a kind of rationalizing in which the way to cover the event has become 'obvious' and the narrative uncertainty that accompanies breaking news is lost. However, one way to witness news making is by taking advantage of one of the few places reporters can be seen gathering information: press briefings. Here, interaction between reporters and officials is direct and unmediated. Here, officials' efforts to guide reporters to a preferred framing is revealed, and here, reporters' instincts and expectations about the form the news product should take emerge in the questions they ask. If memory of the Challenger accident guided reporting of the Columbia accident, reporters' questions at the seven NASA briefings conducted during the five days following Columbia's crash should reveal that influence.

They do. Based on transcript space, those giving the briefings spent approximately 15 percent of their time answering questions that enacted the 'lessons' of Challenger. This figure would rise if only the question-and-answer portion of the briefings were used. Nearly one quarter of all the questions posed at the briefings invoked memories of Challenger. Figure 1 shows the proportion of Challenger-derived questions that were asked each day from 1–5 February. On both 3 February and 5 February, two press conferences were held, one by the shuttle program manager and one by high-ranking NASA administrators. Briefings held the same day contained similar proportions of Challenger-derived questions, so we offer overall proportions for those days here.

The pattern that emerges is not, perhaps, what one would expect. On the Saturday Columbia failed to reach home, reporters were probably expecting a routine day and may have been struggling to get a handle on the story. Yet they are not terribly effective at using Challenger memories to structure their reporting; questions based on the Challenger accident are neither particularly sophisticated nor particularly critical. The most pointed question involved whether NASA had

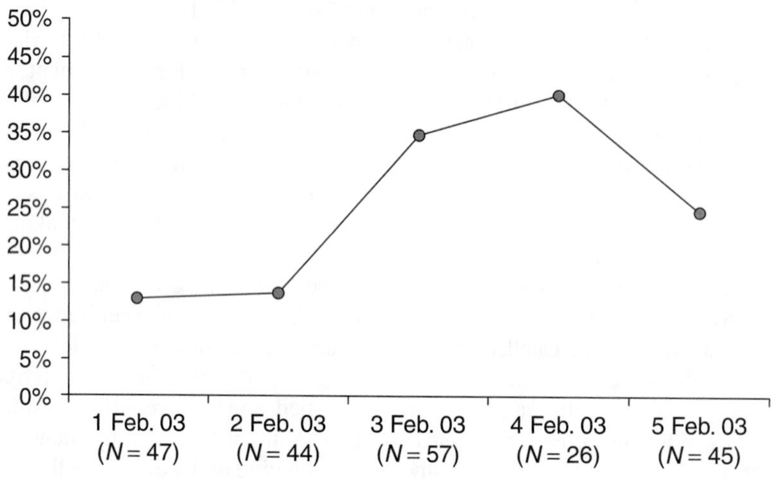

Figure 1 Percent of Challenger-derived questions.

learned anything from past investigations, such as the one into the Challenger accident that would speed the present investigation. Questions like this seem unlikely to provide an interpretive framework for reporters trying to craft facts into story. Further, they account for only six (12.8%) of all the questions posed at the briefing.

By early the following week, Challenger questions were not only more frequent, they raised issues that were much more likely to provide a narrative framework for coverage of Columbia's accident. At the same time, overt references to the Challenger crash became less common. Still, collective memory of the Challenger shuttle was hard to mistake, particularly in the questions about decision-making that would come to dominate the briefings by the middle of the week. In one case, reporter Seth Borenstein made a direct connection between the decision-making process for Columbia's safety-of- flight and the decision-making associated with Challenger's crash: . . . And are you looking into the decision-making process as an issue, sort of like Challenger looked into overall management problems of decision-making?' (National Aeronautics and Space Administration News Briefing, 3 February 2003). Elsewhere, reporters clearly refer to the infamous Monday night meeting where the decision to launch Challenger was made:

- Can you flesh out for us a little bit more the discussions that took place about the possible consequences of the foam impact on the shuttle? How many people were involved? Was it NASA? Contractors? And also, can you address that here have been some reservations expressed. Were those reservations expressed at any stage of the discussion process? (National Aeronautics and Space Administration News Briefing, 4 February 2003).

- There were reports this morning that some shuttle engineers were very alarmed by the post launch films of debris hitting the wing and thought that was a very grave problem and said that it was sugar coated before reaching top management. Could you address that please? ('Major General Mike

Kostelnik Holds News Conference at NASA Headquarters', 5 February 2003).

- [G]iven the fact that there were some reservations, but those reservations didn't reach the management team, do you see anything wrong with that? Is that a problem that should be addressed should the process be changed there? ('Major General Mike Kosternik Holds News Conference at NASA Headquarters', 5 February 2003).

These questions all reproduce key elements of the Monday meeting, such as the idea that dissent was ignored, that engineers' concerns were overridden by managers, and that concerns regarding safety were not effectively communicated through the command hierarchy. Many other questions contain similar references to details of the Challenger disaster.

Our interview with Seth Borenstein (personal communication, 12 May 2004) confirmed that as an experienced space reporter, he was quite knowledgeable about the Challenger accident and that it played an important role in his coverage of the story. Unaware that collective memory was the focus of this research, he himself introduced the Challenger crash into the conversation and mentioned it at least five times in the interview before he was asked about it. Of course, it is possible that at least some of the reporters who asked such questions were not themselves familiar with Challenger's story but were instead following the lead of their better-informed colleagues, as seems to have been the case with Traci Watson of *USA Today* (personal communication, 21 May 2004), but this would not lead one away from the conclusion that Challenger memories were an important part of Columbia's coverage. In fact, it could be an important element of the mechanism that transforms specific knowledge of a particular past into a typification (Berkowitz, 1992; Tuchman, 1972).

Reporters asked few questions about weather or contractors, but here, too, the fact pattern of Challenger can be discerned. Weather questions all involved cold weather and the build up of ice, an aspect of the Challenger launch. Such questions were odd given that the overnight low on the night before Columbia's launch was 43F degrees, well above freezing and significantly warmer than the 18F degree morning of the Challenger launch. While the weather in the weeks preceding Columbia's launch might have provided independent cause for concern and some of the fuel is chilled to subzero temperatures so that ice is always a possibility, it is likely that well-informed reporters were recalling Challenger. Almost all of the questions that mentioned contractor performance included references either to safety-of-flight decisions or longstanding problems. The few that did not (four, to be exact) picked up other elements of Challenger's fact pattern in that they focused on propulsion systems or contract renewal.

By Monday, Challenger-derived questions were not only becoming more common, they were being asked earlier in the briefings, suggesting that more reporters were using the Challenger accident as a thinking tool. Shuttle Program Manager Ron Dittemore answered 6 Challenger-derived questions (30% of the total) in his Monday briefing, 3 about how the decision was made that Columbia was safe to fly despite being struck by debris during launch and 3 that asked whether foam striking the orbiter was a long-standing problem. The first of these questions was the sixth of the session. On the previous day, the first Challenger-based question was the 13th that he answered. For Bill Readdy (Administrator of Space Flight) and Michael Kostelnik (Deputy Associate Administrator for the Space Shuttle and International Space Station Program), Challenger was an even more dominant theme in their Monday briefing. The second question they were asked applied the 'lessons of Challenger', and they answered 14 questions derived from Challenger's fact pattern (almost 38% of all questions asked), 7 of which dealt with NASA's decision-making processes.

The questions quickly became a dominant theme. On Tuesday, 4 February, 6 of 10 Challenger-derived questions put to Readdy and

Kostelnik were about decision-making (in a briefing where a total of 25 questions were asked). By Wednesday, five of the seven Challenger-derived questions Readdy and Kostelnik answered were about NASA's decision that Columbia was safe to fly.

Five of the seven briefing transcripts identify the reporters asking questions and the organizations they represent. They reveal that major media reporters were much more likely to ask Challenger-derived questions than were reporters working for less-well-known organizations. Almost 37% of all the questions asked by reporters for major media alluded to the Challenger accident (25 of 68), while only 16.4 percent of those asked by representatives of smaller organizations did (11 of 67). Reporters for the major media were especially interested in the post-launch review process. Almost half of the Challenger-derived questions asked by major media inquire into how the decision that the debris-hit had not compromised flight safety was reached.

The atmosphere at the briefings moved over the course of the five days from information seeking to relatively confrontational. In part, this was because reporters homed in on NASA decision-making processes over the course of the week, and questions in this vein necessarily questioned the competence of the organization itself and also of the people doing the briefings because all of them were involved in the shuttle program. Another reason for the uncongenial atmosphere was that Challenger-derived questions about decision-making began to fall closer together. Rather than responding to diverse requests for information, the people giving the briefings found themselves being interrogated as reporters followed up each other's questions with more calls for NASA to explain its procedures for determining safety-of-flight. Finally, the questions began to evolve into the classic formulation of the 'Watergate' question: what did they know and when did they know it (Schudson, 1992), pushing the idiom of the briefings from information provision to cross-examination.

As the Challenger memory became a more effective tool for structuring reporters' questions about Columbia's destruction, mentions of Challenger itself became progressively rare. On Saturday, three of six questions at the first briefing specifically mentioned Challenger. By Wednesday, none of the Challenger-derived questions did. Immediately after Columbia's crash, then, one easily recognizes the Challenger connection, but it seems relatively innocuous. Soon afterward, however, one must be familiar with the fact pattern of the Challenger accident to recognize the memories at work in the Columbia press conferences, even as these references to Challenger seem much more likely to have an impact on Columbia's story. Indeed, were one unfamiliar with the Challenger story, the questions asked at the Columbia press conferences might simply seem like the 'normal' and 'common sense' questions that would be asked in light of any space-related accident.

Reporting

We considered the reporting of journalists working for large and influential news organizations who made use of Challenger memories in formulating questions at the briefings. Two reporters work for individual newspapers: Kathy Sawyer of the *Washington Post* and Tracy Watson of *USA Today*. The other reporters work for wire services. Marcia Dunn reports for the Associated Press. Seth Borenstein, Sumana Chatterjee, and Phil Long work for Knight Ridder, which provides wire copy as part of the Knight Ridder/Tribune news service. Most of these journalists are experienced space reporters. Dunn has been a space reporter since 1990, Borenstein began as a space reporter in 1994 (personal communication, 2004), and Sawyer began covering space with the Challenger launch (McDowell, 1987).

Reporters who provide wire copy, like Borenstein and Dunn, are potentially very influential in at least two ways. First, their reporting is likely to appear in whole or in part in a large number of smaller newspapers that do not have a full-time space reporter or the resources to assign a staff reporter to cover the event. Second, their stories will be some of the first filed in the wake of the event. Their choice of narrative frame thus has great potential to influence the reporting of other journalists with later filing deadlines. A number of scholars have noted that reporters for the major wires are often a source of comparison for reporters looking for 'the story' of an event. Because wire service reporters file stories on the day of the event rather than the day after, as print reporters would, we consider the stories they filed between 1–5 February. The Associated Press (AP) offers a variety of services to subscribers, but the content of stories across services proved quite similar. Thus, we use only the stories Dunn filed for the main AP wire, a total of 11 stories over the five days. The Knight Ridder reporters also produced 11 stories over the first five days, although they did not produce any stories datelined 1 February. We consider the work the print journalists published between 2–6 February. Each had three stories published in that time.

Our analysis reveals the variety of ways memories of Challenger insinuate themselves into coverage of the Columbia accident. Quotes obtained at the briefings as responses to Challenger-based questions appear in the stories, and there is some evidence that memories of Challenger governed the search for information in other ways, particularly in the search for whistle-blowers whose warnings about safety had been ignored. Challenger memories also influenced the narrative frame of the stories. Chronicles of events were less apparently affected by memory, but those stories that attempted to interpret or contextualize (see Barnhurst and Mutz, 1997) the event and the ongoing investigation almost invariably included Challenger-driven perspectives with regard to decision-making at NASA. Finally, there is evidence that the growing frequency of Challenger-derived questions at briefings helped drive reporters' narrative choices, for the persistence of the journalists' questions itself became news.

Marcia Dunn: The Associated Press

Marcia Dunn seems to have been the primary Associated Press reporter assigned to cover the Columbia disaster. While she may not have had personal memories of Challenger in her capacity as a professional journalist, she was more focused on collective memories of the Challenger decision-making process than any other reporter whose questions can be identified in the press conferences. All three of the questions she is credited with demand explanations of NASA decision-making processes and rely on Challenger memories, including,'. . . do you have any idea of how many engineers were involved in all these various meetings? And during this time, and even after that, was there any concern expressed by even a single individual, any reservations, to the conclusion that was ultimately made?' ('National Aeronautics and Space Administration News Briefing', 3 February 2003b). Answers to her questions would be repeatedly quoted in stories produced by the reporters included in this study.

Two of Dunn's early stories (written with Pam Easton and carried on the wires 1 February and 2 February) are best described as round-ups of the day's events, collating information from a wide variety of sources including NASA officials, people who had witnessed Columbia's disintegration, and surviving relatives of the astronauts. As is the case in the earliest press conference, Challenger memories are present but are not used to give structure to the story. For example, in their second round-up story, they observe, 'The tragedy occurred almost exactly 17 years after the Challenger exploded' (Dunn and Easton, 2 February 2003).

Dunn's stories on the investigation into Columbia's crash appear much more influenced by memories of Challenger, but as in the press conferences, it is the fact pattern of the Challenger accident rather than explicit references to the earlier event that gives shape to the story. For example, in this passage she includes most of the key elements of the Monday night meeting:

> High-level officials at NASA said they agreed at the time with the engineers' assessment . . . 'We were in complete concurrence', Michael Kostelnik, a NASA spaceflight office deputy, said at a news

> conference Monday with NASA's top spaceflight official, William Readdy . . . 'The best and brightest engineers we have who helped design and build this system looked carefully at all the analysis and the information we had at this time, and made a determination this was not a safety-of-flight issue.' . . . No one on the team, to Dittemore's knowledge, had any reservations about the conclusions and no one reported any concerns to a NASA hot line set up for just such occasions. (Dunn, 4 February 2003a)

She goes on to report Dittemore's claim that NASA only later heard that some had reservations about the conclusion, quoting Dittemore's response to a Challenger-influenced question asked by reporter Kathy Sawyer.

Elsewhere, Dunn's stories on the investigation include the idea that the problems with Columbia were longstanding and that warnings about them had been ignored. On 4 February, the lead of one of her stories read: 'NASA was warned nine years ago that the space shuttle could fail catastrophically if debris hit the vulnerable underside of its wings during liftoff—the very scenario that may have brought down Columbia' (Dunn, 4 February 2003b). Many of her stories included the fact that foam had come off of the external tank and hit space shuttles during earlier missions.

The Challenger accident also seems to have influenced Dunn's search for other sources of information. On the day of the crash, Dunn quoted a NASA retiree who claimed that safety-of-flight had been compromised by budget cuts and had, according to her story, taken his concerns to the president without result. In later days, she would find other officials, scientists and engineers whose Cassandra-like warnings had been ignored, along with some whose analysis had in fact affected shuttle procedures. Within three days of the crash, Dunn's stories about the investigation into its cause are not reports on the progress of the investigation but instead are investigations themselves into decision-making practices at NASA. Because she is an experienced space reporter and the AP's representative, her work may well have served as a model for that of her colleagues.

One might ask at this point if Dunn's questions at the briefings and the stories that she wrote are not simply the standard trope of coverage for this type of event. Luckily, the Columbia accident was only the third in the history of U.S. manned spaceflight to result in loss of life, so there probably is no 'standard' way to cover space disasters. Moreover, Dunn's coverage little resembles the AP's early coverage of the Challenger accident. Early coverage of Challenger focused on the main clues and key information sources likely to be important in the investigation, explanations of how key systems worked and how they might have failed and, where it apportioned blame at all, questioned the performance of a variety of contractors. NASA decision-making was rarely discussed and where it was, the issue was the agency's decision to send a teacher, Christa McAuliffe, into space. Interviews with Cassandras who had warned of trouble to come are also quite rare.

Seth Borenstein, Sumana Chatterjee, and Phil Long, Knight Ridder

The work of the Knight Ridder team was influential not just because it was shared throughout the newspaper chain but because the coverage was a finalist for the Pulitzer Prize for spot news. This was reporting that the industry itself upheld as a model. At the briefings, the Knight Ridder reporters were responsible for several questions based on memories of Challenger. When it came to reporting the event, Borenstein claimed that there were two basic stories (personal communication, 12 May 2004): 'How did it happen?' and 'How could it happen?' The latter, he said, was 'the better story', and it was also, he argued, where Challenger memories came into play. Asked why Challenger memories were important, he responded, 'Because the past is always repeated', and went on to say that there were always warning signs that were missed, that this 'was the story' with Challenger and that it 'was the story' with Columbia.

Both his comments and his reporting suggest that Challenger memories helped Borenstein to decide what kinds of information to gather and what kinds of stories to tell. The lead in one of the first stories he wrote on the accident was: 'Scientists have warned Congress for years that the space shuttle program needed more money and newer equipment or else it faced dangerously rising safety risks, and six NASA scientists were fired in March 2001 after issuing such warnings for years' (Borenstein, 2 February 2003). Borenstein also quoted a variety of sources who claimed to have known about and warned about longstanding problems with key shuttle systems, including one who said he had warned engineers about the debris-hit during Columbia's flight:

> About two days after the Jan. 16 launch, NASA engineers realized from flight videos that the shuttle's wing area was hit by a sizable piece of insulation from the shuttle's external fuel tank. One of them immediately told Reyes [a former safety official at NASA and expert on the thermal tiles], who replied: 'Oh man, you're going to have trouble on re-entry.' (Borenstein, 4 February 2003)

One source, Bob Hotz, who appears in multiple stories, is a member of the Rogers Commission that investigated the Challenger accident. Hotz offered several parallels between the Columbia investigation process and that of Challenger, including a prediction that the investigation would focus on decision-making processes and a comment that the management attitudes that had led to the Challenger accident seemed to have persisted in the decision-making regarding Columbia.

In several stories, the Knight Ridder team employed an approach reminiscent of Watergate-style scandal reporting: they began by reporting the claims of NASA officials from the briefings, then used resources generated by enterprise reporting to challenge the official story. Borenstein, who was especially given to this technique, described the key question of the Columbia investigation as 'What did they know, and why didn't they know it?' (personal communication, 12 May 2004), a close variation of the key Watergate question, 'What did they know and when did they know it?' The work of the Knight Ridder reporters suggests that more than one collective memory may influence the development of a story but still does not suggest typification since the reporters are not categorizing the Columbia crash as one of a generic class of events-as-news but are rather employing specific collective memories to give structure to their search for information and their storytelling.

Kathy Sawyer, *Washington Post*

Kathy Sawyer asked one of the harshest Challenger-derived questions during the briefings: '[T]here's a memo that surfaced this morning that . . . suggests that somebody in your operation knew about extensive tile damage, wrote a memo two days before the accident . . . Can you give us a chronicle of how that memo was handled and how high in the organization did it reach?' Watson and Dunn both made use of the response in stories filed on 3 February and 4 February.

Although her question speaks to NASA's decision-making, her reporting does not make much of this issue. Nevertheless, memories of the Challenger disaster do influence Sawyer's reporting of Columbia's crash. Her long tenure as a space reporter means that she has 'personal' memories of the Challenger accident. While the collective memory of Challenger focuses on poor decision-making, as her question implies, in her reporting she recalls the Challenger accident as a time when NASA was 'defensive' and 'secretive' with reporters, recollections of her own experiences as a reporter trying to cover the story.

Tracy Watson, *USA Today*

Tracy Watson is credited with asking three questions based on Challenger memories, one about decision-making, one about weather, and one about longstanding problems. She never really uses the answers to her own questions in her reporting, but she does use responses provoked by the Challenger-derived questions of Dunn and Sawyer in her stories.

Watson's second story, printed 3 February, demonstrates how the tenor of the briefings themselves, rather than the responses to particular questions, began to leak into the finished stories. She observes:

> The re-examination [of the post-launch assessment of the foam hit] comes as more questions are being asked about whether NASA officials made the right judgment call in determining that the Columbia was safe and without risk of burning up in the atmosphere as it attempted its re-entry. (Watson and O'Driscoll, 2003: 4A)

Of course, it is reporters who are asking the questions at the news briefings, though they remain invisible in order to satisfy the demands of 'objectivity'. The story goes on to detail not the investigation process but the decision-making process that concluded the debris strike had not significantly damaged the shuttle. Watson then describes evidence from the crash itself to suggest that this decision might have been wrong. Her fellow reporters have helped to make her story newsworthy by focusing on NASA's decision-making processes in their reporting.

Watson's story provides an excellent example of the potential benefits and problems of reporters invoking collective memory as they gather information and report the news. On the one hand, memories of Challenger give journalists a perspective on the Columbia accident that is somewhat independent of NASA's claims about the event without sacrificing claims to objectivity (after all, the Challenger crash *really* happened). Such alternative perspectives may make reporters less vulnerable to officials' news management. Even if no official or 'legitimate' source were willing to criticize NASA's performance, the memory of Challenger makes it possible to pursue this story angle without violating professional norms. Indeed, if enough reporters take this approach, it will be hard for other reporters to ignore it. The quest itself becomes newsworthy, as Watson's story shows. On the other hand, collective memory can lead news astray, encouraging the pursuit of inappropriate questions that will not hold officials accountable or otherwise benefit citizens and democratic practice (Schudson, 1992). Did collective memories of Challenger help reporters be critical, or did they encourage reporters to jump to conclusions and lead the public astray with them? In our conclusion, we consider the role and importance of Challenger memories in structuring reporting of the Columbia accident and whether it improved or impaired reporting in those first, crucial days.

Conclusion

The early coverage of the Columbia crash examined here was not just 'common sense' coverage of a space disaster. The 'common sense' knowledge that problematic practices at NASA might have contributed to the crash was itself a product of the Challenger investigation, and there were a variety of alternative trajectories the stories might have taken. For example, they might have developed along the lines of a debate over the future of manned space flight, a question that has come up repeatedly over the years. They might have evolved as scientific stories about improving the technologies involved in space flight. An investigative narrative about the performance of NASA's outside contractors was possible (and would have more closely resembled early Challenger coverage). A political story about NASA's budget future might have emerged.

Instead, collective memory of the space shuttle Challenger's crash played an important role in structuring reporting of Columbia's destruction for these journalists, but not right away. In the chaos of the first few hours following Columbia's crash, reporters recognized Challenger as a relevant past but did not use it effectively as a tool for gathering information or structuring narrative.

Only after they had been on the story for a day or two were reporters able to use Challenger as a means of making sense of Columbia's demise. By the third day, its 'lessons' became a dominant theme in press briefings and the published reports examined here.

However, Challenger's role in reporting on Columbia's accident is not obvious. Indeed, anyone unfamiliar with Challenger's 'lessons' would have a difficult time detecting memory's influence in the briefings or the articles, for reporters very rarely made manifest the link they were constructing between present and past. Nevertheless, collective memory influenced reporters' search for information and thus the material available for constructing stories. It also helped to shape the deep structure of stories by influencing the narratives used to present information. Thus, Bennett's (1983) complaint that news lacks a sense of history may be valid not in the sense that context is absent from reporting but rather in the sense that the context driving the reporting often remains invisible to the audience.

One might argue that reporting on the Columbia accident owes its narrative frame not to Challenger but to the more general trope, common in reporting, of governmental venality and incompetence. While this explanation does not account for the specific and distinctive Challenger fact pattern that emerges in the briefings and the stories, and therefore does not represent a fundamentally appealing alternative explanation, it does raise an interesting possibility with regard to the role of Watergate in Columbia's coverage. Both Borenstein and Watson overtly referred to Challenger as an influence on their coverage of the Columbia crash, suggesting collective memory at work. However, despite his reliance on Watergate-style reporting techniques and questions, Borenstein never mentioned Watergate as an influence on his coverage. This suggests that while Watergate memories continue to shape reporting, they are evolving into a genre of reporting that is no longer linked to the specific past that gave rise to it. That is, this collective memory is taking on the characteristics of a typification.

Collective memory can, under certain circumstances, offer reporters alternatives to the frames and stories promulgated by officials and elites by helping them customize their professional practices. That is, typifications and other generalized reporting rules offer only broad guidelines about the kinds of information to seek and what sort of story to tell, and may make reporters dependent upon officials' structuring of the issue or event. A particular past offers more specific direction about what kinds of information may be relevant and what 'the story' is, and, because it is 'real', allows reporters to resist official frames without giving up their claim of objectivity. The Columbia crash briefings and stories reveal that more general norms and practices were refracted through collective memory of a specific past, and the interaction of the two gave Columbia's coverage its particular flavor and made it difficult for NASA officials to exert effective control over the story. The coverage of Columbia's destruction may not have qualified as counter hegemonic, but it almost certainly did not reflect the space agency's preferred framing of the event.

In addition to resisting the version of events given in briefings, reporters using collective memories of Challenger sought out sources likely to dispute the official story. Lawrence (2000) argues that accidental events like the Columbia crash offer opportunities for unofficial perspectives to enter the news as groups compete to define the event. Early coverage of Columbia's crash reveals that reporters sometimes identify the relevant groups using collective memories of previous events.

Yet using collective memory also represents a risk. Was collective memory of the Challenger accident helpful in holding officials accountable in Columbia's case, or did the memory of the earlier crash distract reporters from vital aspects of the more recent one? Challenger memories encouraged reporters early on to focus as much on NASA's decision-making processes as on the immediate causes of the crash. Reporters repeatedly held officials to standards of consensus decision-making and quickly abandoned accident stories (implying an unforeseeable outcome) for malpractice stories (implying a preventable failure). The official accident report, released in late August 2003, upheld this conclusion, for it made a point of holding organizational failures at NASA as responsible as the technological failure of the foam strike and subsequent heat shield collapse for Columbia's destruction. If we applied Best's (1993) conservative approach to social constructionism, we could say that Challenger memories were effective, since two different groups of observers with different perspectives and goals reached the same conclusion. However, it is also possible that Challenger memories distracted investigators and reporters alike and that the 'true' cause of Columbia's crash will never be known. Another important consideration is that the risk associated with this application of collective memory may have been especially low since the two accidents involved the same organization and occurred less than 20 years apart. Relying upon a more ambitious historical analogy might well prove more problematic.

More research is needed to tease out the implications of using collective memory as a reporting resource, but one final observation should be made here: since reliance on the past is not apparent in finished reports, news consumers are incapable of assessing for themselves the risks of reporting through the lens of the past.

References

Barnhurst, K. G. (2003) 'The Makers of Meaning: National Public Radio and the New Long Journalism', *Political Communication* 20(1): 1–22.

Barnhurst, K. G. and D. Mutz (1997) 'American Journalism and the Decline of Event- centered Reporting', *Journal of Communication* 47: 27–53.

Bennett, W. L. (1983) *News: The Politics of Illusion.* New York: Longman. Bennett, W. L. (1990) 'Toward a Theory of Press-state Relations', *Journal of Communication* 40: 103–25.

Berkowitz, D. (1992) 'Non-routine News and Newswork: Exploring a What-a-story', *Journal of Communication* 42: 82–94.

Best, J. (1993) 'But Seriously Folks: The Limitations of the Strict Constructionist Interpretation of Social Problems', in J. A. Holstein and G. Miller (eds) *Reconsidering Social Constructionism: Debates in Social Problems Theory,* pp. 129–47. New York: Aldine de Gruyter.

Borenstein, S. (2 February 2003) 'Explosion or Damage to Insulation may have caused Shuttle's Disintegration', retrieved 19 March 2003 from Lexis/Nexis database.

Borenstein, S. (4 February 2003) 'NASA "blew it" by Downplaying Hit from Foam, 2 ex-managers say', retrieved 19 March 2003 from Lexis/Nexis database.

Darnton, R. (1990) *The Kiss of Lamourette: Reflections in Cultural History.* New York: Norton.

Dunn, M. (4 February 2003a) 'NASA Looking for Mistakes in Analysis of Insulation that may have harmed Columbia', retrieved 19 March 2003 from Lexis/Nexis database.

Dunn, M. (4 February 2003b) 'NASA Warned Nine Years Ago that Shuttle Wing Underside Especially Vulnerable', retrieved 19 March 2003 from Lexis/Nexis database.

Dunn, M. and F. Easton (2 February 2003) 'Authorities Probe Cause of Shuttle Disaster that Killed Seven and Stunned a Nation', retrieved 19 March 2003 from Lexis/Nexis database.

Edy, J. A. (1999) 'Journalistic Uses of Collective Memory', *Journal of Communication* 49(2): 71–85.

Edy, J. A. (2001) 'The Presence of the Past in Public Discourse', in Roderick F Hart and Bartholomew H. Sparrow (eds) *Politics, Discourse, and American Society: New Agendas,* pp. 53–70. Lanham, MD: Rowman and Littlefield.

Entman, R. M. (1991) 'Framing U.S. Coverage of International News: Contrasts in Narratives of the KAL and Iran Air Incidents', *Journal of Communication* 41(4): 6–27.

Esser, J. K. and J. S. Lindoerfer (1989) Groupthink and the Space Shuttle Challenger Accident: Toward a Quantitative Case Analysis', *Journal of Behavioral Decision Making* 2(3): 167–77.

Gitlin, T. (1980) *The Whole World is Watching: The Mass Media and the Making and Unmaking of the New Left.* Berkeley: University of California Press.

Hirokawa, R. Y., D. S. Gouran and A. E. Martz (1988) 'Understanding the Source of Faulty Group Decision Making: A Lesson from the Challenger Disaster', *Small Group Behavior* 19: 411–33.

Lang, K. and G. E. Lang (1989) 'Collective Memory and the News', *Communication* 11: 12 3–9.

Lawrence, R. G. (2000) *The Politics of Force: Media and the Construction of Police Brutality.* Berkeley: University of California Press.

Lule, J. (2001) *Daily News, Eternal Stories: The Mythological Role of Journalism.* New York: Guilford Press.

Major General Mike Kostelnik Holds News Conference at NASA Headquarters (5 February 2003), retrieved 19 February 2003 from Lexis/Nexis database.

McDowell, M. (1987) *Challenger: A Major Malfunction.* New York: Doubleday.

National Aeronautics and Space Administration News Briefing (3 February 2003), retrieved 19 February 2003 from Lexis/Nexis database.

National Aeronautics and Space Administration News Briefing (2003b, 3 February) Re: Space Shuttle Columbia (OV-102) Accident, retrieved 19 February 2003 from Lexis/Nexis database.

National Aeronautics and Space Administration News Briefing (4 February 2003) Re: Space Shuttle Columbia (OV-102) Accident, retrieved 19 February 2003 from Lexis/Nexis database.

Novick, P. (1999) *The Holocaust in American Life.* Boston, MA: Houghton Mifflin Company.

Schudson, M. (1992) *Watergate in American Memory: How We Remember, Forget, and Reconstruct the Past.* New York: Basic Books.

Sigal, L. V. (1973) *Reporters and Officials: The Organization and Politics of Newsmaking.* Lexington, MA: D.C. Heath.

Tuchman, G. (1972) 'Objectivity as Strategic Ritual: An Examination of Newsmen's Notion of Objectivity', *American Journal of Sociology 77(4):* 660–79.

Vaughan, D. (1997) *The Challenger Launch Decision: Risky Technology, Culture and Deviance at NASA.* Chicago, IL: University of Chicago Press.

Watson, T. and P. O'Driscoll (2003) 'That Missing Link is Out There', *USA Today* (3 February): 4A, retrieved 19 March 2003 from Lexis/Nexis database.

Zelizer, B. (1998) *Remembering to Forget: The Holocaust through the Cameras Eye.* Chicago, IL: University of Chicago Press.

Source: From "Reporting Through the Lens of the Past: From Challenger to Columbia," 2006, by J. Edy & M. Daradanova, *Journalism* 7(2), 131–151. Reprinted by permission of Sage Publications, Ltd.

21

Memory in Journalism and the Memory of Journalism

Israeli Journalists and the Constructed Legacy of Haolam Hazeh

Oren Meyers

Within the rapidly growing corpus of research on collective memory, relatively modest attention has been dedicated to the simultaneous operation of journalists as narrators of both the memories of the societies for whom they report and the memory of their own professional community. The numerous books and articles focusing on collective recollections rarely address journalism and journalists as primary goals of inquiry and most of the works written within this sub-field of collective memory research were authored by communication scholars (Edy & Daradanova, 2006; Kitch, 2002; Meyers, 2002; Schudson, 1992; Zelizer, 1992). Furthermore, the existing literature on the topic has mostly looked at the construction of journalistic memory as the derivative of the journalistic coverage of "general" past public events.

This article accordingly probes the role of journalists as collective memory agents via an exploration of the interplay between the stories journalists tell as professionals and the stories they tell about their profession. In order to do so, the article investigates the stories that Israeli journalists narrate about their own work, its significance, and its relevance to larger cultural and social narratives. Specifically, this exploration of the Israeli journalistic community focuses on the construction of the memory of the radical and sensational weekly *Haolam Hazeh* (in Hebrew: *This World,*[1] 1937–1993; hereafter referred to as *HH)* seen here as a phenomenon that illustrates the ways in which the journalistic past and present are inherently intertwined. Thus, the heart of this investigation lies in the stories Israeli journalists have narrated about *HH* across time and the ways in which such stories reflect and shape the professional self-perceptions of the Israeli journalistic community.

The article illuminates a community and a process that were understudied within the larger bodies of both collective memory research and journalism studies. By looking at journalistic accounts that shape a longitudinal narrative of a professional coming of age, the article delineates the intersection between several realms of inquiry: It points at how professional—rather than ethnic or national—communities construct their understanding of their past according to changing present perceptions and within the context of larger cultural narratives; it probes the work of journalists as agents of collective memory and offers an insight on how commemorative and noncommemorative recollections interact within this process of communal narration. Finally, the article offers a first-of-its-kind investigation of these themes within the context of the study of Israeli journalism. Although previous studies have offered rich organizational, institutional, and linguistic explorations of Israeli journalism, existing research does not adequately address the role of Israeli journalists as cultural interpreters and memory agents and the communal and longitudinal dimensions of their work. Hence, by addressing these areas, this study advances our understanding of the workings of Israeli journalists.

The article consists of five sections. The first section conceptualizes journalistic collective memory within the context of both journalism studies and collective memory research. Correspondingly, it explores the reasons for the marginalization of journalistic memory within the larger field of collective memory studies and points at the ways in which the reported inquiry addresses this lack. The second section explores the dynamics through which *HH* became the functional transgressor of Israeli journalism during the 1950s and 1960s. The next two sections investigate the current construction of HH as a constituting memory of Israeli journalism: The third section looks at the complementing commemorative and noncommemorative components of this retrospective tale of professional triumph and explains *how* this narrative is advanced in current Israeli journalism. The fourth section addresses the *why* question. It looks at the conditions and circumstances that made this transformation in the weekly's public reputation possible. Together the two sections offer an integrative view of both the ways in which various "reputational entrepreneurs" (Fine, 2001, p. 12) promote this specific narrative of *HH*'s memory, and the ways current Israeli journalists use this transformation to reinforce their professional and critical ethos. The concluding section discusses the transformation of journalistic reputations via memory work as a key concept in journalism studies.

Journalists as Memory Agents

Social groups shape their understanding of the past in ways that fit current goals and challenges. And so, the group reproduces this common past by constantly renegotiating the meaning of events (Halbwachs, 1951/1992). Correspondingly, past events and shared experiences shape the ways communities understand the present. Therefore, collective memory contains two complementary components: the common consciousness shared by members of social groups regarding their past and the system of mnemonic signifiers placed across time and space in order to publicly narrate and affix these perceptions (Bar-On, 2001).

The significance and effectiveness of news journalists as collective memory agents may be best explained by means of observations made by journalism scholars who have probed day-to-day journalistic practices, routines, and norms. Their findings point to fundamental similarities between journalistic professionalism and memory work: They emphasize that the main task of journalists is to select socially "marked" events out of the neverending flow of occurrences, place those events within a context, and construct around them a meaningful continuum (Harcup & O'Neill, 2001; Molotch & Lester, 1975). Furthermore, most of the formal and informal guidance journalists receive from peers and superiors revolves around these exact qualifications, which apply to the documentation of the present and to the interpretation of the past:

being able to select, define, and make sense of events in accordance with a set of professional guidelines. Another dimension of journalistic practice that situates journalists as qualified memory interpreters is their heavy reliance on the past as a guiding context. The volume of journalists' work, their fear of being sued, and their trust in the credibility of former journalistic work leads them to frame the new within the context of the old (Tuchman, 1973). Moreover, good journalism is defined as a story that incorporates a new development into a familiar (and thus consumer-friendly) framework.

Hence, when journalists act as memory agents they engage in three complementary dimensions of their work. On a basic level, they do what they always do: tell the public stories about realities that are beyond the public's immediate reach. On a second level, the journalistic coverage of the past always situates it within larger cultural and social contexts. Third, when journalists narrate the past, they tell stories about their own work and the role they have played and still play in shaping social memories.

Despite the omnipresence and assumed influence of the news media, and the documented growing role and authority of journalists in the shaping of our understanding of collective pasts (Zelizer, 1993b), the operation of journalists as memory agents has been clearly marginalized within the larger field of collective memory research. Several factors could explain this phenomenon: First and foremost, the way in which collective memory researchers perceive journalism and journalists might be influenced by the way journalists perceive themselves. The endurance of the objective—natural—factual paradigm in journalism contributes to the understanding of news work as a transparent process of information transformation. So, although collective memory studies often base their arguments on reports and views that have appeared in the press, the overwhelming use of these data tends to overlook the role of journalists as social storytellers and members of an interpretive community (Roeh, 1989; Zelizer, 1993a). Journalistic work tends to be depicted in such studies as a general *Zeitgeist* somehow concretized into the language of headlines and follow-ups. Following that line, journalism seems to figure within the prevailing discourse of collective memory studies as a mediating entity: It lacks the stature and authority of the academic establishment, the formal power of the state, and the extended reach of popular-commercial culture.

Finally, the relatively minor focus on journalists as agents of collective memory might be attributed to conceptual and methodological factors: The most prevalent method of investigating the presence and influence of collective memories explores the ways present perceptions shape understanding of the past. This attitude underlies studies that look at concrete and intended commemorations, those that seek to decode the changing ideological givens that constitute shifting views of the past. The second, less common, method of addressing collective recollections aims to trace movement from the past into the present. This attitude is evident in studies of noncommemorative and unintended influences of past phenomena (Schudson, 1997). The increased analytical focus on commemorative memory contributes to the relative understudy of journalists as agents of collective memory. This is because most journalistic work is routine and noncommemorative by nature. The ways in which the past and present are continuously constructed via routine journalistic work is harder to track down and to conceptualize than the study of state-sponsored rituals, commemorative museums, or lucrative popular culture productions.

Therefore, the following look at *HH* narratives broadens the existing discussion of the role journalists as memory agents as it offers a notable shift in the relations between centerstage and backstage in the process by which communal journalistic memory is constructed. Previous explorations of the role of journalists as agents of collective memory focused on the ways in which journalists narrate past public events while establishing their own status as authoritative interpreters of the past. Thus, when journalists recollect JFK's assassination or Watergate, the general (American) past is usually at the center of the stories, whereas the construction of journalistic authority is mainly an interpretive byproduct.

The following research complements existing scholarship by offering a reverse perspective: The reported case study focuses on the unique and significant occasions in which the journalistic past and present are positioned at the center of the stage of routine media coverage while the general past provides the contextual background. In other words, although previous studies probed the ways in which journalists construct the past of their professional community as they narrate the *biographies* of the societies to which they belong, the study of the shaping of the memory of HH looks at how journalists operate as communal *autobiographers.* This difference bears analytical significance for the study of journalists as members of interpretive memory communities: Journalists' operation as an interpretive community mostly takes place as journalists cover routine events. The fact that journalistic inner discourse is conducted largely in public—in contrast to many other professional communities—and within the context of dealing with various other topics, complicates the conceptualization of the journalists' inner discourse. Hence, journalists' self-reflexive recounting of the "private" story of their professional community clarifies the inner interpretive process that is so rampant among journalists.

Haolam Hazeh as the "Functional Transgressor" of Israeli Journalism

The assumption guiding this exploration is that journalistic communities define their boundaries, set normative standards, and distinguish between good and bad journalism through the functional narration of professional tales. Within this context, news reports in which journalists recall the past offer a unique occasion for studying journalistic interpretive communities: Comparing the ways by which journalists position themselves within news stories when they first report them with the way they view them and their coverage of them in retrospect provides an insight into how communal journalistic perceptions are both maintained and changed over time.

Thus, what I basically tracked down were stories that have been told by Israeli journalists about *HH* since Uri Avnery and Shalom Cohen started editing the weekly in 1950, up until 2003, 10 years after it closed. I searched a computerized database going back to 1987 for the keywords *"Haolam Hazeh"* and the names of prominent staffers as primary and secondary topics. In addition, I searched the archives of the Israeli dailies *Ma'ariv* and *Ha'aretz* for all journalistic items published there and other print media since 1950 about *HH* and its staffers. I also searched *HH's* own issues for items referring to other newspapers that wrote about the weekly.

Next, I examined other relevant materials in the archives of the Israeli Press Council, the Federation of Israeli Journalists, and the Israel Defense Forces; *HH's* self-commemorative coverage; and autobiographies of prominent Israeli journalists. I also studied discussions about *HH,* the legacy of the Israeli journalistic community, and key debates on journalistic norms and values that appeared in trade magazines, media criticism columns, and especially the Yearbook of the Association of Tel Aviv Journalists (YATAJ), first published in 1943 and for many years the only venue for Israeli journalists' self-reflexive discourse. Supplementary data were gathered from interviews with two groups of veteran Israeli journalists: four ex-staffers of HH and four veteran prominent journalists who did not work for the weekly. Beyond my own interviews, I gained access to those conducted by the filmmaker Yair Lev for his 2002 documentary *Ha-Nidon: Uri Avnery* (The topic of discussion: Uri Avnery). Lev's extensive research included interviews with individuals whose paths had crossed Avnery's through the years, including of course many *HH* staffers.

To encapsulate this process of communal–professional sense making, my analysis followed the principles of interpretive research (Lindlof, 1995). Hence, the data were explored using four interpretive frames, or "layers" that are not mutually exclusive, but rather complementary in their discussion of *HH*'s place within Israeli journalism: The first frame addressed the "straightforward" chronological story of *HH* and thus explored the background against which the weekly shaped its agenda, and what characterized the alternative it offered. The second frame addressed the discourse surrounding *HH,* and so, it explored the ways the Israeli journalistic community and *HH* itself constructed its changing images through the years.

The third frame endeavored to point out "gaps" between the first and second levels. Hence, it addressed the strategies used over time to narrate stories about *HH* in ways that served the changing professional ethos of Israeli journalists. This interpretive frame illuminates the changing roles designated for *HH;* the ways different presentations of *HH* were constructed and validated; and the ways in which such narratives assisted the mainstream journalistic community, as well as *HH* itself in defining their values and fortifying their (often opposing) storytelling statuses. The fourth interpretive frame dwelled upon the interrelations between the communal memory of the Israeli journalistic community and "general" Israeli collective memory. Such accounts provide a salient example of how Israeli journalists position themselves within present critical perceptions of Israel's past.

In 1937, the journalist Ouri Kessary established the weekly *Tesha Baerev* (9 p.m.) that changed its name to *Haolam Hazeh* in 1946. Kessary's paper published literary works alongside lighter sections dealing with Tel Aviv nightlife. In April 1950, Uri Avnery and Shalom Cohen, two young combat veterans of Israel's 1948 war, bought *HH* from Kessary. Following the buyout Avnery, who became the weekly's editor, and Cohen, who became the chief of its editorial staff, recreated *HH* as a newsweekly different from other Israeli newspapers of that time.

Two major tendencies influenced Israeli journalism of the state's formative era: On the one hand, most Israeli journalists of that time, especially those who entered the profession before the establishment of Israel, were unable to position themselves as critical observers of the young state. The mainstream journalistic community of the 1950s was supportive of the Zionist ideal and viewed itself as an integral part of the fulfillment of its vision. Hence, in most cases publication policies were restrained and attentive to the authorities' requests (Nossek & Limor, 1998). Of course, different journalists had different ideas regarding what was actually good for the Zionist endeavor, but it is important to note that in that era ideological justification was an essential element in the journalistic discourse on professional excellence. On the other hand, the Israeli journalistic community of that era was also engaged in an initial effort to define its independent professional identity. For instance, a review of YATAJ issues reveals a steady shift, throughout the 1950s and 1960s, from a focus on the achievements of the new state to the discussion of professional issues such as journalistic ethics, editing styles, freedom of speech, and journalism education.

The tension between these two tendencies ran through all the major issues facing the Israeli journalistic community during the 1950s (Meyers, 2005). In this sense, *HH* was an integral part of the journalistic community: Through its messages and practices, it, too, negotiated the tension between affiliating with an ideological agenda and committing to an ethos of professional and critical journalism. But this was also where *HH* differed from other Israeli media of the time. Until 1965 when the *Haolam Hazeh—Ko'ach Hadash* (This World—New Power) party was established, the weekly was indeed an ideologically identified publication, but unlike other Israeli ideologically identified newspapers, it did not serve a political party or a labor union from which it could recruit readership and financial support.

Moreover, the convictions advocated by *HH* were in many respects beyond the sphere of legitimate political discussion of the time. When mainstream Israeli journalists debated the pros and cons of party versus private journalism, the assumption was that all types of Israeli journalism ought to promote Zionist ideals and goals (Carlebach, 1951/1992). In contrast, most of the ideological stands of *HH,* like acknowledging the existence of a Palestinian people, accepting the Palestinian refugees' right of return (to Israel), the struggle to eliminate Jewish theocratic elements from Israeli law, or its personal attacks against Israel's first prime minister David Ben-Gurion, were clearly far beyond the consensual journalistic discourse. At the same time, unlike other radical political publications of the time, *HH* was determined to reach wide audiences.

The combination of these three factors—nonconsensual ideology, lack of institutional backing, and the aspiration to appeal to mass audiences—led *HH* to develop a journalistic formula that was nontraditional yet alert to the existing "blind spots" of Israeli journalism of that era. The most salient component of the formula was a combination of "harder" and "softer" journalistic contents most clearly expressed in the initiation of the two-cover system in 1959: the front cover related to hard news topics, including the weekly's famous investigative reporting crusades, whereas the back cover displayed sensations, usually of a blatantly sexual nature.

HH represented a complex or rather paradoxical mix of Israeli realities; on the one hand, its reports and op-eds aspired to voice the discontents of disenfranchised sectors of Israeli society, namely new Jewish immigrants from Middle Eastern countries and the Arab citizens. On the other hand, *HH*'s lighter sections extensively covered, if not invented Israeli glamour; its issues depicted Tel Aviv nightlife and Israeli popular culture stars with fervor unheard of in Israeli journalism. At the core of *HH*'s journalistic style lay its language. The headlines were brief, dramatic, and often cynical. *HH*'s texts aimed to reflect a renunciation of the cumbersome, awkward "Jewish" writing of the founders of Hebrew journalism. The language sought decisiveness and thus was often blunt and aggressive. For instance, in 1960, the Editors' Committee (composed of the editors of Israel's mainstream dailies) advised newspapers to replace the term "committed suicide" with "died in tragic circumstances" and "raped" with "attacked" (Symposium, 1964, p. 26). The committee even sent a special written request to *HH* asking it to adopt this terminology but the weekly refused (Tel Aviv Journalists Association archive, 1960). Moreover, discontent with the limited vocabulary of Hebrew journalism was answered by the invention of new Hebrew words now commonly used by Hebrew speakers.

HH's journalistic vision was sustained through questionable practices. The weekly's hegemonic analysis of Israeli reality was the basis of its disputed claims to objectivity and fairness: According to *HH,* all other Israeli media were coconspirators with the ruling elites. And since the weekly was supposedly the only reliable, truth-telling Israeli media outlet, it did not include in its investigative reports the responses of the people and the establishments it targeted. Correspondingly, *HH* staffers' methods of gathering information and captioning photographs were ethically questionable (Bar-Am, 1996, p. 206; Berkowitz, 1997, p. 35)

Predictably, most mainstream Israeli journalists of the formative era who publicly discussed *HH* were appalled, to say the least, with such content and style. Public journalistic disdain was so prevalent that on several occasions mainstream journalists argued that the only effective way to combat *HH* was to ignore it altogether (Carlebach, 1955; Shamir, 1957). A typical reference by *Ha'aretz*'s prominent columnist Amos Elon argued:

> *Haolam Hazeh* has a unique writing style that is enforced upon all of its sections, in an almost totalitarian manner . . . this style appears to be [written] in one octave above normal prose, a trick that keeps the reader in a state of constant tension, and induces him to share the editors' hysteria . . . This style brings us every week articles that increase [the weekly's] circulation through well-known methods such as fanning ethnic, party, and cultural differences, combined with large doses of pornography and coffee-shop gossip. . . . Letters written by minors are published alongside propaganda campaigns that serve only to undermine morale in high schools, and increase

> the tension between teachers and pupils. (1954, p. 5)

The political, professional, and moral public criticism of the journalistic mainstream against *HH* during those years was comprehensive, to the extent that it defined the mainstream's own journalistic vision: The strategic positioning of *HH* as the designated "other" of Israeli journalism was articulated in order to define the boundaries of the journalistic community, enforce normative standards, and establish what was considered good and bad journalism. Hence, *HH* was positioned publicly as the ultimate contrast against which the journalistic community could define its positive and constructive ethos.

However, precisely when *HH* was being used to define everything that legitimate Israeli journalism opposed, it also served in many cases as a source of professional inspiration, a de facto journalism school and an unofficial channel for exploring topics and approaches unacceptable to the mainstream Israeli media, as explained by Eli Tavor, a former chief of *HH*'s editorial staff:

> Many professional reporters were actually [de facto] staffers of *Haolam Hazeh* that worked without pay, just because of their journalistic obligation. They had a good story, they wanted it to get published but they could not publish it in their newspapers. So they gave it to *Haolam Hazeh.* (E. Tavor, personal communication with Y. Lev, 2001)

The weekly played a similar role within the context of the Editors' Committee, which met routinely with state officials who informed the editors about sensitive information in return for the editors' promise not to publish it. Because committee membership was formally reserved for editors of daily newspapers, *HH* was excluded. Correspondingly, *HH* argued that it opposes the mere existence of such a body (Avnery, 1959). But this is only part of the story: In many cases, soon after the officials met with the editors, *HH* would submit reports leaked from the meeting to the military censor (Bar-On, 1981, p. 77). Because this information was banned for publication by voluntary agreement, the censor had to try to convince *HH* to join this agreement retroactively. In some cases, *HH* did so but in others its insistence on publishing the material forced the censor to inform mainstream newspapers that they could do so because *HH* was going to publish the story (U. Avnery, personal communication, March 21, 2003).

HH, therefore, allowed mainstream journalists to maintain the impression of adherence to strict ideological directives (i.e., cooperation with state officials) while at the same time, it enabled mainstream journalists to follow their professional calling and publish these stories either through *HH* or because the weekly was going to publish them.

Thus, *HH*'s paradoxical existence as a functional transgressor underscored the major inner contradictions between ideological loyalties and professional consciousness within the Israeli journalistic community during that formative era, and some of the ways such contradictions were appeased. *HH*'s criticism of the mainstream journalism, countered by the mainstream's fierce public denunciation of the weekly, might seem to reflect a struggle between two clear-cut alternatives. With that, the ways in which these two archrivals used one another, and conducted their overt and covert dialogues, suggest a more nuanced picture of their relationship.

The Transformation of Disputed Journalistic Reputation through Memory Work

Through the late 1960s and onwards, *HH* lost its status as the most significant transgressor of Israeli journalism due to a combination of internal and external dynamics: The establishment of the *Haolam Hazeh—Ko'ach Hadash* party (1965–1973) and Avnery's overall focus shift form journalism to party politics made the weekly less effective and more vulnerable.

Ongoing personal disputes and financial difficulties also weakened *HH.* At the same time, new developments within Israeli journalism made it less relevant to the extent that the journalistic mainstream no longer needed the weekly as its defining "functional transgressor." In addition, changing professional journalistic perceptions and practices facilitated this process. A review of the journalistic discourse of the last three decades shows a gradual movement toward the view of journalism as a profession and the adoption of a critical journalistic approach. The decline in the status of the Editors' Committee and the growing tendency of the journalistic community to award prizes to investigative journalists rather than to commentators attest to this change. This shift was also fueled by the influence of foreign (mainly American) journalism and the effect of key events in the history of Israeli journalism. For instance, journalistic discourse positions the reporting of the 1973 Yom Kippur war as a professional failure that served as a critical lesson internalized in the far more critical and thus professionally successful reporting of the 1982 war in Lebanon (Meyers, 2004, pp. 215–234).

Correspondingly, *HH* became increasingly significant as a functional memory of the Israeli journalistic community. In the final decade of the weekly's existence, and still more after it closed in 1993, numerous articles published in the Israeli press addressed *HH* and its legacy. The current construction of the memory of *HH* is articulated through three interconnected discursive moves: The first component of *HH*'s retrospective tale of triumph positions it as the ultimate maverick of Israeli journalism in the state's early years. Thus, most current journalistic and academic references to it tend to emphasize the elements that the weekly itself used to highlight through its ongoing self-commemoration. The second component of this tale attributes to *HH* a definitive influence on the professional maturation of Israeli journalism. According to this interpretation, Israeli journalists learned from *HH* how to investigate scandals, critique officials, take powerful photographs, and more. In his 1997 autobiography Margalit, a 1960s' *HH* reporter and a current prominent political columnist, clearly emphasized this notion:

> Avnery initiated a successful journalistic revolution. He slaughtered sacred cows. A whole generation of journalists learned from him how to fight corruption and how to investigate it, to irritate authorities without fearing them. He published on *Haolam Hazeh's* cover the slogan "Without fear or favor." There was "favor" in his newspaper. But he himself was "fearless," and he could be rightfully declared the father of the Israeli school of investigative journalism. (p. 213)

A final component of the retold *HH* tale positions it as a tragic victor. Journalistic accounts that discuss the gradual regression in terms of readership and journalistic significance argue that, paradoxically, it was caused by its very success: Over the years, the weekly's competitors adopted some or most of its journalistic formulae. Because those competitors were all better off financially than *HH,* the weekly stood no chance. This concluding component of *HH*'s narrative seems to provide a dramatic, even an epic ending: *HH*'s true greatness could be proven only through its tragic demise.

Like all functional narrations of the past, this retelling requires construction and selection. And so, this selective storytelling downplays some elements of *HH*'s agenda that do not coincide with current professional self-perceptions of Israeli journalists: the weekly's aggressive and one-sided rhetoric, its problematic ethics, and the fact that by its own admission *HH* never aspired to practice "only" professional, objective journalism. Rather, *HH* knowingly harnessed its journalistic coverage to the advancement of ideological goals in a way that would be unacceptable to current Israeli journalists who define themselves as balanced and fair professionals. Moreover, some recollections of *HH* reject the dominant glorifying portrait of the weekly's memory:

> A general and selective view *of Haolam Hazeh's* public struggles . . . could actually create the fairly common image of the weekly that articulated, more than others, the dissonant and nonconformist voice in the Israeli society of the 1950s . . . But this is a fictitious image. A fastidious examination of the weekly's stands would reveal that in many cases, its guiding ideology and journalistic line lead it to change its positions on various issues in a way that was clearly "with favor" . . . The farewell articles [to the weekly] were mostly nostalgic and rather supportive. In this way, *Haolam Hazeh* became, paradoxically, a kind of a "sacred cow" of Israeli journalism that represents the weekly as it pretended to be, rather than what it really was. (Shavit, 1994, p. 21)

As can be seen, even though Shavit, an Israeli historian takes issue with the widespread mythologization of *HH,* his criticism actually sustains the claim that *HH* lies, in retrospect, at the heart of the collective memory of Israeli journalism.

The shaping of *HH*'s current narrative delineates the reinforcing nature of commemorative and noncommemorative journalistic memory: The commemorative construction repositions *HH* at the center of the story that Israel journalists narrate about their community's past. It is evident on anniversaries, and when other media outlets or the professional community formally acknowledge the weekly's contribution to Israeli journalism (Marmari, 2000). For instance, in 2004, Avnery received the prestigious Sokolov prize from the Association of Tel Aviv Journalists for his lifetime achievements. In the same vein, *HH* is commemorated in the personal histories of Israeli journalists. This glorifying memory narrative fits logically into the autobiographies of former staffers. However, the dominance of this tale is most clearly illustrated in its inclusion in autobiographies (Shilon, 1998, pp. 35–36) and biographies (Ben Porat, 1998, p. 59) of veteran journalists who never worked for *HH.*

Correspondingly, the memory of *HH* is constructed via routine and noncommemorative journalistic coverage. Hence, some of the most revealing examples of the current positioning of *HH* as a significant point of journalistic reference occur when the designation is made in passing. Such cases demonstrate the infiltration of journalistic memory from the past into the present, as the legacy of *HH* is utilized—while addressing some other matter—to point out the supposedly consensual perceptions of the Israeli journalistic community (Haber, 2006). For instance, the editorial column of the concluding 2002 photographic issue of the bimonthly journal of the Israeli Police opened thus:

> "You know," I was told by an old acquaintance, a veteran photojournalist working since the days when *Haolam Hazeh's* covers were considered the bon ton of investigative journalism: "The best photographs are always the ones that touch banal, seemingly ordinary human details." (Shayowitz, 2002)

This casual comment highlights the process whereby *HH* became a common signifier of journalistic quality. It also creates the inaccurate notion that during *HH*'s heyday its covers (or any other feature) were publicly considered "the bon ton of investigative journalism." As mentioned, the common public perceptions of HH's journalism during the 1950s and 1960s were quite different.

Similarly, *HH* is routinely referenced through the use of its vocabulary and terminology, such as the reoccurring usage of its slogan "without fear or favor" as a commendation of current muckraking and critical Israeli journalists (Green, 2002); by crowning *HH*'s alleged successors (Sheleg, 1994); and when Israeli journalists address the challenges facing their professional community. In such cases, *HH*'s veterans are asked to comment on timely issues such as the murky boundaries of journalistic ethics in covering the private lives of public figures, journalism education, violence against journalists, and journalistic confidentiality (Kotas-Bar, 2000; Muzikant, 1999; Rosenthal, 1997).

HH's memory is therefore functional for current Israeli journalists in two complementary ways: It enables them to construct the past of their community in ways that match their current professional self-perceptions, while correspondingly Israeli journalists mobilize the memory of the weekly as a source of inspiration, or a point of reference that fortifies their professional status. Of course, these are not absolute categorizations because many journalistic accounts integrate the two perspectives. Rather, it is a functional distinction that illuminates the different processes through which journalistic collective memories are articulated and sustained. Furthermore, the distinction between *HH*-focused stories that are intended to deal with the past and journalistic stories that deal with the present and use the memory of *HH* as a way of contextualizing their contemporary arguments delineates the circular and self-affirming nature of this process: The more *HH* is commemorated and positioned at the center of the retrospective story of early Israeli journalism, the more it is legitimate to use it as a point of reference in the discussion of current journalistic debates. At the same time, the more *HH* is addressed within contemporary contexts, the more its retrospective significance within the story of past Israeli journalism increases.

The Ongoing Functionality of a Journalistic Maverick

The sharp contrast between mainstream Israeli journalism's earlier harsh public denunciation of *HH* and its current glorification demands a comprehensive explanation. So, does the very choice of *HH* as a vehicle for narrating the past of Israeli journalism: In the state's early years there were various other "others" that deviated from the template of veteran Hebrew mainstream newspapers committed to Zionist ideology. However, neither Arab newspapers, nor the ultra-orthodox Jewish press, nor the Communist Party's Hebrew daily of that era, occupy the memory of Israeli journalism in a way remotely similar to *HH*.

An explanation of the current prevalence of *HH*'s tale of retrospective triumph ought to consider this phenomenon via three components of this constructed narrative: the plot elements used to narrate the tale and their availability for current narrators; the identity of the narrators of this memory version, and the factors that facilitated their rise as influential agents of journalistic memory; and the larger cultural narratives that frame and contextualize the narration of this specific journalistic memory. By looking at these three interrelated elements, this exploration points to the conditions that allow the "repair" of disputed journalistic reputations via memory work. Furthermore, investigating the nature of this shift could illuminate the relations between the shaping of journalistic memories and the changing modes of broader national memories.

The first set of factors that enabled and facilitated this shift is related to the qualities of *HH* as a journalistic narrative. The fact that the weekly frequently dealt with sensational materials and sparked heated debates makes it an attractive subject matter. Few Israeli commentators are indifferent to *HH,* and the mere mention of the weekly produces powerful responses. Furthermore, *HH* makes a good story because it dealt with questionable materials; discussing *HH* provides a legitimate reason for current discussions of ever-popular themes like gossip and sex. Within this context, many descriptions of the history of Israeli journalism position *HH* as the originator of various journalistic phenomena (investigative journalism, advanced graphic design etc.):

> The first signs of sex journalism appeared (like everything else in Israeli journalism) in *Haolam Hazeh.* Uri Avnery, the founder of modern Israeli journalism in the Holy Land, was the first who dared to insert some erotic moisture into the press. (Feldman, 1996, p. 54)

Another characteristic of this memory narrative that contributes to its widespread popularity among Israeli journalists is that it has one clearly identified, articulate, and eager protagonist.

Although dozens of Israeli journalists worked in *HH* through the years, and a number took part in shaping its agenda, the retrospective story, as featured in current Israeli journalism has one protagonist—Uri Avnery. The perception of *HH*'s story as a memory channeled mainly through Avnery is a major factor in the story's clarity and simplicity because journalistic presentations of reality tend to focus on distinct human protagonists rather than abstract themes (Bird & Dardenne, 1988). The frequent appearances of Avnery as a popular historian of Israeli culture, who often comments on Israeli humor, graphic design, youth culture, and more, further promote the construction of the memory of *HH.* In such appearances, Avnery stresses the role played by the weekly in the evolution of various cultural and social processes. Moreover, such appearances promote the retrospective glorification of *HH* once Avnery's credentials as the former editor of weekly are featured as the source of his current interpretive authority.

Similarly, the narration of HH's memory is made easy by the existing "memory infrastructure" laid by the weekly itself. *HH* was heavily invested in shaping its own image and stressing its uniqueness in comparison to other Israeli newspapers. It did so through means such as the marking of the anniversaries of both the original and the new *HH,* the arrival of the 3,001st letter to the editor and more. Also, its editors adopted a salient self-reflexive approach by sharing many behind-the-scenes decision-making processes with their readers. Facing outward, *HH* aspired to refute all attacks and constantly compared its contents to the offerings of the competition—an uncommon attitude in the journalism of Israel's first decades. Moreover, *HH* was heavily involved in the long-term shaping of its own memory via means such as the regular column "That was *Haolam Hazeh"* detailing the main stories it published that same week in previous years. Naturally, most stories selected for the column highlighted *HH*'s accuracy and journalistic boldness in retrospect. Through such memory-preserving activities, *HH* facilitated and directed its own commemoration at the hands of current Israeli journalists leafing through its issues.

Finally, the fact that the weekly itself is a non-threatening memory site aids and abets the retrospective glorifying narrative. Placing *HH* within the recollections of Israeli journalism moved in parallel with the weekly's decline in depth and intensity. Hence, it became easier to address *HH*'s contribution to Israeli journalism when it no longer posed a threat to current competitors. Furthermore, in terms of storytelling strategies the folding of *HH* made commemoration easier, as it provided a sense of (tragic) closure.

The second set of factors that enabled and facilitated this transformation in the way mainstream Israeli journalism narrates *HH* relate to gradual shifts within Israeli public opinion, especially among Israeli journalists, toward the political stands promoted *by HH.* Parts of its agenda, and especially the acknowledgment of a Palestinian people with a right to its own independent state, once viewed as extremely radical, are now more generally accepted. Furthermore, Israeli journalists have often been declared to be more dovish in their political beliefs than the general public. To date, there are no empirical data to support this assumption, but it is compatible with the fact that Israeli journalists generally belong to the more dovish social sectors—the educated, the secular, and the middle class (Tsfati, 2004).

Beyond the mere affinity of many Israeli journalists toward *HH*'s politics is the fact that during its supposed "golden age" between 1950 and 1965, the weekly was not affiliated with a political party. Because the party press model has practically vanished, *HH*'s formative era struggles to advance worthy social causes without party patronage seem to fit the current professional self-perceptions of Israeli journalists. Furthermore, *HH*'s entrance into the parliamentary realm signifies for current journalists the beginning of its end:

> [*HH*'s] shift to [party] politics was viewed, at first . . . as part of its rebelliousness and movement forward. But soon it shifted from "civil" investigative journalism dealing with

> corruption, with the police and with healthcare . . . to strictly political issues. And this is where he [Avnery] made a huge mistake as an editor. Mainly because this shift [to party politics] left all of us alone . . . because [at the time] he was the only one who conducted such [journalistic] work. (R. Zror, personal communication with Y. Lev, 2002)

The third set of factors that enabled and facilitated the transformation in *HH*'s reputation is embedded in the ongoing functionality of the weekly for mainstream Israeli journalism. Through the years, Israeli journalists constructed their communal self-perceptions via a negotiation between the norms and values of their professional community and those of Israeli society. The nuanced ways by which mainstream Israeli journalists have narrated stories about *HH* through the years underlines the complex nature of the weekly itself as well as the professional community's constant need to assert its changing self-definitions.

As noted, *HH* acted as a "functional transgressor" in Israeli journalism throughout the 1950s and 1960s. It was publicly ostracized by the journalistic mainstream and the political establishment as an ultimate "other." At the same time, the weekly was used by that mainstream to accommodate opposing journalistic and ideological impulses. The same was true for *HH* itself offering a seemingly contradictory agenda of "hard" and "soft" contents. Moreover, this mix was created by journalists who were social insiders in many ways—they worked alongside the younger mainstream news reporters, belonged to the same social circles (native Israelis, secular, urban, educated) and in many cases held the right social credentials by virtue of their combat experience in the Israeli army (D. Rubinger, personal communication, December 12, 2002). This inherent in/outsider duality embedded in the weekly itself and corresponding with its dual relations with mainstream Israeli journalism, is pivotal to understanding what enabled the transformation of *HH* into such a significant site of memory. That duality allowed *HH* to be an outcast publicly, although it operated as a de facto journalism school for young reporters who later advanced to more prominent media outlets. And so, many of *HH*'s veteran staffers and avid readers are now firmly rooted in mainstream Israeli journalism and act as its reputational entrepreneurs.

Finally, in order to provide a "thicker description" of the conditions that facilitated this reputation transformation, it is essential to explore this process within the context of the larger narrative Israeli journalists tell about the maturation of their professional community. Within this context, it is important to look at the relations between this narrative and the general cultural move toward a critical reevaluation of the Israeli past. This is a narrative of a professional community coming of age, and *HH*'s role in it is that of a retrospective forefather of contemporary Israeli journalism that is positioned in sharp contrast to the "old journalism" practiced by the actual, chronological founders of Israeli journalism, who wrote and edited the major mainstream newspapers of the formative era.

By bestowing upon *HH* the status of a worthy forefather, contemporary Israeli journalists adopt and utilize *HH*'s original hegemonic perception of mainstream Israeli journalism, claiming that whatever their differences and disputes, all major Israeli media of the 1950s and 1960s were fundamentally similar in their support of Zionist ideology and the political establishment. Nowadays, commemorators use this analysis to describe early mainstream Israeli journalism, as well as the ways *HH* differed from it. This contrast between *HH* and the mainstream is stressed in a way that demonstrates the assumed progress of Israeli journalism from almost total submission to the prevailing ideology and its political proponents, to a professional consciousness guided by the example set by the ultimate transgressor during the formative era:

> *Haolam Hazeh* was the first Israeli newspaper that routinely exposed and covered the corruption and stupidity of some of the heads of the state. It was revolutionary. It undermined the blind faith that people had in their leaders. By doing so, *Haolam*

> *Hazeh* served [Israeli] democracy. Most of the newspapers saw themselves as a part of the Zionist struggle to establish the state, and their editors saw themselves as an integral part of its leadership. *Haolam Hazeh* was not the first or the only newspaper that represented an opposition to Ben Gurion's rule, but it was the first to sustain its stands through investigative journalism. This gave birth to the notion that those who read *Haolam Hazeh* knew more than those who only read the other newspapers. Often, this was true . . . *Haolam Hazeh* published what others did not know, or even worse, what others did not want to publish. (Segev, 1987, p. 23)

Positioning *HH* as such a retrospective journalistic founding father also illuminates one means by which Israeli journalists place themselves within the context of current critical rereadings of Israel's history in popular culture, art, and academia (Ram, 2006). This critical evaluation of the past and those who created the common memory of that past were most extensively discussed throughout the debate over Israel's "new historiography," a term coined to define the generational and analytical shift in the study of Israeli history (Morris, 1988; Shapira, 1997). The current positioning of *HH* as a worthy professional forefather therefore enables Israeli journalists to construct a narrative that corresponds with these critical tendencies. The tale of *HH*'s greatness and influence became so dominant because it enabled the creation of an "alternative" journalistic history. And so, the narration of *HH* provides Israeli journalism—again—a significant tool in its interplay with the changing values of Israeli culture.

Conclusion

Scholars of social deviance explain that the definition of an act or a person as deviant is always embedded within some larger cultural—political background that gives rise to this vilification, and it always answers certain social needs. Or as Goode and Ben-Yehuda (1994) put it: "the important point is, to the sociologist, the characteristic of deviance as defined not by the quality of the act but by the nature of the reaction that the act engenders or is likely to engender" (p. 70). Accordingly, this article probed the functionality embedded in the positioning of *HH* as a designated other, or deviant of early Israeli journalism. This exploration of the overt and covert relations between the journalistic mainstream and *HH* revealed the inner contradictions that characterized the work of early Israeli journalists and some of the ways by which such contradictions were reconciled.

But this study goes beyond the analysis of *HH*'s functionality for Israeli journalism at one specific historical period. Rather, it offers the study of a transformed journalistic reputation over time, as a conceptual framework for the exploration of the development of communal journalistic consciousness. The investigation of the positioning of *HH* during the 1950s and 1960s as a "functional transgressor" alongside its contemporary use as a means of fortifying the professional status of Israeli journalists points to the significance of looking into the processes by which the reputations of journalistic mavericks are sustained and altered. The study of the constructed "careers" of news organizations, individual journalists or journalistic trends that are publicly defined as outliers thereby emerges from this study as critical for the exploration of the professional identity of journalistic communities.

Beyond the suggestion of transformed journalistic reputations as a key concept in journalism studies, this article also points to the conditions, or requirements, that enable and fuel such processes. As can be seen in this case study, what facilitated the transformation of *HH*'s reputation via commemorative and noncommemorative memory work were elements that are related to the qualities of the narrative and its accessibility, the abilities and status of its protagonists and promoters, and the ways in which this transformative professional memory narrative fits within the context of changes in "larger" memories. Thus, the study of changing journalistic reputations enables us to delve into the simultaneous operation of journalists as members of both professional and national memory communities.

Finally, the exploration of the processes by which journalistic reputations are transformed could be further advanced via the incorporation of a comparative perspective. It is beyond the scope of this study to dwell upon this issue, but within the context of American journalism, a similar study of the construction of the memory of the *I.F. Stone Weekly* might offer relevant insights. Current accounts of Stone's maverick journalism seem to illuminate the gap between his previous marginalized positioning by mainstream American journalists as an irrelevant radical to a retrospective commemoration of his achievements as a "vital troublemaker" (Marro, 2006). Furthermore, Stone's journalism is currently suggested as a guiding context or pedagogical lesson for journalists covering events such as the war in Iraq (Navasky, 2003). Such depictions seem to parallel the processes discussed in this study, and so, they stress once again the significance of studying the ways by which the reputations of journalistic mavericks are shaped across time.

Acknowledgments

The author thanks Barbie Zelizer, Eitan Bar-Yosef, Tamar Katriel, Michael Keren, Zvi Reich, Vered Vinitzky-Seroussi, Eyal Zandberg, and the two anonymous reviewers for their comments on earlier versions of this article. Research for the article was supported by grants from The Hubert Burda Center for Innovative Communications, the Memorial Foundation for Jewish Culture and the University of Haifa.

Notes

1. All translations from Hebrew to English are mine.
2. *HH*'s famous motto *Bli morah - bli maso panim* ("without fear or favor") first appeared on its cover on May 19, 1955. It is not clear whether *HH's* editors were familiar with the historical origins of the phrase used by Kipling, Emerson, and Adolph Ochs in his 1896 statement on *The New York Times'* journalistic vision (Konner, 1996, p. 3).

References

Avnery, U. (1959, March 18). Dear reader [Hebrew]. *Haolam Hazeh,* p. 2.

Bar-Am, M. (1996). *The last war* [Hebrew]. Jerusalem: Keter.

Bar-On, A. (1981). *The untold stories: The diary of the chief censor* [Hebrew]. Jerusalem: Edanim.

Bar-On, M. (2001). *Smoking borders: Studies in the history of the State of Israel, 1948–1967* [Hebrew]. Jerusalem: Yad Yitshak Ben Tsvi.

Ben Porat, Y. (1998). *Conversations with Moty Kirschenbaum* [Hebrew]. Tel Aviv, Israel: Sifriat Poalim Publishing House.

Berkowitz, E. (1997, September 19). Big mama [Hebrew]. *Ma'ariv's Weekend Supplement,* pp. 33–36.

Bird, S. E., & Dardenne, R. (1988). Myth, chronicle and story: Exploring the narrative qualities of news. In J. W. Carey (Ed.), *Media, myths, and narratives: Television and the press* (pp. 67–86). Beverly Hills, CA: Sage.

Carlebach, E. (1951/1992). What is a newspaper? [Hebrew]. *Kesher,* 11, 4–6.

Carlebach, E. (1955, June 7). Freedom of the press [Hebrew]. *Ma'ariv,* p. 4.

Edy, J. A., & Daradanova, M. (2006). Reporting through the lens of the past. *Journalism, 7,* 131–151.

Elon, A. (1954, May 28). The weekly meaty portion [Hebrew]. *Ha'aretz,* p. 5.

Feldman, B. (1996, April 5). The embarrassment effect [Hebrew]. *Iton Tel-Aviv,* pp. 54–55.

Fine, G. A. (2001). *Difficult reputations: Collective memories of the evil, inept, and controversial.* Chicago: University of Chicago Press.

Goode, E., & Ben-Yehuda, N. (1994). *Moral panics: The social construction of deviance.* Oxford, UK: Blackwell.

Green, S. (2002, February 9). Good Shely, hello [Hebrew]. *Ha'aretz,* p. A14.

Haber, E. (2006, April 30). No time to cry [Hebrew]. *Yedioth Aharonoth,* p. B4.

Halbwachs, M. (1951/1992). *On collective memory.* Chicago: University of Chicago Press.

Harcup, T., & O'Neill, D. (2001). What is news? Galtung and Ruge revisited. *Journalism Studies,* 2, 261–280.

Kitch, C. (2002). Anniversary journalism, collective memory, and the cultural authority to tell the story of the American past. *Journal of Popular Culture,* 36, 44–67.

Konner, J. (1996). Without fear or favor. *Columbia Journalism Review,* 35(2), 4.

Kotas-Bar, C. (2000, February 4). In the depths of corruption [Hebrew]. *Ma'ariv's Weekend Supplement,* pp. 8–14.

Lindlof, T. R. (1995). *Qualitative communication research methods.* Thousand Oaks, CA: Sage Publications.

Margalit, D. (1997). *I have seen them all* [Hebrew]. Tel Aviv, Israel: Zmora-Bitan Publishers.

Marmari, H. (2000, October 5). Sir Uri (Hebrew]. *Ha'air,* pp. 32–33.

Marro, A. (2006). *The vital troublemaker.* Retrieved on September 20, 2006, from http://www.cjr.org/issues/2006/5/Marro.asp

Meyers, O. (2002). Still photographs, dynamic memories: An analysis of the visual presentation of Israel's history in commemorative newspaper supplements. *Communication Review,* 5, 179–205.

Meyers, O. (2004). Israeli journalists as an interpretive memory community: The case study of Haolam Haze (Doctoral dissertation, University of Pennsylvania, 2004). *Dissertation Abstract International.* (AAT 3125874).

Meyers, O. (2005). Israeli Journalism during the state's formative era: Between ideological affiliation and professional consciousness. *Journalism History,* 31, 88–97.

Molotch, H., & Lester, M. (1975). News as purposive behavior: On the strategic use of routine events, accidents, and scandals. *American Journal of Sociology,* 81, 235–260.

Morris, B. (1988). The new historiography: Israel confronts its past. *Tikkun,* 3(6), 19–24.

Muzikant, R. (1999, June 18). Journalists under fire [Hebrew]. *Zman Tel-Aviv, pp.* 40–42.

Navasky, V. (2003). *I.F. Stone.* Retrieved on July 2, 2003, from http://www.thenation.com/doc/20030721/navasky

Nossek, H., & Limor, Y. (1998). Military censorship in Israel: An ongoing compromise between clashing values [Hebrew]. In D. Caspi & Y. Limor (Eds.), *Media in Israel* (pp. 362–390). Tel Aviv, Israel: Open University of Israel.

Ram, U. (2006). *The time of the "post": Nationalism and the politics of knowledge in Israel* [Hebrew]. Tel Aviv, Israel: Resling Publishing.

Roeh, I. (1989). Journalism as storytelling, coverage as narrative. *American Behavioral Scientist,* 33, 162–168.

Rosenthal, R. (1997, January 27). The question of journalistic confidentiality [Hebrew]. *Ma'ariv,* p. B5.

Schudson, M. (1992). *Watergate in American memory: How we remember, forget, and reconstruct the past.* New York: Basic Books.

Schudson, M. (1997). Lives, laws and language: Commemorative versus non-commemorative forms of effective public memory. *Communication Review,* 2, 3–17.

Segev, T. (1987, May 20). Dear reader [Hebrew]. *Koteret Rashit, pp.* 20–23.

Shamir, M. (1957, June 4). "One has to know how to cheat" [Hebrew]. *Al Hamishmar,* p. 4.

Shapira, A. (1997). Politics and collective memory: The debate over the "new historians" [Hebrew]. In Y. Weitz (Ed.), *From vision to revision: A hundred years of historiography of Zionism* (pp. 367–391). Jerusalem: The Zalman Shazar Center.

Shavit, *Y.* (1994). Haolam Hazeh—A perspective [Hebrew]. *Kesher,* 15, 19–21.

Shayowitz, R. (2002). Moments in a year [Hebrew]. *Maraot Hamishtara,* 191, 2.

Sheleg, *Y.* (1994, June 29). The chasm is the limit [Hebrew]. *Bamachaneh,* pp. 28–33.

Shilon, D. (1998). *Live broadcast* [Hebrew]. Tel Aviv, Israel: Yedioth Aharonoth.

Symposium: Trial by the press. (1964). *Yearbook of the association of Tel Aviv journalists* [Hebrew]. 24, 16–38.

Tel Aviv Journalists Association archive. (1960, January 24–25). Correspondence between the Editors' Committee and HH. File 52. [Hebrew].

Tsfati, *Y.* (2004). Exploring possible correlates of journalists' perceptions of audience trust. *Journalism and Mass Communication Quarterly,* 81, 274–291.

Tuchman, G. (1973). Making news by doing the work: Routinizing the unexpected. *American Journal of Sociology, 79,* 110–131.

Zelizer, B. (1992). *Covering the body: The Kennedy assassination, the media, and the shaping of collective memory.* Chicago: University of Chicago Press.

Zelizer, B. (1993a). Journalists as interpretive community. *Critical Studies in Mass Communication,* 10, 219–237.

Zelizer, B. (1993b). News: First or final draft of history? *Mosaic,* 2, 2–3.

22

Making Memories Matter

Journalistic Authority and the Memorializing Discourse Around Mary McGrory and David Brinkley

Matt Carlson

Introduction

The death of a notable journalist invites a recollection—a discourse of memorialization—that both details his or her accomplishments and situates these accomplishments in a broader context that gives these actions meaning to working journalists and to news audiences. It is from the present, located in the actual act of memorialization, that these contributions are ascribed, re-created, examined, highlighted and elided. While past research has looked at paradigm repair and attempts to bolster authority in the face of journalistic violations (Bennett et al., 1985; Reese, 1990; Berkowitz, 2000; Hindman, 2005), this article examines how journalistic success, embodied by the deceased eminent journalist, is used to promote journalistic authority. The discourse around these figures shapes the collective memory of journalism by retelling the journalist's career through a framework that positions the deceased journalist as evidence for the merits of journalistic values and norms. This discourse further occasions a public evaluation by journalists of the defacement of those values and norms in an attempt to support the cultural authority of journalism. In this way, memorialization simultaneously engenders an active affirmation and signaling of journalistic values among working journalists.

The forms of memorializing surrounding the deaths of two highly respected and popular journalists—television anchor David Brinkley in June 2003 and newspaper columnist Mary McGrory in April 2004—are examined.[1] This article focuses on the ways in which contemporary journalists construct the memory of preceding 'significant' journalists. Specifically, what are the traits or events that cause a journalist to be remembered? Both instrumentally and symbolically, how does memorializing discourse strengthen or consolidate journalistic authority in the present and in what ways does it expose fissures? Finally, in what ways do the memorializing of McGrory and Brinkley correspond and in what ways do they diverge? In order to address these questions, a systematic textual analysis was made of news stories discussing the deaths of McGrory and Brinkley appearing in newspapers, magazines, network and cable television, and radio programs using the Factiva and LexisNexis Academic databases. The breadth of available sources and transcripts, including wire stories, comprises major news sources as well as many smaller outlets. The journalism trade press was also examined, yet articles on McGrory or Brinkley did not differ in tone or substance from the mainstream press outlets.

Questions of Authority

The act of memorializing elite deceased journalists can be contextualized as a strategy employed by living journalists in maintaining the cultural authority afforded to them to perform their specific societal function—broadly speaking, to gather, process, construct, and disseminate presumably veridical stories about society to society. Not simply messengers, journalists create a widely distributed rendering of reality intended to provide a common ground for otherwise largely disconnected people. Gans notes that 'one of journalists' prime functions is to manage, with others, the symbolic arena, the public stage on which national, societal, and other messages are made available to everyone who can become an audience member' (1979: 298). The power inherent in this function contributes to the contestation over journalism's social role generally and its specific renderings of 'the way it is'. The prevalence of media criticism underscores the point that journalistic authority is not assured automatically, but rather must be continually upheld, recreated, and negotiated (Eason, 1988; Zelizer, 1992). In order for journalism to perform its function, journalists must be recognized by news audiences, fellow journalists, and managers of news organizations as possessing the requisite cultural authority to legitimate their work. Strategies to procure authority occur through an established set of journalistic practices, as authority is 'a source of codified knowledge, guiding individuals in appropriate standards of action' (Zelizer, 1992: 2). In this view, authority is not an abstract idealist notion separate from the material workings of journalism but instead imbricated with practice (see Bennett et al., 1985). Manoff and Schudson (1986) note that 'Journalism, like any other storytelling activity, is a form of fiction operating out of its own conventions and understandings and with its own set of sociological, ideological, and literary constraints' (p. 6). It is through these conventions that journalists seek to cultivate their authority to news audiences who consume the news and managers who control resources in the profit-oriented U.S. media system.

Journalistic authority is complicated by ambiguity surrounding the labeling of journalism as a profession (see Singer, 2003). Tunstall (1971) questions efforts to establish a unifying professionalism due to the fragmentary nature of journalistic careers—'can a non-routine, indeterminate, and segmented occupation like journalism ever be a profession?'—and settles on the label of 'semi-profession' (p. 69). Unlike doctors or lawyers, no formal accreditation exists for U.S. journalists, nor is there a standard pre-professional educational track, widespread union, or professional group (Weaver and Wilhoit, 1986). Johnstone et al. (1976) found that this lack of membership in professional organizations 'reinforces the heterogeneity, segmentation, and lack of unity found within the field as a whole' (p. 111). Additionally, the boundaries of journalism are fluid, overlap with other professions, and are prone to challenges from new technology. Consequently, even if a degree of professionalism is admitted, tension forms over who qualifies as a *professional* journalist.

Zelizer (1993: 219) sets aside professionalism to present journalists as an 'interpretive community, united through its shared discourse and collective interpretations of key public events'. Such a view de-emphasizes formal factors of journalistic identity by stressing cultural factors that create collectivity among journalists. Similarly, '"professional identity" refers to a wider frame of reference—an ideology—not so much carried by the members of a clearly identifiable organization, but rather by an imaginary community, that stretches across organizations' (De Bruin, 2000: 229). This view invokes Anderson's 'imagined community' (1983), wherein group members are brought together through the diffusion of common cultural elements, including a shared history. Key to the journalistic community is a shared sense of purpose that Johnstone et al. (1976: 110) label the 'prominent public service orientation'. This view promotes the social value in collecting, organizing, and disseminating information while avoiding a focus on news as a commercial enterprise (see also Gans, 1979; Kovach and Rosenstiel, 2001; Gardner et al., 2001). This sense of purpose for working journalists extends backward from the present by employing collective memory to celebrate past achievements and provide a continual narrative of journalism's accomplishments.

Collective Memory

Collective memory provides a useful conceptual tool for connecting the construction of the past with authority in the present. Schudson provides a functional definition of collective memory as 'the ways in which group, institutional, and cultural recollections of the past shape people's actions in the present' (1992: 2). The centrality of the present in memory studies can be traced to Halbwachs (1992), who identified notions of the past as constructed to serve contemporary interests. Similarly, Connerton (1989: 3) notes that 'images of the past commonly legitimate a present social order'. This is a self-reinforcing process: collective memory aids in sustaining authority in the present even as the construction of collective memory can only be made legitimate through an act of authority in the present. It is a constant process of reproduction and alteration as authority perpetuates itself through its own narratives that justify that very authority. 'Patterns of authority are worked out in collective memory, where they take on specific preferred forms that are determined by their retellers' (Zelizer, 1992: 3). Importantly, the right to retell is a prerequisite to defining collective memory. Not everyone is in a position to do memory work—varying levels of cultural authority legitimate some voices while excluding many others.

With a lack of formal professional boundaries in journalism, collective memory connects the present with the past to reinforce group beliefs and a shared historical narrative. It plays a crucial role by providing a reminder to the public of the press's triumphs while facilitating discourse among journalists regarding their mission and efficacy. Journalists are able to perpetuate a shared history through actively contributing to the discourse. This has been true for the Kennedy assassination (Zelizer, 1992) and Watergate (Schudson, 1992). Memorializing discourse, the focus here, is a component of collective memory that frequently invokes shared norms and values through a construction of the dead journalist as an embodiment of both history (via her experiences) and norms (realized in the professional response to these experiences). The discourse must be constructed in a way that contemporary journalists are able to identify and connect with the memorialized as an emblematic figure.

With the memorialization of a figure from a past era, collective memory can take the form of nostalgia for the figure as well as for her specific era. As cultural producers, journalists have the ability to invoke what Davis labels 'collective nostalgia' or the

> . . . condition in which the symbolic objects are of a highly public, widely shared, and familiar character, those symbolic resources from the past that under proper conditions can trigger wave upon wave of nostalgic feeling in millions of persons at the same time. (1979: 122)

Nostalgia creates a normative-centered narrative of the past through the strategic activation of particular shared memories (and omission of others). In its construction of an ideal past moment, nostalgia indicts the present as a deviation. From this perspective, nostalgia can be either 'restorative'—aiming to bring again what ostensibly was—or 'reflective'—content with the past as past, even if embellished (Boym, 2001: 41). In the discourse below, journalists often use McGrory and Brinkley as emblems of earlier time periods and lament the distance the field has moved from these models.

The peculiarity of journalism as an institution is that it presents discourse about itself publicly. Certainly, memory work occurs in both formal and informal internal newsroom relations, as well in other quasi-public venues such as journalism classrooms and textbooks. However, journalists produce widely distributed cultural texts in which they grant themselves the right to retell journalism's stories. Through a mediated memorializing, events of the past are reinterpreted in a present with its own context, and therefore its own needs related to authority. Thus, which aspects of a journalist's life come to be remembered and how they are remembered, as well as the converse of which aspects are purposely forgotten and omitted, is of real consequence to the shape of journalistic practice.

McGrory and Brinkley in the Context of Contemporary Discourse on News

Memory work reflects the conditions of the present in its construction of the past. Thus, it is necessary to contextualize the memorialization of McGrory and Brinkley in contemporary discourse on U.S. journalism. The championing of McGrory and Brinkley occurs as journalists are routinely criticized for bias, inaccuracy, careerism, and elitism. The Pew Research Center for the People and the Press reports precipitously declining public trust in media over the past two decades. In 1985, 83 percent of those polled believed either all or most of ABC News, Brinkley's network. In 2004, this number fell to 58 percent. With newspapers, the percentage believing all or most of their local paper dropped from 80 percent in 1985 to 50 percent in 2004. A majority of poll respondents—53 percent—'often don't trust what news organizations are saying' (Pew Research Center, 2004). This decline occurs amidst public assaults on the news media from groups with a diverse range of motivations. It also comes following a broad reduction in newsroom resources and staff sizes as managers look to maintain profits in the midst of shrinking audiences and erratic advertising revenues.

Criticisms of the news media flow from disparate quarters, including from the right's assertion of liberal bias, chronicled in Bernard Goldberg's *Bias* (2001) and Ann Coulter's *Slander* (2003). The left has responded with a critique of the press as conservative minded and reinforcing of inequalities, including Eric Alterman's *What Liberal Media?* (2003), as well as with a critique of ownership structures and growing commercialization. Meanwhile, the explosion of Internet news sites complicates the boundaries differentiating journalists from nonjournalists. The growing influence of blogs prompts a discussion on their relationship with established journalism and whether bloggers should be considered journalists or whether the concept of a journalist and the norms of journalism should expand to meet them (Smolkin, 2004). A final—and less ideological—strand of critique centers on the violations of trust as famously perpetrated by Jayson Blair with *The New York Times,* Jack Kelley with *USA Today,* and Stephen Glass with the *New Republic.* These highly publicized cases foreground the issue of trust placed in journalists to deliver accurate representations of the world.

This context of technological change, declining trust, and contestation of authority frames the two case studies of this article: David Brinkley, who died 13 June 2003 at the age of 82, and Mary McGrory, who died 22 April 2004, at the age of 85. McGrory and Brinkley share a number of traits: both lived to be octogenarians and continued to work late in their lives. Both were associated with political coverage and Washington journalism. Both gained recognition working for one outlet and then eschewed retirement with a lateral move in 1981 *(Washington Star* to *Washington Post* and NBC to ABC, respectively). Additionally, their careers as major journalistic figures overlap considerably: McGrory from 1954 to 2003, Brinkley from 1956 to 1996. Conversely, three key differences separate them. First, they worked in different media: Brinkley in network television news and McGrory in newspapers. Second, with regard to gender, McGrory was remembered as a pioneering woman in the male- centric newspaper business while Brinkley belonged to the then exclusively male fraternity of network news anchors. The third difference is the divide between Brinkley as an anchor (with its attendant norms of detached neutrality) and McGrory as a left-leaning columnist. The similarities permit us to look across the memorializing discourse for commonalities while simultaneously noting divergences emerging from their differences. The following sections trace the coverage of the deaths of McGrory and Brinkley along several dimensions of memorialization.

Specified Traits of McGrory and Brinkley

McGrory was widely associated with a persistence in going out in the field to get a story—a norm central to reporters and not regularly associated with columnists. However, in most of the obituaries, McGrory is acknowledged on some level for her insistence at bearing witness in person, as in a *Washington Post* editorial:

> From the Army-McCarthy hearings to the approach of the Iraq war, she found it her good fortune to be able to get out and see the city's principal actors in the flesh, to take in the grand scenes that are staged here almost daily, to observe and weigh and assess and do the drama justice. (*Washington Post,* 2004)

The value of getting out from behind one's desk reinforces the idea of the ever-present reporter fulfilling her role as the Fourth Estate rather than relying on press releases or the reporting of others—even as a columnist not conventionally bound by reporting norms. The value of first-hand reporting was made even more salient in the *Washington Post* a few days later: 'To do this job right, you must speak truth to power; you must name and blame the bad guys; you must get out of the office, as she did far more than reporters one-quarter her age' (Fisher, 2004). Bearing witness is presented as absolutely intrinsic to the central normative role of journalism as a check on power and the discourse represents McGrory as the literal presence of the press in holding leaders accountable.

Recognition as a pioneer for her gender was a second widely addressed dimension of McGrory memorializing. The discourse on gender often emerged in explicit ways. The *Washington Post* began a story on her life with: 'Mary McGrory, a great writer, an abundant soul and a hell of a gal' (Von Drehle, 2004). On the NBC morning news program *The Today Show,* Willard Scott described McGrory as 'A real princess in the journalism world. One of the great newspaper ladies', to which anchor Katie Couric remarked, 'Had the pleasure of meeting her several times and she was quite a lady' (*The Today Show,* 2004). When discussing McGrory's gender, a contrast was often made between femininity (presented as a usual female trait) and tenacity (presented as an unusual female trait). Thus, *Newsweek* magazine referred to her as 'Part her ladyship, part street fighter' (Thomas, 2004). Instead of being incongruent opposites, the feminine/tenacious dichotomy functioned advantageously: 'It was always a treat to watch Mary McGrory buttonhole a lawmaker or cabinet secretary in a Washington corridor and present a punishing question or two in her disarmingly sweet way' (Clines, 2004). The contrast of femininity and tenacity manifested itself when McGrory traveled. Her determination to bear witness informed her tenacity, yet she would insist that male journalists carry her bags and open doors. National Public Radio's Scott Simon, himself a McGrory porter, notes: 'You could stock a Journalism Hall of Fame with the people who had once carried Mary's luggage' (*Weekend Edition Saturday,* 2004). In these discussions, gender is inextricably bound up in McGrory's professional identity: she is independent and demanding of others while maintaining an old-fashioned sense of decorum. Her femininity is central to understanding her as a successful journalist in an industry dominated by men. Rather than overcoming the male-centric newsroom, McGrory remained an aberration, using her gender to succeed as a journalist. Similarly, McGrory's particular writing style was singled out as having feminized qualities.

Brinkley's most recognized trait as a journalist was his presentational style. He was admired for writing his own scripts, which he meticulously edited to suit his staccato speaking style. Former CBS news anchor Dan Rather contrasts Brinkley with other broadcast journalists: 'David, unlike a lot of people in television then and now, wrote a great deal of his own material' *(Larry King Live,* 2003). Brinkley's ABC colleague Sam Donaldson compares his style with Lincoln: 'I think he was the Abraham Lincoln of our day . . . Brinkley knew how to take simple words, short declarative sentences and go to the main line and he'd entertain us all' (*Special Report with Brit Hume,* 2003). Brinkley is positioned as a skilled, witty writer—in contrast to the image of news anchors as simply attractive readers.

Memory work around Brinkley is made more difficult by a pair of controversies at the end of his life. First, during ABC's Election Night coverage in 1996, Brinkley referred to the newly re-elected President Clinton as a 'bore' on the air, expediting his retirement. In 1998, Brinkley became the spokesperson for Archer Daniels Midland (ADM), which was recovering from a price-fixing scandal. The commercials ran during his former show, *This Week,* sparking criticism from many journalists, including Walter Cronkite, that Brinkley behaved inappropriately. Daniel Schorr responded harshly: 'What is money in this stage of my life, and in this stage of David's life? I frankly cannot understand it. He is a role model for young people. I was dismayed and shocked' (quoted in Kurtz, 1998). Columnist Maureen Dowd wrote about 'David Brinkley's sad transformation from revered to skuzzy' (Dowd, 1998). Five years later, some of the same journalists provided positive assessments following Brinkley's death. Many articles mentioned the gaffe about Clinton while fewer mentioned the controversy over ADM. While these incidents stand as blemishes and make it more difficult to present Brinkley as a journalistic model, they do not negate the importance associated with Brinkley throughout the discourse.

Constructing and Contextualizing Influence

Beyond listing recurring traits, the discourse around McGrory and Brinkley locates their achievements within a framework that interprets their importance to journalism. In this way, the traits above are meant to resonate and inform journalistic norms that exist independently of a temporal context. Brinkley was consistently presented in the memorializing discourse as a formative figure—a 'pioneer'—of television journalism. The Associated Press noted Brinkley's humility over this role:

> David Brinkley always downplayed his pioneering role in TV news, insisting, 'I didn't create anything. I just got here early.' But during a half-century on the air, he helped write the rules of TV journalism while becoming one of its biggest stars. (Moore, 2003a)

Instead of a focus on the collaborative nature of journalism institutions, Brinkley is considered a creator of the television news, as by NBC News's Tim Russert:

> So if you step back and look at *one person* inventing the nightly news, bringing forth a new form of campaign convention coverage and re-inventing Sunday morning, what a legacy. (*Capital Report,* 2003, emphasis added)

Brinkley was also contextualized as belonging to a bygone era of influential network news: 'In their heyday, Huntley and Brinkley were simply bigger than anyone who occupies an anchor chair today' (*Nightline,* 2003), and 'It was an era in which network television enjoyed a hold on public attention it no longer possesses' (Cooper, 2003). Brinkley is cast as the ideal of television journalism, and therefore as an object of reverence. Bob Schieffer on the political talk show *CBS Sunday Morning* placed Brinkley in the broadcast news pantheon: 'First there was Ed Murrow, who invented broadcast journalism, Walter Cronkite, who gave it credibility, and David, who gave it style, wit and grace' (*Sunday Morning,* 2003). Occasionally, Brinkley was described in parental language—for example, as the 'father of the modern television newscast' (*US News and World Report,* 2003).

Brinkley is also regarded as a cultural icon. Many articles referred to a 1965 poll showing Brinkley to be more recognized than John Wayne or the Beatles. His cultural role was evident in mentions of the Huntley–Brinkley Report signoff—'Good night, David, good night, Chet'—as a widely recognized and mimicked slogan. At least 25 news stories used the expression 'Good night, David' at some point in the text or headline. In a nostalgic tone, Cokie Roberts recalls the impact of the *Huntley–Brinkley Report:*

> Our families would wait for it to come on at night. We'd sit around the television set. It really defined the news for a whole generation of Americans. And we learned what to think from them, what was going on in the world from them, and David Brinkley understood that. (*Morning Edition,* 2003)

Roberts presents Brinkley as responsible provider of social cohesion, albeit from a past era. Rather than viewing journalism as detached, the cultural resonance of the *Huntley–Brinkley Report* reflects the reality of news as a mass event, experienced simultaneously by millions. The evocation of the ritualized farewell highlights news as cultural performance. With Brinkley, journalistic authority arises out of repetitive rituals in news presentation.

For McGrory, emphasis was also placed on contextualizing her as an influential figure—an object of reverence. Because of the nature of newspapers, McGrory did not enjoy the cultural stature Brinkley possessed, which required her role to be defined to a potentially unfamiliar audience. The Associated Press explicitly noted her influential status:

> A tireless reporter well into her 80s, McGrory was a *revered and influential figure in journalism.* Her career spanned five decades, from the McCarthy era of 1950s [*sic*] to the Iraq war last year. (Kerr, 2004, emphasis added)

The language is unequivocal and explicit in signaling McGrory's importance. Such an opening orients the reader as it makes its argument for this reverence and influence. On CNN, her *Washington Post* colleague Dana Bash offered a short message: 'There was a lot of respect for her as a journalist, as a writer, and as somebody who was an institution in Washington' (*On the Story,* 2004). McGrory is remembered most for winning a Pulitzer Prize for her *Washington Star* columns on the Watergate scandal and the twin acknowledgment of being on President Richard Nixon's 'enemies list'—two items connecting her to the purported paragon of U.S. journalistic success, Watergate (see Schudson, 1992).

When discussing the careers of McGrory and Brinkley, memorializers used memorable news stories as markers of occupational duration. These extraordinary stories displaced quotidian news work, and the importance of the memorialized subjects is bolstered by having been central to the telling of multiple major events that spanned generations. For example, *Time* magazine's economical capsule obituary of McGrory relies primarily on big events:

> DIED. MARY McGRORY, 85, liberal, no-nonsense columnist for the *Washington Star* and *Washington Post* whose career stretched from the 1954 Army-McCarthy hearings to last year's Iraq war; in Washington. She wrote eloquently of President Kennedy's assassination ('Write short sentences in the presence of great grief,' she said) and won a Pulitzer Prize in 1974 for her columns on Watergate—which had already earned her a spot on President Nixon's notorious enemies list. (August et al., 2004)

In the space of 72 words, the obituary evokes a series of major stories as a means of conveying a 49-year career. Similarly for Brinkley, the *Denver Post* offers an example:

> Name almost any major news event in the second half of the 20th century, and you know that David Brinkley brought the story into America's living rooms. JFK's assassination. The Vietnam War. The murders of Robert Kennedy and Martin Luther King Jr. The first human steps on the moon. The Kent State shootings. Watergate. The Reagan era. The first Gulf War. The Clinton years. (*Denver Post,* 2003)

This excerpt illustrates another point: journalists become enmeshed with the memory of the stories that they cover. As an anchor, Brinkley had the responsibility of relaying events that entered both into history and into the culture's collective memory. His role in delivering these events weaves Brinkley in with their narratives.

Agents of Memorializing

The agents of memorialization called upon to speak to the importance of the news work or personal traits of the memorialized subjects (or a combination) take on a double role of constructing the memorialized subject as an elite figure while affirming, through their authority to speak, their own status as elite figures and authorities. While memorialized and the memorializer can be synchronous contemporaries, such as when Walter Cronkite comments on David Brinkley, because both McGrory and Brinkley lived to be in their 80s, memorializers are more often either younger journalists who worked with them or working journalists who felt influenced. Frequently, memorializers occupy comparable positions, such as Dan Rather or *New York Times* columnist Maureen Dowd. For example, former ABC news anchor Peter Jennings reinforces his position as heir to a tradition fostered by Brinkley by describing their relationship as having 'father-son qualities to it' (quoted in Bark, 2003). Jennings also invokes the patriarchal qualities of network news anchors. In a *New York Times Magazine* piece, Maureen Dowd recalls the impact McGrory had on her career: 'I first realized that writing a column could be a good gig when I saw all the cute guys clustered around Mary McGrory's desk in the back of *The Washington Star* newsroom' (Dowd, 2004). Dowd credits McGrory as a model columnist while also recognizing their feminine kinship in male-dominated Washington reporting.

Agents of memorialization can also be the subjects of journalism: politicians and celebrities. ABC's *This Week* memorialized Brinkley with a montage of old tape interspliced with remembrances from Newt Gingrich, Bob Dole, Ted Kennedy, Kweisi Mfume, Donald Rumsfeld, Jesse Jackson, Rudolph Giuliani, Alan Greenspan, and John McCain. These guests displayed reverence at being interviewed by Brinkley. Former senator Bob Dole recalled, 'When I was on David Brinkley's show, I felt like I had really, really arrived' (*This Week,* 2003). The use of non-journalists as agents of memorializing reinforces the mutual dependence between journalists and elite sources that especially marks Washington journalism. Senator Ted Kennedy demonstrated the overlapping nature of collective memory by recounting the admiration of John Kennedy and Robert Kennedy for Brinkley. In a double act of memory work, Kennedy evokes his familial history while adding to the collective memory of Brinkley. His position at the nexus between the two allows him the authority to speak for and about the deceased, which underscores the agency involved in the construction of collective memory.

Contrast With the Present

The narratives arising in the memorializing discourse can be contextualized by their relationship to the contemporary news media environment. Many articles on McGrory and Brinkley contrasted a declining state of journalism with the integrity of the deceased. Shrinking audiences, declining trust, fabrication scandals, economic constraints, and competition from new media were all concerns for journalism at the time of McGrory's and Brinkley's deaths. McGrory died the same week that Karen Jurgensen, executive editor of *USA Today,* resigned over the scandal caused by reporter Jack Kelley's fabrications. Brinkley's death came less than two weeks after the resignations of *New York Times* editor Howell Raines and managing editor Gerald Boyd in the wake of the Jayson Blair scandal.

Emphasis was placed on McGrory's work ethic—defined by her propensity for getting out of the office—as divergent from contemporary punditry. Columnist Mark Shields said: 'She was never a pundit, she was a reporter who pounded the pavement, haunted the halls of Congress, and instead of private lunches with cabinet secretaries, Mary McGrory interviewed ordinary Americans' (*Capital Gang,* 2004). Elsewhere: 'McGrory didn't pontificate, she worked, unlike studio-addicted Washington, D.C., pundits' (Connelly, 2004). McGrory's work ethic functions dually as a timeless journalistic norm and as a timely counter to pundits and high-profile fabrication scandals. The situating of McGrory as a model against contemporary transgressions promotes an individualized response as a means to repair journalism rather than a broader examination and alteration of journalistic practices. In this view, good journalism comes from good journalists and the inverse stems from individuals deviating from the norms. This view persisted throughout the discourse as other writers situated McGrory and contemporary scandals as models, respectively, of the highs and lows of the profession. On CNN, anchor Aaron Brown made this contrast explicit in a conversation with Bob Woodward:

> [T]his has been a tough time for the craft of journalism in some respects. Scandal at *New York Times* over Jayson Blair, at *USA Today* over star reporter Jack Kelley have [*sic*] been painful. It is therefore good to remind the world of journalism and you too that we are not simply the Blairs and the Kelleys. There are also the Mary McGrorys. (*Newsnight with Aaron Brown,* 2004)

Again, journalism's problems are situated as individualistic rather than systemic. Similarly, *Boston Globe* columnist Thomas Oliphant countered newspaper editors' attempts to 'focus on process as their salvation' in light of publicized scandals and budgetary stress by endorsing McGrory as a model: 'Mary's uniquely influential, rich life—based not on her ideology, by the way, but on her integrity—would have been a more useful object of contemplation' (Oliphant, 2004). To fix journalism's problems, Oliphant argues, journalists should rely on individualized emulation.

Despite the proximity of Brinkley's death to the resignations of Raines and Boyd, the memorializing discourse touched less often on journalistic scandal. One exception was *USA Today* (pre-Kelley scandal), which contextualized Brinkley's death in light of declining trust similar to the above assessments accompanying McGrory's death:

> Brinkley's death comes at a time of loud lamentations and sad-eyed self-assessment in the news business. The shameless fabrications of Jayson Blair at the *New York*

> *Times* inevitably call into question the central tenet of journalism: an unswerving commitment to truth. (Shapiro, 2003)

Associated Press writer Frasier Moore used Brinkley as a contrast to the competition over access to Jessica Lynch, the Army private captured by Iraqis and later rescued in an initially misreported story (see Project for Excellence in Journalism, 2003):

> There's a certain irony to this journalistic gold rush, considering the recent death of David Brinkley at age 82. A founding father of TV journalism, Brinkley was memorialized by every news outlet for embodying the highest standards of the profession he helped invent. (Moore, 2003b)

In *The New York Times,* media writer Bill Carter used the occasion of Brinkley's death to enter into a discussion of the end of the 'anchor era' and the waning importance of network news in the contemporary media environment (Carter, 2003). Several journalists took a nostalgic turn by contrasting Brinkley's appearance and manner with the norm as it has developed over time: 'We're also mourning the passing of an era when journalistic savvy and experience meant more than square-jawed, pretty-boy good looks' (Dawidziak, 2003). Critic Tom Shales wrote: 'The qualities Brinkley embodied, though, are not exactly prized in broadcast journalism today. They belong to a more civilized, less frenzied time' (Shales, 2003).

The most often discussed contrast between the work of Brinkley and the contemporary state of broadcast journalism centers on the increase in volume and contestation in television discourse—a contrast between Brinkley and the 'blabbermouth age' in media critic Howard Kurtz's words (*Reliable Sources,* 2003). Columnist and former Brinkley colleague George Will makes the contrast explicit: 'Long before high-decibel, lowbrow cable shout-a-thons made the phrase "gentleman broadcaster" seem oxymoronic, Brinkley made it his business to demonstrate the compatibility of toughness and civility in journalism' (Will, 2003). Brinkley is transformed into the archetype for discussion-based broadcast journalist, but in a nostalgic manner unfamiliar to contemporary broadcast journalism. On CNN, Aaron Brown lauds Brinkley's manner for its combination of style and effectiveness:

> So much of TV has become about volume, who talks the loudest or is the most outrageous. Mr. Brinkley was the mirror opposite. In a soft voice and with just a few words he could make the larger, more important point than all the shouters and the screamers combined. (*Newsnight with Aaron Brown,* 2003)

Fox News talk show host Bill O'Reilly counters the above assessment in a column that praises Brinkley for his career before positioning his reporting style as antiquated in a critique of contemporary broadcast news:

> Thus, the good old days when the Brinkleys, the Cronkites and even Tom, Dan and Peter could simply introduce stories in measured tones are coming to an end. The audience for dispassionate TV news is shrinking; the demand for passionate reporting and analysis is on the rise. (O'Reilly, 2003)

O'Reilly's memory work around Brinkley presents Brinkley as worthy of respect but also as outdated, which reduces the contemporary usefulness of Brinkley as a journalistic model. McGrory and Brinkley can only be recognized as models if the norms and practices they represent are viewed as timeless—otherwise they become historical rather than pertinent or useful.

Conclusion

Externally, declines in both audiences and credibility combine to signal a decrease in journalistic authority while, internally, journalists face reductions in newsgathering resources, the uncertainties of changing ownership patterns, and a growing imperative toward greater convergence across media. Additionally, the ambiguity of journalism as a profession results in contention over the borders between journalism and non-journalism. In the face of these challenges, Gardner et al. (2001) find optimism among journalists in their linking of the past with a continuity that informs the pertinence of journalism's role and values:

> When journalists look to the future, they see no miracles, but many believe that good work in their domain will prevail. They have faith that, with persistence and consciously wrought strategies, the domain of journalism will *return to its traditional high standards,* promoting truth and freedom for an open society, despite all current temptations and pressures toward corruption of its noble mission. (p. 204, emphasis added)

The use of the word 'return' in this passage suggests a narrative that glorifies past journalistic practice, even if this is nostalgia for a past that may bear little resemblance to journalism as it has actually been practiced. Journalism has continually struggled over sensationalism and the quality of its practice of veridical representation (see Stephens, 1988). This return, then, is not to an actual practice or an environment, but to a normative construct. On the occasion of the death of an eminent journalist, these normative attributes find their grounding in an interpretation of the individual as an embodiment of these elusive norms and values.

By presenting the deceased as models, the memorializing discourse examined above possesses an instrumental function for working journalists. The collective memory of journalistic accomplishment creates bonds of purpose, reinforces norms, and creates models for emulation through constructing, supporting, and recalling a recognized tradition of journalistic success and its intrinsic role in society's functioning. Memorializing also works to secure the boundaries between journalist and non-journalist through a focus on the value of journalistic success and the cultural role of elite journalists. McGrory and Brinkley come to represent the heights of the profession, and, in doing so, the discourse promotes an individualistic rather than systemic approach to addressing journalism's ills. In this view, improvement stems from the emulation of timeless model journalists rather than a broader re-evaluation of contemporary journalistic norms and practices.

Yet memorializing discourse extends beyond its subject to speak about the state of contemporary journalism. Journalists reiterate and interpret the careers of their deceased colleagues, but they also create representations of journalism in the present. With McGrory and Brinkley, the discourse engendered discussion of general trends (e.g., the ascension of punditry on television) and specific occurrences (e.g., the Jayson Blair scandal). The connection to the present transforms the memorializing discourse from a theoretical or historical undertaking to a response by working journalists to the material conditions of practicing contemporary journalism. This is the performative aspect of journalistic reaffirmation—through discursive acts, journalists publicly construct and signal their allegiance to a shared normative narrative of what journalism ought to be.

In the space of the news product, journalists retell and construct their own story. By tapping into the cultural resonance of journalism through the evocation of past journalistic successes, memorializing discourse seeks to strengthen the cultural place of contemporary journalism with its audience. McGrory and Brinkley are touted as admirable, which produces an inference that journalism itself deserves respect. The discourse serves a 'double duty by re-affirming professional ideology in both the mind of society and in the minds of journalists who belong to and believe *in* that professional culture' (Berkowitz, 2000: 125). McGrory and Brinkley not only stand out as models for journalists but also act as models of journalism at a time of diminishing trust in the journalistic product.

Memorializing discourse, which acts on the collective memory of journalism, is, in the end, an attempt to bolster the cultural authority journalists possess. In the face of contemporary challenges—some continual and some emergent—journalists may look to the past to find ways to talk about themselves in the present.

Note

1. Brinkley co-anchored the *Huntley—Brinkley Report,* the nightly newscast on the NBC network, from 1956 to 1970 and continued to work for NBC through the 1970s. In 1981, he became host of the Sunday morning political talk show *This Week* on the ABC network until his retirement in 1996. McGrory served as a political columnist in Washington, DC, for the *Washington Star* from 1954 until the paper closed in 1981. She then became a *Washington Post* columnist until a stroke ended her career in March 2003. McGrory received a Pulitzer Prize in 1975 for her columns on the Watergate Scandal and the resignation of President Nixon.

References

Anderson, B. (1983) *Imagined Communities.* New York: Verso.

August, M. et al. (2004) 'Milestones', *Time,* 3 May, p. 20.

Bark, E. (2003) 'TV News Veteran David Brinkley Dies at 82', *Dallas Morning News,* 13 June.

Bennett, W. L., L. Gresssett and W. Haltom (1985) 'Repairing the News: A Case Study of the News Paradigm', *Journal of Communication* 35(1): 50–68.

Berkowitz, D. (2000) 'Doing Double Duty: Paradigm Repair and the Princess Diana What-a-story', *Journalism* 1(2): 125–43.

Boym, S. (2001) *The Future of Nostalgia.* New York: Basic Books.

Capital Gang (2004) CNN, 24 April.

Capital Report (2003) CNBC, 12 June.

Carter, B. (2003) 'Don't Call it Gravitas; David Brinkley was a Brand unto Himself', *New York Times,* 15 June, p. D3.

Clines, F. (2004) 'A Singular Voice from Washington', *New York Times,* 23 April: A22.

Connelly, J. (2004) 'Bushies' Ad Buy Hints at State's Value in Campaign', *Seattle Post-Intelligencer,* 26 April, p. A2.

Connerton, P. (1989) *How Societies Remember.* Cambridge: Cambridge University Press.

Cooper, R. (2003) 'David Brinkley 1920–2003', *Los Angeles Times,* 13 June, p. A1.

Davis, F. (1979) *Yearning for Yesterday: A Sociolgy of Nostalgia.* New York: The Free Press.

Dawidziak, M. (2003) 'Goodnight, David: Giant among TV Journalists, Brinkley would not be Hired Today', *Cleveland Plain Dealer,* 13 June, p. A1.

De Bruin, M. (2000) 'Gender, Organizational and Professional Identities in Journalism', *Journalism* 1(2): 217–38.

Denver Post (2003) 'Editorial: David Brinkley, 1920–2003', 13 June: B6.

Dowd, M. (1998) 'Good Night, David', *New York Times,* 7 January, p. A19.

Dowd, M. (2004) 'A Star Columnist', *New York Times Magazine,* 26 December: 30.

Eason, D. (1988) 'On Journalistic Authority: The Janet Cooke Scandal', in J. Carey (ed.) Media, Myths, *and Narratives: Television and* the *Press,* pp. 205–27. Newbury Park, CA: Sage.

Fisher, M. (2004) 'Honored to Have Known Mary McGrory', *Washington Post,* 27 April: B1.

Gans, H. (1979) *Deciding What's News.* New York: Vintage.

Gardner, H., M. Csikszentmihalyi and W. Damon (2001) *Good Work: When Excellence and Ethics Meet.* New York: Basic Books.

Halbwachs, M. (1992) *On Collective Memory,* trans. by Lewis Coser. Chicago, IL: University of Chicago Press.

Hindman, E. B. (2005) 'Jayson Blair, *The New York Times,* and Paradigm Repair', *Journal of Communication* 55(2): 225–41.

Johnstone, J., E. Slawski and W. Bowman (1976) *The News People: A Sociological Portrait of American Journalists and Their Work.* Urbana: University of Illinois Press.

Kerr, J. (2004) 'Columnist McGrory Won Pulitzer during Watergate', *Milwaukee Journal Sentinel,* 23 April: 9B.

Kovach, B. and T. Rosenstiel (2001) *The Elements of Journalism.* New York: Three Rivers Press.

Kurtz, H. (1998) 'A Tough Sell for David Brinkley; Colleagues Are Uneasy with Ex-Newsman's Enterprising Role', *Washington Post,* 8 January: B1.

Larry King Live (2003) CNN, 12 June.

Manoff, R. and M. Schudson (1986) *Reading the News.* New York: Pantheon.

Moore, F. (2003a) 'Retired TV Newsman Brinkley Dies at 82', *Associated Press Newswires,* 13 June.

Moore, F. (2003b) 'TV News in an Age of Big Media: Just Viewer Come-ons?', *Associated Press Newswires,* 26 June.

Morning Edition (2003) National Public Radio, 12 June.

Newsnight with Aaron Brown (2003) CNN, 12 June.

Newsnight with Aaron Brown (2004) CNN, 22 April.

Nightline (2003) ABC, 12 June.

Oliphant, T. (2004) 'A Journalist's Truth and Beauty', *Boston Globe,* 25 April: D2.

On the Story (2004) CNN, 24 April.

O'Reilly, B. (2003) 'Brinkley's Style Old News Nowadays', *Chicago Sun-Times,* 24 June: 27.

Pew Research Center (2004) 'News Audiences Increasingly Politicized', URL (consulted August 2005): http://peoplepress.org/reports/display.php3?ReportlD=215

Project for Excellence in Journalism (2003) 'Jessica Lynch: Media Myth-Making in the Iraq War', URL (consulted August 2005): http://www.journalism.org/resources/research/reports/war/postwar/lynch.asp

Reese, S. (1990) 'The News Paradigm and the Ideology of Objectivity: A Socialist at the *Wall Street Journal', Critical Studies in Mass Communication* 7: 390–409.

Reliable Sources (2003) CNN, 15 June.

Schudson, M. (1992) *Watergate in American Memory.* New York: Basic Books.

Shales, T. (2003) 'Good Night, David: America's Solid Anchor', *Washington Post,* 13 June: C1.

Shapiro, W. (2003) '"Twinkley" Brinkley a Sad Loss for News, Politics', *USA Today,* 13 June: A6.

Singer, J. (2003) 'Who Are These Guys? The Online Challenge to the Notion of Journalistic Professionalism', *Journalism* 4(2): 139–63.

Smolkin, R. (2004) 'The Expanding Blogosphere', *American Journalism Review,* June/July: 38–43.

Special Report with Brit Hume (2003) Fox News Channel, 12 June.

Stephens, M. (1988) *A History of News.* New York: Penguin.

Sunday Morning (2003) CBS, 15 June.

The Today Show (2004) NBC, 24 April.

This Week (2003) ABC, 15 June.

Thomas, E. (2004) 'Transitions', *Newsweek,* 3 May: 10.

Tunstall, J. (1971) *Journalists at Work.* Beverly Hills, CA: Sage.

US News and World Report (2003) 'Good Night, David', 23 June: 3.

Von Drehle, D. (2004) 'The Pointed Pen of Mary McGrory', *Washington Post,* 23 April: C1.

Washington Post (2004) 'Mary McGrory', 23 April: A22.

Weaver, D. and C. Wilhoit (1986) *The American Journalist.* Bloomington: Indiana University Press.

Weekend Edition Saturday (2004) National Public Radio, 24 April.

Will, G. (2003) 'Journalism's Gentleman Giant', *The Washington Post,* 13 June: A29.

Zelizer, B. (1992) *Covering the Body: The Kennedy Assassination, the Media and the Shaping of Collective Memory.* Chicago, IL: University of Chicago Press.

Zelizer, B. (1993) 'Journalists as Interpretive Communities', *Critical Studies in Mass Communications* 10: 219–37.

23

Memory Studies

"We Were All There": Remembering America in the Anniversary Coverage of Hurricane Katrina

Sue Robinson

In late August 2005, Hurricane Katrina destroyed New Orleans, a catastrophe exacerbated by inadequate federal, state and local response. The press descended upon that south-eastern city, braving fetid conditions, calling officials to task and organizing fund-raisers. In the days that followed, the media promptly named itself the hero of the entire crisis (Fry, 2006). Soon after, however, the news organizations pulled their reporters from the cities, only returning to do the occasional story about recovery progress (Donze, 2006; Grace, 2006; Kurtz, 2006). The press came under attack for abandoning the city as it turned its attention to the budding presidential campaigns and continuing Iraqi war. When the press did check in, it was accused of 'missing the "real" story' (Heitman, 2006). That is, until the anniversary of the terrible hurricane approached. In late August 2006, the press once again took up its post in New Orleans, and began the process of turning the event into collective memory.

Collective memory making is a ritual of the press that has been well documented by scholars of journalism (Davis, 1988; Kammen, 1993; Kitch, 2005; Schudson, 1992; Zelizer, 1992). These first anniversaries correct and solidify the prior year's first drafting of the nation's history writing according to present-day situations. In commemorating, the press (re)establishes itself as an American institution with the authority to tell society about itself (Davis, 1988; Zelizer, 1992). With the chaos of the event behind them, journalists seek to separate reality from illusion and contemplate the lessons learned (Kammen, 1993). Davis suggested that such events are meant to reassure society that our 'human institutions within the flow of time are permanent' (Davis, 1988: 134). But what happens when our societal institutions such as the government and the press are still failing in their roles a year after the initial chaos? What form can the re-remembering take? The study of this coverage in a dozen mainstream outlets as well as six books written by national and local journalists explored how the press overcame criticisms of abandonment in the past year, and whether the anniversary reporting followed the 'typical' commemorative patterns that journalism historians have described.

The findings in this article suggest a template for the collective memory that will endure about Hurricane Katrina and the devastation of New Orleans. The journalism provided an arena for an institutional power stand-off between government, the press and the community of New Orleans. The press seized the opportunity to contrast itself with the government, which failed the public in this crisis. Nationally, the press demonized New Orleans as an example of what the country needed to avoid—politically, economically, structurally, morally. Locally, the press did not set agendas, but rather focused on the importance of ritual in re-creating a lost community. Instead of creating a mnemonic quagmire, though, these seemingly disparate national and local narratives depoliticized and then repoliticized Hurricane Katrina memory in a way that restored a certain faith in American redemption, collectively, at a time of national unrest.

Beyond the specific case of this disaster, this study also offers an opportunity to document how collective memory is formed according to national ideals and local interests. Such research exemplifies the tension between dominant institutions, how authority is asserted and the process by which all of this plays out in the press.

Meaning Making for America's Institutions

The press has evolved into one of America's political institutions with the authority to tell people about their worlds (Cook, 1998; Schudson, 1995; Sparrow, 1999; Zelizer, 1990). Their standardized news stories tend to reaffirm the existing institutions, including government, school, the Church and the press according to society's political hierarchy of power relations (Cook, 1998). Scholars have also acknowledged that the rituals of newsgathering and then news consuming help in the 'creation, representation, and celebration of shared even if illusory beliefs' (Carey, 1992 [1989]:43). Together, journalists exercise an interpretive community through reflexivity and repair-work in news stories; their stories tend to mirror each other, rendering a cultural practice that creates and perpetuates a continually evolving societal identity for America (Bennett et al., 1985; Zelizer, 1997 [1993]). All of this is done through source selection, story placement, word choice, visual effects, tone, labeling, amount of exposure, nuance and innuendo (Parenti, 1993).

Ultimately, the stories of any particular issue, taken together, help people decide what to think about (Cohen, 1963) and set an agenda for society politically, economically, culturally, socially and even individually (McCombs and Shaw, 1972). News coverage helps resolve ambiguity in people's lives and functions as a part of their institutional foundation (Ball-Rokeach and DeFleur, 1976; Cook, 1998; Sparrow, 1999). In academic literature, journalists have been dubbed the nation's storytellers, amateur psychologists, patriots, shapers of events, soothsayers, watchdogs and custodians of fact (Bird and Dardenne, 1988; Jamieson and Waldman, 2001; Zelizer, 2005).

Memory of Crisis in American News Media

When a crisis happens in America, these standardized practices of the press are engaged (Tuchman, 1997 [1973]). In some ways this has meant that journalists lose perspective and 'can't see the crisis for all the crises' (Maher and Chiasson Jr, 1995: 221). The implicit role for the press is as much to stabilize society in the wake of crisis as it is to report on it:

> While we think of the press as geared to crisis and sensationalism, often its task is just the opposite, dedicated to the graying of reality blurring popular grievances and social inequities. In this muted media reality, those who raise their voices too

> strongly against the bland tide can be made to sound quite shrill. (Parenti, 1993: 203)

When the crisis becomes problematic for the power elite, these officials try to spin the information or otherwise engage in 'redressive actions' that redirect the story frame (Turner, 1975: 39–41).

When the anniversary of these crises approaches, the press begins a process of re-remembering (Edy, 1999; Sturken, 1997). This is done largely through a ritualized narratizing (Edy, 1999; Kitch, 2005; Lambeck and Antze, 1996; Schudson, 1992; Zelizer, 1992). 'Through acts of memory, (people) strive to render their lives in meaningful terms. This entails connecting the parts into a more or less unified narrative in which they identify with various narrative types—hero, survivor, victim, guilty perpetrator, etc.' (Lambeck and Antze, 1996: xviii). Lambeck and Antze were referring to how people reconstruct memories with psychologists and for historians, but the same holds true for journalists (Edy, 1999; Kitch, 2005; Zelizer, 1992). In this process, only a fraction of the event is remembered, and it is done so in a political or at least a hegemonic way (Pennebaker, 1997; Sturken, 1997). This narrative is meant to help people move forward, by reformulating the past according to present culture in a way that will anticipate the challenges ahead (Archibald, 2002; Halbwachs, 1992; Rosenzweig and Thelen, 1998; Sturken, 1997).

Scholars have argued that bringing up the past is sometimes a way of avoiding the blame or accountability for current atrocities. It is a way of keeping the current societal machine functioning *sans* chaos. Thus, these tales of the past are also 'framed' in that they call on past and current symbols, metaphors and images to reflect the crisis in a way that offers redemption and hope—or at the very least, explanation (Schwartz, 1998). For example, Carolyn Kitch (2005) documented how the heroic firefighter came to symbolize American resurrection in the aftermath of the September 11, 2001, terrorist attacks. The juxtaposition of the heroic, honorable firemen with stories of the (politically problematic) Iraq War in American magazines justified a contemporary crisis.

A Study of Hurricane Katrina

When Hurricane Katrina hit, killing some 1,500 people, researchers found that mainstream journalism rushed to reassure people that societal institutions such as government, the Church, or the press, were intact (Kitch and Hume, 2008). For example, Meehan (2006) found a certain 'rational religiosity' permeated coverage of Bush's visits to Katrina shelters, where the president was cast as the shepherd or savior to the flocks seeking comfort from a higher power. In other scholarship on Katrina, the press was found to have portrayed itself as heroic (Fry, 2006) and as authoritative (Littlefield and Quenette, 2007). But by August 2006, the city remained a pit of despair, with criticism being levied at both the government and the media. The moment of the crisis had yet to pass, though the moment of the first anniversary—traditionally a time to reconfigure the meaning of that crisis—was at hand. This dichotomy offered a chance to explore memory making during a particularly challenging situation. This article sought to explore the ultimate lessons of Hurricane Katrina, the resilience of stumbling institutions, and the press' role in memory construction of a particularly ambiguous crisis—one that called into question American strength and competence.

Informed by the literature review, the following research questions guided the study: (1) What were the collective memories of Hurricane Katrina a year after the event? (2) What role did the press play in the formation of the collective memory, particularly in relation to America's other institutions? (3) What were the agendas posed in this collective memory for society to stabilize and move forward, if there were any? After a preliminary analysis revealed distinct differences between local and national collective memories, a final research question was added to nuance the discussion: (4) How did local reporters write about this anniversary differently from national journalists?

The sample for this article comprised both national and local news coverage of the first anniversary of Hurricane Katrina between 24 August 2006 and 10 September 2006: Anniversary articles in CNN, National Public Radio, *The New York Times, USA Today, The Los Angeles Times, Time Magazine, Newsweek, US News & World Report, The Times-Picayune,* and New Orleans television stations WWLTV, and WDSU—in all, about 200 news articles, video and radio broadcast stories. In addition, the sample included six journalist-generated anniversary publications. Three of the books were authored by national reporters (*Dallas Morning News,* 2006; CNN, 2006; *Time Magazine,* 2006), and three by local reporters (*The Times-Picayune* Staff, 2006; Horne, 2006; McQuaid and Schleifstein, 2006).

The study entailed textual analysis, which reveals the social production of meaning and the strategic discourse. The method focuses on the representations captured in the words, visuals, sounds or other media elements that form the text. Within textual analysis, researchers employ narrative analysis to uncover structures and themes. The main goal is to discover all the possible interpretations of the text's meaning for society at large. In narrative analyses of the news, researchers have defined common themes (i.e., Lule, 2001), identified sources of credibility (i.e., Zelizer, 1992) and connected the journalistic narrative with cultural trends (i.e., Kitch, 2005).

Specifically, this research followed Gamson and Lasch's understanding that news coverage represents a signature matrix. 'The idea elements in a culture do not exist in isolation but are grouped into more of less harmonious clusters or interpretive packages', explained Gamson and Lasch (1983: 198). The idea elements for Gamson and Lasch and for this article included:

- Metaphors/catchphrases/imagery: How was the information relayed and characterized? For example, 'Helluva job, Brownie' politicized the anniversary because it evokes the ironic praise of the President to the director of the botched emergency response to the catastrophe. An image of a 'flag' symbolizes patriotism; an image of 'Jesus' indicated rebirth or sacrifice.
- Past/present exemplars: A 9/11 terrorist attack reference connected the natural disaster with a man-made one that led the nation into war.
- Character depictions: What sources were included? How active/passive were they? What did they say?
- Roots: Inferences about the cause of the hurricane such as the 'sins of New Orleans'.
- Consequences: Inferences about the results of policy or action taken; what blueprint for the future is implied?
- Appeals to principle: Values in the narrative such as faith in God or American ingenuity.

The resulting matrixes composed a meta-discourse of the anniversary coverage as well as a blueprint for how collective memory is formed. Each sample story was read through three times: once to distinguish the main theme according to the matrix, once to discern the role of the press as an institution in the narrative and once to note the local or national agenda being proposed. The next three sections of this article reveal the results of these analyses as answers to the research questions; the overall signature matrix is depicted as a table in the conclusion.

Katrina's Collective Memories: 'The Storm That Changed America'

The ultimate memory that tends to endure after a specific tragedy or crisis is colored by the politics of the current era and its culture, as well as the particular social group performing the remembering (Halbwachs, 1992; Kitch, 2005; Sturken,

1997; Zelizer, 1992). The overall story arising from the anniversary coverage was reflective of American values such as determinism and pluck. In all, the analysis uncovered 18 different themes, including 'rebirth,' 'politics,' and 'ritualization.' Many of the themes present in the Hurricane Katrina anniversary coverage related to Gans's (1979) categories of American values such as individual ingenuity, democracy and responsible capitalism, as in this *US News & World Report* article: 'If there's anything that's come out of this whole enterprise that has major significance, it's this whole concept of democratic process and self-determination' (Mulrine, 2006: 44). Strong themes throughout the coverage included that the individual American embodies the power to control his or her own fate.

> You know; it's beyond humbling just to know that we really do live in the greatest country in the world . . . we don't need the government to step in and do that—I mean we do need certain aspects of their help, but that at the grass roots level, you know, we get our hands and knees dirty and we do it. (Simon, 2006)

Here, the press substitutes a concept—that of American ingenuity—for an institution that failed—the government. Retelling individual survival stories was ubiquitous (CNN, 2006; *The Times-Picayune* Staff, 2006). *Newsweek* tracked down baby Faith Figueroa, who had been on the 19 September 2005 cover, and recorded her celebrating her second birthday with a cake and two lit candles:

> Starting anew: Tiny Faith Figueroa was on our Sept. 19, 2005 cover, her tears a reminder of the suffering endured by so many . . . When we found them again, Faith was back home in the Ninth Ward, in time to celebrate her second birthday. (Thomas et al., 2006: 35)

Faith's story represents the narrative of all survivors: it matters that her name is Faith, and that she is a child growing up and 'starting anew'. This form of ritual reflects the third stage of the grief process described by researcher Carolyn Kitch (2003): society reminds itself what is most important in the wake of tragedy and renews its faith in age-old values. Little Faith is a symbol of this opportunity for redemption by her perseverance—a major theme in both sets of coverage.

Indeed, it was the people (of New Orleans, of America) who formed an institution that worked effectively and in an orderly way. One iconic image of the tragedy exemplified this point as it appeared over and over in the anniversary coverage: The feet of Jeremiah Ward, shod with makeshift shoes made from two cigar boxes that read 'Keep Moving' (*Dallas Morning News,* 2006: 37). This photo depicted the narrative symbolism of the collective memory being constructed here: (1) The plight of the people reflected by the bare, dirty feet; (2) the ingenuity needed to resolve the situation; and, finally, (3) the ironic message to the country to 'keep moving,' despite inadequate support. Several stories explained how to prepare for the next hurricane in a way that highlighted the American characteristic to survive (Grissett, 2006). Over and over, the press assured its audiences that the American community would step in when other institutions failed: 'Still other campaigns were the work of outsiders, many with religious affiliations, who assembled civilian armies to feed and clothe countless hurricane victims . . .' (Krupa, 2006). In this article, the reporter even likened individuals to 'armies'—a word connoting an institutional machine, a tool for the country's power.

But local and national reporters differed in the way they presented their ideas of community and America. Note the disparate emphasis as depicted in the bar graph in Figure 1 comparing local and national themes in the anniversary coverage.

The national press suggested that New Orleans represented America, as in the *Time Magazine* book titled *The Storm that Changed America:* 'When Hurricane Katrina came to the city of Fat Tuesday on a stormy Monday morning, it attacked not just homes and buildings: it also attacked an idea of a city that is deeply rooted in America's history and culture' *(Time Magazine,*

2006: 32). And yet this and other national accounts actively distanced New Orleans and what was happening there from the rest of the country. The people of New Orleans should never have built there in the first place (Thomas et al., 2006); they were not adequately prepared with flood insurance or escape routes (Ripley, 2006). The national press implied that New Orleans did not measure up to the American ideal:

> The crisis in New Orleans has now been reduced to a matter of government financing for rebuilding homes while reviving the business community. But the real rebuilding project on the Gulf Coast requires bringing new energy to confronting the poverty of spirit. Because that's what was tearing down the city, long before Hurricane Katrina. (Williams, 2006)

Indeed, many national stories portrayed New Orleans as a problem child whose morals had long been decaying (Konigsmark, 2006; *Time Magazine,* 2006). This mirrored Jack Lule's 2001 cataloguing of the 'flood' narrative, in which the press helps its audience find some reason for the catastrophe, usually in the form of a scapegoat, in order to make sense of the incomprehensible. Reporters writing for national press used words such as 'you' to refer to New Orleans, rather than the 'us' and 'we' found in coverage of other national atrocities, such as 9/11 (Kitch, 2005).

Instead, the national press used the anniversary as a way to politicize what happened in order to discuss current political affairs (Kornblut and Nossiter, 2006; Nossiter, 2006b; Rich 2006). In these stories, the press was the watchdog, separating reality from illusion (Gordon, 2006c; Jackson, 2006); 23 percent of the national stories contained this theme compared to 6 percent of local stories:

> Mr. Mayor, everyone has been watching you over the course of the last three days. I'm no exception . . . You've talked about being ready and prepared if another hurricane comes through. But it seems to me, even looking at it from its most optimistic point, it's hard to believe that you'd be ready for yet another hurricane with the devastation you've suffered. (Gordon, 2006c)

This resulted in the construction of two stories: the political one and the 'real' one, according to the press. 'President Bush travels to the Gulf Coast this week, ostensibly to mark the first anniversary of Hurricane Katrina. Everyone knows his real mission: to try to make us forget the first anniversary of the downfall of his presidency' (Rich, 2006: 10). Another story combined politics with the ritual of the anniversary:

> As bells rang out through the streets, citizens gathered for prayer services and residents hung banners in front of their tattered homes to commemorate the anniversary of the storm, Mr. Bush sought to do what he had not accomplished a year earlier: Demonstrate his depth of understanding about the emotional and physical toll Katrina took on New Orleans. (Kornblut and Nossiter, 2006: 1)

When people were quoted as refusing to participate in the official commemoration ceremonies, the reporters framed their choice as a political one (Chadwick and Brand, 2006; Lipton, 2006). Reporters cued readers with metaphors and exemplars when a political re-remembering was at hand: 'Illuminated by lights fit for a Hollywood movie set, President Bush stood in New Orleans' Jackson Square on Sept. 15 and tried to reassure Americans that the darkened and flood-ravaged city would be saved' ('Or help the nation's poor,' 2006). Another reporter discussed the importance of uncovering the 'full picture' of the tragedy:

> As we look back a year later . . . news accounts don't always give you the full picture, and I think at some point people were of the belief that New Orleans was making a comeback . . . often when you see these

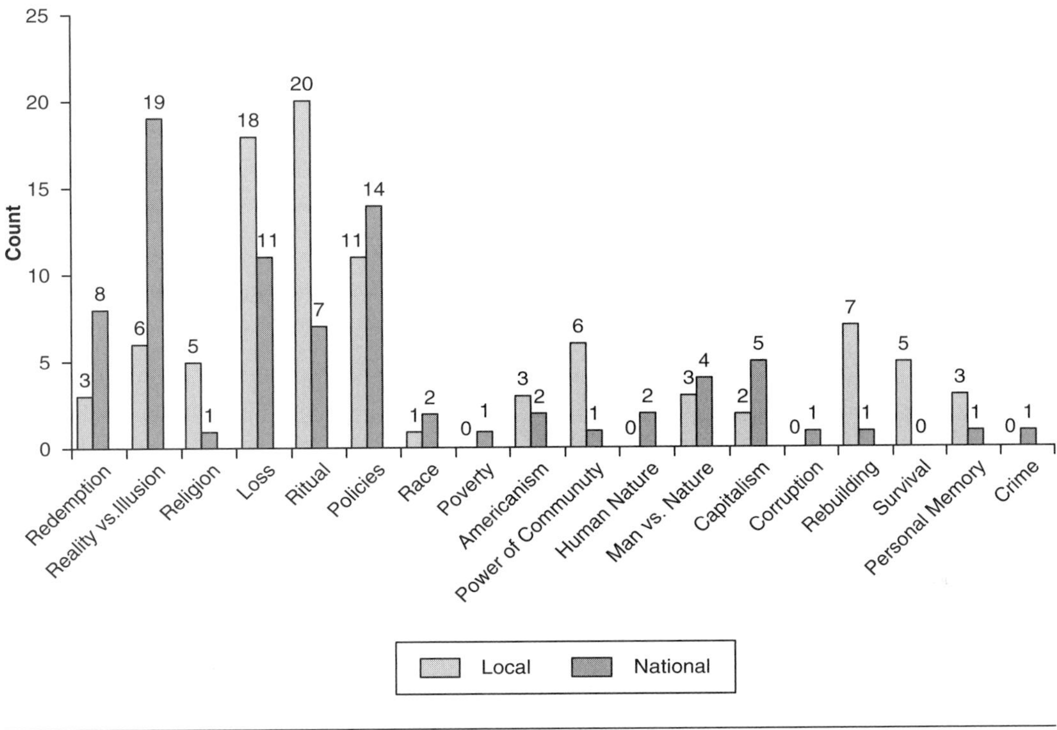

Figure 1 Katrina anniversary themes: national vs. local coverage.

Stories contained multiple themes/agendas, and were counted as such.

> little 10-second snippets, you see the best of New Orleans, but there is still a lot of work to do. (Gordon, 2006a)

At first, it appears that the press is undermining its own coverage by suggesting that the news accounts do not reflect reality. In actuality, though, CNN Anchor Ed Gordon was reminding the public that the very purpose of anniversary coverage is to show the real story. Thus, the piece served to reinforce the notion that the system polices itself.

Reality versus illusion was also a significant theme of the local anniversary coverage, but New Orleans's writers steered clear of political memory making for the most part (Pope, 2006). Local reporters dedicated much more space and time to the content of the rituals than they did national political situations (21 percent versus 12 percent). Decisions to stay away from the formal commemorative events were characterized as a way to mourn privately or to rebuild (Nolan, 2006). They named the dead, for example, and recorded specific personal memories of loved ones. A *Times-Picayune* story used the anniversary to say 'thank you' (Wolfram, 2006). The local anniversary coverage contained more references to God: 'Others rest on blind faith, refusing to believe the place they call home will die in the face of adversity. 'God wouldn't destroy what he intends on restoring" (Lee, 2006a). The local coverage used the musical heritage of New Orleans to create new rituals within the journalism, as in these WSDU videos called 'Katrina Songs by Kids' (Allen, 2006) and 'Song for New Orleans' (WDSU, 2006a).

In another difference, the local press rejected the national press's evocation of 9/11 terrorist attacks and the Iraq War. For example, several nationally published articles made note of how many New Orleans guardsmen were unavailable to help in the recovery process because they are were in Iraq (Gordon, 2006b; *Time Magazine,* 2006); yet not one local story in this sample mentioned the lack of guardsmen. Instead, the local press addressed negative impressions of the city, its people, its looters, its wayward police officers and its actions a year prior. The pillaging, read one article, 'could be forgiven, only more so as the week dragged on without the federal government figuring out how to mount an effective relief effort' (*The Times-Picayune* Staff, 2006: 63). Police officers who had been accused of abandoning their posts were given a chance to explain themselves (Lee, 2006b; Moran, 2006). Even the rapists at the convention center were given a pass: 'The men driven to rape were themselves victims of the chaos in which the whole city found itself . . . They were not the monsters of depravity evoked in media accounts' (Horne, 2006: 116). Such stories reminded people that New Orleans was worth saving, but also that the institutions consisted of 'real' people.

Such declarations shifted the discussion of the hurricane, and repositioned memory of the crisis toward resolving the uncertainty and fear that came with the government's inadequacy.

The Role of the Press: 'The Important Thing Here Was to Tell the Story'

In a time of crisis, the press is meant to resolve ambiguity (Ball-Rokeach and DeFleur, 1976); a year later, its job as a key witness is to help the nation process its grief in a way that allows the country to move forward (Carlson, 2007; Kitch, 2003; Zelizer, 1992). The anniversary coverage of Hurricane Katrina followed similar patterns, despite the fact that media faced accusations of abandoning their posts in the intervening months.

In this Katrina anniversary coverage, reporters became the mediators of the remembering—a reflection of Kitch's concept of news coverage as the grieving process itself: 'You wake up in the morning and I used to just read the comics in the newspaper. Now I run out to see what the front page news is' (Elliott, 2006). Anniversary stories embodied the ritual: WWL-TV published 750 names of people whose deaths were attributed to Hurricane Katrina. In this National Public Radio interview, a man expressed an intensely private piece of information something he refused to share with any friend—in a radio broadcast: 'Staying up there, laying on the concrete, many nights I cried. I didn't let nobody see me cry, but it was nothing nice' (Elliott, 2006). In this way, people seemed to consider the press as a national 'counselor' for that which could not be endured alone. These findings demonstrate how the press had become an integral, internalized part of the commemorating process for these citizens.

But even within these depictions of the press as an institutional champion, there were differences between local and national narrative roles. The national press used self-reflexivity to remind people that it had been a witness to the crisis (Kurtz, 2006; Leibovich, 2006; Lukas, 2006; Stanley, 2006). 'If you had been with us in the Superdome, Matt', the anchor of *The NBC Nightiy News* replied, 'this would be your cause' (Stanley, 2006: 19). This provided a sense that the press was qualified to tell this story. Other reporters portrayed themselves as impartial yet caring helpers whose gumption would bring people the story. 'One of my cameramen has worked with a broken foot since 9:00 o'clock this morning to try to get this story to you' (Cooper, 2006b). And, later in the same anniversary special: 'They'd come up to you, begging to use your cell phone, your satellite phone . . . We tried to give it to as many people as possible' (Cooper, 2006b). In these pieces, the reporters made themselves out to be omniscient narrators and rescuers from the outside world—in contrast to the 'victims' of the hurricane who had to wait for somebody else to help them (O'Brien et al., 2006).

Meanwhile, the local press actively positioned itself as a member of the New Orleans community (51 percent of the local stories depicted reporters as either witnesses, heroes or victims, compared to

33 percent in the national coverage). On the anniversary, WDSU (2006b) published interviews with the reporters who covered the tragedy, confiding in a darkened room, crying and relating personal anecdotes of their own losses. They expressed pride at helping to save lives. They discussed rebuilding. These journalists transformed into New Orleans citizens first, simultaneously heroes (in need of praise) and victims (in need of therapy) (Hoss, 2006). In these local reports, coverage of Katrina's anniversary was not a 'cause' so much as a therapeutic exercise. These reporters struggled in a very public way to explain the tragedy (Arredondo, 2006):

> The journalists who covered Katrina and who wrote, illustrated and created this book are better chroniclers for having experienced the tragedy firsthand, for having seen the devastation in their own homes and neighborhoods. Though impassioned, they have never lost sight of the facts. They vigilantly debunked myths and exaggerations about New Orleans after the storm. They investigated the causes of the levee failures, a civil engineering disgrace of historic dimension. And they have made themselves experts in explaining the complexity of our reordered world. (*The Times-Picayune* Staff, 2006: 1)

Journalists found meaning from within the institution of the press—which did not falter in the face of chaos (CNN, 2006; *The Dallas Morning News,* 2006; Horne, 2006; *Time Magazine,* 2006; *The Times-Picayune* Staff, 2006).

In both sets of coverage, reporters were able to repair the impression that they had abandoned the city during the previous year. They wanted to prove to people that they had returned (as opposed to the government) (Gold, 2006; Thomas et al., 2006). Their absence in the previous months was explained in terms of keeping their audiences' attention (Kurtz, 2006). The lesson of this tragedy's anniversary for Americans is that the press can be relied on in times of crisis: 'Soledad, tonight a year since Katrina, trailers wasted, deadlines unmet, money unspent or misspent and promises not kept. Still, we're keeping them honest, looking for progress' (Cooper, 2006a). Reporters had to reiterate that their role was to reassure people not only that society's core values remained intact, but also that the press is pivotal in keeping them as such

> What happened in New Orleans last year was that rare event in which truth outstripped human imagination, a clear before and after in the ongoing story of a great American city, an event that gave every New Orleanian a story, a thread in our common narrative . . . A disaster is a story, the editors tell us, one that inspires different narratives—narratives of resilience, redemptive narratives, occasionally toxic narratives. (Larson, 2006)

In other words, the press will always be there to tell the story that matters, this last quote implied. 'People will tell and retell their story now and in the years to come. 'Where were you? Did you leave? Did you stay? What happened?' The important thing here was to tell the story' (Kemp, 2006).

The Agendas Set: 'We're Basking in Joy, Rebirth and the Future'

Upon reflection of crises, the media strive to craft the story with a beginning, middle and end so that the whole asserts an agenda, reinforces a particular ideological social control and positions coverage of a new story (Altheide, 2002). In all, the coverage contained a dozen different agendas, as laid out in Figure 2, with discernible differences between local and national coverage

The local press reconnected the community of New Orleans by producing morals about the strength of home, family and community identity. (About 33 percent of the local stories asked people only to remember in some manner, and 18 percent contained no discernable agenda whatsoever.) The national press, however, set a political agenda to fix the New Orleans mess—a lesson for the rest of America. (A quarter of the national stories called for federal money to rebuild New Orleans.)

The main goal of the local reporters was not to set agendas, but rather to reconnect people with the community that was New Orleans, and themselves along with it. 'We all have the chance to do it right this time in so many aspects of our personal and community lives' (Farris, 2006). In other stories, the local press concentrated on memory repair. Anniversary stories showed local officials fixing the impressions left from coverage a year prior. For example, police officers held well-publicized ceremonies to honor their ranks, actively downplaying or refuting that some of their ranks had abandoned their post (Moran, 2006; Nolan, 2006). Other stories concentrated on the day's ceremonies, without setting a particular agenda:

> Serio acknowledged the irony of starting the new school year on Katrina's anniversary, and the emotional significance of the date, given the losses endured by many of his students over the past year. 'The hurt is incredible,' he said. 'You cannot help but reflect on a day like this.' School officials planned a Mass in conjunction with the abbey community to recognize the anniversary. But Serio also stressed the need for students to move forward and celebrate the beginning of a new year and a new chapter in Hannan's 20-year history. 'We're not basking in hurt,' he said. 'We're basking in joy, rebirth and the future . . . They're not thinking about the hurricane anymore.' (Hurwitz, 2006)

In one story, the anniversary rituals were likened to a 'day-long funeral' (Chapple, 2006). All of these stories served to counter national coverage that New Orleans was somehow lost: 'Set against the backdrop of Hurricane Katrina', went one promotion for a local television station's video on the hurricane, 'these one-of-a-kind specials reveal how everyday people responded gallantly and heroically in the midst of one of the worst natural disasters in American history. Their sense of loss gave birth to a new sense of community and a renewed feeling of hope. In the face of overwhelming odds, New Orleans prevailed' (WSDU, 2006a).

As in past atrocities (Sturken, 1997; Zelizer, 1992), the national press vowed to 'never forget' (Cooper, 2006b). The anniversary was a time to remind people of American character in the face of adversity:

> Part three, that's the story that isn't finished yet. What's going to happen to this city? We're going to rebuild . . . We will survive. I know that, but we need to do more than that. We need to go back to living with faith, and with hope. (Cooper, 2006b)

And though the remembrances of Katrina were political in nature for the national press, the agendas tended to be individually focused except for when they were discussing other parts of the country that were vulnerable.

> As Amanda Ripley writes in her investigation of America's curious and dangerous reluctance to prepare for the next disaster, the question a year after Katrina is not who will save us the next time but how will we save ourselves . . . But it turns out in times of crisis, our greatest enemy is rarely the storm, the quake or the storm itself. More often, it is ourselves. (Ripley, 2006: 51, 56, 57)

Those who do not prepare, who dismiss faith, who lose their American spirit or forget their American values, open themselves up to such devastation—or so the coverage went.

CONCLUSION

In the end, the story did not appear to be about a storm that changed America, as that *Time Magazine* book title *Hurricane Katrina: The storm that changed America* proclaimed. The national press discussed politics, capitalism, and how other American cities (and politicians) could

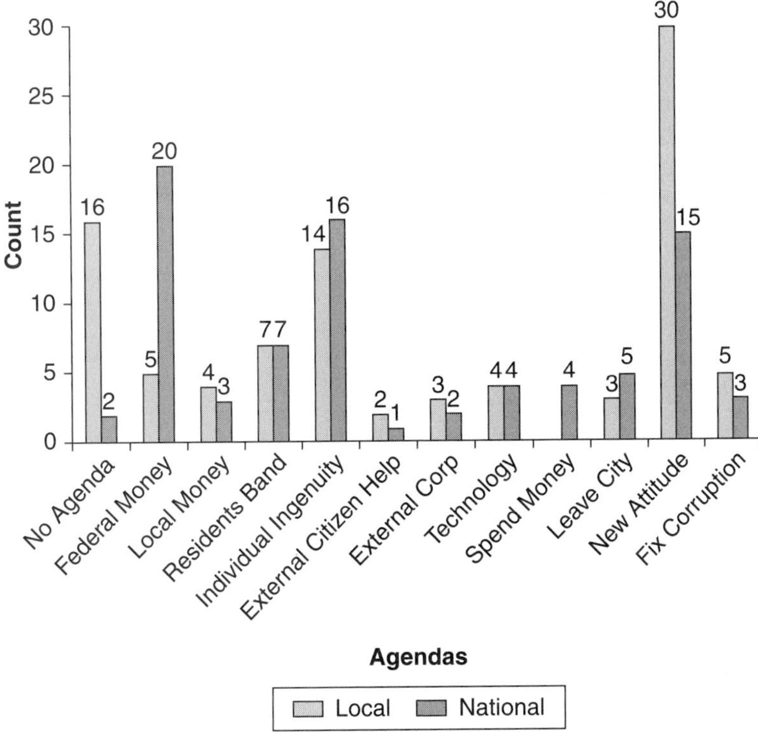

Figure 2 Katrina anniversary agendas: national vs. local coverage: Stories contained multiple themes/agendas, and were counted as such.

avoid being a New Orleans (CNN, 2006; *The Dallas Morning News,* 2006; Nossiter, 2006a; *Time Magazine,* 2006). But for the local press, the collective memory was much more about the community of New Orleans and the loss of home and identity (Horne, 2006; McQuaid and Schleifstein, 2006; *The Times-Picayune* Staff, 2006). Table 1 lays out the resulting signature matrix from these different findings

But just as interesting as these differences were the similarities. Neither set of coverage addressed race or poverty (despite the predictions that these issues would garner a national spotlight) in any in-depth manner (Kurtz, 2006). Instead, the coverage in this sample emphasized the steadfast belief in America's righteousness and its ability to conquer even nature while reaffirming very traditionalistic notions of the nation's dominant institutions and the power of individual ingenuity and community.

In doing this, this research showed that even within a situation as problematic as Katrina, news coverage of anniversaries help construct a collective memory that will benefit society in some way. For the local press, this active memory repair reconnected New Orleans to the people and its press, giving reason to rebuild. For the national press, the country learned political and patriotic lessons from a city scapegoat. Both ways of remembering reconfigured the crisis according to the present needs of the communities. Of course, these separate aims created a tension between the national and local coverage, where the former sacrificed New Orleans for the greater national stability, and the latter stubbornly clung to life by advocating its worthiness for salvation. Here,

American values of responsible capitalism and democratic, institutional ideals sparred with equally strong American characteristics of ingenuity, community and individuality.

And yet, taken collectively, the sample indicates an adhesion to the nation's entrenched institutions. For example, the press promoted the community—either American or New Orleans specifically, depending on the audience—or itself in place of the failed government. Past scholarship has found that journalists become self-reflexive as one method to 'bolster the cultural authority journalists possess. In the face of contemporary challenges . . . journalists may look to the past to find ways to talk about themselves in the present' (Carlson, 2007: 180). In this case study, nationally, journalists touted their watchdog skills, reminding the world that a press is essential to crisis recovery. Locally, reporters assumed an integral role in commemorative rituals and modeled their own recovery as an exemplar for communal behavior. These substitutions encouraged audiences to resolve any feelings of ambiguity or uncertainty arising from a year of institutional failings. This specific memory reconstruction came at a time of general unrest in America, embattled with the Iraq War and a diminishing reputation for competence around the world. This examination of a specific collective memory formation demonstrates that even in the wake of a disaster that uncovered massive institutional inadequacies, the press works actively to reconstruct stability, even using itself as the frame so that the power hierarchies of America remain intact. Thus, this storm, this case study suggests, did not change America much at all (in contradiction to that *Time Magazine* (2006) book title).

Table 1 Katrina's Signature Matrix

Idea Elements	Local Coverage	National Coverage
Metaphors/catchphrases	'We will rebuild'	'Helluva Job, Brownie'
Exemplars	Past destructive hurricanes	9/11 terrorist attack
Character depictions	Individual heroes/victims; gov. workers are individuals too	N.O. is scapegoat; gov. is villain
Roots (of hurricane)	Mother Nature	Incompetence of N.O., Gov.
Consequences	Community is resurrected	N.O. dies without America's help
Appeals to principle	God, faith, individual ingenuity	Patriotism, democracy rules
Main themes	Ritual, loss, rebuilding	Politics, loss, capitalism
Press role	N.O. resident; counselor	Watchdog
Main agendas set	Rebuild	Federal gov. should step in

It should be noted that this study lacked generalizability across other anniversary coverage if only because of the extraordinary nature of Hurricane Katrina. However, both sets of memory construction nationally and locally offered a glimpse of how America will remember Hurricane Katrina—at least in the present. 'We were all there. Because of a revitalized press that allowed us to be, we were there' (CNN, 2006: 173). And 'being there' meant citizens could survive and be redeemed together using the institutions of the world they had built, with the press as their leader—or at least so the story went. It would be interesting to revisit the Hurricane Katrina memories at the five-year anniversary to see whether the overall story has changed in the press as societal conditions have changed (including the very role of the press with new technologies). A scholar might nuance this research by examining the audience reaction to these stories—particularly the portrayal of both government and the press—especially as new tragedies call upon the lessons from Hurricane Katrina, which may well become an exemplar of its own accord.

Acknowledgments

The author extends her gratitude to the editors, the anonymous reviews and Dr. Hemant Shah of the University of Wisconsin–Madison for their suggestions for this article.

References

Allen, H. (2006) 'Katrina songs by kids' (video), 29 August, WDSU.

Altheide, D. (2002) *Creating Fear: News and the Construction of Crisis.* New York: Aldine De Gruyter.

Archibald, R. (2002) 'A personal History of Memory', in J. J. Climo and M. G. Cattell (eds.) *Social Memory and History: Anthropological Perspectives,* pp. 65–80. Walnut Creek, CA: Aha Mija Press.

Arredondo, C. (2006) 'Arredondo: Personnel Shortage, Katrina SENT WEATHER DEPT. SCURRYING' (transcript), 27 August, WWL-TV.

Ball-Rokeach, S. J., and M.L. DeFleur (1976) 'A dependency Model or Mass-media Effects', *Communication Research* 3: 3–21.

Bennett, L., L.A. Gressett and W. Haltom(1 985) 'Repairing the News: A Case Study of the News Paradigm', *Journal of Communication* 35(2): 50–68.

Bird, E., and R.W. Dardenne (1988) *Myth, Chronicle and Story,* in J. W. Carey (ed.) *Media, Myths and Narratives: Television and the Press, pp.* 67–86. London: Sage.

Carey, J. (1992 [1989]) *Communication as Culture.* New York: Routledge.

Carlson, M. (2007) 'Making Memories Matter: Journalistic Authority and the Memorializing Discourse around Mary McGrory and David Brinkley', *Journalism* 8 (2): 165–83.

Chadwick, A. and A. Brand (2006) 'New Orleans Readies for a Somber Anniversary' (transcript), *Day to Day,* 24 August. National Public Radio.

Chapple, C. (2006) 'A Day to Remember: Parish Events Mark Katrina Anniversary', *The Times-Picayune,* 30 August, p. A1.

CNN (2006) *Katrina: State of Emergency.* Kansas City: Andrews McMeel Publishing.

Cohen, B. (1963) *The Press and Foreign Policy.* Princeton, NJ: Princeton University Press.

Cook, T. (1998) *Governing with the News: The News Media as a Political Institution.* Chicago: University of Chicago.

Cooper, A. (2006a) 'Katrina Victims Still Cutting Through Red Tape' (transcript), 28 August, CNN.

Cooper, A. (2006b) 'One Year Later: Dispatches from Katrina' (transcript), 28 August, CNN.

Davis, S. (1988) '"Set your Mood to Patriotic": History as Televised Special Event', *Radical History Event 42:* 122–43.

Donze, F. (2006) 'Mayor Soaks up Media Spotlight: Gaffes No Bigger, but Stage Is', *The Times-Picayune,* 30 August, p. A1.

Edy, J. A. (1999) 'Journalistic Uses of Collective Memory', *Journal of Communication,* Spring: 71–85.

Elliott, D. (2006) 'Katrina Victims Still Struggling to Find Way Home' (Transcript), *All Things Considered,* 27 August, National Public Radio.

Farris, M. (2006) 'Farris: An Open Letter to Those Whose Lives have been Turned Upside Down' (transcript), 27 August, WWLTV.

Fry, K. (2006) 'Hero for New Orleans, Hero for the Nation', *Space and Culture* 9(1): 83–5.

Gamson, W. A. and K. Lasch (1983) 'The Political Culture of Social Welfare Policy', in SE. Spiro (ed.) *Evaluating the Welfare State,* pp. 397–415. New York: Academic Press.

Gans, H. J. (1979) *Deciding What's News: A Study of* CBS Evening News, NBC Nightly News, Newsweek *and* Time. New York: Vintage Books.

Gold, M. (2006) 'After the Storm; Katrina left Brian Williams Shaken but Defined his Role as Anchor', *The Los Angeles Times,* 29 August, p. E1.

Gordon, E. (2006a) 'Politics and Automakers, Black Dads at School' (transcript), *News and Notes,* 28 August. National Public Radio.

Gordon, E. (2006b) 'Rebuilding New Orleans' (transcript), *News and Notes with Ed Gordon,* 28 August. National Public Radio.

Gordon, E. (2006c) 'A Conversation with Mayor Ray Nagin' (transcript), *News and Notes with Ed Gordon,* 29 August. National Public Radio.

Grace, S. (2006) 'Beyond Aug. 29', *Times-Picayune,* 24 August, p. A7.

Grissett, S. (2006) 'Safety Must Come First, Panel Urges: Levees "Urgent Call to Action" Presented', *Times-Picayune,* 26 August, p. A1.

Halbwachs, M. (1992) *On Collective Memory.* Chicago: University of Chicago Press.

Heitman, D. (2006) 'The Media's Post-Katrina Flaw: Boredom', *The Christian Science Monitor,* 29 August, p. A9.

Horne, J. (2006) *Breach of Faith: Hurricane Katrina and the Near Death of a Great American City.* New York: Random House.

Hoss, M. (2006) 'Hoss: MOMENTS of Bravery, Courage' (transcript), 27 August, WWLTV.

Hurwitz, J. (2006) 'Hannan High School Emerges from Ruin: School Marks its First Day at Temporary Location on the North Shore', *Times-Picayune,* 30 August, p. A1.

Jackson, D. (2006) 'Katrina Plan Enacted on Some Fronts, Not on Others', *USA Today,* 28 August, p. A8.

Jamieson K.H. and P. Waldman (2001) *The Press Effect: Politicians, Journalists, and the Stories that Shape the Political World.* Oxford: Oxford University Press.

Kammen, M. (1993) *Mystic Chords of Memory: The Transformation of Tradition in American Culture.* New York: Vintage Books.

Kemp, J. (2006) 'Even Less-afflicted have Stories to Tell', *The Times-Picayune,* 24 August, p. A2.

Kitch, C. (2003) 'Mourning in America: Ritual, Redemption, and Recovery in News Narrative after September 11', *Journalism Studies* 4(2): 213–24.

Kitch, C. (2005) *Pages from the Past: History and Memory in American Magazines.* Chapel Hill, NC: The University of North Carolina.

Kitch, C. and J. Hume (2008) *Journalism in a Culture of Grief.* New York: Routledge.

Konigsmark, A. R. (2006) 'New Orleans' Recovery Slow and Slippery Process; Rebuilding Underway but in the Same Flood-prone Places', *USA Today,* 23 August, p. A1

Kornblut, A. and A. Nossiter (2006) 'Gulf Coast Marks a Year Since Katrina', *The New York Times,* 29 August, p. A1.

Krupa, M. (2006) 'Katrina Generates Wave of Activism: Myriad Groups Aim to Reshape Region', *Times-Picayune,* 27 August, p. A1.

Kurtz, H. (2006) 'Media Returns to New Orleans' (transcript), 3 September, CNN.

Lambeck, M. and P. Antze (1996) 'Introduction', in P. Antze and M. Lambeck (eds) *Tense Past: Cultural essays in trauma and memory,* pp. xi–xxxviii. New York: Routledge.

Larson, S. (2006) 'Wordstorm: Just One Year after the Storm, There Are Already Enough Katrina Pages to Buckle a Bookshelf', *Times-Picayune,* 30 August, p. A1.

Lee, T. (2006a) 'Houston no Substitute for Home', *The Times-Picayune,* 30 August, p. A1.

Lee, T. (2006b) 'Eddie Compass Breaks his Silence', *The Times-Picayune,* 25 August, p. Al.

Leibovich, M. (2006) 'A Punch Line who Refuses to Fade Away', *The New York Times,* 25 August, p. A11.

Lipton, E. (2006) 'Despite Steps, Disaster Planning Still Shows Gaps', *The New York Times,* 25 August, p. A1.

Littlefield, R. S. and A. M. Quenette (2007) 'Crisis Leadership and Hurricane Katrina: The Portrayal of Authority by the Media in Natural Disasters', *Journal of Applied Communication Research* 35(1): 26–47.

Lukas, B. (2006) 'Lukas: Katrina through the Eyes of a Photojournalist' (transcript), 29 August, WWL-TV.

Lule, I. (2001) *Daily News, Eternal Stories: The Mythological Role of Journalism.* New York: Guilford Press.

Maher, M. and L. Chiasson Jr (1995) 'The Press and Crisis: What Have We Learned?', in C. Lloyd Jr (ed.) *The Press in Times of Crisis,* pp. 219–24. London: Greenwood Press.

McCombs, M. and D. L. Shaw (1972) 'The Agenda Setting Function of the Mass Media', *Public Opinion Quarterly* 36(2): 176–87.

McQuaid, J. and M. Schleifstein (2006) *Path of Destruction: The Devastation of New Orleans and the Coming Age of Super storms.* New York: Little Brown and Company.

Meehan, E.R. (2006) 'Sheltering Politics', *Feminist Media Studies* 6(1): 104–9.

Moran, K. (2006) 'Hats Off: Ceremony Pays Tribute to Storm's First Responders', *The Times-Picayune,* 30 August, p. A1.

Mulrine, A. (2006) 'Freret Street Revisited: Throughout New Orleans Residents Band Together to Regroup and Rebuild', *US News & World Report,* 4 September, pp. 38–44.

Nolan, B. (2006) 'Death. Loss. Rebirth. As the Nation Watches, Thousands Mark the Day that Changed Lives', *The Times-Picayune,* 30 August, p. A1.

Nossiter, A. (2006a) 'Anniversary Brings out the Politics of Commemoration', *The New York Times,* 28 August, p. A12.

Nossiter, A. (2006b) 'Bit by Bit, Some Outlines Emerge for a Shaken New Orleans', *The New York Times,* 26 August, p. A1.

O'Brien, M., S. O'Brien, J. Carroll, R. Dornin, C. Myers, A. Velshi, A. Serwer and S. Callebs (2006) 'One Year Later, Katrina Victims Still Cutting Through Red Tape' (transcript), *American Morning,* 28 August, CNN.

'Or Help the Nation's Poor' (2006) *USA Today,* 28 August, p. A14.

Parenti, M. (1993) *Inventing Reality: The Politics of News Media.* New York: St Martin's Press.

Pennebaker, J.W. (1997) 'Introduction', in J. Pennebaker, D. Paez and B. Rime (eds) *Collective Memory of Political Events: Social Psychological Perspectives,* pp. 1–19. Mahwah, NJ: Lawrence Erlbaum Associates.

Pope, J. (2006) 'Leaders Hopeful about Recovery: But Restoring Coast is the Key to Security'. *Times-Picayune,* 29 August, p. A1.

Rich, F. (2006) 'Return to the Scene of the Crime', *The New York Times,* August 27, p. 10.

Ripley, A. (2006) 'Floods, Tornadoes, Hurricanes, Wildfires, Earthquakes . . . Why We Don't Prepare', *Time Magazine,* 26 August, pp. 55–8.

Rosenzweig, R. and D. Thelen (1998) *The Presence of the Past: Popular Uses of History in American Life.* New York: Columbia University Press.

Schudson, M. (1992) *Watergate inAmerican Memory: How We Remember, Forget and Reconstruct the Past.* New York: Basic Books.

Schudson, M. (1995) *The power of News.* Cambridge, MA: Harvard University Press.

Schwartz, B. (1998) 'Frame Images: Towards a Semiotics of Collective Memory', *Semiotica* 121(1/2): 1–40.

Simon, S. (2006) 'Weighing Charity Work in Katrina's Wake' (transcript), *Weekend Edition,* 26 August, National Public Radio.

Sparrow, B.H. (1999) *Uncertain Guardians: The News Media as a Political Institution.* Baltimore, MD: The John Hopkins University Press.

Stanley, A. (2006) 'An Anniversary With Strong Images, Sorrow, Self-Congratulation and Blame', *The New York Times,* 30 August, p. A19.

Sturken, M. (1997) *Tangled Memories: The Vietnam War, the AIDS epidemic, and the Politics of Remembering.* Berkeley, CA: University of California Press.

Thomas, E., J. Darman and S. Childress (2006) 'New Orleans Blues', *Newsweek,* 4 September, pp. 28–38.

The Dallas Morning News (2006) *Eyes of the Storm: Hurricanes Katrina and Rita: The Photographic Story.* Lanham, MD: Taylor Trade Publishing.

Time Magazine (2006) *Hurricane Katrina: The Storm that changed america.* New York: Time Books.

The Times-Picayune Staff (2006) *Katrina: The Ruin and Recovery of New Orleans.* New Orleans: The Times-Picayune.

Tuchman, G. (1997 [1973]) 'Making News by Doing Work: Routinizing the Unexpected', in D. Berkowitz (ed.) *Social Meanings of News: A Text-reader,* pp. 173–92. London: Sage.

Turner, V. (1975) *Dramas, Fields, and Metaphors: Symbolic Action in Human Society.* New York: Cornell University Press.

WDSU (2006a) 'Song for New Orleans' (video), 25 August, WDSU.

WDSU (2006b) 'Duffy Lavigne Rescues People In Plaquemines' (video), 21 August, WDSU.

Williams, J. (2006) 'Getting past Katrina', *The New York Times,* 1 September, A17.

Wolfram, C. (2006) 'Thank-yous Still are Appropriate', *Times-Picayune,* 24 August, p. A2.

Zelizer, B. (1990) 'Achieving Journalistic Authority through Narrative', *Critical Studies in Mass Communication* 7: 366–76.

Zelizer, B. (1992) *Covering the Body: The Kennedy Assassination, the Media, and the Shaping of Collective Memory.* Chicago: University of Chicago Press.

Zelizer, B. (1997 [1993]) 'Journalists as Interpretive Communities', *Critical Studies in Mass Communication* 10: 219–37.

Zelizer, B. (2005) 'Definitions of Journalism', in G. Overholser and K.H. Jamieson (eds.) *The Press,* pp. 66–80. Oxford: Oxford University Press.

Source: From " 'We Were All There': Remembering America in the Anniversary of Hurricane Katrina," 2009, by S. Robinson, *Memory Studies, 2*(2), 235–253. Reprinted by permission of Sage Publications, Ltd.

EPILOGUE

Reflecting on Cultural Meanings of News

This book began with three questions:

- What is news?
- Why does news turn out like it does?
- What does news tell us about the professional culture and the society that produces it?

Throughout the book, the reading selections have provided answers that focus on the third element—culture—while also addressing the first two questions from that perspective. The Introduction offered some ways of thinking about journalism and news, including a table that highlights six key dimensions for understanding research. Each of the parts of readings that followed offered a different answer. In Part I, the quest began with big-picture ideas to build a framework for thinking about journalism through levels of analysis while also introducing the notion that the profession of journalism represents a set of beliefs—a professional ideology—that is mutually agreed upon by those who practice it. Essentially, journalism becomes a culture that shapes news journalists produce. This way of thinking about news moves away from the professional perspective that focuses on norms and judgments about quality and "good" journalistic practice, placing news as a cultural construction instead of a literal rendering of what has happened.

Part II then began to expand on how journalistic culture surfaces through different media and different societies. Part III moved toward a specific perspective on journalistic culture—interpretive community—to show how meanings become shared across journalists, including both the meanings of news and the meanings of *doing* news. Part IV demonstrated how the practice of journalistic culture sometimes goes awry and how journalists and news organizations move to correct understandings about practice and the meanings that are produced. Part V presented an argument that contrasts sharply with beliefs of the professional culture, showing how news narratives represent not something new but a series of old, familiar stories cloaked in new details. Finally, Part VI depicts how news narratives are more than just generic stories but instead are anchored in a collective memory that a culture constructs about itself and its values.

Taken altogether, these parts of readings provide different yet compatible answers to the book's core questions, with culture lying at the center of each. As the Introduction suggested, working with these kinds of answers requires a shift in thinking that moves from the professional to the sociological to the cultural. For somebody coming from the journalistic profession, these kinds of answers might seem difficult to grasp since they are counterintuitive to the professional culture of journalism. At times, these readings might even seem dissonant or wrong because of that clash. In other cases, though, the challenge might come from finding a new answer about news, embracing it, and then moving on to yet another answer that appears equally plausible. Regardless of how you encounter these concepts, the goal is to help think about news from a fresh perspective.

Applying Answers About News Back to News

This Epilogue takes on one last task—to revisit the readings and apply cultural perspectives to examples of news situations.

In June 2009, *The New York Times* published a news item that its reporter, David Rohde, had just escaped along with an Afghani reporter after being kidnapped by the Taliban in Afghanistan seven months earlier ("Times Reporter Escapes," 2009). "Until now, the kidnapping has been kept quiet by The Times and other media organizations out of concern for the men's safety," the newspaper reported. It further turned out that other media organizations had followed suit.

Once the escape story surfaced, media organizations began to offer commentary on the decision to hide the news of Rohde's capture. For example, *Editor & Publisher* (*E&P*) (Mitchell, 2009) stated that at least 40 news outlets knew about the kidnapping but did not report it:

> In fact, what I witnessed in the six months after we found out about it was the most amazing press blackout on a major event that I have ever seen: at least in the case of a story involving such a prominent news outlet and a leading reporter. I wonder how strongly, if at all, this non-reporting will be criticized in the weeks to come.

This *E&P* article went on to mention two other prominent reporters who had been kidnapped in the past, one a *Christian Science Monitor* reporter with the news successfully kept quiet only over a weekend, while a second reporter—Daniel Pearl, who was ultimately beheaded—was also found out quickly. The writer of this *E&P* piece further speculated:

> I wonder now if a great debate will break out over media ethics in not reporting a story involving one of their own when they so eagerly rush out a piece about nearly everything else. I imagine some may claim that the blackout would not have held if a smaller paper, not the mighty *New York Times,* had been involved.

A columnist at Poynter Online (McBride, 2009) went further with criticism, directing comments at *Times* editor Bill Keller:

> The next time you are challenged by a newsworthy kidnapping, I believe you'll put journalism first. You'll return to your role of holding the powerful accountable and

> informing the citizens who count on the *Times* to deliver the most important, accurate stories of the day. And when critics point out the inconsistency, they will accuse *The New York Times* of creating a special standard that applies only to journalists, maybe only to journalists working for the *Times.*

Bloggers were more critical yet in their commentary. "The *Times* has a well-known addiction to double standards," charged one writer (Ambrose, 2009). In an online column titled "What was the real reason for the NYT David Rohde kidnapping news blackout," a writer speculated that the *Times* blackout was a move to keep any potential ransom price low, because publicity of the kidnapping would drive up Rohde's "market value" (Cook, 2009).

This case can be considered through the lens of professional ideology of journalism, in which case the discussion becomes one about ethics. A journalist could ask, for example, if the *Times* acted ethically by hiding the story—would the public's right to know about what had happened supersede the need to protect Rohde's safety? Likewise, did the *Times*' blackout represent a double standard where they likely would have reported on another newspaper's reporter?

But these kinds of ethical questions can also be taken to the cultural dimension. For example, when other media organizations wrote critically on the *Times*' decision, they were really suggesting that the *news paradigm* had been breached. These comments, then, were used to single out the *Times* as behaving inappropriately, thereby suggesting that the rest of the news institution had behaved in a paradigm-appropriate fashion.

Another cultural answer draws on *collective memory,* pointing specifically to how the event had been put into perspective of other Middle East kidnappings. When a writer mentioned other kidnappings of reporters, he called upon society's memory of these occurrences for perspective. Likewise, for journalists, this was a chance to recall an important cultural moment for journalists, performing a professional ritual to demonstrate how journalists put themselves into dangerous situations for the good of the society they serve.

These examples show how the story of Rohde's escape can be examined through multiple lenses. From a professional perspective, the story becomes an ethics discussion. Looking deeper, though, suggests that these ethics concerns grow from the *culture* of journalism, raising concerns about how the paradigm that the culture reveres might have lost credibility because of the *Times*' chosen course of action.

Collective memory serves as a helpful concept for understanding news of Neda Soltan, who was shot and killed in Tehran, Iran, in June 2009 during a rally protesting the outcome of the recent presidential election. Some people in the crowd took cell phone video footage of her last moments of life, which was then spread to Internet sites such as YouTube and picked up by mainstream news media. Some media sources took the opportunity to parallel the video images of Neda to specific events from the past, such as this report from CNN (Ravitz, 2009):

> A 14-year-old girl stoops and screams above the body of a Kent State University student killed in 1970 by an Ohio National Guardsman.
>
> A police chief aims his gun at a Vietcong prisoner's head in 1968, while executing him on a Saigon, Vietnam, street.
>
> And in 1989, an unarmed man in Beijing, China, stands defiantly in front of a column of tanks as they rolled into Tiananmen Square.

These are iconic images, the writer explains, the photographs that signify "rallying cries" for social movements. An AOL Online report made much the same point, bringing up the videotaped beating of black motorist Rodney King by Los Angeles police officers (Varin, 2009). That writer mentioned the Kent State and Tiananmen Square images, too, as well as making mention of President John F. Kennedy's funeral along with the failed iconic image of President George W. Bush standing on an aircraft carrier in front of a banner proclaiming "Mission Accomplished"—far from the reality of the situation in the ongoing Iraq War.

From a conceptual approach, collective memory works for both society and journalists. For *society,* we carry a remembrance of events of the past that helps put a fresh event into perspective of the past. By presenting this perspective in the news, society gains a sense of meaning for the unfolding present. For *journalists,* collective memory serves a dual purpose, at once helping find meaning in a new occurrence while also revisiting the meaning of the journalistic culture that reflects on that culture's high points and sacred moments. For *all,* drawing on collective memory of past news coverage signifies the importance and likely consequence of what has just taken place. Thus, in the case of the shooting of Neda Soltan, collective memory of past events casts the shooting into a story construction that we all can share and make sense of—although it is likely that the cultural contexts of these meanings present a somewhat distorted vision of the outcome.

Toward Future Cultural Meanings of News

This book is not intended to be a comprehensive survey of cultural meanings of news. Instead, the goal has been to identify some key threads in the study of news as a cultural phenomenon and guide the reader through key points that the readings offer. As you will recall, this book's Introduction provided perspective for the study of news, contrasting journalistic, sociological, and cultural answers to the question, "What is news?" Another part of the Introduction offered a basic sense of what is meant by cultural, including the global, the human phenomenon, and the critical. Finally, the Introduction provided a framework for an organized approach to studying news from a scholarly perspective. Altogether, these tools provide a systematic means of studying research about news.

So what lies ahead? As a consumer of news content, this book provides a fresh way of understanding what news is all about—what it means to the culture of journalists and to the culture of its society. As a scholar of news, this book provides concepts and a basic working bibliography through the selections it offers and the references that those works cite. Through an understanding of how the authors developed their data and analysis, a scholar should be able to begin work in this area of research. By doing so, readers can develop a keen eye for analyzing new instances that build a conceptual argument and test out new ideas through encounters with journalists and the news that they produce.

References

Ambrose, J. (2009, June 23). Ambrose: Double standards at the Times [Editorial]. *ScrippsNews.* Retrieved June 25, 2009, from http://www.scrippsnews.com/node/44091

Cook, J. (2009, June 23). What was the real reason for the NYT David Rohde kidnapping news blackout? *Gawker.* Retrieved June 25, 2009, from http://gawker.com/5301151/what-was-the-real-reason-for-the-nyt-david-rohde-kidnapping-news-blackout

McBride, K. (2009, June 24). Journalists can't uphold standard set by news blackout of Rohde kidnapping. *Poynter Online.* Retrieved June 25, 2009, from http://www.poynteronline.org/column.asp?id=67&aid=165629

Mitchell, G. (2009, June 23). Why "E&P" went along with media blackout on kidnapping. *Editor & Publisher.* Retrieved June 25, 2009, from http://www.editorandpublisher.com/eandp/columns/pressingissues_display.jsp?vnu_content_id=1003986498

Ravitz, J. (2009, June 24). Neda: Latest iconic image to inspire. *CNN.com.* Retrieved June 25, 2009, from http://www.cnn.com/2009/WORLD/meast/06/24/neda.iconic.images/

Times reporter escapes Taliban after 7 months. (2009, June 21). *New York Times.* Retrieved June 25, 2009, from http://www.nytimes.com/2009/06/21/world/asia/21taliban.html

Varin, A. (2009, June 25). Will "Neda" video become icon for ages*? AOL News.* Retrieved June 25, 2009, from http://news.aol.com/article/neda-iconic-images/542973

Author Index

Subject Index

About the Editor

Daniel A. Berkowitz is a professor in the School of Journalism & Mass Communication and an associate dean in the Graduate College at the University of Iowa. He earned his PhD in mass communication from Indiana University in 1988 and his master's from the University of Oregon in 1985. His previous book, *Social Meanings of News: A Text-Reader,* was published in 1997, and he is the author or coauthor of more than 30 journal articles and book chapters, as well as more than 50 conference paper presentations. His research interests include sociological and cultural approaches to the study of news and news production and also the interface between media and terrorism.